The Sea Is My Country

THE HENRY ROE CLOUD SERIES ON AMERICAN INDIANS AND MODERNITY

Series Editors:
Ned Blackhawk, Professor of History and American Studies, Yale University,
and
Kate W. Shanley, Native American Studies, University of Montana

Series Mission Statement
Named in honor of the pioneering Winnebago educational reformer and first known American Indian graduate of Yale College, Henry Roe Cloud (Class of 1910), this series showcases emergent and leading scholarship in the field of American Indian Studies. The series draws upon multiple disciplinary perspectives and organizes them around the place of Native Americans within the development of American and European modernity, emphasizing the shared, relational ties between indigenous and Euro-American societies. It seeks to broaden current historic, literary, and cultural approaches to American Studies by foregrounding the fraught but generative sites of inquiry provided by the study of indigenous communities.

THE SEA
IS MY COUNTRY

The Maritime World of the Makahs,
an Indigenous Borderlands People

Joshua L. Reid

Yale
UNIVERSITY
PRESS
New Haven & London

Published with assistance from the Kingsley Trust Association Publication Fund
established by the Scroll and Key Society of Yale College.

Yale University Press books may be purchased in quantity for educational,
business, or promotional use. For information, please e-mail sales.press@yale.edu
(US office) or sales@yaleup.co.uk (UK office).

An earlier version of portions of this book was previously published in
"Marine Tenure of the Makahs," in *Indigenous Knowledge and the Environment
in Africa and North America*, edited by David M. Gordon and Shepard Krech III
(Athens: Ohio University Press, 2012), 243–58. This material is used with permission
of Ohio University Press, www.ohioswallow.com.

Set in PostScript Electra with Trajan display type by Westchester Book Group.
Printed in the United States of America.

Endpapers: map by Bill Nelson.

Library of Congress Control Number: 2014957518
ISBN 978-0-300-20990-7
ISBN 978-0-300-23464-0 (pbk.)

A catalogue record for this book is available from the British Library.

Contents

FOREWORD

Joshua L. Reid is a true scholar and educator. Born and raised in Washington State, he is currently a professor at the University of Massachusetts, Boston, and a former middle school teacher with an undergraduate degree from Yale and a Ph.D. from the University of California, Davis. Josh approached the Makah Tribe with his research proposal and requested access to the extensive archival records held by the Makah Cultural and Research Center (MCRC). The proposal was of interest to the Makah Tribe and pertinent to current issues on both the tribal and national levels. His proposal was approved, and he began his inquiries. At the MCRC, he delved into the recordings of our elders who have gone before us. He held interviews with Makah individuals to gather additional details on historic and current Makah practices, events, and perspectives. He researched the written records within our archives; then he travelled—extensively—throughout the U.S. and Canada to track down all he could find relating to Makah control and management of marine space. His research and analysis of this material provide the most comprehensive source of Makah history ever published.

As Makahs, we know our ancestors took calculated and heroic measures to protect our water, land, and resources that provide for our way of life. Many of us know the stories of whale and seal hunters, fishermen, and warriors. The descriptions of the battles and alliances with other Tribes, Washington State, the federal government, and Canada are not new to us. Josh's book immortalizes Makah efforts to remain steadfast in our claims to ownership and control of this pivotal Northwestern territory throughout time, while highlighting some of the individuals who played key roles.

Other books have been published that help readers understand the complexity of Makah history, but nothing else published to date goes to these lengths to uncover and chronicle the ebb and flow of our struggles to maintain our unique position in this world. *The Sea Is My Country* is an uncompromising examination of Makah history that illustrates how Makahs affected early explorers' efforts to exploit the riches of the Pacific Northwest, how Makahs inserted our preexisting sovereignty to continue to be important players in the changing economy, and how we sustained cultural traditions and values throughout these changing times.

Josh has approached this project with unequivocal scholarship, portraying an unbiased look at crucial portions of Makah history. His investigation has brought forward a number of less commonly known historic facts, statistics, and unpublished research to present a variety of perspectives. *The Sea Is My Country* reconstructs a robust record of Makah use of marine space throughout the last two centuries. And while Josh is not a Makah tribal member, he has provided for the Makah voice to be heard within his work, something that is often missing in publications. He has pieced together our history in a truthful light which has the capacity to educate readers in developing an understanding of the complex history of Makah people.

So much misleading or inaccurate information is available to the public. Josh reveals Washington State's past efforts at providing the media with inaccurate information in order to lead the public to believe that Indians were responsible for overfishing salmon. Ironically, Indians were catching approximately six percent of the salmon at that time. These sentiments still exist. Josh's independent research provides the reader with evidence of these underlying themes throughout historic times and captures the Makah response. We commend his methodical research and efforts to document our history in this way.

This publication chronicles the periods where Makahs thrived both before and after contact, and struggled against governmental policies that were designed to strip our identity and take the wealth of our resources. *The Sea Is My Country* enlightens readers, disabling stereotypes with valid facts, figures, and an extensive bibliography. The timing of Josh's publication will benefit the tribe as we maneuver through the government's newest attempts at marine spatial planning and ocean policy. We expect this book will quickly become a treasured resource for both Makah readers as well as the broader academic community.

As a modern tribe we continually work to protect our treaty rights and way of life by utilizing the existing political and legal systems, all the while immersing our children in cultural traditions. We have been working through the federal government's procedures to resume our treaty-secured right to hunt whales for more than twenty years. This battle continues while another generation of whalers comes of age. Josh's compilation reminds us of how our forefathers maneuvered within both traditional and non-Indian systems to retain our identity and access to important resources that allow us to live and thrive as Qʷidičča?a·tx̌.

Makah Tribal Council
Makah Cultural and Research Center

ACKNOWLEDGMENTS

I have accrued many debts in researching and writing this book. Without the help of numerous individuals and institutions, I could never have embarked on this path, much less completed it. Fortunately, others found this project interesting and provided significant financial support. During graduate school at the University of California, Davis, I received support from the university and the Ford Foundation with both the Predoctoral Diversity Fellowship and the Dissertation Diversity Fellowship—they were even kind enough to support me with the Postdoctoral Fellowship after I completed my doctorate. The American Philosophical Society's Phillips Fund Grant for Native American Research financed several trips to the Makah Nation to conduct oral history interviews and a trip to the National Archives in Washington, DC. Without these substantial awards, I would not have had the luxury to focus solely on researching and writing.

UC Davis proved to be an outstanding place to earn my doctorate. Louis Warren was an ideal advisor and continues to be a valued mentor and friend. I have greatly appreciated his guidance since I met him at Yale years ago where he taught the Studies in the Environment Senior Colloquium, in which I first began exploring some of the ideas that took shape in this book. Alan Taylor was a patient teacher and careful proofreader. I enjoyed our many conversations about the overarching concepts and minutiae of this project. Steve Crum is probably one of the best-read historians I know, and his advice helped me connect the themes of the project to larger historiographical discussions and debates, especially as pertaining to American Indian history. Ari Kelman listened to and read my haphazard ideas and drafts and brought clarity to them. He also responded immediately to numerous phone calls and queries at all hours. Together, the members of my dissertation committee exemplified the best for which a fledgling historian could wish. While at Davis, I had the good fortune of being part of a smart, dynamic graduate cohort. Many of them responded to earlier versions of this project and have remained engaged throughout the process.

While working in various archives, I received assistance from many archivists and librarians. Carla Rickerson, Gary Lundell, and Nicole Bouché assisted me in navigating through the University of Washington's collections. At the regional branch (Pacific Alaska Region) of the National Archives, Patty McNamee's expertise streamlined my time both at Sand Point and the DC branch. While in Washington, Mary Francis Ronan saved me valuable time and gave me a tour of the archive's stacks, which made me much more appreciative of the work the archival technicians at NARA do for us researchers. I am also very grateful to George Miles, Curator of the Western Americana Collection at Yale University's Beinecke Rare Book and Manuscript Library, for ferreting out obscure documents and images I had only dreamed to exist. The staffs at the Washington State Archives, the British Columbia Archives, and the Mystic Seaport Collections Research Center also deserve my thanks, especially because I usually appeared unannounced, with a long list of requests in my fist.

I enjoyed all of my research visits, but my favorite ones took me to Neah Bay, Washington, in the Makah Nation. Janine Ledford, Director of the Makah Cultural and Research Center (MCRC), has earned my deepest thanks. Her interest and support in my project from the beginning provided invaluable access to the wealth of Makah sources on the subject. Janine helped organize oral history interviews, and she gave me valuable feedback on several ideas just as they began to take shape. Keely Parker, archivist at the MCRC, has proved unflagging in her efforts to locate documents, images, and earlier oral histories that illuminate parts of the story I have tried to tell. I have enjoyed sharing with both Keely and Janine my findings from the many archives I have been fortunate to visit. Maria Pascua patiently helped me with the Makah language terms that appear in this book . . . and put up with my efforts to pronounce words my mouth found difficult to form. I am most grateful for the time several Makahs have taken to share their oral histories with me. I learned an enormous amount from Greig Arnold, Ed Claplanhoo, Charles "Pug" Claplanhoo, Mary Ann Claplanhoo-Martin, Dan Greene, Dale Johnson, John McCarty, Maria Pascua, and Dave Sones; I hope they enjoyed the time they spent with me at least half as much as I did with them. Marc Slonim and Russell Svec also provided valuable feedback on portions of the manuscript. During my visits to Neah Bay, I benefited from many informal conversations, but most especially the late-night sessions with my friend Micah McCarty, whether we sat around a fire with his family or in his backroom as he carved a mask. I am greatly indebted to the stunning art he provided for the cover. Various iterations of the Makah Tribal Council have also provided assistance over the years, carefully reading portions of this book and offering valuable suggestions and feedback. Any mistakes here are solely mine.

I have presented and published portions of my work and received excellent feedback and advice from colleagues at a host of conferences and other venues. An earlier version of a portion of chapter 5 was published in *Tribal Worlds*, edited by Brian Hosmer and Larry Nesper (State University of New York Press, 2013); an earlier version of portions of this book were previously published in "Marine Tenure of the Makahs," in *Indigenous Knowledge and the Environment in Africa and North America*, edited by David M. Gordon and Shepard Krech III (Ohio University Press, 2012). I gratefully acknowledge the publishers and editors for their support of my work. At the risk of leaving out any of the countless individuals who offered invaluable suggestions and assistance, I will not list everyone here. Just know that I greatly appreciate the support and input I received from you all, whether we were sitting around a campfire, sharing some grilled reindeer, talking between sets in a New Orleans jazz dive, swapping stories while kayaking in Puget Sound or Doubtful Sound, or skulking in a hotel bar long after conference sessions had ended. However, I would especially like to express my gratitude to Jay Gitlin for setting me on this course years ago in a history seminar I took at Yale University. His continued support and encouragement have helped to maintain my own excitement.

The University of Massachusetts, Boston, has proved an outstanding academic home for me over the past several years. My colleagues in the History Department, the Native American and Indigenous Studies program, and various workshops and seminars have been especially supportive, attending talks, responding to ideas, reading chapters, and helping out where they can. Everyone has been generous with their time and hospitality. A very special thank-you is due to Conevery Bolton Valencius, who carefully read an entire draft of this work and provided advice that improved every chapter—I am hard pressed to think of a better critic. I have also had the good fortune to work with outstanding graduate research assistants, including Nicole Breault, Krystle Beaubrun, Deirdre Kutt, and Phill Marsh. They transcribed oral history recordings, scanned through gobs of newspapers online, and performed other invaluable research tasks. The College of Liberal Arts has also been generous with time off from teaching and research funding that has allowed me to complete this book.

During my second year at UMass Boston, I took a Ford Foundation Post-Doc Fellowship at Yale. The Howard R. Lamar Center for the Study of Frontiers and Borders kindly offered me a home, where I worked under the guidance of Ned Blackhawk as I began revising the dissertation into this book. His engagement with my project at this time helped prepare it for publication in the Henry Roe Cloud Series on American Indians and Modernity, something for which I am greatly appreciative. While at Yale, I benefitted from participation in the Yale Group for the Study of Native America and from involvement with the Native American Cultural Center, then under the supervision of Ted Van Alst. Being back at Yale long after my undergraduate years was an invigorating experience, especially as I got to be a part of the increasingly supportive place it has become for Native students and scholars.

Yale University Press has been delightful to work with on my first book. Editorial Director Chris Rogers took an interest in this project years ago, and his advice and careful reading have improved the book through every stage of the process. Erica Hanson patiently provided assistance with the images and interfacing with the press on various issues. I must also thank the two readers, David Igler and Colin Calloway, for their careful insights on an earlier version of this manuscript. They pushed me to clarify my thinking and fine-tune my arguments for the final version. Thanks are also due to Bill Nelson for his prompt attention to my various map requests and to Laura Jones Dooley for her careful copyedits. I cannot imagine finding a better home than Yale University Press for this book.

I have benefitted from the support and hospitality of friends outside the academic world. Many have maintained a constant interest in the project, asking good questions that have encouraged me to avoid convoluted explanations when something more straightforward makes better sense. For years they have been telling me that they are looking forward to "the book."

I reserve my closing acknowledgments for my family. My grandfather, Marvin Dailey, first introduced me to the ocean and the notion that it is a site rich with history. Stories of his grandmother, smoking a corn-cob pipe as she paddled her canoe through local waters, fired my young imagination as we sat around driftwood campfires on the Pacific coast. My parents, Gary and Virginia Reid, also sparked my connection to the sea by taking my sister Lisa and me on our first backpacking trip to Ozette, a former Makah village and archaeological site just south of Cape Flattery. Lisa and her family have offered welcome support and distractions, reminding me that there is more than just my narrow academic world. Last, I would like to thank my wife, Maya Reid. I have truly appreciated her patience as I relocated us from Seattle to Davis, then back to Seattle, and now to Boston—I know that the peripatetic life of the academic can be challenging. She has been a constant companion, whether exploring the wine country of northern California, jazz scene of Seattle, state parks in Vermont, the ghosts of old London, or winding roads of the Olympic Peninsula. I dedicate this book to my family.

A NOTE ABOUT WORDS AND NAMING

Words have power. I have taken care with the specific terms I use in *The Sea Is My Country*. When writing about indigenous peoples, it is most precise to use specific names, such as "Makahs." I have tended to minimize the use of "the Makah" because there really is no single entity that speaks for all individuals who ascribe to this identity. Occasionally, I have needed to use this term, usually in reference to the political body of the tribal nation. I have also used "the People of the Cape," an Anglicized gloss of what they call themselves, Qʷidiččaʔa·tx̌ ("kwi-dihch-chuh-aht"). When referring to more general groups of indigenous peoples, I have used a range of terms interchangeably, including "Natives," "American Indians," and "Indians." All these terms have histories of their own that highlight unequal dynamics of power, racial rhetoric, and identity politics, but alternating them allows me to do more than craft language that flows better. At times, I employed a specific term to invoke the perspectives of a particular group in that historical moment. In addition, I avoided "tribe," instead using "tribal nation" to highlight Native sovereignty and the special political relationship American Indians have with the United States.

Another term worth explaining is "fisher," a word that sounds clunky and awkward to many, including some Makah readers. For this I apologize—in no way am I implying that women who fish today or fished in the past were something less than "fishermen," their male family members. However, the term "fisher" is useful because it helps us acknowledge and discuss how gender shapes the kinds of techniques and gear choices used by different people at specific times in history. I also make an active decision to employ this term here because, as one of my environmental historian colleagues casually noted, "We don't call 'em farmermen or minermen or loggermen." Many younger readers, such as students in our classrooms, comfortably use "fisher," so in hopes that this book speaks to future generations who will find the term "fisherman/men" anachronistic, I have used "fisher."

I include a large collection of Makah language terms. Part of the Wakashan language family of the Northwest Coast, Makah is closely related to Nootkan languages of Vancouver Island, particularly Nitinat and Pacheena. Like many Native North American languages, Makah includes sounds that do not appear in English, which is why I have used words in an orthography that looks unfamiliar to many readers. This vocabulary is integral to broadening our understanding of Makah culture and their relationship with marine space, so I have included many words that highlight the Makahs' environmental and geographical knowledge. On first use of these terms, I have italicized common nouns and followed them with the phonetic pronunciation and English equivalent in parenthesis, like this: *čitapuk* ("chih-tuh-pook," whales). I also included many Makah proper nouns, such as names of people and places. These are capitalized and not set in italics. For these proper nouns, I include a phonetic pronunciation, like this: Čaqa·wiλ ("tsuh-kah-wihtl"). I am not fluent in Makah—not even close! However, I worked carefully with Maria Pascua, language specialist at Neah Bay, who patiently explained these terms, helping me sound them out. Any mistakes here are my own. For those interested in learning more about the Makah language, Pascua recommends William H. Jacobsen Jr., *First Lessons in Makah* (Neah Bay: Makah Cultural and Research Center, 1999).

Last, I would like to point out that as a historian writing about events in the past, I have largely stuck to the past tense, except where the present or future tense was necessary. Many of these past conditions have persisted into the present, however, and affect the future. Makahs continue to shape marine space as the primary site of their identity, and their work and advocacy influence politics and policies in the Northwest Coast. In using the past tense, I am in no way arguing that Makahs no longer exist or are irrelevant today. Similarly, when discussing environmental conditions, I have employed the past tense because I wish to emphasize that past environments were in many cases different from those today. As with human cultures, environmental features and conditions have their own histories. Like the Makahs themselves, these past environments will continue to change and influence circumstances today and in the future.

Introduction: Just Where *Does* One Get a License to Kill Indians?

On the morning of May 17, 1999, eight Makah men paddled the *K̓ʷiti·k̓ʷitš* ("kwih-tee-kwihtsh," *Hummingbird*) up to the three-year-old gray whale. Ignoring the drizzling rain, buzz of news copters above, and watchful eyes of a National Marine Fisheries biologist, Theron Parker thrust the harpoon. Unlike his misses on the prior two days of hunting, this throw sank into the thirty-ton leviathan and stuck. From a nearby support craft, a modified .577 caliber rifle roared three times. Fired by an experienced game hunter and decorated Vietnam War combat veteran, the third shot lanced through the water and into the whale's brain, killing it within seconds. As the female whale died off Washington State's Pacific coast, harpooner Theron led the crew in prayer, thanking her for offering herself to the Makahs. Surrounded by a small fleet of canoes from neighboring American Indian nations, the *Hummingbird* brought the whale ashore at Neah Bay about twelve hours later. Hundreds of men pulled on two heavy chains, hauling her onto the beach where generations of whalers had beached them before. Theron sprinkled eagle feathers on the whale's head while the community welcomed her—the first in seventy years—to the Makah nation.[1]

A coalition of indigenous peoples and non-Natives throughout the world supported the hunt at several critical stages. When the United States removed the gray whale from the list of endangered wildlife in 1994, the tribal nation expressed interest in resuming customary whale hunts. With the support of the National Oceanic and Atmospheric Administration, in 1997, the Makah petitioned the International Whaling Commission (IWC) for approval of annual subsistence hunts. After negotiating with other North Pacific indigenous groups, the IWC granted the tribal nation a yearly quota of five whales, one for each ancestral Makah village near Cape Flattery, the northwesternmost tip of the contiguous

United States. As part of this deal, Alaska Inuits traded twenty bowhead whales
to the Chuktchis, a Siberian people, for five gray whales. Chuktchis have an annual quota of two hundred grays, and this reallocation undercut the potential
criticism that Makah hunts would add stress on the species.[2]

Indigenous peoples continued to provide encouragement during the 1999 hunt
and afterward. A few years earlier, several Vancouver Island Nuu-chah-nulth carv-
ers, relatives of Makahs, helped to make the *Hummingbird,* and American
Indian communities and Canadian First Nations from across North America offered prayers for the hunters' success. After landing the whale at Neah Bay,
members of the community stripped blubber and meat from the carcass and
hosted a large feast, reminiscent of potlatches from earlier centuries. Makah
elder Dale Johnson remembers that getting the whale "brought a gathering of
people; tribes from all over came in" as the whalers shared the catch. In addition to American Indians from Alaska, the Great Plains, and the West Coast,
indigenous peoples from across North America, the Pacific, and Africa were
honored guests at the celebratory feast. Billy Frank Jr., a Nisqually elder, president of the Northwest Indian Fisheries Commission, and veteran of the Indian
fishing wars of the 1960s and 1970s, spoke passionately about the importance of

Hauling the whale ashore, May 17, 1999. After the power winch failed, the
community worked together to pull the whale ashore. Photograph by Theresa Parker,
courtesy the Makah Cultural and Research Center, Neah Bay, WA.

exercising treaty rights. A Maasai warrior from Kenya expressed the need to preserve unique cultural characteristics in the world today. Many non-Natives also supported the hunt because whaling is a treaty right that Makahs reserved for themselves in the 1855 Treaty of Neah Bay, which the tribal nation signed with the United States. The 1999 hunt has inspired self-determination struggles by others. Currently negotiating treaties with the Canadian government, Nuu-chah-nulths point to the Makah whale hunt to support their efforts to re-sume a customary lifestyle based on whaling.[3]

Coming at the close of the twentieth century, however, the whalers' actions drew passionate opposition. Longtime foes of American Indian treaty rights, such as Congressman Jack Metcalf (R-Washington), railed against the federal govern-ment's bias of "giving Indians special rights," a statement exhibiting his igno-rance that Native negotiators, not the government, reserved rights for their tribal nations in the treaties.[4] A vocal minority argued that whaling is barbaric and out of step with today's more "enlightened" views. Racism peppered much of their rhetoric, echoing criticisms levied against Washington's American Indians during the fishing rights conflict of earlier decades. Makah commercial fisher Dan Greene observed that "the same people who are racist against the Indian tribes are still there" since the treaty fishing wars of the 1960s and 1970s, "and that this [the 1999 whale hunt] just brought it to the surface again." After the May 17 hunt, "the floodgates of hate were opened."[5] Calling Makahs "'Red' necks with rifles" and accusing them of "playing Indian," non-Natives revealed strong anti-Indian sentiments still present in mainstream society. Phillips Wylly, an ac-complished film and television producer, wrote to the editor of the *Seattle Times*, asking, "I am anxious to know where I may apply for a license to kill Indians. My forefathers helped settle the west and it was their tradition to kill every Red-skin they saw. 'The only good Indian was a dead Indian,' they believed. I also want to keep with the faith of my ancestors." Protestors blocked the road to Neah Bay, issued bomb threats, and harassed gray whales in local waters in order to chase them away from Makah hunters. Anti-Indian sentiment became so vocif-erous that the governor deployed the National Guard to the reservation to pro-tect Makah lives. The US Coast Guard defended the whalers at sea from activist organizations such as the Sea Shepherd Society.[6] These critics were racist, and they were also wrong. This kind of criticism of the Makahs' continuing whaling efforts reveals a deep lack of understanding about the issue. They have overlooked—and continue to ignore—the historical and cultural connections Makahs have to the ocean.

Calling themselves the Qʷidičča?aʔtx̌ ("kwi-dihch-chuh-aht"), meaning "the People of the Cape," Makahs shaped marine space in and around the Strait of

Juan de Fuca, rather than terrestrial spaces, as the primary locus of their identity. They placed marine space at the center of their culture. Strategic exploitation of customary waters enabled the People of the Cape to participate in global networks of exchange, to resist assimilation, and to retain greater autonomy until the early twentieth century, later than many other land-based reservation communities in North America. When explorers and maritime fur traders entered the Pacific Northwest at the end of the eighteenth century, Makah chiefs protected their control over customary waters and resources. During talks for the 1855 Treaty of Neah Bay, Makah negotiators forced Territorial Governor Isaac Stevens to alter the treaty language to fit the tribal nation's maritime needs. Networks of exchange, kinship, and conflict made the waters around the Strait of Juan de Fuca, today an international border that separates the state of Washington from the Canadian province of British Columbia, into a space of connections. Indigenous whalers, sealers, and fishers combined customary practices with modern opportunities and technology to maintain Makah identity amid the cultural and environmental changes of the nineteenth and twentieth centuries. Challenges included overfished marine species, environmental degradation, rising state power, and assimilation and conservation efforts. By understanding the contours of the Makahs' connection to the ocean, we can see more easily why reviving the active practice of whaling is critical to the People of the Cape today.

THE ENVIRONMENTAL AND CULTURAL CONTEXT
OF THE NORTHWEST COAST

As a marine people, Makahs developed a deep understanding of and relationship with the waters around them. Oceanographic features created what some scholars call a bioregion, acknowledging that powerful forces of the natural environment are more important than divisions created by borders. As in other places such as the Medicine Line country of the Alberta-Montana borderlands, environment and geography—rather than gender, age, ethnicity, or nationality—dictated community bonds in this region. Unpredictable and difficult forces of nature exerted a "constant push and pull" on the lives of those living in the Medicine Line country. Similarly, natural forces such as the ebb and flow of tides, winds and currents, powerful storms, spawning salmon, breaching whales, and gamboling seals and sea otters exerted a constant push and pull on the lives of the People of the Cape and other indigenous inhabitants of the Northwest Coast. Environmental features made these marine waters a complex, rich space that drew many peoples to this region and encouraged a spectrum of exchanges from violence to trade.[7]

Surface and submarine geological features bound this marine space in three dimensions. At the seascape's edges, the watersheds of mountainous Vancouver Island and the glaciated ramparts of the Olympic and Cascade Ranges sent mineral-laden freshwater into inshore coastal waters. Separating Vancouver Island from the Olympic Peninsula, the Strait of Juan de Fuca funneled cold seawater into the warmer waters of Puget Sound.[8] Underwater west of the Olympic Peninsula and Vancouver Island, the continental shelf kept the seafloor shallow farther offshore and worked with seasonal currents to prevent winter waters from becoming too frigid, thereby improving conditions for marine organisms during the cold months. Numerous reefs, rocky outcrops, and other localized submarine features attracted many types of fish.

Possessing a detailed indigenous knowledge of the local seascape, Makahs understood that distinct water masses in the region circulated in a complex yet regular manner as currents interacted with seasonally changing winds and geological features.[9] Within a larger geographic context, permanent ocean currents moved water masses into and out of this region. Flowing east across the Pacific Ocean, the North Pacific Current split when it drove into the coast of North America. One branch, the Alaska Current System, headed north along the west coast of Vancouver Island. Pushing warmer water northward, it moderated conditions in the southeast Bering Sea. A second branch, the California Current System, headed south along the Washington coast to the Baja Peninsula. These currents deposited flotsam on beaches in front of Makah villages, bringing giant redwood logs from northern California in the winter and carrying bamboo and other tropical flora from Asia in the summer. More important, these water masses affected the marine biology of local waters, making species available at regular times. When the California Current System swung closer to the coast each spring, it brought fur seals, migrating to their breeding grounds on the Pribilof Islands in the Bering Sea, within safe reach of Makah men hunting from canoes. Observing these natural cycles helped coastal indigenous peoples understand that these larger currents affected local marine space and the resources within it.[10]

The effects of regional movements of water also benefited the People of the Cape. Rivers discharged nutrient-rich water into local marine space. Freshwater from the numerous smaller watersheds of Vancouver Island and the Olympic Peninsula carried minerals into this environment. Large outlets such as the Strait of Juan de Fuca and the mouth of the Columbia River funneled plumes seaward. Draining an approximate area of 258,200 square miles, the Columbia River discharged nutrients that moved north along the coast as the Davidson Current picked them up. In the Strait of Juan de Fuca, estuarine runoff from the Fraser River mixed with deep, nutrient-rich seawater before being discharged

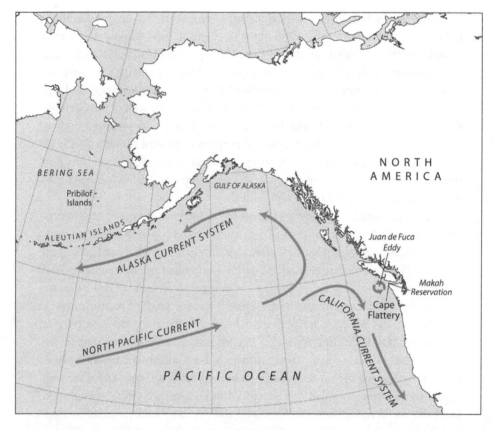

Currents of the northeastern Pacific. Map by Bill Nelson. The California Current System was a complex, three-dimensional mass of water. The surface component of this current system meandered southward, pushing cold water from the Subarctic Current down the coast. Possessing greater concentrations of oxygen and phosphates, this mass of water from the higher latitudes helped marine life and the human societies dependent upon it thrive. Another component of the California Current System, the deeper and northerly flowing Davidson Current, transported warmer, equatorial water along the slope and outer continental shelf. It appeared off the Washington coast in September and was well established by January. From the middle of November to mid-February, this was the dominant inshore transporter of water and suspended material along the coast. Most important for marine life, the Davidson Current helped to keep inshore water temperatures warmer than water farther offshore during the winter months. It diminished in the spring when the offshore surface current of the California Current System swung closer to the coast. This change resulted in the seasonal upwelling of colder, nutrient-rich water, fueling a rich marine environment. A third component of the California Current System, the California Undercurrent, flowed northward along the upper continental shelf at 660 feet and deeper.

into the ocean. This mixture contributed substantially to the nutrient supply and the resultant production of phytoplankton—microscopic, single-cell plants—around Cape Flattery. The wide continental shelf off the west coast of Vancouver Island created an extensive foundation for spreading this nutrient-rich water mass into ocean waters farther offshore. Experienced Makah mariners used the strong tidal current around Cape Flattery to get to and from fishing grounds off the cape and to travel among villages. Oral histories highlight Makah knowledge of local currents and tides and relate how indigenous mariners used them to their advantage.[11]

Because they could literally see it through the resultant high concentration of sea life, the People of the Cape also knew about one of the most important regional oceanographic processes, upwelling.[12] This raised cold, nutrient-rich water into the photic zone where sunlight fueled photosynthesis, which created a highly productive biomass. Promontories and capes such as Cape Flattery and the related Juan de Fuca Eddy created "upwelling centers" in the surrounding waters. The deep California Undercurrent and the outflow from the strait interacted with the submarine canyon system off the cape to facilitate upwelling from an extreme depth. The Juan de Fuca Eddy made this marine space into a dense biomass of phytoplankton (microscopic single-celled plants), which, in turn, enhanced the quantity of larger marine species. During its peak, the eddy propelled dissolved inorganic nutrients about sixty miles from the mouth of the Strait of Juan de Fuca and marked the water with a dark stain as it literally "boil[ed] with bait." It also facilitated the mixing of fresh- and salt-water in the strait and flushed the inlets of the west coast of Vancouver Island.[13]

The physical features of this complex marine environment supported a rich food web, which radiated out from the phytoplankton. These microorganisms got energy from sunlight and dissolved inorganic nutrients. In the spring, the Juan de Fuca Eddy facilitated an explosive bloom of these phytoplankton, which fed the large amount of krill at the coastal-oceanic interface along the Washington coast. A type of zooplankton, krill was a keystone species, the primary food source for most other marine life. This included fish, seabirds, and marine mammals, especially whales, all significant to Makahs and Nuu-chah-nulth peoples of Vancouver Island. Found throughout the Strait of Juan de Fuca and along the coast, kelp beds formed dense marine forests that supported fish, invertebrates, marine mammals, and seabirds.[14]

Keeping temperatures warmer in the winter and cooler in the summer, the ocean also shaped the weather patterns experienced by the Makahs. Driven by the Aleutian Low, an atmospheric pressure cell that dropped south from the Bering Sea during the winter, wet storms often swept in from the ocean, annually depositing from 90 to 110 inches of precipitation, most in the form of rain due to the temperate climate. Calmer and warmer, summer was rarely hot. Cloudy weather, foggy conditions, and variable winds bedeviled many a non-Native mariner and at times presented challenges for Makahs when on the water. The latitude, various ocean currents, and climate kept the waters off Cape Flattery cold, yet warm enough to support the rich marine life of the region.[15] Together, winds, geological features, the circulation of water masses, and marine biology composed the oceanography of marine space in which the People of the Cape and neighboring indigenous peoples lived.

Located on the shores of the Pacific Northwest, the People of the Cape are part of the Northwest Coast culture. This cultural area extends along the Pacific coast from the Copper River delta on the Gulf of Alaska to the Oregon-California border and inland to the Coast Mountains of British Columbia and the Cascade Mountains of Washington and Oregon. Speaking forty-five separate languages that scholars have organized into thirteen language families, the many distinct peoples of the Northwest Coast composed the second most diverse (after California) linguistic area of indigenous North America in the fifteenth century. Despite this diversity, these peoples shared several commonalities differentiating them from the interior peoples east of the Cascades, far northern peoples of the Pacific, and those in California.[16]

Northwest Coast peoples exploited a range of natural resources, but most relied on cedar and salmon. Natives used cedar, an evergreen tree found throughout the region and valued for its durability and decay resistance, for so many necessities that some referred to the spirit of the tree as "Long Life Maker" or "Rich Woman Maker." They spun, wove, and plaited its fibrous bark into clothing, baskets, and rope. Northwest Coast peoples split cedar into planks for longhouses, steamed boards into bentwood boxes, carved totem poles and masks, and fashioned canoes from logs. They fished for five species of salmon, an anadromous fish that hatches in freshwater streams, swims to the ocean to spend most of its life fattening up, and returns to natal streams to spawn and die. Using reef nets, seines, weirs, lines, and spears, families took from three hundred to a thousand pounds of salmon per person each year. Because the separate species return to spawn at different seasons and only for limited durations, Native women developed a range of methods for preserving and storing salmon. The differential availability of cedar and particular species of salmon—and other food and natural resources—fueled a vast trade network encompassing this culture area and beyond. Makahs had unique access to enormous amounts of halibut, whales, and seals, which they traded to other Northwest Coast peoples for salmon and cedar, two resources that they did not have in abundance in comparison to peoples living on major river systems.[17]

Indigenous communities formed around villages situated to exploit marine resources. Makahs resided at five primary villages—Biʔidʔa ("bih-ih-duh"), Diʔya ("dee-yuh," Neah Bay), Waʔač ("wuh-uhch"), Čuʔyas ("tsoo-yuhs"), and ʔuseˑʔił ("oo-sa-ihlth," Ozette)—located near Cape Flattery. During the spring and summer, families dispersed to residences located to access seasonal resources more easily. During the late eighteenth century, many Makahs annually relocated to the summer village on Tatoosh Island, about half a mile northwest of Cape Flattery, to fish for halibut and hunt whales. Others lived in smaller communities such as Q̓idiˑqabit ("kih-dee-kuh-biht")—called "Warm Houses" in English because of the many smokehouses for drying fish—and fishing camps along the Hoko River, where they caught and preserved various fish. During the stormy winter months, they relocated back to sheltered, more permanent villages.

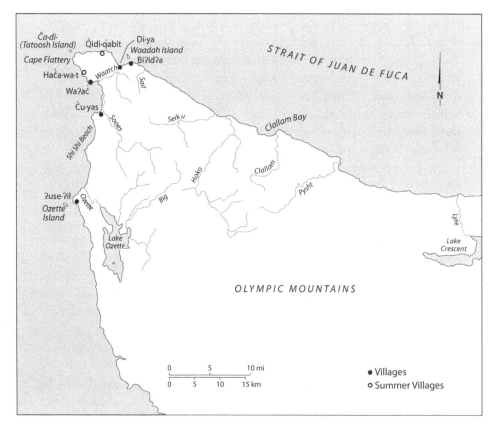

Cape Flattery, homeland of the Qʷidičˇčaʔaˑtx̌ ("kwi-dihch-chuh-aht"), the People of the Cape. Map by Bill Nelson.

Families moved from one area to another because they had ownership and usufruct rights (the right to use something owned by someone else) based on kinship to specific resources. These rights shifted as social connections changed due to marriages and divorces, births and deaths, and the waxing and waning power of particular individuals and communities. Because of these changes, and periodic fluctuations in the availability of particular species, families did not always follow the same particular pattern of seasonal movements.[18]

Before the appearance of non-Natives in the eighteenth century, Northwest Coast peoples recognized the status of individuals within a three-tiered system of social stratification, which included chiefs, commoners, and slaves. A range of ranked leaders occupied the highest social stratum in each village. Claiming ancestral ties to supernatural ancestors, chiefs owned the rights and titles to leadership positions within communities. Titleholders owned lucrative fishing and hunting grounds and other resource areas. "Outside resources"—called such because they were in marine spaces outside bays, inlets, and rivers—were the most important property rights, and only the highest-ranking chiefs owned them. Among the People of the Cape, the most powerful chiefs were whalers. In addition to tangible property such as cranberry bogs, freshwater streams, driftwood, game, timber, and wild plants, chiefs owned intangible items, like names, dances, songs, and stories. Sometimes sold but usually given as gifts, these propertied items passed within kinship networks and crossed gender lines, which meant that women occasionally held positions of authority.

Except for personal items such as canoes, clothing, and fishing gear, commoners did not own any culturally significant property like resource areas and titles. However, they did have access to hunting and fishing grounds because chiefs extended these rights to people who respected their authority. In return, commoners often gave a portion of what they hunted, harvested, and caught to the high-status owner. Slaves, seized during conflicts between communities and traded throughout the Northwest Coast, occupied the lowest social stratum and made up 20 to 40 percent of a village's population. Slave status was hereditary—the children of slaves inherited this condition. Because they did a range of labor and augmented an owner's wealth, slaves were both valuable property and status items. High-status Makahs kept many slaves, and the People of the Cape were key traders in the regional slave trade.[19]

Ownership of important titles and rights provided Northwest Coast chiefs with their foundation for leadership within villages and sometimes across larger sociopolitical spaces. Chiefs exercised authority through influence rather than coercion. Although titles, rights, and privileges passed from one generation to the next through kinship networks, an individual had to maintain his—and sometimes her—noble status by providing for the people. Within a Makah village, whaling chiefs who harvested several thirty-to-forty-ton whales each year provided a wealth of subsistence and trade goods. This system of leadership made authority competitive both within villages and across larger areas. The wealthiest chiefs—those who could provide the most for their people—had more influence than others with less. These leaders could muster hundreds of warriors from several villages. They protected their people from raiders or led war expeditions against neighboring villages to seize slaves and lucrative resources such as salmon streams or marine fishing and hunting grounds. Chiefs strengthened their social status by marrying members of other noble families throughout the region; for similar reasons, they married their sons and daughters into other high-status families. Marriages often brought more property items, including fishing rights, slaves, titles, and other tangible goods, although these privileges ended on divorce.[20]

Chiefs displayed and distributed wealth through rituals and feasts, which scholars often lump together under the name "potlatch." These events ranged from simple affairs, during which a chief shared a substantial catch of salmon, to more elaborate celebrations such as a marriage between two noble families. The largest events involved hundreds of guests, whom the host would feast for several consecutive weeks. Potlatches incorporated speeches, dances, songs, and other ritual activities. These feasts featured the giving of gifts ranging from food to valuable commodity trade items. Within the framework of leadership rivalries in the Northwest Coast, potlatching became competitive when chiefs expanded their influence over people by demonstrating the ability to provide increasing amounts of wealth for supporters. The People of the Cape were renowned throughout the Northwest Coast for their feasts. S'Klallams, a separate people living to the east of Cape Flattery, called them *Makahs*, a name that means "generous with food," probably because of the abundance they harvested from rich marine resources, which allowed them to host lavish events.[21]

Northwest Coast characteristics of marine resources, hierarchy, competitive power, and potlatches worked together to allow influential Makah chiefs to produce tribal space. As human geographers have demonstrated, spaces are products of societies. Makah society produced marine and terrestrial spaces—made them Makah spaces—through the ways they thought about, organized, and lived in these spaces. Many factors shaped the historical process of producing space in the Northwest Coast, including the environment, competing Native and non-Native societies and polities, the actions of individuals and groups, differing attitudes on how to best make a living, and connections to other spaces. Makah marine space became a social reality through the actions of distinct borderlands peoples and through the networks of kinship, trade, and violence drawing them together.[22] The availability of whales, seals, and halibut made the People of the Cape different from others, and Makahs funneled these unique resources into Native and non-Native trade networks. Influential chiefs exploited these resources to expand and maintain their power, which allowed them to interrupt imperial processes such as trade and colonization. Much like an interruption in a conversation pauses the flow of words, registers a counterpoint, or inserts a missed perspective, these interruptions of imperial processes questioned, suspended, or redirected non-Native plans for a time, served as bold reminders that newcomers were in Native spaces layered with specific protocols, and on occasion shaped the unfolding trajectory of empire by interjecting indigenous priorities in ways that could not be ignored. Makah leaders recognized the foundation of their power and identity, an understanding captured in the words of Čaqa·wiƛ ("tsuh-kah-wihtl"), a Makah chief, during the negotiations for the 1855 Treaty of Neah Bay. He told the Euro-American treaty negotiators, "I want the sea. That is my country."[23]

The Sea Is My Country explains the historical meaning of Čaqa·wiƛ's statement, before, during, and after the treaty negotiations. The chief's words require us to take a marine-oriented approach, a different historical perspective on American Indians and the North American West. Nearly all of these histories problematically end at the coastline, keeping oceans "relegated to the saltwater margins of human history."[24] Terrestrial extractive industries, such as mining and timber, are a common focus of Western history. One historian has characterized these industries as "get in, get rich, get out."[25] But similar patterns first appeared in the Pacific Northwest during the late eighteenth-century maritime fur trade and were repeated in later marine-oriented extractive industries such as whaling, sealing, and fishing. Indigenous peoples had a large role in these maritime activities. Other themes characteristic of narratives of the US West—such as the role of the federal government, industry, and capital in shaping the region—also display new dimensions when applied to marine spaces and industries west of the continent's coastline.[26] The nineteenth-century whaling, sealing, and fishing industries helped to bring new places such as the Pacific Northwest, Hawai'i, and Alaska into the United States. A few scholars have begun to look at the extension of the US West into and across the Pacific Ocean and the reciprocal role of Pacific peoples, places, and industries on the development of the nation. But these narratives present a traditional story of non-Native commercial interests overwhelming and replacing indigenous economies. Native peoples, if they appear at all, only seem to react to more dynamic Europeans and Euro-Americans.[27] This narrative interrogates the standard assumptions, exploring the critical role of marine-oriented indigenous peoples—specifically Makahs—in the settler-colonial processes shaping the North American West from the eighteenth through twentieth centuries.

Some might wonder why settler-colonialism is an appropriate concept relative to investigating historical Makah marine space because the sea did not attract settlers in the ways that land did. However, historical processes that happened on land affected the People of the Cape even though they were primarily a marine people. Often overlooked by historians, marine spaces were integral to settler-colonialism in the Pacific Northwest from the very beginning. Many traders, settlers, and government officials engaged in or benefited from such maritime pursuits as shipping, fishing, whaling, and sealing, all activities that took place in indigenous spaces on the water or along the shoreline. Additionally, settler-colonial officials applied to marine spaces laws, treaties, and boundaries that attempted to circumscribe the autonomy and mobility of Northwest Coast Natives. Yet what unfolded on these waters was no simple set of processes that spelled unequivocal doom for Native peoples. Like other historical processes, settler-colonialism in this region unfolded in contingent ways that indigenous historical actors attempted to shape for their own purposes and to benefit their own communities. For Makahs such as Čaqaʔwiƛ, this meant keeping the sea as their country.[28]

Understanding how the People of the Cape transformed and maintained the sea as their country also requires us to think outside some of the traditional boundaries of histories of American Indians and the West. Histories about interactions between Native and non-Native peoples in the North American West often limit narratives to their respective national framework. For example, histories of interactions among First Nations and British (and then Canadian) peoples in the Canadian West rarely stray south of the current boundary separating the United States and Canada. Similarly, narratives about American Indians and Euro-Americans in the US West often confine themselves to the geopolitical space of the present nation.[29] From the perspective of Northwest Coast peoples, however, confining scholarship to one side of the border appears odd because non-Native empires (American and British) and nation-states (the United States and Canada) did not come into existence until late in indigenous histories, which span thousands of years. Living around Cape Flattery, just south of Vancouver Island, Makahs have long been a part of both the US and Canadian Wests. This book examines the way Makahs and other indigenous peoples of the Northwest Coast engaged settler-colonialism through non-Native trade, settlement, treaty-making, law, bureaucracy, and property.

In order to take a Makah-centered, regional perspective, *The Sea Is My Country* draws on borderlands concepts to examine the complex interactions of local peoples—both Native and non-Native—with one another, with regional spaces broader than nations, and with sociocultural networks engaging capital, trade, kinship, and identity. These interactions defined the specific characteristics of what I call the ča·di· ("cha-dee") borderland, after the Makah name for Tatoosh Island, a key location in the region.[30] Although it changed over time, in the eighteenth and early nineteenth centuries, the ča·di· borderland stretched nearly five hundred miles, as a canoe might travel, from the mouth of the Columbia River to the northern tip of Vancouver Island and east into Puget Sound. Characterizing Makah marine space as part of an indigenous borderlands is more than an academic exercise or historical conceit. Indeed, many of the places within this borderland remain relevant to Makahs today.

This analysis of the ča·di· borderland differs from the standard borderlands approach, highlighting that borderlands are spaces shared and contested by distinct peoples. Specific social, economic, political, cultural, and environmental networks crossed these spaces, binding together borderlands inhabitants and specific places. Because two or more societies constructed these networks, they changed over time and across space, making borderlands products of history. Like frontiers, borderlands are messy social creations of amalgamation, accommodation, and contention. But unlike frontiers, borderlands have defined—yet contested—geographic and cultural borders.[31]

The story of the maritime world of the Makahs complicates the current approach to borderlands, frontiers, and boundaries. Many scholars agree with the formulations of these three concepts as expressed by historians Jeremy Adelman and Stephen Aron, who argue that borderlands, unlike frontiers, are defined by the competitive nature of European imperialism. They define *frontier* as a "meeting place of peoples in which geographic and cultural borders were not clearly defined." Frontiers are "borderless lands" marked by cultural and ethnic mixing and accommodation. They reserve *borderlands* for "contested boundaries between colonial [European] domains." Natives exploited both frontiers and borderlands when resisting submission to a single European power and to negotiate more favorable intercultural relations. Adelman and Aron argue that when borderlands turned into borders, indigenous peoples lost their ability to play off imperial rivalries. Once borders separating nation-states emerged, these political entities could then better dictate and control property rights, citizenship, and population movements.[32]

The Sea Is My Country presents an alternative borderlands history. The actions of Makahs and other indigenous peoples challenge the problematic formulation that only *European* imperialism produces borderlands.[33] They also complicate the borderlands-to-border process Adelman and Aron describe. Although Britain and the United States settled on the northern border of Oregon Territory in 1846, dividing what became Washington State and British Columbia along the forty-ninth parallel and Strait of Juan de Fuca, well into the twentieth century the People of the Cape and neighboring communities continued to cross this boundary line marked by the strait. The precise nature of this porous marine border meant that frontierlike conditions continued long after the borderlands-to-border transition that Adelman and Aron detail. Borderlands qualities of contestation and sharing among distinct peoples interfered with settler-colonial efforts to create first imperial and then national spaces in the Pacific Northwest.

To demonstrate how this happened, the first two chapters discuss the ča·di· borderland and its indigenous, marine characteristics in the late eighteenth century both before and during encounters with non-Natives. Chapter 1 opens with the 1788 encounter between Chief Tatoosh, the highest-ranked Makah titleholder at the time, and John Meares, a British maritime fur trader. Focusing on the web of regional trade and kinship ties, this chapter explains that borderlands networks and related diplomatic protocols already existed when Europeans and Euro-Americans arrived in this corner of the Pacific. Indigenous networks and protocols shaped the initial period of Native and non-Native interactions on the Northwest Coast from the late eighteenth century into the 1800s. Makahs used customary marine practices, such as hunting sea otters and fishing, to engage expanding networks of exchange. Providing sea otter pelts and provisioning ships were the first examples of this pattern that recurs throughout Makah history. By exploiting networks of trade and kinship, Native chiefs controlled spaces on their own terms and frustrated imperial processes. Their ability to do so reveals that the broader processes of encounter, resistance, and conquest reshaped the indigenous world.

Chapter 2 explores the role of violence and theft within the ča·di· borderland during the maritime fur trade. Although these activities marked encounters among Natives and non-Natives, they were much more than the simple conflicts and acts of plundering that ship captains and crews perceived. Violence marked encounters because rival chiefs competed with each other to control space, resources, and people in the borderlands. When imperial actors entered the borderlands, they exacerbated older lines of tension, created new opportunities for conflict, and applied their own tools of violence. In the indigenous borderlands where distinct peoples contested over and shared spaces and resources, violence and theft were neither anomalous nor a result of miscommunication: threats and violence were mechanisms central to both Native and imperial processes of this period. Indigenous leaders such as Tatoosh used these to expand their influence and to frustrate imperial designs for domination of tribal space. The first two chapters explore how these networks and protocols changed to accommodate and incorporate non-Natives into Northwest Coast societies.

As the maritime fur trade shifted its focus farther north along the Northwest Coast during the early nineteenth century, Makah men used another customary marine practice—whaling—to engage the Hudson's Bay Company (HBC), a new commercial and colonial force in the region. Chapter 3 opens with Makahs "pillaging" a shipwrecked HBC vessel and concludes with the smallpox epidemic, two critical events in the early 1850s. These incidents resulted from the changing nature of the mid-nineteenth-century ča·di· borderland, specifically the transition from maritime to land-based fur trade, the rising power of the Hudson's Bay Company, and the arrival of British and US settlers. The region also underwent a geopolitical change as the United States and Britain maneuvered to define their colonial claims to the Oregon Country, an area of joint occupation in the Far North American West until 1846, when the two nations divided the region along the forty-ninth parallel. In the process, a more traditional borderlands between two colonial empires emerged, yet conditions of the preexisting indigenous borderlands continued long after the two nation states settled the boundary question. Amid these changes, the supposed pillaging of the ship and the smallpox deaths highlight the ways indigenous peoples such as Makahs experienced, interacted with, and responded to settler-colonialism. The actions of Makah chiefs maintained their control and ability to influence others. By engaging new opportunities, the same chiefs also made colonialism possible in this region.

The rise of Euro-American power in the region brought new challenges and opportunities to the People of the Cape, and they responded by continuing to exploit and protect tribal marine space. Focusing on Makah engagement with Euro-American officials, settlers, and traders, chapter 4 begins by examining the 1855 Treaty of Neah Bay. Despite the emerging imbalance of power between Natives and newcomers, Makahs used the treaty to protect their rights to customary marine space. By calling the sea his country during the treaty negotiations, Chief Čaqa·wiλ articulated a Makah perspective on marine space, namely that local waters were sovereign tribal space. Post-treaty data drawn from a portion of the diaries of James Swan, the first Euro-American teacher at Neah Bay, illustrate that this seascape remained a space of Native connections, despite the 1846 creation of a US-British borderline along the Strait of Juan de Fuca.[34] Statements made by Makah chiefs during the treaty negotiations and actions of Native borderlanders demonstrate that the People of the Cape were trying to find a place for themselves in the settler-colonial world. Chapter 4 also reveals that the Makah perspective on marine space challenged the emerging Euro-American view on coastal waters as both a resource commons and an appropriate boundary line dividing colonial spaces.

With their access and rights protected in the Treaty of Neah Bay, Makah whalers and sealers continued to bring wealth to their people during the second half of the nineteenth century. Chapter 5 focuses on these industries, demonstrating that Makahs pursued a "moditional economy" (a combination of *mod*ern and trad*itional*) by combining customary marine practices and indigenous borderlands networks with modern technology and opportunities to succeed at a time when many American Indian communities fell into poverty.[35] Their successes and capital investments in North Pacific extractive industries allowed Makahs to mitigate some of the worst assimilation efforts while expanding access to marine space. Wealthy Makah sealers bought schooners, began hunting seals as far abroad as northern California and the Bering Sea, and made large profits, which, in turn, they invested in regional industries and used to finance cultural practices that federal officials were trying to prohibit. Swan's diary entries later in the century illustrate that the People of the Cape and others continued to experience the reservation's coastal boundary line as a permeable zone and space of connections rather than one of confinement.

But the end of the nineteenth century proved to be a turning point for Makahs. At this time, national conservation laws, international agreements, and the growing ability of nation-states to enforce boundaries began to constrict Makah marine space and to cut them out of the commercial industries of the North Pacific while privileging Euro-American users. Early conservation efforts codified into law the non-Native assumption that indigenous peoples only hunted for subsistence purposes, thereby strengthening the stereotype of the Ecological Indian and cutting Makahs out of commercial opportunities. Although Makahs suspended an active whaling practice in 1928—a decision they made for their own reasons—they maintained the whaling tradition through other means and kept a strong connection to the sea.

Within this context, the People of the Cape found their halibut and salmon fisheries under increasing pressure from non-Natives. Chapter 6 examines the Makah fisheries of the late nineteenth and twentieth centuries, explaining that overfishing by better capitalized non-Native fishers and local, state, and international conservation regulations and agreements undercut the initial success experienced by Native fishers. These factors also separated Makahs from marine foods, as tribal fishers needed to sell their dwindling catches to buyers for cash and to satisfy bureaucratic regulations. When the tribal nation's economic and political economy eroded in the early twentieth century, it became more susceptible to the increased assimilation efforts of government officials then bent on controlling Native peoples. However, we should not see this narrative as one of decline, a simplistic framing that often characterizes histories of American Indians.[36] The story of the Makahs and the relationship to their marine space does not end there. Beginning in the 1930s, Makahs—through a newly formed tribal council—fought back with various legal and political strategies to reclaim access to marine space.

Returning to the current controversy over Makah whaling, the Conclusion revisits the themes of indigenous borderlands and ways that the People of the Cape have combined customary marine practices with new opportunities and technology. Opponents of Makah whaling denigrate the tribal nation for being motivated by a naive and antimodern desire to live in the past. Makah history, however, reveals that this tribal nation has continuously exploited marine space and borderlands networks to chart a traditional future. Modern Makah whaling illustrates that this tribal nation is living in the present and moving into the future while retaining what is best about its traditions. The current whaling efforts exemplify how Makahs are using customary practices to reclaim their marine space while protecting their sovereignty and charting a course for a particular identity in the modern world.

"THE POWER OF WICKANINNISH ENDS HERE"

The clear, sunny June afternoon made it easy for Makahs to spot the sails of a non-Native ship approaching one of their seasonal villages. Chief Tatoosh had anticipated the vessel's arrival since it had begun to creep down the west coast of Vancouver Island three weeks earlier, after spending a month at Nootka Sound. These strangers had been in Nuu-chah-nulth communities, trading for furs with neighboring rival chiefs, Maquinna (Mowachaht) and Wickaninnish (Clayoquot), and the outsiders had recently agreed to an exclusive trading arrangement with Wickaninnish. In preparation for the strangers' arrival, Tatoosh's warriors clothed themselves in the skins of *tiˑčaq* ("tee-chuhk," sea otters), painted their faces with red and black ocher, and armed themselves with bows, barbed arrows, and mussel shell–tipped harpoons. In order to show his stout, courageous heart, Tatoosh painted his face black and added glittering sand.[1] When the vessel entered Makah waters in 1788, Tatoosh led his warriors in numerous large war canoes as they surrounded the intruding ship, the first of its kind to visit his people.

Tatoosh boarded the vessel, the *Felice Adventurer*, captained by John Meares, a British Royal Navy veteran who had seen action during the Revolutionary War. Meares noted this encounter in the official account of the voyage, writing, "The chief of this spot, whose name is Tatootche, did us the favour of a visit, and so surly and forbidding a character we had not yet seen. . . . He informed us that the power of Wicananish ended here, and that we were now within the limits of his government, which extended a considerable way to the Southwest."[2] Meares gave the imposing chief a "small present." This insulted Tatoosh, and he ignored it and failed to reciprocate with a gift as he might normally have done. The Makah chief departed and did not allow his people to trade with the newcomers.

After leaving the *Felice*, Tatoosh watched the British send out their longboat to look for safe anchorage for the evening. Meares hoped to sail deeper into the Strait of Juan de Fuca, which opened up east of Tatoosh Island, in order to determine whether it was the fabled Northwest Passage. A firm believer in the existence of this desired waterway, Meares wanted to find it so he could claim it for the glory of his nation—not to mention the £20,000 reward the British Parliament had offered since 1745 to the first captain who discovered and sailed through the elusive body of water. Canoes surrounded the longboat heading toward the shore. Knowing their chief's dissatisfaction with these strangers, Makah men intimidated them, jumping into the longboat from their canoes and stealing whatever they could pry loose. These brazen thefts enraged the crew, but Meares and his officers maintained order throughout this tense encounter. Fearing violence, the sailors rowed the longboat back to the *Felice*, and the vessel sailed three leagues into the Pacific Ocean to prevent a Makah ambush under the cover of darkness.

The following morning, Tatoosh led four hundred warriors in canoes out to the vessel. They circled the *Felice*, demonstrating the sea power that the chief could deploy. Tatoosh paired this show of force with a peaceful overture as his warriors sang a song similar to the ones of friendship that Meares and his crew had heard previously at Nootka Sound. But Meares ignored the gesture and compounded his earlier insults by failing to reciprocate in any manner. Keenly aware of their isolation, Meares decided to withdraw his vessel and crew of fifty sailors, smiths, carpenters, and artisans from Makah waters. The British captain's exploration of the Strait of Juan de Fuca would need to wait: the *Felice* fled on the first wind.[3]

After sailing south of Cape Flattery, Meares met few Indians. But those he did meet—such as the father and son who paddled out from Shoalwater Bay (Willapa Bay) and offered sea otter skins for exchange—had probably heard of the non-Native trade vessel's presence. As Meares wrote in his account, "It is more than probable that some of the natives of Tatootche's district may have occasionally roamed this far, and communicated the intelligence of strangers arriving in ships to trade for furs."[4] Meares's impression of communication in this region was accurate—news spread quickly along this stretch of the indigenous North American coast.

Less than two weeks later, the *Felice* returned to the Strait of Juan de Fuca. Meares and his crew spent several more weeks at the entrance to the strait, but on the Vancouver Island side to avoid any further encounters with Tatoosh. Still hoping to discover the Northwest Passage, the captain sent the longboat out to explore the strait. However, Makah and Pacheedaht warriors attacked the small craft and sent the crew limping back to the *Felice*.[5] Fearing the pos-

Chief Tatoosh. His hat depicts a whaling scene,
highlighting his status as a whaler. Drawing by
José Cardero, 1789–94, who accompanied the
Alejandro Malaspina expedition to the Pacific.
Image courtesy the Museo de América, Madrid.

sibility of more attacks, Meares returned to the safety of Nootka Sound, where
he hoped that Chief Maquinna's authority would protect him from any hostile
Natives.

Meares and his contemporaries during the early encounter era (1774–78)
through the maritime fur trade (1778–1840s) found themselves in an indigenous
seascape defined by particular borderlands networks and protocols. Alongside
oral histories and written accounts of other explorers and maritime fur traders,
the story of this encounter on the Northwest Coast reveals that Meares had ventured into an indigenous borderland that existed long before the arrival of
Europeans in this far corner of the Pacific Ocean. Non-Native interactions
with the distinct peoples of this region went well when they conformed to indigenous expectations. But outsiders encountered befuddling and often violent

resistance—or felt the need to resort to violence themselves—when they ig-nored or misunderstood the cultural rules of this particular borderland.

Like any borderland, a combination of diplomatic protocols and overlapping networks defined the specific characteristics of the ča·di· ("cha-dee") borderland. By interacting with each other and with outsiders from beyond the borderlands, the distinct peoples inhabiting this region developed protocols to guide these interactions and unfolding encounters. These networks connected peoples and places within this dynamic region, revealing how indigenous borderlanders shared and contested marine space. A series of trade networks facilitated the distribu-tion of goods while providing opportunities for chiefs to compete over control-ling the terms of exchange. Similarly, an intricate web of kinship networks drew families and communities together across the ča·di· borderland. Yet even these intimate connections could be tense because high-ranking families competed for kin throughout this region. During the generations before the arrival of non-Natives in the 1770s, indigenous leaders and groups had shaped and contested these protocols and networks of trade and kinship in the ča·di· borderland.[6]

During the late eighteenth and early nineteenth centuries, those living in the ča·di· borderland engaged the related protocols and networks in meaningful ways. More important, individuals such as Chief Tatoosh had enough power to inter-rupt imperial processes. He prevented Meares from exploring the Strait of Juan de Fuca and from expanding British claims even further in the area. Meares and his contemporaries wanted to impose imperial corridors of transportation and trade through Makah marine space. Drawing on his mastery of local net-works of exchange and kinship, however, Tatoosh resisted these attempts, except when such processes conformed to his own agendas and priorities. Through chiefly influence and authority, he decided who could trade and under what con-ditions. More dramatically, Tatoosh deployed his sea power to control the move-ment of others in and through Makah marine space.

The arrival of non-Native navigators and traders in the ča·di· borderland re-sulted in clashing perceptions of both terrestrial and marine spaces. Northwest Coast societies rooted their spatial perceptions in locality and historically con-tested boundaries separating distinct peoples. Yet non-Natives saw these same spaces through the lens of an "imaginative geography," a representation of a dis-tant, "alien" region ripe for exploitation by European—and only European—empires.[7] These differing spatial perceptions applied to both terrestrial and marine spaces; water, like land, acquires significance because it "is saturated with the ideas, meanings, values, and potentials that [societies] have conferred upon it."[8] While Meares and his fellow ship captains of the late eighteenth century saw the ocean simply as a space to traverse, their freedom to do so, especially in the "imaginative" waters of the Native Northwest Coast, ought to have gone un-contested, they believed. For a Royal Navy veteran such as Meares, the sea—specifically Great Britain's hegemony over it—constituted a critical component of his English identity and his role in imperial design.[9]

Although Tatoosh probably did not understand all the intricacies of particu-lar imperial visions, he understood that Meares and his men were attempting to impose their own rules and control over this indigenous marine borderland. He knew that keeping his leadership status in the borderlands depended on the abil-ity to control customary waters while expanding his authority. Within this in-digenous marine borderland where titleholders competed for influence over others, Chief Tatoosh and his followers understood the importance of using power to produce and control social spaces by making them uniquely Makah through the imposition and enforcement of culturally specific protocols and practices that both shaped and reinforced identity. Perhaps he would have understood French sociologist Henri Lefebvre's argument that a society that fails to produce its own space disappears. Traditional historical narratives assume that a Euro-pean imperial vision quickly crushed indigenous configurations of space. But the history of the Makahs reveals that influential chiefs followed Tatoosh's lead and produced customary marine space long after Meares departed the Strait of Juan de Fuca for good.[10]

DISTINCT PEOPLES OF THE ČA·DI· BORDERLAND

Most people characterize the Northwest Coast region as a bountiful environ-ment; the reality, however, is more complex. Local oceanographic features, sea-sonal variations, and long-range cycles and fluctuations in marine life made specific places and times richer than others. When non-Natives began sailing into the Pacific Northwest, Makah waters off Cape Flattery were among the most abundant of all nearshore microenvironments in the ča·di· borderland. This nat-ural wealth of the sea attracted many distinct peoples, Natives and non-Natives, to the region and helped to ensure that this would be a borderland. By 1788, when Chief Tatoosh confronted Meares and his imperial vision, the Makah leader and his ancestors had already spent generations strengthening their control over these rich waters and transforming them into Makah marine space.

In the ča·di· borderland, particular peoples became known by their locations and the natural wealth tied to these places. Before the appearance of non-Natives on the Northwest Coast, Makahs already possessed the beginnings of what be-came their tribal identity in the mid-nineteenth century. They called themselves Qʷidičča?a·tx̌ ("kwih-dihch-chuh-aht"), "the people who live by the rocks and the seagulls," or as it has been glossed in English, "the People of the Cape." Across the strait, related Nuu-chah-nulth peoples knew them as Kla-iz-zarts, which means "southerly people." During the late eighteenth century, non-Natives came to know Makahs as Classets, which is what they heard when Nuu-chah-nulth peoples such as the Mowachahts said Kla-iz-zarts. But Kla-iz-zarts also has the important connotation of "outside, toward the sea," owing to their access to oceanic resources such as whales, seals, and halibut, which they considered "outside resources." The S'Klallams, unrelated neighbors on the Olympic Peninsula, called them Makahs, the name they are known by today. Meaning "generous with food," this term reflected the abundance Makahs could reap from customary waters. The People of the Cape likely earned this name because of the many extravagant feasts they threw, some which lasted for weeks. Oil and whale sinew were important trade goods; they exchanged these commodities with peoples throughout this marine borderland. Non-Makahs depended on them to provide both the greatest quantity and highest quality of these goods, and this productivity became a central component of Makah identity.[11]

When Meares and other non-Natives arrived in the čaꞏdiꞏ borderland, they entered a zone already contested by many ranked leaders, each representing a distinct people and controlling a specific area. In the north section of the borderlands, Europeans and Euro-Americans encountered Maquinna, the most powerful leader of the Mowachahts during the maritime fur trade era. In the mid-eighteenth century, Maquinna had begun to unite several villages in Nootka Sound into what scholars have called the Yuquot-Tahsis confederacy. Southeast along the Vancouver Island coastline, non-Native traders encountered Wickaninnish, who had recently consolidated his chiefly authority through violent conquest of Clayoquot Sound's villages.[12] On the southwestern entrance to the Strait of Juan de Fuca lay the Cape Flattery villages over which Tatoosh held authority.

As non-Native navigators and traders sailed from one village to another, they crossed indigenous boundaries. These lands and waters were geopolitical spaces over which leaders such as Maquinna, Wickaninnish, and Tatoosh exercised a type of Northwest Coast indigenous sovereignty. When examining indigenous sovereignty, we need to remember that "sovereignty is historically contingent" because it is "embedded within specific social relations in which it is invoked and given meaning."[13] In the late eighteenth century when Meares and other non-Natives appeared on the scene, Northwest Coast societies rooted sovereignty in chiefly power and authority. Although leadership emanated from lineage-based titleholders, belonging to a high-ranking family did not guarantee that lower-ranked people would respect one's authority. Leaders maintained authority by providing for their people through the management of resources, by throwing potlatches, and by challenging outsiders. Chiefs such as Tatoosh controlled sovereign spaces, both marine and terrestrial, in this manner.

The highest-ranked individuals within their respective societies, Maquinna, Wickaninnish, and Tatoosh saw themselves as equals. They owned lucrative outside resources, such as whales and halibut banks. The fact that these resources were owned challenges a core assumption of encounter narratives, namely the idea that property-oriented Western societies claimed lands and resources that Natives only held in common and did not fully use. From the Northwest Coast perspective, the non-Native vessels laden with trade goods represented new, outside resources for chiefs to own and manage to the advantage of their people. Seeking to fit the new floating resources within their own cultural framework of property, perhaps they conceived of these ships as something similar to drift whales, leviathans that had died at sea and drifted ashore. When a dead whale drifted into a community's waters or onto a beach, it became the property of the ranking whaling chief, who held the title to these places and resources. Northwest Coast people believed that drift whales did not appear by chance; they resulted from the power and rituals of chiefs, so they belonged to these individuals. Therefore, as owners of these types of resources, titleholders took actions to monopolize trade with ships when they appeared in sovereign Native waters.[14]

Although Europeans did not understand the complexities of indigenous property rights, they did witness and experience tensions related to their appearance in Native waters. From the beginning of his 1778 sojourn at Friendly Cove in Nootka Sound, Captain James Cook and his crew witnessed Chief Maquinna's efforts to control access to the British vessels. When several canoes of "Strangers" arrived to trade with the British, Maquinna marshaled his people to take up arms to defend his right to monopolize access to the ships. Ten years later, Wickaninnish deployed many canoes to capture men from a neighboring village who had visited Meares's *Felice* without the chief's consent. Wickaninnish's warriors dragged one of the "intruders" into the woods and executed him. As they did with other important resources, chiefs moved quickly to establish and maintain control over the new sources of wealth.[15]

Rivals in the ča·di· borderland contested other leaders' efforts at control. When Meares sailed from Friendly Cove to Wickaninnish's village at Clayoquot in 1788, the chief's brothers, Hanna and Detootche, paddled out to the *Felice* and attempted to entice the captain to anchor at their villages instead.[16] Although boundaries separated the sovereign spaces of particular leaders—and indigenous peoples understood these demarcations—in reality, these were fuzzy zones of shared and contested opportunities, where one person's authority overlapped with another's. Sailing through these zones, non-Natives attempted to transform

these microborderlands into clearer sovereign spaces, thereby heightening indigenous competition in the ča·di· borderland.

Tatoosh's confrontation with Meares provides one of the strongest expressions
of Northwest Coast sovereignty in the late eighteenth century. When the Makah
chief boarded the *Felice,* he made it clear to the captain—despite the vagaries
of English speakers trying to understand Qʷi·qʷi·diččaq ("kwih-kwih-dihch-
chuhk," the Makah language) statements—that they were now in his waters,
which differed from Wickaninnish's waters, and that his authority extended a
considerable way down the coast. Tatoosh also exercised his authority over his
sovereign waters by not allowing his people to trade with Meares's party. Additionally, Tatoosh deployed his sea power of four hundred warriors from several
Cape Flattery villages to intimidate the British into leaving his marine space.
Tatoosh had the strength to curtail imperial efforts at transforming this space
into a transportation corridor and trade zone controlled by non-Natives. These
actions by Maquinna, Wickaninnish, and Tatoosh reveal some of the dimensions of indigenous Northwest Coast sovereignty at this time and illustrate that
these societies thought of themselves as distinct peoples.

DIPLOMACY IN THE ČA·DI· BORDERLAND

Before non-Natives appeared in the late eighteenth century, the inhabitants
of this borderland had developed some standard protocols, forms of ceremony
and etiquette observed by diplomats and peoples, when engaging in some activity in the spaces of others. Borderlanders employed a particular protocol
when entering a titleholder's sovereign space. Although he provided few details,
British trader James Colnett observed the protocol at work north of Cape Flattery when indigenous outsiders entered Muchalaht waters in eastern Nootka
Sound, where he had anchored for several days in July 1787. A non-Muchalaht
chief in a large canoe approached the village, stopping "almost out of hearing,
& sight of the usual Song & gestures, which are perform'd on their passage
when going a visiting." Colnett's comment implies that outsiders performed a
standard type of song and set of gestures when coming into the space of another
group. Other non-Natives also noted that animated speeches were an important component of this protocol. In 1817, the French trader Camille de Roquefeuil observed what he characterized as a "violent speech" that Maquinna
delivered when a Clayoquot canoe entered Nootka Sound to investigate the arrival of the *Bordelais.* Although we do not know precisely what Maquinna said,
the Clayoquots did not trade with the *Bordelais* while in Nootka Sound, probably
because the local ranking leader did not grant them any trading privileges at the

time. So, part of this protocol established permission from the owners of the area to approach. If outsiders did not receive permission—indicated by either verbal denial or a violent reaction—they had to keep away.[17]

This protocol was central to the production and maintenance of indigenous space in this region. Through it, visitors recognized the sovereign authority of the local titleholder. Chiefs engaged in the protocol to affirm the production of their space, to exercise leadership responsibilities, and to confront outsiders. By respecting the protocol, lower-ranking chiefs and commoners affirmed an owner's title. When non-Natives entered indigenous spaces in the ča·di· borderland, Native leaders used this protocol to exhibit indigenous property rights to the outsiders and to frustrate the extension of imperial visions of space and control.

Although the historical record has failed to capture the full details of the protocol that indigenous peoples of the ča·di· borderland used when entering another's space, oral and archival sources have memorialized adapted versions employed in several first encounters with Europeans. Nuu-chah-nulths in the early twentieth century recalled that sometime in the late eighteenth century, Nanaimis and Tsaxawasip—now remembered by history as Chief Maquinna—spotted an approaching object in the distant ocean off Nootka Sound. They wondered whether it might be an island rising from the ocean. As it grew larger, they saw that it was a kind of watercraft that moved quickly and made great waves. Some thought that its power came from *x̌ix̌i·ktu·yak* ("hih-heek-too-yuhk"), the lightning snake cast by Thunderbird when he hunted whales, and that the supernatural snake must be working underwater to propel the vessel forward with such speed. Because others guessed that it might be an enchanted salmon transformed by magic, one of the canoes that went out to greet it carried Hahatsaik, a spiritual specialist who had power over all kinds of salmon. Donning a red cedar bark cap and apron, she sang to the unknown watercraft while shaking whalebone rattles with each hand. Tsaxawasip and Nanaimis also approached in their own canoes. They brought with them several high-quality sea otter skins and discovered that the vessel contained men, not enchanted salmon people. Wearing a fine, gold-braided hat, one of the strangers offered blankets and his hat to the two chiefs, who, in return, gave him the skins they had brought as a gift. Then the people welcomed the newcomers to their village by performing the wolf dance on the beach.[18]

Other oral versions of first encounters between peoples of the ča·di· borderland and Europeans include additional details. In some stories—such as this one from Winifred Davis, a Clayoquot whose grandmother was from Nootka Sound—Mowachaht warriors, not spiritual specialists or chiefs, first approached the ship. They received pilot bread (hardtack) from the captain, an act that

Northwest Coast peoples greeting Captain Cook's *Resolution* at Nootka Sound. Orators in three or four canoes are initiating the diplomatic protocol by welcoming outsiders into their space. Mowachahts and Europeans appear to be engaged in possibly clandestine trade out the stern of the ship. Engraving by John Webber, 1778. © The British Library Board, Add. 15514 B, f10.

would have indicated the strangers' friendliness. The warriors in the canoe kept repeating the Nootkan word *nu·tka·ʔičim* ("noo-tka-eecheem"), telling them to go around the harbor. Misunderstanding this as the name for the place, the strangers named it Nootka Sound. In another oral account of this first encounter, Peter Webster (Ahousaht) relates that the vessel became stuck when entering the sound. Mowachahts sent a whaling canoe out to direct them around the point. Mistaking the blocks (wooden pulleys) on the masts for skulls, Hesquiahts of Vancouver Island believed that the dead crewed these vessels. But they quickly discovered that these strangers were just humans.[19]

Europeans also tell their own stories of first encounters in the ča·di· borderland. These begin with the Spanish, the first Europeans to sail into this corner of the Pacific. Concerned about Russian and British expansion in the North Pacific, Antonio María de Bucareli, the viceroy of New Spain, ordered some secret expeditions to chart Spanish claims along the western coastline of North America. Off the entrance to Nootka Sound in 1774, several canoes came out to investigate the *Santiago*, the first Spanish vessel to enter the ča·di· borderland. Fray Tomás de la Peña, one of the Franciscan priests accompanying the expedition, noted that the canoes remained "a musket-shot from the ship," their occupants sometimes crying out in a "mournful tone of voice." The other Franciscan, Fray Juan Crespi, wrote that they seemed to be making gestures for the Spaniards to go away. In the morning, the Spaniards found themselves surrounded by fifteen canoes carrying one hundred men and women, and the paddlers appeared to give them advice on good anchorage. Captain Juan Pérez ordered the longboat into the water so it could go ashore in order to take possession of the land. But high winds and rough seas prevented them from entering the sound. In the meantime, the crew aboard the *Santiago* conducted a brisk trade, exchanging clothes, Monterrey shells, and knives for sea otter furs, herring, and clothing made from woven cedar bark. When the weather became too rough and pushed the ship toward a nearby rocky point, Pérez ordered the anchor cut free, and the vessel sailed south away from Nootka Sound.[20]

Captain Cook and his crew left a much more complete and extensive record of their first encounter in the ča·di· borderland. When the *Discovery* and *Resolution* entered Nootka Sound on March 29, 1778, they made a less-than-impressive entrance. Approaching the entrance to the sound, the ships became becalmed, and they had to lower all the boats to tow in the ship. On their arrival, more than thirty canoes surrounded them. The first to pull alongside the *Discovery* held an orator who "stood up and held forth a long while." He pointed farther into the inlet, indicating that he wanted them to approach the village and anchor in front of it. Midshipman Edward Riou described the speech as a "harangue," while surgeon David Samwell emphasized the orator's "strange Motions." Afterward, the occupants of the canoes "all sung in a wild Manner, which some of our sailors compared to that of a Brother Tar on board who it seems in his time had cryed Potatoes about London." Then the orator presented his cedar bark hat and other objects as a gift; in return, he received a large ax, which appeared to make him content. After completing this initial exchange, other Mowachahts then exchanged various articles for iron goods. When non-Mowachahts came to trade with the British during Cook's monthlong sojourn in Friendly Cove, the "strangers" repeated similar versions of these performances.[21]

How would Northwest Coast peoples have conceptualized the appearance of Europeans? Before the arrival of Europeans in the 1770s, these borderlanders did have experience with people from beyond their village communities. Possibly they would have categorized outsiders as belonging to one of three groups.[22]

Local outsiders came from villages within the ča·di· borderland, and they knew one another very well through previous networks of trade, kinship, and violence. Distant outsiders came from beyond this indigenous marine borderland, yet they, too, were recognized—but not as well known as fellow borderlanders—from previous interactions. For example, people in this region knew of and took precautions against Haida slave raiders who paddled their large war canoes from the Queen Charlotte Islands of northern British Columbia to strike at villages in the ča·di· borderland and Puget Sound.[23] Other distant outsiders of this time would have included the Nimpkish Kwakwaka'wakw, with whom the Mowachahts traded oil from eulachons, a type of smelt, via overland trails.[24] A third category of outsiders encompassed powerful nonhuman peoples, denizens of the supernatural world with whom Northwest Coast peoples interacted regularly. According to Northwest Coast worldviews, the physical dimension was a manifestation of the spiritual realm, and communication and travel between the two worlds was not unusual.[25]

When Mowachahts first encountered Pérez and Cook, they knew that they were dealing with outsiders. But were they distant outsiders from somewhere far away or transformed nonhuman people? When the first canoes went out, Mowachahts appeared to hedge their bets by sending out a woman with power over salmon people and an orator who could greet them with the proper protocols for human outsiders. Just minutes into these encounters, Mowachahts concluded that the newcomers were not supernatural beings—they were strangers from someplace far from the ča·di· borderland. Indigenous peoples quickly abandoned the idea that these were supernatural or transformed beings for several reasons. First, when they got close enough to or boarded the vessels, they saw that the blocks on the masts were not skulls. Second, the brisk trade that arose between Natives and non-Natives indicated their shared humanity. These strangers then became a fourth category of outsider, mamáni, a Nootkan term that meant "those living on the water and floating around, like they have no land"— Makahs called them babałid ("buh-buh-lthid").[26] Late eighteenth-century inhabitants of this indigenous marine borderland knew that outsiders—local, distant, mamáni or babałid, and supernatural—fell somewhere along a spectrum of exchange ranging from contestation to sharing. Protocol helped them determine where on the spectrum to situate an unfolding encounter.

By 1787, when Meares's Felice sailed into the ča·di· borderland, Natives had codified the protocol for greeting babałids when they entered indigenous spaces. Meares would have known what to expect because he had spoken with others who had visited the Northwest Coast previously. He even brought with him charts and logs from earlier voyages.[27] Maquinna and Callicum, the ranking chiefs of

Yuquot, employed this protocol when welcoming the *Felice* to Friendly Cove. The vessel had already been there for three days before the chiefs, who were visiting Wickaninnish when Meares sailed into their waters, made their appearance. They approached the vessel in twelve canoes, each holding eighteen men. The canoes paraded around the ship while the occupants sang "a song of a pleasing though sonorous melody," gestured toward the north and south, and cried out *wacush, wacush*, which meant "friends." The two chiefs then came aboard, and one of them likely made a speech. Knowing the rudiments of Northwest Coast protocol, Meares—an outsider in their waters—gave the chiefs presents of copper, iron, and several other items. They reciprocated by throwing off their sea otter garments and presenting them to the British captain. On completion of the formal gift exchange, Maquinna allowed Meares to anchor the *Felice* in Mowachaht waters.

Maquinna employed a separate protocol to open formal trade relations with the captain and crew of the *Felice*. After the vessel anchored off Yuquot, he invited Meares to his longhouse—a structure whose enormous size impressed the British guests—where he and Callicum initiated an exchange of presents. In front of a "great number of spectators," the two chiefs ceremonially gave the captain some sea otter skins amid "great shouting and gestures of exultation." The audience quieted when Meares presented the chiefs with his reciprocal gifts. Despite Meares's efforts to conduct a "common barter" between his crew and lower-ranked Mowachahts—and one based on the values of articles exchanged—Maquinna managed the exchanges at Yuquot as one of "reciprocal presents."[28] During the *Felice*'s sojourn in Nootka Sound, exchanges were often conducted in the ceremonial manner described above. Meares and other traders found the notion of reciprocity familiar because it had been a guiding principle in the land fur trade in northeastern North America for more than a century.[29]

When Meares arrived in Clayoquot Sound the following month, he relied on Wickaninnish's local knowledge of the waters to navigate a safe anchorage. Accompanied by a fleet of canoes, the chief greeted the *Felice* and then boarded the vessel to pilot it into the harbor. As Meares noted, "Wicananish proved an excellent pilot, and was not only indefatigable in his own exertions, but equally attentive to the conduct of his canoes, in their attendance upon us" by helping the larger vessel avoid dangerous reefs and submerged rocks.[30] When the *Felice* anchored in front of Clayoquot village, Wickaninnish remained on board while Meares "entertained" him—probably presenting him with small gifts, feeding him, and showing him around the vessel—for most of the day. Meanwhile, many Clayoquots came out to the ship to trade fish, wild onions, and berries for small bits of iron and other items.

The following day, the chief invited them to his longhouse. Arranged to display his power and authority, Wickaninnish sat at the upper end of the house, surrounded by other high-ranking individuals and chests overhung with bladders of oil and large slices of whale flesh and blubber. Notably, "Festoons of human skulls, arranged with some attention to uniformity, were disposed in almost every part where they could be placed, and were considered as a very splendid decoration of the royal apartment." The estimated eight hundred guests inside the longhouse were enjoying "the most luxurious feast we had ever beheld."[31] Wickaninnish's brother escorted the British guests to seats near the leader. When the feast ended, Meares presented gifts of blankets and two copper teakettles to the chief, who reciprocated with fifty jet-black sea otter skins. These he gave to Meares with an accompanying speech. After this grand spectacle, Wickaninnish managed the trade of sea otter skins with Meares, whereas he allowed his people to continue exchanging goods of lesser value, such as fish, berries, and greens, with the crew.

These separate but related protocols conformed to indigenous practices and engaged several distinct audiences for a variety of purposes. In the first protocol on the water, Maquinna and Wickaninnish demonstrated to Meares that he had entered their sovereign spaces, the waters in front of Yuquot and Clayoquot villages. The fleets of canoes that accompanied these titleholders when they first approached the vessel exhibited the sea power each chief could put on the water, a display that Meares, a veteran of the Royal Navy, understood. Wickaninnish affirmed that the *Felice* was in his sovereign waters by literally bringing the vessel into his marine space. Piloting the ship also illustrates how, at these crucial moments of encounter, indigenous local knowledge trumped the imperial conceit of simply navigating wherever captains ordered their vessels. Indigenous assistance in navigating unknown waters also facilitated imperial processes such as exploration and trade.[32] Through the giving of gifts aboard the ship, Meares thought he had guaranteed Clayoquot compliance with his terms; to Northwest Coast chiefs and their followers, however, he had acknowledged their sovereignty and payed for the privilege to anchor in their waters. When Maquinna and Callicum reciprocated by giving the captain their garments—which had a much greater value in both societies than the gifts the captain had presented—they demonstrated their hospitality, influence, wealth, and chiefly authority. Similar to the logic that underlay the potlatch tradition, titleholders displayed power by giving away their wealth. According to the sociocultural standards of the Northwest Coast, they demonstrated that they were of a higher status than Meares by giving more valuable gifts.[33]

Similar dynamics shaped the second protocol in the longhouse. Unlike the shipboard performances, these occurred in the chiefs' longhouses, spaces that belonged to Maquinna and Wickaninnish. The Clayoquot chief demonstrated his influence and ownership of the region around Clayoquot Sound through the size of his longhouse—the larger the structure, the more important the chief, and one that could hold eight hundred people indicated the scale of his power—and the prominent display of whale products he had hunted and skulls of warriors he had vanquished. The skulls also served to warn both his followers and visitors about what could happen if they crossed the powerful chief. At Yuquot, the Mowachaht chiefs presented their gifts first, demonstrating to Meares that by the power of their wealth, they held authority in this part of Nootka Sound. Meares acceded to their authority by reciprocating with gifts of appropriate value. Although the order was reversed in the performance in Wickaninnish's longhouse, the effect was the same. The Clayoquot chief's gift of fifty prime sea otter skins outstripped the blankets and teakettles Meares offered first, thereby demonstrating Wickaninnish's superiority over the British captain. But these performances also targeted an indigenous audience, the lower-ranked Mowachahts, Clayoquots, and any local outsiders present. Through these protocol performances, Maquinna and Wickaninnish affirmed their authority over their marine waters, villages, and exchanges with mamáṅis. Most important, the chiefs demonstrated to Natives and non-Natives alike their power to control space and people on their terms.

Unknowingly blundering among chiefs competing for authority, influence, and power, Meares inflamed these tensions by being rude to Chief Tatoosh, explaining simply why his encounter with the Makah chief differed from his interactions with other ranking Mowachaht and Clayoquot leaders in the čaˑdiˑ borderland. Similar to Maquinna and Wickaninnish, Tatoosh approached the babałid vessel with his large fleet of canoes and warriors. Unlike the previous two encounters, however, Tatoosh presented a more formidable and antagonistic appearance—his warriors brandished threatening-looking weapons, and the chief himself had blackened his face in a "surly and forbidding" manner. The initial conditions of this encounter off Cape Flattery differed from those on Vancouver Island, which accounted for the confrontational reception that the British trader received. When Meares sailed into Nootka Sound, he had brought with him Comekala, one of Maquinna's brothers who had spent more than a year exploring the Pacific, visiting the Sandwich Islands and China.[34] The inhabitants of Yuquot welcomed Comekala home with an extravagant feast of whale blubber and oil. Meares sailed into Clayoquot Sound on Wickaninnish's express invitation. Conversely, the British trader brought the *Felice* into Tatoosh's sovereign waters with no invitation or beloved relative; instead, Meares arrived after having spent weeks engaged in gift and commercial exchanges with Tatoosh's rivals. Wickaninnish had even warned Meares that Tatoosh and his people were a "subtle and barbarous nation," probably hoping to limit and control Meares's trading activities within the čaˑdiˑ borderland.[35]

When Tatoosh boarded the *Felice*, Meares unknowingly insulted the powerful Makah chief twice. First, he offered only a "small present." Although Tatoosh had not been present at Yuquot or Clayoquot when Meares exchanged gifts with Maquinna and Wickaninnish, Tatoosh had likely heard about the gifts they had received from others who were present. Because he ranked as high as Maquinna and Wickaninnish in the čaˑdiˑ borderland, the trifling present failed to show him the respect he was due. Second, Meares sent his longboat into Tatoosh's waters without having paid for this right, as he had done at Friendly Cove and Clayoquot. The British were fortunate the chief's warriors harassed them only with thefts rather than with a full-fledged attack. The following day, Meares compounded his earlier insults. When Tatoosh and his warriors returned to the *Felice* the next day, they initiated the basic greeting protocol by singing the familiar welcoming song—the British had heard something similar at Yuquot and Clayoquot. Instead of inviting the chief aboard and offering appropriate gifts, the babałid crew unfurled the sails and left. As we will see in the next chapter, this insult had serious consequences for the crew.

TRADE NETWORKS IN THE ČAˑDIˑ BORDERLAND

The variable distribution of resources fueled an extensive trade network, one of the defining qualities of the čaˑdiˑ borderland. This network exemplified exchanges that linked peoples across geographic, cultural, and linguistic boundaries and were central to the social and economic patterns of American Indians before the appearance of Europeans.[36] Stretching from southeast Alaska to northern California and east to the western foothills of the Rocky Mountains, the core of this trade network centered on three, smaller overlapping regions of exchange. An analysis of the indigenous exchange of slaves, an important trade item during the eighteenth and nineteenth centuries, identifies the three trade regions: a northern network, stretching from Vancouver Island northward; a southern nexus focused around the mouth of the Columbia River, dipping south along the Oregon coast and extending north to Cape Flattery; and a third series of connections among the Coast Salish peoples of Puget Sound.[37] These networks of exchange bound indigenous borderlanders together but also provided opportunities for some to control weaker or less-advantaged peoples.

Due to their location midway between the northern and southern networks and at the entrance to the Strait of Juan de Fuca that opens to the east into Puget

Sound, Makah traders connected these three networks. As Makah historian Greig Arnold describes it, every person or good had to pass Cape Flattery if going up or down the coast or into or out of Puget Sound.[38] Access to larger quantities and a broader range of desirable trade goods processed from the sea enabled Makahs rather than neighboring peoples to dominate the nexus of these three trade networks. By leveraging their superior location and unique resources, Makahs controlled space and neighboring peoples who lacked these advantages. Their success as middlemen before the arrival of Europeans positioned them to become a critical component in expanding commercial markets in the Pacific from the late eighteenth century on. After they began trading with babałids, Makahs leveraged their control over these exchanges to extend Makah marine space at the cost of weaker neighbors.

From the early encounter era (1774–78) through the maritime fur trade (1778–1840s), non-Native captains witnessed many exchanges between Makahs and inhabitants of Vancouver Island. Although Cook never recorded the names of any of the "strangers" who came to Friendly Cove to trade with him and his crew, Makahs probably did come to Nootka Sound during the weeks he was there. After having anchored there for two weeks, a group of Indians residing to the southeast and outside Nootka Sound arrived, and accompanied by Mowachahts, they traded with the ships. They differed from other Northwest Coast peoples by a scar made across the bridge of the nose, a little below the eyes. More than sixty years later, during the US Exploring Expedition that visited the Northwest Coast in 1841, naval lieutenant Charles Wilkes met George, a Makah chief at Tatoosh Island, who had a similar scar on the bridge of his nose. Wilkes noted that it was a Makah custom to cut the nose when they had caught a whale. So perhaps these scarred "strangers" who came to trade with Cook during his sojourn at Yuquot were Makahs who had heard of the newcomers.[39]

Makah traders connected the northern and southern trade networks. After Meares had spent nearly a month among the Mowachahts at Friendly Cove, a Makah canoe—yet another "strange canoe"—arrived to trade. These people stood out from the other local outsiders who had come to trade because the British crew noticed that one of the Indians had adorned himself with a metal seal that had once belonged to Mr. Millar, an *Imperial Eagle* crewmember "murdered" by Quileutes at the mouth of the Hoh River about a year earlier. Although the sailors assumed that these were the perpetrators and urged retribution, Maquinna convinced Meares to stay their vengeful hands by explaining that the visitors were traders living north of the Quileutes and had received the item in exchange from them.[40]

Overlapping networks of communication brought news of non-Native vessels and the trade opportunities they represented to distant chiefs. Indigenous borderlanders across the region used the same network of signal fires that alerted neighboring communities to the presence of Haida raiders to broadcast news of vessels in the region.[41] Meares's account of his time on the Northwest Coast highlights several incidents that demonstrate the spreading news of trade opportunities. From his village at Clayoquot Sound, Wickaninnish had heard about the mamáni vessel's presence at Yuquot—this was why he came to Yuquot in early June to invite Meares to bring the *Felice* to his village. During Meares's sojourn at Clayoquot, news of their presence brought many visitors from the south, Makahs and other Nuu-chah-nulth groups, who came to trade; however, Wickaninnish would not allow it. As more mamánis and babałids entered the čaꞏdiꞏ borderland, chiefs kept close tabs on their movements and activities. In 1792, Don Cayetano Valdés, the Spanish commander of the *Mexicana*, noted that Chief Tatoosh could name all the English and Spanish captains who had visited the coast, Clayoquot, and Yuquot; he also knew about the other vessels present in the strait even though they had not yet stopped at Cape Flattery.[42]

Even as an increasing number of non-Native vessels shuttled back and forth between villages, a thriving indigenous exchange between Cape Flattery and Vancouver Island continued throughout the maritime fur trade. En route to Tatoosh Island to trade with Makahs, the Clayoquot chief Tootiscoosettle visited the crew of the Boston vessel *Columbia Rediviva* in the Strait of Juan de Fuca in 1791. A year later, Maquinna told the Spanish naturalist José Mariano Moziño that he traded with peoples to the south but never went any farther than Cape Flattery and Neah Bay. In the early nineteenth century, Makahs were still among the most important traders in the region, and they provided many slaves, the finest sea otter skins, great quantities of oil, whale sinew, salal cakes, ornamented canoes, haꞏykʷa ("hai-kwuh," dentalia shells used as currency), red ocher, elk skins, and mica to neighboring peoples.[43]

Trade networks also connected Makahs to indigenous peoples living south along the coast and to those in Puget Sound. Makahs traveled to the mouth of the Columbia River about two hundred miles away to trade whale products, slaves, and canoes with Chehalis, Clatsop, and Chinook Indians. In addition to making canoes, Makahs purchased some from Nuu-chah-nulth villages on Vancouver Island. They kept the new ones and sold the used canoes to people farther south after chiseling off old wood to make them look better.[44] Makahs also made regular trips into Puget Sound. In the late 1780s, Chief Tatoosh told Charles Duncan, captain of the *Princess Royal*, that the Haꞏčʔiq Tuṗał ("hah-tsihk too-puhlth," meaning "the long saltwater," the Strait of Juan de Fuca) extended east, where it branched north and south, opening into C̓a·bap ("tsah-buhp," Puget Sound) that ran inland a considerable distance. Nearly four years later, Tatoosh impressed Valdés with his detailed navigation knowledge of the entire one hundred miles of the Strait of Juan de Fuca. The Makah chief also described the entry to Puget Sound and shared with the Spanish accurate information regarding its extent. He had gained this knowledge through trading voyages that he and other Makahs made deep into Puget Sound. Peter Eggers, a Euro-American who lived at Neah Bay at the end of the nineteenth century, noted that Makah families paddled in their "big canoes" to trade dried halibut for clams and spring salmon with the Puyallups near Tacoma. He also detailed Makah trips to Squaxin Island, located at the farthest extent of Puget Sound's inland extension, to trade for clams that the Squaxins specifically dried for them. These were regular trade excursions that had occurred for many generations, not recent trade connections generated by the growth of settlement in Puget Sound.[45] As today's Makah recall, "the ocean was a big highway" used by their ancestors to connect regional trade networks. These regularly used marine routes created a historicized and known waterscape of economic and social networks radiating out from Cape Flattery.[46]

Already in place when non-Native maritime fur traders came to the region, an efficient and wide-ranging indigenous trade network fueled the newcomers' hopes of quick and easy profits. Russian *promyshlenniki*, entrepreneurs who combined hunting and trapping with trading, had worked the far northern portion of the Northwest Coast since 1743, but the global exchange in furs did not penetrate into the čadi· borderland until the 1770s. The Spanish expeditions of 1774 and 1775 collected some sea otter skins, but their primary purpose was to extend their imperial claims farther along the North American coast to prevent Russian intrusions from the north. Historians traditionally credit Captain Cook's third Pacific voyage for establishing the true commercial potential of the maritime fur trade, citing the oft-quoted example of a broken metal belt buckle that a midshipman traded for a sea otter skin that he sold for $300 in China.[47] During the weeks that Cook's *Resolution* and *Discovery* spent at Friendly Cove in 1778, the indigenous trade network brought canoes of "strangers" from outside Nootka Sound to exchange sea otter skins for European trade goods. The enormous bounty of "soft gold," which Indians brought to non-Indians, gave the impression that traders simply needed to anchor in front of a village to receive such valuable goods for mere trifles.

Competing imperial claims of sovereignty and the enormous profitability of the maritime fur trade nearly brought the Spanish and British Empires to war in an incident now known as the Nootka Sound Controversy. In 1789, Manuel

Nootka Sound, 1778. The Mowachahts on the left have a pile of salmon for which the English sailor holding the rifle is negotiating. Engraving by John Webber, 1778, in James Cook's *A Voyage to the Pacific Ocean.* University of Washington Libraries, Special Collections, NA3917.

Antonio Florez, then viceroy of New Spain, ordered Esteban José Martínez to establish a fort at Nootka Sound to declare Spanish sovereignty there in light of Russian and British activity in the North Pacific. Martínez then seized several British ships that came into Nootka Sound to trade. He reconditioned and re-named several of these vessels and arrested their crews, even sending some to the nearest Spanish prison, a facility in San Blas, New Spain, southeast of the southern tip of Baja California. Martínez responded so aggressively because he believed that Britain was attempting to establish a colony at Nootka Sound. Be-cause of treaties from the fifteenth through eighteenth centuries and the Span-ish voyages along the Northwest Coast in the 1770s, Spain considered the entire western coast of the Americas as its sovereign territory. Seeing an opportunity to undermine Spanish claims to Pacific sovereignty, British prime minister Wil-liam Pitt protested Martínez's actions, and the two empires prepared to go to war. The conflict dissipated when King Carlos IV, new to Spain's throne, de-cided that he could not go to war without their usual ally, France, then embroiled in the French Revolution. Through a series of conventions in the 1790s, Spain—then an empire in decline—eventually abandoned its three-hundred-year-old claim to exclusive sovereignty in the Pacific.[48]

Euro-Americans sailing from New England ports came to dominate the Pacific's maritime trade by the turn of the century, despite the fifty-year lead Russians had at the time. The Russian method of setting exchange prices in distant Saint Petersburg meant that they could not respond quickly enough or competitively to British and US captains who could adjust prices on the spot. The resolution of the Nootka Sound Controversy in the 1790s removed Spain as an imperial competitor in the region. British traders faced their own economic impediments. They had to work within the confines of two monopolies, purchasing privileges from the South Sea Company to gain permission to get furs in the Pacific and paying the East India Company for the ability to sell furs in Canton. To dodge the monopolistic practices, most British vessels involved in the maritime fur trade flew a foreign flag. Meares sailed under a Portuguese flag, which allowed him to land his furs at Macao before selling them to Chinese merchants in Canton. The South Sea Company would not allow maritime fur traders to export Chinese goods to England, thereby cutting entrepreneurs out of another profitable leg of the England–Northwest Coast–China global trade circuit. This arrangement gave a significant commercial advantage to US maritime traders, drawn into the Pacific by John Ledyard's reports of the lucrative commerce found along this coast. A corporal of marines on the *Resolution*, Ledyard had accompanied Cook and had tried to persuade New England shipowners and merchants to invest in this commercial enterprise since 1783.[49]

When Robert Gray and John Kendrick, commanders of the Boston vessels *Columbia Rediviva* and *Lady Washington*, arrived on the Northwest Coast midsummer 1788 shortly after Meares, they found a trade into which they could insert themselves. Experienced Indian traders eagerly exchanged furs for their goods. Kendrick and Gray encountered an efficient indigenous trade network that funneled skins to a handful of key chiefs, who, in turn, managed the exchanges with non-Native traders. While trading with Wickaninnish, they discovered that he had already collected skins from more remote villages inland and elsewhere on the coast. Similarly, in their first exchange with Tatoosh the following spring, they found that he had bought all the skins from neighboring peoples.[50] But perhaps the Northwest Coast indigenous trade network was too efficient. When Gray brought his furs to Canton after stopping at the Sandwich Islands, he received a lower price than expected because British traders, fresh from the Northwest Coast, had already flooded the market with furs.

The efficiency of the trade network also facilitated the near extinction of sea otters as skilled indigenous hunters exacted a lethal toll. Some places rapidly became destitute of these sea mammals. Spaniards noted that by 1792, sea otters were "scarce" in Nootka Sound. From 1788 to 1826, American ships made at least

127 voyages from the United States to China via the Northwest Coast as part of the maritime fur trade. Filling the cargo holds of so many vessels with the skins of *Enhydra lutris* year after year nearly drove the species extinct.[51]

From the beginning of the maritime fur trade, Northwest Coast societies desired a range of non-Native articles. In 1774, when several canoes of inhabitants from Nootka Sound paddled into the ocean to trade with the Spanish explorer Juan Pérez, the first European to venture into the ča·di· borderland, they exchanged sea otter skins, herring, and garments made from woven cedar bark for knives, clothing, and abalone shells from Monterrey. Four years later, when Cook spent a month anchored off Yuquot, Maquinna's village at Friendly Cove in Nootka Sound, Indians rejected beads and cloth offered by the British, instead trading a wealth of sea otter skins for metal items, including knives, chisels, buttons, nails, and pieces of iron and tin. Northwest Coast peoples used the metal tools to carve cedar canoes, make planks for longhouses, and craft artwork. They desired smaller pieces of metal to use as decorative items, wearing some as jewelry and incorporating others into clothing and art. As Cook noted, "Before we left the place, hardly a bit of brass was left in the Ship, except what was in the necessary instruments."[52] Already consummate traders rich in material goods, indigenous borderlanders desired new exchange items. They had specific wants, which changed over time and from one village to the next.

In 1788, Meares traded a wide range of items with numerous inhabitants of this indigenous marine borderland. In addition to the usual metal goods, he traded blankets, which would become a mainstay in Pacific Northwest exchanges for more than a century afterward. Meares also purchased indigenous labor, which he paid for daily with iron beads. These laborers supplemented the work of his Chinese carpenters who built a fortified post at Yuquot and the *North West America*, the first non-Native vessel constructed in the ča·di· borderland. As Meares departed Nootka Sound for China, Callicum, a Mowachaht leader second only to Maquinna, asked him to bring shoes, stockings, hats, and other European clothing when he next visited.[53]

But the most desired goods that Meares made available to Maquinna and Wickaninnish were weapons, including swords, firearms, and ammunition. These chiefs employed the new weapons in their campaigns against neighboring peoples. In August 1788, Maquinna and Callicum filled twenty of their larger canoes with warriors armed with muskets—on loan from Meares—and set out to strike a village about twenty leagues up the coast. More than two weeks later, they returned victorious with a "great booty of sea-otter skins" and baskets full of the heads of thirty of their enemies. Northwest Coast peoples took the heads of their enemies in order to display them as warnings to others and to prevent the vanquished from burying warriors killed in battle—they believed that, if buried, slain enemies would come to life and attack, so removing their heads kept this from happening.[54] Maquinna traded some of these skins for more firearms from Meares. After the introduction of firearms to this region, Wickaninnish withheld furs unless traders offered muskets for exchange. His strategy worked: in 1792, the American trader John Kendrick exchanged a swivel gun, two hundred muskets, powder, and shot to the Clayoquot chief for his supply of furs.[55]

Those muskets probably brought Wickaninnish some victories. Although they were inaccurate weapons that commonly misfired, muzzle-loaded muskets worked well when employed in large volleys. After gaining the firearms from Kendrick, the Clayoquot chief used them to drive away the British vessel *Butterworth* after its crew had stolen some furs. But when these weapons were not used in a coordinated volley, they were no more effective than indigenous arrows, harpoons, and clubs. This became evident when Meares's first officer, Robert Duffin, ordered the crew of the longboat to defend themselves from the attacking Makah and Pacheedaht warriors. Due to the chaos of the attack and limited number of men Duffin had, it appears that they could only discharge their firearms singly rather than in a coordinated volley. In this incident, the attackers were not intimidated because the firearms failed to harm a significant number of Indians.[56]

What eighteenth-century firearms lacked in lethality, they made up for in cultural significance among indigenous peoples of the ča·di· borderland. Northwest Coast peoples believed that the supernatural being Thunderbird caused thunder and lightning and that he employed them when whaling.[57] Perhaps they believed that firearms harnessed the Thunderbird's supernatural powers and bestowed them on one who carried these weapons. This could explain why Wickaninnish, a whaling chief, desired his own brace of pistols. Tatoosh, a rival whaling chief, likely wanted his own set, which helps to explain why Meares's trifling present had angered him—he, too, desired this type of access to Thunderbird's power. Possession of firearms signified to a chief's enemies that he had direct access to a wider range of trade goods. This enhanced the influence of a leader and displayed to his rivals that his commercial connections made him a more powerful leader than others in the ča·di· borderland.

Northwest Coast chiefs also desired other status items to employ militarily. For example, Wickaninnish endeavored to purchase a non-Native vessel. In 1793, he struck a deal with Josiah Roberts, the Bostonian commander of a two-ship expedition to the Northwest Coast, to purchase the smaller of his two vessels, the ninety-ton *Resolution*, for fifty prime sea otter skins. Roberts reneged on the deal. Instead of turning the schooner over to Wickaninnish, he sent it south to

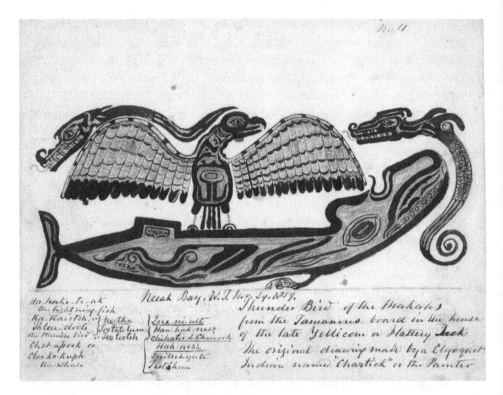

Thunderbird, 1859. According to Makah beliefs, Thunderbird taught them to whale. In this image, a sketch of a painting by a Clayoquot artist on a *tame·nawas* ("tuh-ma-nah-wuhs," supernatural power) board in the longhouse of Yelaḵub (Flattery Jack), two *x̌ix̌i·ktu·yak* ("hih-heek-too-yuhk," lightning snakes) flank Thunderbird. Drawing by James Swan from a painting by "Chartick" (the Painter), from the Franz R. and Kathryn M. Stenzel Collection of Western American Art. Image supplied courtesy of the Beinecke Rare Book and Manuscript Library, Yale University.

trade at the Columbia River. Three years later, when the American Charles Bishop declined Wickaninnish's offer to exchange his *Ruby* for an entire cargo of furs, the chief gave Bishop a significant amount of furs to purchase in advance a ship fifty-four feet long with six carriage guns and a schooner rigged with a gig whaleboat. However, Bishop never delivered the ship after receiving payment.[58] As with the possession of firearms, owning a vessel would have indicated to Wickaninnish's rivals his stronger ties with and better access to European traders. Moreover, having his own vessel would have given him better control over trade in the ča·di· borderland and increased the space he controlled.

After the confrontation with Meares, Tatoosh courted other traders who came into Makah marine space. A month after Tatoosh had intimidated Meares into fleeing Makah waters, the chief spent three days in 1788 exchanging all the skins he had with Charles Duncan, the British captain of the *Princess Royal*. Already positioning himself as the preeminent trader of the strait, the chief told Duncan that Makahs were the only people in the area who had anything worth trading.[59] Tatoosh had previously secured most of the sea otter skins from weaker neighbors, including S'Klallams, Quileutes, and Pacheedahts.

Although Duncan had easy success with Tatoosh, subsequent traders left Makah waters in frustration because he would not exchange all his furs for whatever they offered. In April 1789, Robert Haswell, second mate on the US vessel *Lady Washington*, complained about getting only thirty furs from Tatoosh because they lacked enough iron chisels, the sole item the Makah chief wanted at that time. After the *Lady Washington* had exhausted its supply of chisels, Makahs paddled off, taking their other seventy furs with them to save for trading with another vessel. Compounding the non-Native traders' disappointment was the fact that no other furs could be found in the strait because Tatoosh had already collected them from neighboring peoples. When traders failed to offer competitive prices, Tatoosh would allow his people to trade only a handful of furs, knowing that he could get a better price from another vessel.[60] With so many traders frequenting the coast, Tatoosh and other indigenous leaders could afford to wait.

Once they received non-Native goods in exchange for furs, Northwest Coast leaders circulated them both within their communities and to neighboring peoples. Meares saw Wickaninnish turn over to his brothers Hanna and Detootche the prized copper teakettles he had given the Clayoquot chief two weeks earlier. Wickaninnish did this in exchange for their furs, which he then traded to Meares for more goods, including firearms, powder, and shot. During his brief encounter with Tatoosh off Cape Flattery, Meares and his crew saw a Makah man in "possession of a complete set of coat buttons, which was very familiar to the memory of us all."[61] This individual could only have received them in exchange from someone on Vancouver Island.

In addition to trading these new goods within the čaꞏdiꞏ borderland, Northwest Coast peoples used them as important gifts. Meares noted that "[Wickaninnish] had lately given a splendid feast to a large number of his principal subjects; and from the great quantity of those articles he had received from us . . . there was every reason to suppose that he had added to the splendour of his banquet, by dividing his treasures among those who had the honour of being invited to it."[62] By the early nineteenth century, every chief needed to include non-Native goods among the gifts given away at a potlatch.[63] In 1803, Maquinna held a potlatch to commemorate a new name, Sat-sat-sok-sis, for his favorite son. The chief gave away a significant amount of the plunder he had taken by force from the *Boston*, including one hundred muskets, a hundred mirrors, four hundred yards of cloth, and twenty casks of powder. By the nineteenth century, chiefs also began incorporating European goods into indigenous funerals. After the death of his nephew, Maquinna burned ten fathoms of cloth and buried him with a combination of Native and non-Native goods.[64] Considered as a whole, these exchanges within and across indigenous communities reinforced relationships, status, and chiefly power.

Although manufactured items became important within Northwest Coast societies, they did not replace indigenous trade goods in a wholesale way. Instead, American Indians "interacted with [Europeans] and their materials in ways that were consistent with their own customs and beliefs."[65] Some maritime fur traders became important transporters of indigenous trade goods within and beyond the ča·di· borderland. When the Boston trader Josiah Roberts wintered his vessel, the *Jefferson*, in Barkley Sound in 1793–94, he collected 160 fathoms of dentalia and 210 "moose" (elk) skins from various indigenous peoples.[66] He knew that Indians along the Columbia River would trade sea otter skins for dentalia, while Haidas in the Queen Charlottes wanted elk skins to use as armor. Well into the twentieth century, whale oil, varieties of dried seafood, cedar logs and products, and other customary items continued to circulate throughout the region.

In the ča·di· borderland of the late eighteenth century, a handful of indigenous leaders—Maquinna, Wickaninnish, and Tatoosh—used their control over local trade networks to produce Mowachaht, Clayoquot, and Makah space on their own terms. All three were among the highest-status individuals in areas that possessed unique advantages over other places. This enabled them to exercise their power over larger spatial areas than others. In Tatoosh's case, he held sovereignty over the strategically located Cape Flattery and Tatoosh Island and owned a wealth of valuable marine resources. These advantages enabled him to gather furs from neighboring peoples with fewer resources. Once he had their furs, he limited their access to non-Native vessels and trade goods. But he also limited non-Native access to other peoples in the ča·di· borderland. Because he had a bulk of the furs in the region, there was little reason for them to engage or trade with other peoples. In addition, by holding such a large volume of furs, he could manipulate the terms of trade, holding out for better prices and desired items. After exchanging furs for non-Native goods, he possessed a wealth of trade articles that he could spread throughout the ča·di· borderland in order to gather even more furs. In this way, Tatoosh quickly came to monopolize the fur trade in an extensive portion of this indigenous marine borderland, although rival leaders certainly contested this. He controlled it to strengthen his authority and influence in the region and to extend Makah marine space deeper into the Strait of Juan de Fuca and south along the coast.

KINSHIP NETWORKS OF THE ČAˑDIˑ BORDERLAND

While trade created a web connecting borderlands peoples and communities of the late eighteenth-century Northwest Coast, a network of kinship knitted them together in more intimate ways. Marriages between different villages helped to expand a high-ranking individual's access to resources, important titles, and other status items. Kin in nearby communities could provide critical allies in the čaˑdiˑ borderland. So when outsiders arrived in this region, influential leaders such as Maquinna, Wickaninnish, and Tatoosh drew on kin networks to frustrate and resist the imperial efforts of newcomers. Non-Natives noticed kinship ties most readily among the upper ranks of the indigenous societies they encountered. Members of families at the top of the social hierarchy married similarly ranked individuals from neighboring villages and even from other ethnolinguistic areas. This gave many non-Native traders the impression that most of the chiefs in the čaˑdiˑ borderland were related.[67]

The Clayoquot chief Wickaninnish exemplified these connections. One of his sisters was married to a Makah. When her husband died, Tootoocheeticus, one of Wickaninnish's brothers, adopted her Makah son and brought him to Clayoquot. After the chief's twelve-year-old son took his adult name and earned the right to head his own whaling canoe, Wickaninnish betrothed him to Maquinna's daughter, the Mowachaht leader's oldest child. Although this betrothal nearly resulted in violence in the 1790s, when Maquinna stalled on surrendering his daughter to the Clayoquot chief, tensions appear to have abated afterward. Maquinna's wife a decade later was one of Wickaninnish's sisters, perhaps the same one who had been widowed when her Makah husband died in the 1780s. Women often remarried after a husband died or after leaving a spouse.[68]

Common peoples and younger siblings of chiefs also married across boundaries in the čaˑdiˑ borderland. The extant, sparse observations about Northwest Coast family networks in the late eighteenth and early nineteenth centuries provide only a glimpse of families and individuals at the top of the social hierarchy. Yet although traditional archival materials fail to note family networks among commoners, Makah and Nuu-chah-nulth oral histories recall a long history of marriage ties connecting the villages of Cape Flattery to communities on the Olympic Peninsula, south to the mouth of the Columbia River, and north across the strait. Children of these unions often had identity claims to both Makah and Vancouver Island communities. A broad web of family ties within communities and across the region meant that individuals' group affiliations were multifaceted, a borderlands characteristic that explorers, traders, and later colonial officials—British and US—had difficulty understanding.[69] With the great number of distinct peoples and their associated customs and languages in the Northwest Coast, those who married into other communities played central roles as intermediaries in the indigenous borderland. Most often women and slaves, these individuals spoke several languages and traveled regularly and freely between their new homes and natal villages.[70]

In an effort to strengthen their influence in the region, titleholders occasionally extended kinship ties to non-Native traders. Some chiefs attempted to tie European traders to them in more intimate ways by exchanging names. During one of James Hanna's two voyages to the Northwest Coast in the 1780s, the Clayoquot chief Cleaskinah—another of Wickaninnish's brothers—took the British trader's name, and the chief promised to save all his furs for him, the first maritime fur trader on the coast after Cook's voyage of 1778.[71] Cleaskinah appears in the accounts of subsequent traders as Chief Hanna, a familiar identity that he presented to encourage trade.

Although he misunderstood it, Meares also experienced an event that was probably a name-exchange ceremony. Before leaving Friendly Cove, Maquinna honored him with a special ceremony witnessed by many of his people: "Maquilla [Maquinna] thought proper . . . to do obedience to us as his lords and sovereigns. He took off his tiara of feathers, and placed it on my head; he then dressed me in his robe of otter skins; and, thus arrayed, he made me sit down on one of his chests filled with human bones, and then placed himself on the ground. His example was followed by all the natives present, when they sung one of those plaintive songs, which we have already mentioned as producing such a solemn and pleasing effect upon our minds.—Such were the forms by which he intended to acknowledge, in the preference of his people, our superiority over him."[72] Meares interpreted the Mowachaht chief's action as an acknowledgment of British sovereignty over them. In general terms, this would have fit with Meares's worldview, which characterized indigenous peoples as inferiors. More specifically, though, Maquinna's seeming expression of submission had important geopolitical ramifications in the subsequent Nootka Sound Controversy. If Maquinna had submitted to Meares and King George, then Britain's claim to Nootka Sound would be stronger than that of the Spanish Empire.

But it appears to have been an adapted ceremony that extended some of Maquinna's titleholder privileges to the British trader. Maquinna dressed Meares in robes worn only by ranking chiefs and sat the captain on a chest that held the skulls of prominent Mowachaht whalers. Meares inaccurately believed that these skulls and bones belonged to individuals who had fallen prey to Maquinna's cannibal appetite. Instead, these were talismans of power that strengthened Maquinna's whaling prowess. Bones and corpses of prominent whalers figured in ritual preparations made by Northwest Coast whalers.[73] By doing this in front of other Mowachahts, Maquinna demonstrated that he had tied Meares to him through kinship. A similar desire to create familial connections lay behind Wickaninnish's request for Meares to take the chief's nineteen-year-old son with him when he left the Northwest Coast. Meares declined the offer, despite the youth's "amiable and docile disposition" and his "very quick and sagacious" appearance. The captain felt that his presence would give the crew anxiety, an effect they felt even with Ka'iana, a respected Sandwich Islands prince who had accompanied them on the entire voyage. In addition, Meares was under instructions to not pick up any more Natives.[74]

During the late eighteenth and early nineteenth centuries, the few non-Natives who lived among indigenous peoples in the ča·di· borderland benefited from attempts to anchor them to specific families through kinship. However, the quality of their experiences depended on their ability to meet the expectations of indigenous leaders. At the end of the summer trading season in 1786, British trader James Strange departed the Northwest Coast and left behind the ship's surgeon, John Mackay. Strange intended to return the following spring, and Mackay volunteered to stay behind in order to gain a more intimate knowledge of Mowachahts. The trader ordered the Irish surgeon to commit "to Paper every Occurrence, however trivial, which might serve to throw light on our hitherto confined knowledge of the Manners, Customs, Religion, & Government of these people."[75] He hoped that Mackay's knowledge would then give him an edge over other traders the next year.

Maquinna offered to take the surgeon into his family, even promising him a wife. The chief vowed to feed him so well that Mackay would become "as fat as a Whale." Mackay had already gained the Mowachaht chief's respect when he had cured one of his children of scabby hands and legs, a complaint common among children of Nootka Sound.[76] Strange honored Maquinna's request of arming the surgeon with a musket, pistol, and two hundred rounds of ammunition. Maquinna expected the Irishman, like any other member of his family, to fight his enemies. To complete Mackay's "Warlike appearance," Maquinna requested a red coat to wear, explaining that this color would intimidate enemies.[77] Many societies in this indigenous borderland rubbed themselves with red ocher when they went to war. When the chief offered to incorporate the surgeon into his family, he had expected to gain someone who would strengthen his influence over rivals on his borders.

But Mackay spent a rather unsuccessful fourteen months as a member of Maquinna's family because he failed to meet the leader's expectations. His troubles likely began even before Strange left. The captain supplied Mackay with presents so that he could continue to influence his indigenous hosts by giving gifts. The surgeon also received seeds for a garden and a pair of goats. While the Mowachahts watched, the Irishman sowed the seeds. The captain hoped that Mackay's cultivation of the soil and livestock—ways Englishmen established their claim to lands in North America—would bolster Strange's claim to Yuquot.[78] Mowachahts would have interpreted Mackay's actions very differently. They probably saw his labor as the actions of a slave, so perhaps this was ironically the beginning of his loss of status.

Mackay continued to undermine his position. Just days after Strange's departure, Maquinna held a potlatch in Mackay's honor. Several hundred guests from neighboring communities attended the feast, and the Mowachaht chief displayed his newest relative. Probably dressed in his red coat, Mackay displayed—and likely gave away, at the chief's urging—the rich presents he possessed. Maquinna also cajoled the surgeon into demonstrating his musket, which failed to impress the guests when Mackay missed his target. To salvage this poor exhibition of marksmanship, Maquinna urged the surgeon to disassemble the musket to reveal its power. Unfortunately for the young Irishman, he passed around the musket's springs and screws, and these were never recovered; perhaps a rival of Maquinna palmed them. As surmised by Alexander Walker, a military commander employed by the East India Company who had debriefed Mackay on his return to Bombay, "[Mackay], by an Act of the greatest indiscretion, in this manner disarmed himself. Deprived of this powerful Weapon of respect and defence, he became less formidable, and less secure. He was no longer able to assist the Savages as they expected, against their Enemies, and in their projects for revenge, which it was too evident they had in view by his stay amongst them."[79] Mackay nullified his most significant advantage as a member of Maquinna's family.

Despite this setback, Mackay refused to leave Yuquot when James Hanna visited Nootka Sound for the second time, a month after Strange's departure, and offered to take the surgeon back across the Pacific. He told the British trader that "he began to relish dried fish and whale oil, was satisfied with his way of life, and perfectly contented to stay 'till next year." When Hanna threatened to take Mackay away by force because he resented the advantage the Irishman would give to Strange, Maquinna and his Mowachaht warriors warned the British trader that they would resist. At this point, they still valued Mackay's presence and believed that it would come to some advantage in the future.[80]

The Irishman's situation worsened, however. After the botched musket demonstration, Maquinna refused to give Mackay a wife. The goats starved to death that winter. Even worse, Mackay lost Maquinna's friendship when he stepped over the chief's favorite infant, an action that Mowachahts believed presaged misfortune. When the infant died less than a fortnight after the incident, the chief's warriors beat the surgeon, and Maquinna expelled him from his longhouse. The outcast Irishman suffered at the hands of other Mowachahts. Although he attempted to keep the journal that Strange had requested, Callicum destroyed his writing materials, fearing that these items possessed supernatural powers and could cause sickness and even death.[81] Mackay traded his remaining clothes for food and stayed alive only through handouts.

When the British trader Charles Barkley sailed into Friendly Cove the following summer, Mackay must have felt relieved. It surprised Barkley's young bride when a "dirty" Indian "clothed in a greasy sea-otter skin" boarded their vessel and spoke to them in fluent English, offering his services in securing furs.[82] Although some derided Mackay's limited command of Nootkan, he had learned enough of their language to benefit Barkley—his invaluable assistance helped the trader fill the vessel's hold with eight hundred furs, which he sold for $30,000. When Barkley sailed west across the Pacific after a successful trading season, he took Mackay with him.[83]

Although Mackay had disappointed Maquinna and his plans for using him in borderland political struggles, the Mowachaht chief later found two other mamᦓnis to be of greater value. In 1803, when he seized the *Boston* and executed most of the crew, Maquinna saved two of the more useful crewmembers, the blacksmith John Jewitt and the sail maker John Thompson. He incorporated these two captives into his family as prized slaves. As in 1786, when he had ceremonially displayed Mackay to neighboring chiefs, Maquinna hosted a large potlatch to exhibit Jewitt and Thompson along with the rest of the booty he had seized from the *Boston*.[84]

Unlike Mackay, Jewitt and Thompson became useful members in Maquinna's household. As two individuals among the larger pool of unfree people in the chief's household, both men worked hard, doing menial work such as cutting firewood, drawing water, hauling goods, building and repairing longhouses, and fishing. Putting his professional skills to use, Jewitt made bracelets, copper ornaments, fishhooks, and daggers for the chief to trade with other borderland peoples. After a difficult whaling season, Maquinna had Jewitt make him a steel harpoon head, and the "delighted" chief experienced immediate success with it. Probably in appreciation for Jewitt's valuable contributions, Maquinna gave him a young woman to take as his wife.[85] The way that Maquinna benefited from

Jewitt's enslavement illustrates the advantages that could be gained from resisting imperial incursions. By attacking the *Boston* and seizing the vessel's goods and two men with useful skills, the Mowachaht chief increased his personal wealth, his status, and the well-being of his community for the short term.

Although Maquinna's white slaves increased the Mowachaht chief's influence, Jewitt became the object of jealousy among other Northwest Coast leaders in the ča·di· borderland. Wickaninnish attempted to purchase the blacksmith from Maquinna on at least four occasions. Years later, Jewitt noted—and probably exaggerated—that the Clayoquot chief offered a wealth of goods, including four young male slaves, two highly ornamented canoes, numerous sea otter skins, and many fathoms of cloth and dentalia. Perhaps realizing that the Mowachaht chief would never sell his valued property, Machee Ulatilla, a Makah chief who frequented Yuquot and had also offered to buy Maquinna's favorite white slave, helped free Jewitt. Ulatilla conveyed a letter the captive wrote to Samuel Hill, captain of the brig *Lydia*. This prompted the Bostonian to go to Jewitt's aid.[86]

Several years after finagling Jewitt's and Thompson's release from Maquinna, Ulatilla himself kept white slaves. In 1808, the Russian schooner *Sv. Nikolai* wrecked along Quileute shores just south of Cape Flattery. Four of the Russian survivors, including Timofei Tarakanov, became the property of Ulatilla in 1809. Ulatilla treated Tarakanov and his peers well; the Russian even claimed that he was "treated . . . as a friend, not as a prisoner."[87] In 1810, Ulatilla brokered a sale of his Russian slaves, an Englishman, and four Aleuts that Makahs held in captivity to Thomas Brown, then captain of the Boston ship *Lydia*. Although they could be members of ranking indigenous Northwest Coast households, non-Native slaves were also valuable status items and important commodities. Chiefs such as Ulatilla appeared to profit by selling their white slaves to non-Native captains eager to redeem "civilized" men from "savages," even when they possibly acted from more sympathetic motives.[88]

Indigenous leaders such as Maquinna, Wickaninnish, and Tatoosh used trade and kinship networks to produce sociopolitical spaces they could control. Naturally, they extended more intimate connections to mamánis and babałids. Perhaps the chiefs had hoped that exchanging names would discourage specific captains from trading with rival chiefs—at the very least, this would strengthen a leader's authority by demonstrating to his rivals that he had a direct connection to these newcomers. Marrying into another family often resulted in gaining conditional access to that family's usufruct and proprietary rights. Similarly, marriage and other kinship practices such as adoption allowed titleholders to extend these rights to others. In societies where leaders earned and maintained authority through influence, building extensive kinship ties was beneficial—chiefs could expand the space over which they held authority by developing familial relationships in other villages, even those separated by ethnolinguistic boundaries. Contested and shared, overlapping trade and kinship networks defined the ča·di· borderland.[89]

By exploiting networks of trade and kinship, titleholders such as Maquinna, Wickaninnish, and Tatoosh controlled space and interrupted imperial processes. Their ability to do so reveals how the broader process of encounter, resistance, and conquest reshaped Native worlds and indigenous spaces. Chiefs allowed vessels into their waters because it gave them the opportunity to fill them with whale oil, fish, and sea otter furs. They found that they could exchange customary indigenous goods for valuable objects that allowed them to maintain their authority. In the ča·di· borderland of the late eighteenth and early nineteenth centuries, Northwest Coast chiefs—not non-Native navigators, traders, and distant imperial officials—were the primary historical actors. Their understanding of local networks gave them enough power to control customary marine and terrestrial spaces during initial imperial struggles over the Pacific Northwest.

When mamảnis and babałids began sailing into these waters, they did not find empty marine and terrestrial spaces on which they could simply inscribe their cartographic and geopolitical fantasies of empire.[90] In the waters stretching from the west coast of Vancouver Island down to the Columbia River and into Puget Sound through the Strait of Juan de Fuca, non-Native explorers and traders found a borderland space shared and contested by distinct peoples. Similar to all borderlands, diplomatic protocols and overlapping networks of trade and kinship drew together its various societies in complex and intricate ways. The arrival of Meares and his contemporaries did not create these borderland networks—they found them in place when they arrived.

Non-Natives in the ča·di· borderland witnessed and participated in the protocols and networks through which distinct peoples of the Northwest Coast shared and contested this marine space. Networks of trade united borderland communities by distributing the products of variable marine and coastal environments within the region. But the process itself could at times become competitive when indigenous chiefs wrestled over the best trade terms and controlled exchanges and distribution to benefit themselves and their people. Similarly, kinship networks intertwined borderland families at all levels of society in intimate ways. As titleholders competed for kin in both their village communities and across ethnolinguistic boundaries, however, kinship could also become a point of conflict.

Borderland strategists such as Tatoosh, Maquinna, Wickaninnish, and Machee Ulatilla extended these protocols and networks to non-Natives during the late eighteenth and early nineteenth centuries.[91] Europeans and Euro-Americans became valued trade partners. Chiefs controlled access to traders and their vessels and competed—even fought—over trading privileges. In a few cases, chiefs incorporated mamáṅis or babaɬids into their households. Individuals such as Mackay, Jewitt, Thompson, and Tarakanov seemed to be included in high-ranking families only as slaves or in a similar position. Occasionally, captains received honored names from chiefs, which was a way titleholders attempted to tie them to their families and communities.

Yet the adaptation of indigenous protocols to encounters with non-Natives illustrates that the čaˑdiˑ borderland remained a region where strong chiefs continued to control space on their own terms and to meet their own priorities and agendas throughout this period. Loosely codified into a recognizable form by 1788, when Meares sailed throughout the borderland waters, these protocols demonstrated continued indigenous sovereignty and chiefly authority to both Native and non-Native audiences. Those who ignored these protocols did so at their peril.

2

INVETERATE WARS AND PETTY PILFERINGS

Less than two weeks after Captain Meares and his fifty crewmembers fled Makah waters in 1788, the *Felice* returned to the *čaˑdiˑ* ("cha-dee") borderland but avoided Tatoosh's space around Cape Flattery. Instead, Meares anchored in Barkley Sound, located north across the Strait of Juan de Fuca from Tatoosh Island. Although the ship lay miles away from either Tatoosh or Wickaninnish, the two chiefs learned of the *Felice's* return by those visiting the ship. The British stayed for ten days, trading with Makahs, Clayoquots, and other Natives who brought fish, berries, and the occasional sea otter fur. While anchored in Barkley Sound, Meares deployed the longboat under the command of First Officer Robert Duffin to determine whether the Strait of Juan de Fuca was the Northwest Passage. While waiting for the return of Duffin's expedition, the situation of the longboat, which carried their "hopes of success, or the fears of calamity," weighed on the minds of the crew.[1]

Once again, Tatoosh thwarted British ambitions. Four days after setting out, Duffin brought the longboat into a small cove in San Juan Harbor on Vancouver Island. The Pacheedaht inhabitants claimed Tatoosh as their leader, and Duffin found them a "bold, daring set of fellows." The following morning, several canoes carrying forty to fifty warriors—a coalition of Makahs and Pacheedahts—attacked. As the adversaries prepared to board and seize the craft, a Pacheedaht chief readied his harpoon to impale the coxswain. Instead, one of the crew fired first and dropped the chief with a single shot to the head. Warriors lining both sides of the shore rained arrows and stones onto the vessel. One barbed missile struck Duffin in the head—only his thick hat prevented mortal injury. Arrows wounded an Italian in the leg, a Chinese sailor in the side, and a third crewmember in the chest. The longboat "was pierced in a thousand places by arrows," and the survivors felt that the conflict had been "close" as they "fought for their lives."[2]

Duffin ordered the crew to the oars, and they pulled the little vessel out of the cove. After fleeing the coalition of Makah and Pacheedaht warriors, Duffin named the location Hostility Bay because he believed that he had done nothing to provoke the attack. While limping back to the *Felice*, a small canoe paddled by two of Wickaninnish's people approached. They sold the bruised and battered crew some fish and offered two freshly severed heads "still streaming with blood." They told Duffin that these were two of Tatoosh's warriors whom they had killed because the Makah chief had declared war on Wickaninnish. Duffin declined the grisly offering, and the crew continued creeping along the coast. On their reunion with the *Felice*, Meares concluded, "We were now obliged to give up all hope of obtaining any further satisfaction concerning the extent of the strait," which he still believed was the Northwest Passage. Instead, they left the strait and returned to Nootka Sound. Their arrival relieved the shore crew of English and Chinese laborers who had stayed behind at Yuquot in order to build a small vessel that Meares intended to use for accessing trading opportunities in the innumerable shallow inlets dotting the coast. By then, indigenous messengers had already brought news of the attack on the longboat. Some reports exaggerated, telling how the entire crew of the *Felice*—not just the longboat—had been "cut to pieces" and the principal officers had perished. Other details were accurate and described specific wounds.[3] The ambush by Tatoosh's people and allied Pacheedaht warriors delayed British exploration of the strait until George Vancouver's expedition four years later.

Meares's interpretation of the attack on the longboat exemplifies the perspective of many non-Native traders who experienced threats or violence in the čaˑdiˑ borderland. Ignoring relevant details, he characterized the antagonists as inherently savage. In the voyage's official account, Meares wrote, "Though we had never had any intercourse or communication with the inhabitants of the straits, we had . . . hope[d] that our friendly conduct toward their neighbours, might, by some means have reached the district of their habitation and given them favourable impressions of us: but their conduct marked the most savage and bloody hostility."[4] But his first officer, and therefore Meares, knew that they had communicated with those who had attacked them: the warriors had told Duffin that Tatoosh was their chief. However, by stating that he "had never had any intercourse" with the antagonists, Meares could claim the higher moral ground and characterize the violence as an unprovoked attack by hostile savages. Many, but not all, maritime fur traders parroted similar claims.

The belief in the inherent savageness of some indigenous peoples reflected a common assumption of racial violence in a colonial world. Many explorers, navigators, and trading captains categorized Natives as noble or ignoble savages.[5] Meares believed that Tatoosh and the Makahs lacked the civilized and noble qualities he found present among other peoples of this borderland. First, Wickaninnish, a leader whom Meares respected, had warned him about Tatoosh and Makahs. From Meares's perspective, then, even the local savages deemed the People of the Cape ignoble. Second, the Makah chief refused to trade, unlike non-Makah chiefs. This seemed to confirm what Wickaninnish had told him about their hostility. Third, Maquinna and Callicum, who both shared geographical information about the coast, helped Meares's Chinese and British carpenters build a smaller vessel at Yuquot. The assistance of these two chiefs supported British efforts to explore the region. By contrast, Tatoosh's warriors had foiled Meares's attempts to map empire onto Makah waters. While most traders and navigators found these obstructions baffling and frightening, some understood the reasons behind indigenous attacks on their vessels. Non-Natives criticized the competition, accusing rivals—often from other nations—of being provocateurs of violence.

In the ča·di· borderland, most first contact encounters and maritime fur trade exchanges included violence because of the competitive nature of producing space by imposing and enforcing culturally specific protocols and practices that both shaped and reinforced identity. Not merely reactive, violence was part of group interactions and politics long before the arrival of European ships. Natives and non-Natives harassed, intimidated, stole from, punished, attacked, and murdered one another. Beyond its immediate destructive qualities, however, violence could be productive when leaders and communities claimed space and power at the expense of others. Indigenous borderlanders maintained protocols and reciprocity by force—what Europeans often called "theft" or misconstrued as violence inherent to Natives—when they were not followed or offered voluntarily. Moreover, violence in this borderland had a multidimensional quality because distinct indigenous peoples also committed these acts against one another. Yet violence itself operated on the metaphorical knife's edge—too much violence or conflict at the wrong time had counterproductive results and weakened a leader's influence and authority.[6]

This understanding of violence differs from previous interpretations of maritime fur trade conflict that have downplayed its violent qualities, arguing that traders capitulated to Native chiefs who "vigorously asserted their demands."[7] Some posit that both sides had goods wanted by the other, thereby fueling peace and accommodation. Violence emerged only after the fur trade era when settlers failed to accommodate Native demands and came to the frontier to transform it to meet their needs. However, oral histories and documents report many incidents of theft, intimidation, and violence, which have prompted some to characterize the maritime fur trade as a "looting of the coast."[8] In these histories, greedy traders resorted to pawning off poor-quality goods, theft, hostage-taking, and violence when competition increased and sea otter furs became scarce. Native health deteriorated with the introduction of alcohol, nontraditional foods, venereal diseases, and smallpox. The proliferation of firearms made Indian warfare deadlier and fueled an increase in Northwest Coast slavery. The commodification of sea otters disrupted the ecology of the coast, thereby reducing fish numbers and increasing Native dependence on non-Native foods. Assuming the inevitability of racial conflict, this assessment of fur trade violence casts indigenous peoples as victims whose simple natures precipitated trouble with rapacious European and Euro-American traders. A more recent study counters the assumption of indigenous victimization by explaining that traders became entangled in Native agendas and rivalries because the maritime fur trade "inflamed old grievances and encouraged new conflicts."[9] This reassessment, however, misses the larger and more important dynamics characteristic to the ča·di· borderland because it ignores the region's transnational characteristics and confines its subject to Canadian boundaries, which did not exist at the time. Previous scholarship simplifies the complex local dynamics that transcended simple racial antagonisms between Natives and non-Natives and often resulted in violence between indigenous peoples and imperial actors.

If we examine the violence of this era from the indigenous perspectives, a different picture emerges. Violence marked early encounters because of competition among rival chiefs in the ča·di· borderland. When imperial actors entered the region, they exacerbated older lines of tension, added new opportunities for conflict, and applied their own tools of violence and terror. In this indigenous borderland where distinct peoples shared and contested spaces and resources, violence was not anomalous or the result of miscommunications: threats and violence were central to both the borderlands and imperial processes of this period. More important, indigenous leaders such as Tatoosh employed violence to foil imperial designs for domination of tribal marine space. To non-Natives during the maritime fur trade, these dynamics created a geography of fear that came to characterize the ča·di· borderland. Sometimes inscribed onto maps with place-names like Hostility Bay, stories of earlier incidents of violence and theft shaped the expectations of subsequent encounters. And indigenous peoples were anything but passive in the creation of this geography of fear. Chiefs manipulated *mamáni* and *babałid* ("buh-buh-lthid," non-Natives) anxieties to the advantage of themselves and their people.

PREENCOUNTER VIOLENCE
IN THE ČA·DI· BORDERLAND

Native and non-Native interactions of the maritime fur trade did not introduce violence to the ča·di· borderland. Before the arrival of Europeans along this stretch of the Pacific shore, indigenous leaders such as Maquinna, Wickaninnish, and Tatoosh employed violence to extend their authority and shape outcomes. Thus, violent incidents had a productive quality; they were not simply aberrations resulting from misunderstandings or breakdowns in normal relations. Nor were these incidents part of a cycle of revenge, reflecting an inherently violent Indian mentality. In some ways, episodes of violence on the Northwest Coast shared similarities with those described by European historian David Nirenberg in his examination of the medieval persecution of minorities in neighborhoods where violence was also part of the negotiations of space and social place. He argues that perpetrators and recipients of violence "were tightly bound in a wide variety of relations that enmeshed moments of violence and gave them meaning," a conclusion that also fits the ča·di· borderland of the eighteenth and early nineteenth centuries.[10]

Nirenberg identifies five categories of violence—quotidian, cataclysmic, strategic, controlled, and stabilizing—which offer a useful framing for similar acts along the Northwest Coast. In this indigenous region, violence committed against slaves illustrated the most common acts of quotidian violence.[11] During the maritime fur trade, cataclysmic violence was not a relevant category. From the perspective of Northwest Coast peoples, this type of violence would have applied only to large-scale violence related to the supernatural world, such as the time when Transformer changed the world and gave nonhuman people the forms they wear today.[12] Once they concluded that mamánis and babałids were not from the supernatural world—a determination they quickly made during the initial first encounter period—violent interactions with Europeans better fit the other analytical categories. Chiefs used violence strategically, attacking their rivals to seize slaves, resources, land, and sea space. Violence could also be a stabilizing factor used by one or more titleholders to keep a rival from becoming too powerful. Finally, chiefs deployed violence and threats to control areas over which they held authority.

For generations before the arrival of non-Natives, indigenous leaders and peoples competed over marine resources and access to them, and their struggles often became violent. As some of the best locations to harvest the sea's riches, the villages of Cape Flattery and Tatoosh Island were the focal point of repeated, violent contests. Some Makah oral histories relate that the Qʷidičča?a·tx̌ ("kwih-dihch-chuh-aht"), "the People of the Cape," have always been there, while other accounts date their arrival from Vancouver Island to 3,500 years ago.[13] Northwest Coast societies commonly have different versions of stories about how they came to occupy specific places because various lineages came together to form today's tribal nations.[14] Although Makahs have called Cape Flattery and its nearby waters home for a very long time, other indigenous peoples have contested their tenure. These historical conflicts help us better understand the competitive nature of violence in the late eighteenth and early nineteenth centuries.

Recorded in the early to mid-twentieth century, oral histories explain that possibly during the late sixteenth or early seventeenth century, Makahs fought Ditidahts, related kin from Vancouver Island, for ownership of Neah Bay, Tatoosh Island, and the adjacent marine space. The former held Wa?ač̓ ("wuh-uhch"), Ćuʔyas ("tsoo-yuhs"), and ?use·?ił ("oo-sa-ihlth," better known as Ozette) villages, while the latter claimed Tatoosh Island and Neah Bay. In earlier times, a great flood had brought Ditidahts to the southern side of the strait, where they then claimed former Makah lands and waters. For a while, the two related peoples lived in a tense peace. However, tensions between them intensified when a Ditidaht strongman pulled the head off a Makah in a strength contest and when Ditidahts enslaved five Makah girls after a storm had pushed their canoe to Tatoosh Island. Makahs attacked Tatoosh Island, and after a "great slaughter on both sides," Ditidahts retreated to Neah Bay. In a war council, Makahs agreed to continue fighting until they had pushed the Ditidahts back to Vancouver Island. Remembered as a cultural hero, Whacwad ("wuhts-wuhd"), son of an Ozette chief, assassinated one Ditidaht chief, and then Makahs slew another chief during a subsequent battle. With their two highest-ranking chiefs dead, the surviving Ditidahts packed their belongings and left the Cape Flattery region, returning north across the strait. This left the ancestral Makah lands and waters in Makah hands once again, prompting some People of the Cape to argue that Neah Bay and Tatoosh Island belong to them "because we have shed blood here." Conflicts between these two peoples in the ča·di· borderland continued for some time as Makahs raided Ditidaht villages in order to take salmon runs.[15]

In an effort to fashion claims to Cape Flattery and valuable marine resources, non-Makahs also tell their own stories about fighting the People of the Cape for control over the Makahs' ancestral home. A nineteenth-century Quileute oral history—generally discredited by Makahs today—claims that their warriors had once pushed the People of the Cape north across the strait.[16] The victors then claimed Cape Flattery, Tatoosh Island, and the surrounding waters. The exiled Makahs—then living with Ditidaht kin on Vancouver Island—continued fishing the halibut banks stolen by Quileutes. Fearing that the People of the Cape were preparing to reclaim ancestral villages and marine waters, Quileute warriors paddled in one hundred war canoes across the strait and raided a Ditidaht-Makah village while the men were absent. The Indian agent who sensationally recounted this incident wrote, "With whale bone and stones and clubs, clam shell knives, and yew wood daggers [the Quileutes] dealt death on every side." The victors took women and children captive, cut off the heads of the old men, and returned home. While Quileutes reveled in their victory, Makahs and Ditidahts retaliated against the Cape Flattery villages still held by their enemies. Arriving at Neah Bay, they turned it into a smoldering ruin. Then they moved around the cape, slaughtering all Quileutes they could find. A Makah whaling chief slew one of the most powerful Quileute "medicine men" by harpooning him through the head. The victors dragged the bodies of their enemies to the low tide mark so the sea would carry them away because "all Indians whose bodies are claimed by the sea turn into owls, the worst thing that could happen to anyone."[17] Makahs finished with a "terrible battle" at Ozette, the premier whaling village of the coast. They pushed Quileutes south and thereafter excluded them from the waters and marine resources around Cape Flattery and Tatoosh Island.

At this time, chiefly rivalries centered on controlling lucrative marine resources and the best sites for harvesting them. For example, when Ditidahts laid claim to Neah Bay, Tatoosh Island, and the nearby waters, they temporarily transformed this area into Ditidaht space. This meant that Ditidahts and those with kinship ties to them resided in these villages, fished the nearby halibut banks, harvested shellfish along the foreshore, and hunted sea mammals off the northern corner of the Olympic Peninsula. Ditidaht chiefs claimed authority over this space and benefited from the resources, which gave them trade goods and potlatch gifts to spend strengthening their influence in the borderlands. The People of the Cape retaliated with strategic violence to reverse this situation and to turn this area back into Makah space.

The lingering effects of violent struggles affected non-Natives when they arrived in the 1770s and 1780s. Wickaninnish was an expansionist leader who had moved his people from the interior to the coast in the decade before the appearance of Europeans. Oral histories collected in the early twentieth century explain that the population of Wickaninnish's inland village grew so large that they had outstripped local food resources. With superior numbers, the chief and his people declared war on the Kelsamites, who lived on the coast, in order to obtain their waters and resources. Wickaninnish drove the Kelsamites out of Opitsit, and from there he conquered neighboring villages and expanded his influence throughout Clayoquot Sound. Through this conquest, Wickaninnish gained access to marine resources, especially salmon, halibut, and whales. His success brought this portion of the ča·di· borderland under his control and gave him access to whale oil, an important commodity in the regional trade network. The new wealth allowed him to host lavish potlatches, which secured his influence among the conquered people in the sound and within the region. By the time Meares came to trade, Wickaninnish had expanded his influence over thirteen thousand people living in eleven villages throughout Clayoquot Sound.[18]

These episodes of violence over ocean waters, marine resources, and the best sites to access them illustrate that the ča·di· borderland was a region spatially contested long before the arrival of mamánis and babałids. When Meares sailed into Makah marine space in 1788, he entered an indigenous borderlands crisscrossed by historic and contemporary lines of conflict and violence. Europeans and Euro-Americans did not introduce violence into a peaceful Native Eden. Instead, the newcomers exacerbated existing lines of tension and added new possibilities for conflict, especially when Northwest Coast chiefs incorporated mamánis and babałids into established and competitive trade and kinship networks.[19]

VIOLENCE AND EARLY ENCOUNTERS
IN THE ČA·DI· BORDERLAND

During the late eighteenth century, distinct peoples—locals and outsiders, Natives and non-Natives—sought control over the ča·di· borderland. Yet amicable exchange characterized the first encounter between indigenous borderlanders and Europeans. In 1774, when Pérez and his Spanish crew exchanged clothing, shells, and knives for sea otter furs, fish, and cedar bark clothing, bad weather— not threatening or violent Natives—drove the *Santiago* away. This first contact encounter in the region had a peaceful outcome because both sides "sought to minimize danger and maximize opportunities."[20] Beyond these practical considerations, however, the dynamics of the ča·di· borderland better explain why violence did not mar this particular meeting. Unlike later navigators who coasted from one village to the next and traded with competing chiefs, Pérez appeared off the entrance to Nootka Sound. This was also Pérez's sole stop in the borderlands, and he stayed for less than two days, which left little time for rivals chiefs to appear. Additionally, Pérez's encounter off Nootka Sound involved only a single group of people. After leaving Nootka Sound, the *Santiago* sailed south along the Washington coast. Although the crew saw the "smokes of many great fires, so that we know this coast to be inhabited," they did not linger to meet any other indigenous borderlanders.[21]

Subsequent first contact encounters, however, did include intimidation, theft, and conflict as borderlands violence shaped cross-cultural interactions and created a geography of fear in the minds of newcomers. This became evident during the 1775 Spanish expedition along the western edge of North America. Captaining the frigate *Santiago*, Bruno de Hezeta y Dudagoita commanded the expedition. A second vessel, the schooner *Sonora*, captained by Juan Francisco de la Bodega y Quadra, also accompanied them. On their way north, the vessels became separated somewhere along the Washington coast. Early the following morning, July 14, nine Indians in a canoe approached the *Santiago* and offered sea otter skins and fish to trade. Afterward, Hezeta and an armed party went ashore and performed the customary possession ceremony—erecting a cross and reading the *requirimiento*, which ordered Indians to accept Spanish rule and Christian conversion—as Spaniards had done all over North and South America. They kept this one quick because they feared that the deteriorating weather would beach the *Santiago*. Naming the sheltered anchorage Rada de Bucareli (Bucareli's Roadstead), Hezeta described the landing site as being "choked with brush and branches so that any object at a distance of four *varas* [twelve feet] can not be seen by anyone outside," a condition that heightened his anxiety and hastened their return to the *Santiago*.[22]

On sailing farther north along the coast, his crew spotted the *Sonora* near the mouth of a river and heard the firing of shots. They later learned that a host of Indian warriors had killed several Spanish crewmembers. The bloodshed resulted from a chain of events that had begun the evening before. A canoe of Indians had approached the *Sonora*, and Bodega y Quadra invited them aboard and gave presents. The Indians reciprocated with fish and whale flesh and invited the crew to come to their village to feast and dance. The following morning, Bodega y Quadra sent seven crewmembers ashore in a launch to collect water and to cut a topmast. According to the Spanish witnesses, when they arrived at the mouth of the river, two to three hundred Indians ambushed them. They "cut to pieces" five of the crew as another two "escap[ed] from their hideous cruelty by throwing themselves into the sea," only to tire and drown.[23] The attacking Indians stripped the launch of its iron, salvaged what boards they could, and set the remainder afire.

As the boat smoldered on the shore, the attackers retreated into the woods, appearing to take the dismembered Spanish bodies with them, an action that convinced the seven remaining crewmembers aboard the schooner that the attackers were cannibals. At the same time, nine canoes of Indians who had visited them the evening before returned. A sailor on the *Sonora* alerted the crew that the newcomers had armed themselves, yet as they drew nearer, the Indians made signs of friendship. The Spanish offered glass beads to entice them to approach. When a canoe came within range, the Spaniards fired their muskets and a swivel gun (small cannon)—these were the shots the *Santiago* crew heard. The fusillade "killed seven of the nine [Indians in the lead canoe], thus making them pay for life for the seven Spaniards they had slain," and the canoes retreated hastily. When the Spanish ships reunited, Bodega y Quadra urged Hezeta to land a party onshore so they could punish the "treacherous" Indians. The commander, however, decided against vengeance. Not only did he have instructions to limit violence to cases of self-defense, but the crew were also outnumbered and would be fighting in overgrown terrain that the enemy knew well. He recognized that if he lost any more men, he would need to turn back. Instead, he ordered the vessels to leave the coast and to push north.[24]

During the return voyage south several days later, they again encountered Indians while sailing near the waters where they had lost the seven crewmembers. A canoe carrying ten Indians came out to the *Santiago*, offering pelts and dried smelt for trade. One of the sailors told Hezeta that he recognized two as part of the group that had come onboard the *Sonora* the evening before being attacked. The commander plotted to lure the canoe close enough to take them hostage. The Indians evaded his efforts and skillfully kept the canoe positioned into the wind, making it impossible for the Spanish to overtake them. Hezeta lost sight of them at sundown, and the following day, he sailed south away from the Northwest Coast.[25]

Unlike the earlier Pérez voyage, Hezeta's 1775 expedition illustrates that competition between distinct peoples of the ča·di· borderland could lead to violence. While exploring the Washington coast, the vessels had sailed into the waters of two competing tribal nations, the Quileute and Quinault, both just south of the Makahs. Although the Spanish were unable—or unwilling—to distinguish one group from another, the concurrent incidents of trade and violence indicate that they had encountered two different peoples. The peaceful interactions were likely with Quileutes, whereas the violent ones involved Quinaults, an understanding corroborated by Quinault oral histories. Those who visited the *Sonora* on the evening of July 13 had exchanged whale flesh and fish for "trifles" offered by the Spanish—these were Quileutes because they had better access to whale meat, something that Quinaults would have been unlikely to have because they only harvested the occasional drift whale.[26] When seven of the *Sonora*'s crew went ashore, they landed at the mouth of the Quinault River, within Quinault territory and near Taholah, one of their villages.[27] When the Quileute canoes returned after the Quinault ambush, they had armed themselves to fight the Quinault, not to attack the Spanish aboard the *Sonora*. With emotions running high after witnessing the death of seven crewmembers, the Spaniards fired on the Quileutes, assuming that they had been the attacking Indians and misunderstanding that they offered support against a common enemy, the Quinault.

This incident also reveals clashing efforts among Quileutes, Quinaults, and Spaniards to produce and control space in the southern corner of the ča·di· borderland. The position of the Spanish vessels suggests that the Quileute traders had trespassed in Quinault waters when they offered sea otter skins and fish to exchange. By trading in Quinault waters, Quileutes challenged the Quinaults' control over this marine space. Quileutes probably armed themselves in an attempt to ally with the Spanish against their rivals. On a voyage of exploration, the Spanish engaged in producing space for empire. They took "possession" of the land by planting a cross, an action which some Quinaults possibly witnessed from the safety of the woods that had made the Spaniards nervous.[28] However, the Quinault attack on their shore party demonstrated the fiction of this space being Spanish. Complex indigenous dynamics fueled the Quinaults' violent reaction. They attacked the Spaniards onshore to punish them for trading with the rival Quileutes in Quinault waters. Spanish attempts at taking timber and freshwater from woods and rivers owned by titleholders also would have concerned Quinaults. This attack exemplified Quinault efforts to control interactions within tribal space, illustrating that from the beginning of imperial efforts at producing space in the Northwest Coast, indigenous peoples frustrated this process.

Scholars often emphasize the peaceful quality of the region's next mamáni-indigenous encounter, Captain Cook's monthlong sojourn at Friendly Cove in April 1778. But tensions of violence particular to the ča·di· borderland marked that episode, too. What Europeans perceived as theft provoked initial anxieties among the British crew. After just one day among the Mowachahts of Nootka Sound, Cook concluded that "they were as light fingered as any people we had before met." Indians pilfered many small items, including nails, chisels, and other pieces of metal. Some of these petty thefts went unnoticed by the British at the time, but others seemed threatening to voyagers so far from home, especially when important equipment went missing. Someone stole a thirty-pound iron hook used to pull up the main anchor. Cook also complained about the Natives' sharp trading practices. Some cheated his crew by mixing water in with the whale oil they sold. Subsequent traders complained of Mowachaht chiefs who blackened sea otter pelts with charcoal to make them appear of a higher value.[29]

We should understand these thefts and apparently unscrupulous trading practices within the context of the Northwest Coast culture and of sociocultural dynamics specific to the ča·di· borderland. Many accounts noted supposed incidents of theft between distinct, unrelated peoples. John Rickman, a lieutenant on the *Resolution,* one of the two vessels on Cook's third voyage, described an incident where Mowachahts "took everything" from a non-Mowachaht "stately youth" who had visited the ship and traded. To British eyes, it appeared that the inhabitants of Friendly Cove had stolen these goods. From the perspective of the indigenous inhabitants of the ča·di· borderland, however, the young chief had committed the theft by trading with the mamánis without the Mowachaht chief Maquinna's permission. Mowachahts simply confiscated the goods he had received illicitly. Non-Native explorers' and traders' accounts rarely recorded thefts among the inhabitants of one village or within a confederation of communities. In 1787, the British trader James Colnett believed that the inhabitants of any one village in Nootka Sound were "strictly honest among themselves."[30] Theft was unusual within a village where everyone shared real or fictive kinship.

The fact that nearly all the mamánis and babałids lacked kinship connections to local indigenous communities made them fair targets for theft. Nuu-chah-nulths and other ča·di· borderlanders saw non-Native property as up for grabs because Europeans were outside the established kinship and trade networks of the region. Perhaps the inhabitants of Nootka Sound saw non-kin Europeans as potential enemies and therefore legitimate marks for theft. Chiefs might have found the property threatening if it fell into the hands of a rival who might use it against enemies or to enhance status. Perhaps this concern encouraged leaders to overlook thefts of non-Native property, especially when the valued goods ended up in their village rather than a rival's.[31]

Social status also shaped these incidents. In the ča·di· borderland, trade often happened between high-ranking equals who ritualized exchanges through formal diplomatic protocols. Trade across status ranks, though, was more of a free-for-all. Chiefs often had the right to seize what they wanted from the lower ranks when commoners operated in leaders' owned spaces. Colnett noted that Oughomeize, a Muchalaht chief along the eastern shores of Nootka Sound, intercepted canoes returning from his fishing grounds, and he took a percentage of the catch. The same dynamics shaped incidents of supposed "theft." Natives probably classified many sailors and laborers aboard vessels as slaves because they did the work ascribed to the lowest-ranking members of society. Eighteenth-century Europeans and Euro-Americans would have understood this assumption because some compared a sailor's lot—most of whom had been impressed into service—to that of black slaves. Many of the accounts of theft occurred when an Indian stole something from a non-Native who was not an identifiable officer. Cook noted an early incident where a pair of Indian men worked together to steal from one of his sailors; one individual "amused" the crewman while another stole from him.[32]

To Natives, these incidents inscribed class and status along indigenous terms. From the British perspective, however, they exemplified theft. Although crew comments written in hindsight described indigenous hosts who "offered the least violence" while Cook's vessels were at Friendly Cove, at the time, the British found theft and underhanded trading practices threatening and believed that they portended violence. When their hosts armed themselves against potential antagonists about to enter Friendly Cove, some crewmembers feared they might be preparing to attack.[33]

Non-Native captains found these thefts galling. Eighteenth-century captains possessed "near-dictatorial powers [that] made the ship one of the earliest totalitarian work environments."[34] All captains relied on physical force to keep the sailors—men in a lower social class than the captain and his officers—in line. This included beatings, curses, and threats to kill, especially if any sailor raised a hand in self-defense. Kanakas (Native Hawaiians) and non-Anglo sailors received more disciplinary actions than Anglo crewmembers.[35] Captains meted out punishments such as keel-hauling, running the gauntlet, and flogging with the cat-o'-nine-tails in front of the crew in order to intimidate the rest into following his orders.[36] Recognizing the point beyond which one should not push the crew, shrewd captains combined rewards, promises, and kind words with brute strength, curses, and threats to maintain authority and prevent mutiny.

This disciplinary model influenced how captains and crew dealt with Natives whom they believed had done them wrong. Drawing on the early eighteenth-century experience in which authority and discipline stabilized the merchant shipping industry and empire, maritime fur trade captains of the late eighteenth century believed that they needed to establish discipline over indigenous peoples in the Northwest Coast.[37] They deployed violence to create imperial spaces in the ča·di· borderland. As on their ships, captains believed that punishments were most effective when conducted in front of an audience of potential offenders. Some captains struck chiefs in front of their people, fired on canoes with other warriors watching, and destroyed villages while Natives hid in nearby woods. Shrewd traders understood that a combination of enticements and violence best intimidated potentially dangerous trade partners.

British crewmembers and officers expressed their anxieties by employing violence to punish thieves. Cook noted that an Indian thief "generally relinquished his prize with reluctancy and sometimes not without force."[38] One midshipman also wrote about a fellow sailor who threw a piece of wood at one thief with such force that it cracked a canoe it hit instead to the waterline. Those in the canoe became angry and drew their bows to fire at the sailor, but another crewmember intervened, firing an arrow from a bow he had just purchased from an Indian man.[39] Even Cook himself, often viewed as a paragon of restraint, attempted to punish indigenous thieves. After having been at Friendly Cove for nearly a month and suffering from what he perceived as theft, the exasperated Cook fired a musket loaded with small shot at a canoe carrying someone who had stolen a small piece of iron. He injured four men in their backs and "made the whole party leave us rather apparantly in an ill Humour with us."[40] The crew and officers exerted their authority to extend British space in this corner of the ča·di· borderland. But continued thefts indicated their failure.

Much as Hezeta's 1775 expedition had triggered conflict off the Washington coast, at Nootka Sound, Cook's presence in 1778 also exacerbated tensions among distinct peoples with a history of mutual hostility. Charles Clerke, commander of the *Discovery*, reported that the local Indians had many disputes with neighboring peoples. At one point, three to four hundred Mowachahts paddled across Nootka Sound to attack enemies on the opposite shore. On their return, they exchanged with the British some sea otter pelts they had seized from their rivals.[41] This and other longstanding conflicts demonstrate that this was a region contested long before the arrival of Europeans. With the influx of new goods, Maquinna employed violence to maintain his authority and to expand Mowachaht control. His indigenous methods of warfare and politics complicated imperial designs to transform this into European zones of safety, order, and free trade.

MARITIME FUR TRADE VIOLENCE IN THE ČA·DI· BORDERLAND, 1786–1803

Similar dynamics of theft, intimidation, and conflict pervaded the maritime fur trade throughout the ča·di· borderland. When a growing number of non-Native traders came to the area during the late eighteenth century, relations of violence expanded along existing lines of tension in the region, encompassing a greater variety of peoples. Increased Native contacts with mamánis and babałids provided numerous opportunities for misunderstandings, insults, and new violence. Some incidents of violence had a productive quality because borderlands dynamics allowed rivals to benefit from discord elsewhere. Chiefs such as Tatoosh used conflict to their advantage to expand their influence in this indigenous marine borderland.

Earlier incidents of violence shaped subsequent interactions between indigenous peoples and non-Natives. In 1787, twelve years after Hezeta's voyage of violence along the Washington coast, Captain Charles Barkley brought the four-hundred-ton, twenty-gun *Imperial Eagle* to the region seeking sea otter skins.[42] Because East India Company employees had surreptitiously financed the voyage, the twenty-six-year-old Barkley renamed the *Louden* the *Imperial Eagle* and flew the Austrian flag as a subterfuge to avoid the expensive licensing fees that they were supposed to pay to the company. Barkley and his crew spent more than a month at Nootka Sound trading for furs. After other licensed trading vessels arrived, Barkley completed his transactions at Yuquot and sailed south along the Vancouver Island coast, stopping at Clayoquot Sound and Barkley Sound to collect furs from Wickaninnish and related peoples. Later, he headed south across the strait, identifying and naming this the "long lost strait of Juan de Fuca."

Sailing south along the coast of the Olympic Peninsula, Barkley ran into serious trouble near where Indians had attacked Hezeta's Spanish crew. The British captain anchored off the mainland and sent thirteen men in two boats to travel up the Hoh River to trade with Indians. Because the river was too shallow for the longboat, the smaller craft with six men took a sheet of copper for trade and rowed upstream, never to be seen again. When Barkley sent an armed party ashore the next day, they discovered clothes and linen, "mangled and bloody," but they found neither bodies nor boat. Drawing on a common fear of Pacific Natives consuming Europeans, they concluded that the sailors had been eaten and set a nearby Hoh village afire in retribution.[43] Afterward, Barkley sailed for China, where he sold his eight hundred furs for $30,000, which fueled dreams of wealth despite news of hostile Natives.

Barkley had brought the *Imperial Eagle* into waters already bloodied by an earlier cross-cultural encounter. Other Native peoples told babałid captains that Quileutes had attacked Barkley's crew.[44] Quileutes would have had at least two reasons to do so. First, they recalled the encounter from twelve years earlier when babałids (Spaniards) fired on them without cause, slaughtering a canoe-load of their people who had offered support against the attacking Quinault warriors. Second, Quileute chiefs desired to keep non-Natives away from the Hoh village that Barkley approached. With the competitive dynamics of this indigenous borderland, Quileute titleholders would have blocked a rival Hoh chief's access to valued trade goods. From the Quileute perspective, they had seen the *Imperial Eagle* sail past their village. Rather than stopping to offer trade—and to make up for the murderous actions of the earlier non-Native visitors—the vessel anchored in the waters of their closest competitors. The attack on the crew of the *Imperial Eagle* exemplified strategic violence, which Quileutes used to discourage the British from trading with rivals.

Especially when these incidents resulted in dead Europeans, indigenous power created a geography of fear for non-Native visitors to the Northwest Coast. Non-Native reactions to and memories of the Spanish and British deaths along the Olympic Peninsula illustrate this process. After Quinaults killed members of his crew, Bodega y Quadra mapped this violent incident into the imaginations of Spaniards and other Europeans by naming the location of the "massacre" Punta de los Mártires (Martyrs Point). He also named a nearby island Isla de Dolores (Isle of Sorrows).[45] The names Bodega y Quadra bestowed on these features appeared on late eighteenth-century maps of the Pacific Northwest. Similarly, Barkley named the waterway where he lost thirteen men Destruction River and renamed Bodega y Quadra's Isla de Dolores with an English name, Destruction Island, the name it carries to this day.[46] The act of naming transforms a space "symbolically into a place . . . a space with history."[47] For both of these Spanish and British captains, violence would forever mark the histories of these places.

Captured on maps, the geography of fear made non-Natives anxious and fearful when on the Northwest Coast. This can be seen throughout Meares's time in the region. The "massacre" of the sailors of the *Imperial Eagle* weighed on the minds of Meares and his British crewmembers, and it shaped many of their actions and interactions with various indigenous peoples. Erecting a trading base and crude shipyard at Yuquot, Meares enclosed them within a strong breastwork and defended it with a cannon. Revealing his anxiety, he explained that they "wished to operate on [Indian] fears as well as their gratitude." Meares also overlooked most thefts, even of important items such as the ship's pinnace, a small boat handy for shore landings. Someone in Friendly Cove had stolen and broken it apart for its iron and nails. Although both Maquinna and Callicum professed to know nothing about its theft, Meares chose not to confront them about this very serious loss. He feared that a confrontation might jeopardize their trading activities or lead to a more serious conflict in this remote corner of the Pacific.[48]

Thefts prompted Meares to take precautions, which often insulted indigenous leaders. When they first anchored off Wickaninnish's village in Clayoquot Sound, Meares feared the chief's power to do "mischief" against the vessel and its crew. The captain always kept armed crewmembers on deck and curtailed the number of Indians on the *Felice* at any one time. This constant vigilance angered the

Clayoquot chief, who left the ship and refused to allow his people to trade. Meares then had to assuage the chief's feelings by giving him a sword, a large copper dish, and a pistol, an item Wickaninnish had desired for some time.[49]

Meares's anxieties heightened when he crossed into Makah marine space. Wickaninnish had already warned the captain that Tatoosh and his people were "subtle and barbarous." Coming from the chief of the Clayoquot, a bold people who appeared less civilized than those he had met at Friendly Cove, Wickaninnish's warning must have commanded the captain's attention. After Tatoosh's confrontation with Meares aboard the *Felice*, the British dispatched the longboat to look for secure anchorage. Fear kept the longboat crew from retaliating when a "great crowd of canoes" surrounded the small boat and when intimidating Makah men leapt aboard and stole various articles. For Tatoosh and his warriors, taking goods from total outsiders, these babałids, was justified under cultural norms, especially after the captain had insulted the Makah chief. Fortunately for the longboat's crew, the People of the Cape stopped short of an all-out assault, probably because they hoped that intimidation would encourage Meares to make up for the insult by giving gifts. Just before departing Makah waters the next day, Meares wrote of their isolation "on a wild and unfrequented coast, in a distant corner of the globe, far removed from all those friends, connections, and circumstance which form the charm and comfort of life, and taking our course, as it were through a solitary ocean."[50] Fear hurried them out of Makah waters, despite Tatoosh's efforts to make amends for his earlier confrontational behavior.

The crew's anxieties intensified when they entered the waters where Barkley's *Imperial Eagle* had lost six of its crew. Coming within sight of Destruction Island, the weather became "thick and gloomy" and then turned to rain. The wind died, forcing Meares to anchor off a Quileute village, which "distress[ed]" the crew, who feared becoming a meal for "cannibals." The captain's account captured the crew's anxiety: "The wretched fate of the people belonging to the *Imperial Eagle*, evidently predominated in the minds of our crew; and being on the very coast where such an act of barbarity was committed, the infectious apprehension of a similar destruction spread amongst them. It was the common subject of their discourse, and had such an influence on their spirits, as to endanger the loss of the ship."[51] Fortunately for the crew, a wind kicked up, and the *Felice* tacked out of the frightening waters by nightfall. Meares's impressions illustrate the geography of fear through which he and his crew sailed.

For their part, indigenous borderlanders remained ambivalent about the mamánis and babałids. Chiefs and their followers desired the trade goods that vessels brought. The non-Native scramble for furs even encouraged some chiefs to raid other indigenous peoples possessing "soft gold." Late in the summer of 1788,

Meares witnessed Maquinna, Callicum, and Comekala lead a Mowachaht navy north to wage war on a distant people. Although Maquinna told Meares that they were retaliating against those who had attacked a village under the leadership of his grandmother, the battle netted a "great booty of sea-otter skins."[52] Some chiefs tried to gain mamáni allies in conflicts against others. When Bodega y Quadra's cabin boy turned up dead in 1792, Maquinna attempted to convince the Spaniards that a rival on the other side of Nootka Sound had ordered the murder. Maquinna offered to have his brother Comekala take a Spanish launch, armed with several swivel guns, to punish the murderer. Maquinna wanted this to be a joint Spanish-Mowachaht expedition so that his enemies would know that "Maquinna is the same as Quadra, and Quadra is the same as Maquinna."[53] A common pattern throughout the eighteenth-century North American West, displaced violence was often the result of imperialism: one group of indigenous peoples committed violent acts against others for reasons related to the expanding colonial world.[54] In the čaˑdiˑ borderland, displaced violence happened along indigenous lines of tension. Maquinna, for example, took this opportunity to strike at longtime enemies. For these influential chiefs, the ability to wage war and plunder others indicated their power to control areas distant from home villages.

Sometimes, a chief manipulated the borderlands' dynamics of rivalry and conflict to expand his influence. Tatoosh did so in the late eighteenth century. When Meares agreed to the exclusive trading arrangement with Wickaninnish in 1788, this action exacerbated existing tensions within the borderlands, and Tatoosh maneuvered himself into a position to extend his influence deeper into the Strait of Juan de Fuca. After Meares demonstrated that he would not offer the Makah chief a similar trading arrangement, Tatoosh became worried that Wickaninnish's exclusive agreement with the babałid trader would give his Clayoquot rival an inordinate amount of regional influence. Therefore, when the *Felice* returned to the area and sent its longboat deeper into the strait, Tatoosh seized the opportunity to strike at the Meares-Wickaninnish alliance. Leveraging ties with Pacheedahts on Vancouver Island, Tatoosh convinced them to join his warriors in attacking the British longboat just as the Makah chief declared war on Wickaninnish. Pacheedahts preferred an alliance with the powerful chief from Cape Flattery to falling prey to Wickaninnish's expansion. Neighbors of the conquest-minded Clayoquot chief, the Pacheedahts worried that they might be next, especially now that he had strong ties to a non-Native trader who provided him with firearms and metal weapons.

The alliance with Tatoosh came at a cost, however. Instead of conquest at the hands of the Clayoquots, Pacheedahts needed to provide furs to the Makah chief. When the *Lady Washington* sailed into the Strait of Juan de Fuca a year later, the American crew complained that Pacheedahts and others along the strait had no furs because "Tatooth of Clahaset" had already procured them. It also appears that Tatoosh used this foothold on Vancouver Island to expand his authority even farther into the borderlands. Probably through a combination of trade opportunities, kinship ties, intimidation, and violence, Tatoosh held sway over a village on the southwest corner of the island by 1792. At this time, Spaniards noted that the Makah chief "was one of the most feared of all the chiefs who live on these shores, and that he had won the greatest respect and authority among [the inhabitants of this village], on account of his bravery, ability and character." In 1793, after Tatoosh had finished trading furs with the Boston vessel *Jefferson* at Barkley Sound, he "took the opportunity to plunder the [local] natives." What the captain mistook as plundering was Tatoosh exerting his titleholder's privilege to collect furs and other goods from people over whom he held authority. But Tatoosh's influence, and that of subsequent chiefs, over non-Makah villages and peoples did not go uncontested. By 1825, the People of the Cape were engaged in an "inveterate war" with the Clayoquots and Ditidahts, enslaving many to sell to indigenous communities as far south as the Columbia River. Neighboring peoples rankled at Makah influence in the čaꞏdiꞏ borderland. At times, S'Klallams along the northern edge of the Olympic Peninsula and Quileutes to the south maintained antagonistic relations with Makahs through the mid-nineteenth century.[55]

Violence enabled some powerful chiefs to maintain or enhance their status; mamáni and babałid attacks against their people and neighbors, however, made them wary. One contemporary observer worried that the "hot tempered character" of his fellow sailors sparked altercations with Indian men.[56] In many ways, this observation was an understatement. Non-Native intimidation, theft, and violence created an atmosphere of fear and even terror within indigenous villages and among certain groups. And mamánis and babałids committed plenty of violence to make indigenous peoples cautious. Some of this violence was possibly a strategy on the part of ship captains to maintain "advantage" over indigenous peoples.[57] Perhaps this was one way that captains attempted to mitigate the geography of fear.

While non-Native captains and crew complained about indigenous thefts, many of the mamánis and babałids also stole from Indians, who then retaliated. In 1787, Captain Barkley angered the Nootka Sound chiefs when he ignored indigenous trading protocols by intercepting canoes and seizing sea otter skins, offering Indians only what he thought proper. In 1803, Maquinna complained to his "white slave" John Jewitt that Captain Tawnington entered Maquinna's longhouse when the chief was gone and stole forty of his best furs at musketpoint from his women and slaves. This plundering especially insulted Maquinna because the Mowachahts had treated the captain well when he wintered at Nootka Sound.[58] Non-Natives committed actions that indigenous peoples perceived as theft yet non-Natives saw differently. Northwest Coast societies believed that everything had an owner. So when mamảnis and babałids entered sovereign spaces of titleholders and helped themselves to water, driftwood, timber, fish, sea mammals, game, and wild plants, the rightful owners saw this as stealing. These thefts encouraged reciprocal takings by indigenous peoples.

While chiefs perceived theft of property and kidnappings as affronts to their authority, they saw attacks on themselves and their people as more serious challenges requiring forceful responses. The first mamảni after Captain Cook to bring a vessel into the ča·di· borderland, the British trader James Hanna, had what other traders called "a very serious Engagement with the Natives."[59] In September 1785, Hanna sailed the *Sea Otter* into Nootka Sound. After a few days of amicable trade with the Mowachahts, a dispute arose. Hanna fired on a canoe carrying an Indian blamed for stealing a chisel, which the accused thought he had received in exchange for a fur. This fusillade killed twenty men, women, and children. On the schooner at the time, Maquinna escaped by ignominiously leaping into the water from the quarterdeck.[60] After avoiding the *Sea Otter* for a few days, several canoes approached the schooner, and a herald stood in one and "solemnly declared" the "reasons for war," informing Hanna that they would attack the following day. The next day, a fleet of canoes surrounded the schooner and fired a "shower of arrows and darts," but "Captain Hannay's musquetry and small guns did great execution among them, and they drew off."[61] Afterward, a Mowachaht came forward and begged for peace. Trade commenced once again and continued until the British trader sailed for China.

Also during this voyage, one of Hanna's sailors played a practical joke on Maquinna, a stunt with long-lasting consequences. Still upset by this incident four years later, the Mowachaht chief told the Spanish captain Esteban José Martínez about it. Eager to highlight the poor behavior of a British captain, Martínez recorded the incident in his journal: "One day, when Macuina, the principal chief of the village in this port where we are lying, went on board [Hanna's] ship to visit him, and when they had seated him near the binnacle, they sprinkled a little powder under his chair, giving him to understand that this was an honor which they showed to chiefs. He supposed that the powder was dark colored sand, but he soon felt its effect, when one of the Englishmen set off the charge. Poor Macuina was raised from the deck by the explosion and had his buttocks scorched; he showed me the scars."[62] Unlike violence directed at lower-ranking Indians, this insult struck at the chief. Compounded by Hanna's killing of twenty Indians for a petty theft, the practical joke prompted Maquinna to limit the flow of furs. Although violence did not shut down trade at this time, it did limit it—Hanna complained that Maquinna only traded half the furs his people had. Perpetrated by low-status sailors, this prank demonstrated that sailors were not completely controlled by their captains. Indeed, their actions could help set, or sometimes harm, the terms of trade and interactions in ways that commanders did not intend. More important, this incident demonstrated that chiefs controlled the rules of exchange and could frustrate non-Native commercial desires.

Rival chiefs could turn violence against another group of indigenous people in the ča·di· borderland to their advantage. Cleaskinah, an Ahousaht chief and lesser rival to Maquinna, exchanged names with Hanna during his 1785 voyage to the Northwest Coast.[63] Hearing of the conflict between Hanna and Maquinna, Cleaskinah recognized the opportunity to gain trade goods from the British vessel rather than mediated through the more powerful Mowachaht chief. Hanna welcomed the Ahousaht chief's offer because Maquinna had curtailed trade with the *Sea Otter.*

The fact that mamáni̇s and babałids struck indiscriminately at chiefs and commoners alike concerned many titleholders. In 1789, Martínez established a settlement and fort at Nootka Sound to strengthen Spanish sovereignty in the face of Russian, English, and US encroachments along the west coast of North America. Martínez was an unpopular commander—the expedition's naturalist, José Mariano Moziño, described him as a "ferocious pirate whose avarice did not respect a single thing." Martínez's confrontational actions in seizing several English trading vessels precipitated the Nootka Sound Controversy, which nearly brought England and Spain to war and resulted in the loss of Spanish claims to the Northwest Coast. More concerning for Native peoples in Nootka Sound, brutal violence marked his time there. When Callicum, the second highest-ranked chief in Nootka Sound, boarded the *Princessa* and called Martínez a "wicked man" for seizing the vessels of the Mowachaht's British friends, the captain had him killed for his impertinence as the chief departed. When Martínez's weapon misfired while shooting at the retreating chief, another Spaniard shot Callicum dead. His body tumbled into the sea and sank. Afterward, the chief's father begged Martínez for permission to "creep for the body beneath the water," but the captain refused the request until presented with a sufficient quantity of sea otter pelts. Moziño noted that Callicum's "blood with which the sea was tinted, saddened the natives beyond measure" and prompted Maquinna to flee Nootka Sound to seek safety among Wicka-ninnish.[64]

Nuu-chah-nulth oral histories reveal a darker side to the Spanish time at Nootka Sound. Martínez's Yuquot fort included a blacksmith shop to manufacture small metal trade items and to supply the garrison with arms. Nuu-chah-nulth histories remember that some Spaniards mistreated young Indian girls, pulling them into the blacksmith's shop "without any romance." The blacksmith always had a red-hot iron ready for those who refused. According to an oral account, the smith would poke the hot iron into a girl's vagina if she refused his unwanted advances; some died from their injuries.[65] Colonial sexual violence such as this "establishe[d] the ideology that Native bodies [were] inherently violable—and by extension, that Native lands [were] also inherently violable."[66] Even if this example of horrifying violence has been exaggerated over centuries of oral histories, what is important is that Spaniards created a social environment in which such abuses were possible.

Spaniards in positions of power attempted to produce imperial space by controlling Natives through violence and intimidation. Martínez killed Callicum because the chief had shown disrespect for him in front of his men on his own vessel. Already unpopular among his crew, perhaps Martínez feared that allowing such disrespect would encourage his crew to do the same or even mutiny. He also demonstrated his spatial control over the very waters of Friendly Cove by prohibiting Callicum's father from recovering his son's body. In this violent environment shaped by the "ferocious" Martínez, his men felt that they had the power to deploy sexual violence against Native women. From the male Iberian perspective, Mowachahts needed to learn the value of hierarchy in Spanish spaces such as the blacksmith's shop and the *Princessa*. Far from disapproving official eyes, some Spaniards deployed such violence to demonstrate their control over Yuquot.

Spanish abuse of Mowachahts affected cross-cultural interactions in other parts of the ča·di· borderland when news of the atrocities spread. A year after Martínez abandoned the Yuquot outpost, Makahs resisted subsequent Spanish efforts to control Cape Flattery. In late July 1790, Manuel Quimper sailed the *Princesa Real* into Neah Bay, took possession for the Spanish Empire, and named it Nuñez Gaona. Although he noted the excellent shelter the bay offered and that the surrounding country appeared fertile with several level spots for settlement, the People of the Cape discouraged him from staying long. Before his arrival, he had certainly heard firsthand from Bodega y Quadra about the troubles the 1775 Hezeta expedition encountered on the Northwest Coast—the two sailed together from Cádiz, Spain, to New Spain in 1789—which established Quimper's expectation to experience a geography of fear. Makahs confirmed this when they told him that they "pride[d] themselves on having killed the captain" of a fur trading vessel. Much to Quimper's horror, they ambushed and left for dead one of his sailors when a group of Spaniards went ashore and used a Makah stream—owned by a chief—to wash their clothes.[67] As some Spaniards accrued a nasty reputation, so Makah resistance earned them a reputation for fierce independence that endured for the next century.

Despite the People of the Cape's warlike reputation, the viceroy of New Spain—gazing at a map while sitting in Mexico City more than a thousand miles away from Cape Flattery—concluded that Nuñez Gaona (Neah Bay) was a suitable spot for a new Spanish garrison. In 1792, he ordered Salvador Fidalgo to fortify the port by establishing a permanent Spanish presence there. Fidalgo's *Princessa* anchored at Nuñez Gaona in late May. After taking possession of the site with the customary formalities, Fidalgo's crew began building the outpost, which consisted of a shed, bakery, provisional barracks, blacksmith's shop, corral for cattle, and garden.

Spanish outpost at Nuñez Gaona (Neah Bay) and "grand war canoe" of Chief Tatoosh. On the right is the Spanish frigate *Princessa*; the *Mexicana* and *Sutil* of the Galiano exploration of the Strait of Juan de Fuca lie astern. Drawing by José Cardero, 1789–94, who accompanied the Alejandro Malaspina and Galiano expeditions to the Pacific. Image courtesy the Museo de América, Madrid.

Relations among the Spanish and the People of the Cape remained tense. Recalling the earlier Makah assault on a sailor from Quimper's expedition and the fate of Hezeta's crew who put ashore just south of Cape Flattery, Fidalgo took precautions. He kept a longboat close to shore to evacuate the garrison if Makahs attacked. The Spaniards fortified the outpost and protected it with six small cannons. Fidalgo allowed only chiefs on board to trade, and he refused to provide them with arms or even knives. At sunset, Fidalgo's crew fired a cannon to warn the People of the Cape to stay away from the *Princessa* and the outpost until dawn. Not only did these actions highlight the geography of fear that must have weighed on Fidalgo's mind, but they also indicate that Fidalgo understood the tenuous hold imperial Spain had over Makah space.

At the beginning of July, Antonio Serantes, the *Princessa*'s pilot, disappeared while hunting in the woods behind the outpost. The following morning, twenty men and several dogs searched the woods in vain. Meanwhile, a Makah told Fidalgo that Chief Tatoosh had killed the Spanish pilot. Although the Spanish sources do not note what would have caused Tatoosh to kill Serantes, Makah oral histories from the 1860s relate that the People of the Cape had killed Serantes for committing several rapes.[68] In a fit of rage, Fidalgo fired on two canoes of Makahs, killing all within except a boy of fifteen and a girl of six.[69] Several days later, Spaniards found Serantes's body in the woods. When interviewed by Bodega y Quadra not long after this incident, Tatoosh related that non-Makahs had murdered and robbed Serantes before fleeing the area. Although the commander did not believe Tatoosh, he realized the precarious nature of the tiny Spanish settlement and decided to befriend the powerful chief by giving gifts for sharing this information.

While Makahs continued trading with the Spanish, tensions remained high. Canoes of warriors intimidated passing vessels, and chiefs exchanged sea otter pelts with British and American vessels, something that frustrated Fidalgo because these competitors took valuable furs away from him. The People of the Cape told any non-Spanish captain who would listen that they disliked the intruders. Constant Makah threats, coupled with the inability of Bodega y Quadra and George Vancouver—empowered by the British crown to resolve the Nootka Sound Controversy—to settle the Pacific boundary claims between their respective empires, encouraged the viceroy to abandon Neah Bay.[70] Less than four months after Fidalgo sailed the *Princessa* into Nuñez Gaona, Bodega y Quadra ordered him to abandon the fledgling outpost and remove his garrison to Nootka Sound. Once the Spanish retreated from Neah Bay, Makahs dismantled the outpost as if to eradicate its former presence. They burned what they could not use, threw the bricks in a nearby creek, and transformed the site into a refuse heap.[71]

The People of the Cape had stymied Spanish efforts at producing imperial space in their customary territory.

LEGACIES OF VIOLENCE IN THE ČA·DI· BORDERLAND

As chiefs struggled to maintain their influence in the changing dynamics of the early nineteenth-century ča·di· borderland, they occasionally struck at maritime fur trade vessels in dramatic incidents that became infamous examples of "savage" violence and confirmed non-Native assumptions about indigenous peoples of the region. Two specific incidents, the Mowachaht capture of the *Boston* in 1803 and the Clayoquot attack on the *Tonquin* in 1811, clarified for non-Natives a geography of fear for the west coast of Vancouver Island, which contributed to reorienting the maritime fur trade away from these coastal villages and ended the diplomatic protocol that once structured encounters. These changes altered the indigenous sociopolitical dynamics of the ča·di· borderland, strengthening the Makahs' position at Cape Flattery.

On March 22, 1803, Maquinna and his warriors attacked the crew of the *Boston* after Captain John Salter had offended the Mowachaht chief. Salter had given Maquinna a double-barreled musket, which broke after a few days' use. When the chief complained about the defective weapon, Salter angered Maquinna by calling him a liar and snatching away the musket. A few days later, the Mowachaht chief returned. He lured away some sailors, encouraging them to fish for salmon some distance from the *Boston*. Then he and his warriors killed those remaining on the vessel and lined the quarterdeck with their severed heads. Maquinna spared the lives of John Jewitt and John Thompson, the ship's blacksmith and sail maker, and enslaved them. They remained as his "white slaves" for almost twenty-eight months. After their period of captivity, Jewitt published the journal (1807) he kept of his time at Nootka Sound and later adapted it into a narrative (1815) and a play (1817) in which he starred. At the time, Jewitt's captivity narrative sold well, and it has shaped our view of the Northwest Coast and its indigenous peoples for the past two centuries.[72]

Questions remain about why the Mowachaht chief attacked the *Boston*. Historian Anya Zilberstein has noted that scholars characterize Maquinna's action as an episode "in what had become a cycle of Indian retaliation for incidents of Euro-American misconduct and guile." She correctly critiques this standard assumption for simplifying the complex dynamics of the maritime fur trade and for "relying instead on the well-worn stereotypes of natives as bloodthirsty or victimized primitives."[73] Recent examinations of the maritime fur trade have set this incident within other contexts. Geographer Daniel Clayton, for example,

Maquinna's attack on the *Boston* at Nootka Sound, 1803. The Yuquot chief likely hoped that seizing the vessel would result in a wealth of trade goods that would bolster his waning influence in the ča·di· borderland. Illustration from the 1816 edition of *A Narrative of the Adventures and Sufferings of John R. Jewitt*. Oregon Historical Society, #cn 086321.

argues that "chiefly power and prestige" motivated Maquinna's actions.[74] However, Clayton limits his sociopolitical analysis to neighboring chiefs on Vancouver Island and does not encompass the more relevant dynamics of the larger ča·di· borderland.

Acknowledging the status issues Clayton notes, Zilberstein problematically argues that Maquinna resorted to violence out of desperation caused by food shortages. According to her analysis, she concludes that those living at Yuquot produced few consumables and had to import most of their food. Zilberstein posits that with the advent of the maritime fur trade in the late 1780s, Mowachahts redirected their labor from meeting basic subsistence needs toward hunting sea otters.[75] In turn, they exchanged goods procured from non-Native traders for foodstuffs from indigenous neighbors. When the supply of foreign products dried up with the collapse of overhunted sea otter populations, those living at Yuquot became susceptible to periodic food shortages and subsequent spells of hunger. Citing Jewitt's account of his time at Yuquot, Zilberstein argues that hard times hit the Mowachaht village in the early nineteenth century. On April 9, 1804, Jewitt complained that "we cannot get any thing to eat except what we are obliged to sell our wearing apparel for. The natives eat only once a day, and their meal consists of cockles, muscles, &c."[76] Even Maquinna worried about the food shortage. Concerned that his people might kill him if he could not provide, the chief ordered Jewitt to arm himself with a brace of pistols and a cutlass to keep watch at night.

But did an increasingly desperate subsistence situation at Yuquot provoke Maquinna's attack on the *Boston*? Probably not. Zilberstein is misreading the evidence when she cites Jewitt's observation of imported foodstuffs as proof that Mowachaht labor had reoriented to such a degree that they could no longer provide their own sustenance. Because local environments provided unequal kinds and quantities of resources, indigenous borderlanders regularly exchanged large amounts of different types of salmon, berries, other fish and shellfish (dried and fresh), and whale oil. Zilberstein bases her conclusion on the assumption that before the maritime fur trade, Mowachahts labored only to provide for their own subsistence. These Vancouver Islanders were one of many groups who fished and hunted for commercial purposes long before Europeans came to the Northwest Coast. By 1795, trade in sea otter skins had dropped precipitously at Yuquot, and fewer vessels visited as they began acquiring furs from Haidas on the Queen Charlotte Islands of British Columbia.[77] It seems improbable that Maquinna or any other leader at Friendly Cove allowed his people to go hungry from 1795 until 1803, when the chief eventually had an opportunity to seize the *Boston*'s supply of trade goods that could then be exchanged for needed food from neighboring peoples. Finally, periodic food shortages on the Northwest Coast were not uncommon. A Makah oral history recounts a time of famine caused by a lengthy period of rough weather that made fishing dangerous and difficult. Similarly, Mackay suffered food privations during his time at Nootka Sound from 1786 to 1787.[78] Concluding that Mowachahts reoriented their practices so radically away from basic subsistence needs in order to secure European goods exemplifies the problematic trope of classic dependency theory in American Indian history, namely that Native desires for whatever non-Native traders offered caused Indians to neglect critical subsistence and cultural activities.[79]

Analyzing Maquinna's decision within the context of the ča·di· borderland reveals a different possible conclusion and complex motives for his assault on the *Boston*. The Mowachaht chief desired to strike back at mamȧnis because of earlier violence perpetuated against his people. While Salter's rudeness over a broken musket sparked the actual violence, Maquinna later confided to Jewitt that earlier incidents, such as the Spanish killing of Callicum and other transgressions, had made the Mowachahts "resolved to have revenge on the first ship they should fall in with." Nuu-chah-nulth oral histories from Nootka Sound blame Spanish violence for angering Mowachahts to the point of attacking any mamáni vessel when the opportunity presented itself.[80]

But more than the chief's desire for revenge caused Maquinna's attack on the *Boston*. By 1803, few furs could be found in parts of the čaꞏdiꞏ borderland such as Friendly Cove. Much to the disadvantage of some chiefs, the dearth of sea otter pelts was not uniform throughout the borderlands. Tatoosh and Wickaninnish had access to sea otter pelts well into the nineteenth century, a situation that must have rankled their rival, Maquinna.[81] The small amount that he had came from distant villages. These numbers had been dwindling since the late 1790s, when traders began collecting furs from the supplier villages, thereby cutting out Maquinna as the middleman. The Nimpkish Kwakwaka'wakw, who once sent their furs to Maquinna via the overland "grease trails," began exchanging the valuable pelts directly with non-Native traders in the early 1790s. By the turn of the century, the Nimpkish encountered non-Native traders frequently enough that they no longer sent furs to Maquinna.[82] Fewer furs meant that the Mowachaht chief secured a smaller quantity of trade goods, which resulted in his waning influence in the čaꞏdiꞏ borderland. During this time, the dwindling number of vessels that stopped at Friendly Cove only sought supplies: fresh and dried fish, whale oil, freshwater, and timber to repair ships. These provisions brought fewer goods than what had once come to Maquinna and his people. Therefore, his desire to reestablish his influence by seizing a wealth of trade goods contributed toward the decision to attack the *Boston*. Maquinna was desperate; but his desperation lay in his declining influence with respect to neighboring chiefs such as Wickaninnish and Tatoosh.

The Mowachaht chief exploited his victory to enhance his status and that of his son. At Maquinna's invitation, a great number of canoes from twenty tribal nations to the north and south arrived at Yuquot a few days after taking the *Boston*. The Mowachaht chief arranged to awe his visitors with his rejuvenated chiefly power. He assembled his warriors on the beach, each man carrying at least one loaded musket and wearing clothes pillaged from the vessel. Years later, Jewitt recalled, "Nothing could be more ludicrous than the appearance of this motley group of savages collected on the shore, dressed, as they were, with their ill-gotten finery, in the most fantastic manner, some in women's smocks, taken from our cargo, others in *Kotsacks*, (or cloaks,) of blue, red, or yellow broadcloth, with stockings drawn over their heads, and their necks hung round with numbers of powderhorns, shot-bags, and cartouch-boxes, some of them having no less than ten muskets a piece on their shoulders, and five or six daggers in their girdles."[83] One of Maquinna's new white slaves, Thompson, readied a cannon that the chief had mounted in front of his longhouse. When the visitors approached, Maquinna leaped to the roof of his longhouse, began drumming on the boards, and then ordered the muskets and cannon fired. Afterward, he invited his guests into his longhouse, where he feasted them for days on whale blubber, smoked herring spawn, dried fish, and whale oil. In a grand potlatch, Maquinna gifted part of the seized loot to his guests, all in the name of his son, Sat-sat-sok-sis. These crafted displays illustrated to all that Maquinna and his lineage still held enough power to control space on his own terms.

Yet Maquinna had his critics, and their views even shaped some Nuu-chah-nulth communities' memories of the chief. At the time, the attack on the *Boston* angered some because it had driven away the valuable trade vessels. More than a year after the seizure of the *Boston*, rumors of borderlanders "massacre-ing one another for want of cloth, muskets, &c." reached Nootka Sound, and Maquinna worried that neighboring peoples held him responsible and intended to kill him.[84] Similarly, a few late twentieth-century oral histories remember Ma-quinna unflatteringly as "the first white man" among their people and charac-terize him as arrogant, aggressive, and high-handed. They criticize him for acting on his own decisions rather than consulting his people and keeping their best interests in mind, damning criticisms that would have resonated with the Mowachaht chief in the early nineteenth century.[85]

Eight years after Maquinna's seizure of the *Boston*, another successful attack on a maritime fur trading ship seemed to confirm to non-Natives the violent nature of Indian peoples in the ča·di· borderland. After insulting a Clayoquot chief, Euro-American captain Jonathan Thorn lost his life and the *Tonquin* in June 1811. The German-born New York financier John Jacob Astor had hired Thorn to transport one of the two parties headed west to establish the Pacific Fur Company in Oregon Country. During the eight-month voyage from New York to the mouth of the Columbia, Thorn had earned a reputation for irasci-bility and stubbornness, especially when dealing with indigenous peoples and his inexperienced crew. On March 22, 1811, his poor judgment cost the lives of eight crewmembers when he sent them into treacherous waters at the mouth of the Columbia to seek a channel for the *Tonquin*. Before sailing into Clayoquot Sound, Captain Thorn had demonstrated characteristics that made him unsuited for cross-cultural negotiation.[86]

Thorn's disrespect sparked the Clayoquot attack on the *Tonquin*. The dispute began when Thorn and Nook-a-mis, an elderly chief from Echachis village, dis-agreed over the low price of two blankets that the captain would pay for each sea otter skin. Exploding in anger, Thorn kicked aside Nook-a-mis's pile of skins, verbally abused the chief in front of his people, and struck him across the face with one of the pelts. After the insulted Nook-a-mis and his people left the

Tonquin, Shee-wish, the youngest son of Wickaninnish, returned the next day with a large number of Clayoquots, offering furs to trade. Shee-wish negotiated for a rate of three blankets and a knife per skin, a deal to which Thorn agreed. The captain allowed many Clayoquots onboard, despite warnings from Joseachal, the Quinault interpreter Thorn had hired for the voyage. As a brisk trade ensued—and armed each Indian man with at least one knife—the crew became anxious, especially when they noticed that the few women present stayed in the canoes. Thorn scorned their anxieties, believing that they could repel any attack. But moments later, he became afraid when Clayoquots crowded close and cut him off from the crew. At this point, he ordered the Indians back to their canoes and sent his crew scurrying to ready the ship to sail away. Instead of departing, the Clayoquots grabbed their recently acquired knives, pulled other weapons from the furs, and attacked. Striking crewmembers unconscious, they threw them into the sea, where women in canoes dispatched them with their paddles. After Thorn stabbed Shee-wish and cast him down a hatch, Wickaninnish's brother, an "uncommonly strong Indian," constrained the captain while warriors clubbed him to death. Leaping overboard, the interpreter surrendered himself to the women. Because his sister was married to a Clayoquot, they did not kill him.[87]

Four to six survivors, including a few Native Hawaiians, ignited some black powder, and in the ensuing fire, they made their escape. Several slipped away in a small boat and set out for the mouth of the Columbia River, but a gale drove them aground at Cape Flattery, where Makahs executed them.[88] The other survivors (probably the Native Hawaiians) swam ashore, where they died at the hands of Clayoquots. Believing that they had put out the fire, Clayoquots began to tow the *Tonquin* to Tin-Wis, a nearby village; however, the still smoldering fire ignited the ship's magazine, nine thousand pounds of gunpowder the vessel was carrying to the Russian-American Company outpost at Sitka. The resultant explosion destroyed the ship and killed between eighty and two hundred Clayoquots.[89] A possible eyewitness recalled decades later, "The noise of the explosion made the earth tremble, and . . . fragments of the ship were flying through the air everywhere."[90] After the *Tonquin* incident, the Clayoquot community closed in on itself. Some saw the explosion and the deaths of many warriors as a sign that their people should withdraw from the maritime fur trade. One grandmother even took her family away from the oceanside village, returning to the Clayoquots' ancestral home at Kennedy Lake. Today's Tla-o-qui-ahts (Clayoquots) remember this as a "grim event" in their history.[91]

Unlike Maquinna's seizure of the *Boston*, the attack on the *Tonquin* did not result in a wealth of looted goods. However, similar motivations appear to have precipitated this incident. In both cases, captains had disrespected a ranking titleholder. Like other indigenous peoples in the region, Clayoquots had suffered earlier insults from non-Native captains and crew. Two Americans had upset Wickaninnish separately in 1793 and 1796 when they failed to turn over vessels the chief had paid for with down payments of prime sea otter skins.[92] Fresh on the minds of Clayoquots in 1811 was the more recent affront, when the Bostonian Captain Ayres had hired and then abandoned a dozen seal hunters earlier that year on the Farallon Islands off the northern California coast. This angered Wickaninnish, who vowed to "avenge themselves on the first white men who appeared among them."[93] The *Tonquin* turned out to be that ship. Clayoquot Sound communities also suffered from smaller amounts of furs than they once had, although the declining number of available sea otter pelts was less severe than the situation in Nootka Sound because Wickaninnish still had suppliers from distant villages on Vancouver Island. This meant that Clayoquot chiefs would have also worried about their waning influence in the borderlands.

Word of each vessel's loss traveled throughout the Pacific and beyond, fueled by a combination of Northwest Coast peoples spreading the news and maritime ship captains carrying it to distant ports. Four days after the capture of the *Boston*, two ships, the *Juno* and the *Mary*, entered Nootka Sound and fled after Mowachahts fired on them with the captured muskets. In mid-August 1803, visiting Clayoquots informed Jewitt that a captain anchored in the Columbia River had told Chinooks that he knew of the two survivors. By the end of that month, Spanish officials in Monterrey first heard about the loss of the *Boston* when John Brown, captain of the *Alexander* (Boston), reported that he had almost suffered the same fate. News of the cannon battery Maquinna had set up in front of the village and the existence of a few survivors traveled on to Mexico City and Madrid via San Blas and cooled any plans the Spanish had about reoccupying Nootka Sound. By April 25, 1804, word had reached Boston, probably via Canton or the Sandwich Islands, when a brief report appeared in a local newspaper; but it took another three years for a more complete recounting of the loss of the *Boston* to become known in the Northeast. Similarly, within a matter of weeks, local Indians brought rumors of the demise of the *Tonquin* to Fort Astoria at the mouth of the Columbia River and to maritime fur trade vessels collecting sea otter skins at Nahwitti village located in Tlatlasikwala Kwakwaka'wakw lands on the northern tip of Vancouver Island. Based on news from vessels returning from the Pacific, the first published account of the loss of the *Tonquin* appeared in a New York newspaper on April 22, 1812. By the fall of 1813, papers in the Northeast had published versions of the interpreter Joseachal's eyewitness account and at least one periodical in London had duplicated it.[94] This reportage made clear that despite decades of encounters, non-Native navigators and traders had failed to turn these into Spanish, British, or US spaces.

The 1803 and 1811 attacks on these two US vessels cast a long shadow over the ča·di· borderland and changed the local contours of the maritime fur trade. For some time after Maquinna's seizure of the *Boston*, vessels avoided Nootka Sound, fearing that they, too, would suffer the same fate. With fewer ships visiting Yuquot, Maquinna had to rely on indigenous trade networks to send the few sea otter pelts that he did procure to other trading ports, such as Nahwitti village and Fort George (what the British renamed Fort Astoria after the Northwest Fur Company of Montreal took it over during the War of 1812), probably through Makah connections at Cape Flattery. This represented a critical reversal of the earlier pattern where Maquinna received furs from others and benefited from monopolizing the exchanges with traders. Wickaninnish and Clayoquots experienced a similar outcome because trading ships shunned their villages for several years after the losses of the *Boston* and *Tonquin*. Just as conflict among indigenous peoples and Spaniards had made non-Native crews afraid when stopping on the Washington coast in the 1780s, Nuu-chah-nulth attacks on these two vessels created a geography of fear along the entire west coast of Vancouver Island. Now that captains had more knowledge of the region, they realized that they could trade with friendlier Indian peoples to the north and south and still procure furs while avoiding villages now seen as dangerous. This situation privileged Makah chiefs because ships stopped at the Cape Flattery villages in lieu of Yuquot and Clayoquot. The *New Hazard*, a trading brig from Salem, Massachusetts, deliberately sailed past Nootka Sound about two weeks after hearing rumors of the loss of the *Tonquin*. Instead, the *New Hazard* headed south to Cape Flattery, where the crew purchased whale oil and slaves from Makahs.[95]

When vessels began visiting Vancouver Island villages once again, high-ranking chiefs kept a low profile. In 1817, when the French *Bordelais* sailed into Nootka Sound, Maquinna approached in a small canoe. Unlike his conduct during previous visits by non-Native ships, Maquinna did not announce his presence with a parade of canoes. Captain Camille de Roquefeuil noted, "There was no ceremony that announced the presence of their chief, but the natives having pointed him out to me, I invited him to come on board." Once aboard, the captain gave the Mowachaht chief a small meal, a present, and a seven-gun salute. Maquinna reciprocated with three small sea otter furs, but he demanded immediate payment for them. Worried that Maquinna might mount an attack on the *Bordelais*, the captain deployed the boarding nets, which prevented people from climbing aboard anywhere along the vessel, and kept the ship a fair distance away from Yuquot. Eight years later, a Hudson's Bay Company ship, the *William and*

Ann, sailed into Nootka Sound. This time, a small flotilla of canoes greeted them, but Maquinna was absent; he did not board the vessel until it anchored off Yuquot. Unlike previous encounters with traders, the Mowachaht chief had no sea otter pelts to offer because Native hunters had nearly wiped out the species in waters over which Maquinna controlled. As with the *Bordelais,* the HBC ship took extra precautions to prevent an attack.[96]

Diplomatic protocols also changed in high encounter areas outside Nootka Sound because chiefs questioned their safety aboard vessels. When the *Bordelais* made a second visit to Nootka Sound in 1818, a delegation from Clayoquot—minus Wickaninnish—tried to lure the French vessel away from Maquinna's space. The French did not trust the offer, and they sailed south for California instead of visiting Clayoquot Sound. Similarly, when the *William and Ann* entered Makah waters after its visit to Nootka Sound, no diplomatic protocol took place. Canoes carrying fish greeted the vessel, but Chief Tatoosh was not among the passengers. Instead, he sent a lower-ranking chief, one of his brothers, to facilitate the exchange of fish for trade goods.[97] The highest-ranking chiefs, Maquinna, Tatoosh, and Wickaninnish, no longer felt safe leading delegations to trading vessels. They feared that captains might take them hostage to extort furs from them or to punish them for attacks on non-Native vessels. The diplomatic protocol that had once provided structure for encounters between Natives and non-Natives appears to have become a casualty of violence. Abandoning the diplomatic protocol eroded the authority and influence that some chiefs had accrued through monopolizing the maritime fur trade exchanges.

Maquinna, Wickaninnish, and Tatoosh dominated much of the maritime fur trade in the čaˑdiˑ borderland. The manners of their deaths in the 1820s illustrate the consequences of their responses to the changing dynamics of the indigenous marine borderlands in the early nineteenth century. Of the three, we have specific information only about the death of Maquinna. The last archival reference to Maquinna comes from an HBC trader in 1825—he described the infamous Mowachaht chief as an "ageing man." Oral histories report that in the late 1820s, Maquinna planned to raid his uncle's Muchalaht village to take their salmon stream. Muchalaht women living at Yuquot warned their people after overhearing the chief's plan. When Maquinna and his warriors paddled upriver toward the target village, his uncle led an ambush and killed Maquinna by holding his head underwater until he drowned.[98]

The situation and manner of Maquinna's death reveal that the desperation of this maritime fur trade chief continued to mount after the 1803 capture of the *Boston.* When naturalist John Scouler visited Nootka Sound in 1825, he noted the scarcity of European goods among the Mowachaht.[99] Now that the maritime fur trade had long shifted away from Friendly Cove and Maquinna's control, the Mowachaht chief believed that he needed to do something dramatic, on the scale of what he had accomplished more than two decades earlier with his attack on the *Boston*—the aged leader decided to seize a valuable indigenous resource, a nearby productive salmon stream owned by his uncle. With the paucity of non-Native vessels stopping at Nootka Sound and the Mowachahts' limited supply of sea otter pelts, Maquinna turned to a common strategy in the ča·di· borderland: seizing a lucrative resource site from a rival in order to augment one's influence.

The deaths of Tatoosh and Wickaninnish were neither dramatic nor violent. No oral histories tell of these leaders dying at the hands of rivals while making desperate gambles to maintain or reestablish influence. This suggests that these chiefs died of old age or by other normal means. When Scouler sailed into Makah waters in 1825, he met an elderly brother to the still-living Tatoosh. This is the last archival reference to the Makah chief. By 1841, when Wilkes's US Exploring Expedition lingered at Neah Bay, they encountered Chief George, then the ranking titleholder. Wickaninnish also seems to have died of old age sometime after 1820.[100]

In contrast to the violent death of Maquinna, the quiet passings of Tatoosh and Wickaninnish illuminate the changing borderlands conditions that privileged the People of the Cape and Clayoquots. First, the villages of Cape Flattery and Clayoquot Sound were better positioned to benefit from valuable indigenous trade goods harvested from whales and other sea mammals. From his time at Nootka Sound at the beginning of the century, Jewitt noted that Kla-i-zarts (Makahs) and Wickaninnish's people (Clayoquots) provided great quantities of whale oil and other sea mammal products. During the same period, he described Maquinna's concern over his lack of whaling success, a significant problem because Tatoosh and Wickaninnish could then maintain their influence in the borderlands more easily than Maquinna once the maritime fur trade shifted away from Nootka Sound.[101] Second, unlike the inhabitants of Nootka Sound, Makahs and Clayoquots still had access to sea otter pelts, albeit in smaller quantities than before. This meant that non-Native vessels traded greater quantities and higher-quality goods with the People of the Cape and Clayoquots for the valued furs. Again, this gave Tatoosh and Wickaninnish an advantage over their rival Maquinna. Finally, because the dramatic attacks on vessels at Nootka and Clayoquot had encouraged vessels to anchor at Neah Bay instead, this also benefited Tatoosh over his Nuu-chah-nulth rivals. Together, these advantages meant that Wickaninnish and especially Tatoosh did not need to resort to desperate and dangerous violence against neighbors or relatives to maintain or reestablish their authority in the borderlands. Violence—or the lack thereof—continued to play a pivotal role in the political dynamics of the ča·di· borderland well into the nineteenth century.

Maritime fur trade accounts and logbooks confirm that theft, intimidation, and violent conflict characterized this industry. Many—but not all—traders believed that Indian attacks on them were unprovoked and due to the inherently "savage" nature of Natives. This was not the case. Borderlands dynamics and previous incidents established the context of subsequent encounters and made violence multidimensional as Natives clashed with other indigenous peoples and mamánis or babaɬids. Colonialism and imperial processes did not create this violence. Instead, they exacerbated existing, indigenous lines of tension and conflict, characteristics of the ča·di· borderland where distinct peoples contested and shared spaces and resources as they had for generations before and after the arrival of Europeans.

But violence also had its benefits. Certain chiefs and their people gained from conflict and tension in other parts of the borderlands. Direct violence against weaker rivals resulted in the expansion of tribal spaces, alliances, and resources. Some chiefs manipulated the dynamics of conflict to expand their influence, such as when Tatoosh allied with Pacheedahts to stop both Meares's exploration and the growth of Wickaninnish's influence. This extended Makah space deeper into the Strait of Juan de Fuca. Dramatic incidents of violence, such as Nuu-chah-nulth attacks on the *Boston* and *Tonquin*, indirectly benefited the People of the Cape by making Neah Bay a safer port of call than Vancouver Island villages. This situation shaped the dynamics of the land fur trade, which came to eclipse the maritime fur trade in the Pacific Northwest.

Indigenous chiefs such as Maquinna, Tatoosh, and Wickaninnish used violence to produce and control space on their own terms. They deployed violence strategically to gain or protect resources and spaces. Chiefs also used violence as a stabilizing factor to confront rivals who became too powerful. Additionally, they employed violence to control people within the spaces over which they held authority. Most important, indigenous leaders applied violence to interrupt Europeans and Euro-Americans from making imperial spaces in the region. Some individuals and peoples—especially Makahs and their various chiefs—disrupted imperial efforts at least through the early 1850s. However, several important events and the establishment of colonial borderlands began to challenge the power of indigenous leaders in the ča·di· borderland in the decades following the maritime fur trade.

"Depending on the Success or Good-Will of the Natives"

On December 24, 1851, the Hudson's Bay Company's brig *Una* wrecked at Neah Bay after having sheltered there for a few days. Even with both anchors down, the ship was blown by strong winds into Waadah Island at the opening of the bay. Bound from Fort Simpson, about five hundred miles to the north, to Fort Victoria at the southern end of Vancouver Island, the *Una* carried a load of furs and £300 worth of gold that the crew had collected from the Queen Charlotte Islands along the northern coast of British Columbia. Makahs salvaged stores, rigging, and other flotsam from the wreck of the 187-ton vessel. According to Northwest Coast ownership standards, chiefs of the People of the Cape (Makahs) owned whatever washed ashore at Neah Bay. Conflict erupted, however, when the *Una*'s crew and passengers attempted to prevent Makahs from exercising their salvage rights. In the fray, someone stabbed a passenger, Sudaał, daughter of a Gispaxlo'ots (Tsimshian) chief and wife of Fort Simpson's chief trader, John Kennedy. A prominent individual in Northwest Coast and Hudson's Bay Company societies, Sudaał was probably known by some of the People of the Cape; perhaps she was injured while attempting to use her high status to protect the ship's cargo. Two American trading vessels, the *Damariscove* and *Susan Sturges*—also anchored in Neah Bay—intervened and took aboard the *Una*'s crew, passengers, and valuable cargo. As the survivor-laden ships departed, someone set fire to the wreck's remains, demonstrating that the foreshore and sea around Cape Flattery was still Makah space.[1]

Two Makah leaders, Chiefs Yelakub ("yeh-luh-koob") and x̣isi·t ("klih-seet"), knew that they needed to make some effort to appease the King George men (British) of the Hudson's Bay Company and officials of the nearby Vancouver Island Colony. The chiefs would have been eager to avoid having British gunboats shell Makah villages in reprisal. More important, they would have desired to maintain cordial relations with the company, which provided them with valuable trade goods that they used to maintain their authority among the People of the Cape and neighbors in the ča·di· borderland. They sent messages to James Douglas, HBC chief factor and governor of the colony, apologizing for their people's conduct and offering to pay for the stolen and damaged property. As one of the chiefs explained, they were absent at the time of the incident, so they could not control the villagers. Recognizing an opportunity, Yelakub and ƛisi·t attempted to turn this incident to their advantage. By claiming their absence when the aggressive actions and violence occurred, they could point to the perpetrators as "bad" Indians while positioning themselves as the "good" chiefs with whom Douglas could work.[2]

In fact, one Makah leader—probably Yelakub—performed his version of the "good" chief when the Hudson's Bay Company's *Cadborough* sailed into Neah Bay a month later, seeking restitution for damage to British property and pride.[3] Instead of being cowed by this symbol of empire, he contained the threat by deploying customary Northwest Coast diplomacy. The Makah chief told Charles Dodd, the commander of the expedition, that he had already executed ten of the plunderers and burned alive the one accused of setting the vessel on fire. In reality, this leader had probably done nothing of the kind. If he had executed or immolated anyone, the individual would have been a slave. Within Northwest Coast societies, high-status individuals occasionally used slaves as proxies to pay for murders, property damage, and theft, a fact that Dodd, an experienced HBC employee, might have known. Although the Makah leader never offered up any physical evidence of the grisly justice, the *Cadborough*'s commander quietly accepted the chief's assurances about punishing the perpetrators, thereby acknowledging this leader's authority to punish his people for supposed crimes against British citizens and property. Yelakub then restored to the King George men every article of value that his people still possessed from the *Una*. Additionally, he offered an annual payment of whale oil as restitution. This leader had guessed that the expiations would result in the *Cadborough*'s departure from Makah waters without incident.[4]

While positioning himself as a broker of peace between King George men and the People of the Cape, Chief Yelakub followed indigenous protocols of Northwest Coast justice rather than acquiescing to British intimidation. A Native leader, not British officials, had "executed" the guilty Indians, and he paid the aggrieved party for the loss of property, as if making peace with another chief rather than suffering extortion from a coercive imperial agent. At this time, neither Great Britain nor the United States could apparently exercise Max Weber's essential power of the state at Cape Flattery—neither could "lay claim to the monopoly of legitimate physical violence" at Neah Bay.[5] Makah chiefs still held this power, despite Britain's commercial hold on the area through the land-based fur trade and US territorial claims to the region. Yet Natives such as X̌isi·t and Yelaku̓b valued the trading relationship they had with the King George men, and they worried that the aggressive actions of some of their people jeopardized opportunities to benefit from the settler-colonial world of the mid-nineteenth century. Similarly, HBC employees, settlers, and colonial officials found themselves balancing retributive violence with reliance on local Indians, who provided the furs, supplies, and food that made colonialism possible in the Northwest Coast. Together these various stakeholders engaged one another and the new opportunities and challenges presented by the expanding settler-colonial world to meet differing needs of authority on the shifting grounds and waters of the borderlands.

One set of changes revolved around the geopolitical claims to the region. From the 1770s through the 1840s, competing empires—including Russia, Spain, France, Great Britain, and the United States—drew boundary lines throughout the Pacific Northwest and attempted to reconfigure preexisting indigenous spaces, such as the ča·di· borderland, into places of commerce and empire. By the early 1820s, these overlapping colonial claims had simplified into the Oregon Country, a region whose joint occupation the United States and Great Britain made official through the Anglo-American Convention of 1818. According to the dominant historical narrative, the Pacific Northwest went from a borderland to a bordered land in 1846 when these two nations settled the boundary issue by creating a border from the Rocky Mountains to the Pacific Ocean along the forty-ninth parallel and extending through the Strait of Juan de Fuca, cutting through Makah marine space. This transformation supposedly meant that the messy complexities of the colonial borderlands—embodied through the jointly occupied Oregon Country, the ambiguous identities of people living there, and the ethnic diversity and mixed-race world of the fur trade—settled into a tidy division between the US and British Wests.[6] But the reality was not as neat as non-Native colonial and territorial officials desired because of the persistence of the ča·di· borderland's characteristics.

Considering this period from a Makah perspective highlights not only continued indigenous agency and power but also the palimpsest nature of this borderland.[7] New international boundaries, such as the one that separated the two halves of the Oregon Country, "remained dotted lines that took a generation to solidify."[8] When nation-states consolidated their power in the hinterlands, indigenous borderlanders supposedly lost autonomy. The metaphor of the palimpsest, however, allows us to uncover competing histories, such as those of the People of the Cape, whose actions demonstrate that the indigenous dynamics of the ča·di· borderland persisted longer than a single generation and after nation-state control grew. Paddling in canoes, trading, marrying, and fighting among the many villages of the Olympic Peninsula and Vancouver Island, Northwest Coast peoples demonstrated that the indigenous ča·di· borderland continued to exist alongside the colonial borderlands. Instead of there being one border-land zone with conditions shaped and controlled by newcomers and distant colonial officials, two layers of overlapping and interacting borderlands defined this space.

These geopolitical changes unfolded within the context of the land-based fur trade, an industry that shaped the lives of ƛisi·t and Yelak̓ub much as the mari-time fur trade had done for previous chiefs in the ča·di· borderland. The new industry resembled its maritime antecedent because both depended on the com-plex, interconnected relationships among numerous peoples—both Native and non-Native—of the Northwest Coast. From the beginning of the land-based fur trade in the early nineteenth century, indigenous contributions allowed for non-Native survival and success, highlighting the way that different peoples, societ-ies, and practices "imbricated" into the regional fabric of the Northwest Coast.[9] Similar to the maritime fur trade, the land-based industry depended on safe, ordered spaces for profitable exchanges. But different strategies for creating safety and order marked the greatest contrast between the two trades, influenced the lives of local indigenous peoples, and altered the dynamics of power in the re-gion. The land-based fur trade established long-term, terrestrial toeholds for non-Natives in the Pacific Northwest. Kernels of settlement, the HBC forts and the trade goods they provided made the company influential and drew new kinds of non-Natives to the region. During the 1840s, US and British settlers began establishing sawmills, fishing operations, farms, and small settlements in the re-gion. Eager to protect these newcomers, the colonial governments of the United Kingdom and the United States grappled with policies for managing the large populations of Indians who still outnumbered whites.

Influential Makah chiefs engaged trade and colonization in personal ways to maintain their ability to control space, and their actions helped to make colo-nialism possible in this region.[10] By the 1850s, two Neah Bay chiefs—Yelak̓ub and ƛisi·t—emerged as the Makah Nation's faces to the settler-colonial world. Born in 1818 or 1819 to a prominent Makah trader, Yelak̓ub worked as a kitchen scullion at the Hudson's Bay Company's Fort Langley, located about thirty miles up the Fraser River, which empties into the eastern waters of the ča·di· border-land. There he learned English and lived among King George men who gave him a new name, Flattery Jack, and likely treated him poorly due to his age, race, and position in the kitchens. After someone murdered his father in 1831, the teenage Yelakub took over the family trading activities, traveling throughout the borderlands and beyond to exchange animal skins, ha·ykʷa (dentalia shells used as currency), and slaves. Largely through trading, Yelakub rose to power among the People of the Cape, and he cultivated ties with several HBC personnel, who commonly called the village at Neah Bay "Flattery Jack's Village." There, he and his extended family lived in a longhouse that was about a hundred feet long by 1850, an indication of his high status.[11]

Known to non-Natives as "the White Chief" because of his light complexion and Russian heritage through his father, ƛisi·t competed against Yelakub and other chiefs for authority among the People of the Cape. Born sometime between 1807 and 1812, he came of age as a whaler just as US and British coastal traders began purchasing large quantities of whale oil from Makahs. After the 1846 death of George, the previous ranking Makah titleholder, ƛisi·t used the wealth garnered from whale oil to secure his position as the highest chief among the People of the Cape. He also married the sister of S'Hai-ak ("s-hay-uhk"), a prominent chief among the neighboring S'Klallams, a move that restored peaceful relations between the two tribal nations. Probably to counter the influence of Yelakub, ƛisi·t sought closer ties with Bostons (Euro-American officials and traders) by the early 1850s.[12]

During the second quarter of the nineteenth century, Yelakub's and ƛisi·t's actions reveal aspects of Makah politics. The People of the Cape employed customary Northwest Coast leadership strategies to maintain their people's autonomy in the face of mounting settler-colonial pressure, such as the racialized nature of power in this emerging colonial borderland. During the mid-nineteenth century, however, Native deaths from epidemics combined with increasing numbers of non-Native immigrants to change the demographics of the region and undercut the ability of Indians to define and control space on indigenous terms. In the years following the burning of the Una, a suite of diseases hammered the People of the Cape and other Native borderlanders. These catastrophes threatened to unravel the networks of kinship and trade that bound together the many peoples of the ča·di· borderland; that this did not occur is a testament to the resilience of the Makahs and their neighbors.

THE LAND-BASED FUR TRADE AND RISE
OF THE HUDSON'S BAY COMPANY, 1811–1848

Native responses to the rising presence of King George men and Bostons transformed the ča·di· borderland into the sociopolitical region in which ƛisi·t and Yelakub emerged as Makah leaders. Beginning in the 1810s, Makahs and other indigenous peoples of this marine borderland encountered more people from outside the Northwest Coast. Provided to non-Natives by various indigenous peoples, a wealth of natural resource commodities—furs, fish, whale oil, timber, and coal—drew newcomers to the region during the first half of the nineteenth century. Both ƛisi·t and Yelakub developed ties to the most powerful newcomer, the Hudson's Bay Company, as the People of the Cape became one of the key indigenous peoples central to the company's regional success. When HBC forts appeared in the Northwest Coast, the young ƛisi·t and Yelakub confronted the company's efforts to produce and control space in and around the outposts. During this period, HBC officials at the forts employed retributive violence against Indians for supposed depredations on whites and their property. This established a precedent for the racialized nature of settler-colonial power that emerged in the mid-nineteenth century.[13] Yet Makah chiefs such as ƛisi·t and Yelakub retained enough power to interrupt imperial processes at least until the early 1850s.

From the beginning, the new iteration of the fur trade presented Makahs with competition and opportunity, a pattern that carried through many of the later changes the People of the Cape faced. Although established during the maritime fur trade, Fort Astoria became the first land-based fur trade outpost at the edge of the ča·di· borderland. Having made his fortune in the Northeastern fur trade after emigrating from Germany to the United States, John Jacob Astor financed the Pacific Fur Company (PFC), whose employees erected Fort Astoria at the mouth of the Columbia River in 1811. Astor planned to collect furs from Indian hunters around the Columbia basin, ship the pelts to China, and exchange them for valuable products that could then be sold to US consumers. But Astor focused even more on attempting to monopolize provisioning the Russian-American Company's settlements to the far north, thereby undercutting the incentive for potential competitors in the North Pacific. His plans went far beyond "calculations of profit"—he sought to extend US political and economic dominion beyond the Rockies, which would inhibit the expansion of his primary competitors, the North West Company and the Hudson's Bay Company, into the Pacific Northwest. But the early loss of the *Tonquin*, en route to the Russian outpost of New Archangel (Sitka, Alaska) to deliver a load of gunpowder and additional goods, and other difficulties stymied Astor's plans. By the fall of 1813, in the midst of the war between Britain and the United States, the Pacific Fur Company's partners at Fort Astoria decided to abandon the enterprise. They sold the fort and the company's goods and furs to the North West Company, and many of the personnel stayed on with the new owners. With no other land-based operations to contend with at this point, the newly renamed Fort George continued to be an important hub during the waning years of the maritime fur trade.[14]

Drawn by the trade's opportunities for goods and labor, indigenous peoples both local and from farther away proved central to the success of the land-based fur trade. The *Tonquin* brought a dozen Kanakas (Native Hawaiians) to the Columbia River basin, and the Pacific Fur Company's *Beaver* brought another sixteen to Fort Astoria in May 1812. In addition to helping to construct and maintain the fort, these men played a critical role in sustaining the Astorians by crewing vessels, felling trees, clearing land, tending livestock, maintaining the post garden, foraging for edibles, hunting deer and elk, and fishing.[15] The Astorians and their Kanaka employees would have failed from the beginning had they not received the consent and assistance of local Native leaders, such as Chiefs Concomly (Chinook) and Coalpo (Clatsop). Already adept at handling non-Natives through the maritime fur trade and Lewis and Clark's Corps of Discovery, which wintered at the mouth of the Columbia River from 1805 to 1806, Concomly and Coalpo understood the advantages to be gained from a local fort to which they could control access. Chinooks, Clatsops, and other Lower Columbia peoples protected the Astorians from hostile Indians, piloted ships across the treacherous sandbars of the river, passed on news and intelligence of regional events, and guided trade and reconnaissance expeditions into the interior and along the coast. They also performed more quotidian assistance as porters, hunters, gatherers, and fishers; women sold Astorians hats, moccasins, and baskets. As Alexander Ross, one of the fort's clerks, complained, they "had to depend at all times on the success or good-will of the natives." The Astorians' amicable relationships often depended on their intimacy with Native women of rank and power. Daughters of prominent chiefs married white employees of the fort, and these exogamous relations fostered commercial ties and strategic alliances vital for the outsiders' survival and success.[16]

Although they lived two hundred miles away, Makahs saw Fort Astoria as a potential trade competitor and just another small polity, one of several "little sovereignties" that composed indigenous Oregon from 1792 to 1822.[17] During a reconnaissance to lands and peoples along the coast, Robert Stuart, a junior partner in the Pacific Fur Company, received warnings from Quinaults of a numerous and "wicked" nation to the north that "kill a great many Beaver & dispose of them (as well as the Quinhalt people, of their sea otter, of which they kill a considerable number) to the Neweetians for Hyquoyas." Quinaults were likely referring to Makahs, who leveraged exchange and kinship networks to control the flow of furs, slaves, haᐧykʷa, and other goods from peoples living between the mouth of the Columbia River and Nahwitti, a Tlatlasikwala Kwakwaka'wakw village at the northern tip of Vancouver Island. During the summer months, Indians from the north visited Baker's Bay on the northern side of the Columbia's mouth to fish and trade. Concomly warned PFC officials that these visitors were trying to encourage Chinooks to assist them in destroying the fort. Astorians conflated most northern Indians into "Neweetie Indians" and assumed that they were from Vancouver Island, although these northern visitors were more likely Makahs. Not only did they have marriage ties with Concomly's Chinook family and make regular trips to the Columbia River, but they also would have had a significant motivation to attack interloping competitors.[18]

Although initially plotting to attack Fort Astoria, by 1816, Makahs had decided that without Chinook support, they were better off selling furs to these white traders on the Columbia, who by then were Nor'westers, employees of the North West Company. Peter Corney, an English sailor, noted that a group of Indians from Classet (Makahs) often camped at Baker's Bay from June to October to cure salmon and sturgeon and to sell beaver and sea otter skins to Fort George, formerly Fort Astoria. Despite their decision to trade with the King George men, Makahs made it clear that they were a powerful people whom the outsiders should respect. Corney noted that "they are a very warlike people, and extremely dangerous, taking every advantage if you are off your guard." Makahs continued to exchange furs with non-Native traders at the mouth of Columbia throughout the first half of the nineteenth century.[19]

With the support of the British government, the Hudson's Bay Company absorbed the rival North West Company in 1821 and acquired Fort George. The company then began an aggressive expansion in the Pacific Cordillera stretching from the Columbia River to northern British Columbia, establishing fourteen posts between 1821 and 1846. Reflecting the shifting geography of the fur trade, in 1825 the company replaced the coastal Fort George with Fort Vancouver, located ninety miles upriver along the northern bank of the Columbia River, to better access inland exchange networks and the beaver skins they provided. The new fort became the Hudson's Bay Company's administrative headquarters and supply depot west of the Rocky Mountains. It also became home to an increasingly diverse population. After a visit in the winter of 1846–47, the Canadian artist Paul Kane described Fort Vancouver as "quite a Babel of languages, as the inhabitants are a mixture of English, French, Iroquois, Sandwich Islanders, Crees and Chinooks."[20] Like its predecessor, Fort Vancouver lay at the southern extent of the ča·di· borderland, "dropped into . . . [the] fully formed system of Chinook and Salish trade and culture," by which it continued to receive furs from coastal peoples.[21]

Although the Hudson's Bay Company set out to monopolize the industry in the Pacific Northwest, US competition provided indigenous peoples with even more trade options. Based out of New England ports, small "coasters" frequented the southern side of the Strait of Juan de Fuca, Puget Sound, and the Pacific shores to the mouth of the Columbia River. The brig *Owhyhee* entered the Columbia River in 1827, even sailing up to Fort Vancouver in an attempt to intercept furs bound for the HBC headquarters. Fearing potential losses from American coasters, Chief Factor John McLoughlin sent a crew to the mouth of the Fraser River at the eastern end of the ča·di· borderland to establish a new post, Fort Langley, in the fall of 1827. Reflecting a pattern typical of HBC workforces, this construction crew included one Abenaki from northeastern North America, two Native Hawaiians, one "York Factory Indian" from the shores of Hudson Bay, two Iroquois from upstate New York, and one "Canadian Half breed." The Hudson's Bay Company began collecting beaver skins from local Coast Salish peoples, Vancouver Island communities, and S'Klallams on the southeastern edge of the Strait of Juan de Fuca. Fort Langley also drew Native laborers to the Fraser River area. They cleared land, provided large quantities of fish, cut timber and firewood, and performed other tasks important for the fort's survival. Shortly after the establishment of Fort Langley, an influential Makah trader arranged to have his ten-year-old son, Yelaḱub, work in the kitchens.[22] Yelaḱub's father probably wanted his son to learn English and to gain a better understanding of the culture of King George men in order to benefit his people's commercial dealings with the newcomers.

Other goods that Native peoples brought to Fort Langley outpaced the value of furs collected there and became commodities in the developing transnational exchange networks crossing the Pacific. In the early nineteenth century, Americans were the first to pursue a strategy of diversification that catalyzed an economic transformation for the northeastern Pacific. Beginning in the mid-1810s, maritime fur traders from New England traded sailing vessels with Kamehameha I, first king of the Kingdom of Hawai'i, for sandalwood, which they exported to Canton, where Chinese craftsmen made incense, medicines, and carvings from the wood. During the 1820s, US coasters carried spars from the Northwest Coast to Oahu and supplied Russian outposts in Alaska and Spanish missions in California with provisions. Eyeing the success of these small competitors, George Simpson, the Hudson's Bay Company's administrator of the Columbia Department, urged the company to diversify its economic activities by expanding into provisioning these growing Pacific markets, and Fort Langley occupied an important role in the efforts. When Honolulu became the base of the North Pacific whaling fleet during the second quarter of the nineteenth century, the company was well positioned to supply specialized naval stores and hardware—including sheet copper, sheathing nails, anchors, anchor chains, rolls of canvas, tar, black and white paint, pitch, varnish, paint brushes, iron hoops, copper bolts, salted pork, arrowroot, charts, and nautical almanacs—to vessels that visited the Oahu agency. This outpost in the Kingdom of Hawai'i became the primary supplier of produce, cured salmon, and spars, commodities collected from Northwest Coast peoples. The outcome of Simpson's plan pleased company officials in the Pacific Northwest. In 1832, Archibald McDonald, chief trader at Fort Langley, reported, "Our Salmon . . . is close upon 300 Barrels, & I have descended to Oil & Blubber too. . . . I am much satisfied with its proceeds myself." In return for indigenous goods, HBC traders such as McDonald provided standard trade items like tea, rice, tobacco, molasses, sugar, and salt. More exotic goods requested by Northwest Coast chiefs included coral and Chinese-made sandalwood and camphor boxes, which became popular potlatch gifts. Native demands illustrated the complexity of early nineteenth-century Pacific trade networks. Not only were indigenous peoples suppliers of commodities, but they also were savvy consumers of Asian and European goods.[23]

By the second quarter of the nineteenth century, the regional economy depended on the trade among indigenous peoples and newcomers. Much as powerful chiefs had monopolized exchanges with vessels during the maritime fur trade, prominent Northwest Coast leaders controlled access to forts after they had been built on their lands or those of a weaker neighbor. Concomly, the ranking Chinook chief, and members of his family mediated many of the exchanges between Natives and traders at Forts Astoria and George during the first part of the nineteenth century. Cowichans, a powerful people at the eastern edge of the ča·di· borderland, controlled Native access to Fort Langley and prevented others, such as Makahs, from trading there, even though the Hudson's Bay Company had built the post in Stó:lō territory.[24]

The People of the Cape circumvented Cowichan control over exchanges at Fort Langley by trading with HBC vessels when they stopped at Neah Bay. Shortly after the post's founding in 1827, Cape Flattery emerged as "the critical spot" in Fort Langley's trading area.[25] Captain James Scarborough, who worked for the company for twenty years, so frequently visited Neah Bay that some colonial records called this body of water Scarborough Bay.[26] Located between Nuu-chah-nulth peoples to the north and Coast Salish peoples to the east and south, the early nineteenth century Makahs continued to attract indigenous trade from all corners of the ča·di· borderland. Compared to surrounding parts of the Northwest Coast, valuable sea otters could still be found off Cape Flattery, where Makah men such as Yelaḳub and his father hunted them from canoes in the open sea and from behind blinds on coastal beaches. In addition to sea otter pelts and beaver skins from other parts of the borderlands, Makahs provided whale oil and bone, fresh fish, slaves, and haʸykʷa, shells they harvested from the deep seafloor by means of a long pole. Indicating its importance as a commodity, the chief traders at Fort Langley tallied the acquisition of "Cape Flattery oil," whale oil that HBC ships often purchased at more than one hundred gallons at a time. They shipped much of it to London, where it was distilled into benzene to light homes and businesses.[27]

Despite the rising presence and power of the Hudson's Bay Company, the wealth of goods provided by Northwest Coast peoples continued to draw US coast-ers to the region through the 1830s. The presence of these small, private traders backed by New England capital frustrated HBC traders and strengthened the position of Indian traders who could—and did—hold out for more favorable prices. Many of these coasters stopped at Neah Bay to purchase furs, fish, and whale oil, thereby intercepting commodities that normally went to Fort Langley.[28] The overall trade in Cape Flattery oil increased, and by 1852, Makahs sold more than thirty thousand gallons of whale oil (valued at more than $20,000) to passing HBC and American vessels, and the People of the Cape kept a similar amount for personal consumption and exchange with neighboring Indians. According to whaling returns provided by a Makah chief in the late 1850s, sixty thousand gallons of oil represented approximately twenty-six whales killed annually.[29] At times, Makahs had so much whale oil on hand that the visiting ships lacked enough casks and had to turn away Indian traders.[30] A successful whaler such as ƛisiˑt would have been a primary supplier and overseen his people's interac-tions with the Bostons and King George men when exchanging whale oil for trade goods at the cape.

The HBC answer to increasing competition—the building of more forts— entangled Makahs more closely with the company after the establishment of Fort Victoria in 1843. Earlier forts had appeared at the čaˑdiˑ borderland's edges; Fort Victoria, however, was located squarely within the borderland, or "in the midst of the Natives' world." By 1843, the company had grown concerned about the boundary issue. Hudson's Bay Company officials worried that the United States and Britain would place the border north of Fort Vancouver, which would leave their primary Pacific depot in US territory. They wanted a depot situated far-ther north in order to supply more easily the majority of their outposts in the northern Pacific Cordillera. During the 1820s and 1830s, several ships wrecked at the dangerous mouth of the Columbia River, resulting in the loss of years' worth of trade goods, thereby undercutting the company's ability to compete with American coasters. These reasons encouraged the HBC to erect a new outpost at the southern end of Vancouver Island. In addition to its advantages over Fort Vancouver, Fort Victoria lay close to the important fisheries in the Strait of Juan de Fuca, Puget Sound, and the Fraser River. The new outpost also had easy access to ample lumber for construction, to good-quality land for expansion, and to a large Native population. The company assumed that Indians throughout the ča·di· borderland would construct the fort, sell food to HBC employees, supply goods for export, and provide a market for British imports.[31]

The establishment of Fort Victoria and its early operations highlight the way indigenous peoples were the cornerstone of HBC growth in the region. When charged with the task of constructing the fort in the Strait of Juan de Fuca, Chief Factor James Douglas chose Camosun, a sheltered harbor on the southern tip of Vancouver Island, where Indians could beach their canoes easily. To Douglas, this site appeared appealing—even Edenic—because the Coast Salish Lekwungen set regular fires to maintain this as one of the region's prime camas fields. After disembarking at Camosun, Douglas told the Lekwungen chiefs who owned the site that he desired to build a trading post on their land. Knowing that Fort Langley had benefited neighboring indigenous peoples along the Fraser River, the chiefs gave Douglas permission to build the fort and provided labor to help in its construction. Later that summer, the company brought to the new outpost wild Spanish cattle and workhorses from Fort Nisqually in Puget

Fort Victoria, 1854. The artist captured the post's marine connections with local Native communities by including Northwest Coast canoes, some with sails, traveling to and from the fort. Drawing by unnamed artist. Image A-04104 courtesy of Royal BC Museum, BC Archives.

Sound. Lekwungens helped to care for the livestock, even taking them into their longhouses during severe winters. In the beginning, non-Natives often called Fort Victoria by its "Indian" name, Camosun, delaying the immediate tendency of Europeans to replace indigenous place-names and illustrating that early colonial places often occupied spaces where indigenous peoples continued to exercise power.[32] Fort Victoria thrived because of the consent, labor, and support provided by nearby indigenous villages.

Even more than they had with Fort Langley, the People of the Cape played a key role in Fort Victoria's survival and early success. After construction began at Camosun, Makahs became regular visitors at the new HBC outpost, located just a short canoe paddle across the strait from their Cape Flattery villages. During Fort Victoria's first summer and fall, Makahs and Nuu-chah-nulth peoples provided salmon and potatoes that fed the King George men and the Kanaka and Lekwungen laborers constructing the outpost.[33] Just as important to the fort's success, though, were the commercial products brought there by the People of the Cape and other indigenous communities. Makah chiefs, such as Yelaḱub and ƛisi·t, visited the fort with their people to sell fish, furs, and whale oil.[34] Other borderlanders also brought goods to the fort, including enormous quantities of salmon, cedar shingles by the thousands, and canoe-loads of blueberries. The Hudson's Bay Company earned a substantial margin of profit from these indigenous commodities by funneling them into the Pacific market that provisioned miners in California and the growing urban center of San Francisco. Douglas estimated that in 1854 Fort Victoria exported ten thousand gallons of Native-produced oil to California, where it fetched two to three dollars per gallon.[35] Acknowledging the advantageous location of Fort Victoria and its rising importance in the provisioning trade, the Hudson's Bay Company made it the company's Pacific depot and headquarters in 1849. The commodities that ƛisi·t, Yelaḱub, and others exchanged at Fort Victoria helped to transform this outpost into a prosperous commercial hub and provisioned colonial activities throughout the Pacific.

While providing commercial opportunities for Native traders, the presence and actions of the Hudson's Bay Company in the ča·di· borderland exacerbated existing tensions among the indigenous peoples, much as the maritime fur trade had done earlier. Unlike the previous industry, in which vessels—sometimes several at a time vying for the attentions of Native traders—anchored for short periods of time off villages, the land-based fur trade established long-term trading opportunities in the homelands of specific indigenous groups. Throughout the year and over decades, these forts repeatedly drew a range of Native leaders, families, and warriors to the same places. This meant that when tensions escalated into violence, they often coalesced outside fort walls on the same Native lands time and again. Fortunately for Makahs, no forts were located at Cape Flattery, so they did not suffer from this violence at home. Instead, they found themselves in conflict with neighboring groups often on the lands of another people with whom they were not at war.

Company officials lacked the power to control intertribal conflicts for most of the first half of the nineteenth century, so no consistent policy with respect to this type of violence emerged. At times they desired to curb indigenous violence in order to create a safe and ordered environment for profitable exchanges. From the perspective of Chief Trader James McMillan at Fort Langley in 1828, violence among Indians was not the problem; instead, it was that conflict hampered Native abilities to collect furs. He wrote, "The poor tribes of this quarter Cannot attend to any thing like hunting [for furs] while their Powerful Neighbours from Van[couver] Island are allowed to Murder and Pillage them at pleasure."[36] McMillan believed that the commercial existence of the fort required order and safety. But company officials ignored intertribal violence when it did not inhibit trade. At least one official, Roderick Finlayson, even promoted conflict among communities, noting years later, "The policy of the Company was honesty—and also to keep the several tribes divided and at enmity among themselves. This plan followed for purposes of protection to ourselves—in short to keep up a jealous feeling between the respective tribes."[37] In charge of Fort Victoria from 1844 to 1849, Finlayson ignored the murder of Chief George, a Makah titleholder, just outside Fort Victoria in 1846. Visiting from the Columbia River, several Chinooks murdered the Makah chief after watching him exchange a sea otter skin for trade goods from Finlayson. While robbery might have partly motivated the killers, the reasons for attacking him were probably more complex. One British observer noted, "[George] had doubtless in his time played many tricks of the same kind as that to which he now fell a victim; they usually act and react one upon the other."[38] Although this comment is steeped in white assumptions of vengeful Natives, it speaks to the underlying reality that complex indigenous reasons—probably a combination of economic competition and a protest against Makah control of regional trade networks, in this case—provided the motivations for violence.

At other times, however, intertribal conflict made Finlayson anxious. During the fall of 1846, S'Klallams took possession of a drift whale Makahs had harpooned but lost. When the People of the Cape demanded a share of the whale and, more important, the return of their whaling gear, S'Klallams refused. This resulted in a "great battle" between the two peoples, and the S'Klallams "had suffered very severely." S'Klallams retaliated by killing Chief Yelakub's brother and some of his people when the Makah traders were paddling home after visiting Fort Victoria. Yelakub set out in twelve canoes with more than one hundred warriors and attacked a S'Klallam village. He took eighteen slaves and the heads of eight warriors that he "stuck on poles placed in the bows of the canoes[. . . ,] carried to their village and placed in front of the lodge of the warriors who had killed them."[39] A year later, the tensions between the two peoples still simmered and concerned those living at Fort Victoria. In 1848, Captain George Courtenay soothed Finlayson's anxiety by bringing the fifty-gun HMS *Constance* into Victoria Harbor to defuse a Makah-S'Klallam conflict unfolding just outside the fort's gate.[40] This incident reflected the Hudson's Bay Company's minimal ability to control indigenous peoples in the spaces beyond the walls of forts.

The company did use its limited power to exercise retributive violence against Indians for perceived depredations on non-Natives and their property. This ad hoc policy established a racialized precedent that haunted the čaˑdiˑ borderland for decades. In January 1828, S'Klallams killed HBC employee Alexander McKenzie and his companions along Hood Canal. As with many interracial acts of violence in this borderland, the S'Klallams had numerous reasons for attacking the HBC party. An experienced fur trader, McKenzie had married the "Princess of Wales," the daughter of Concomly, the powerful Chinook chief who kept slaves, including several S'Klallams. McKenzie's wife accompanied the party, and S'Klallams took her hostage, perhaps to bargain for their people's freedom from Concomly. S'Klallams were also upset that the company traded with their longtime borderlands enemies, the Cowichans of Vancouver Island. S'Klallam chiefs had made several efforts to dissuade McKenzie and others from trading with Cowichans. Adding insult to injury, the company had established Fort Langley north of S'Klallam space. This benefited indigenous rivals and prevented S'Klallam chiefs from serving as intermediaries. Last, indigenous oral accounts point to earlier injustices traders had committed against these people: McKenzie's party could have been killed in retaliation.[41]

Chief Factor John McLoughlin decided that the Hudson's Bay Company needed to employ a policy of retributive violence against Indians who murdered company employees. Writing from Fort Vancouver to his superiors in London about the killing of McKenzie, McLoughlin argued, "To pass over such an outrage would lower us in the opinion of the Indians, induce them to act in the same way, and when an opportunity afforded kill any of our people, and when it is considered the Natives are at least an hundred Men to one of us it will be conceived how absolutely necessary it is for our personal security that we should be respected by them, & nothing could make us more contemptible in their eyes than allowing such a cold-blooded assassination of our People to pass unpunished & every one acquainted with the character of the Indians of the North West Coast will allow they can only be restrained from committing acts of atrocity & violence by the dread of retaliation." He believed that conditions unique to the Northwest Coast at this time—Indians outnumbered whites, these Natives only respected vengeance—necessitated a violent response.[42]

Although the punitive expedition targeted ethnic S'Klallams rather than all Indians in general, this action illustrated an early example of the racialized nature of colonial power that whites used to control indigenous peoples, something that officials noted at the time. Led by Chief Trader Alexander McLeod, a force of about sixty men left Fort Vancouver in June, entered Puget Sound from the south, and set out in canoes for S'Klallam villages. McLoughlin instructed McLeod to find the "murderous tribe, and if possible, to make a salutary example of them, that the honour of the whites was at stake." On the way to rendezvous with the HBC schooner *Cadborough*, McLeod's party encountered two S'Klallam lodges. They fired on those sleeping inside, killing at least two families. After meeting up with the *Cadborough*, the expedition set out for the distant S'Klallam village at New Dungeness on the south side of the Strait of Juan de Fuca. Under cover of fire from the schooner, the expedition's forces landed. After recovering the Princess of Wales and some articles from McKenzie's party, they looted what provisions and whale oil they could carry. Then they burned the village and destroyed the rest of the S'Klallams' property, including nearly thirty canoes, while the inhabitants watched from the forest's safety. Although critical of McLeod's leadership, Frank Ermatinger, an HBC clerk accompanying the expedition, reported that the extensive destruction of property would "be seriously felt for some time to come."[43] He believed that news of this retribution would travel among regional Indians. Makah chiefs certainly heard of this incident, and this story of HBC vengeance likely made the rounds among Indians such as young Yelakub, then working at Fort Langley. A year later, McLoughlin exacted a similar punishment on Clatsops for pillaging the wreck of the company's *William and Ann* at the mouth of the Columbia River.[44] Together, these responses illustrated the desire of some HBC officials to use collective violence when they could in order to punish Indians for perceived wrongs.

During the 1830s and 1840s, Makahs and others challenged HBC efforts at controlling Indians. One area of contention involved Northwest Coast slavery, specifically the enslavement of non-Natives by indigenous peoples. Company employees found it necessary to adhere to indigenous protocols when redeeming slaves from Makah leaders. During the winter of 1833, a storm drove a "junk" laden with rice and fourteen sailors out of sight of the Japanese coast. They drifted east across the Pacific for three months and came within sight of Cape Flattery.

Makahs paddled out to the vessel and found a man and two teenage boys who had survived on rice and freshwater collected from rain. After enslaving the Japanese survivors, Makahs seized the vessel and its goods and broke it apart to salvage the useful materials. Chinook Indians brought the news of the unusual slaves to McLoughlin at Fort Vancouver; although he wanted to free the captives as soon as possible, he could not address the issue until later that year. Captain William McNeill, master of the HBC brig *Llama*, redeemed the captives by purchasing them from Chief George, the same chief whom Chinooks murdered a decade later outside Fort Victoria. After spending several months at Fort Vancouver waiting for a ship, the Japanese survivors caught one headed to London; from there the survivors attempted to return to Japan. Diplomatic tensions between the United Kingdom and Japan, in addition to the Japanese attitude that regarded anyone who left the country—even accidentally—as contaminated, prevented them from returning home.[45] In the mid-1840s, the Hudson's Bay Company also redeemed a white sailor whom Chief George had enslaved; much to the consternation of other whites, this sailor voluntarily returned to Chief George after his release. Stories of powerful Makah chiefs who kept non-Native slaves continued to color white opinions of the People of the Cape throughout the mid-nineteenth century.[46] These incidents demonstrated that Makahs had the ability to control space on their terms. King George men could not enter Makah villages and simply demand the release of non-Native slaves—they had to accede to indigenous protocols and purchase them from the owner.

Even in spaces closer to forts, the Hudson's Bay Company had only slightly more ability to punish Indians for perceived depredations, especially theft. At Fort Victoria, some Makahs ran afoul of the company's efforts to control Natives and protect HBC property. In 1847, an HBC employee whipped a Makah man caught breaking into one of the outpost's warehouses; when "a body of Cape Flattery Indians . . . threatened to attack the Post in retaliation," Lekwungen warriors took up arms to protect the fort, Douglas noted to his superiors. But the theft of company livestock vexed Douglas more. In 1848, he complained of this "mischievious practice which must be checked by the punishment of the Offender, an object in which we have partly succeeded." By 1850, "wandering Tribes" became such a problem that he appointed four guards to stand permanent watch over company livestock. Although he did not name the "wandering Tribes," Makahs frequented the lands around the fort and were likely part of this group.[47]

A range of experiences during the decades of the land-based fur trade shaped λ̓isi·t's and Yelakub's strategies for interacting with the growing presence of King George men and Bostons in the ča·di· borderland. They learned about the many ways they could use trade and new labor opportunities to the advantage of them-selves and their people. But Makahs also participated in, witnessed, or heard about the kinds of violence that these opportunities drew, especially when the outsid-ers established permanent operations in Native homelands. So when non-Natives intruded on Makah spaces, the People of the Cape responded aggressively.

SETTLERS AND INDIGENOUS PEOPLES, 1845–1855

British and American settlers began arriving during the 1840s, thereby chal-lenging indigenous sovereignty while providing more opportunities for Natives to engage the expanding settler-colonial world. The newcomers no longer simply needed small islands of security and order—forts—within an indigenous world; by the mid-nineteenth century, they required larger spaces of safety and order for pioneer enterprises, such as lumbering, farming, mining, and settling. This brought the newcomers into conflict with indigenous peoples, especially those living in places where outsiders wanted to build sawmills, open mines, and es-tablish farms and towns. In order to ensure the newcomers' safety, US and Brit-ish officials drew from HBC strategies to attempt to control Indians.[48] As in previous encounters, early settler-colonial processes depended on the participa-tion and support of Native peoples. Without the labor provided by Natives who cut down trees, cleared land, tended livestock, and dug up coal, many early ven-tures would have failed. Northwest Coast peoples provided fish, potatoes, ber-ries, and sea mammal oil to nascent settlements, critical commodities that sustained many of the first settlers who arrived in the mid-nineteenth century. More important, Native leaders interacted with settlers and colonial officials in order to strengthen their own authority over rivals and neighboring peoples.

During the mid-nineteenth century, the US and British empires began carv-ing up the čaʼdiʼ borderland into supposedly discrete colonial spaces, yet these changes did not affect indigenous polities immediately. Coming along the Oregon Trail, increasing numbers of American filibusters settled south of the Columbia River. Supported by politicians with dreams of a continental nation, these newcomers agitated for US control over the entire Oregon Country. Dur-ing the 1844 presidential contest, the Democratic Party embraced expansionist ideology and campaigned on the slogan "Fifty-Four Forty or Fight!" Once elected, President James K. Polk—who had never taken the slogan very seriously—abandoned the assertion that the western US boundary should ex-tend north to the Russian frontier. Compromising instead on the forty-ninth parallel, his administration settled the boundary issue in 1846 through the Ore-gon Treaty. This ended nearly three decades of joint occupation in the Pacific

Northwest and placed the boundary between US and British claims in the Far North American West "along the said 49th parallel of north latitude to the middle of the channel which separates the continent from Vancouver's Island, and thence southerly through the middle of the said channel, and of Fuca's Straits, to the Pacific Ocean." In 1848, the US Congress created the Oregon Territory, comprising the current states of Washington, Oregon, and Idaho. A year later, Britain created the Colony of Vancouver Island. In 1853, Congress separated Washington Territory from Oregon Territory; six years later, Oregon became the thirty-third state in the union.[49]

Although the Oregon Treaty had defined the border between colonial claims, government officials quickly discovered what the People of the Cape and other borderlanders already knew—by nature, the marine portion of the boundary along the Strait of Juan de Fuca was permeable. Makahs probably learned of the new boundary quickly. If crewmembers of HMS *Herald* neglected to tell them when visiting Cape Flattery in 1846 while surveying the marine borderline, then HBC officials at Fort Victoria would have informed Makah visitors and traders. Throughout most of the 1850s, the Hudson's Bay Company remained the Makahs' top trading partner, with company vessels stopping at Neah Bay and the People of the Cape traveling to Victoria. Indiscriminate trade between Makahs and the company concerned US officials. George Gibbs, a member of the Pacific Railroad Exploration and Survey of 1852, noted that it was impossible to "check this traffic," and he advised Congress that "in any treaties made with them, it should enter as a stipulation that they should confine their trade to the American side." In 1858 an Indian agent surveying the region complained that "all the money paid out by [our] government and citizens [to the Makah] goes immediately over to Victoria to be invested in blankets, muskets, etc." Both US and British officials complained of citizens from the other side crossing the border to sell liquor to Indians, "an evil which endangers the peace of the frontiers." One Puget Sound Indian agent, G. A. Paige, noted in 1857 the impossibility of controlling this traffic because of the many small trading vessels plying local waters. Like those living in other borderlands in North America, local residents—both Native and non-Native—exploited the boundary for their own economic advantage.[50]

At this time, mobile Indians who ignored the border were part of a larger colonial concern about local borderlanders who disrespected official boundaries. For much of the mid-nineteenth century, the British worried about American squatters. Despite the demarcation of the boundary line in 1846, the potential for squatters north of the borderline concerned colonial and company officials. In response—and to support their economic diversification efforts—the Hudson's Bay Company decided to encourage British emigration to Vancouver Island.

Based on information provided by Douglas, the company believed that the island would be an ideal place for a colony because it offered cultivable lands in the south, sheltered harbors for a naval depot, and abundant timber and coal. Sir John Pelly, HBC governor, secured permission from the British crown to allow the company to establish a colony on Vancouver Island in 1849. The first settlers arrived by the barque *Harpooner* on May 31, 1849, and included coalminers, workmen, carpenters, bakers, a shipwright, and their families. These would have been the first settlers to interact regularly with the People of the Cape.[51]

The experience of Walter Colquhoun Grant, the first non-Native to settle independently of the Hudson's Bay Company on Vancouver Island, illustrates that early emigrants needed assistance from both local Indians and company officials. A Scottish native, Grant arrived on Vancouver Island in the fall of 1849. He planned to manufacture prefabricated house frames to sell in California for $250 each. From the beginning, his venture encountered difficulties. Concerned about Grant's "destitute means"—he came with no money—the company paid for his passage from California to Fort Vancouver, gave him company credit, and provided him with livestock. The men Grant hired for this venture arrived at Fort Victoria two months before him, and Douglas had trouble preventing them from leaving for more lucrative work on American vessels or for the California gold fields. When Grant arrived, Douglas took him along the coast to point out potential sites for his sawmill and to introduce him to local Indians. Against Douglas's recommendation, Grant chose a location twenty-five miles from Fort Victoria because it offered an abundant supply of timber and a stream for his sawmill. Douglas "endeavoured strongly to impress on the minds of Captain Grant and his followers, the invaluable importance, both as regards the future well being of the Colony, and their own individual interests, of cultivating the friendship of these Children of the forest." The experienced fur trader worried that settlers such as Grant would antagonize local Indians.[52]

But Natives and settlers had many motivations for interacting in productive ways. Grant relied on indigenous labor and information. While at Neah Bay during a survey of the region, he asked Chief Yelakub for advice on where to settle and locate his sawmill. Already exhibiting a proclivity to direct settlers away from Makah space, Yelakub told him about large tracts of arable land and timber resources across the strait on Vancouver Island.[53] Men from nearby Nuu-chah-nulth villages helped in felling trees and building Grant's sawmill, which he had located on indigenous land. Like those living near Fort Victoria, Grant and his men bought salmon and potatoes from their indigenous neighbors. Many Native borderlanders welcomed the new markets in commodities and labor that settlers provided. Others, however, worried about newcomers taking land and resources, and resistant Indians stole from and threatened the outsiders. Echoing the complaints of other settlers, Grant accused Indians of "depredations"—the contemporary term for theft—and claimed that they caused everything to go "to ruin" during his absences.[54] As interracial tensions mounted, colonial officials on both sides of the new boundary became concerned.

Those governing the Colony of Vancouver Island worried that the presence of British settlers made it all the more important to control Indians. After founding the colony in 1849, the Hudson's Bay Company intensified its policy of inflicting devastating retribution for violence against whites and their property. Unlike previous attempts to develop a coherent policy, these efforts worked because official colonization brought with it the military backing of the British crown. On the Northwest Coast, this power manifested itself in the gunboats (sloops-of-war, corvettes, and frigates) of the Royal Navy, which local officials deployed against Indians. The resultant gunboat diplomacy approved by Douglas left "the smouldering ruins of a village and a scattered village tribe" as "the telling testaments of the process of keeping Northwest Coast Indians 'in awe of British power.'"[55] These destructive expeditions illustrated the growing colonial ability to project power into indigenous spaces.

The People of the Cape kept a wary eye on the Royal Navy vessels sailing—then steaming—through local waters to shell other villages. During 1850 and 1851, the fledgling colonial government at Victoria found itself needing to respond in kind to the murder of three deserters from the company ship *Norman Morison*. Believing that the Newitty (Tlatlasikwala Kwakwaka'wakws) near Fort Rupert on the northern edge of Vancouver Island had murdered the deserters, colonial officials called on the Royal Navy's corvette *Daedalus* to punish the offenders. Echoing sentiments expressed by HBC officials in previous decades, they believed that "if we make no demonstration the Indians will lose all respect for us and may make an attack on [Fort Rupert]." As in the earlier incidents against the S'Klallams and Clatsops, the British burned longhouses and canoes at Nahwitti village, deciding that if the community would not surrender the murderers, then the whole group deserved punishment. The Newitty sued for peace on their own terms by bringing three mangled Indian bodies to Fort Rupert, telling the British that these were the offenders.[56] Colonial officials felt that they had accomplished their goals. Douglas reported to William Tolmie at Fort Nisqually, "The Indians [are] all quiet and civil, being greatly awed by the example made of the Neweetees."[57] In what would become a pattern for Douglas, however, he ignored the way in which the Newitty chiefs confronted British retributive violence. Newitty actions demonstrated that Native leaders still had enough power to control some outcomes of conflicts within indigenous spaces. Native chiefs, not British officials or soldiers, executed the offenders.

Less than six months later, at the beginning of 1852, British colonial officials again faced Natives—this time Makahs and their aggressive salvaging and burning of the *Una*—exercising sovereignty over indigenous spaces. The way colonial officials responded reveals the limitations of colonial power while highlighting the emerging racial divide in the region. When initially reporting on the brig's loss and Makah actions, Douglas highlighted the fledgling colony's inability to protect British lives and property: "The Natives . . . gathered about the wreck in vast numbers, and behaved with great barbarity towards such of the 'Una's' crew as were landed from the wreck. They broke open and rifled the Seamens' chests, stript them of their clothes, and maltreated those who attempted, unarmed as they were to defend their property." In fact, only the intervention of the Americans—fellow whites—prevented "greater atrocities" from happening and kept the valuable furs and gold out of Makah hands.[58] Incidents such as this supported his argument that the colony needed even more naval support to protect it.

Most especially, though, the incident frustrated Douglas because there was little he could do immediately about this affront to British authority and property. For one, he did not have ready access to a company vessel that he could use to punish Makahs. The *Cadborough* was on a trading voyage in the north, while US customs officials in Olympia detained another two—the brigantine *Mary Dare* and steamer *Beaver*—for alleged duties violations. It was not until the end of January that he could deploy the *Cadborough* and "a well appointed force" to Neah Bay to bring the Indians "to a serious account for their barbarous conduct on that occasion, in order to repress the mischievous consequences likely to arise from their evil example, and deter other Savage Nations from committing wanton outrages on the persons and property of Her Majesty's subjects." Seeming more appropriate for a purposeful attack on the *Una* than a vigorous salvaging of a shipwreck, Douglas's rhetoric indicated the mounting pressures he felt at securing white property against aggressive and still powerful Indians. Second, he could not ignore the fact that Neah Bay was in US territory. Unlike dealing with Native peoples north of the border, he could not simply shell this village of American Indians as he had responded to the Newitty. Instead, he was careful to inform Edmund A. Starling, the federal Indian agent for the Puget Sound District in Oregon Territory, of his actions against the Makahs.[59]

When reporting back to his superiors in both the colonial and company offices, Governor Douglas downplayed the fact that a Makah chief had handled the threat of British violence in his own manner. The governor condemned the chief's "barbarous actions" of the summary execution of ten Makahs and the immolation of another while reassuring his superiors that deploying gunboat diplomacy—even without the firing of any shots—had achieved a suitable result. He explained that this expedition "produced the desired effect of alarming the Natives" and "has made a deep impression in the minds of the Natives, who were intently watching our proceedings."[60] Douglas's threat of gunboat diplomacy reflected Lord Palmerston's mandate from several years earlier: "Wherever British subjects are placed in danger . . . thither a British ship of war ought to be . . . for the protection of British interests." But it also exemplified an even longer HBC effort of "keeping the Indians in awe" of British power in the Pacific Northwest.[61] Although he framed the outcome of this incident as a success of personal, HBC, and colonial policies, the governor appeared too embarrassed to admit that Cape Flattery was still Makah space under the sovereign power of influential chiefs. Neither the British nor the Americans were in control—the People of the Cape were. For the time being, Douglas had to acquiesce to Makah authority because HBC operations in this region still depended on the consent and support of local chiefs.

But the balance of power was shifting. During the winter of 1852–53, Douglas confronted the Cowichans and Nanaimos for the murder of a company shepherd stationed just five miles from Victoria. Again with Royal Navy assistance, the governor took more than 150 men into Cowichan territory to capture the two accused murderers. After Douglas gave the tribal nation an ultimatum, they turned over a man the governor believed to be the suspect; actually, he was a slave offered instead as compensation. In this encounter, Cowichans handled British intimidation on customary indigenous terms by paying for a murder with a slave. But this incident did not conclude on Cowichan terms. Colonial forces caught a second suspect, the son of a Cowichan chief, after Douglas took the father hostage. The governor had both suspects—the slave and the chief's son—tried in the colony's first trial by jury. Naval officers found the two men guilty and hanged them in front of their people. In personal correspondence with Tolmie, Douglas cast his success in almost biblical terms, writing, "We had a good deal of trouble in effecting our object, and had to carry their villages sword in hand, but the Almighty disposer of events favoured the just cause, and the land is now cleansed from the pol[l]ution of innocent blood." He argued that God sided with innocent, Christian Anglos against violent heathens. Once again, Douglas reported to his superiors that the scene "appear[ed] to make a deep impression" on the assembled Cowichans.[62] Chiefs Yelakub and x̓isi·t certainly heard about the execution of a Cowichan chief's son and likely worried about the shifting dynamics of power in the region.

From the late 1840s on, both chiefs would have noticed the growing number of Bostons arriving in the region. The first Americans to claim lands north of the Columbia River, the African American Bush family and their white friend Michael Simmons, whom Makahs came to know as the territorial Indian agent, settled near Tumwater in 1845 after emigrating along the Oregon Trail. George Washington Bush, the patriarch of the family and key leader of this group, was the wealthy son of a black sailor and an Irish American servant. A former HBC employee, he had been to the Pacific Coast in the 1820s.[63] These emigrants chose lands along the southern shores of Puget Sound over the more popular Willamette Valley because the provisional government of Oregon Territory had passed discriminatory laws prohibiting African Americans from settling south of the Columbia. During the second half of the 1840s, an increasing number of lumbermen came to the Puget Sound region to establish more than a dozen sawmills. They harvested the seemingly "inexhaustible forests of . . . rich timber," which they shipped aboard the "large number of ships that are now constantly arriving and departing, heavily laden," as one early settler noted.[64] Many of these vessels would have stopped at Neah Bay to trade with Makahs for salmon and oil used to grease the skids of their logging operations. By 1849, C. T. W. Russell settled in Shoalwater Bay (Willapa Bay), north of the mouth of the Columbia River, where he started an oyster business. Several years later, he reported to Isaac Stevens, the territorial governor, that he had induced others—"the right kind of settlers, not hunters and trappers, but good old farmers with their families"—to take up residence in the area. While reports from early settlers such as Russell, Bush, and Simmons encouraged more Americans to come to the region, the Donation Land Act of 1850 further promoted settlement in Oregon Territory. In November 1851, the Denny Party landed at Alki in Puget Sound; by 1852, they had relocated to an indigenous Duwamish site, Little Crossing-Over Place, and founded Seattle.[65]

Before the 1850s, few non-Natives came to Neah Bay to settle, and any who did—or even gave the appearance of considering appropriating Makah space—received a chilly welcome. In 1838, HBC traders at Fort Nisqually heard from visiting S'Klallams that a vessel had visited the "Clasits" (Makahs) and that some passengers had purchased land for a settlement. However, these settlers did not stay long. Similarly, in 1845 the People of the Cape chased away company employees who left their vessel to explore Waadah Island at the mouth of Neah Bay. The logbook of the *Cadborough*, which regularly stopped at the Makah village to trade, noted, "The Captain & four men went in the jolly boat to sound, & whilst on Neah [Waadah] Island observed 6 canoes evidently in pursuit of them. The Captain instantly embarked and pulled toward the ship pursued by the canoes, in the foremost of which was a man standing up with a musket leveled at the Captain, as were, several bows & arrows. When the Captain got near the ships laying in the bay, the Indians landed & pursued the ships back, along the shore for some distance, but did not fire." As they had during the maritime fur trade, Makahs discouraged non-Native efforts to encroach on their spaces. In 1849, when Grant spoke to Yelakub about locations for settling and cutting timber, the chief directed him away from Makah land. Several years later, the Scottish settler complained that "Flattery Jack . . . seemed to have delighted in telling the most atrocious falsehoods," specifically lying about the "beautiful prairie-land" at Barkley Sound. Considering the number of complaints explorers and settlers have made regarding similar Indian "lies," this appears to have been a common strategy used by Natives to get rid of unwanted outsiders.[66]

Makahs discouraged settlement around Cape Flattery while taking advantage of opportunities presented by the increasing number of non-Natives in the region. Since the maritime fur trade, Neah Bay had been an important anchorage and trading spot for many vessels, a condition that continued throughout the nineteenth century. When HMS *America* visited the Strait of Juan de Fuca in 1845, Captain John Gordon described Neah Bay as "a secure place for small ships" and a common anchorage for US whalers. Three American whaling vessels even asked the HBC barque *Cowlitz* for a barrel of powder and some stores so they could trade with Makahs, a request the captain denied. The People of the Cape regularly encountered ships sailing through their marine waters. When HMS *Herald* entered the strait in 1846, Makahs visited the vessel in canoes launched from Tatoosh Island. They offered fish and skins for trade and boarded the *Herald* "without the least fear," indicating that this was a normal occurrence. By the early 1850s, Makah slaves were raising more than a hundred tons of potatoes annually from seed obtained from the Hudson's Bay Company. Makah families consumed some of this harvest and traded the rest to nearby company posts and passing vessels.[67]

Although many Makahs benefited from trade with Bostons and King George men, they resisted initial attempts to establish permanent trading posts at Cape Flattery. In 1849, the Euro-American Samuel Hancock failed to establish one at Neah Bay. Keenly aware of his "isolated situation," Hancock worried that Makahs would steal his trade goods. He wrote that they "seemed dissatisfied with my presence" and described numerous Makah threats and entreaties for him to leave. In fact, a "large deputation" of two hundred Makahs surrounded his post, broke his canoe into pieces, and forced him to depart within three days. Neither Chief λisi·t nor Chief Yelakub interceded on Hancock's behalf at this time. Between the growing number of vessels anchoring at Neah Bay and the burgeoning port of Victoria, the Makah leaders likely felt that they had plenty of trade options and did not need a Boston trader in a Makah village. Not wanting to kill the trader, which might result in a loss of trading opportunities with non-Natives and unite white officials on both sides of the border against Makahs, they still worried that this outsider might compete with them by ignoring chiefs' prerogatives to manage trade. Therefore, he needed to go.[68]

But competition between Chiefs Yelaḱub and X̌isi·t brought Hancock back to Neah Bay in 1851. The growth of Fort Victoria and proliferation of Puget Sound towns likely began to siphon away trade from local Indians, so Makah chiefs without privileged connections to non-Native traders would have begun losing their position as middlemen in regional exchange networks. If Yelaḱub had successfully positioned himself as the Makah leader of influence in dealings with the Hudson's Bay Company, X̌isi·t would have been eager, for example, to explore new trade opportunities such as having a Boston trader under his authority at Neah Bay. In his memoir written less than a decade later, Hancock did not name any particular Makah chief, much less the one who invited him to return to Cape Flattery. He did note, however, that the community welcomed him as a trader, which would have only happened if one of the ranking chiefs had approved of the outsider's presence. Perhaps Hancock received an invitation to return to the Makah village when he went to Neah Bay on business earlier that year.[69] As these powerful chiefs competed to enhance their authority in the ča·di· borderland, they offered new commercial opportunities to settlers such as Hancock.

The trader's second venture began well and benefited both him and the sponsoring chief. This time, Hancock came better prepared. He hired two assistants and chartered a vessel from the new Puget Sound town of Olympia to take them and an adequate quantity of trade goods to Neah Bay. With a chief's support, Hancock received a better reception from the People of the Cape. By October, he and his men had built a small compound; they also hired a Makah cook. He traded for furs, oil, and salmon with Makahs and others to the north and south. In 1852, the commander of the US Pacific Coast Survey noted that Makahs "maintain trade with the Indians on the west of Vancouver [Island], forcing them to dispose of their oil and skins to themselves directly, and not the traders. By this means they make a large profit as intermediate traders."[70] Following longstanding practices that had served titleholders well during the maritime fur trade, Hancock's sponsoring chief mediated trade between non-Makahs and the American trader.

However, the presence of Hancock and other intrusive outsiders displeased other Makahs, especially someone such as Chief Yelaḱub, who would have resented the competition. After the trader's arrival, several people stole some of his goods. Hancock also worried that tensions between the People of the Cape and ships carrying goods from San Francisco to Puget Sound towns would make him a target for Indian anger. Many ships stopped at Neah Bay to trade liquor and other goods for fish, furs, and whale oil. Although Hancock railed against the evils of selling liquor to Natives, he also appeared to engage in this illicit trade—at least one set of trade goods he bought from San Francisco included more than two hundred gallons of whiskey. While the People of the Cape welcomed the trade brought by these vessels, they resisted those who failed to show proper respect. During the winter of 1851–52—the same season as the wreck of the *Una*—Makahs threatened Captain Pinkham's schooner *Franklin*. Evidently the captain had angered someone, and when several canoes of warriors painted for battle approached his vessel, he fired his cannons at them. Fearing that Makahs might retaliate against him after suffering violence and insults from other whites, Hancock built a ten-foot-high palisade and breastwork around his post in early 1852.[71]

While tenuously accepting Hancock's presence, the People of the Cape resisted when other non-Natives encroached on their sovereign spaces. This became evident when the US Pacific Coast Survey expedition established a base camp at Neah Bay while Hancock still traded there. Having heard that the People of the Cape antagonized whites who set foot on Makah land, the survey's leader, Lieutenant George Davidson, worked through Hancock to convene a council with Chief x̌isi·t. With Hancock translating, Davidson explained to the large group assembled in the chief's longhouse that the survey crew was not there to "take away their lands, or interfere with their rights in any way; that our mission was for the benefit of shipping, and that in this they would share by having a trade with the whites." But he also warned them that "if any attack was made upon us, or injury inflicted, a retribution was sure to follow."[72] Taking his cue from British and US officials, Davidson indicated his willingness to deploy retributive violence against aggressive Indians.[73] Yet Davidson's desire to secure x̌isi·t's permission for being on Makah land revealed that some indigenous leaders still possessed power that government officials respected.

The presence of the survey crew at Cape Flattery heightened the mounting tensions between competing Makah chiefs. Although one high-ranking titleholder, x̌isi·t, allowed Hancock and the Pacific Coast Survey crew to occupy his people's land temporarily, other chiefs were less welcoming. At the council, Chief Yelakub warned Davidson that his people were "equally willing to come to blows" if need be. Davidson's crew worried about Yelakub, having heard that he was "a most incorrigible scoundrel, who by force of mental power and rascality had made himself of some importance to the tribe." After setting up their camp in mid-

July, the steamer *Active*, which had brought them to Neah Bay, left to survey the eastern part of the strait. They worried that the local Indian population greatly outnumbered them. James Lawson, topographical aide to Davidson, wrote, "All told in camp there were but nine of us, and when it is considered that in 24 hours about 500 Indians could be mustered against us, this might be considered a small force. But while we feared no danger we deemed it well to be prepared. We had in camp sufficient arms, rifles, revolvers, cavalry pistols and shotguns, to fire over sixty shots without stopping to reload." Lawson's assessment that superior fire-power and military training could overcome overwhelming Native numbers seems to reflect Victorian era assumptions about racial violence.[74]

Leveraging his influence within the borderland, Chief Yelakub demonstrated to expedition officials, Chief ƛisi·t, and other Makahs his willingness and ability to strike at intruders. After the survey crew established their tent camp, "a large fleet of canoes" carrying around two hundred Nuu-chah-nulths from Vancouver Island came to Cape Flattery to exchange oil with Hancock via Yelakub. The trader overheard a conversation among the Indians regarding a plan to attack the survey crew. Darting over to the camp, Hancock informed Lawson and Davidson of the impending attack. The crew erected a breach work of logs, prepared their firearms for action, and posted guards at both the camp and Hancock's post. The Nuu-chah-nulth did not camp on the beach that evening, instead staying in their canoes positioned in a kelp field to which they could anchor their craft. Throughout the night, two Indian men periodically sauntered by the camp to reconnoiter its defenses. In the morning, the fleet departed for home back across the strait. In hindsight, Lawson wrote in his autobiography that "the Mak-Kahs, on account of threats of punishment, were afraid to commit the deed, but the Vancouver [Island] Indians were to do so, and after sharing the spoils the latter would return home." A keen borderlands strategist, Yelakub probably manipulated his kin on Vancouver Island to be his proxy. If these "northern Indians" had attacked, US authorities would have questioned Yelakub, who could have then accused the Nuu-chah-nulths instead of taking the blame himself.[75]

Much to Lawson's frustration, Makahs resisted the US government's effort to map colonial spaces on indigenous lands. They stole survey markers and ran off, with a pistol-wielding Lawson in pursuit. Eventually Lawson took out his frustration by shooting a village dog and threatening to kill any men or whip any women and children who interfered with the survey. Davidson drilled the small crew with weekly target practices, which he scheduled for times when large groups of Makahs watched. He hoped to create in them a "wholesome dread" of firearms. Instead, Makah chiefs just wanted the weapons even more, offering "fabulous price[s]" for the guns. After an absence of ten weeks, the *Active* returned on October 1 to collect the survey crew at Neah Bay, and the US intruders left.

Interactions between Makahs and whites—the US Pacific Coast Survey expedition, Hancock, visiting maritime traders, and the HBC—shaped contemporary impressions of the People of the Cape and their chiefs as formidable and aggressive. Newspapers carried this impression to a wider audience. The *New York Daily Times* informed readers that Makahs had been "exceedingly troublesome" to the US surveyors, who had only "finished their labors at imminent risk of their lives at this inhospitable point."[76] These events demonstrated that Makah chiefs still had substantial power and influence within the čaˑdiˑ borderland. Working with allied kin from across the strait, Makahs could intimidate non-Native intruders, forcing them to leave or accommodate to some Native protocols. Chief Yelakub possibly hoped that these displays of power would impress both rival titleholders in the borderlands and the newcomers. These incidents illustrated that indigenous leaders still possessed enough power to frustrate imperial processes during the early 1850s.

US intrusions did exacerbate tensions between these Makah chiefs. Lawson's account drew from the dichotomy of Native stereotypes of the vanishing noble Indian and the hidebound savage in the way of progress.[77] He presented ƛisiˑt as a leader willing to accommodate the expanding settler-colonial world. After ƛisiˑt witnessed one of the survey crew's rounds of target practice, Lawson noted, "[ƛisiˑt] walked to the target, and placing his thumb and forefinger at an average distance of the shots from the bull's eye, he measured off how many times it required to pass across his breast; then dropping his hand, and shaking his head as though to say, 'Poor chance for an Indian there' he walked slowly and sedately back, and without a word, seated himself. It was one of the most expressive movements I ever saw."[78] Although Lawson represented this action as a performance staged for the survey crew, he missed ƛisiˑt's intended audience: the People of the Cape. He was trying to illustrate to his people the futility of violence against the Bostons, a path that his rival, Yelakub, had threatened to lead them down. As he had been doing for years, Chief ƛisiˑt was arguing that his strategies and leadership would provide for the best opportunities to profit from non-Natives.

Lawson mistakenly portrayed Chief Yelakub as the stereotypical savage who inhibited progress and hated all whites. Having been a kitchen scullion at Fort Langley as a boy, Yelakub was probably used to these aspersions. For years, patronizing HBC traders had lectured him for being "impudent" and castigating his followers as "ugly customers."[79] Yet he still appeared eager to engage with the expanding settler colonial world, albeit on indigenous terms. Drawing on an earlier practice from the maritime fur trade, at some point during 1851 or 1852, Yelakub either exchanged names with Albert or Lafayette Balch, two New England traders who had relocated to the West Coast in the mid-nineteenth century, or gave his son Sixey their surname; throughout the rest of the century Sixey also carried the name "Captain Balch" or "Billy Balch." During the early 1850s while based out of San Francisco, Albert had engaged in the whale oil and salmon trade with West Coast Indians, while his brother Lafayette took out the first coasting license issued in Puget Sound. Lafayette established the town of Steilacoom, Washington, where he operated a trading post and sawmill, the latter of which would have required whale oil to lubricate its machinery. One of their employees, E. M. Fowler, was mate aboard the *George Emery*, a ship Lafayette captained—Fowler eventually captained his own ships, the *Cynosure* and the *Potter*, and both ships and captain became frequent visitors to Cape Flattery.[80] Based on this evidence, it seems likely that both brothers stopped regularly at Neah Bay in the early 1850s. Trade with visiting, not resident, Bostons such as the Balch brothers gave Yelakub an opportunity to expand his authority among his people and throughout the region.

But neither chief spoke for the entire tribal nation. In fact, there were certainly other Makah titleholders, ones who do not appear in the archival record, jockeying for authority. Before the continuing rivalry between ƛisiˑt and Yelakub could develop into an intratribal conflict, however, a new crisis hit and transformed the balance of power in the čaˑdiˑ borderland forever.

CONFRONTING DISEASE AT NEAH BAY, 1853

Increased engagement with settler-colonial peoples brought Eurasian pathogens to the Cape Flattery villages. In the mid-nineteenth century, multiple afflictions hit the People of the Cape, compounding mortality as epidemics struck a people already weakened by earlier maladies. While Makahs suffered the severest effects of disease and their population plummeted, the number of non-Natives living in the region grew. These conditions combined to reverse the demographics of the borderlands: newcomers then outnumbered indigenous peoples. The smallpox epidemic of 1853 was particularly catastrophic because it killed the highest-ranking chiefs, including ƛisiˑt and Yelakub. Not only was this a severe emotional blow to Makahs, but it also meant that less experienced chiefs became the leaders forced to confront the expanding power of settler-colonial governments to control Indians. The high mortality and loss of experienced chiefs threatened to undermine the ability of the People of the Cape to control the čaˑdiˑ borderland.[81]

Numbering around 5,400 individuals before the arrival of Europeans, Makahs had suffered from Old World diseases before the mid-nineteenth century. At some point between 1775 and 1782, smallpox struck the People of the Cape and others in the borderlands, killing many.⁸² Although no maritime fur traders noted evidence of Makahs having suffered from this epidemic, members of the American *Columbia* observed smallpox scars among Ditidahts in 1791. Local borderlanders blamed the Spanish for introducing the disease. Because networks of kinship, trade, and warfare crossed the strait and connected Nuu-chah-nulths such as the Ditidahts to Makahs, if one group contracted smallpox, others did, too. By the mid-nineteenth century, the indigenous borderlands population had risen substantially but had failed to recover to the pre-smallpox level. When Natives confronted settler-colonial power during the mid-nineteenth century, they did so with fewer people than when they had encountered maritime fur traders.⁸³

Some non-Natives took advantage of the "heritage of confusion and fear" the late eighteenth-century epidemic left behind. Duncan McDougall, head of the Pacific Fur Company's Fort Astoria at the mouth of the Columbia River, reportedly told local Chinooks, "'The white men among you,' said [McDougall], 'are few in number, it is true, but they are mighty in medicine. See here,' continued he, drawing forth a small bottle and holding it before their eyes, 'in this bottle I hold the smallpox, safely corked up; I have but to draw the cork, and let loose the pestilence, to sweep man, woman, and child from the face of the earth.'" The chiefs were struck with horror and alarm.⁸⁴ Known as "the Great Smallpox Chief" after this 1811 speech, McDougall exploited indigenous fears of this Old World disease after hearing of the demise of the *Tonquin* in Clayoquot Sound. He hoped that this fear would help him control local Indians who might be emboldened to attack Fort Astoria. Natives and white traders spread the theory of bottled diseases that angry whites could uncork at will. In 1830, Captain John Dominis of the Boston brig *Owyhee* threatened to uncork a bottle full of disease, unleashing it among Makahs if they refused to trade beaver skins. Compounded by the "fever and ague" (malaria) that Dominis's *Owyhee* brought to the People of the Cape and other indigenous borderlanders that season, this inaccurate explanation for disease shaped Makah understandings of pathogens into the 1850s.⁸⁵

Northwest Coast peoples became part of a broader disease pool during the 1830s and 1840s. However, Makahs avoided many maladies that struck the region, including the influenza and smallpox outbreaks of 1836–38 and dysentery in 1844. Some evidence indicates that Makahs perhaps limited their contact with sick locations and affected peoples. The Fort Nisqually records indicate that from

1833 to 1836 Yelakub led annual Makah trading delegations there, arriving in the late fall and staying until January. But after January 1836, he no longer came to the fort. That fall, Makahs avoided Puget Sound possibly because they had heard about the influenza outbreak in March and April 1836 that struck Indians living near Fort Nisqually. The increasingly interconnected nature of the Northwest Coast, however, meant that the People of the Cape could not avoid all outbreaks of Old World diseases. In the spring of 1848, measles arrived at Fort Victoria, where Makahs contracted it. That summer, white passengers carried influenza to the fort, and Makahs, already weakened by measles, caught this, too. By the mid-nineteenth century, the People of the Cape regularly suffered from scrofula, a form of tuberculosis affecting the lymph nodes.[86]

During the summer or fall of 1853, the year following the US Pacific Coast Survey's sojourn at Neah Bay, smallpox ravaged the indigenous communities of the ča·di· borderland. Mortality from this epidemic was higher than previous ones because Makahs had spent the months before the outbreak fighting off a bevy of other ailments, including malaria. During his time at Neah Bay with the survey expedition, Lawson suffered from "chills and fever" and took quinine. Malaria then spread to the People of the Cape. Lawson noted incidents of "serious illness" among the villages and even complained of their "avidity" for applying for and taking "Boston drugs"—Chief ƛisi·t made the most frequent requests.[87] Having seen his people suffer for the past five years from measles, influenza, and now malaria, ƛisi·t sought non-Native cures to these afflictions.

But the US Pacific Coast Survey did not bring smallpox to Neah Bay. Instead, passengers and clothing on Captain Fowler's brig *Cynosure* carried the disease north from San Francisco, infecting indigenous peoples along the Columbia River, at Willapa Bay, and at Cape Flattery. By November, the epidemic had reached deep into Puget Sound and was "raging" at the Puget Sound Agricultural Company's farm at Tlithlow, near Steilacoom. When the *Cynosure* arrived at Neah Bay, two sick Makahs disembarked and infected their people. One of the returning men died, but the other survived. Many People of the Cape fled into the borderlands, crossing the strait to live among relatives at Ditidaht and other Vancouver Island villages. British Indian agent William Banfield reported that smallpox had "nearly annihilated" the Pacheedahts in the early 1850s. They likely contracted the disease from fleeing Makahs or neighboring Ditidahts who had taken in smallpox refugees from the Cape Flattery villages.[88]

From his trading post at Neah Bay, Hancock witnessed Makah efforts to combat the epidemic. In the beginning, when someone became sick in a longhouse, all the occupants fled to live in other houses after leaving behind some dried fish and water for the afflicted person. As the epidemic spread, sick people pulled themselves out to the beach to die. Many begged Hancock for help, promising to become his slaves for life if they survived. Beyond providing food and water, however, he believed he could do little. Many People of the Cape died in front of the trader's post. Hancock had survivors dig large holes to deposit fifteen to twenty bodies at a time. When he tired of bodies filling his yard, he dragged them down to the beach at low tide, hoping they would drift away. In a matter of six weeks, the disease burned its course, taking almost two thousand Makahs, or three-quarters of the People of the Cape.[89] Hancock reported that "the beach for the distance of eighteen miles was literally strewn with the dead bodies of these people, presenting a most disgusting spectacle."[90] What disgusted Hancock devastated Makah society.

Survivors hypothesized about whom to blame for the 1853 smallpox epidemic. Still believing that whites kept diseases in bottles, some blamed the US Pacific Coast Survey because they had left behind bottles to mark a coastal astronomical station. Fearing future outbreaks, some Makahs dug up and destroyed these bottles.[91] Others blamed the survivor who had returned to Neah Bay aboard the *Cynosure*. Hancock observed, "Being determined to have satisfaction from some quarter for the loss of so many of their people, [they] apprehended the Indian who contracted the disease on the schooner, but recovered: as a punishment he was taken out in the middle of the Strait of Juan de Fuca, and placed in a small canoe barely large enough to hold him and set adrift, without a paddle or anything else. They thought he would drift out to sea and perish, but the night was calm and favorable, and paddling with his hands he succeeded in reaching by morning, Nerah Island [Waadah Island in Neah Bay], where he was discovered by the natives who went after him and shot him with their muskets."[92] Many Makahs also blamed Hancock, and he taxed his limited communication skills to convince them otherwise.

Despite his reassurances, Hancock never regained the Makahs' goodwill. Before the 1853 epidemic, the presence of the Pacific Coast Survey had exacerbated tensions among Makah chiefs and with Hancock. He had lost his patron to the smallpox epidemic, and some continued to blame him for the catastrophe. The trader's actions during the epidemic would have upset many. Not only had he failed to help those in need, but he also had dragged the dead to the waterline. From the Makahs' perspective, this was a terrible insult because this was a common way to dispose of dead slaves. The People of the Cape made their feelings for Hancock known. He later recalled that hostile Makahs "threatened at various times to kill me if I did not leave the place." After the epidemic, he concluded that he was no longer safe. By the end of 1853, he abandoned his trading post, exchanging the remainder of his goods with neighboring S'Klallams for passage to Whidbey Island in northern Puget Sound, where he lived "the quiet life of the farmer."[93]

The high mortality from the 1853 diseases dealt a severe blow to the People of the Cape. Hancock reported, "It was really distressing to look at those who had survived this sad occasion, some of whom had lost all their near and dearest friends, and whose countenances showed their distress more plainly than words could have told; all seemed to realize their forlorn situation, and be ignorant what to do with themselves." Makahs also appeared either reluctant or still too sick to engage in regular trade with vessels that came to Neah Bay that winter. A year later, Territorial Governor Isaac Stevens and his treaty commission visited Neah Bay. "Klah-pe at hoo" (Captain John Claplanhoo), younger brother of Chief Halicks—one of the three highest-ranked chiefs—told Stevens, "Since his brother died, he had been sick at heart."[94] Coming on the heels of previous afflictions, the combined onslaught of malaria and smallpox led to a demographic and social catastrophe unmatched by previous epidemics.

The loss of their most prominent leaders compounded the Makahs' sadness. Among the casualties buried in pits around Hancock's post, abandoned on the beach, or dragged to the waterline at low tide were X̱isi·t, Yelaḵub, and Halicks. Smallpox struck them down at the peak of their lives. A year earlier, Lawson had remarked on X̱isi·t's physical health after witnessing the whaler at work: "Perfectly naked he stood in the bow of the canoe, one foot on each gunwale, a perfect specimen of an athlete, and never failed to strike his mark."[95] In his mid-thirties, Yelaḵub was a renowned war chief in the ča·di· borderland. Seeing these accomplished and healthy whalers and warriors—literal paragons of their people—waste away in a matter of weeks must have devastated the People of the Cape. Their loss also necessitated a reshuffling of leadership among the Makahs. Self-described "small chiefs" such as Q̱alču·t ("kuhl-choot") of Neah Bay became the ranking titleholders. These less experienced leaders then became the ones to confront the US treaty representatives in 1855. At this point, only about a quarter of the Makahs remained—all demoralized survivors—to resist the outsiders.

Throughout X̱isi·t's and Yelaḵub's lives, conditions in the ča·di· borderland began to shift in a way that challenged indigenous control of the region. They experienced the emergence of terrestrial colonial and settler spaces within the borderlands and non-Native attempts to intrude on Makah lands. New commercial competitors appeared, including fur trading enterprises such as the Pacific Fur Company, North West Company, and Hudson's Bay Company, along with an increasing number of smaller, private US outfits operating ships sailing along the coast. Throughout the rising commercialization of the region, Makahs made conscious efforts to hold onto their position as middlemen by transforming these potential competitors into trade opportunities. Chiefs Yelakub and λisi·t were able to do this because of their ability to exploit customary marine resources, a prime location along the Northwest Coast, and borderlands dynamics and networks. But they also became concerned about the growing power of colonial entities to deploy retributive violence along racial lines. A series of geopolitical changes began to transform the region and gave rise to a colonial borderlands and eventual boundary line separating US and British claims in the Pacific Northwest. However, many of the conditions and dynamics of the ča·di· borderland persisted alongside the colonial borderlands, even after it hardened into a borderline between nation-states.

The year 1853 was crucial for the People of the Cape. They began that year from a position of relative power in the ča·di· borderland. Leaders had reversed their people's waning trade influence in the borderlands by bringing a non-Native trader to Cape Flattery. Selling tens of thousands of gallons of whale oil to this trader and the HBC had made chiefs such as λisi·t and others wealthy. For the time, Makahs remained integral to the success of the HBC and early settler industries and processes. Their "pillaging" of the *Una* and purported "barbarous" punishment of those Makahs who preyed on helpless whites encouraged newcomers to the region to respect—even fear—them. Chiefs λisi·t and Yelakub embodied the power of indigenous leaders to both interrupt and enable colonial processes such as trade, surveying, and settlement. The Northwest Coast of the early 1850s was a complex region where indigenous power, people, and commodities simultaneously worked with and against the governments, settlers, and markets of two of the most powerful empires of the time, the United Kingdom and the United States. At the beginning of 1853, Makah chiefs such as λisi·t and Yelakub still possessed the ability to control space.

Part of this strength came from the competitive nature of authority in systems of Northwest Coast leadership. Influential Makah chiefs engaged colonialism in various ways in order to maintain or strengthen personal influence in the Northwest Coast. Colonialism did not create rivalry among titleholders; nor did these tensions represent a detrimental and growing schism within tribal communities such as the People of the Cape. Chiefs λisi·t and Yelakub were not simply colonial collaborators or resisters.[96] Instead, they both embraced and encouraged precise aspects of the emerging settler-colonial world to meet culturally specific Makah needs. Usually missing this dynamic, non-Natives such as HBC employees, American traders and ship captains, and government surveyors often became embroiled in these rivalries. Most important, though, competition among Makah chiefs had a productive quality, fueling non-Native respect for the power of the People of the Cape, who continued to be known for their formidability. During the crucial years of the mid-nineteenth century when settler-colonial pressures increased, this reputation helped to protect Makah sovereignty.

As 1853 unfolded, however, catastrophic challenges threatened the People of the Cape. A deadly smallpox epidemic hammered a population already weakened from an earlier affliction of malaria, reducing the Makahs from about 2,500 individuals to several hundred. Adding to the devastation of death on such a massive scale, other Makahs temporarily fled the Cape Flattery villages, deepening their desolation. The epidemic, moreover, claimed the lives of the two most powerful chiefs, x̌isi·t and Yelak̓ub, and other ranking titleholders. The high disease mortality rate of 1853 contributed to a dramatic demographic shift as increasing numbers of non-Natives began arriving. On February 8, 1853, Congress organized Washington Territory, which intensified non-Native emigration to the Northwest Coast. Unlike earlier non-Natives, these newcomers came with the intention of establishing homes and communities that would substantially limit indigenous sovereignty. How the People of the Cape recovered from one challenge to confront the next would determine their fate for future generations.

4

"I WANT THE SEA"

One winter morning in 1855, Makahs at Neah Bay village awoke to find a vessel anchored in the shelter of the bay. They recognized the schooner *Potter* and knew its captain, E. M. Fowler. During the past several years, Fowler had visited Neah Bay to trade, and, ominously, his *Cynosure* had brought smallpox to the Makahs in 1853. As on its previous visit, the *Potter* brought some Bostons (Americans) on government business. Earlier, Colonel Michael Simmons, the territorial Indian agent, had stopped at Neah Bay and tried to impress upon the People of the Cape the importance of signing a treaty with the United States.[1] This time the *Potter* carried Washington's territorial governor Isaac Stevens and members of his treaty commission, including Simmons, Benjamin F. Shaw (interpreter), and George Gibbs (surveyor and secretary). Stevens believed that he had tapped the best talent in the territory for his commission. "Old frontiersmen" and some of the earliest settlers to the region, Simmons had been described by his admirers as the "Daniel Boone of Washington Territory," while Shaw was a noted translator of Chinook jargon, the local trade language. Gibbs had also lived in the area for some time, coming west after studying law at Harvard and working for the American Ethnological Society in New York.[2] The commissioners had come to this remote corner of the United States to negotiate a treaty with the residents of Cape Flattery.

After warily observing the governor and surveyor map out reservation boundaries, six leaders from Neah Bay and other nearby Makah villages boarded the *Potter* to learn about the proposed treaty and to state their concerns. With the help of Captain Jack—a neighboring S'Klallam chief who translated from Chinook jargon, a language spoken by Captain Fowler and Shaw, into Makah—the chiefs listened while Stevens explained that the Great Father had sent him to watch over them. To open the negotiations, Governor Stevens explained his per-spective on the proposed treaty. Like the treaties Stevens had signed with Puget Sound tribal nations, this one would transfer Native land to the United States. In return, the federal government would provide a reservation, school, farms, and a physician, among other items.[3]

The chiefs cared little for what Stevens offered. Instead, each one emphasized the importance of retaining their marine tenure. Five of them spoke about the need to reserve their fishing and whaling rights. Q̓alču·t ("kuhl-choot"), one of the two chiefs representing Neah Bay, stated, "I ought to have the right to fish, and take whales and get food when I like. I am afraid that if I cannot take hali-but where I want, I will become poor." Governor Stevens acknowledged this position by replying that he wanted them to continue fishing and whaling; he only wanted whites to do so, too. Q̓alču·t conceded that he "would live as a friend to the Whites and they should fish together." Except for the 1853 smallpox epidemic, the past several decades of interactions with King George men

Biʔidʔa ("bih-ih-duh") Village, 1862. Neah Bay lies beyond Biʔidʔa, and the cedar longhouses of Neah Bay village can be seen on the far shore. Watercolor by James Swan, from the Franz R. and Kathryn M. Stenzel Collection of Western American Art. Image supplied courtesy of the Beinecke Rare Book and Manuscript Library, Yale University.

(British) and Bostons had gone well because the People of the Cape had profited by selling oil, sealskins, and fish to traders and vessels.

But Makah statements also articulated a marine space connection broader
than fishing and whaling rights. Individuals spoke of specific marine locations
they owned. K̇a·baksaɫ ("kuh-buhk-saht") from Ċu·yas ("tsoo-yuhs"), a coastal
village at the mouth of the Sooes River, spoke of an estuary as his property. Q̇i·čuk
("kee-chook") of Tatoosh Island explained that his holdings encompassed the
island and extended through marine waters to the Hoko River's mouth, about
fifteen miles away. More important, these Makah leaders identified the ocean
as the homeland of their people. In describing his holdings, Q̇i·čuk told the Bostons that "he did not want to leave the saltwater." Another chief, ʔitʔa·ndaha·
("iht-ahn-duh-hah"), echoed his words, repeating that he, too, did not wish to
leave the saltwater. Appointed "head chief" by Governor Stevens, Ċaqȧ·wiɬ
("tsuh-kah-wihtl") of Ozette stated it clearest: "I want the sea. That is my
country." Wanting to impress upon the governor the importance of this statement, Ċaqȧ·wiɬ refused to even consider the terms of the treaty until Stevens
joined him in a canoe on the saltwater. As the two leaders paddled around, the
Ozette chief explained that the sea was his country. Although it is tempting to
imagine this exchange as literally one where the two men were alone in a small
canoe on the water, Captain Jack and Fowler probably accompanied them to
help Stevens understand Ċaqȧ·wiɬ.[4]

Representing their people, forty-two Makahs signed the treaty by marking an
"X" next to the approximations of their names that Gibbs noted. As their ancestors had done for generations, Makah chiefs protected their marine tenure and
reserved their rights to the waters they claimed. Specifically, they secured their
continued rights to fish and hunt whales and seals. This time, however, they used
a non-Makah tool of diplomacy—a treaty—instead of indigenous protocols. From
the perspective of the People of the Cape, Governor Stevens appeared to understand and acknowledge their tenure claims to customary marine space. They
would not have signed the treaty otherwise.

The historical context of local power dynamics in the mid-nineteenth-century
ča·di· borderland shaped the treaty negotiations between Bostons and the People of the Cape. At this time, the Makah held a better negotiating position than
other American Indians west of the Cascade Mountains in Washington Territory, despite the recent mortalities from diseases that had burned through their
communities. Not only were Makahs an important part of the settler-colonial
economy, but whites still feared and respected them. Governor Stevens recognized that this tribal nation retained enough power to complicate the new territory's development. Most important, though, Makah chiefs—the ones newly

elevated to their positions due to the deaths of more experienced leaders—used the treaty to protect what was important to their people: the sea. Their ability to force Stevens to negotiate was significant because the governor appeared unwilling to do so with other tribal nations, even when it resulted in failed negotiations. Stevens's negotiations south of Cape Flattery with the Quinaults, Queets, Satsops, Chehalis, Chinooks, and Cowlitz unraveled when he refused to grant them all their own separate reservations.[5]

The Makahs' connection to the ocean and its resources shaped the concerns the chiefs expressed during the treaty negotiations. By describing the sea as his country, Čaqá·wiƛ articulated cultural values central to his people's relationship to customary marine space. First, his words reveal that the People of the Cape owned specific marine waters and resources. This contradicts the assumption underlying most narratives about settler-colonial expansion into indigenous spaces, namely the idea that property-oriented societies claimed lands and resources that Natives held in common and did not fully use. Second, the Ozette chief's words and those of his peers also invoked the ways that Makahs made the sea their country through customary practices, such as whaling, sealing, and fishing. These practices enabled Makahs to exploit marine resources, which provided them with the wealth and power that better positioned them when they needed to negotiate with non-Natives.

Captured by calling the sea their country, the Makahs' worldview highlights how they conceptualized marine space differently from whites. Shaped by a common European geographical conceptualization that divided water from land, British and US officials in 1846 had used the Strait of Juan de Fuca, which separates Vancouver Island from the Olympic Peninsula, to make a convenient and natural boundary between colonial claims in the Oregon Country. When Governor Stevens and his treaty commission drew up the boundaries of the Makah reservation, they assumed that the coastline made a natural boundary to the north and west, like some invisible fence that would keep Makahs inside and other Indians and non-Native settlers outside. However, those on either side of the international border frustrated both British and US colonial officials who desired to keep Natives in their respective political, social, and economic places.

Unlike Europeans and Euro-Americans who saw marine water as a boundary separating one colonial space from another, Makahs and other indigenous borderlanders continued to experience these waters as a space of connections. Preexisting indigenous networks of trade, kinship, and violence endured. The continuation of these networks confounded the efforts of officials on both sides of the border to create a more traditional boundary line between nation-states.

By engaging in regional indigenous networks, peoples such as Makahs and neighboring Nuu-chah-nulths illustrate that characteristics and processes of the čaˑdiˑ borderland endured throughout the nineteenth century. The indigenous borderlands persisted not only into the period when a separate but related colonial borderland emerged but also after 1846, when Britain and the United States established what they considered a definitive boundary between their respective claims. The continuation of čaˑdiˑ borderland dynamics shaped the development of Washington Territory and the British colonies of Vancouver Island and British Columbia to the north.[6] These borderland characteristics also enabled Makahs to resist the growing power of the United States even as they continued to engage with settler-colonialism to benefit their people.

LOCAL POWER AND NEGOTIATING
THE TREATY OF NEAH BAY, 1855

The ability to exploit lucrative marine resources left the People of the Cape in a better position than other American Indians when negotiating with the United States. Because the US treaty negotiators valued Makah contributions to the nascent settler-colonial economy, Governor Stevens was willing to negotiate a few key points in the Treaty of Neah Bay. As they had been for decades, the Makah were the most feared tribal nation west of the Cascades in the new territory, and officials worried that this group could cause them trouble, even after having lost three-quarters of their people to Eurasian diseases. In North America "every land transfer of any form included elements of *law* and elements of *power*."[7] When examining treaty making, land sales, and theft of indigenous spaces, most scholars have limited their scope to explaining that settler-colonial societies possessed more power than indigenous peoples. Looking back in time with a wide-angle lens, we can see that US treaty negotiators in Washington Territory acted from a "position of assured dominance," believing that they possessed more power than Indian tribes in the mid-nineteenth century.[8] For instance, the population of the United States outnumbered American Indians in the territory; an entire legal framework of treaties, laws, and courts supported the taking of Indian land and control of Natives; and the nation could deploy its military might against tribal nations. Without denying these facts, however, we should consider local dynamics of indigenous power that shaped specific negotiations, such as the Treaty of Neah Bay. Due to the aggressive actions of the People of the Cape and their leaders in the period before the treaty negotiations, Bostons and King George men continued to respect Makah power. So even within the framework of a process predisposed to work against indigenous peoples, Makah chiefs in 1855 had enough power to alter the treaty to protect what was most important to their people—continued access and rights to the sea and its resources upon which they had relied for generations.

At the time of the treaty negotiations, whites depended on the contributions the People of the Cape made to the settler-colonial economy. Makahs provided whale oil, fish, furs, information, and labor to the British colonies in the region and Washington Territory, a fact the treaty commissioners appreciated and respected. Having lived in Puget Sound for nine years before Stevens appointed him Indian agent in 1854 and to the treaty commission, Michael Simmons wrote in a local paper, "[The Makah] are altogether the most enterprising within the Territory. In industry, thrift, and enjoyment of the comforts of life they are not approached by any neighboring tribe southward. They take the whale with harpoon, spears, etc., of their own invention and venture in their whale excursions in their light canoes an almost incredible distance from land." Other observers informed the governor that the Makah technique with indigenous equipment was "vastly superior" to American whaling methods, which lost many whales each voyage. George Gibbs, surveyor for the commission, understood the scale of contribution Makah whalers made to the settler-colonial economy—in the 1850s, he had reported to Congress that Makahs annually traded tens of thousands of gallons of oil.[9] The fact that most of these anecdotal observations of Makah contributions to the settler-colonial economy were written after diseases had severely reduced the tribal nation seems to indicate that local whites still believed that the People of the Cape had an important economic role to play in the new territory.

Since the maritime fur trade, Makahs had participated in making colonialism possible in the Northwest Coast. A product harvested and processed into a vital commodity for both indigenous peoples and newcomers, whale oil was a key ingredient non-Natives used to expand colonial spaces in the region. Makah oil heated and lit homes and businesses in nearby towns such as Victoria and Port Townsend. Victorian era colonialists prided themselves in bringing light—a central component to imperial projects across the world—to the Pacific Northwest. Many Victorians believed that wherever the British flag flew, they had a "responsibility to import the light of civilization (identified as especially English), thus illuminating the supposedly dark places in the world."[10] Little did these Victorians expect, though, that indigenous oil would fuel English lamps. Large quantities of Makah oil also greased the skids of local logging operations. By removing trees, newcomers tamed an otherwise threatening wilderness by clearing the land for towns and farms. Proud of transforming wilderness spaces into civilized places, non-Natives ignored the irony that indigenous oil expedited the processes of settler-colonialism. Although this seemed lost on Stevens, Gibbs, and Simmons, these individuals knew and appreciated the products provided by the People of the Cape. These treaty negotiators expected to hear Makah statements that insisted on their continued rights to whale and fish in customary waters. During the negotiations, Stevens acknowledged Makahs' contributions to settler-colonialism when he told the chiefs, "I know what great whalers you are," and when he promised that "[the Great Father] will send you barrels in which to put your oil, kettles to try it out, lines and implements to fish with."[11] But the federal government never kept these promises after local officials gained enough power to ignore Makah demands later in the nineteenth century.

Acknowledgment of the ways American Indians supported settlers provided a problematic tension in the treaty process advocated by the federal government and territorial officials. During the third quarter of the nineteenth century, whites possessed a "deep ambivalence about the place of Indians in urban life."[12] But

Makah Indians towing a whale ashore at the Tatoosh Island landing, 1861. Just as they did in 1999, the Makahs depicted in this sketch are pulling the whale onto the beach. Sketch by James Swan. National Anthropological Archives, Smithsonian Institution [NAA INV 09037900].

settlers living outside urban spaces felt this ambivalence, too. Non-Natives wanted to continue benefiting from indigenous products, trade, and labor. Local Indians, and even those from as far north as Alaska, provided a wealth of goods that fed early settlers and fueled commercial enterprises. Native men, women, and children cleared forests and broke ground; harvested crops; delivered mail, cargo, and people in their canoes; piloted non-Native vessels through unknown and dangerous waters; and provided companionship to white men far from home. Yet many newcomers desired to separate Indians from white society.

The actions of territorial officials such as Governor Stevens and the treaty commissioners often reflected this ambivalence. Stevens believed that Washington Territory urgently needed Indian treaties, and he set out to put Natives in their place. By 1855, American settlers had already filed thousands of land claims under the Donation Land Act and the Preemption Act, which Congress had extended to Washington Territory the previous year. Often located on indigenous lands, these claims brought newcomers into conflict with local American Indians. In the winter of 1846, Indians shot and butchered a bull owned by an American settler who had taken up a claim near Fort Nisqually, and conflicts such as these became common when more outsiders arrived.[13] Just before Congress created Washington Territory in 1853, separating it from the northern half of Oregon Territory, the number of whites killed by American Indians had increased from thirteen in 1850 to fifty-eight in 1852, including thirty-nine emigrants.[14] Although many of these deaths occurred in areas south of the Columbia River, which separated Washington and Oregon territories, the statistics pointed to a disturbing regional trend of rising interracial conflict. Natives also complained of violent whites who failed to pay for work or services.[15] These incidents weighed on the mind of the new governor.

A Jacksonian Democrat, West Point graduate, veteran of the Mexican War, and ardent expansionist, Isaac Stevens initially believed that he had the power and personal ability to impose the government's reservation policy on Indians. Characterized as a "young man in a hurry," Stevens felt pressured to negotiate treaties quickly to open the land for settlers, economic development, and roads. On February 28, 1854, in his address to the first session of the territorial legislature, the governor promised to take the "promptest action" at terminating Indian title to lands. He also hoped that peaceful settlement with tribal nations would enable white citizens and businesspeople in the territory to continue benefiting from the indigenous labor and goods critical to settler-colonial processes.[16]

One strain of Stevens's ambivalence about the place of Indians in Washington Territory emerged from the federal government's entwined reservation and treaty policies. George W. Manypenny, commissioner of Indian affairs, had committed his agency to a strategy of using treaties to assign tribal nations to small reservations where federal agents would work to "civilize" American Indians, training them to develop "such habits of industry and thrift as will enable them to sustain themselves." Manypenny believed that this strategy was a viable alternative to extermination. Before beginning the territory's treaty negotiations, Stevens met with Manypenny and the commissioner's second-in-command, Charles Mix, in the nation's capital. These officials directed the new territorial governor to concentrate Washington's American Indians onto as few reservations as possible. Mix advised Stevens to minimize the number of treaties in the territory, encouraging him to unite bands into tribes and to concentrate multiple tribes onto each reservation. Manypenny and Mix were concerned about creating many small reservations because this strategy had caused the Senate to deny ratification of the nineteen earlier treaties Anson Dart (first superintendent of Indian affairs for Oregon) had negotiated with Indians in Oregon Territory in 1851. Agreeing with their recommendations, Stevens left Washington, DC, hoping to consolidate all the territory's Natives onto two reservations, one west of the Cascades and another east of the mountains. He did not plan on making the same mistake Dart had made in giving each tribe its own reservation. Stevens assumed that this strategy would reduce administrative costs and curb "mischievous" Indian dispositions.[17]

To facilitate the process, Stevens adopted a treaty template that reflected the federal government's philosophy and the policy advocated by the Office of Indian Affairs. Before treating with any of Washington's tribal nations, he asked Gibbs to develop a uniform treaty that reflected local conditions and could be used with all groups. This template included a key provision protecting indigenous fishing at "usual and accustomed places" both on and off the reservations. The treaty commissioners believed that if they allowed tribal nations to continue normal subsistence practices, American Indians could support themselves, which would save the government money. Besides, Native fishing would not compete with settler-colonial land uses, such as farming, lumbering, mining, road building, and town establishment, the commissioners assumed. The fishing clause embodied the other strain of Stevens's ambivalence over the place of Indians in the social and economic life of the territory. By protecting the right of tribal members to fish at "usual and accustomed places," the treaties—documents designed to remove indigenous peoples from their lands and keep them separate from white spaces and society—encouraged Natives to leave the reservation in order to pursue customary practices that kept them engaged with Euro-Americans.[18]

The treaty commission then attempted to follow a reservation policy designed to draw lines around American Indians, removing them from territorial society to prepare them for eventual assimilation. Ardent supporters of this policy, Stevens and the commissioners assumed that physical reservation borders would contain Indians. In an 1858 annual report, Commissioner of Indian Affairs Mix explained the goal of the reservation policy to the secretary of the Interior, writing, "Great care should be taken in the selection of the reservations, so as to isolate the Indians for a time from contact and interference from the whites." Also, "No white persons should be suffered to go upon the reservations." And further, "There should be sufficient military force in the vicinity of the reservations to prevent the intrusion of improper persons upon them . . . and to aid in controlling the Indians and keeping them within the limits assigned to them."[19] When marking out the reservation at Cape Flattery, commissioners believed that borderlines drawn across the land and along the coast would keep Makahs in and non-Makahs—both Natives and non-Natives—out.

Territorial officials reinforced the physical reservation border with additional boundaries designed to keep Makahs and other Washington Natives in their place. Controlling American Indians lay at the heart of these efforts.[20] Some officials, such as Governor Stevens, advocated military control over the territory's indigenous peoples. A longtime supporter of using the military to monitor Natives in the frontier, Stevens tried and failed to get support for a strong territorial militia. Without this type of military power at his disposal, Stevens turned to the treaties to encode some method of control. Along with other territorial officials, Stevens wanted to control Indian trade, redirecting it to benefit US rather than British interests. Although the Hudson's Bay Company went unnamed, article 13 of the Treaty of Neah Bay dealt implicitly with the company by prohibiting Makahs from trading "at Vancouver's Island or elsewhere out of the dominions of the United States." While foreclosing indigenous economies if enforced, this provision reflected Stevens's desire to undermine the Hudson's Bay Company's influence over the territory's Indians. In his instructions to the officers in charge of surveying the territory, Stevens wrote, "The Indians must look to us for protection and counsel. . . . I am determined, in my intercourse with the Indians, to break up the ascendency of the Hudson Bay Company and permit no authority or sanction to come between the Indians and the officers of this government." The treaty provision prohibiting American Indians from trading outside the nation's boundaries struck at the heart of čaˑdiˑ borderland dynamics that ignored nation-state boundaries yet echoed concerns expressed by Edmund Starling, an earlier Indian agent, who complained about Natives crossing the border to trade for blankets and other goods.[21] As the colonial entities of Vancouver Island and Washington Territory took shape in the mid-nineteenth century, each set of officials worked to make this trade benefit their colony and not the other's. Ironically, this treaty provision redirecting Indian trade toward Americans strengthened the connections between the territory's indigenous peoples and non-Native society precisely when the federal government was attempting to separate the former from the latter through reservation policies. If enforced to the letter of the provision, the People of the Cape could no longer trade with their most important partners, the indigenous communities on Vancouver Island, instead needing to establish and enhance ties with newcomers living south of the strait.

The treaty commissioners also sought to control another troubling crossing of social boundaries, the captivity of non-Natives. Article 12 in the Treaty of Neah Bay ordered Makahs to free all slaves and not acquire any more. On the surface, this provision reflected national concerns over the expansion of slavery in the US West, and Congress had established Washington as an antislavery territory.[22] Euro-Americans—especially those such as Stevens who had strong abolition backgrounds—characterized Northwest Coast Indian slavery as a backward institution that should be prohibited in the progressive territory.[23] Even though the number of these incidents was small, white fears of Natives enslaving non-Natives underscored the importance of prohibiting slavery. In the decades before signing the Treaty of Neah Bay, Makahs had drawn the attention of HBC, British, and US officials intent on combating slavery because wealthy chiefs had purchased or captured Japanese, Russians, and white Americans, in addition to indigenous peoples from other communities. During the mid-nineteenth century, Neah Bay continued to be the center of the indigenous slave trade, and whites still feared becoming the property of Indians.[24] Therefore, when the US treaty commission came to Neah Bay, prohibiting slavery—especially across racial lines—was a top priority. Yet in the decades after signing the treaty, federal agents at Neah Bay made few efforts at ending Makah slavery of Natives, thereby revealing that officials at the time only desired to prevent Indians from enslaving whites and other "civilized" peoples.[25]

The territorial legislature also used laws to erect legal boundaries controlling interracial relations. In 1854 and 1855, the legislature passed and amended a law voiding all solemnized marriages—unions officiated by clergymen or government officials—between whites and Indian men and women and making it illegal for anyone to solemnize such unions. During the land-based fur trade, interracial unions had been common.[26] When settlers and colonial officials came to the region in the 1840s, they expressed their distaste for these relationships, especially when they resulted in mixed-race children. Berthold Seemann, botanist aboard the British survey vessel HMS *Herald*, described his "disgust" at the "half-castes" he saw at Fort Victoria in 1846, surmising that they "appear to inherit the vices of both races." Five years later, the first schoolteacher in the Colony of Vancouver Island complained about HBC officers living with Native women.[27] Through these laws and others (such as barring Indians from testifying in civil and criminal proceedings), US territorial officials sought to separate Natives from most aspects of white society.

Of all the tribal nations west of the Cascade Mountains, Governor Stevens worried most about the Makahs at Cape Flattery. He knew of their reputation for violence and intransigence. In his report on Indians in the US West, Stevens predicted, "The superior courage of the Makahs, as well as their treachery, will make them more difficult of management than most other tribes of this region. No whites are at present settled in their country; but as the occupation of the territory progresses, some pretty stringent measures will be probably required respecting them." Characterizing them as "the most formidable [tribe] to navigators of any in the American territories on the Pacific," Stevens worried that the People of the Cape could interfere with his dream of transforming the territory into a strategic trade link to Asian markets. Situated at the entrance to Puget Sound, angry Makahs could disrupt maritime traffic. But Stevens also knew that he had a timely opportunity to negotiate with the People of the Cape because smallpox had killed the leading chiefs and had left survivors despondent. If he was ever going to badger such a formidable people onto a reservation with other coastal Natives, he felt that this was the moment.[28]

But Makahs and other Puget Sound Indians were neither as cooperative nor despondent as Stevens hoped. Even before the *Potter* arrived at Neah Bay, the commissioners had abandoned the goal of placing all American Indians west of the Cascades onto one reservation. Stevens began his treaty negotiations with Puget Sound peoples, who forced him to concede to several reservations rather than one. Like the indigenous leaders Anson Dart had negotiated with previously, the Puget Sound chiefs refused to give up ancestral lands, convincing Stevens that doing so would lead to war. The most dramatic example of this was when Chief Leschi (Nisqually) told Stevens that if he could not get his home, then he would fight. One eyewitness to the incident reported "Leschi then took the paper out of his pocket that the Governor had given him to be sub-chief, and tore it up before the Governor's eyes, stamped on the pieces, and left the treaty ground, and never came back." Eventually, Simmons forged the chief's mark on the treaty.[29] Makahs had already refused to join the S'Klallams for the negotiations with Stevens; they insisted on having their own treaty with the United States. Expecting complications, Stevens tried to frighten the Makah chiefs, warning them that "many whites were coming into the country, and that he . . . did not want the Indians to be crowded out."[30] His threat failed to intimidate the chiefs into leaving Cape Flattery, and the leaders informed him that they would not sell or abandon ancestral lands and waters. Eager to leave Neah Bay with some kind of settlement and fearing the repercussions of angering the People of the Cape, Stevens conceded to Makah demands.

In 1855, Makah chiefs still held enough power to force Stevens to alter a critical clause in the Treaty of Neah Bay. At their insistence, he changed article 4, which detailed their fishing rights, to include whaling and sealing rights (the addition is emphasized): "The right of taking fish *and of whaling or sealing* at usual and accustomed grounds and stations is further secured to said Indians in common with all citizens of the United States."[31] This small but important alteration made this the only treaty to protect indigenous whaling rights in the continental United States. With the exception of this addition in the Treaty of Neah Bay, all the Stevens treaties contained the same exact language detailing tribal fishing rights.[32] The fact that Stevens made this change is important because Makahs forced him to alter his treaty template, something he loathed doing. The Treaty of Neah Bay was the only Stevens Treaty to have this—or any—tribally specific condition beyond particular reservation boundaries.

The smallpox deaths did encourage Makah chiefs to negotiate with Stevens, but not in the way that the governor had hoped. The recent disease mortalities still affected Makahs. Klah-pe at hoo (Claplanhoo), a Neah Bay chief, told Stevens that "he had been sick at heart" since his brother's death.[33] Others also explained that the losses of the ranking chiefs had resulted in their promotion to leading titleholders. But instead of undercutting Makah power, the recent disease experience encouraged the chiefs to approach the treaty negotiations as an opportunity to protect what was important to the People of the Cape. They knew that the dynamics of the ča·di· borderland had changed. The recent smallpox epidemic had slashed Makah numbers, reducing their power and influence among neighboring indigenous peoples, King George men, and Bostons. Perhaps they believed that US acknowledgment of Makah marine tenure in a treaty would protect customary marine space not just from white settlers but also from indigenous rivals.

Makah chiefs appeared to know what to expect from a treaty negotiation. Although this was their first treaty with a colonial authority, indigenous networks of trade and kinship had brought news of other such negotiations. Between 1850 and 1854, James Douglas, as governor of the Colony of Vancouver Island, negotiated fourteen treaties with Natives north of the Strait of Juan de

Fuca. On the surface, these were little more than land purchases. Douglas paid the "Swengwhung" (a band of Lekwungens) of Victoria Peninsula HBC blankets valuing £75 for their land in April 1850. Through these negotiations, these Lekwungens secured for themselves a small reserve and hunting and fishing rights in customary areas.[34] Makahs would have also known of the 1851 Dart Treaties, particularly the Tansey Point Treaty, signed with Quinaults and neighbors to the south.[35] These earlier British and US treaties gave Makah chiefs certain expectations for their own treaty: payment for lands they conceded, protection of key ancestral lands, and guaranteed fishing and hunting rights. These earlier negotiations provided Makahs with the notion that treaties could benefit their people.

Makahs today remember the treaty negotiations as a time when ancestors fought for their way of life. This conclusion aligns with oral histories kept by other tribal nations that were parties to Stevens's treaties. Ted Strong (Yakama) speaks of his people's belief that their chiefs saw the 1855 Yakama Treaty as "an instrument to preserve life for our tribal nation. . . . Our treaty was looked upon by our leaders as a way of preserving what tribal members were left after decimation by war, by diseases and a reduction in the quality of life because of the encroachment of a new order of people and society that was coming to the Northwest." Makahs still speak of the treaty as a document in which they "kept the sea" for themselves.[36]

MAKAH MARINE TENURE IN THE
MID-NINETEENTH CENTURY

In 1855, Makah chiefs believed that keeping the sea for the People of the Cape was paramount. By calling the sea his country during the treaty negotiations, Čaqá·wiƛ expressed Makah tenure over customary marine waters and resources. During the mid-nineteenth century, *tenure* meant ownership of land, according to the doctrine of property that predominated in the United States and Britain.[37] Americans and Britons understood that ownership was exclusive and gave the owner the right to buy and sell her or his property and to manage the land as he or she saw fit. But ownership was not absolute within the context of modern nations. Through legal institutions and political bodies, societies have exercised constraints over both the use and allocation of property, including taxation and regulatory powers, such as policing and zoning. The existence of tribal marine tenure extends traditional scholarship on indigenous peoples that limits Native tenure concepts to terrestrial spaces. Many studies on American Indians examine the relationship of a particular people to its land and

related resources, defining land as the foundation of tribal identity.[38] This terrestrial perspective overlooks those indigenous peoples, such as Makahs, who
vested marine rather than terrestrial spaces and resources with their most valued tenure rights.

Settler-colonial nations and empires have used tenure concepts to their advantage in order to dispossess indigenous peoples of land and terrestrial resources.[39] During the North American colonial period, expanding empires
acknowledged varying degrees of indigenous tenure rights to enable them to purchase Native lands or to seize vast tracts through "just wars." During the treaty
era, the United States recognized American Indian tenure in order to negotiate
for land cessions, just as Governor Stevens did during the 1855 Treaty of Neah
Bay. Congressional legislation, such as the Dawes Severalty Act of 1887, granted
ownership rights to individuals to fragment tribal holdings and to transfer more
land out of American Indian hands. Like other Western concepts applied to indigenous peoples, tenure has a long history of being used to the advantage of
the colonizer.[40] Therefore, when discussing *indigenous tenure*, we must differ-
entiate it from the version of market capitalism–style tenure that predominated
in the United States. For Makahs of the mid-nineteenth century, *tenure* included
sentimental and spiritual components and entailed rights and responsibilities
that owners possessed and maintained.

In North America, indigenous tenure concepts and protocols varied from one
society to the next and over time. Like their Nuu-chah-nulth relatives, Makahs
observed a complex system of ownership rights encompassing nearly every cultural and material item, including propertied spaces. When Europeans and Euro-
Americans encountered Northwest Coast peoples during the late eighteenth and
early nineteenth centuries, many complained that everything—driftwood, fish,
shellfish, game, sea mammals, timber, wild plants, and freshwater—appeared to
have an owner. In the early 1940s, Makah elder Henry St. Clair explained that
ownership rights were tied to specific marine and terrestrial places. Called
tupaˑts ("too-pahts"), these property items included intangible objects, such as
songs, names, and stories, and places like fishing or hunting grounds, beaches,
and other identifiable spots. No one was allowed to remove or harvest anything
from someone's tupaˑt unless they had permission. Anything that came into a
tupaˑt belonged to the owner of that place. If someone found something of value,
such as a drift whale, in another person's tupaˑt, he or she was supposed to tell
the owner, who in turn paid the informant. People with tupaˑts threw regular
feasts in order to remind everyone where their property was and who owned it.
Tupaˑts continued to be relevant to the People of the Cape until at least the early
twentieth century.[41]

As non-Natives became more familiar with indigenous societies of this corner of the Pacific, they learned that ownership rights extended to cultural property. These included names, songs, dances, games, stories, rituals, and privileges to practice particular occupations, such as whaling. Northwest Coast peoples embedded ownership rights within social hierarchies. Chiefs held the most important resources and hunting, fishing, and gathering areas, including cranberry bogs, locations for fishing weirs, and offshore fishing grounds. They managed and monitored use of these resources and extended usufruct rights—the right to use something owned by someone else—to family members and others, even possibly to non-Makahs on an occasional, case-by-case basis. Makah oral histories differ on this point. Some recall hearing elders mention that they allowed non-Makah Indians with kinship ties to a Makah family to fish propertied grounds on an occasional basis, whereas others state that non-Makahs never fished tribal grounds. Regardless, when the People of the Cape occasionally allowed non-Makah Natives to fish in customary waters, they did not transfer ownership rights to these people; nor did it make these sites part of the collection of "usual and accustomed grounds" non-Makahs could claim under a treaty.[42] In 1941, Makah elders explained to an attorney connected to the federal Indian Office that their ancestors never fished an area that did not belong to them unless the owner invited them to do so.[43] While Makahs of the mid-nineteenth century owned many terrestrial resources and lands, the ocean around Cape Flattery was their most valuable property.[44] They rooted their marine tenure rights within the very fabric of what made them Makah—cultural practices and performances related to the marine environment.

A combination of natural forces made Makah home waters off Cape Flattery a complex marine environment. Fluctuating winds, nearby mountains and watersheds, submarine geological features, circulating water masses, and a rich marine ecosystem interacted to create Makah marine space. Located just off the cape, the Juan de Fuca Eddy drew rich nutrients from the cold ocean depths to the surface. This upwelling fueled a food web that included a wide variety of fish, seabirds, and marine mammals—especially whales—which were culturally significant to Makahs. While scholars characterize the entire Northwest Coast region as a rich marine environment, substantial variations occurred from one place to the next and over time. Because of the Juan de Fuca Eddy, customary Makah waters were some of the most consistently plentiful marine environments in the region.[45]

Societies conceptualize spaces as more than a collection of places people use. We can best understand spaces as social realities with sets of forms and relations; societies use culturally specific processes to transform "amorphous space into articulated geography."[46] Focusing on the maritime space of Torres Strait Islanders between the Australian continent and New Guinea, one geographer argues that "sea territories are not just bounded sea space but areas named, known, used, claimed and sometimes defended. A social group's familiarity with an area creates a territory. A territory, whether terrestrial or marine, is more than simply spatially delimited and defended resources for the exclusive use of a particular group. A territory is social and cultural space as much as it is resource or subsistence space. Sea space becomes an entity because a social group establishes and recognizes the location, pattern and interaction of marine things and processes."[47] These ideas confirm what Chief Umeek (Richard Atleo), a hereditary chief of the Ahousaht First Nation, has explained about his people today: "There is a direct relationship between membership in a community and the resources of that community."[48] The People of the Cape, then, expressed membership within their community through the ways they experienced local marine space and related to and relied on the resources within their waters.

Makahs expressed tenure over these bountiful waters through indigenous knowledge of local spaces. During the treaty negotiations, Q̓alču·t, the first Makah leader to speak on behalf of his people, connected knowledge to tenure rights. When introducing himself to Governor Stevens, Q̓alču·t stated, "I know the country all around and therefore I have a right to speak" about Makah ownership of the sea and their fishing rights.[49] One of the highest-ranking chiefs, he owned important marine resources, such as specific halibut fishing banks just off the coast, and his family had fished them for generations. The "country" he and other Makahs described was the ocean around the Cape Flattery villages, which provided access to lucrative fishing, whaling, and sealing grounds. Their familiarity with the area transformed this portion of the Pacific into Makah home waters to which they held title.

Like other societies, Makahs articulated their ownership and knowledge through place-naming. Using examples from Western Apaches, anthropologist Keith Basso explains how the process of place-naming invests spaces with social meaning by invoking stories that teach culturally specific values. Place-names also encode cultural knowledge that reflects subsistence patterns and a people's understanding of geography and natural forces. Among Torres Strait Islanders, "Names acknowledge familiarity with places. . . . Place names provide traditional title to land and sea territory. History and tenure are confirmed by places named." Stó:lō scholar Albert McHalsie reminds us that place-names "transform our landscape from what others consider a *terra nullis* ('empty land') into a place where our ancestors continue to live in spirit." Makahs also employed place-names in ways similar to Apaches, Stó:lös, and Torres Strait Islanders to transform the sea into their home.[50]

Archival records before, during, and after the nineteenth century illustrate the importance of marine place-naming to Makahs. During the 1792 Galiano and Valdés expedition to the Strait of Juan de Fuca, Spaniards noted several Makah names for harbors, river mouths, islands, passages, and other marine features. The geographic breadth of these names demonstrates that Makah mariners knew the entire Strait of Juan de Fuca and northern Puget Sound. Makahs still remembered many of these place-names into the late twentieth century, reflecting the continued importance of these sites both off-reservation and on the Canadian side of the border.[51] While residing at Neah Bay in the decades after the Treaty of Neah Bay, James Swan, the first Euro-American teacher on the reservation, noted many Makah place-names for marine locations. Some identified fishing grounds over which specific families and villages held particular usufruct rights. In his unpublished manuscript on Makah geography of the early twentieth century, anthropologist T. T. Waterman recorded 144 marine place-names (64 percent) out of a total 224 from the Cape Flattery region. Examples ranged from named sea stacks (vertical columns of rock formed by coastal erosion) to submerged rocks to particular spots on beaches. The high densities of place-names demonstrate the People of the Cape's long-term occupation and intimate knowledge of these places.[52]

The naming of Tatoosh Island exemplifies how Makahs used names to articulate indigenous knowledge, history, and values. The island actually has several names. *Hupačakt* ("hoo-puh-chuhkt," island) was one of the original Makah names for the island.[53] But from the eighteenth century, the People of the Cape have referred to it more frequently as *Tatoosh Island*, its current name. Ditidahts, a group of Vancouver Island Nuu-chah-nulths and close relatives of Makahs, named the island *Too-too-tche*, the Nootkan word for Thunderbird, a powerful, supernatural being. According to John Claplanhoo, a mid-nineteenth-century Makah chief, "[Thunderbird] is in all aspects like an Indian and feeds on whales. When he is hungry he clothes himself with wings and feathers, as he would put on a blanket and soars away like a vast cloud over the ocean. When he sees a whale he throws down the Ha hake to ak—an animal like the sea horse—who with his red tongue causes the lightning by thrusting it out like a snake. This stuns or kills the whale when the Thunderbird seizes it with his talons and carries it home for food. The rustling of its wings causes the thunder."[54] Accounts such as this illustrate the cultural belief that Thunderbird taught Makahs and Nuu-chah-nulths to whale. To mid-nineteenth-century Makahs, Thunderbird was not a mythological relic of the past—he was still physically present. George Gibbs spoke with one Makah whaler who encountered Thunderbird while chasing a whale. Thunderbird appeared and plucked the whale from the water, "causing a great commotion . . . and nearly capsizing the canoe."[55] Therefore, when Ditidahts named Tatoosh Island, they were recognizing this as one of the premier whaling sites in the ča·di· borderland. The People of the Cape accepted this name, even though Ditidaht oral histories purport that they once claimed the island.[56] Makahs adopted *Tatoosh* as an honored name that prominent whaling chiefs earned the right to hold as any other ceremonial property.

More than just expressing ownership, indigenous knowledge of this named marine country allowed Makahs to navigate it safely and to exploit its resources. When on the water, they used both landmarks and seamarks to pinpoint their location. Fishers located fishing spots by referencing features along Vancouver Island and the Olympic Peninsula. To help them locate usual places where migrating fur seals slept, sealers noted the difference between shallower inshore waters and the deeper "blue sea" above the submerged continental shelf. They also knew the locations of regular kelp beds and used them as overnight anchorages when away from their villages, just as the Nuu-chah-nulth canoe fleet did in 1852 when intimidating the US Pacific Survey at Cape Flattery. Whaling crews occasionally lost sight of land and stayed out on the *tupał* ("too-puhlth," ocean) for days. On clear evenings, they steered by the pole star. Combinations of regular swell patterns and winds enabled them to fix their approximate location, even in the regular fogs that conceal the coast. Experienced Makah mariners also used the water's appearance and the set of the riptide to approximate their location when out of sight of land.[57]

Spending so much time on the water, the People of the Cape also needed to understand and be able to predict local weather. Individuals with the most developed weather-prediction skills were "broadcasters" who advised fishers, sealers, and whalers when to go out. Makahs embedded this indigenous knowledge in cultural terms. They had two months that they named after the changing weather conditions. *λułačaktpał* ("kloo-lthuh-chuhkt-puhlth"), their equivalent of February, marked the beginning of good weather, indicating that it was safe to canoe alone. *Ćaċa·ʔuqšpał* ("tsuh-tsah-ooksh-puhlth") began in late November, and its name means "month of winds and screaming birds." They also differentiated between certain weather phenomena on land and at sea. *Łutka·batid* ("lthoot-kah-buh-lthihd") means "thunder on the ocean."[58] For Makahs, this term not only recognized that thunder sounds different on the ocean, but it also signified the whaling power of Thunderbird, who causes thunder on the ocean when he whales.

Makah ability to predict the weather impressed non-Indians. In 1863, James Swan reported that Makahs recognized that the clamor of birds and a particular type of swell preceded storms. The swell caused "strange noises" to emanate from the rocky caverns on Cape Flattery; Makahs believed that "Indians who have been drowned about the Cape, whose office it now is to warn other Indians of impending danger," made these sounds. When fishers and sealers on the water heard these noises, they had just enough time to round the cape and seek safety in Neah Bay before the storm hit. In a separate account, Swan also recorded the ability of Makahs and neighboring peoples to predict upcoming seasons of especially unpleasant weather. Toward the end of September 1865, he wrote in his diary, "Capt. John [Claplanhoo] tells me that the Indians predict a very cold winter. There will be according to his statement, very high tides, violent gales, great rains, much cold and snow. The Arhosetts [Ahousahts on Vancouver Island] predict rain from an unusual number of frogs in a particular stream at their place. The Oquiets [Ohiahts on Vancouver Island] predict cold from the fact that great numbers of mice were seen leaving an island in Barclay Sound and swimming to the mainland." His entries that winter noted the conditions his "informants" had predicted. This level of familiarity with their home illustrated ways the People of the Cape made the sea their country.[59]

Makah knowledge of their marine environment also extended to the biological resources within it. This allowed them to adapt gear and techniques to harvest a range of oceanic foods and materials. Similar to indigenous knowledge of the local environment, the work they did in these waters also expressed tenure. Statements made by Makah chiefs during the treaty negotiations demonstrate that they understood the connection between labor and ownership. In the same breath as they spoke of their ownership of the sea, they detailed the importance of maritime work, such as catching halibut and hunting whales. By mixing their labor with the ocean through customary marine practices, Makahs transformed the sea into their country.[60]

Makah sealers drew upon indigenous knowledge to hunt two species of seals, *k̓iƛaduˑs* ("kih-lthuh-doos," fur seals) and *kaˑščuʔu* ("kahsh-choo-oo," hair seals), the former at sea and the latter in caves dotting Cape Flattery. The customary practice of sealing, something they had done for generations, also expressed Makah tenure of their marine country. Sealers embarked from winter villages at 2:00 a.m. to take advantage of the east wind that propelled their canoes, rigged with sails woven from cedar bark, out to the ocean. They went ten to forty miles into the Pacific, reaching the hunting grounds at daylight in order to catch herds of sleeping fur seals. From January to May, the Davidson Current, which carries warmer, equatorial-type water along the Washington coast, brings migrating seals close to shore. In fair weather, sealers stayed on the water for more than twenty-four hours, lighting fires in their canoes to stay warm.[61]

Sealers used specially designed silent canoes to approach the sleeping herd, getting close enough to hear individual fur seals snore.[62] Twenty-four feet long, these canoes held a three-man crew—a harpooner and two paddlers—and up to fifteen carcasses. Canoe makers constructed these vessels to ride high in the water so that the harpooner could more easily see his prey, and they scorched the bottoms to burn off splinters that might make noisy ripples and wake sleeping seals. Paddlers approached from the leeward side of the herd so that the seals could not smell them coming. When the canoe got within twenty feet of the prey, the hunter hurled a fifteen-foot harpoon shaft mounted with two barbed spearheads. The best harpooners sometimes only needed one throw with the double-headed harpoon to strike two seals sleeping side by side. Attached to lines sixty feet long and to buoys made from inflated sealskins, the harpoon heads detached from the shaft when they struck. Then the hunters hauled the seal toward the canoe and clubbed it dead. In the afternoon, they took advantage of the west wind to carry them home.[63]

Pelagic (oceanic) sealing entailed a certain amount of manageable danger. Like other wild animals, injured seals bite. When dragged close enough to club, seals lashed out, biting limbs and sometimes even gouging canoes. A combination of thrashing fur seals and turbulent waters occasionally overturned canoes. One Makah sealer recounted a time when his canoe overturned and dumped him, his brother, their little white dog, and bleeding seal carcasses into the ocean off Tatoosh Island. This attracted nearby sharks that circled and made "savage runs" at them and the dead seals.[64] Sudden storms could sweep sealers far out to sea. In 1874, a ship bound for Asia picked up a canoe of Makahs that a storm had forced far offshore; the sealers switched to another vessel bound for San Francisco and returned home two months later.[65] Indigenous knowledge allowed Makah sealers to minimize these dangers and to hunt this marine resource with some predictability and safety.

Of all their customary practices, whaling best demonstrates how the People of the Cape combined indigenous knowledge with labor to express marine tenure. Makah whalers have relied on their knowledge of the marine environment to hunt leviathans for the past two thousand years. Through the mid-nineteenth century, most whalers caught one or two *čiłapuk* ("chih-tuh-pook," whales) annually and as many as five in good years. Primarily hunting *sixʷawix̌* ("sih-hwah-wihk," California gray whales) and *čičiwad* ("chih-chih-wuhd," humpbacks), whalers also occasionally harvested *kuˑcqi* ("koots-kee," sperm whales), *ʔiˑčup* ("ee-choop," right whales), *kaˑʔaˑp ʔapaˑwad* ("kah-uhp uh-pah-wuhd," fin whales), and even *ʔiʔišpał* ("ih-ihsh-pulth," blue whales). They also took

Makah rock art at Ozette, 1905. Photograph by Edmond S. Meany.
University of Washington Libraries, Special Collections, NA1274.

k̫ak̫ʔaqƛi· ("kwuhk-uhk-klee," porpoises), *čitku·* ("tseelth-koo," dolphins), *saba·s* ("suh-bahs," sharks), and *kawad* ("kuh-wuhd," orcas).[66]

Successful whalers possessed knowledge and experience specific to particular species of whales, information guarded and passed from father to son, just as whaling gear was. The Claplanhoo family remembers a harpoon that fathers had passed to sons since the mid-eighteenth century. In 1907, this device had 142 notches on it for the whales Claplanhoo whalers had killed with it. The crew of eight, assembled by the harpooner, sometimes remained on the ocean for days at a time, fifty to a hundred miles away from shore, pursuing čitapuk. A whaler harpooned his prey several times and then bled it to death with a lance amid "great fountains of crimson spray." In extreme cases, a whaler would leap onto a harpooned whale that took too long to die. He held onto the lines connecting the whale to the canoe while stabbing the leviathan to dispatch it. Whalers even practiced holding their breath underwater in case they needed to hold onto submerging whales in these situations. Once the whale was dead, a naked diver sewed

Canoes at Neah Bay, 1900. The canoe in the foreground is filled with sealskin floats used in whaling. Photograph by Anders B. Wilse, courtesy Museum of History and Industry, Seattle.

shut its mouth to prevent it from sinking. Then the crew towed the whale back to the coast, sometimes taking three days to get it ashore. Staying out for this length of time and paddling across such great distances required Makah whalers to rely on their knowledge of the ocean environment and their navigational and weather-prediction skills within a large marine area.[67]

Laboring in their country, the sea, Makah families harvested enormous quantities of marine products during the mid-nineteenth century. The wealth they earned from these products allowed them to wield significant authority and power in the ča·di· borderland. Abetted by indigenous knowledge, access to unique trade goods harvested from halibut, seals, and whales enabled the Makah to establish their middleman position in regional trade networks before the appearance of Europeans. The People of the Cape maintained their influence by exchanging customary marine products with non-Native traders during the postcontact decades. In the early encounter years, non-Natives desired sea otter pelts; other products increased in importance during the first half of the nineteenth century. Seals provided Makahs with several valuable subsistence and commercial products. The People of the Cape ate the flesh, rendered the blubber into oil, used the skin for bedding, and employed the bladder to store sea mammal oil. From entire hair sealskins that they inflated, whalers made floats used when hunting. They often employed thirty to forty of these buoys to slow down and tire out harpooned whales, and these prevented the heavy carcass from sinking. During the second half of the nineteenth century, fur sealskins became an important commodity that Makahs traded with whites on both sides of the strait.[68]

Mid-nineteenth-century Makahs profited most from the trade of whale products. Popular assumptions about indigenous peoples emphasize the subsistence aspect of hunting, fishing, and gathering while minimizing or ignoring the commercial importance of these customary practices in the past. However, archaeological analysis of sea mammal remains at Ozette demonstrates that Makah whalers took far more whales than they could consume—whaling during the centuries before the arrival of Europeans and global markets in whale products was nonetheless a commercial activity. Indigenous peoples of the ča·di· borderland prized whales for their flesh, sinew, blubber, oil, and bones. As with halibut and seal meat, women smoked whale flesh, which spoils more quickly than blubber. Makahs ate blubber fresh and hung the remainder in smoke to cure it like bacon. Non-Natives who tried dried blubber thought it tasted like sweet pork. The People of the Cape used the bones as tools—spindle whorls, bark shredders, bark beaters, mat creasers, clubs, wedges, and tool handles—and structurally in water diversion efforts and as retaining walls to help stabilize small mudslides. But whale oil was the most important subsistence and commercial product harvested. After stripping the blubber from a carcass, women boiled it and used clamshells to skim off the oil as it rose to the surface. Makahs stored processed oil in bladders and consumed it like butter, dipping dried fish, potatoes, and berries in it. In earlier times, the People of the Cape traded whale oil among themselves and with neighboring peoples, measuring out precise quantities of this valuable commodity with a two-and-a-half gallon bucket made from a pelican's beak.[69]

While Makahs valued the material goods the sea provided, their marine country and the resources within it had an importance beyond economic terms. Unlike forms of tenure that predominated in the United States during the first half of the nineteenth century, Makah tenure had sentimental—even spiritual— components. By mixing their labor with the sea, they communicated a "bond of belonging."[70] In writing about Hispano loggers' belief that they owned the forests of northern New Mexico, anthropologist Jake Kosek reminds us that "sentimental arguments over nature are often considered the antithesis of rational discourse about property rights." Applied to American Indians, scholars mistakenly dismiss these sentiments as stereotypes of the Ecological Indian.[71] For Makahs, their bond with the sea has been and continues to be far more complex. When Čaqá·wiƛ described the sea as his country, he invoked the Makahs' spiritual bond with the waters around Cape Flattery. His words referenced the ways they owned marine space, used customary practices to express tenure rights, and exploited the ocean's bounty to gain wealth and power.

During the nineteenth century, Makahs recognized that tenure often entailed both rights and responsibilities.[72] These rights included usufruct rights, and high-ranking leaders decided who else could share the property in question and on what terms.[73] Makahs embedded tenure concepts within a larger worldview that recognized "numinous forces" in their environment and that the spiritual and physical realms are one, so they understood that ownership also entailed responsibility.[74] The People of the Cape believed they were responsible for maintaining a balanced relationship with a community that included the very animals and fish that they harvested. For most indigenous cultures, the "community extends beyond human relationships."[75] But we should not misconstrue this as Makahs acting like proto-ecologists. Hunting thousands of seals and harpooning dozens of whales annually illustrate that Makahs cannot be stereotyped as Ecological Indians. More than anything else, their belief that marine tenure entailed responsibility differentiates the Makahs' understanding of ownership from similar concepts that predominated in the nineteenth-century United States.

The worldview of the People of the Cape related spirituality with responsible stewardship. From their perspective of a "sacred ecology," most animals, plants, and prominent landmarks were nonhuman people.[76] Billy Balch, one of Swan's "informants" and Chief Yelakub's son, told Swan that Makahs believed that everything—including trees, animals, birds, and fish—were "formerly Indians who for their bad conduct were transformed into the shapes that now appear."[77] Balch told Swan that Seal was once a thief, so the brothers Sun and Moon shortened his arms and tied his legs. They then cast him into the sea and told him to eat only fish. Sharing a common origin and designation as people, everything deserved respect, which Makahs demonstrated through protocols, laws governing the relationships between human and nonhuman beings. Northwest Coast peoples continue to believe that "the land, the plants, the animals and the people all have spirit—they all must be shown respect. That is the basis of our law."[78] Through stories elders told, Makahs learned that protocols kept relationships balanced and that violating these laws had consequences. Makahs also embedded their worldview in the marine-oriented, spatial context of the geography around

Cape Flattery. "Se kar jecta" was an "evil genius"—probably a powerful shaman—who had transformed into a large rock off the coast south of the cape. On two separate canoe trips, Swan observed Makahs throwing offerings of bread, dried halibut, and whale blubber at Se kar jecta in order to ensure their safe passage.[79]

Like other Northwest Coast peoples, Makahs believed that the nonhuman members of their community possessed power and punished those who failed to observe protocols correctly. Cedakanim, a mid-nineteenth-century Clayoquot chief whose son was married to a Makah woman, told Swan about a time when sea otters had vengefully drowned the son of a chief, who was a successful hunter of the species. The chief exacted his revenge by killing a great number of sea otters and feeding their dried hearts to his dogs, a serious sign of disrespect. This severe protocol violation insulted the otters, and they left the coast. Although Nuu-chah-nulths and Makahs had hunted sea otters to near extinction in the ča·di· borderland during the maritime fur trade, some blamed a high-ranking chief's behavior for the dearth of otters. His disrespectful behavior to nonhuman people resulted in both personal (a drowned son) and society-wide (sea otters abandoned the coast) consequences. Therefore, chiefs were most responsible for maintaining respectful relationships with nonhuman members of the community.[80] Makahs blamed the poor salmon and sealing seasons in 1879 on a chief who had allowed his pregnant wife to eat of the first salmon of the season. This resulted in the deaths of her and their unborn twins and caused salmon to leave the rivers and seals to flee.[81] For commoners, it appears that the consequences for disrespectful behavior were personal, whereas the actions of chiefs had both personal and societal consequences, explaining why leaders took seriously their responsibilities to follow correct protocols.

The spiritual dimensions of the whaling practice best exemplify how Makahs honored and propitiated the nonhuman members of the marine community. To become a "skookum whaleman" (strong whaler), a harpooner—who was also the captain of a whaling crew—needed supernatural powers. Because a harpooner's success at whaling relied on his ability to interact with a nonhuman person possessing greater spiritual strength, he needed additional powers. Makahs believed that humans normally possessed limited supernatural power and ability, especially in comparison to a powerful being such as a whale. Whaling included both physical and spiritual hazards. To meet these challenges, whalers sought spiritual assistance through ceremonial practices. Prayers could help someone attain a power, and dreams could also grant a power or reveal how to earn it. To secure these supernatural powers, an individual performed specific actions, such as ritual bathing, or scoured the woods and beaches for signs of power. Whalers also sought guardian spirits whose supernatural strength would protect the crew.[82]

Makahs believed that acquiring "whale medicine" ensured one's success at sea and augmented an individual's authority within the community. A spar that waves had thrown to the top of a nearby sea stack enticed many whalers for years. They devised methods to retrieve the inaccessible spar because they believed that they could craft it into a harpoon shaft that would bring its owner immense whaling luck. John Claplanhoo told Swan several stories of whale medicine he or his family members had received. One time, "raven lit on a stone a few feet off and ruffling up his feathers as they do when angry, first uttered a hissing sound and then a croak, and opening his beak wide twice to vomit up something," a bone, three inches long. Claplanhoo believed that this was a bone of the x̌ix̌i·ktu·yak ("hih-heek-too-yuhk"), the lightning snake that Thunderbird uses to hunt whales. About a week before Swan left the reservation—he had resigned from his teaching position at Neah Bay—Claplanhoo showed him his best whale medicine: the bone of a x̌ix̌i·ktu·yak; a goose egg–sized rock that had come from a dead whale and that he had bought from a Ditidaht whaler; and the dried blow-hole of a whale carcass that his father had found in the mountains, thought to have been carried there by Thunderbird.[83] Whalers guarded these relics and passed them on to their sons. The People of the Cape knew that humans rarely received supernatural powers, so these individuals became important leaders within the community. Spiritual power enabled the acquisition of resources for the well-being of their people. This explains why chiefs—those who acquired numerous spiritual powers—owned these resources, held the rights to hunt whales, and passed them from one generation to the next.

In addition to accumulating supernatural powers, whalers exercised ownership and tenure responsibilities through ritual preparations for a hunt. Sometimes lasting for eight months, pre-hunt rituals were the most important aspect of preparation. The rites included fasting, swimming, and purification through ritual bathing conducted at secret bathing ponds. Similar to other forms of ceremonial property, families owned specific rituals; many consisted of ceremonially washing the body and scrubbing oneself with twigs, leaves, and hemlock branches. While bathing, some harpooners imitated the whale, making slow movements so that it would act this way when hunted. Members of the whaling crew abstained from normal food and sex. If someone had not gone through these ritual preparations, he was not allowed in the canoe. Before embarking on a hunt, the whaling captain sang to the whale, asking it to give itself to his people. When a whale damaged or capsized a canoe, it indicated that the whaler or his crew had failed to observe the necessary protocols.[84]

Ritual practices continued during the hunt and after the whale's death. Once the harpooner struck the whale, he sang to his prey in order to encourage it to come ashore easily. Descendants of whalers recall hearing elders discuss that a whale "accepted the harpoon" if the harpooner had followed the correct protocols, thereby affirming the relationship between hunter and prey. Harpooner's wives also played an important role while the crew was at sea because her behavior affected the whale her husband hunted. She had to remain still in the dark and fast for the duration of the hunt. The People of the Cape believed that her spiritual power helped to draw the whale safely to the village. As they brought the whale ashore, the village welcomed it into their community. The harpooner acknowledged the whale's special status by placing eagle down and feathers on its hump and blowhole. Then he demonstrated his whaling power through a special performance. The whaler's wife danced, while his father and an uncle sang songs thanking the whale for giving itself to their people.[85]

Through his whaling success, a harpooner proved that he had received these powers, gained the protection of guardian spirits, and followed the protocols. Whalers marked their success by taking important names they had earned through their whaling accomplishments, such as when the whaler John Claplanhoo took the name Łutka·bałid ("lthoot-kah-buh-lthihd," thunder on the ocean) later in life. Makahs believed that the most successful whaling chiefs had accumulated so much power that they could call whales to shore without even hunting them. Hiškʷi·sa·na·kši·ł ("hish-kwee-sah-nahk-sheelth," He Makes the Whale Blow on the Beach) is a propertied name owned by a prominent whaling family. The ancestral Hiškʷi·sa·na·kši·ł had so much spiritual power, he could get whales to beach themselves at his village. For this reason, drift whale landings validated a chief's power. Chiefs guarded their rights to drift whales, even going to war with neighboring villages over these beached carcasses.[86]

As owners of the proprietary right to harvest this rich resource, whaling chiefs also had to satisfy responsibilities within the human community. After welcoming a whale ashore, they butchered it, a process that took an entire day and unsettled the weaker stomachs of some non-Native observers. Butchers observed specific rules when dividing the meat and blubber. Richest in oil, the hump went to the harpooner. The whaling crew received large strips of blubber and divided the tongue, an organ that contained a large amount of oil. Through feasts during which they distributed blubber and whale meat, whalers fulfilled their spiritual and material responsibilities of ownership. Chief Umeek (Ahousaht) notes, the "sumptuous feasts reflect[ed] well upon the host chief's ability to provide for the well-being of his community," while "overflowing feast tables [were] an indication that [he had] been favoured with spiritual power." When chiefs shared whales through feasts, they reaffirmed their authority, validated their spiritual prowess, and demonstrated ownership over specific resources.[87]

Butchering a whale on the beach at Neah Bay, 1910. Each member of the whaling
crew received a share of the whale, with the choicest selections going
to the harpooner. Photograph by Asahel Curtis, courtesy the Makah
Cultural and Research Center, Neah Bay, WA.

The material and spiritual importance of whaling also influenced customs
that took place off the water. When a whaler wanted to marry, he had to demonstrate his prowess to his potential bride and her father, who was often another
whaler. This included a mock whale hunt in front of the longhouse where the
desired bride lived with her family. Swan witnessed one such engagement in December 1863: "A canoe was hoisted on the shoulders of some 8 or 10 Indians and
in it were two men and two boys. In front crawling on all fours was an Indian
dressed to resemble a whale although the resemblance was very small. Every
now and then he would raise his head to blow like a whale. This he did very
exact. The Indians in the canoe kept their paddles going as if she was in the
water and went through all the performances of killing a whale except darting
the harpoon at the fellow ahead." Instead of harpooning the individual imper-
sonating a whale, the whaler hurled his harpoon at the door of the longhouse,
"splitting the door in two." More than a decade earlier, Samuel Hancock, the
first Euro-American trader to reside briefly at Neah Bay, also observed this performance, noting that the groom threw the mussel shell–tipped harpoon with
such force that it went clear through a three-inch-thick cedar board. During the

mock hunt, the groom's family heaped blankets in front of the longhouse. A successful performance—indicated by breaking down the door and piling up enough blankets as gifts—demonstrated the whaler's spiritual, physical, and financial ability to provide for his potential bride and her family.[88]

Čaqá·wiƛ's position as a prominent whaling chief framed his perspective on the words he spoke during the treaty negotiations. When describing the sea as his country, he stated Makah ownership of customary marine space. His words articulated tenure rights expressed through indigenous knowledge of local spaces. Through their ability to navigate the ocean and predict its conditions, Makah familiarity with the sea transformed local waters into their home and country. They embedded knowledge, history, and values in their culture via place-naming, and the density of marine place-names reflected ownership over this space.

The People of the Cape also mixed their labor with the ocean. Through customary practices such as fishing for halibut and hunting seals and whales, Makahs made the sea their country, reaped a wealth of subsistence and commercial goods, and expressed a sentimental bond of belonging. Shaped by a common Northwest Coast worldview, Makah tenure over marine space also had a spiritual component. Rituals and protocols connected to marine practices best exemplified this, specifically the responsibility to maintain balanced relationships with the non-human people of the region. Although the treaty commissioners did not understand the Makahs' perspective on marine space, this was what the whaling chief meant when he called the sea his country.

DIFFERING CONCEPTS OF MARINE SPACE IN THE MID-NINETEENTH CENTURY

When Makahs characterized the sea as their country, they highlighted a perspective on marine space that differed from mid-nineteenth-century Euro-American views of the ocean. Stevens and the other treaty commissioners thought of the sea as a commons for American Indians and non-Native citizens of the territory to share. They held a belief common to that time—coasts and bodies of water make for convenient, natural boundaries—that emerged from a "Western" notion that terrestrial and marine spaces are separate.[89] The 1846 demarcation of the border between British and US colonial spaces in Oregon Country reflected and reinforced this concept. The People of the Cape saw local waters as sovereign Makah space and larger marine bodies as a medium of connections. During the decade after signing the treaty, Makah actions in local marine waters revealed that their connection to the sea remained strong, and their perspective on marine space remained dominant for much of the nineteenth century.

While at Neah Bay, Stevens sought to create boundaries around the Makah. The most important one would be the borderline demarcating the reservation. On his first morning there in 1855, Stevens and the commission's surveyor, George Gibbs, hastily surveyed Cape Flattery for the reservation's boundaries. At this point, they had not yet met with the Makah chiefs, and Stevens still hoped that this location would become the reservation for all the territory's coastal peoples if none of the tribal nations agreed to leave the coast for reservations in Puget Sound.[90] From his perspective, the coastline surrounding Cape Flattery made a convenient boundary around part of the reservation.

Before Stevens became governor of Washington Territory, his experiences shaped his view of coastlines as boundaries. After he graduated from West Point, the army assigned him to the Corps of Engineers, where he oversaw the rebuilding and fortification of coastal forts in New England from 1839 to 1846. Increased tensions with Mexico and the Maine–New Brunswick boundary dispute between the United States and Britain heightened national concerns over coastal defenses. After returning from the Mexican War, Stevens accepted a position in Washington, DC, as assistant to the director of the US Coast Survey from 1849 to 1852. With the recent acquisition of Alta California through the Treaty of Guadalupe Hidalgo, which ended the Mexican War, this department focused on surveying the Pacific coast. Stevens oversaw the production, publication, and distribution of new, detailed maps of the coastline from California to the Pacific Northwest.[91] A decade of experience in the Army Corps of Engineers and in the Coast Survey office meant that when Stevens strolled the beach at Neah Bay that January morning in 1855, the governor believed that he was walking the reservation's boundary.

Despite seeing the waterline as a part of the proposed reservation's boundary, Stevens expected Makahs to continue relying on customary marine waters to make a living. This was the reason why article 4, which guaranteed Indian fishing rights, was in the Treaty of Neah Bay and the other Stevens treaties. However, the governor's perception of marine space shaped his understanding of the fishing rights the People of the Cape would have. Stevens thought of the waters around Cape Flattery as a marine commons for American Indians and the territory's citizens. Similar to other whites of this time, Stevens reduced the sea to a "homogenized commons" for all to share.[92] With a background in coastal issues and previous aspirations for a career in law, the governor had some familiarity with the US legal perspective on water rights as articulated by Joseph Angell in A Treatise on the Common Law, in Relation to Water Courses. In this treatise, Angell argued that "a man might be restrained from fishing in the sea by contract or argument, although the sea was considered as open and common to all."[93]

By using the treaty's article 4 to impose common-property status on indigenous fisheries, the governor did what officials in other settler-colonial societies were doing at the time—attempting to extinguish exclusive indigenous tenure on land and sea.

The People of the Cape, however, did not believe that the treaty had extinguished their marine tenure. Like Stevens, Makahs drew from their cultural perception of marine space to understand the treaty. Indigenous negotiators such as Q̓alč̓uʔt and Ċaqá·wiƛ believed that the same waters that the governor saw as a marine commons instead belonged to the People of the Cape as sovereign space. From the Makahs' perspective, "commons" fisheries did not exist as US treaty commissioners assumed.[94] Individuals and families who fished at someone else's spot paid in some manner for the privilege.

By extending fishing rights to whites of Washington Territory during the treaty negotiations—noted by the phrase "in common with all citizens of the United States" in the treaty—Makah chiefs did not believe that they had surrendered ownership over their "usual and accustomed" fishing sites or had turned these into a propertyless commons. During the treaty negotiations, when Q̓alč̓uʔt stated that he "would live as a friend to the Whites and they should fish together," he likely assumed that Makah owners would grant specific, case-by-case fishing rights to whites just as they had done in the past to other non-Makahs.[95] This meant that newcomers fishing in customary Makah waters would need to gain permission from the rightful owner and pay for the privilege of fishing there. Q̓alč̓uʔt and the other chiefs did not believe that granting whites the right to fish Makah-owned grounds abolished indigenous ownership or weakened Makah control over this critical resource.

During the first post-treaty decade, Makah chiefs enforced their understanding of article 4 over non-Natives who fished customary indigenous waters. In 1863 a Makah chief from Ċu·yas ("tsoo-yuhs") village punished Captain Thomas Stratton, master of the schooner *Brant*, for fishing without the titleholder's permission. Tsat-tsat-wha set the captain's skiff adrift because he was "angry with Stratton over some fish." Later that year, Stratton returned to Neah Bay to fish, but this time he went out with several Makah men, whom he paid by giving them half his catch. When they returned to the beach, several older Makahs took fish from the seine Stratton had used. Swan noted in his diary that those taking the fish "inquired what right we had to catch their fish. I told them the fish belonged to whoever caught them and if they wanted to fish to go and catch them. I soon restored them to good humor by giving each one a present of a fish and they promised that hereafter they would keep out of the net and not crowd round so much." These elders possibly owned rights to the oceanic banks that Stratton had fished, so they believed that they were entitled to some of the catch. Although Swan lectured them on the Euro-American concept of individual property harvested from a commons, they would have seen his eventual gift of fish as payment for fishing Makah grounds.[96]

The People of the Cape participated in the first non-Native commercial fishing venture in their waters, although they likely saw participation as confirming their ownership over local waters. On June 15, 1865, Captain Stratton's schooner, the *Brant*, returned to Neah Bay to take Makahs halibut fishing. Agent Henry Webster had arranged for tribal fishers to go with Stratton so they could learn how to fish from a schooner, which he told them that he would try to get the government to provide. They returned from their "fishing cruise" several days later with five barrels of halibut. Until at least 1879, Makah men often accompanied whites fishing customary waters. Each time, the non-Native fishers shared their catch with the People of the Cape, an action that Makahs continued to see as payment for allowing others to fish propertied marine spaces.[97] Ironically, both Makahs and non-Natives alike believed that these actions confirmed their respective and divergent understandings of marine space.

Makahs also continued to believe that the sea was a medium of connections rather than a boundary of confinement. After signing the Treaty of Neah Bay and agreeing to live on the reservation, the People of the Cape continued to travel into and across the čaˑdiˑ borderland. By the 1860s, these interactions had grown to incorporate different types of vessels from a variety of nations and to include nearby settler-colonial towns such as Victoria and Port Townsend (on the British and US sides of the boundary, respectively) and distant Pacific ports. The coastline bounding the northern and western edges of the reservation did not keep Makahs in and non-Makahs out. Instead, it remained a permeable zone in which canoes, steamships, and sailing ships arrived, landed, or departed and across which people, information, clandestine goods, and valued commodities crossed. The coast continued to be a site of cultural interaction among diverse Native and non-Native peoples.[98]

In the marine waters of the čaˑdiˑ borderland, the actions and travels of Makahs, other indigenous peoples, and non-Natives mapped the contours of engagement and relationships in the years following the Treaty of Neah Bay. Although the People of the Cape did not make or need any literal maps in this period, it is possible to approximate what such a map might have looked like if we turn to the diaries of James Swan. Born in Medford, Massachusetts, in 1818, Swan began living along the southern shores of the Strait of Juan de Fuca in 1859 after having spent a brief period in San Francisco and then several years in Shoalwater Bay (Willapa Bay) north of the mouth of the Columbia River. He first en-

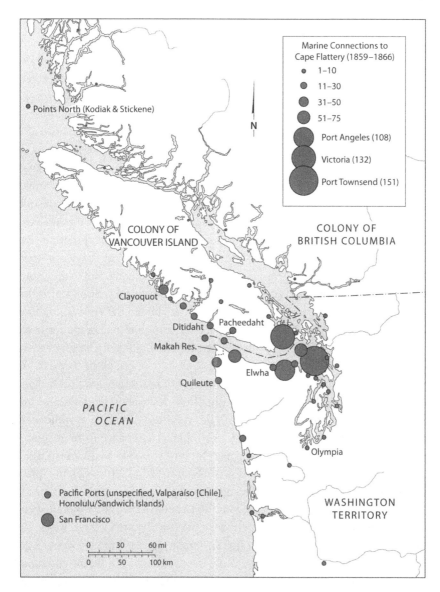

Map of the frequency of marine connections to Cape Flattery, 1859–66.
Map by Bill Nelson.

countered Makahs at Neah Bay that March, and over the next few years, he made
many trips to the Cape Flattery villages. He wrote articles about the People of
the Cape for local and regional newspapers and did various jobs for local Indian agents. In 1861, George Paige, Indian agent for northern Puget Sound,

asked Swan to take the first federal census of the Makah. The following year, the Office of Indian Affairs appointed him teacher at the Neah Bay agency, a position he held until 1866. From 1859 until 1866, he kept a daily diary of his time at Neah Bay.[99] Many of his entries include information about Makahs leaving the reservation in canoes or aboard vessels and about non-Makahs—Natives and non-Natives—visiting the Cape Flattery villages. Although Swan certainly failed to note every time someone came to or left the reservation, his observations of 951 such events in a seven-year period reveal some basic patterns charted on this map. Mapping these travels and interactions underscores the conclusion that the People of the Cape continued to perceive the ocean as a space of connections.[100]

The high number of visits to or from villages, towns, and cities demonstrates that the Makah reservation boundaries remained permeable during the decade following the signing of the treaty. Just under half (46 percent) of these interactions involved travel between Neah Bay and San Francisco or the nearby towns of Port Townsend, Port Angeles, and Victoria—both Makahs and whites, sometimes together, made these trips. With ties to all four places, Swan noted most of these interactions, especially when non-Natives visited the reservation. Since the maritime fur trade, Neah Bay had been a common anchorage for vessels passing by Cape Flattery. Ships often stopped there to ride out a storm or to wait for more favorable winds that would bring them into or out of the Strait of Juan de Fuca. They also anchored there to resupply with freshwater and fish; to deliver or pick up mail; and to get the news, either from reservation employees or from old newspapers. For many voyages, Neah Bay was the destination, as whites came to trade for whale oil, to deliver cargo or people, or to engage in reservation or territorial business. A few, such as Captain Stratton, came to Neah Bay to fish.

In canoes and non-Native vessels, Makahs traveled to settler-colonial places for their own reasons. The primary purpose of many trips was to exchange indigenous products for non-Native goods. To the consternation of Indian agents, Makahs often crossed the border to trade at the British port Victoria, where they purchased blankets, muskets, and liquor, sometimes with money the US government had paid the People of the Cape for ceded lands. In his annual report, one agent complained that "all the money paid out by government and citizens goes immediately over to Victoria to be invested in blankets, muskets, etc." British traders offered lower-priced, superior-quality goods that Makahs and other American Indians preferred to purchase. Henry Webster, the first Indian agent assigned to Neah Bay, reported, "The contrast between the 'King George' and the 'Boston' blanket, when good, is sadly against us, but when 'cultus' [poor quality] we are *humiliated* before the Indian."[101] Makahs visited towns for specialized services only found there, such as when Willub took his brother, Captain

Balch, to Victoria to see a surgeon. Following a tradition practiced by HBC officials, reservation employees hired Makahs to deliver mail, cargo, and people throughout the region. Makahs also labored aboard non-Native vessels. When Swan conducted his census in 1861, he met Jackson, a Makah who told stories about his travels to the Sandwich Islands, San Francisco, and the Columbia River. Proud that he had worked as a cook, Jackson knew how to prepare hash and fries. During the mid-nineteenth century, Q̓iˑtap ("kee-tuhp," David Fischer) had worked on several whaling vessels, which took him to places as distant as Africa. Making use of intimate knowledge of local marine waters and currents, Makahs also gained occasional employment piloting vessels entering or leaving Puget Sound.[102]

More important, this map reveals that Makahs continued interacting with other indigenous peoples in the čaˑdiˑ borderland during the immediate post-treaty years. Twenty-eight percent of Swan's observations show that the People of the Cape regularly visited or received visitors from more than eleven indigenous villages beyond the reservation boundaries. Five of these—Ahousaht, Clayoquot, Ditidaht, Ohiaht, and Pacheedaht—were villages on Vancouver Island, and another six—Clallam Bay, Dungeness, Elwha, Ozette, Quileute, and Quinault—were on the Olympic Peninsula.[103] Most likely, Swan kept an even less complete record of Makah interactions with other indigenous peoples. First, these incidents did not interest him as much as encounters with whites. Moreover, Swan was not everywhere on the reservation at all times, especially at the coastal Makah villages. There were interactions between Makahs and non-Makah Natives that he neither observed nor deemed important enough to note. The number of times Makahs traveled to or received visitors from these villages was substantially higher. (I am analyzing only the major points of interaction revealed on this map. The other 26 percent of encounters included people from many indigenous communities throughout the Northwest Coast and with individuals and vessels from a handful of other early settlements in Puget Sound and global ports such as Valparaiso, London, and Honolulu.) Interactions among distinct indigenous peoples reveal that Natives sustained the borderlands networks that existed before the arrival of Europeans, even when new networks tied to settler-colonial places emerged and became important. Exchange of indigenous and non-Native products continued to bring together Native borderlanders, and Neah Bay maintained its position as the hub of regional trade. Whale oil, fresh and dried seafood, animal skins, slaves, liquor, and finished products such as canoes and carved items continued to circulate along indigenous exchange networks throughout the region. Makah men, women, and children also funneled Native products valued by white traders into non-Native markets. At Ohiaht on

Vancouver Island, Peter Brown (a Makah whaler) purchased sixty gallons of oil to resell to white traders.[104]

Kinship and violence—sometimes interconnected—continued to bind various communities throughout the ča·di· borderland. Cedakanim, a prominent Clayoquot chief and grandson of Wickaninnish, often visited the Cape Flattery villages because his son Frank was married to Totatelum, daughter of Q̓alču·t. They had an infant daughter who unfortunately died. Swan noted that if the child had been a boy and had lived, he would have become a very powerful chief in the region as the grandson of two of the highest-ranking families among both Clayoquots and Makahs.[105] These family ties remained important during the 1860s because they conferred sociopolitical advantages, ownership claims, and usufruct rights. In March 1863, Frank informed Swan of a potential incident of borderlands violence against the Makah that Cedakanim had defused. In retribution for a chief a Makah had murdered earlier, Ahousahts, a Nuu-chah-nulth people, had asked Clayoquots to assist in an attack on the People of the Cape. Ahousahts promised Cedakanim that he and his people would receive one hundred blankets and twenty Makah slaves after the attack. After much debate, "old Cedakanim told them he would not fight the Makahs nor did he want any pay from the Arhosetts [Ahousahts] as he was much richer than they and to prove this he ordered 100 pieces of blubber to be given them, each of which was worth a blanket. This . . . made the Arhosetts so ashamed that the sweat ran off of their faces so they took the blubber and left without saying anything more."[106] As they had done for generations before the arrival of Europeans, the indigenous peoples of the Northwest Coast engaged one another for various reasons and on their own terms. Rather than acting as a confining boundary for the People of the Cape, the coastal edges of the reservation facilitated Makah and non-Makah interactions.

Despite the rising presence of settler-colonial governments based out of Victoria and the territorial capital, Olympia, indigenous chiefs—not just colonial officials—still possessed enough power to shape the outcomes of events in the ča·di· borderland after signing the Treaty of Neah Bay. Both within and beyond the boundaries of the reservation, the interactions of Makahs and non-Natives illustrated the ambivalent relationship between Indians and whites in the immediate post-treaty years. Native peoples, such as Makahs, continued to engage settler-colonial society on both sides of the border, and whites were becoming an increasing part of the social lives of the People of the Cape. Although colonial officials crafted reservation boundaries designed to separate indigenous and settler societies, all groups sought out each other for many reasons. Marine waters did not make for effective boundaries separating peoples. The sea continued to be a medium of connections facilitating various interactions and opportunities. These connections followed pre-encounter borderlands networks, tying together indigenous communities and newer settler-colonial networks encompassing non-Natives and their settlements.

In the 1860s, a series of incidents involving several indigenous peoples, King George men, and Bostons demonstrated how complex these relationships were. Metsonak, an Elwha living to the east of Cape Flattery, killed Wha-laltl as sá buy (known to local whites as Swell), a Makah chief in 1861. Wha-laltl had earned the Elwhas' enmity after stealing away his sister, whom Metsonak beat. When Wha-laltl traveled to Port Townsend in his canoe to pick up some goods for an American trader at Neah Bay, Metsonak shot him in the back.[107] Michael Simmons, one of the treaty commissioners and then the Indian agent for Washington Territory, asked the People of the Cape to allow him to punish the murderer. But the agent did not act quickly enough for the Makah chiefs, who decided to punish the Elwhas according to standards of Northwest Coast indigenous justice. That September, a war party of twelve canoes carrying eighty warriors armed with guns struck the Elwhas. They returned three days later with the heads of two they had killed. Cobetsi, the leading Makah war chief, told Swan why they had attacked: "We think Mr. Simmons has made fools of us and the Indians on Vancouver's Island, the Nittinats and the Clyoquots laugh at us, and call us old women. It is for this that we have gone up and killed these two men. Swell went up to Port Townsend for the Bostons, and he was killed; and the Bostons promised to hang his murderers, but they have not done so, and now we will look out for ourselves."[108] Cobetsi also told Swan that "before Mr. Simmons came, the Mackahs had strong hearts and were brave. If any Indians killed their people, they at once resented it, but Mr. Simmons gave them papers and told them not to fight. They promised him and they kept their word. When the Clallams found that Mr. Simmons did not do as he agreed they laughed at the Mackahs and recently killed two of their slaves. It was for this additional insult of the Clallams that they had gone."[109] As a testament to the persistence of Makah power, Cobetsi displayed the heads in front of his longhouse at Cuʹyas for months afterward. His intended audience—Natives and non-Natives who visited the cape—could not miss Cobetsi's message. With empty eye sockets staring out to sea, the desiccated heads cast a morbid fascination on white visitors to Cuʹyas.[110] Elwhas asked Swan to recover the heads, offering ten blankets for each one. However, the Makah chief declined to surrender them, stating that "this could not be done till he had added [Metsonak's] head to the number and then he would be ready to talk about peace."[111] At one point, Makah chiefs appeared willing to try Boston-style justice. When they experienced the impotence of territorial officials at keeping the peace and were ridiculed by neighboring peoples, they did not hesitate to settle conflicts by indigenous rules.

But the conflict between the Elwhas and Makahs did not end there. The following March, an Elwha chief, Kachin, secured a tentative peace with Makahs after agreeing to execute Metsonak. When Kachin neglected to follow through on his promise, many Makahs became angry. In July 1863, one of Wha-laltl's cousins stabbed Metsonak's brother in vengeance, which prompted the Elwhas to declare that they would retaliate by killing Peter Brown, Wha-laltl's brother. The intertribal conflict continued to simmer, and anytime Elwhas visited Neah Bay, tensions threatened to escalate. Even Metsonak's death from consumption in February 1864 did not end the tension. Two years later, while trading at Victoria, Brown killed an Elwha, which prompted the aggrieved community to threaten Makahs and whites passing their village at the mouth of the Elwha River. This time, the territorial government intervened by coming to Neah Bay and arresting Brown. After Webster, the Indian agent at Neah Bay, placed Brown on the schooner *Westin* to transport him to Fort Steilacoom for imprisonment, a group of Makahs staged a daring rescue. Following the schooner in a canoe, they boarded the vessel and freed Brown. During the rescue, another set of Makah warriors, led by John Claplanhoo, one of Swan's closest Makah friends, held Swan hostage in case something happened to Brown in the interim. After the rescue party returned to Neah Bay, Claplanhoo released Swan, and the People of the Cape began debating whether they should kill all the whites on the reservation. A few days later, a steamer bearing two howitzers and thirty-three US soldiers arrived at Neah Bay to quell the potential uprising and to apprehend Brown and thirteen other Makahs.[112] The belligerent Makahs did not remain in prison at Fort Steilacoom for very long. By the fall of 1867, Brown was back at Neah Bay, ironically employed as a reservation policeman by the same agent who had arrested him a year earlier.[113]

The People of the Cape continued to possess the ability to subvert settler-colonial efforts at establishing control over the region and indigenous peoples. Typical borderlands conflicts in which kinship intermingled with violence, these events illustrate that regional rivalries still meant something to indigenous peoples. Makah chiefs worried that letting Wha-laltl's murderer go unpunished jeopardized their standing among other peoples in the region, thereby provoking them into action. Although the settler-colonial governments had established bordered spaces in 1846, indigenous networks of the ča·di· borderland continued to cross imperial boundaries. These Native networks were more than subtle connections running parallel to and separate from non-Native networks. The incidents reveal that indigenous borderlands dynamics sometimes took place in non-Native places and involved—even threatened the lives of—whites. Individuals such as Brown attempted to take advantage of the boundary separating imperial domains. Perhaps he killed the Elwha on the north side of the borderline because he believed that US officials might overlook this action if it happened on British soil and that British officials would not cross the border to arrest an American Indian once he had returned home.

These incidents illustrate another degree of complexity in the Northwest Coast, the nature of violence and justice in a region where indigenous peoples still had the power to interrupt imperial designs. Settler-colonial officials eagerly enforced peace and imposed British and US legal systems in their respective domains; however, this remained difficult in an indigenous region where Native chiefs could still enact their own systems of justice and power. Even when the territorial government apprehended belligerent Natives who had broken out of reservation boundaries and subverted US attempts at punishment, justice seemed elusive. It appears ironic that Brown became the reservation policeman shortly after his imprisonment for committing a murder, flaunting US authority, and threatening white lives. But this result reveals that Indian agents at Neah Bay had to rely on Makah chiefs, even some who resisted Euro-American hegemony. Brown came from a high-ranking family that had enough influence with white officials that he not only spent little time in prison but also secured a position as a person with power recognized by non-Native bureaucrats. During the 1860s, Euro-American authority on the Makah reservation still relied on indigenous power.

As at other Washington Territory reservations, the confinement aspect of reservation policy at Cape Flattery was a resounding failure through at least the 1860s.[114] The ambivalent relationship between Indians and whites undermined the policy itself. More important, powerful Native peoples such as the People of the Cape refused to abide by settler-colonial efforts at confining them to reservations. Coastal and marine borders that non-Native officials perceived as firm boundaries were instead permeable zones of interaction. The Makahs' view of the sea as a medium of connections prevailed during the second half of the nineteenth century. Their perception of the sea as their country enabled financial success in the face of the expanding settler-colonial world. Put into action, these understandings allowed them to continue subverting federal attempts at control. By employing successful, customary marine practices, Makahs convinced some colonial agents entrenched in the philosophy of assimilation that indigenous methods worked.

5

"AN ANOMALY IN THE INDIAN SERVICE"

In June 1865, Henry Webster, US Indian agent at Neah Bay, composed the agency's annual report for the commissioner of Indian affairs, characterizing his Makah charges as "an anomaly in the Indian service." From his vantage at the most northwestern point of the United States, the people living in a collection of cedar longhouses hugging the rugged shore of Cape Flattery must have appeared this way. Violent storms swept across heavily forested, mountainous terrain and regularly dumped more than a hundred inches of rain each year. With the nearest US settlement several days away by Indian canoe, Neah Bay felt isolated from the world. After one of his earliest visits to Cape Flattery, James Swan described Webster as living an "almost Robinson Crusoe residence on this bleak, extreme northwest portion of the domain of the United States . . . the farthest west of any settlers on American soil."[1] But in this seemingly isolated and unwelcoming environment of Cape Flattery, Makahs anomalously thrived.

This was no "bleak," remote edge of the world for the indigenous people who made this their home. Networks of trade, kinship, and conflict knit together village communities and growing non-Native towns in the ča·di· borderland and Puget Sound. Makah whalers, sealers, and fishers harvested a wealth of resources from customary waters. Agent Webster reported that they did not "procure a scanty and temporary supply, but have abundance to dispose of in trade with the Indians and whites." He advised the commissioner that the federal government should encourage their fisheries so that they could remain self-supporting and attain a "state of civilization." This also made them anomalous to the Indian service: rather than civilizing Makahs by transforming them into Jeffersonian yeoman farmers, Webster contradictorily believed that the federal government should support customary marine practices to help them progress.[2]

Perhaps the People of the Cape appeared anomalous to Agent Webster in a third way, for he came from a culture that defined whites and Indians as opposites.[3] Euro-Americans pictured themselves as modern, civilized, prosperous, masculine, and dynamic, believing themselves to be agents of the future who would usher in progress and develop the Northwest Coast wilderness. Conversely, American Indians were supposed to be traditional, uncivilized, impoverished, feminine, childlike, and static. Nearly all non-Natives saw Indians as a part of nature, relics of the past, and impediments to the inevitable progress and economic development of the continent. Men like Webster regarded Makahs as anomalous because they did not fit the Indian stereotype.[4] During the second half of the nineteenth century, the People of the Cape bought and used expensive vessels and prospered as dynamic actors in regional and international markets of exchange. Their labor in modern extractive industries of the North Pacific strengthened their ability to continue living as Makahs even though the United States attempted to tighten control over indigenous peoples in the West. They labored and engaged in new economic experiences in order to maintain cultural practices, thereby establishing new paths to capitalist development.[5] Agent Webster witnessed the beginning of a Makah version of economic development that was part of the rise of indigenous entrepreneurs in Gilded Age America.

Some historical narratives that detail the rise of regional and global markets continue to cast indigenous peoples as either tragic victims or ignorant dupes who could only accept or react to European and Euro-American actions and changes. These narratives simplify the role of indigenous peoples in commercial exchanges. Natives appear at the fringes, as peripheral hunters or fishers swept aside or exploited by dynamic non-Natives, "the utmost antithesis to an America dedicated to productivity, profit, and private property."[6] These characterizations obscure the way indigenous entrepreneurs created roles for themselves within market societies in order to maintain and strengthen distinct cultural identities. Reports such as those written by Agent Webster perpetuated this false conclusion and framed successful Makahs as anomalous, as the exception to the rule.

A marine-oriented approach to Makah history of the late nineteenth century reveals that these whalers, sealers, and fishers combined new opportunities and technologies with customary practices to maintain their identity, much as other Native peoples of North America did as they confronted settler-colonialism and growing capitalist markets.[7] Rather than allowing expanding networks of capital to overwhelm and replace indigenous practices, these fishers and sea mammal hunters engaged markets of exchange and attracted—even made—capital investments in North Pacific extractive industries. When examined from a Makah perspective, these actions reveal dynamic, indigenous actors who exploited new opportunities within their own cultural framework. The subsequent success of the People of the Cape stemmed from measures Makah chiefs had taken to protect access to customary marine space while negotiating the 1855 Treaty of Neah Bay.

During this period, the Claplanhoo family exemplified Makah prosperity. Prominent patriarchs such as John, James, and Jongie emerged as indigenous entrepreneurs and occupied the ranks of tribal leadership for more than a century, from the early 1850s to the late 1950s. Although James engaged in the pelagic sealing industry and Jongie both sealed and fished commercially, all three Claplanhoo chiefs whaled. Similar to other Northwest Coast whaling chiefs, these men married women from prominent families around the ča·di· borderland, which enabled them to maintain close ties with influential in-laws. In 1860, John married Ši·ʔa·štido ("shee-ahsh-ti-do"), sister to Chief Quistoh (Ditidaht of Port Renfrew) and originally betrothed to Chief ƛisi·t ("klih-seet"), a casualty of the 1853 smallpox epidemic. James married Mary Ann George, daughter of Tsat-tsat-wha (Makah chief of Tatoosh) and Mei-ye-te-tidux (Ahousaht). In 1897 Jongie married Lizzie Parker, daughter of Wilson Parker and Babitsweyklub, two Makahs. James married his daughter Minnie to Chestoqua Peterson, the son of Peter Brown and nephew of Wha-laltl as sá buy, the Makah chief whose murder in 1861 perpetuated the conflict with the Elwhas.[8]

Claplanhoos first appear in the documentary historical record during the negotiations of the 1855 Treaty of Neah Bay with Territorial Governor Isaac Stevens. Early in the treaty council, a Neah Bay chief named Klah-pe at hoo (John Claplanhoo) spoke about his continuing sadness at the death of his brother, Halicks—whom he identified as the third-highest chief—from smallpox.[9] After Halicks died, his chiefly position, titles, and other property passed on to his brother. But John also inherited his brother's responsibilities. This meant that during the treaty negotiations, a distraught John still focused on what his people needed: access to customary marine waters, whales, seals, and fish.

To varying degrees, all three Claplanhoo chiefs during the post-treaty decades engaged new opportunities—schools, local and global markets, influential whites, and non-Native technologies—that accompanied settler-colonialism in the region. Yet they continued to participate in cultural practices ranging from lengthy potlatches to ritual preparations for customary hunting and fishing practices. Other Makahs also succeeded during this period; the Claplanhoos were not unique among their community. These accomplishments, tracked through archival and oral sources, reveal that the People of the Cape combined customary practices with new opportunities to attain high standards of living. Their participation in the expanding settler-colonial world supported their ability to continue forging a unique Makah identity and to resist the cultural assault of federal assimilation policies.

However, Makahs of the second half of the nineteenth century experienced enormous challenges that eventually undercut their success and autonomy. These challenges illustrate the limits of Makah agency in the face of unequal power held by non-Natives and historical trends outside their control.[10] The People of the Cape and other indigenous peoples of the Northwest Coast were not the only ones who hunted whales and seals. The growing number of non-Native whalers and sealers in local waters and the larger Pacific Ocean devastated marine species that provided for Makah subsistence and commercial economies. As more users overhunted Pacific resources, nation-states established conservation measures that legally privileged non-Natives over Natives and large over small operations. By the early twentieth century, Makah hunters of the sea found themselves excluded by law from once-lucrative fisheries then collapsing. Without the wealth and subsequent power Makahs accrued from customary marine harvests, the People of the Cape became susceptible to assimilation and poverty.

MAKAH WHALERS, 1850–1928

A customary practice for more than two thousand years, whaling had secured substantial wealth and power for the People of the Cape, but this situation began to change in the second half of the nineteenth century. As non-Native commercial whalers depleted Pacific stocks, Makahs experienced greater difficulty finding *čitapuk* ("chih-tuh-pook," whales) in local waters. Subsequently, these indigenous whalers petitioned the federal government for new technologies to expand their Pacific hunting range. Yet Makahs received inconsistent levels of support for these requests, which prevented them from securing access to modern technologies for whaling to the degree that they wanted. Troubled by the dearth of whales migrating past Cape Flattery, Makahs suspended the active practice of whaling in 1928 until stocks rebounded at some point in the future.

Whaling had always provided the foundation of the subsistence and commercial economies of the People of the Cape. They hunted many species of leviathans found in the Pacific. In 1852, they caught more than two dozen whales, which provided them with more than 60,000 gallons of oil, an amount exceeding the average take of a whaling ship returning to its northeastern port after a two-year voyage. A ship returning to New Bedford, Massachusetts, that same year carried an average number of 1,343 barrels, which represented between 40,290 and 47,005 gallons, of oil harvested during a two-year period.[11] Makahs exchanged oil for a wide range of Native and non-Native goods, which made whalers wealthy individuals within the community and the ča·di· borderland. One Makah elder today recalls stories of his grandfather Hišk^{w}i ("hish-kwee"), a Waʔač ("wuh-uhch") chief born in 1845 who had earned substantial wealth from whaling. When federal Indian agents in the late nineteenth century forced him to give up two of his three wives, Hišk^{w}i provided these women with enough money to live in comfort for the rest of their lives.[12] But overhunting by non-Natives in the Pacific Ocean eventually changed the fortunes of Makah whalers.

Initially, the arrival of non-Native whalers to the Pacific brought further wealth to Makahs, much as maritime fur traders did. In the late eighteenth century, these outsiders sailed into the Pacific as they sought new hunting grounds, and their numbers grew rapidly. In 1787, the English whaler *Amelia* took the first sperm whale in the Pacific, and by 1791, Yankee whalers from Nantucket and New Bedford hunted in the ocean, too. Maritime historians sometimes aggrandize the role of white whalers, characterizing them as "part of the advance guard of civilization" because they explored uncharted seas and brought unknown areas and peoples—unknown at least to the United States and Europe—into global markets. But this assessment becomes complicated when we consider the role of indigenous peoples in these pursuits. The *Butterworth*, one of the earliest ships to return to England after trading along the Northwest Coast and generally credited for commencing North Pacific whaling, brought back about twenty thousand gallons of whale oil in 1795. The *Butterworth*'s crew, however, did not procure this oil from whales they had hunted; they had purchased it from indigenous whalers in the ča·di· borderland. By the early nineteenth century, a few whaling vessels from England and New England told port authorities that they were bound for the Northwest Coast to hunt leviathans.[13] After making the long trip around Cape Horn, these ships needed fresh provisions, which encouraged them to interact with indigenous peoples along the Northwest Coast. Savvy Native traders also offered whale oil to these outsiders, meaning that perhaps indigenous whalers harvested and processed a substantial portion of oil landed in Atlantic ports by these ships.

After the War of 1812, the Pacific whaling industry grew as the fleet expanded and engaged new ports along the northeastern seaboard of the United States. Whalers targeted sperm whales because of the high quality of their oil, which was used for illumination. The "golden age" of whaling began in 1835 with the taking of the first right whale—called this because it was the "right" whale to hunt due to its high oil content and ease of capture—off the Northwest Coast above 50°N latitude. This coincided with a booming demand for whale oil lubricants used by textile factories filled with power looms. In 1851 alone, one factory in Lowell, Massachusetts, used 6,772 gallons of whale oil, which represented the harvest of three sperm whales.[14] By 1846, more than seven hundred barks, brigs, and schooners from US ports whaled in the Pacific, most of them cruising right-whaling grounds in the Gulf of Alaska and off Kamchatka and the Kuril Islands.[15]

Whaling vessels often came into the ča·di· borderland, where they interacted with Makahs and other indigenous peoples. Whalers anchored at Neah Bay to procure fresh provisions and whale oil from the People of the Cape. But because of the legacy of violent encounters during the maritime fur trade, some feared Makahs and neighboring communities. In September 1843, the *Caroline* (US) and *Réunion* (French) fled Cape Flattery despite a brief and friendly encounter. After whaling together off Alaska's Kodiak Island, the two vessels approached the cape to seek provisions and new hunting grounds. Seven canoes of Makahs greeted them, offering fresh fish and whale oil for sale. An English-speaking chief tried to persuade them to come into Neah Bay where they could sojourn for several weeks until whales migrating north came into the strait. But Captain Daniel McKenzie of the *Caroline* "d[id] not like the appearance of things" and feared a trap. Over the strenuous objections of the French captain, whose crew needed provisions, McKenzie departed the area and sailed for San Francisco. Fearing to anchor alone at Neah Bay, the *Réunion* followed the *Caroline* south. Although anxiety marked this encounter, enough whaling ships visited Neah Bay that Makahs knew what crews needed and wanted.[16]

Some vessels came into the Strait of Juan de Fuca looking for new whaling grounds or for locations to establish shore whaling operations. In the fall of 1847, the *General Teste*, a French whaler from Le Havre, cruised into the strait to hunt in the Gulf of Georgia and northern Puget Sound, sixty to eighty miles east of Cape Flattery. But the *General Teste* did not do well—the crew killed only one whale and lost even that one—and they had left by early 1848. Non-Native shore whaling operations in this region also faltered in the beginning. From 1867 to 1871, just under a dozen companies—all operating from shore stations on the British side of the border—formed and collapsed, and none lasted longer than two seasons. They suffered from stormy weather, lack of proper equipment, low oil prices, vessel losses, and perhaps unskilled workers. In the dense fogs characteristic to the area, these nonlocal hunters often lost slain whales, which drifted off or sank. The most successful venture captured only nineteen whales and produced about thirty-three thousand gallons of oil in 1869, about half of what Makahs had processed a decade earlier.[17]

As with similar expansions of the settler-colonial world into the region, Makahs engaged in the non-Native whaling industry. Along with other Pacific peoples, some, such as Q̓i·tap ("kee-tuhp," David Fischer) and General Jackson, labored on non-Native whaling ships and explored the larger world. Shipping out of Neah Bay in the 1850s, Fischer joined cruises lasting years in length and even traveled as far abroad as Africa.[18] A few indigenous borderlanders also labored at local shore whaling stations, although white operators ignored the whaling expertise of these people, limiting them to tasks such as towing carcasses to shore and stripping the flesh and blubber. Native women lived with some non-Native men working at the shore stations and probably contributed by rendering blubber into oil, a customary activity back in their home villages. Indigenous whalers often picked up the prey struck but lost in the fog by their non-Native counterparts. Although whites complained in local papers that Indians "appropriated to their own use" carcasses belonging to shore whaling operations, Natives probably sold to traders oil processed from these "losses."[19] Through this wage work and by harvesting drift whales that had escaped from white shore whalers, Natives continued to mark historical and cultural places in the ča·di· borderland as theirs.[20]

The eastern Pacific whale fisheries followed a similar pattern of declining returns as non-local, commercial whalers depleted a given stock within a decade and then moved on to another species. During the 1840s, whalers targeted right whales in the North Pacific, and by the 1850s, returns had plummeted to a quarter of those from the previous decade. These whalers often lost many they harpooned. In 1841, the *Superior* struck fifty-eight whales along the Northwest Coast but only recovered twenty-six, noting that another five sank before retrieval. After examining numerous logs from whaling's golden age, one historian concluded that the death of unrecovered whales was high because nearly every logbook made references to encountering the carcasses of right whales that had died from harpoon strikes.[21] After discovering bowhead grounds in the Bering Sea in 1849, whalers shifted to this baleen whale, and by 1865, they had reduced the bowhead population by more than half. Due to decreasing numbers of bowheads—and the actions of the *Shenandoah*, a Southern privateer steamship that burned thirty-four Yankee whaling vessels in the Bering Sea toward the end of the Civil War—non-Native whalers shifted their focus to hunting gray whales in calving grounds off Baja California. Intense commercial whaling also caused this fishery to collapse, and the gray whale population plummeted from a high of twenty-four thousand at the beginning of the century to two thousand by the 1880s.[22]

Overhunting of Pacific whale populations caused the New England whaling industry to wither and die during the 1870s. Decades of fluctuating prices for oil and baleen made it difficult for investors to sustain steady returns. Profitable years resulted in the growth of the fleet and new ports, which in subsequent years flooded markets with whale products and drove prices down. This situation meant that voyages were too expensive for the meager returns. Once lasting just two years, cruises in the 1870s stretched from four to six years, yet amounts of oil and baleen decreased. Longer voyages required a more substantial outfitting of vessels, an expense that grew out of proportion with profits. Only the Northern Pacific and Arctic fisheries—"where disasters were the rule and immunity from them the exception"—retained any hope of profit. The whaling fleet in the Arctic suffered a catastrophe in 1871, when ice crushed thirty-four ships. The financial losses from this numbered in the millions of dollars. More than a thousand survivors eventually made it to Honolulu, where they languished while seeking employment in a dwindling industry. As whaling profits plummeted, the output from the nation's petroleum wells increased, providing a plentiful, high-quality, and cheap alternative to whale oil for lighting and lubricants.[23]

For New England laborers and investors, other industries beckoned. By the 1870s, whaling captains, experienced sailors, and "green hands" were earning little; crewmember income averaged between $3 and $7 a month. These laborers felt that "a strenuous and dangerous voyage of a year yielded not a penny besides the food." They found better wages in the booming manufacturing industry of the Northeast. Pacific Rim gold discoveries encouraged desertions as whaling became less profitable. Sailors—and even captains and officers—joined whaling ships simply to get to the region. Profits also diminished for shipowners. After the 1871 catastrophe in the Arctic, insurance premiums rose to "almost prohibitive heights." The transition from sail-powered ships to more successful steam-powered vessels was too expensive for many who had already invested their capital in sailing ships.[24]

Although the end of the industry in the Northeast was not the end of US whaling, the demise of Yankee whaling in the 1870s affected the People of the Cape, illustrating just one way that larger trends undercut Makah opportunities. After the Civil War, San Francisco grew into the leading port for whalers, and competition from this new center of the industry contributed to the waning influence of Northeastern ports, whose vessels had once frequented the Cape Flattery villages. By 1883, San Francisco had whale oil refineries and sperm candle works. Instead of shipping oil and other whale products around Cape Horn—an arduous and long voyage, at best—merchants used new transcontinental railroads to transport commodities east. By 1893, thirty-three whaling ships were based out of the Pacific port, and twenty-two of these were steamers. Instead of anchoring at Neah Bay to resupply, steamships put in at other ports, which had access to abundant coal. With no Yankee whalers stopping at Cape Flattery and the new steam-powered whaling fleet bypassing Makah villages, the People of the Cape lost an important market for whale oil. The shift to expensive floating factory ships at the turn of the century moved whaling even farther from the coast and indigenous whalers. Twentieth-century whaling focused less on whale oil, a commodity easily provided by Makahs, and more on goods indigenous peoples could not provide, such as fertilizers, bone meal, animal fodder, glue, cosmetics, and other products requiring expensive industrial processes.[25]

Most important, the overall decline of whales in the Pacific affected Makah whalers such as John Claplanhoo. Known as Captain John by whites, this patriarch was a whaling chief. But he seemed to doubt his whaling ability when he measured his kills against those of other hunters. To bolster his hunting prowess and prove his lineage as a whaler, he made theatrical shows of his ancestral "whale medicine," pieces of dead whales and a bone of the x̌ix̌i·ktu·yak ("hih-heek-too-yuhk"), a sea horse–like snake that stuns whales with lightning. According to Northwest Coast legends, Thunderbird uses the x̌ix̌i·ktu·yak when he comes down from his alpine nest to hunt whales. When John had trouble hunting in the mid-1860s, he underwent extra ritual preparations, including fasting, sleep deprivation, and bathing in saltwater with his whale medicine.[26]

Others who noticed the declining number of whales attributed it to various causes. In 1858, Makahs complained to an Indian agent that they objected to the government lighthouse at Tatoosh Island not only because it was built on land that belonged to the tribal nation but also because "it keeps the whales from coming as usual." Several decades later, Lighthouse Jim (Makah) joked to James Swan that they had a harder time catching čitapuk "as [they] now drink coffee at each breakfast before going out as the whales smell their breath." However, John's poor whaling skills, the new lighthouse, and Lighthouse Jim's coffee breath probably did not make it harder to catch whales. Instead, their experiences reflected the changing ecology of the Pacific, namely the removal of vast numbers of leviathans by non-local commercial whalers.[27]

Despite the increasing difficulty of securing whales throughout the second half of the nineteenth century, whaling remained important to the People of the Cape. The continued prominence of whalers among tribal leadership indicates that these chiefs must have provided tangible benefits. John Claplanhoo maintained his position as a recognized leader of his people, and detailed census records of the 1860s show his longhouse as one of the largest. From 1861 to 1865, average longhouse populations fell from 18 to 12.6, whereas the Claplanhoo longhouse grew from 22 to 24 individuals. In the first American-style election held on the reservation, the residents of Neah Bay chose John as one of their four chiefs, who, in turn, elected him tribal chairman in 1879. Although Claplanhoo drew his profits from a variety of economic activities—his slaves cut wood, cleared land, and did chores for the Neah Bay Agency; he fished; and he engaged in regular trade with Native villages and colonial towns—he continued to value his identity as a whaler. In 1878, during a grand ceremony, he took the name Łutka·bałid ("lthoot-kah-buh-lthihd," Thunder on the Ocean), which tied him to his family's whaling heritage.[28]

Whaling statistics from the second half of the nineteenth century are difficult to ascertain because no one kept complete returns for the entire community, yet available evidence indicates that Makahs regularly landed around a dozen whales each year. Based on statistics provided by the whaling chief Wha-laltl as sá buy (Swell) in 1859, Swan noted that thirty canoes of Makah whalers harvested thirteen whales that year and produced about thirty thousand gallons of oil.[29] During his tenure at Neah Bay as the agency teacher, Swan noted occasions when Makahs hunted whales; but these numbers were less accurate than the 1859 statistics provided by Wha-laltl because Swan could not be everywhere on the reservation at all times. He never heard of some hunts—especially those from the coastal villages of Waʔač, Ću·yas, and Ozette—and there were probably times when he did not report whaling about which he did hear. Yet some of Swan's numbers are close to those reported by Wha-laltl, as are those reported by Indian agents who also occasionally noted the number of whales taken that year. Agents' numbers are lower than they actually were because they, too, were not in a position to report every hunt.

These whaling returns compared favorably to contemporaneous non-Native operations along the West Coast. In 1872, Makahs hunting in canoes produced an estimated 20,700 gallons of oil from the nine whales the agent reported among

Table 1. Snapshot of Makah whaling returns during the second half of the nineteenth century

Year	Swan estimate	Agent estimate
1862	13	—
1863	8	—
1872	—	9
1888	—	9
1891	6 (just for July)	12
1897	—	10

Sources: From Swan's Diaries, 5–7, 55, Swan Papers, 1833–1909; E. M. Gibson, Agent Report, *ARCIA* (1873), 308; W. L. Powell, Agent Report, *ARCIA* (1888), 225; John P. McGlinn, Agent Report, *ARCIA* (1891), 448; Samuel G. Morse, Agent Report, *ARCIA* (1897), 292.

this community of 604 individuals. Two years earlier, San Francisco, a growing city with nearly 150,000 people, landed 4,013 barrels (or about 130,423 gallons) of whale oil from six vessels that identified the city as their homeport. This oil resulted from four-to-six-year cruises in the Bering Sea and Arctic Ocean, and 1870 saw one of the highest oil returns recorded by the city's port officials until the advent of steam-powered whaling ships later that century. When we consider that this non-Native oil came from leviathans harvested during voyages lasting several years, this statistic represents an average of 27,590 gallons per year, an amount not much higher than what Makahs produced in 1872.[30]

As whale oil returns dwindled at similarly sized white operations, Makah harvests remained high during the last two decades of the nineteenth century. In 1888, Makahs again harvested at least nine whales, which produced approximately 20,700 gallons of oil. In comparison, a shore whaling station occupied by Portuguese at San Simeon Bay, California, took seven gray and humpback whales in 1888 and the same amount in the following year. From these whales, this station produced only 180 and 260 barrels (or 5,850 and 8,450 gallons) of oil, respectively. With twenty-one men and nine boats at the time, this operation was "one of the principal whaling stations on the Pacific Coast" and had operated since 1865.[31]

Comparing the oil returns of Makah whalers to a similar whaling operation along the coast of California reveals two important conclusions. First, during a period when leviathans were "disappearing from the Pacific Ocean," as reported by the *New York Times*, Makah whalers harvested more whales than non-Natives engaged in the same industry. Second, Makah women were more then twice as efficient when it came to processing oil—either that or Makahs hunted larger specimens than their Portuguese counterparts in California did. The fact that the People of the Cape on average rendered 2,300 gallons of oil from each whale is significant. This number might appear unusually high because scholars commonly assume that commercial whalers in the nineteenth century harvested between 20 and 30 barrels (anywhere from 600 to 1,050 gallons) of oil per whale. Butchering a whale on the high seas was dangerous because it produced a large amount of blood and oil, making the deck of a whaling vessel slick. Sailors slipped in the mess and sometimes ended up overboard in waters filled with sharks drawn to the carnage. Add to this the way large waves or storms would rock a ship, and it is easy to see that whalers probably sacrificed thoroughness for speed when it came to butchering a whale, which could take many hours or even days. When compared to Long Island shore whaling stations of the eighteenth century, Makah returns appear reasonable. Lord Cornbury, the British governor of New York and New Jersey (1702–8), reported in 1708 that two-year-old whales often yielded nearly

2,000 gallons of oil, with the largest specimens resulting in more than 3,000 gallons. Industrial whaling of the early twentieth century sometimes resulted in yields of 7,500 gallons of oil from the blubber of large whales.[32]

Despite their success as whalers, the People of the Cape could do little about the impact of modern whaling on sea mammal populations in the Pacific. Claplanhoo oral histories recall that 1909 marked the last whale hunt completed by a family member. Jongie, grandson to John Claplanhoo, killed this whale and added the one-hundred-and-forty-second notch to the harpoon that his forebears had used for four generations. Makahs took the occasional whale during the second decade of the twentieth century, but by this time, they rarely saw čitapuk in local waters. A whale sighting resulted in tremendous excitement and the immediate launch of whaling canoes. In 1928, nineteen years before non-Natives

Charles White harpooning a whale. The whale has already been harpooned; White is making a second thrust and has a sealskin float attached to the harpoon line. This is thought to be a photo of the hunt in 1928, the last one for more than seventy years. Photograph by Asahel Curtis, courtesy the Makah Cultural and Research Center, Neah Bay, WA.

decided to suspend the hunt of gray whales, concern over the dearth of whales caused the tribal nation to suspend the active practice of whaling until populations had rebounded. Makahs took their responsibilities to nonhuman kin such as whales seriously, and this tough decision made sense. To provide the youngest generation with the experience of welcoming a whale to Neah Bay, whalers held a final hunt. The tribal nation always intended to revive an active whaling practice at some point in the future.[33]

Before deciding to suspend whaling, the People of the Cape looked to new technologies that would allow them to expand their hunting grounds deeper into the Pacific, much as non-Native commercial whalers were doing at the time. In 1862, John Claplanhoo spoke with Swan about the possibility of purchasing a schooner from a local trader. Already finding it more difficult to locate whales along the coast, John hoped to use the larger vessel to hunt far from the safety of the coast. In 1884, a hundred Makahs met in council with an Indian inspector and urged him to convince the government to provide them with a steamship so they could more easily haul in whales from the Pacific. Some of these individuals had been present at the 1855 treaty negotiations, and they recalled that Governor Stevens had promised to support tribal marine industries. By making these requests in the decades following the treaty, the People of the Cape attempted to hold the government responsible for its promises.[34]

Some officials supported Makah requests for modern vessels, despite federal efforts to transform all American Indians into farmers. In his annual reports for 1865 and 1867, Henry Webster, the Makah agent, forwarded the tribe's requests to his superiors, as did agents Elkanah M. Gibson (1873) and Charles A. Huntington (1876). They questioned the department's wisdom in sending agricultural implements to coastal peoples such as the Makah, who found the intended purpose of these tools nearly pointless. Instead, the People of the Cape fashioned them into fishhooks, blubber knives, and points for whaling lances.[35] During the 1860s and 1870s, the Indian Affairs Department ignored Native entreaties for vessels. In the 1880s, however, the department agreed to finance the Makah request for a steamship due to a favorable review by an Indian inspector. Unfortunately, the final decision rested on the advice of the current Makah agent, Oliver Wood, who apparently thought that all American Indians, including those living on the Pacific Coast, should abandon fishing in favor of farming. Even though many Makahs were experienced deckhands aboard local steamships plying Northwest Coast waters, Wood considered the request unreasonable because a steamer would cost $8,000, plus the cost of fuel and wages for white crewmembers. If they had acquired either of these vessels earlier, Makah whalers could have possibly met the challenge of a dwindling number of whales migrating past Cape Flattery by expanding their hunting range farther into the Pacific.[36] Instead, they spent more time seeking fewer whales that swam into coastal waters. In this way, a combination of environmental (non-Native overhunting) and policy (federal policies and assimilationist agents) factors outside their control curtailed a fundamental Makah practice.

Although customary whaling methods endured throughout the nineteenth century and into the twentieth century, the People of the Cape sought more efficient ways to hunt whales. In 1861, James Swan observed Peter Brown—an individual from a long line of whalers—use a rifle during a casual hunt. Eighteen years later, after seeing a mortar fired, older whalers expressed interest in acquiring one to use for whaling. When the opportunity presented itself, whaling crews hired powered ships to haul harpooned whales into Neah Bay. In 1905, two vessels, the *Wyadda* and the *Lorne*, witnessed a hunt and competed for the opportunity to bring in the carcass. The Makahs chose the *Wyadda*, a tugboat that pulled ships into or out of the strait. Because the federal government had failed to honor Makah requests for a modern vessel, the People of the Cape turned to local ships to assist in their hunts.[37] Using tugboats to tow whales ashore, employing rifles to hunt, and expressing interest in other modern gear did not dilute the customary practice of whaling. Nor did these modifications and participation in local and global markets make these hunters any less Makah. By engaging non-Native tools and opportunities during the third quarter of the nineteenth century, Makah whalers continued what they had been doing for generations—adapting to a changing world in ways that maintained their wealth and distinct identity as the People of the Cape.

MAKAH PELAGIC SEALING, 1871–1897

When Makah families such as the Claplanhoos combined customary practices with modern opportunities and technology in the case of pelagic (oceanic) sealing, they accumulated considerable wealth.[38] This strategy enabled them to better resist assimilation and to control both their marine space and reservation lands. Not only did Makah hunters labor on vessels owned by non-Natives, but they also became important investors in this extractive industry, purchasing expensive, modern schooners that the federal government would not. Sealing from ships allowed this tribal nation to expand Makah marine space substantially as they hunted pinnipeds in local waters, to the south off the coast of California, to the north in the Bering Sea, and eastward to Japan. The environmental cost of this industry—in which Makahs were particularly successful hunters—prompted the United States to focus the nation's first international conservation efforts on fur seals, the target of pelagic sealers. At the end of the nineteenth century, Congress passed laws that ended commercial pelagic sealing for Makahs and other laborers while allowing well-capitalized and politically connected non-Native corporations to continue hunting. When nations grappled with conservation issues on the international stage, diplomats not only shut out indigenous investors from a profitable industry but also denied them compensation opportunities. Wealthy Makah entrepreneurs found themselves shackled to the timeless stereotype of the Native subsistence hunter. The US prohibition on pelagic sealing reversed the fortunes of the People of the Cape, transforming many from wealth to poverty as they entered the twentieth century.

Like his father, John, James Claplanhoo took advantage of modern opportunities to secure and strengthen his leadership position among Makahs. Although James whaled, his financial success in the fourth quarter of the nineteenth century came from sealing rather than whaling.[39] By the 1870s, the skins of *kiɬaduˑs* ("kih-lthuh-doos," fur seals)—a sea mammal long hunted by Makahs for their flesh, hide, and oil—had become a valuable commodity. Skins from the North Pacific ended up in London, where furriers turned them into stylish, ebony sealskin coats worn by the likes of wealthy, urban women and Mark Twain. An early twentieth-century reference book for English women called a sealskin coat a "precious possession" and carefully detailed how to select one, which usually cost around £200.[40] By 1871, Makahs were trading sealskins for clothing, flour, and other items. London merchants prized skins from fur seals caught off Cape Flattery; these skins garnered the best prices in the 1870s. As local traders on both sides of the international border competed for sealskins, Makahs began demanding cash. In 1873, James and about 150 Makah hunters together earned over $10,000 (nearly $200,000 today) selling 1,500 skins from seals they had taken up to forty miles offshore during the first five months of the year. A year later, they sold twice the amount of sealskins and made $15,000.[41]

By the late 1870s, Makah sealers began accumulating substantial cash by joining crews aboard white-owned schooners based out of Victoria, Port Townsend, Seattle, and San Francisco. Nuu-chah-nulths from the West Coast of Vancouver Island had been sealing from schooners for more than a decade before this. For one-third of the catch, schooners took sealers and their canoes and gear out to sea for weeklong voyages. By the mid-1880s, indigenous hunters could make almost twice as much in one sealing season as non-Native laborers in other industries earned in a year because of the high price of sealskins. Some chiefs earned fees for brokering labor agreements with ship captains, traders, and Indian agents. A local trader agreed to pay Lighthouse Jim $30 at the end of the sealing season if he persuaded his friends to sell their skins to him. Occasionally, a sealer's wife joined the crew as cook and skinner. Makah women also processed seal blubber into oil—around 1,500 gallons each season—reserving the cleanest oil for consumption. In 1880, the Makah-organized Neah Bay Fur Sealing Company chartered the *Lottie*, a Port Townsend schooner, and made over $20,000 during the four-month season. Competition for sealskins enabled skilled hunters to command high values for their catches and choose the captains and vessels for which they would hunt.[42]

The People of the Cape understood the benefits of schooner ownership. James Claplanhoo was one of the first Native borderlanders to acquire one of these vessels. After spending the previous year considering several, James purchased the

Nuu-chah-nulth pelagic sealers aboard the Canadian schooner *Favorite*, 1894. For one-third of the catch, schooner owners took Indian sealers aboard their vessels to hunt fur seals in the Pacific, from California to the Bering Sea. This photograph was taken in the Bering Sea. Photograph by Stefan Claesson. National Oceanic and Atmospheric Association/Department of Commerce.

thirty-one-ton *Lottie* from a local trader at the beginning of 1886. He paid $1,200 cash, some of which he borrowed from Ditidaht relatives across the Strait of Juan de Fuca, with another $600 due at the end of the sealing season. Crewing his new ship with Makah sealers, James employed it in the spring hunt along the Washington and Vancouver Island coasts. The *Lottie* transported canoes to sealing grounds up to one hundred miles offshore. At night, the sealers ate and slept on the *Lottie,* which allowed them to stay out on cruises for a week or longer. After purchasing the schooner, James increased his profits from commercial pelagic sealing. That year Makah sealers earned $16,000; although the Indian agent did not record the division of profits, the Claplanhoos and the hunters they took with them on the *Lottie* probably cornered a large share of these profits.[43]

Other Makahs also invested in pelagic sealing. A year before James bought the *Lottie,* the high-ranking chief Peter Brown purchased the *Letitia* for $1,000. In 1886, the same year that James acquired his first schooner, Klahoowik and Haspooey bought the twenty-six-ton *Sierra* from three San Franciscans for $1,500. A month later, Lighthouse Jim paid over $1,000 for the *C. C. Perkins.* These owners recruited Makahs and other Natives from neighboring villages on both sides of the strait to work their vessels, and occasionally they hired white captains and sailors. By 1887, five Makah-owned schooners engaged in sealing out of Neah Bay, and that number more than doubled by 1893. As the People of the Cape integrated schooners more deeply in their society, they made toy schooners for boys so they could envision themselves growing up to become ship captains and owners.[44]

In the 1890s, local whites mistakenly assumed that the motivation—and perhaps even funds—for Makah schooner ownership came from the federal government, not entrepreneurial Native families. A popular history of the time surmised that "somehow the proprietorship of several well known sealing vessels has come to them without any effort on their part; it was something of a parental care on the part of a thoughtful government."[45] Yet the archival record and oral histories prove that the People of the Cape acted on their own initiative when making capital investments in the North Pacific extractive industry of pelagic sealing. By working hard, taking risks, and pooling and investing money, Makah families—not a paternalistic or helpful government—made this possible. Like late nineteenth-century Cherokee farmers and ranchers who had "a passion for building family fortunes in business ventures," Makah schooner owners sought new entrepreneurial opportunity to build their own fortunes. Like Navajo coalminers and weavers, Menominee loggers, and Tsimshian, Tlingit, and Haida fishers and cannery workers, these Makahs exemplify yet another way that indigenous peoples situated their industries in a capitalist marketplace, even operating within capitalist modes of production, while adhering to local values to create unique economic accommodations and outcomes.[46]

By employing schooners as floating bases to hunt seals, the People of the Cape not only earned larger profits but expanded their hunting range. Whereas canoes alone had once limited Makahs to hunting pinnipeds within thirty miles of Cape Flattery and in the strait, schooners allowed them to extend their spring coastal sealing from the mouth of the Columbia River to the northern tip of Vancouver Island. Makah sealing also expanded into the North Pacific. In the summer of 1887, James took the *Lottie* farther north, for cruises in the Bering Sea made the greatest profits. Hunters could harvest many more seals, and these skins fetched high prices on the London market. The Bering Sea voyages were

Makah sealing schooner *Columbia*, with sealing canoes, 1894. Chestoqua Peterson (Makah) purchased this schooner on October 22, 1893, and took it sealing in the Bering Sea. Photograph by Stefan Claesson, 1894. National Oceanic and Atmospheric Association/Department of Commerce.

lucrative, netting James $3,600 in profits during the 1889 season in the Bering Sea. In following years, the *Lottie's* profits from North Pacific pelagic sealing brought the Claplanhoos between $7,000 and $8,000 annually (about $180,000 to $200,000 today).⁴⁷

With these profits, James expanded his investment and purchased a small fleet of vessels. After the 1891 sealing season, he began shopping around for a second schooner, traveling to San Francisco aboard a steamer to inspect vessels. He eventually commissioned a boat builder in Seattle to construct the larger, forty-two-ton *Deeahks*, which he named after an ancestor and sailed back to Neah Bay in January 1893. That year, he also purchased the *Emmett Felitz*, a thirty-ton vessel. And sometime between 1887 and 1893, he bought the fifteen-ton *Puritan*. His son Jongie commissioned a new schooner for $2,500 at the beginning of 1897. James also maintained his vessels regularly. During the stormy winter months, he paid for sheltered moorage at Scow Bay near Port Townsend. He had them repaired by non-Native carpenters in Hadlock, another Puget Sound port, and bought new sails for his ships. The Claplanhoos and other Makahs insured their vessels with local white merchants, such as Frank Bartlett, owner of one of Puget Sound's largest mercantile establishments, and J. Katz, a German immigrant who had become a successful mercantilist.⁴⁸

Although less well documented than shipbuilding, pelagic sealing also supported the canoe-building industry among Northwest Coast peoples because it generated a demand for medium-sized hunting canoes. Sealing required hundreds of canoes across the čaˑdiˑ borderland. Many of these saw hard use; frequently damaged and broken canoes needed constant replacement. In the 1890s, top-quality sealing canoes cost as much as $300. Financial benefits from this industry flowed to more than just the handful of chiefs who owned the growing fleet of sealing schooners.⁴⁹

Makah pelagic sealers such as the Claplanhoos succeeded as entrepreneurial capitalists, an identity that scholars rarely ascribe to indigenous people. As one historian explains in her analysis of "rich Indians," the gaze of historians is drawn away from enterprising Natives by the "seductive paradigm . . . [that] contrasts an egalitarian, spiritual, traditionalist Indian ethos with a competitive, materialistic, activist non-Indian ethos."⁵⁰ Like other successful investors, James diversified his assets in 1890 when he bought out the reservation trader for $3,000, purchasing his inventory and operation. A year later, he deposited $5,000 in Port Townsend's Merchants Bank, where his money earned 6 percent interest. Some Makahs invested their sealing profits in other ventures, including Kobaˑli ("koh-bah-lee"), a "full-blooded Indian" who owned a hotel and had saved $1,000 to erect "a more pretentious building for accommodation of his guests," as one surprised Makah agent reported. The financial actions of the People of the Cape were part of a larger indigenous engagement with settler-colonial economies in the region. Aboriginal entrepreneurs of British Columbia made important contributions to the emerging capitalist economy of the colony—then province— during the second half of the nineteenth century. They traveled from one village to the next, buying Native products such as furs, fish, and oil to exchange in Victoria for goods they would resell up the coast. Indigenous artists created works for sale in non-Native markets, and Indian-owned stores and sawmills dotted the Northwest Coast. The diversity and scale of these financial and commercial activities reveal that many indigenous peoples of the ča·di· borderland were important investors in North Pacific extractive industries. Bucking the stereotype, these American Indians were highly sophisticated venture capitalists.[51]

Although sealers such as James embraced certain elements of non-Native technology and business acumen, they did not abandon Makah hunting methods. Instead, they combined the best aspects of both to increase their success in a customary practice. Even in the dangerous and new waters of the Bering Sea, Makahs preferred using customary gear. As along the coast, they conducted the actual seal hunt from specially adapted canoes. Most used a double-headed harpoon that they hurled with both hands instead of noisier rifles or shotguns that scared away seals. They adapted the harpoon's design, incorporating iron or sheet copper tips instead of mussel shells. The reservation's blacksmith, hired by the Office of Indian Affairs to support the tribe's agricultural pursuits, instead became busy in the weeks before the coastal sealing season, fashioning metal tips for spears, lances, and harpoons. Prominent sealers in the community continued using traditional gear during important ceremonies, thereby indicating their enduring cultural value. By employing traditionally designed gear, Makahs rarely lost seals they struck. Some men used guns to hunt seals, but only when they worked from white-owned schooners in the Bering Sea.[52]

Pelagic sealing in the late nineteenth century supported and complemented other Makah labor and industry. Based out of Neah Bay, the coastal sealing season typically began in mid-January and lasted until early June. Beginning in mid-May some years and usually lasting until early October, Makahs sealers and their vessels hunted in the Bering Sea.[53] In the 1880s and 1890s, sealing was the most important occupation for Makah males. Chestoqua Peterson, a prominent Makah by birth and marriage—he had married James Claplanhoo's daughter—told Swan that 112 Makah males had hunted seals during the coastal season in 1892. This represented about three-fourths of the community's hunting-age males, who began sealing at the age of ten with their older male relatives and continued into their mid-sixties. Unlike whaling, sealing was not limited to high-status

Makah men, so anyone with access to a canoe and hunting gear could participate. During the coastal hunting season that year, these sealers made $21,242 (over $500,000 today), a substantial injection of cash and goods to the reservation community.[54] A smaller percentage of Makah men sealed in the Bering Sea, earning thousands of dollars more during the summer. Those not sealing in the Bering Sea often headed to regional salmon canneries to labor as fishers, earning in the early 1880s nearly $60 per month, which compared favorably to wages of a skilled tradesperson.[55] Seeking to get the most from their investments, indigenous schooner owners chartered their vessels for other purposes when they were not sealing. Makah ships transported goods around Puget Sound, hauled lumber and dynamite, and salvaged shipwrecks. Lighthouse Jim even shipped cargo to Honolulu aboard his vessel, the *C. C. Perkins*. Makahs also made their schooners available for family and friends who traveled around the region, such as groups of hop pickers headed to fields south of Seattle. Part of a larger migration of seasonal indigenous laborers, Makah hop pickers headed into Puget Sound in late August, returning to Cape Flattery in mid-October. Like other indigenous workers of this period, Makahs blended seasonal labor opportunities and extended their maritime customary practices well into the era of assimilation.[56] Makah families spent the profits from their labors on various goods and services, including potlatches, vessels, homes and housing material, clothing, food, and photographs.[57]

As with Pacific whaling, commercial hunting rapidly exacted a catastrophic toll on fur seal numbers. Native and non-Native hunters took pinnipeds from the Pribilof herd, a once-massive population that migrated along the Northwest Coast to their breeding grounds on the Pribilof Islands in the Bering Sea. After the United States purchased Alaska from Russia in 1867, various fur companies flocked to the Pribilofs the following year, slaughtering more than three hundred thousand seals on Saint Paul and Saint George Islands. Concerned that a continued free-for-all would wipe out the herd, Congress designated the islands a government reserve and restricted hunting to a single leaseholder. In 1870, the Alaska Commercial Company (ACC) agreed to pay the US government $500,000 each year for a twenty-year hunting lease, which allowed them to harvest 100,000 fur seals annually. This lucrative arrangement allowed the federal government to net $10 million during the lease period, while the company paid more than $22 million to company shareholders, many of whom were congressmen. During the lease period, ACC hunters clubbed dead an average of 98,823 seals each year in their rookeries. In 1890, Congress awarded the second twenty-year lease to the North America Commercial Company (NACC). Attempting to conserve the Pribilof herd, the Department of Treasury limited the annual quota of seals

Seal fishery, Saint Paul Island, 1895. During the nineteenth century, the Alaska Commercial Company and North American Commercial Company used Aleut wage labor to club and skin seals. Photograph by Stefan Claesson. National Oceanic and Atmospheric Association/Department of Commerce.

killed on land to 60,000. NACC employees harvested well below this number, normally taking between 12,000 and 30,000 seals any given year. In 1892 and 1893, the government limited them to 7,500 seals annually in an effort to relieve hunting pressure on the herd.[58]

Convinced that seals belonged to no one until caught, pelagic sealers plied the North Pacific and Bering Sea, taking their prey from the same Pribilof herd from which the ACC and NACC hunters harvested. During the Alaska Commercial Company's lease from 1870 to 1889, pelagic sealers took 269,276 fur seals, for an average of just over 14,000 seals a year, a number substantially below the lessee's catch. However, this situation reversed in the mid-1880s as more vessels hunted seals in the North Pacific. In 1883, three hunters aboard the American *City of San Diego* caught 900 seals in the Bering Sea, which inspired a geographic expansion of the pelagic industry.[59] By the time the North American Commercial Company assumed the Pribilof lease in 1890, the catch at sea outnumbered the land harvest by nearly three to one. From 1890 to 1897, pelagic sealers took 364,203 fur seals (an annual average of 45,525), while the NACC land hunters caught only 135,976 (an annual average of 16,997). Employing shotguns, non-Native pelagic hunters lost from half to three-fifths of what they shot, a wasteful practice deplored by Makah hunters who largely kept to using spears. Osly, a Makah who had sealed in the Bering Sea three separate times on both white-owned and Makah-owned schooners, complained, "The white hunters who used guns in the Bering Sea were banging away at the seals sometimes all day long, and they would lose a great many of those that they had shot. I do not think that they brought to the schooner one-half of those that they killed." More concerning for conservationists, 75 to 80 percent of the pelagic catch consisted of breeding females, which undercut the ability of the Pribilof herd to sustain its numbers. When considering the additional loss of unborn pups and nursing ones that starved to death after the loss of the mother, pelagic sealing resulted in the loss of nearly two million seals from 1868 to 1897. Hunting pressure at sea and in the terrestrial breeding grounds triggered the collapse of the fur seal population.[60]

Among the first to notice reduced seal numbers in coastal waters, the People of the Cape went farther out seeking seals, which brought them into the ocean where sudden storms could capsize canoes or push them even farther away from home. Seven Makah men died at sea in 1875, and in 1881, on his way from Port Townsend to Honolulu, Captain Rufus Calhoun picked up two exhausted Makahs and their canoe more than fifty miles west of Cape Flattery. The 1883 season appeared particularly dangerous—"West Coast" Indians from Vancouver Island reported that "between 40 and 50 men of the different tribes, who ventured too far out to sea in their frail canoes, in search of seals, have been overtaken by gales and perished." Although maritime accidents were not uncommon, schooner ownership enabled sealers to expand their customary activity from overhunted local waters to the greater North Pacific and into the Bering Sea with relative safety.[61]

Makah hunters faced an even greater obstacle: seal conservation backed by the power of the state and the London fur industry. As pelagic sealers, Makah hunters and shipowners such as the Claplanhoos found themselves on the losing side of a diplomatic struggle over the Pribilof seal herd. When he began investing in schooners in 1886, James Claplanhoo confronted Treasury Department officials keen on discouraging pelagic sealing in the Bering Sea. That year, he asked for permission to take the Lottie to Alaska to hunt sea otters and seals. The acting secretary of the Treasury replied that his department would not authorize any sealing permits for anyone other than the leaseholder of the Pribilofs, the Alaska Commercial Company, so James did not take his schooner into the Bering Sea. Fearing that they were getting cut out of the more lucrative hunting grounds in Alaskan waters, he and other Makahs repeated the request the following year. When federal officials neglected to reply, James took his schooner to the Bering Sea that summer, thereby expanding Makah marine space.[62] Makahs did not extend ownership or control over these far northern waters as they did with more local waters off Cape Flattery. Instead, they began to make this space "theirs" through the shared experience of labor. For many Makah men in the late nineteenth century, sealing in the Bering Sea became an important part of their marine identity.

The People of the Cape brought their vessels into the Bering Sea at the same time that the federal government attempted to make the North Pacific into a more "legible" space. States attempt to arrange populations and resources in ways that simplify functions such as taxation, conscription, and order.[63] From the perspective of the US government administering the District of Alaska, the most orderly and profitable way to benefit from the seal catch was by leasing to a single corporation the rights to hunt fur seals on the Pribilof Islands. Enforcing licensing fees on more than a hundred individually owned vessels and collecting taxes on the sale of skins from these ships was nearly impossible for any single nation-state. Many of the shipowners and individual hunters were not even US citizens—they instead hailed from Russia, Japan, and, most especially, Canada. When shipowners found any one nation's licensing fees or hunting restrictions too onerous, they simply registered their vessel in another country.[64] Schooner captains had numerous places in the North Pacific—many not even in the United States—where they could dock to sell their skins. From the view of US officials, pelagic sealing was anything but orderly, and it threatened the profitability of a lucrative national resource.

To curb the depredations on the American herd by foreign sealers, US Revenue cutters stopped twenty Canadian schooners from 1886 to 1890. They turned five foreign vessels out of the Bering Sea and confiscated the rest. Masters and mates of captured ships were imprisoned and fined, while the hunters were set "adrift several hundred miles from homes, without food or shelter," as one contemporary commentator noted.[65] Harry Guillod, the Indian agent for the West Coast Agency on Vancouver Island, detailed the difficulties Nuu-chah-nulth hunters experienced after US Revenue cutters seized the *W. P. Layward* in the Bering Sea: "These Indians suffered exceptional hardship having to find their way home from Sitka by canoe, it taking them 19 days to Port Simpson where they parted with their canoes for provisions also personal property, being there

26 days finally working their passage to Victoria on the Boscowitz. They lost their sealing gear and everything they had with them." The US Treasury Department auctioned some of the seized vessels, such as the *Anna Beck*, a Victoria schooner that Chestoqua Peterson, the son of Peter Brown and husband to James Claplanhoo's daughter, bought and renamed the *James G. Swan*. The US confiscations of Canadian vessels triggered a twenty-year-long diplomatic struggle between the United States and Great Britain—and eventually Japan and Russia, two other sealing nations—over the Pribilof herd.[66]

The US Revenue cutters also targeted Makah vessels in the Bering Sea. Narrowly escaping the cutters in early July 1889, Claplanhoo's *Lottie* stayed in Alaskan waters for the summer and returned to Neah Bay at the end of August with 600 sealskins for a profit of $3,600. Peterson's newly purchased *James G. Swan* was not as lucky; the Revenue cutter *Rush* seized it with 190 sealskins at the end of July. Fearing that the loss of the schooner and the summer's returns would be a great hardship, Peterson pled ignorance of the law, arguing that he believed that the Revenue cutters had been in the Bering Sea to protect US schooners from foreign competitors.[67] In previous years, the few Euro-American-owned vessels the Revenue cutters had seized had been either released or cleared of all charges by Treasury officials, a fact that infuriated Canadian sealers. At the urging of W. L. Powell, the Indian agent at Neah Bay, the commissioner of Indian affairs asked the attorney general's office to provide legal protection to the schooner's owner and Makah crew. But the Office of the Attorney General refused to offer them legal protection. Unlike Euro-American owners of vessels, Makah schooner owners suffered prosecution from the federal government.[68]

Peterson then hired James Swan, after whom he had named the schooner, as his attorney to help settle the case with the government. Swan petitioned the secretary of the Treasury on Peterson's behalf, but the department declined to intervene in the case. When Judge Cornelius Hanford of the US district court decided against Peterson and ordered him to pay a $350 fine and nearly $100 in court costs, Peterson paid to get the vessel released immediately, and Swan filed an objection. He argued that the Bering Sea was an open sea and that no law of Congress could make it a *mare clausum*, or closed sea. He told the court that the ruling had made Peterson "suffer hardship and consequent loss" and that although the schooner owner would like to appeal the ruling, he lacked the financial means to do so. Swan wanted the district court to forward Peterson's case as a claim for consideration by the court of arbitration in Paris, which would be adjudicating illegal seizures of Canadian schooners by US Revenue cutters. Agent Powell concurred, asking the Office of Indian Affairs to tell him how Makahs could file for their share of the $470,000 award issued by the Paris court.[69] The department ignored this request, however, because the award applied only to British vessels seized by US Revenue cutters. During the tribunal's hearings in Paris, arbitrators made it clear that they would not consider claims of British-licensed vessels owned by US citizens. Closing a potential loophole in the settlement, the tribunal would determine claims to be valid only if British citizens owned these vessels.[70]

At the same time, Makahs of the late nineteenth century encountered local courts and judicial officials increasingly hostile to Native sealers and indigenous vessel owners. In November 1893, Koatslanhoo (Makah) leased the *Mary Parker* to Captain Frank Bangs of Seattle for coastal trading. Bangs insured the schooner and cargo in his name, scuttled it in December, and pocketed the insurance money. When Koatslanhoo sued, the federal court acquitted Bangs because he employed "able counsel" and Koatslanhoo recovered nothing, despite the jury's acknowledgment that the captain had scuttled the ship.[71] In 1895, Judge Hanford—the same official who had decided against Chestoqua Peterson several years earlier in the case of the *James G. Swan*—refused to hear the case of a white sealer, Henry Anderson, accused of murdering Philip Brown (Makah) as the two divided their catch of seals at Ozette. Although a Port Angeles judge ordered Anderson to appear before the US district court and set bail at $5,000, Hanford referred the case back to the local court, whose jury released the white murderer.[72] With growing numbers of Euro-Americans in the new state, officials and colonial juries were more interested in privileging whites over Indians.

But even in this settler-colonial regime growing increasingly hostile to American Indians, not everything hampered the ability of the People of the Cape to continue succeeding in the sealing industry. In 1894, the US and British governments agreed to follow a modified version of the recommendations of the tribunal of arbitration in Paris. Unknowingly echoing James Swan's argument from two years earlier, the Paris tribunal decided against the US claims that the Bering Sea was a mare clausum and that seals swimming in the North Pacific were exclusive government property. Instead, the tribunal made several recommendations to conserve the Pribilof herd. They proposed a closed season from May 1 to July 31 in the North Pacific and Bering Sea and prohibited firearms and other explosive devices in the hunting of seals. These conservation measures provided both confusion and opportunity for Makah sealers and schooner owners.[73]

The closed season caused some trouble for indigenous sealers. Although required to notify schooners of the beginning of the closed season, US Revenue cutters passed the Makah fleet anchored at Neah Bay for weeks without telling them of the upcoming date. Instead, in June the Revenue cutter *Grant* seized two Makah schooners, the *Puritan* and the *C. C. Perkins*, weeks after they had reportedly sealed during the closed season. Citing the fact that the cutters ignored Euro-American vessels in Puget Sound ports, even though everyone knew that they, too, had sealed illegally in the Bering Sea, Agent Powell begged Captain Dorr Tozier of the *Grant* to release the schooners. It appeared that the cutters had unfairly targeted Makah schooners once again. The cutters released the vessels only after Swan petitioned the secretary of the Treasury on behalf of the Makah owners. Makah sealers lobbied federal officials for a partial exemption to the closed season because it prohibited sealing during May, one of the best months for marine conditions off the Washington coast. Although their agent and the acting secretary of the Interior supported this request, the government failed to grant an exemption.[74]

The Paris tribunal's 1894 prohibition on firearms, however, worked in favor of indigenous sealers because they alone were proficient in the use of spears. After learning about the 1894 regulations, a local newspaper noted jealously, "Ten schooners for sealing voyages are being fitted out by the Makat Indians of Neah Bay. The fleet will be worth over $20,000, and will be entirely owned, officered and manned by aborigines. As the regulations as laid down in the Paris tribunal forbid the use of firearms in sealing, the Indians will have a decided advantage in the industry, since at handling the spear they are experts."[75] Anticipating an attitude that would resurface in many US treaty rights debates in the twentieth century, this white Canadian commentator objected to the "special rights" the regulations appeared to confer on Indians. This situation must have been especially galling to non-Natives already suffering from the global depression of the 1890s.

Under the new conservation regulations, Makah sealers did very well. During the first year of the firearms prohibition, the People of the Cape caught more than 2,500 seals off the coast of Washington. In 1895, Jongie took the *Deeahks* to the Bering Sea and brought back nearly six hundred skins after two months of hunting. According to the agent at Neah Bay, this was one of the best years for Makah sealers, who earned over $44,000 ($1.2 million today) during several months of work. The following year, the Claplanhoos hired Henry Hudson, an experienced Quileute captain, as master to take the schooner into the Bering Sea, which netted them over five hundred skins.[76] These returns compared well to those taken from the Bering Sea in the years before the Paris tribunal's regulations. This success demonstrated to the federal government and the North America Commercial Company, the new lessee of the Pribilof Islands, that the firearms prohibition was no disadvantage to experienced indigenous pelagic sealers. Further steps were necessary for conserving the herd from Indian hunters.

The late 1890s were a critical turning point for Makah sealers because national laws privileged powerful and well-connected business interests over small, family-run operations such as the Claplanhoo fleet. Darius Ogden Mills, the principal NAAC shareholder, had strong ties to the Republican Party. His political connections with President Benjamin Harrison likely helped to secure the twenty-year lease in 1890, and they probably served the company well when the Republicans took back the White House and won strong majorities in Congress in the 1896 election. Big businesses such as the North American Commercial Company supported William McKinley and contributed to his victory, so it should come as no surprise that in the first year of his presidency, McKinley backed and signed a congressional act protecting the monopolistic company at the expense of small sealing operations. This measure prohibited all US subjects from pelagic sealing in the North Pacific and Bering Sea.[77] From the perspective of the federal government and the North American Commercial Company, this legislation was necessary because the pelagic catch from 1890 to 1896 was nearly three times higher than the land catch, and pelagic hunters killed more than they caught. Coastal Natives such as the Makahs would be exempt from the prohibition, as long as they hunted seals for subsistence purposes and from canoes with spears. They would not be able to use schooners to support their hunting efforts, nor could they engage in any form of commercial sealing, the cornerstone of the economy of the People of the Cape at this time.

This new law exemplified the confusion over the legal status of American Indians at this time. Ironically, this legislation would treat Makahs as US subjects in an era when other government policies and actions limited their citizenship rights. The logic that the proposed act applied to Makah hunters stemmed from the mid-nineteenth-century assumption that American Indians, similar to slaves, were subject to US jurisdiction despite their lack of citizenship status. United States Attorney General Caleb Cushing stated this clearly in 1856: "The simple truth is plain, that the Indians are *subjects* of the United States, and are not, in mere right of home-birth, citizens of the United States. The two conditions are incompatible." More than four decades later, US Attorney General Judson Harmon came to the same conclusion, arguing specifically on the question of Makah sealers in early 1897 that they fell under the nation's laws "because they owe obedience to our laws as subject." Although some US officials and politicians disputed this legal interpretation, the prevailing opinion in Washington State was that American Indians were under the nation's jurisdiction. This was why the state's original constitution in 1889 specifically barred indigenous people from voting, with language stating "that Indians not taxed [i.e., members of federally recognized tribes, such as the Makah] shall never be allowed the elective franchise."[78] Delegates to the state's constitutional convention worried that without this specific exclusionary language, some county officials might allow members of tribal nations to vote. Technically, American Indians in Washington State could gain citizenship rights and become eligible to vote if they took individual allotments and "had adopted the habits of civilized life," as vaguely stated in the 1887 Dawes Act—indeed, some in Puget Sound did vote in the late nineteenth century.[79] But this option was not open to the People of the Cape in the late 1890s; at this time, their reservation remained un-allotted. Even if any of them did qualify, a Makah voter would then need to satisfy the voting qualifications of amendment 2 (1896), which required fluency and literacy in English.

But their "anomalous legal status" was not what concerned Makah sealers.[80] Anxious about the effects the proposed law would have on their livelihood and likely aware that the attorney general would offer them no protections, Makah leaders took action. In December 1897, the Claplanhoos led a petition effort for an exemption to the impending prohibition. The formal, typed petition and the language expressed in this document illustrated the way Makahs adapted certain non-Native strategies and the rhetoric of progress for their own cultural purposes, specifically the protection of the sovereign right to develop resources as they saw fit.[81] The petitioners began by connecting their contemporary commercial sealing activities to cultural traditions: seals had always furnished them with clothing and food. Then they invoked the specific 1855 treaty "right" to take seals forever and to never have this right limited by the government. Objecting to the meager exemption allowing Natives to seal from canoes, they worried that "permission to hunt seal in open canoe, 50 miles from shore is but permission to go to certain death." For a generation of hunters then used to the safety that schooners offered in deep ocean waters, this anxiety must have appeared all too real. They drew on assimilation rhetoric to demonstrate the progress they had made through sealing: they had invested all their "capital" in schooners and appliances for sealing, a "trade" they understood very well. Seeking the attention of fiscally conservative officials, the petitioners pointed out that they supported themselves without government aid through this industry. The petitioners also cast themselves as Christians, arguing that "God gave us the Seals for our sustenance." Finally, they attempted to appeal to a sense of fairness: "We think we ask only what is justice and equity is due us. You call us your wards and the care of our interest is in your hands, to prohibit us from Sealing would take us our livlihood, and destroy all our capital which is invested in boats and appliances for Sealing. The Misery and want which would come to us would be such as would come to your people if from them were taken at once lands and tools and stock and factories and mines and they were left to face ruin and starvation." Pelagic sealing defined them not only as Makah but also as productive members of a modern, American society. In their minds, the Makah right to seal was no different from a miner's right to extract ore, a rancher's right to raise livestock, or a factory owner's right to manufacture goods.

Despite the concerted efforts of the Claplanhoos and others, the 1897 law that prohibited pelagic sealing by US citizens ended this commercial industry for the People of the Cape. Shortly after the law's passage, Revenue cutters steamed into Neah Bay and confiscated the largest schooners, including three owned by James and Jongie. The cutters towed a dozen Makah ships to the nearby Life-Saving Service station at the western edge of Neah Bay, beaching them there, where they remained until storms and waves destroyed them. Ironically, part of the station was located on Claplanhoo land that Swan had recommended that the Department of the Interior appropriate for this coastal outpost in 1877. It must have been especially upsetting for James and Jongie to see their vessels wasting away just yards from family property. Decades later, the grandchildren of Jongie played in the rotting hulks of stolen Claplanhoo schooners.[82] Those owning smaller schooners fared slightly better. Some Makahs sold them, but with pelagic sealing outlawed, these ships sold under market value.[83]

Others turned to čaˑdiˑ borderland networks to prolong their sealing careers by looking north for employment on Canadian ships. In his first report for the new century, the Makah agent complained of ten "educated, young" Makah men who went to Victoria and shipped out on British schooners to go sealing in the Bering Sea, despite his explicit prohibition on doing so. From his perspective, the fact that they were "educated" meant that they knew they were breaking US law. Ironically, their education enabled them to read the shipping articles Canadian schooner owners in Victoria required Natives to sign, thereby making them desired crewmembers.[84]

The continued decline of the Pribilof fur seal herd at the hands of foreign sealers—and the desire of the federal government and the London fur industry to protect their long-term profits via conservation—resulted in the North Pacific Fur Seal Convention of 1911, the first such international treaty to conserve marine mammals. A year earlier, the federal government declined to renew the NACC lease of the Pribilof Islands, thereby taking over the monopoly of hunting seals on land. Through an elaborate financial arrangement, Japan, Russia, and the United States, countries that held seal rookeries, agreed to pay pelagic sealers a percentage of future annual returns. The majority of these payments went to Japanese and Canadian sealers. The US Department of Treasury bought out the sealing fleets of these two nations for $200,000 each.[85]

Funds for American and, most especially, Makah sealers were significantly smaller and more difficult to secure. When the United States began considering a buyout of foreign sealing fleets in the 1890s, they refused to consider claims made by American citizens.[86] By 1911, the US sealing fleet no longer existed, and compensating the Japanese and Canadian fleets commanded the attention of the negotiators of the Fur Seal Convention. Politicians made no plans to compensate Makah schooner owners because they assumed that they only—and had always only—hunted from canoes and for subsistence. In fact, lawmakers likely believed that Makah schooner ownership derived from government encouragement and funds, not indigenous entrepreneurial activity, a common attitude at this time.[87] In the eyes of non-Native diplomats, American Indians had lost nothing because the 1894, 1897, and 1911 regulations, laws, and conventions had enshrined subsistence hunting rights. But rather than reflecting indigenous practices, this legislation constructed a limited definition of "traditional" activities, thereby stifling innovation and entrepreneurial efforts that could have met the changing needs of the People of the Cape.[88] Under the subsistence exemption, some coastal Natives did continue sealing into the twentieth century, and they were eventually allowed to sell small quantities of skins to the reservation trader, with careful oversight from the agent. But Makah profits were never as high as they had been during the 1880s and 1890s.[89] The stereotype of the Native hunter who only kills enough to feed himself and his family encouraged non-Native officials to ignore the investments—at least more than $20,000 (over $500,000 today) in schooners from 1886 to 1897—Makahs had made in the North Pacific sealing industry.[90]

Government officials in contact with the People of the Cape appear to have known better. After passage of the 1897 law prohibiting pelagic sealing, a "Navy man" had promised Jongie Claplanhoo and other schooner owners that the government would compensate them for their losses. Jongie followed the diplomatic battle over pelagic sealing in the Bering Sea because he hoped to recover his family's financial losses. As a regular and literate visitor to Victoria, Jongie learned about the Anglo-Canadian position in local papers and from other shipowners. Canadians refused to consider any cessation of pelagic sealing unless the US government would buy them out. In 1899, Jongie wrote to James Swan, seeking information on a government plan to buy out the Victoria sealing fleet at $150 per ton, arguing that "we have all the rights to sell our Schooner the same." Years later, officials repeated these promises, albeit garbled and sometimes confusing. In 1919, Schuyler Colfax, another Makah sealer, wrote to federal officials, reminding them that "Government officials" in 1911 had promised that they could continue to hunt annually up to four thousand seals for commercial purposes, perhaps as a new concession that was part of the North Pacific Fur Seal Convention. These same officials had told the People of the Cape that if they could not hunt commercially, the government would compensate them at this amount. Because Makahs had never received any compensation, Colfax wanted permission to use his small, nine-ton *Elsie Allen* as a tender to support eight sealers who would hunt from canoes and with spears. In reply, the Indian office, informed by the commissioner of fisheries, stated that it could not grant Colfax the right to use his schooner to seal commercially.[91]

Although Makah schooner owners could sue for compensation, expensive lawsuits required years of patience and rarely guaranteed success. Thirty-one years after the passage of the 1897 law that ended pelagic sealing for Americans, Chestoqua Peterson's widow received an estimated $20,000 settlement from the government on a sealing claim she filed. However, the lawsuit cost her thousands of dollars, requiring her to borrow $1,500 from the local trader and more than $500 from other individuals. Despite decades of effort, Jongie never secured any compensation for the substantial loss of his property, an unresolved complaint that still angers his descendants.[92] During the first half of the twentieth century, few Makahs had the money to pursue these claims. Any cash they had was invested in gas-powered fishing boats and other expensive, modern gear used for halibut and salmon fishing.

As Makahs still recall, the US prohibition on pelagic sealing was a turning point that undermined their economic security. Samuel Morse, the Neah Bay agent in 1899, reported on the tribal nation's impoverishment: "There was a time once when they had plenty, when whale oil brought a good price and they were permitted to kill seal; then they had money and had everything they wanted that money could buy. At that time they owned several schooners and made regular trips to Alaska sealing, and were very successful. In their native canoes they went many miles out in the Pacific and killed whales of great size, and now the market for whale oil is gone. They are prohibited from sealing, their schooners were seized and sold."[93] Commercial pelagic sealing continued for another fourteen years by Japanese and Russian vessels and the occasional Canadian schooner. Managed by the US government, sealing also continued on the Pribilof Islands. Conservation efforts indeed saved the fur seal species and allowed for continued systematic exploitation. By 1941, the Pribilof herd had rebounded, increasing in population by an order of ten.[94] But conservation diplomacy cut out the People of the Cape from these profits, even though sealing was a customary commercial activity protected by the 1855 Treaty of Neah Bay. After the end of the nineteenth century, they could hunt seals, but now only for subsistence purposes and by using "Native" gear. Laws inaccurately recast entrepreneurial Makah sealers as anachronistic hunters separate from and irrelevant to the commercial economy of the North Pacific.

BEING MAKAH IN THE LATE NINETEENTH CENTURY

During the second half of the nineteenth century, Makah whalers and sealers strove to overcome the environmental challenges and government policies that threatened the livelihood of their people. For decades, they succeeded by combining customary practices and new opportunities to participate in the settler-colonial economy, to maintain their identity, and to push back against assimilation policies and efforts to confine them to the reservation. These labors and industries—operating schooners, hunting seals and whales, processing and selling whale oil, picking hops or fishing for wages, or hiring out their vessels to haul cargo locally or across the Pacific—did not represent a radical departure from earlier Makah economic practices. Much as they had been doing for generations, their lives revolved around the ocean, both as a highway of exchange and as a space from which they created their wealth and identity through work. In fact, the labor and capital investments of the People of the Cape exemplify a "moditional economy" that many Northwest Coast peoples practiced in the nineteenth and twentieth centuries.[95] In this way, they bridged the indigenous Northwest Coast and non-Native cultures and carved out a way to continue being Makah during a time when American Indians seemed to be under assault across Indian Country.

Long after the establishment of the boundary separating US and British territory in the Pacific Northwest, networks crossing and binding together the čaʔdiˑ borderland gave advantages to the People of the Cape as they participated in a moditional economy. Makahs continued to experience the sea as a space of connections rather than a boundary of confinement, even after decades of reservation policies and the residencies of eleven Indian agents from 1861 to the end of the century. The diaries of James Swan sketched out the contours of these networks in the early 1860s. After leaving his post as the reservation schoolteacher in 1866, Swan moved to nearby Port Townsend. Renowned as a "rascally old drunkard" suspected of "debauchery among Indian women," Swan struggled to make a living in this port at the eastern edge of the čaʔdiˑ borderland. He held numerous positions, including working for the Pilot Commissioners of Puget Sound, for the county as a probate judge, and for the Northern Pacific Railroad in helping that company choose a western terminus for its transcontinental line. Drawing on his Native contacts from Puget Sound to the Queen Charlotte Islands north of Vancouver Island, he also collected hundreds of American Indian artifacts for the Smithsonian Institution and was likely the most important collector from the Northwest Coast. In 1878, Henry Webster, a friend and former Indian agent to the Makah (1861–69), appointed Swan as customs inspector at Neah Bay, a position he held until August 1, 1881. Once again, Swan left a voluminous record of daily accounts of his time there, including more than thirteen hundred observations about the comings and goings of people to and from Cape Flattery over a three-year period, which can be plotted to uncover the contours of Makah marine space at this time.[96]

As they had in the first half of the 1860s, the People of the Cape and others in the ča·di· borderland continued to experience the coastline as a permeable zone and site of cultural interactions among diverse peoples, despite the efforts of federal officials at making and enforcing boundaries. Makahs hosted and attended potlatches with many Northwest Coast peoples, including Clayoquots, Ditidahts, Kyuquots, and Ucluelets on Vancouver Island, and Quileutes south along the Olympic Peninsula. Family ties still crossed the marine borderlands, connecting villages in ways that non-Natives sometimes misunderstood. On March 5, 1879, some Pacheedaht in-laws of Tadahie (Hosett George) brought dried salmon and potatoes across the Strait of Juan de Fuca to their Makah relatives at Neah Bay. One of the reservation traders mistakenly accused them of trafficking British goods without paying duties. At other times, Makahs took advantage of the porous nature of the marine border, especially when dealing in indigenous products. Swan suspected Makahs Beershad and Tokeva of illicitly transporting oil from Ditidaht on Vancouver Island to sawmills at Port Blakely in Washington Territory in October 1879.[97]

The frequency of Makahs, other indigenous peoples, and non-Natives coming to and from the Cape Flattery villages attests to the permeability of the reservation's marine boundary and the continuation of indigenous borderlands characteristics. Participating in these fluid borderlands dynamics rather than accepting the confinements of the reservation was a key part of being Makah in this period. More than 38 percent of Swan's observations included Makahs traveling alone, in small groups, or in the company of non-Natives or other Native peoples. This represented a slight drop (7 percent) from the 1859 to 1866 period. Percentages of non-Makah Native visitors to the People of the Cape dropped even less, from just over 15 percent in the first set to slightly under 15 percent in the second. In both cases, these reduced percentages did not result from Native peoples traveling the ocean less frequently. Instead, the number of incidents involving some indigenous maritime traveler rose in both cases during the second set of Swan's observations. Others noted Makah mobility as well. Reports of the People of the Cape traveling off-reservation showed up in local newspapers,

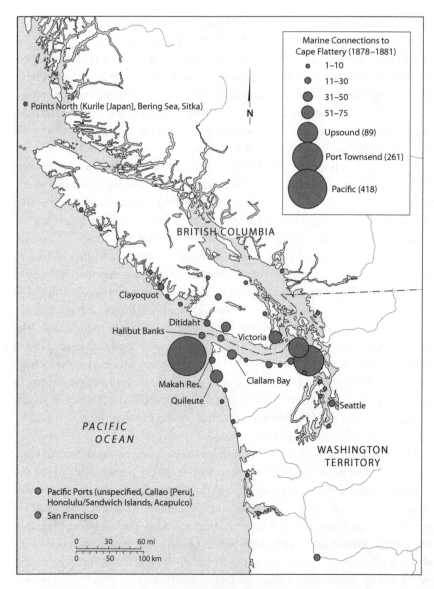

Map of the frequency of marine connections to Cape Flattery, 1878–81.
Map by Bill Nelson.

such as when a young Makah woman drowned when caught by a "large devil-fish" while swimming near Victoria during a family visit with Lekwungens.[98]

A far greater number of incidents of non-Natives crossing the reservation's maritime boundaries outpaced those of indigenous peoples from 1878 to 1881. Nearly

81 percent—and more than twice the number of specific observed incidents from the earlier period—included non-Natives. As in the early 1860s, non-Natives en route to somewhere else continued to use Neah Bay as an anchorage, coming into Makah waters for shelter or to await changing winds. The Cape Flattery villages drew non-Native vessels for trade, cargo shipments, reservation and territorial business, marine resources, and Makah labor. On February 26, 1879, the steamer *Mastick*, owned by the Mastick and Company sawmill at Port Discovery in Puget Sound, delivered to the reservation lumber that Makah laborers unloaded. Later that year, Young Siac (Makah) shipped twenty bushels of potatoes grown at Cape Flattery to Ahousaht aboard the Victoria-based schooner *Anna Beck*. In 1880, Makah hunters shipped out on the US schooner *Three Sisters* to hunt seals and sea otters off Kuril Island, Japan, and Okhotsk.[99] The increase in non-Native vessels coming into Neah Bay reflected the growth in Puget Sound and North Pacific industries and shipping. Taking advantage of these opportunities from their prime location constituted another aspect of being Makah in the late nineteenth century.

Comparing the data from Swan's two extended residencies at the reservation also reveals the changing nature of Makah relationships with settler-colonial places. The connections between the Cape Flattery villages and non-Native ports reoriented as Washington Territory grew in population and capital. The number of trips to or from the nearby British port Victoria dropped from 132 to 71 from one set to the next as local US ports such as Port Townsend (151 to 261 incidents), Seattle (3 to 26 incidents), and smaller towns in Puget Sound grew in importance. These Puget Sound towns replaced the early influence of San Francisco (55 to 22 incidents) as local networks of capital took hold and more settlers moved to the Pacific Northwest. The data also illuminate shifts in local places, as better connected and more profitable ports such as Port Townsend and Seattle eclipsed the settlements of Port Angeles (108 to 4) and Steilacoom (9 to 0).[100]

But more than just local ports connected Makahs to the settler-colonial economy of the region. Although Swan's data from 1878 to 1881 do not represent this well, the People of the Cape also engaged the regional moditional economy through networks of labor. Many Northwest Coast peoples, including Makahs, traveled deep into Puget Sound to pick hops for wages from late summer to fall, thereby illustrating another example of the contradiction between the late nineteenth-century trope of the vanishing Indian and Native workers participating in modern wage labor. Characteristic of a moditional economy, Native hop pickers combined several purposes when traveling upsound, including important pantribal gatherings outside Port Townsend on the way home from the hop fields. On August 30, 1879, Swan noted that a large number of canoes headed upsound; during the first week of October, Makah families returned to the reservation, sometimes aboard the weekly mail steamship *Dispatch* or in canoes laden with goods they had purchased at Port Townsend. Although he did not record at this time why they went upsound, a later entry illuminates the possible purpose—to pick hops. In January the following year, Agent Charles Willoughby lectured Makahs about "going to Nisqually to pick hops and told them if they had remained at home and caught salmon they would have made more money and that they would not be permitted to go to Nisqually this year." Perhaps he worried about the vices whites believed hop pickers engaged in: prostitution, smuggling, drinking, possible collective Indian action or resistance, and participation in customary practices such as Native medicine and gambling. For the rest of Agent Willoughby's time at Neah Bay, Makahs appeared to abide his prohibition on traveling upsound to pick hops. Some even followed his advice and fished for salmon instead, selling four hundred pounds after one day of fishing to a cannery at nearby Clallam Bay. However, they did not let this prohibition prevent them from attending the pantribal gatherings at Port Townsend. Swan's diaries from the autumns of 1880 and 1881 noted numerous Makahs heading to Port Townsend for a few weeks to "visit" their friends. After Agent Willoughby's departure in September 1882, Makahs resumed their travels upsound to pick hops, often stopping in at Port Townsend to see Swan. Picking hops for wages and participating in the pantribal gatherings constituted yet another component of being Makah in the late nineteenth century.[101]

By the late 1870s, competition among several steamship companies serving regular routes connecting Puget Sound and West Coast ports reshaped Makah engagement with the growing settler-colonial economy. In the early 1860s, Makahs often transported cargo, ran errands for the Indian agent, and paddled non-Natives throughout the ča·di· borderland in their canoes. Swan paid four Makah men each four buckets of potatoes—the going rate was 25 cents per bucket—for three days of paddling him around the Cape Flattery villages so he could conduct the annual census in October 1864. These labors accounted for 36 percent of all Makah travels at midcentury but only 5 percent from 1878 to 1881. When shipping rates dropped, non-Natives relied more on steamships. Regular maritime transportation networks kept the reservation traders better supplied, which likely contributed to the decline in Makah trips off-reservation to engage in trade—these incidents dropped from about 15 percent of Makah voyages to 7 percent from one period to the next. The People of the Cape also made use of these growing transportation opportunities, as they took passage or shipped cargo aboard non-Native vessels, such as when a Makah had the steamer *Mas-*

tick deliver a shipment of lumber in 1880. The increase in Puget Sound shipping brought even more ships and their crews to Neah Bay because it was a convenient and safe harbor for waiting tugboats and pilot vessels. None visited Makah villages during the early 1860s, but Swan counted 108 instances of tugboats and pilot vessels anchoring at Neah Bay later in the century.[102]

Swan's data reveal continued, yet important, changes to Makah use of local marine resources that were foundational to their identity. Compared to other maritime industries such as fishing and sealing, whaling experienced a relative decline, dropping from over 4 percent to just under 1 percent from the early 1860s to the late 1870s. This statistic highlights one of the limits of Swan's observations. The People of the Cape indeed continued whaling, which remained a culturally and commercially important activity throughout the nineteenth century, even if it did not capture the attention of this collector of customs. But living at Biʔidʔa ("bih-ih-duh") along the Strait of Juan de Fuca, about five miles from the Pacific coast villages that served as the best bases for launching whaling canoes, Swan was not in a position to note most—much less every—whale hunt. Swan's data, though, do show that Makahs continued to harvest great quantities of halibut from their fishing banks. In two days at the end of May 1880, several canoes of Makah fishers caught over 550 halibut at a time when they regularly pulled specimens weighing more than a hundred pounds from the waters off Cape Flattery.[103] By fishing customary halibut banks, the People of the Cape continued to mark these as propertied Makah places.

As collector of customs, Swan also kept track of sealing vessels during a period when Makah involvement in this industry first grew. In the early 1860s, Swan noted only a single instance of Makahs heading into the Pacific to hunt seals. Similar to the whaling counts Swan made, this number is substantially lower than it actually must have been because the best places for launching sealing canoes were the coastal villages and not Neah Bay. From 1878 to 1881, Swan counted more than 350 separate incidents of Makah sealing, which represented over 70 percent of all Makah trips off-reservation. During the coastal and pelagic sealing seasons in 1879, Swan observed forty-four times that the People of the Cape hunted pinnipeds from canoes and Anglo-owned schooners. In the 1880 and 1881 seasons, this number grew threefold as increasingly more British and US schooners hired Makah hunters. This was likely a conservative estimate because Swan could not observe the even higher frequency of sealing from coastal villages, which pairs of Makahs would have done from canoes. Throughout the rest of the century, as Makahs invested their initial profits into a fleet of schooners, this number only grew.

The Claplanhoos exemplified the ways that the People of the Cape combined new opportunities with customary practices in the moditional economy of Northwest Coast peoples to be Makah during the late nineteenth century. This family fostered ties among neighboring Indians, traders, Indian agents, and other key members of the non-Native community on both sides of the international border. One of the family's most important white contacts was James Swan. As teacher, notary, judge, secret agent for the North Pacific Railroad, deputy collector of customs, and Hawaiian consul, Swan was a useful family friend. He helped the Claplanhoos and other Makahs sort through the legal issues concerning the purchasing and licensing of schooners. When James Claplanhoo bought his first schooner, Swan helped him negotiate the deal with the previous owner, Henry Landes, and file the correct paperwork with the Customs House in Port Townsend. In later years, James and Jongie kept Swan on as the family retainer, having him file bills of sale, apply for licenses, and handle mortgage and insurance paperwork for their vessels. Family ties across the Strait of Juan de Fuca also helped the Claplanhoos in their entrepreneurial efforts, illustrated when James borrowed cash from Native relatives to purchase his first schooner. Captain John still valued recognition from chiefs across the ča·di· borderland, evident when he discussed with Swan some ways to maintain James's authority among the S'Klallams, Ditidahts, and Clayoquots.[104]

Claplanhoo success in the moditional economy of the second half of the nineteenth century relied on their ability to bring benefits and gains to their people while abiding by Makah cultural expectations. John Claplanhoo maintained his chiefly position with elaborate potlatches, some lasting nearly a month. During these ceremonial feasts, the Claplanhoo family organized and performed ritual dances, fed hundreds of guests from villages on both sides of the Strait of Juan de Fuca, and gave gifts. Claplanhoo oral histories recollect the size and scale of the potlatch held at Pacheedaht on Vancouver Island to celebrate John's marriage to Ši·ʔa·štido (Ditidaht). They invited twenty-five tribal nations from around the ča·di· borderland, feasting the guests for more than a week and giving each individual $20 in gold and several Hudson's Bay Company blankets.[105] John also raised James to be prominent in the moditional economic culture of the mid-nineteenth-century Pacific Northwest. When he went to Victoria, he often took James along so he could learn from an early age about the non-Native economy. John supported government efforts to teach his son and other children to read and write in English. He organized fifty men to help raise the schoolhouse and even lectured antsy students when they caused trouble for Swan in school. John's actions complicate the traditional narrative of indigenous resistance to non-Native education. He believed that an American educa-

Ellen + mettis   *Jimmy*   *Peter*   *capt John*

Claplanhoo family and Peter Brown, 1864. Makahs occasionally had their photographs taken when they traveled to nearby towns. This group likely sat for this photograph while visiting Victoria in April 1865. University of Washington Libraries, Special Collections, NA1410.

tion in the fledgling Neah Bay school could provide James with expanded opportunities.[106] Although John pursued opportunities to familiarize James with the settler-colonial world, at the same time he taught the boy Makah dances and saved his powerful whale medicine for him. He even arranged to have more successful whalers teach James how to whale.[107] John knew that in order for James to be a successful leader of his people, he would need to feel comfortable in British, American, and Northwest Coast societies.

Like his father, James pursued similar strategies to satisfy his people's expectations. With some of his sealing profits, he continued to host potlatches, spending an estimated $3,000 on one in 1890. During another held on Tatoosh Island three years later, the family spent $6,000 (over $150,000 today) of "American silver dollars" on food, blankets, flannels, and other goods, which they gave away to the assembled guests.[108] Fulfilling his chiefly obligations, James also spread his profits and influence in the non-Native world throughout the greater Makah

community. Beyond hiring Makah crews and captains, he helped others purchase their own schooners, loaning money and expertise to close deals. James
brought in his son-in-law Chestoqua Peterson as part owner of the *Lottie*, and
three years later, Chestoqua—probably with help from James—purchased the
Anna Beck. Although he invested in the settler-colonial economy, James did not
abandon his obligations as a chief.[109]

As his father did for him, James groomed his son Jongie for leadership in the
late nineteenth-century Northwest Coast. Born in 1877, Jongie attended the reservation school to learn English and accompanied his father to the growing towns
of Puget Sound and the Strait of Juan de Fuca. When James bought out the reservation trader, he put the teenage Jongie in charge of the store, a move supported by the Indian agent on the grounds that the young Claplanhoo would
gain a business education. Most important, James also taught Jongie about his
chiefly responsibilities. He took Jongie and his other children to potlatches and
regional Northwest Coast gatherings. Family histories recall that Jongie learned
to whale from his father, and he inherited the family's whaling gear that
had been passed down for generations.[110] James wanted Makah culture to
shape the upbringing of his children; but he also wanted them to be conversant
with the opportunities of the settler-colonial world. Made across three generations, these efforts exemplified the ways that the People of the Cape participated in a moditional economy to mark out a unique Makah identity in the late
nineteenth-century Northwest Coast.

THE MEANING OF MAKAH SUCCESS
AND THE PRICE OF POVERTY

During the second half of the nineteenth century, the People of the Cape
remained a successful and influential people in the čaꞏdiꞏ borderland. Makahs
continued to benefit from the wealth of the sea and from networks that crossed
marine space to connect them to other Native and non-Native communities.
Families such as the Claplanhoos engaged markets of exchange in a moditional
economy and made significant capital investments in North Pacific extractive
industries. Not only did this strategy make Claplanhoos and others wealthy, but
it also enabled them to strengthen their identity as Makahs in the face of mounting pressure from US assimilation policies.

The success of the Claplanhoos and others convinced various government officials, including Indian agents on the frontline of assimilation, that Makah methods worked and should receive support. Initially, federal agents tried to "civilize"
the People of the Cape by transforming them into farmers, but both the reser-

vation landscape and Makahs frustrated assimilation efforts. Nearly every Indian agent posted to this agency commented on the unsuitability of Cape Flattery for agriculture, a situation common to many reservations but most especially there.[111] Agent Charles Willoughby (1878–82) described the reservation as "mountainous and densely wooded, with a climate proverbial for its moisture, its scarcity of game, limited tracts of land fit for cultivation, and poorness of its soil . . . a country scarcely desirable for cultivation." But he did note that the wealth of the ocean made it "all that can be desired" for a "fishing people."[112] Environmental realities and successful Makahs appeared to create a difficult situation for agents such as Willoughby, tasked with assimilating American Indians through farming. Makah families who accumulated substantial wealth through customary practices—yet in very modern ways—made the case for alternative approaches.

The active participation of Makahs in marine markets of exchange integrated them into Euro-American society better than agriculture ever could. Their maritime profits convinced some agents, such as the Reverend Charles Huntington (1874–77), to recommend to the commissioner of Indian affairs that the government should civilize the Makah by encouraging fisheries and teaching trades that would support customary marine practices. Considering the cultural characteristics of the People of the Cape and their environment, Lieutenant Joseph Hays, Indian agent from 1869 to 1870, put it best when he wrote, "It would be worse than folly to attempt to change these expert fishermen into a tribe of farmers." Many believed that customary Makah marine pursuits were legitimate markers of civilization. In 1885, the agency teacher, an educated Makah, suspended school for two weeks so that the older boys could go sealing. Agent Gibson lauded Makah mariners for the benefits their labors brought the nation: "The products of the waters around Cape Flattery, which amount to many thousand dollars annually, would be lost to the country were it not for these Indians, as there are perhaps no other people who would or could take their places and obtain a support as they do, and beside produce annually what is worth thousands of dollars to the several interests of our country."[113] When families such as the Claplanhoos combined their labor with capital investments in schooners and trading posts, agents saw what they wanted to see—they believed that Makahs were distancing themselves from traditional, "savage" ways.[114]

A few non-Natives even commented that Makahs were more successful than most whites. At the close of the century, Hazard Stevens, son of Territorial Governor Isaac Stevens, reflected back on the last four decades of Washington's history, declaring that "in their remote, rocky stronghold, protected by the strong arm of the government extended over them by this treaty, but depending upon the sea and their own efforts for a livelihood, [Makahs] have prospered greatly, putting up vast quantities of fish, furs, and oil for market; and there are few white communities that have so much wealth per capita, or wealth so evenly distributed, as these industrious and manly Indians."[115] In this passage, Hazard emphasized his perspective on the legacy of his father's treaties, namely that they had protected the territory's indigenous peoples and allowed them to prosper. His assessment of Makah success reveals that many in the state recognized the important contributions this community made to the state's development.

Makah success also allowed them to confront allotment, the cornerstone of assimilation efforts, by adhering to their marine identity. In 1890, when asked by the Indian agent about dividing the reservation into individual agricultural plots, they expressed no interest. Instead, two years later they pushed for—and received—ten-acre allotments, each with frontage on Neah Bay, the Strait of Juan de Fuca, the Pacific Ocean, or one of the rivers flowing into these saltwater bodies. Individuals wanted a "fair distribution of the most desirable location on the water front," according to the Indian agent.[116] Marine-oriented Makahs rejected the pastoral and abstract "imaginative geography" that the Office of Indian Affairs attempted to create across all reservations in the United States.[117] Unfortunately, a subsequent agent voided these allotments after removing the previous agent for corruption. The new 1907 allotments—divided for paltry agricultural purposes and not oriented toward ocean access—angered many Makahs who had been pleased with the earlier division of the reservation.[118] But in the 1890s, the People of the Cape repudiated farming as the only path to civilization and rejected the stipulation that reservation lands should be allotted for agricultural purposes. By asserting their marine identity and engaging in a moditional economy, Makahs articulated culturally specific alternatives that combined customary practices, characteristics of their identity, and new opportunities presented by settler-colonialism. The success of the Claplanhoos and other Makah families even convinced off-reservation bureaucrats that the sea best supported the tribal nation. Concluding that "little can be done" to encourage farming, horticulture, and raising cattle at Cape Flattery, one federal inspector who visited the reservation in 1890 advised the community to continue relying on marine resources. Subsequent federal officials in the Interior Department came to the same conclusions, arguing that "there seems little hope of the Indians doing anything in the way of agriculture" and that they "[get] along very well" from sealing and fishing.[119]

By the close of the nineteenth century, the situation for the People of the Cape had changed. Oral histories recall that the century's end marked a turning point: Congress made it illegal for Makahs to engage in commercial pelagic sealing, Revenue cutters confiscated the best Makah vessels, and families became poor.

The Barker family on the beach at Neah Bay, 1910. Sonny Barker and his family pose with a whale he recently hunted. Photograph by Asahel Curtis. University of Washington Libraries, Special Collections, NA664.

Former sealers and whalers even tried their hand at farming because customary marine practices that had made them wealthy were no longer tenable. Restrictions on maritime pursuits discouraged Makah families from living at some coastal villages, such as Ćuʼyas ("tsoo-yuhs"), Waʔač ("wuh-uhch"), and Ozette. Another government policy accelerated abandonment of these villages. At the end of the nineteenth century, when the reservation school switched to a day school system and required all Makah children to attend, many families from the Pacific villages relocated to Neah Bay to live closer to their children. Those who grew up in Neah Bay while attending school in the early decades of the twentieth century then settled there afterward instead of returning to the old villages. By the 1940s, only a few old people remained at the most distant village of Ozette. The days of suspending school to allow Makah boys to hunt sea mammals were over. Instead, teachers at the Neah Bay day school focused more intently on a curriculum taught at Indian schools across the nation, teaching Makah children farming skills, making and repairing harnesses, blacksmithing, horseshoe making, woodcutting, silversmithing, sewing, keeping house, and staying clean. Increased missionary efforts and a rigid government education system altered customary social and spiritual systems, especially those tied to the ocean.[120]

At a glance, the example of Makah whalers and sealers might resemble a narrative of declension common to most histories of American Indians. Their story, however, complicates many usual assumptions. The example of the Claplanhoos overturns the stereotype that Natives are "traditional" and have no role in a "modern" world. Individuals such as John, James, Jongie, and others combined modern opportunities and technologies with customary marine practices to maintain a Makah identity. They purchased schooners, trading posts, and hotels and deposited money in local banks. Many of their financial dealings and commercial activities followed the older but still relevant networks of the ča·di· borderland, while others took advantage of the more recent international border separating the United States from Canada. With new equipment, they expanded their marine space into the Bering Sea. At the same time, they hosted extravagant potlatches, used their influence and money to help other Makahs, and passed on their cultural values to sons and daughters. During the first four decades after the 1855 Treaty of Neah Bay, many Makahs profited in their moditional economy. They used their success to blunt the harshest edges of federal assimilation policies, even shaping some to fit their unique maritime needs.

Makah whalers and sealers also confronted significant environmental and legal challenges during the late nineteenth century. As whale numbers decreased, they scaled back commercial whaling to a moderate level that they could sustain into the twentieth century. When seals became harder to find in local waters, they took to the high seas in larger vessels. They wrote letters, signed petitions, and hired lawyers to protect rights they had secured for themselves in the treaty. Once again, they pursued strategies that adapted modern opportunities and technologies within their own cultural framework.

But Makah sealers found themselves on the losing side of a battle over a valuable marine resource. The federal government and the London fur industry used conservation measures to cut smaller, independent pelagic sealers out of a profitable industry. The wasteful practices of gun-wielding, non-Native pelagic sealers made the entire industry an easy target on the international stage of conservation diplomacy. At the same time, regulations, laws, and conventions redefined the role of indigenous sealers by limiting them to the stereotype of the Native subsistence hunter. This codified into law the assumption that indigenous peoples could not be modern and denied most Makah sealers compensation rights that were extended to non-Native sealers.

Just how "anomalous" were the Makah of the second half of the nineteenth century? Other indigenous peoples also thrived in complex moditional economies and environments that non-Natives found hostile and challenging. The story of the Claplanhoos and other Makah whalers and sealers forces us to set aside the assumption that Natives cannot be prosperous and dynamic on their own terms. Instead, they exemplify the larger narrative of indigenous peoples who engaged modernity within their own cultural framework and in order to pursue their own ends.[121] Perhaps the only anomaly was the way in which some government officials perceived Makahs as so different from other American Indians.

6

"Everything Is Played Out Here"

In April 1959, Makahs received the bad news. The Indian Claims Commission (ICC) had dismissed the tribal nation's case against the federal government. In *Makah v. United States*, the People of the Cape (Makahs) had filed for $10 million in damages for the curtailment of their halibut fishing rights guaranteed by the 1855 Treaty of Neah Bay. As lawyers for the tribe had argued, the United States had not upheld the Makahs' right to take halibut at offshore fishing banks; instead, it had "virtually destroyed" opportunities at their usual and accustomed grounds in marine space.[1] After decades of overfishing, the halibut industry had reached a critical point. By the mid-twentieth century, Makah participation in this fishery was a far cry from what their fathers and grandfathers in 1855 had envisioned when they reserved fishing rights for the tribal nation in perpetuity.

In his final opinion on the case, Chief Commissioner Edgar E. Witt noted the similarities between the Northern Pacific halibut fishery and pelagic sealing of the previous century. "Both ran the gamut from early superabundance to massive, reckless exploitation bordering upon complete destruction of the species, to government intervention through international agreements and regulation to conserve and rehabilitate seal and halibut," he wrote. But Makahs' experience with conservation regulations in these two North Pacific extractive industries shared another similarity: the legal power of the state limited Indian treaty rights to subsistence. Commissioner Witt ruled that the petitioners (Makah Tribe) had provided no evidence that "in complying with these regulations the Makah Indian is unable to take sufficient halibut to sustain his immediate wants or those of his family." Leaving no room for misinterpretation, Witt wrote, "The Commission, therefore, is of the opinion that the Makah fishing rights reserved under the 1855 treaty are in no sense commercial rights, and on the contrary mean simply that the Makah Indians, as in the case of other west coast fish eating Indians, were to continue to have the right of taking fish and other marine products from the usual and accustomed places in order to satisfy immediate wants and provide the necessary sustenance for themselves and their families consistent with their then subsistence economy." From his perspective, treaty rights belonged in the Native subsistence past and had no bearing on the present commercial fishing activities of the People of the Cape.[2]

As they waited nearly a decade for the ICC decision, Makahs likely hoped that fairness would prevail and that they would receive vindication for the diminishment of treaty fishing rights. The final decision dismissing the case, though disappointing, was not entirely unexpected. Since the 1880s, Makah halibut fishers had faced increasing competition from non-Native commercial fishers. Local fishing banks that had once been Makah-owned property became exhausted in the early twentieth century, and commercial fishers had to expand to grounds farther out to sea and north off the coasts of British Columbia and Alaska. To maintain profits, independent fishers needed larger, faster, and more expensive boats that enabled them to bring catches to market from increasingly distant fishing grounds and that allowed them to participate in other fisheries. With little to no access to cash or loans until after World War II, Makah commercial fishers fought to keep up. Unlike the previous generation, when "Indian babies played on the floor with $20 gold pieces, and individual Indians ha[d] been known to receive at one time for their seals more than $20,000," the Cape Flattery community struggled financially during the first half of the twentieth century.[3]

As halibut and salmon stocks became overfished, Washington State, British Columbia, the United States, and Canada implemented a range of domestic regulations and initiated international efforts to conserve what remained. Indigenous marine property was replaced with a colonial paradigm of a highly regulated commons that favored non-Natives over indigenous people. Facing regulations that privileged white commercial and sports fishing, American Indian fishers such as Makahs found themselves targeted by state fish and game wardens when they tried to access the off-reservation usual and accustomed grounds and stations their ancestors had reserved in the 1855 treaty. On the reservation, impoverished Makahs of the early twentieth century found themselves with far less autonomy than before as a progression of unsupportive and unsympathetic Indian agents—then called superintendents—attempted to control their lives and turn them from the sea.

These assaults on their culture and livelihood galvanized the People of the Cape to fight back. Empowered by the Indian Reorganization Act and an administrative consolidation of western Washington Indian agencies in 1933, Makah leaders pursued legal and political strategies to regain access to and control over tribal marine space and its resources. From the 1940s on, local and federal courts became the tribal nation's new battlegrounds. As one of the plaintiffs in the landmark *United States v. Washington* (1974), Makahs finally gained their fair commercial share of the salmon and steelhead fisheries. However after 1976, Makahs found themselves shut out from their most productive marine fishing banks, Swiftsure and 40-Mile (La Perouse) Banks, which ended up under Canadian jurisdiction after that nation declared an exclusive fishery zone in accordance with emerging international protocols on extending marine jurisdiction farther offshore. This hardening of the international border and Canada's subsequent efforts at keeping Makah fishers out of these waters challenged the ča·di· borderland the People of the Cape had relied on for generations and undermined the way they experienced the sea as a space of connections. Further litigation became necessary for tribal members to secure their treaty-guaranteed share of the offshore, marine halibut fishery in domestic waters. These developments in the twentieth century demonstrate that as Makahs increasingly lost access to their marine space and resources through overfishing by non-Natives, state regulations, and international agreements, they fought back with a variety of legal and political strategies to carve out a future dependent on continued access to the sea.

MAKAHS AND THE COMMERCIAL HALIBUT AND SALMON FISHERIES

Contrary to Commissioner Witt's opinion in the 1959 ICC case, the Makah halibut fishery had long been far more than one simply geared for sustenance. Like other Northwest Coast indigenous communities, the People of the Cape engaged in longstanding efforts to control marine space for both subsistence and commercial purposes.[4] Before outside forces encroached, Makahs had ably balanced these two purposes. This is not to claim that Makahs lived in some Edenic marine wonderland before the arrival of Euro-Americans. Instead, they probably came to this balance through hard-won generations of trial and error, and not without contestation from neighboring peoples throughout the ča·di· borderland. Initially consumer demands for fresh and canned fish from the Pacific Northwest provided Makahs with an opportunity for succeeding financially from a customary practice, much as they had done in the fur seal industry. Yet rising demands of the market economy from the late nineteenth century and competition from better capitalized non-Native fishers in the first half of the twentieth century destabilized the balance, skewing it toward commerce at the expense of consumption, thereby separating Makahs from their marine foods. At the same time, the profits that Makahs could make from commercial fishing became increasingly meager as non-Natives squeezed them off their fishing grounds. These factors undermined the tribal nation's economic foundation.

For at least three thousand years, the People of the Cape exploited numerous fish species for consumption and commerce. Most important were the *šuyuʔ* ("shoo-yoolth," halibut) they took from many fishing banks located offshore in tribal marine space. The North Pacific halibut (*Hippoglossus stenolepis*) is a bottom fish, with both its eyes generally on the right side oriented toward the water's surface. Reaching maturity in eight years, males are seldom heavier than forty pounds, whereas females mature in twelve years and occasionally exceed three hundred pounds; some live past thirty years. Ranging along the continental shelf from Santa Barbara, California, to Nome, Alaska, near the Bering Strait, halibut can be found from fifteen to two hundred fathoms underwater.[5] When feeding, they concentrate in great numbers on specific banks, such as *ƛušuʔaˑ* ("kloo-shoo-ah") and *ƛuƛubaƛid* ("lthoo-lthoo-buh-lthihd"), two of the most important Makah fishing grounds, located fifteen and forty miles respectively from Cape Flattery. These names highlight the indigenous knowledge that Makah fishers possessed: *ƛušˑʔaˑ* means "the dry place on the rocks" or "shallow place," indicating the shallow nature of this bank; *ƛuƛubaƛid* means "fish lying like boards on the surface of the ocean," a reference to halibuts' behavior of feeding on smaller fish close to the surface at night. More commonly, these Makah banks are respectively known as Swiftsure Bank, named after the HMS *Swiftsure*, which surveyed the area in the 1880s, and La Perouse Bank, named in honor of Jean-François de La Pérouse, the French explorer who sounded the bank in 1786 and later disappeared in Oceania.

These and other fishing banks were places embedded in Makah waters within the *čaˑdiˑ* borderland. Native vessels crossed La Perouse Bank when going between Neah Bay and Nootka Sound and traveled over Swiftsure Bank en route to and from Barkley Sound. According to Makah oral histories, ancestors found Swiftsure when returning from whaling. The whalers spotted sea lions feeding on halibut, so they took cross-bearings on Tatoosh Island, Waadah Island in Neah Bay, and the highest peak on Vancouver Island. The next day they returned with their gear and "filled the canoe with halibut in a little while, and came home happy and shouting from far out to sea." Over time, they discovered and named čaʔad(i)łačakt ("tsuh-uh-dih-lthuh-chukt"), the quickest current to Swiftsure. Other important banks included Umatilla Bank, four to five miles offshore from Ozette; the Big Prairie, about thirty-five to forty miles southwest of Cape Flattery; q̓ata·yaq̓a· ("kuh-tai-yuh-kah") offshore south of Cape Flattery; dacša·dit ("duh-chah-diht," Skookum Bank), three miles off Ču·yas ("tsoo-yuhs"); Blue Water Bank, about sixty miles off the coast; and banks east in the Strait of Juan de Fuca, off the mouths of the Hoko and Seiku Rivers, and others close to Pacheedaht and the San Juan Islands. As Makah fisher Charles Peterson recalled in 1949, these banks "were quite heavy with halibut" from mid-April through July in the early twentieth century. Although the grounds in the strait produced fewer halibut than those in the ocean, these were critical fishing banks that Makahs depended on when the ocean was too rough. A 1941 survey of the Makah Tribal Council revealed that they still knew the names of 114 places related to halibut, fishing, and gathering seafood in their marine space and coastal landscape.[6]

Although halibut was more important to the subsistence and commercial needs of the People of the Cape, many families also fished for salmon. Nearly all the millions of salmon that swam up the Fraser River or into Puget Sound first went through the ča·di· borderland and Makah waters en route to their natal streams to spawn and die. Before the advent of the commercial salmon industry in the late eighteenth century, Makah fishers trolled for salmon at specific marine fishing grounds and used nets, gaffs, spears, and traps in local waterways, such as the Hoko, Lyre, Seiku, Pysht, and Clallam Rivers and Lake Ozette.[7]

As in sealing and whaling, Makahs used specific gear and methods that reflected their knowledge of fish species and especially habitat. In a 1905 newspaper article designed to interest prospective shoppers in Puget Sound fish markets, Makah fisher Henry Markishtum explained his people's method of catching halibut. Fishers left the villages and summer camps before dawn in order to reach the banks by noon. On arrival, a fisher cast out his line carrying a sinker and two specially designed hooks made from the knot of a hemlock or yew. Known as a čibu·d ("chih-bood"), these hooks were curved so that yača?a· ("yuh-chuh-ah," dogfish) infesting the halibut banks slipped off when they struck, whereas the intended prey rarely escaped once they bit. They used octopus for bait, knowing that halibut prefer it while dogfish avoid it. In Markishtum's account, the sinker pulled the line sixty fathoms to the fishing bank. Once the halibut—or sometimes two—took the hook, "then [came] the tug-of-war, the halibut has bit the curved genius." After pulling up the sixty fathoms of line, a feat that often required wearing several pairs of gloves to protect the hands, the fisher then clubbed the halibut dead and hauled it over the edge of

Makah *čibu·d* ("chih-bood") recovered at Ozette. Makah fishers preferred
this specially curved design to non-Native gear because it kept halibut on
the hook while dogfish that infest the Cape Flattery banks slipped off.
Photograph by Mike Short, from the Ruth Kirk Collection, courtesy the
Makah Cultural and Research Center, Neah Bay, WA.

the canoe. In an afternoon, several fishers in a canoe thirty to thirty-five feet
long could fill their vessel with ten to forty halibut, depending on the size.[8]

Once ashore, women pulled out "butcher knives, sharp as razors," and cedar
bark mats for cleaning the catch on the beach. According to Markishtum, "Those
dexterous with the knife seize[d] the halibut, chop[ped] the head off with a single

jab . . . , clean[ed] the internal section and wash[ed] it thoroughly" with saltwater. When processing halibut for winter storage and trade with other Indians,
women cut the fish into *pitas*, full-length, ribbon-thin strips. Without the aid of
salt, they first sun-dried the strips on racks and then brought them into the "warm
houses" to smoke when partially dry. Captain J. W. Collins of the US Department of Fisheries steamer *Albatross* described two large warm houses in 1888:
"These are barn-like structures, one of which is 66 feet long, and the other 92
feet long, 42 feet wide, 14 feet high on the walls, and 32 feet to the ridge pole. A
smudge fire of driftwood is kept burning at each end of the building, and around
this is a light lattice framework about 10 feet high, upon which are hung strips
of fish and blubber for smoking. Along both sides of the building, for its entire
length, are raised platforms, about 5 to 6 feet wide, and 1 foot high. These are
covered with matting and skin robes of various kinds, upon which the Indians
sleep or recline. In the center of the warm-house is an earthen floor that is frequently used for dances." In addition to these large structures, Makahs kept "many
small smokehouses," separate from their cottages. Once the strips were dry,
women kneaded the halibut pieces, softening and flattening them before bal-
ing and packing them away in blankets and boxes. When processed this way,
halibut lost three-fourths of their weight but remained edible for a year. Because
this was such a critical source of food and trade good, "Makahs [took] more care
and pains in drying halibut than in the preparation of any other article of food."
The Indian agent at Neah Bay in the early 1870s, E. M. Gibson, noted that Makahs
spent the summer procuring and processing the fish they needed for the winter.
They also preserved the gills, backbones, and heads for soups and oils.[9]

Because it was so important, nearly everyone fished. Hillary "Zab" Irving recalled that he began fishing at the age of seven in the early twentieth century
while living at Ozette. His grandfather started him on salmon, rigging him up,
putting him in a canoe, and sending him out to get his first fish. Irving's gear
likely consisted of a set of bladder floats affixed to lines baited with herring that
drifted behind his canoe, a common method Makah fishers used to catch silver
salmon. When he got older, he started fishing for halibut in the open ocean.
Learning to fish at a young age was common: Henry St. Clair recalled learning
at the age of nine from his grandfather, Old Doctor; Henry McCarty started
fishing halibut on Swiftsure Bank at the age of ten. Men and women fished together, which was something commented on by both Irving and Daniel
Quedessa and captured in photographs. Women also fished on their own, including Nora Barker, who continued after her husband drowned near Destruction Island in 1917. He had showed her the best spots because they had fished
together before his death.[10]

Makahs with their halibut catch on the beach at Neah Bay, 1903. Women hunker down in the foreground, cleaning the fish and preparing it for sale to a fish buyer or for drying for their families' winter supply. Photograph by Albert Henry Barnes. University of Washington Libraries, Special Collections, NA1107.

Working in this way, the People of the Cape harvested and preserved staggering quantities of fish. In 1880, James Swan estimated that the Makah, a community of 728 individuals, annually took more than 1.5 million pounds of fresh halibut. This statistic is a reasonably accurate figure because at this time Swan worked for the Department of the Interior as special agent of the Census Bureau in fish and fisheries. If anything, Swan underestimated the statistic. In separate interviews in the 1930s with Roger Chute, a Stanford economist, Makah elders Henry St. Clair and Sebastian LaChester noted that a family typically dried two hundred to four hundred halibut, depending on their size, for winter use, along with a hundred and fifty to three hundred silver salmon and two hundred to three hundred pounds of dried whale blubber. Assuming a conservative weight of thirty-five pounds per halibut, this meant that Makahs dried just over a million

Young Doctor with his family and a load of black rockfish, ca. 1905. Families often fished together. Photograph by Samuel G. Morse. Bert Kellogg Collection of the North Olympic Library System.

pounds of fresh halibut, along with another three thousand pounds of salmon.[11] And these numbers from Saint Clair and LaChester would have just been for their personal winter stock, not including fish Makahs traded to neighboring Indians or sold to non-Natives. To gain some perspective on an annual of harvest of 1.5 million pounds, consider that in 1891, the entire American fishing fleet, in 129 separate trips, landed over 1.8 million pounds of fresh halibut at Gloucester, Massachusetts, from the Western Bank off Nova Scotia, the most lucrative halibut bank in the Atlantic Ocean off the coast of North America that year.[12]

In addition to the large quantity processed for the winter, Makahs also traded halibut among themselves and to Native communities across the ča·di· borderland and beyond. In 1942, experienced Makah fishers born in the 1870s explained to attorney Edward Swindell, hired by Commissioner of Indian Affairs John Collier to conduct a detailed study on the treaty rights of Pacific Northwest Indians, that "all Makahs did not use all of the various places and as a consequence those from each place would trade their kind of fish for the kind caught at the other places."[13]

Makah couple, Neah Bay, ca. 1900. Husbands and wives commonly fished together.
Photograph by Anders B. Wilse, courtesy Museum of History and Industry, Seattle.

For example, the fishers from Lake Ozette caught a very tasty and long-lasting
salmon, while those who fished at Shi Shi, a Pacific beach located north of Ozette,
also caught smelt. The range of fish Makahs caught facilitated abundant trade
among the Cape Flattery villages. In 1861, the People of the Cape also traded
"great quantities" of dried halibut packed in baskets to other Indians. On the west
coast of Vancouver Island, British Indian agent W. E. Banfield observed that
"the [Makah] halibut fishery forms a great article of traffic with neighboring tribes,
with whom the fish are exchanged for potatoes, blankets, cummasse [camas], and
other articles of food, clothing, or ornament," as they had done for generations.
These neighbors included Nuu-chah-nulths on Vancouver Island, Quinaults and
Quileutes south of Cape Flattery, and S'Klallams to the east. In the late nineteenth and early twentieth centuries, fleets of Makahs regularly paddled deep into
Puget Sound, trading dried halibut with Squaxins for dried clams and with Puyallups for clams, spring salmon, and boxes of dried berries. The fact that halibut
could be converted into durable goods increased the value of this trade item.[14]

Makah fishers chose to work particular banks at specific times in order to get distinctive types of halibut to meet their subsistence and commercial needs. When fishing for their winter supply, Makahs selected a specific fishing bank for the size of halibut they wanted. In July, fishers pulled up thirty-to-forty-pound halibut, ideal for preserving because these lasted the longest. In the fall, they specifically fished the northern portion of Swiftsure for "chicken halibut," small ones from ten to twenty pounds. Because there was not enough time at this point in the season to preserve them properly, families ate this supply of dried fish first. Halibut over one hundred pounds tended to be slimy, with flesh that did not preserve well, so families ate these fresh. Halibut processed for the market differed from what they caught for winter eating, so fishers selected specific banks at particular times to provide fish for immediate trade.[15]

When non-Natives appeared in Makah waters and the c̆a·di· borderland, the People of the Cape offered fresh fish to the newcomers for trade. Crewmembers of Robert Gray's *Columbia* commented on the halibut they purchased from Makahs from 1789 through 1792. Similarly, Hudson's Bay Company vessels such as the *Dryad* and *Columbia* often traded for fresh fish in addition to the whale products they bought from the Cape Flattery villagers in the 1830s and 1840s; many Makah salmon ended up in barrels that the Hudson's Bay Company shipped throughout the Pacific and to London. As increasingly more non-Natives settled in Puget Sound, boats often stopped at Neah Bay and nearby summer camps, trading sugar, pilot bread, molasses, and liquor for fish. Schooners sailing from Hawai'i to Puget Sound ports in the second half of the nineteenth century also stopped at Neah Bay, the first opportunity to fill water casks and procure fresh fish after having been at sea for weeks. Long before non-Native commercial fisheries began, Makahs had been selling halibut and salmon and engaging new markets for it.[16]

The People of the Cape also occupied a central role when non-Natives explored the commercial possibilities of the Pacific halibut fishery. In August 1857, four white Americans from California—including Henry Webster, who later became the first full-time Indian agent assigned to Neah Bay—settled at Bahaada Point to trade for fish, oil, and furs. Halibut was one of the goods they bought and attempted to market elsewhere. In the first month of their operation, they put up a hundred barrels of halibut. A year later, Banfield noted that the Americans, "who located themselves at Cape Flattery, last autumn, for the purpose of curing fish, and establishing a general trade among the Indians, have succeeded far beyond their expectations. They have this summer cured large quantities of halibut, and shipped them to San Francisco and China, for some of which I am credibly informed they netted large profits." Still exerting control over their marine space, Makahs refused to let these traders do the fishing themselves.[17]

By 1862, Webster was Indian agent at Neah Bay, and he lobbied the federal government to support Makah fisheries. Although Webster wanted to profit from marketing halibut, his requests likely reflected the desire of Makahs to sell their fish. In his second annual report, Webster asked the government to provide the tribe with nets, salt, and a cooper to make barrels for "proper[ly] . . . preparing their fish for sale" to non-Native customers. The government never honored these requests, but Makahs continued to sell their fish when they could, such as to two sailing vessels from Port Angeles that anchored at Q̓idi·q̓abit ("kih-dee-kuh-biht") in the summer of 1864 to get cargoes of fresh halibut for local markets in their homeport and Port Townsend. In 1878, the schooner *Letitia* sailed to Neah Bay, and the captain reported that "the Indians brought [halibut] in such number that he with his crew of men could not handle them rapidly enough and consequently they were forced to turn many away. He thought he could have loaded a clipper ship in a few day's time." These scattered anecdotes provide a glimpse of the substantial commercial scale of the Makah fishery well before a white court dismissed the existence of this kind of activity.[18]

Subsequent agents repeated some form of Webster's requests, which actually reflected the Makahs' continued desire to find new markets for their halibut. Agent Charles Huntington lamented in his 1874 report that "if they had the proper appliances for preparing these fish for commerce a large revenue might be derived from them, for the finest salmon and halibut in the world abound in these waters." Two years later, he advocated teaching Makah children trades that would augment their fisheries. The next Indian agent emphasized the Makah desire to learn the latest methods of curing and packaging fish for non-Native customers, concluding in 1881 that "with a little assistance and proper teaching in this branch of industry, but few years would elapse before the Indians of this reservation would rival in wealth any equal number of any nationality in the most favored locality of the older States." The next year, he repeated the Makahs' request, adding that "they have learned that the fruits of their [marine] labors have a market value." With an unlimited supply of halibut, the missing piece was an efficient way to get it to non-Native markets.[19] As in the past, the People of the Cape took the initiative on trying to overcome this impediment. By 1886, Makahs were selling halibut in Victoria and towns farther upsound and supplying fresh fish to sawmills, along with oil for lubricating machinery and greasing logging skids. In the 1880s, a small group of two-man sailing sloops, each carrying up to three thousand pounds of fish to markets in Victoria, Nanaimo, Vancouver, Port Townsend, and other nearby ports, bought from Makahs.[20]

A distinct change came in 1888. The commercial Pacific halibut fishery began shifting from one in which Makahs did all the fishing on tribally and family-owned halibut banks to one dominated by non-Native fishers. That year, three sizable schooners arrived from Massachusetts, encouraged to head to the North Pacific by a series of 1886 letters in the New England *Cape Ann Advertiser*. The *Oscar and Hattie*, *Edward E. Webster*, and *Mollie Adams* came to engage in pelagic sealing and to fish for halibut during the offseason. Headquartered at Port Townsend, the *Oscar and Hattie* docked at Tacoma with 50,000 pounds of fresh halibut from Makah fishing grounds on September 20, 1888; from this Puget Sound port, the fish were iced and shipped to Boston via the Northern Pacific Railroad. But as observers noted, "Little or nothing was realized from the trip" because of the high cost of ice and exorbitant rates charged by the railroad. Earlier that summer, the *Mollie Adams* also fished Makah banks. After four three-day trips to Swiftsure, Captain Solomon Jacobs's schooner landed 145,000 pounds of fresh halibut at Seattle, all bound for East Coast cities. The *Mollie Adams* returned to Cape Flattery that fall for another fresh halibut trip, but poor fishing and storm delays resulted in a low-quality catch on arrival in Seattle. Although Jacobs's schooner earned a modest profit for its crew, the expensive ice, high shipping rates, and long distance from the fishing banks to Puget Sound ports discouraged him. By March of the following year, Jacobs had sold his schooners to a Port Townsend businessman.[21]

Minimizing the earlier Makah attempts at engaging fish markets, most point to the *Oscar and Hattie*'s 1888 halibut shipment to Boston as the beginning of the commercial Pacific halibut fishery. Yet there was a major difference between what Makahs did before and the fishing activities of this year: the exponential increase in gear used, and thereby fish caught, and fishing done by non-Makahs. Both the *Oscar and Hattie* and the *Mollie Adams* fished with dories, small, two-person oared boats deployed on the fishing banks. As in the northwest Atlantic, dory fishers set and retrieved skates of gear on a bank. In the 1880s, skates were composed of ten fifty-fathom lines with gangings—shorter lines connecting the hook to the main line—spaced every nine feet; on the average, each skate carried 310 hooks. The *Oscar and Hattie* fished with six dories, each setting two skates of gear—a total of 620 hooks—per day. The *Mollie Adams* carried eight dories, each setting four skates of gear twice a day, or 2,480 hooks daily. At that time, a Makah canoe averaged 250 pounds of halibut per afternoon. Landing 50,000 pounds of fish after a three-day trip, the *Oscar and Hattie*'s six dories each averaged about 2,775 pounds per day of fishing, an elevenfold increase over Makah fishers. Dory fishing was well suited for the early years of the commercial Pacific halibut fishery, when the Cape Flattery banks still carried abundant quantities of fish.[22]

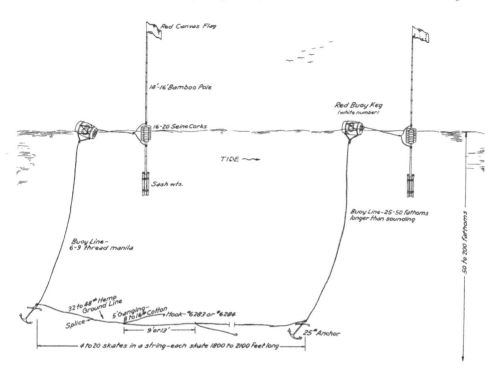

Diagram of halibut gear as set by non-Native fishermen. Dories and then larger vessels themselves set fishing gear in this way so they could retrieve it later once halibut had taken the hooks. Image courtesy the International Pacific Halibut Commission.

Although profits from the first schooners remained minimal, their activities demonstrated the potential for the fishery and encouraged its growth. With Atlantic supplies of halibut dwindling and an increasing demand for this fish in growing East Coast cities, more non-Natives sought Makah banks off Cape Flattery. The reservation agent's 1891 report noted that a "mosquito fleet of about twenty fishing boats, and four or five schooners manned by white men" fished for halibut and caught "enormous quantities of fish." The schooners regularly took 25,000 to 35,000 pounds of fish, which they shipped east by rail from Seattle. The *New York Times* reported that from September through November of 1891, about 600,000 pounds of salmon and halibut from Puget Sound and Makah banks off Cape Flattery had been packed in refrigerator cars and sent east to Chicago and New York City, where they arrived in "perfect" shape and "sold well."[23]

In earlier years, the People of the Cape had kept non-Natives from fishing their halibut banks, so what had changed by the early 1890s? One important factor was demographic. In 1857, the year Makahs prohibited Webster and his

companions from fishing, the Makah numbered around 600; by 1888, the year
that the *Oscar and Hattie* and *Mollie Adams* first fished off Cape Flattery, their
population had fallen to 492. While Makah numbers dropped, the population
of non-Natives in the region had increased from 11,594 in 1860 to 349,390 in
1890.[24] Makahs also faced other threats in 1888 when the first non-Native schooners fished for halibut. Agent Powell noted that they had picked up measles
while laboring in Puget Sound hop fields, and "many children died." Two years
later, disease struck their children again—forty-six of the fifty children attending the agency school caught influenza, and the Makah population dropped to
454. Perhaps Makahs worried more about their sick and dying children than
about non-Natives encroaching on tribal halibut banks. In addition, wealthier
Makahs were focused on building their capacity to hunt seals at this time, whereas
those of lesser means possibly saw the initial arrival of non-Native schooners as
an opportunity to sell fish they caught. Regardless, Makahs came to resent the
presence of whites on their fishing grounds. In 1891, Agent John McGlinn captured their reaction: "The Indians view with jealousy the encroachments of the
white men on what they have always regarded as their exclusive possessions,
and find for the first time in their history that white competition has overstocked,
and will I am afraid eventually take from them a market of which heretofore
they have had almost a monopoly." Unlike Webster more than two decades
earlier, McGlinn cared more about controlling Makahs and suppressing cultural practices such as the potlatch than finding ways to help them develop
their fisheries for self-sufficiency.[25]

Another important change included the scale and intensity of the non-Native
Pacific halibut fishery, which grew quickly from 1888 to 1915. Aggregate annual
landings by US and Canadian fishing vessels went from just under 1.5 million
pounds to nearly 69 million pounds, a forty-six-fold increase over this period.
Technological advances intensified the fishery, and specific ports, such as Vancouver and Tacoma, became leading places for landing and shipping halibut
across the continent. Fishing companies invested in new steamers that overcame
some of the limitations of sail-powered vessels and could carry up to 310,000
pounds of iced halibut, thereby extending the fishing range into waters farther
from homeports and intensifying the harvest on closer ones. The Puget Sound
Fish Company sent the *Francis Cutting* to Cape Flattery twice each week during the summer of 1892, purchasing up to thirty tons of fish each trip from Makah
and white fishers. The halibut were packed on ice, transported to Puget Sound,
and then shipped to New York. Smaller, engine-powered schooners rose in prominence, and by 1900, the gas-powered, owner-operated schooner became the industry standard. With the largest dealers of schooner fish located in Seattle, these

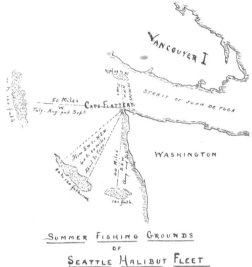

SUMMER FISHING GROUNDS
OF
SEATTLE HALIBUT FLEET

Summer fishing grounds of Seattle halibut fleet,
1906. These fishing grounds were actually
Makah-owned halibut banks that the non-Native
fleet commandeered in the 1890s. Sketch from
Pacific Fisherman Annual, 1906, 79. Image
courtesy the Freshwater and Marine Image Bank
at the University of Washington, Seattle.

independently owned vessels made this port the center of the Pacific industry
by 1905. As halibut numbers declined, crews became less enthusiastic about dangerous dory fishing, and schooners focused on long-lining. Long-liners paid out
lines of six or eight skates of gear at a time over the stern of a vessel and later
collected the skates with motorized gurdies and powered winches. During the
spring and summer, schooners and some larger boats worked Makahs' Cape Flattery banks. In the winter, much of the fleet fished halibut banks in southeastern
Alaska and the Queen Charlotte Islands.[26]

As the halibut fishery grew, so did the region's canned salmon industry, which
came of age in the 1890s. The first canneries on the Fraser River opened in 1870.
Forty-nine canneries—plus one at Clayoquot, close to Makah fisheries—operated
on the Fraser by 1901, and together they packed over a million cases that year.
During the 1870s, various salmon companies opened in Puget Sound, including one at Clallam Bay, just east of the Makah reservation, that put up six hundred casks of salmon, in addition to seven hundred of halibut, during the inaugural

season. The first salmon cannery in Puget Sound opened in 1877, and by 1915, forty-one canneries packed over 1.2 million cases of salmon. Of the five species of Pacific salmon (genus *Oncorhynchus*), sockeye was the best and most valuable for canning, yet large amounts of spring, humpback, silver, and chum also ended up in the stubby tin cylinders.[27]

As in fishing for halibut, increasingly expensive technological advances intensified the commercial salmon fishery and gave non-Natives an advantage when commandeering indigenous resources. Fish traps proliferated in Washington State's Puget Sound waters, growing to 163 by 1900. These traps interfered with American Indian fishers, obstructing Native access and transportation routes, in addition to intercepting salmon before they reached reservation fishing grounds. Although traps posed no immediate problems for the People of the Cape, the growth of the fishing fleet did. Around the turn of the century, purse seines—a large net used to encircle a school of salmon—became a common gear preference, especially aboard US vessels. By 1912, nine purse seiners fished out of Neah Bay, and seven years later, around a thousand operated in Puget Sound, Alaska, and British Columbia. With mechanical power, boats and seine nets increased in size and came to dominate the Puget Sound salmon fishery by the 1920s, intercepting salmon offshore before they reached trap sites or reservation waters. In British Columbia, gill nets—operated both as drift nets and as fixed gear in rivers and estuaries—were the preferred method for taking salmon commercially until the 1910s. Sized so that salmon could swim partway through, net meshes snared the gills and entangled the fish when they attempted to back out. By 1901, the province had issued 4,722 fishing licenses, most for gillnetting. As with purse seining and long-lining, using powered winches to set and draw nets made gillnetting more profitable. Motor power also made trolling commercially practical, and boats added more lines to catch salmon. Until the introduction of gas-powered engines, Natives were the only ones who trolled for salmon. In 1911, 250 trollers worked off Cape Flattery; by 1918, that number had doubled.[28]

During the summer seasons, huge fleets of fishing vessels made Neah Bay their home. Described by the *Pacific Fisherman* monthly as "one of the sights of the coast," this "floating city" of six thousand people included 115 purse seiners, 350 gasoline trawlers (halibut long-liners), and 600 sail and rowboats in 1912. Seattle's Gorman and Company's newly incorporated Neah Bay Fish Company operated an onshore cannery that included a machine shop and long dock with a Standard Oil station for fueling ships. The Seattle Packing Company's floating cannery, the *Amelie*, also anchored there, along with three floating mild cure plants, including an old modified ferry and a converted sternwheel steamboat. A "colony" of floating amenities had sprung up, including machine

Neah Bay harbor with fishing fleet, early twentieth century. During the summer fishing season, a thousand boats turned Makah waters into a floating city. Photograph by Philip Wischmeyer, from the Forks Timber Museum collection.

shops, bakeries, and a restaurant. The article struck a visual tone, noting, "The sight is said to be most impressive at night when most of the vessels are in harbor. Their thousands of lights make the little port look like a large city. In the daytime the bay is often a veritable forest of masts." While some Makahs worked in the canneries during heavy delivery times, others must have worried about this sizable fleet working fishing banks that had until recently belonged to them.[29]

The People of the Cape engaged in these commercial fisheries. In 1888, reservation visitors surmised that forty to sixty Makah canoes fished for halibut and trolled for salmon during the summer months, catching 600,000 pounds of halibut and seven thousand individual salmon. In the 1890s, they sold much of this catch—often five to ten tons daily—to steamships owned by Puget Sound fish companies. When fish buyers were absent, they shipped their catch to Seattle by steamer. By the end of the century, the Euro-American Eggers family had established a commercial dock at Neah Bay and offered free hot coffee, hard tack, and cubed sugar to Makahs to encourage them to sell fish to their operation instead of to outside buyers. The Eggers both sent fresh halibut to Tacoma to be shipped east and smoked some, which they marketed to Midwest farmers. By 1912, the Eggers were mild curing Makah salmon. Other fish buyers also came to Neah Bay in the early twentieth century, paying cash—from 15 to 20 cents per halibut, regardless of the size, and up to 35 cents per salmon—for a day's catch. Indian Agent Samuel Morse noted in 1901 that a "good [Makah] fisherman" could make $20 or $30 a day during the salmon season. The following year, Makah fishers sold over $6,000 in salmon to a Port Angeles cannery. In years with the heaviest runs, they sold over $20,000 in salmon to canneries, but in poor years they struggled to sell even $4,000 in total for all their fisheries. Often spending $5,000 annually on Makah fish, the reservation trader also bought halibut from fishers, although they complained that he paid low prices for a halibut "as large as a table," while charging exorbitantly for his goods.[30]

As they had with pelagic sealing and whaling, Makah fishers combined new technologies and marketing opportunities with customary practices. Well into the twentieth century, many continued to use čibu·ds for halibut. Agent Morse noted in 1897 that Makahs "discard[ed] the hooks made by white men and use[d] an ingenious invention of their own, made of wood and bone, which they aver is far superior to any other." The Eggers delivered pitchforks by the dozen in the early years of their Neah Bay operation; Makahs removed the tines and fashioned these into metal čibu·ds. Some fishers shunned mechanized power for pulling up lines because this tore fish from hooks. While many continued to fish from canoes, in the early twentieth century, increasing numbers of Makahs began purchasing gas-powered vessels, such as Young Doctor's sloop *Wadda*. In June 1906, he brought fresh fish to Tacoma for the American Fish Company and contracted with them to spend the summer halibut fishing off Cape Flattery. By 1930, the Makah fleet had grown to twenty-five powered schooners, with the largest being James Hunter's eleven-ton *Hunter No. 4*. Like pelagic sealing arrangements of the previous generation, Makah owners of powered schooners often "towed out" four to five canoes to offshore fishing banks. On arrival, the canoes were unloaded, and Makah fishers handlined for halibut. At the end of the day, the schooner, which had also fished, picked up the canoes and collected from one-third to one-fourth of the catch before towing the canoes back to shore. Makahs used their fishing profits, which peaked at $32,000 in 1905, to build new homes, repair old ones, purchase powered vessels, loan money and pay bills of extended family members, and engage in "old-time customs," such as multiday potlatches and dances. As they had in the previous century, the People of the Cape relied on the sea to maintain their identity amid early twentieth-century changes.[31]

CONSERVATION, CAPITALIZATION, AND MAKAH FISHERS

Into the 1910s, the Pacific halibut and salmon fisheries remained profitable, especially for non-Natives but only sporadically for Makahs. High and stable net returns for white fishers generated investment capital used to expand fleets and drew more Canadian and US firms into the business. Yet both fisheries began showing signs of severe stress. Overfishing hammered halibut grounds and salmon runs, but the contributing factors proved to be more complex. Conservation policies exacerbated pressures on the halibut fishery, concentrating increasing numbers of commercial fishers into shrinking seasons. The situation for freshwater-spawning salmon was even more complex because of the substantial impact of habitat degradation caused by settler-colonial development in the Pacific Northwest. Stakeholders' false faith in a technological fix, hatcheries that would create more fish to catch, only worsened the situation because it obscured the real factors while various user groups could blame each other for the problem and avoid the necessary regulations and changes that might have made a difference. Within this context, Washington's tribal nations such as the Makah who fished for both consumption and the market found themselves targeted by early conservation laws, legislation, and court decisions that were antagonistic to their economic interests.

In the early years, the commercial Pacific halibut fishery resembled what historian Arthur McEvoy calls "the fisherman's problem." As common property, halibut stocks were not managed in a self-preserving way. Because no one entity owned the fishery, there were no incentives to refrain from fishing for conservation purposes. The fish one left behind would only be caught by another. As McEvoy illustrates in the case of California fisheries of the nineteenth and twentieth centuries, "In a competitive economy, no market mechanism ordinarily exists to reward individual forbearance in the use of shared resources." McEvoy's analysis matches one halibut expert's description of the industry's boom years as "wild and unregulated."[32] But the Pacific halibut fishery off Cape Flattery differed from the marine fisheries McEvoy describes because these fishing banks were owned places belonging to specific Makah families, who subsequently had an interest in conserving their property. Fishers in the second half of the nineteenth century made "management decisions" about where and when to fish for specific types of halibut that "guaranteed that Makahs would distribute fishing activities among the resident halibut populations and habitat, allowing the resource numbers to proliferate despite intensive use."[33] With the halibut's slow growth cycle, the Makah strategy of spreading the fishery out across many banks ensured conservation. Because this was such an important resource, Makahs "would drive away any other tribes which had not been accustomed to fish on the halibut banks."[34] This action, too, helped to conserve the species.

But the non-Native commercial fishers who flooded onto Makah banks shared none of these concerns initially. Some of the first halibut grounds worked because of their proximity to railroad ports, the Cape Flattery banks showed signs of depletion early. In his remarks about the fishery in 1895, A. B. Alexander, an investigator for the US Fish Commission, observed the occasional scarcity of halibut on the Cape Flattery banks and that vessels had to go elsewhere to get their expected catch. More pointedly, Richard Rathbun, assistant secretary of the Smithsonian and a trained ichthyologist, warned that "the grounds in the Gulf of Georgia, Puget Sound, and Strait of Fuca, with those off Cape Flattery, have all together only a relatively small capacity, which has already been overtaxed." Despite these early signs, many involved in the industry continued to believe in an unlimited supply of halibut, even when catches off Cape Flattery were "milky and soft and of poor quality," conditions that indicated that immature halibut were being taken because the stock was being overfished more quickly than the slow-growing fish could mature.[35] By the mid-1910s signs of overfishing became harder to ignore. In 1901, Washington State fish commissioner A. C. Little reported that fishers landed more than 5.7 million pounds of fresh, salted, and smoked halibut in the state. That number increased to over 20 million pounds a year later and then doubled by 1909, only to decline to just over 28 million pounds by 1915. The *Pacific Fisherman*, a monthly industry publication, reported in 1916 that "of recent years there has been a tremendous increase in the fleets operating on the halibut banks, the area covered has been greatly extended, a greater quantity of and more efficient gear is in use, and despite all this the catch to the dory is decreasing, showing that the reserve or capital stock of fish is being steadily depleted." When compared to returns a decade earlier, the 1914 landings reported by the Puget Sound halibut fleet showed a 20 percent decrease in the average catch per dory. The decrease was even more severe when one considers that the fleet in 1904 did not fish year-round like the one in 1914 did. William Thompson, an ichthyologist with the British Columbia Department of Fisheries, reported similar findings north of the border. Analyzing annual halibut returns and fishing activity from many vessels landing catches at Vancouver, he demonstrated that fish caught per unit of gear fell from an average of

42.8 in 1906 to 21.9 in 1912, although specific banks suffered variously. The oldest banks in Puget Sound, including Makah grounds off Cape Flattery, were more depleted than ones farther north.[36]

In the late nineteenth and early twentieth centuries, concerns over the salmon fishery in the North Pacific also grew. Unlike halibut stocks that spawned in the ocean, salmon depended on rivers for spawning, which left them susceptible to habitat degradation from mining, logging, and other development. By the end of the nineteenth century, resource development had already begun taking its toll on most major salmon runs. So the growing number of commercial and sport fishers and canneries in the region exacerbated an already suffering fishery, overwhelming initial attempts to manage the harvest for conservation. As different types of gear proliferated and became tied to specific ethnicities, competition and tensions intensified. User groups relied on simple stories of the catastrophe and blamed each other for the crisis. As early as 1875, businessmen and politicians sought ways to keep the Pacific salmon industry from sharing the same fate as the Atlantic fishery, which had collapsed by 1865. Since the 1870s, sport fishing and hunting organizations had been pressuring western states to establish commissions and agencies to protect, manage, and conserve fish and wildlife, at the expense of other users, including commercial and Native fishers. In 1877, Washington State experimented with closed seasons. A year later, British Columbia began instituting specific regulations and regular closed periods. The situation only became more complicated when salmon fishing moved farther into the ocean, and Washington and British Columbia officials and fishers began arguing over whose fish citizens from the other nation were catching. The emerging crisis even caught the attention of President Theodore Roosevelt, who, in his 1908 State of the Union address, called particular attention to the Columbia River and Puget Sound fisheries as one of several critical issues that deserved congressional attention. However, politicians were reluctant to enforce regulations that hampered the livelihood of their constituents; instead they sank increasing amounts of money and effort into fish culture, believing that if they could just produce more salmon, the problem would resolve itself. This only obscured the real problems and weakened natural stocks.[37]

Signs of depletion encouraged stakeholders to explore conservation options. As with fur seal conservation at the turn of the century, government efforts to regulate fishing also ended up privileging non-Native access to fisheries at the expense of Makahs and other indigenous peoples. Throughout the twentieth century, the fisheries of the People of the Cape ended up in a dizzying array of different and competing regulatory jurisdictions, and not just because halibut and salmon, like other migratory species, ignore political boundaries. As politics and international diplomacy interacted with the oftentimes incomplete yet emerging knowledge of fish biology, Makahs found their livelihood and treaty rights ignored at best, and under assault at worst, by powerful stakeholders and government officials.

In the case of halibut conservation efforts, regulatory powers seemed to ignore Makah concerns and treaty rights because this was an offshore fishery, outside the jurisdiction of Washington State authorities who were often the most antagonistic to American Indian fishers. Even as halibut returns remained high in the 1910s due to the fleet's expansion into northern waters, those in the industry and government branches involved in monitoring the fishery debated what to do about the signs of depletion they saw. In 1914, Alvah Hager, the president of the Canadian Fishing Company, based out of Vancouver, urged the industry to organize an international closed season in the winter and to begin regulating the fishery. Ichthyologist William Thompson disagreed with the appropriateness of a closed season, warning that a closed season was not only incompatible with halibut biology—they mature too slowly for a short closed season to make any difference—but that it would also exacerbate the problem by intensifying fishing on already depleted banks during the shorter open season. Two years later, Thompson drew from his statistical and scientific studies of the industry and halibut to argue that large areas needed to be closed for years at a time to allow depleted grounds to rebound. Halibut fishers on both sides of the border, however, repeated Hager's proposal for a closed season in the winter and urged for an international solution.[38] These differing approaches illustrate that "there was no sharp divide between conservation and anti-conservation but rather a spectrum of opinions on *how* to conserve."[39] Halger, Thompson, and halibut fishers shared a desire to maintain high yields from the fishery, yet they differed on which strategies would work.

Cries for conservation pressured Canada and the United States to hold a joint fisheries conference in 1918, the first official transnational attention to halibut conservation. But the talks focused on a host of fisheries issues relative to the two countries, and the US Senate refused to consider the proposed agreement on halibut, despite evidence showing that "the depletion is everywhere apparent and most serious," and that effective protection measures were needed immediately.[40] In 1922, Canadian and US negotiators began new discussions that resulted in the halibut treaty of 1923, which turned this high-seas fishery from a freewheeling industry to one of "strict, international regulation."[41] This implemented the one provision the industry and politicians agreed on—a closed season from November 16 to February 15—and established the four-member International Fisheries Commission (IFC), an investigative body to study halibut biology and make recommendations for managing the fishery.

The 1923 treaty codified several key principles that shaped halibut conserva-tion in the region for decades, and as the first such agreement dealing with con-servation of a threatened high-seas fishery, it "serve[d] as a precedent for international co-operative control of sea fisheries."[42] First, it emphasized a lim-ited closed season as the primary mechanism of preserving and restoring the fishery. Second, the treaty supported the scientific study of fish biology by estab-lishing the International Fisheries Commission, even if the recommendations this body made privileged the needs of capital over halibut. As in this situation, re-search was a typical early step in international conservation efforts. Third, the treaty ignored a critical stakeholder in the fishery—Native fishers and their com-mercial, subsistence, and cultural needs. No Makahs or First Nations peoples, individuals with some of the greatest experience with halibut and those who probably best knew how to conserve the resource, were consulted during the treaty negotiations or asked to serve on the International Fisheries Commission. These patterns reappeared in subsequent halibut conservation agreements and compounded the difficulties the People of the Cape experienced in exercising their treaty fishing rights.

As Thompson had predicted, the annual winter closed season first instituted in 1924 neither conserved halibut nor reversed the depletion. Instead, it "favour[ed] expansion and exploitation of the stock over restraint and restoration."[43] The initial IFC studies revealed that overfishing was "uneconomical." Commercial fishers caught halibut at an increasingly earlier stage in their life, before they had spawned, "thus endangering the supply of young and the future productiv-ity of the fishery." Based on their investigations, the commission made a range of conservation recommendations in 1928.[44] At the same time, IFC statistics about overfishing provided compelling evidence that more drastic measures were necessary. In their studies, the commission divided treaty waters into three ar-eas. Area 2 included the Makah banks, and returns (see figure on p. 235) show that landings and catch per skate of gear dropped from 1907 to 1930, despite the expansion of halibut fishing from 500 to 2,100 square miles in the area. On some of the first banks exploited, such as those off Cape Flattery, the catch per unit of fishing gear had fallen even more dramatically, from 300 pounds in 1906 to 50 pounds in 1926, just 16 percent of previous returns. One halibut expert interviewed in 1936 described the fishery of the previous decades in damning terms: "The method of exploitation was exactly that now employed by profes-sional exterminators of vermin and varmints—attack from the outside, destroy everything as you go, and keep down the species in cleaned-up ground." Yet with the 1915 opening of Prince Rupert, British Columbia, to US vessels and adapta-tion of the less expensive diesel engine to fishing boats after 1921, the fishery

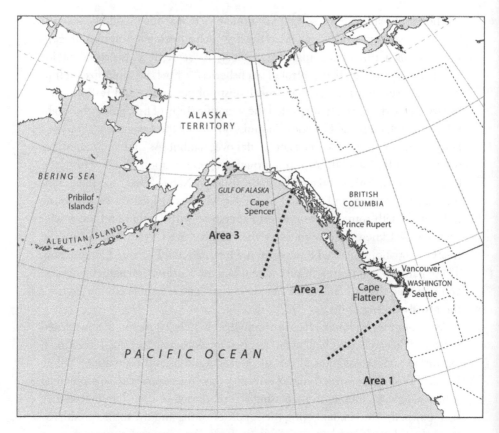

Map of the halibut research—and subsequent regulation—areas as of 1928.
Makah grounds fell in Area 2. Map by Bill Nelson.

remained profitable because ships could efficiently expand into new areas in the Gulf of Alaska. Despite the growing overall catch, many worried that even the newest banks exhibited the same trend of declining returns.[45]

The IFC findings prompted the United States and Canada to negotiate a new halibut treaty in 1930 that adopted their earlier recommendations and expanded the role of the International Fisheries Commission into a regulatory commission. After ratification, the new regulations came into effect for the 1932 fishing season beginning on February 15. The commission divided the fishery into four areas, largely following those used in the studies during the 1920s, and set quotas for each. It also required all halibut vessels, except small ones under five tons, to have licenses. The commission established clearance procedures that all vessels had to satisfy before leaving to fish, including supplying statistical information

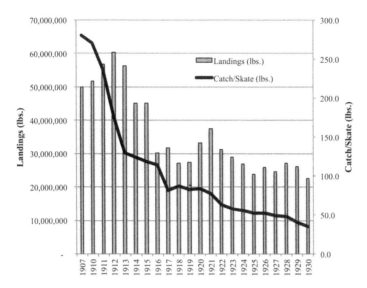

Graph of halibut landings and catch per skate from 1907 to 1930, as
compiled from William F. Thompson and Frederick Heward Bell,
*Biological Statistics of the Halibut Fishery: Effect of Changes
in Intensity upon Total Yield and Yield per Unit of Gear*
(Seattle: International Fisheries Commission, 1934), 12.

about catches for each trip, validating returns through a dealer or buyer, and
keeping accurate fishing logs. Subsequent conventions in 1937 and 1953 added two
more members to the commission to reflect the rising influence of the fishery
in Alaskan waters, renamed it the International Pacific Halibut Commission
(IPHC), and broadened its regulatory purview, resulting in an increasingly
sophisticated system of zones, quotas, size limits, allowable incidental catches,
gear restrictions and prohibitions, and the closure of nursery grounds.[46]

The halibut industry also took steps to establish a system of orderly marketing that complemented the regulatory structure administered by the transnational commission. Fishers complained about a lack of control, noting that
25 percent of the limit in Area 2 was caught in the first two months of the season
and that they filled the quota of halibut in August, forcing the commission to
close fishing in the area three months early. Seeking to spread out the flow of
fish to market and to secure stable and high prices throughout the season, non-
Native vessel owners and members of fishermen's unions in Seattle formed the
Halibut Production Control Board (HPCB) in 1932. It split the US fleet into increasingly smaller parts and staggered start dates for each group. The HPCB also

experimented with various lay-in schedules, individual quotas for each fisher on a vessel, and penalties for not following these strategies. By 1936, Canadian vessels began collaborating with these voluntary HPCB measures, which the province then turned into official regulations. Experts estimated that 95 percent of US vessels and the entire Canadian halibut fleet followed the HPCB control measures by the late 1930s. Non-Native conservationists, commercial fishers, government agencies, and industry boosters lauded the dual management system created by the commission and control board. In 1943, an economist reported that the catch per skate in Area 2 rose by 77 percent from 1930 to 1941.[47]

But how did these regulations and control efforts affect Makah fishers? Their impacts ended up separating the People of the Cape from customary foods such as halibut. Directly, the regulations and controls encouraged the sale of a catch for cash and discouraged fishers from setting aside fish for subsistence and ceremonial purposes. Counting halibut seemed to be at the heart of the regulations and control mechanisms. When fishers sold halibut, fish dealers and buyers kept track of these counts and reported them to the respective commission and board. This meant that Makah halibut schooners, in order to be cleared to leave the port of Neah Bay and go fishing, had to have accurate and up-to-date counts, which could best be kept if they sold fish to dealers and buyers. This accounting system encouraged Makah fishers to sell the large majority of their catch while reserving smaller portions for other uses. In addition, because more Makahs fished from gasoline- or diesel-powered schooners, they needed the cash from a fish sale to pay for fuel. The People of the Cape could bypass these controls by setting out in canoes to go fishing, but as non-Native commercial fishers in larger and more expensive boats cleaned out the nearby halibut banks, an afternoon spent fishing resulted in smaller catches.

Little data remain on returns from Makah halibut vessels in the 1930s, but the available evidence seems to confirm this conclusion. In 1941, the local fish buyer at Neah Bay provided some statistics. Some of what the buyer bought included salmon, but most of these returns were for halibut because Makahs would have sold the former to canneries or cannery buyers, which would not have appeared in this count. These numbers show that after the commission regulations and HPCB controls went into effect, Makahs only kept from 6.6 to 9.1 percent of their catch for noncommercial use and that this percentage decreased over time. Anecdotal evidence from this period also confirms the situation. As early as 1936, some Makahs complained that they were not drying halibut anymore for winter provisions because they had to sell to the buyers. Even though the returns indicate that the local buyer paid cash for halibut, this did not always mean that money stayed in Makah households. As Henry St. Clair noted in 1936,

Table 2. Value of fish sold to fish buyer at Neah Bay, 1937–1940

Year	Total value of fish taken by Makahs	Value estimated for subsistence	Commercial value
1937	$16,500	$1,500	$15,000
1938	$13,282	$1,000	$12,282
1939	$15,988	$1,200	$14,738
1940	$18,837	$1,250	$17,587

Source: Frank D. Beaulieu, clerk, "Fishing Activities of Indians, Makah Reservation," July 18, 1941, File 921.6 Edward Swindell, Jr. Associate Attorney, box 171: Decimal File 921.5-936, TIA, NARA-PNR.

"Those boys out there today will catch only a few fish, which they must sell to the buyer for less than the market price, and when they are paid they will have almost nothing for themselves" after paying for fuel and expenses for operating their vessel, which were increasing as fishers worked increasingly harder on over-fished banks. Because fishing was one of the few ways Makahs could make money that they needed for twentieth-century necessities such as medicine, flour, and clothing, fishers found it necessary to sell their catch for cash instead of keeping more aside for winter provisions.[48]

Trying to wrest the most cash out of their catches—perhaps in the hope of being able to reserve more fish for household use—tribal fishers formed the Makah Boat Owners Association at the beginning of 1938. Its existence indicates that Makahs sought their own voice in marketing fish, likely because the halibut control board ignored them. The association lobbied for the Indian superinten-dent to authorize a permit to the Neah Bay Fish Company so that a buyer would be on site year-round in order to handle more than just halibut, to pro-vide a supply of ice at fair prices throughout the year, and to make available a machine shop that would enable vessel owners to maintain their boats. Associa-tion members laid out plans for the tribe to acquire the company but urged the superintendent to permit it for five years while they figured out how to do this. They also connected the fish company's presence at Neah Bay to other tribal priorities, hinging on keeping the town electrified: without the company's ice plant in operation, the light plant would no longer remain profitable and would shut down periodically. If the light plant shut down, then the school would go dark, preventing children from studying. Plus, the fish plant would supply wage-paying jobs that Makah families needed. That year, the associa-tion also asked the superintendent to help secure federal assistance in getting the fishing fleet in shape, replacing worn-out gear and making improvements so the Makahs could better compete against non-Native fishers working Makah banks. Superintendent Nicholson even assigned a subagent to investigate what Makahs would need: several new engines and some hull repairs, which together came to about $200, an expenditure that appears never to have been made.[49]

In addition to regulations and controls that discouraged fishers from setting aside substantial portions of a catch for winter use, other laws reduced the opportunity for Makah fish to reach household tables. By 1941, at Neah Bay "it was practically impossible to buy fish even when [Makah] fishermen were successful and arriving with large catches."[50] The local buyer lacked a retail license, so fish caught by Makahs could not be sold back to the community; instead, the buyer shipped fish to Puget Sound, where he got a better price, so he had no incentive to apply for a retail license. Market pressures combined with the increasing bureaucratic oversight of commodities and consumption to further separate the People of the Cape from customary foods.

Makahs understood the differences between the commercial and subsistence fisheries, and they tried to get the commission to accommodate these. Even though various families owned small powered schooners by the 1940s, Makahs still largely handlined for halibut from open boats. At the beginning of each season, there was a "tremendous rush" because commercial fishers raced to catch as many halibut as possible. In small boats and canoes, Makahs competed against larger, more expensive vessels that fished all year-round, from South America to Alaska, for different types of fish. At the opening of the season, these outsiders concentrated on the halibut banks off Cape Flattery and quickly filled the IFC quota for the region before Makahs had a chance to procure enough fish for their own livelihood, thereby cutting them out of the fishery. In the early 1940s, "Old men [at Neah Bay] contrast the time when they were boys, when a man could return within a few hours with a canoe load of fish. Now with better equipment and with boats that enable them to cover a greater area, they may fish for hours or even for days and return with nothing or with only a paltry load insufficient to pay for the petrol used in getting to the fishing banks and back." As Makah Charles E. Peterson testified in 1949, "We don't get much chance anymore." The tribal nation asked the International Fisheries Commission for a small season that fit their needs and accommodated treaty fishing rights, but the commission denied the request.[51]

Unlike non-Native conservationists and industry boosters looking for evidence about the improving halibut fishery, the People of the Cape appeared unimpressed with the commission's and control board's efforts. Local fishers possessing deep knowledge and experience with the fishery, Makahs continued to see the effects of overfishing. They blamed white fishers for the decline of this critical commercial and subsistence resource that they had relied upon for generations. In 1936, reflecting back on the way the halibut fishery had changed since he began fishing in 1889, Henry St. Clair recalled that around 1903, when purse seiners adapted the power gurdy to their vessels, was when "they [white fishermen] killed all the fish that were left on Swiftsure Bank in no time." He continued, remembering that "in those days we couldn't fish in the bank because set-lines [were] all over. Lines criss-cross[ed]. Many hooks. Almost every fish [was] caught. When fish [were] gone, boats left. No food for the Indians. And today there are no fish there." That same year, John Markishtum, another Makah fisher, broadened overfishing beyond halibut, even relating the demise of customary resources to cultural practices: "Everything is played out here. The little fish are played out. The herring and smelts and minnows are gone. I used to catch king salmon right here in the mouth of the bay where they followed the herring in, but now we have to go all over the ocean to catch enough to eat. There are no more whales, and no war canoes, and all the old paddlers are dead." Five years later Henry Markishtum expressed a similar sentiment when he opened the meeting Edward Swindell had with the community about their usual and accustomed fishing places. "The white man came west and various species of the animal kingdom and fish soon depleted. The rivers finally became empty, so to say, and again, the ocean."[52] The biases of any particular stakeholder—in this case, Makah fishers—"often stemmed less from selfishness than from substantive differences in how they understood the complex problem of overfishing." From the perspective of users who had heavily exploited these fishing banks for about three thousand years without wiping out the resource, the Makah explanation of white overfishing made sense. Much as Plains Indians blamed non-Native actions for the near extinction of the buffalo in the late nineteenth century, the People of the Cape understood that white commercial fishing had undercut Makah commercial and subsistence marine resources, which, in turn, threatened their culture.[53]

During much of the twentieth century, Washington State's laws and the actions of its officials kept Makah fishing rights and access to fish within state waters under siege. States in the West have a long history of being antagonistic to federal control over lands, waters, and resources even as they rely on federal support for their very existence. Sometimes protected by the federal government through the courts and other bodies, American Indian treaty rights represented a large point of contention for many Westerners. Washington State officials and many non-Native residents resented—and continue to resent—the supposedly "special rights" embodied in the Stevens treaties that American Indians signed with the federal government in the mid-nineteenth century. In the early twentieth century, treaty critics characterized Native peoples as conquered subjects and impediments to white progress. They remained willfully blind to the fact that indigenous leaders in the nineteenth century used the treaties to reserve specific rights for their nations in return for ceding vast amounts of land and for promising to share Native wealth, such as fisheries, with the settlers. Anti-Indian attitudes shaped the state's approach at managing fisheries, while non-Native stakeholders used the power of the state to privilege their uses at the expense of American Indian fishers and families.[54]

Fortunately, many of the most important Makah fishing banks lay beyond the boundary of state waters, which extend just three miles from shore. But anything within state waters, including the important salmon fishing waterways of the Hoko, Lyre, Seiku, Pysht, and Clallam Rivers, along with Lake Ozette, and marine banks close to shore, fell under Washington's jurisdiction. Some of the earliest state fishing laws targeted American Indian men directly and indirectly. Regulations prohibited Native gear, especially nets stretching across rivers and weirs. By 1909, commercial fishers needed state licenses, which were available only to US citizens. Most Washington Indians, especially those living on reservations, remained ineligible for these licenses because they did not gain citizenship until congressional action in 1924. In 1915, the state legislature passed a new fisheries code that struck against Native fishing methods, such as spearing and snaring, while providing partial support for treaty fishing rights. The new regulations affirmed the rights of treaty Indians to fish on their respective reservations for subsistence purposes and guaranteed them access to marine waters within half a mile from the reservation and in rivers up to five miles off-reservation. It limited the nets to no more than one-third the width of a waterway but did not require American Indians to get fishing licenses.[55]

Despite these modest guarantees, state officials interpreted the 1915 fisheries code loosely. The state fish commissioner from 1913 to 1921, L. H. Darwin, an individual who "seemed to have a personal vendetta against Indian fishing," arrested American Indians for fishing during closed seasons and insisted that they needed state licenses, contrary to the law.[56] In his first annual report to the governor, Darwin stated his position: "One of the most vexing problems which has confronted the Department has been the insistence of some of the Indians that they are entitled under their treaty rights to fish for salmon without securing a license from this office, as citizens are required to do, and without any regard whatsoever of the closed season prescribed by law." To justify the arrests, Darwin "examin[ed]" the treaties and determined that "the Indians off their reservations have no rights superior to those of whites." He complained that Native fishing endangered salmon conservation and even blamed some federal Indian agents for "wrongfully advis[ing] those under their charge that they possessed these superior rights to whites." Darwin took to local papers to argue his case after passage of the 1915 fisheries code, warning, "If we cannot make these Indians obey these laws, then there will be absolutely no protection for the salmon in the closed rivers and on the spawning grounds during the closed season." Because the salmon fishing season dates coincided with the commercial open-water fishery, salmon only reached places where Natives could fish for them after the season ended. He never wavered from this anti-Indian position over his eight years as commissioner. Even after Darwin's term ended and the legislature replaced the Fish Commission with the Department of Fish and Game, subsequent officials reflected the non-Natives' antagonism against Indian fishing.[57]

Two state supreme court cases in 1916 confirmed the right of Washington to regulate against American Indian fishers. *State v. Towessnute* and *State v. Alexis* involved Washington Indians—a Yakama and a Lummi, respectively—who had been arrested for violating state fishing laws. The state supreme court ruled against the defendants in both cases, arguing that Towessnute and Alexis were subject to the same state fishing laws as other citizens. Cato Sells, the commissioner of Indian affairs, contemplated appealing these decisions. Yet in his annual report, he noted that a successful decision affirming Indian treaty rights was unlikely to come from the US Supreme Court, which that same year decided in *Kennedy v. Becker*, a case involving Seneca fishing rights in New York, "that the State might enforce within the ceded area against the Indians as well as white people such laws as might be enacted for the preservation of the fish and game within the borders of that State."[58] This case introduced a precedent that shaped subsequent court cases about Indian treaty fishing rights: states can regulate Native fishing for conservation purposes. State officials such as Commissioner Darwin then saw that courts would uphold the arrests of Indian fishers.

Being subject to state fishing laws similar to other Washingtonians did not bring Makah fishers any rights or protections as citizens. Instead, state fisheries patrols cracked down on Washington's Native fishers, and Makahs found themselves targeted within state waters, especially on the Hoko River, just four and a half miles east of the reservation boundary. The People of the Cape felt that local whites got jealous of them and would report to the fish warden when "the Indians [were] back on the beach again," fishing at the mouth of the Hoko with drag seines nets. In 1924, state deputy Jack Warden arrested eighteen Makahs there—including members of the Greene, Irving, Johnson, and Claplanhoo families—and confiscated four gas boats, five canoes, and four drag seines, along with the salmon they had caught. State regulations mandated that within three miles of a river, fish could be taken only with a hook and line. Deputy Warden took the Makahs and their gear to Port Angeles, where the accused wired Carl

Boyd, the superintendent at Neah Bay. Boyd traveled to Port Angeles and found that Chief Deputy Shaw from Seattle had also come out to confer on the incident. Shaw wanted to fine each Makah $10, confiscate their nets, and sell the boats, which would have been a catastrophic blow to the families involved. Boyd talked him into releasing the Makahs and allowing them to keep their boats and gear, as long as they pled guilty and promised to pay the fines.[59]

Reactions to this incident capture the divide that had developed during the first quarter of the twentieth century over Indian treaty fishing rights in the state. On one side lay the non-Native position, as embodied by Shaw. He insisted that the treaty was "null and void and that the present State of Washington did not at this time recognize it."[60] He argued not only that Washington's statehood had nullified the Stevens treaties but also that the 1924 Indian Citizenship Act made Indians "amenable to laws as other people."[61] On the other side lay Makahs and their supporters. In response to his arrest, Albert Irving wrote to the commissioner of Indian affairs in 1925, reminding him that when Governor Stevens asked for Makah land, "the chief of the tribe, said yes you can take the land that belongs to us, but not the fish that goes in and out of the rivers." Irving declared, "All my great great grandfathers lived on fish long before the white men came to America and I am the same. I like fish I can't get along without fish. God give us the fish for our food. The whole tribe of Makah Indians who are living on fish would like their right of taking fish out of rivers given back to them." He also noted that they were "short of food" because the fish deputy bothered them before they could get any salted or smoked. Superintendent Boyd also supported the Makah position, explaining to the commissioner that the salmon caught at the Hoko were for winter use. "They have always, after the regular fishing season is over, laid in a supply of fish food to carry them over the winter time, and they cannot understand why this privilege [sic] and right as they claim, should be taken from them."[62] In a second letter, the superintendent pointed out that Makahs could not afford the expensive larger boats and gear that whites used, so they relied on small nets that two men could handle, but only in river mouths such as the Hoko, to get any salmon.[63]

Other Indian superintendents sympathetic to treaty fishing rights voiced their concern. Evan Estep, superintendent at the Yakima Indian Agency in eastern Washington, had sent a newspaper clipping about the incident to the commissioner because he worried that the arrest, if upheld, would become a precedent used to punish Indians under state laws. He pointed out the inaccuracy of the state officials' position because the 1924 Citizenship Act "specifically states that it does not in any way affect their [Indians'] rights to property either individual or tribe." According to Estep's understanding of the treaties, fishing rights were a property right. He urged the Bureau of Indian Affairs to appeal the decision, warning, "There seems to be a growing tendency in this State by the courts to gain a foothold on the reservations. If this is allowed to go on, or it be held that the State courts do have this jurisdiction, then the end of the Indians' rights and privileges is near at hand. The State courts would probably not go so far as to attempt to deprive him of his allotment but they are making an effort to tie up the products of his allotment and if they succeed in doing that they had just about as well take the whole business and have it over." These letters prompted Charles Burke, then commissioner of Indian affairs, to ask the secretary of the Interior about a course of action. Burke noted that the divergent treaty rights opinions "cause[d] . . . much friction between the Indians and the state officials." Reminding the secretary that many Northwest treaties share the same fishing provision, he urged the Interior Department to make progress toward a "final settlement of this controversy."[64] Although Boyd—one of the few supportive Makah superintendents in this period—appeared to sort out this particular incident with state officials, the battle lines over Indian treaty fishing rights had been drawn, and subsequent incidents would not be settled so easily.

A precursor to the fishing wars later in the century, the Hoko River incident highlights the precarious economic and political position in which the People of the Cape found themselves during the early twentieth century. The Makah economy was not as strong as it had been during the previous century, when profits from whale oil and pelagic sealing allowed them to thrive. A pair of inspection reports from 1916 and 1928 reveals the eroding Makah economy and the various ways tribal members earned cash. In 1916, Otis Goodall compiled labor statistics for the 412-member community. He reported that 65 women made baskets—woven from cedar bark and beargrass, specifically for non-Native consumers—that they sold to the trader for $6,000 the previous year. Sixty Makahs, mostly women, earned 15 to 20 cents an hour at the local cannery, for a total of $2,500 during a fishing season. Goodall thought that 100 Makahs fished part time, while another 60 did this full time; together, fishers earned $25,000 in 1915, and many families owned gas-powered boats. Thirty labored in nearby timber and sawmills and brought home $3,600, while a "good many"—perhaps only 8, as reported in the annual commissioner of Indian affairs report—worked the reservation logging camps, earning just under $200. The agency and school at Neah Bay employed 5 Makahs, who perhaps earned around $1,000. In total, members of the tribe earned around $38,300, or about $93 per person, that year.[65]

Earl Henderson's inspection report for 1928 shows a similar assemblage of labor for the 436 People of the Cape. Once again, women annually earned around $3,000 from their basketry. Although he did not report the total profits earned from Makah fishers, the superintendent at Neah Bay two years later estimated that the tribe earned $19,700 during the fishing season. Henderson did note that two-person operations earned from $50 to $100 from four to six days of fishing for salmon or halibut. He counted fourteen powerboats owned by Makah families; four to five were worth $3,000 each, while the rest were about $1,500 a vessel. Women worked in one of two floating canneries for 35 cents an hour, and a few men occasionally cut firewood for $4.50 to $5.00 per cord. Although neither the inspector's report nor the commissioner's annual report tabulated Makah reservation employees, a handful probably received no more than $1,000 total as assistant teachers and reservation police. Under new pelagic sealing rules, Makahs could hunt seals from canoes, as long as the agency superintendent tagged them before sealers sold them to the reservation trader. The previous year, Makahs sold about $9,000 in sealskins, yet they recognized that these regulations still imposed a "great hardship . . . upon them" because sealing from canoes was dangerous. Makah laborers earned at least $32,700 in 1928, or $75 per person. By the end of the 1920s, the Makah economy had fallen behind that of non-Natives. In 1929, the first year that the US Bureau of Economic Analysis has statistics for this, the per capita income in Washington State was $737, almost ten times that for Makahs the year before. The tribe also possessed comparatively little in the way of capital investments. Worth only $28,500, their fleet of fourteen boats cost about the price of one of the many white-owned purse seiners that came to Neah Bay during the summer.[66]

No longer protected by economic success, the People of the Cape fell under increasing control of the reservation superintendent at a time when these officials were strengthening assimilation efforts and reframing them as blatant policies of control. Previously, nineteenth-century Indian agents focused on ways to make American Indians self-sufficient so they could join "civilized" society. By the turn of the century, superintendents possessed a more pessimistic view of Native abilities, and assimilation policies sought to incorporate American Indians into US society but as a marginalized people. With an emphasis on controlling tribes, early twentieth-century federal officials had abandoned the hopes of the previous generation of humanistic reformers who sought to transform indigenous peoples.[67]

At Neah Bay, the changed policy attitude meant that superintendents had little interest in supporting a marine-based economy that had made Makahs self-supporting and unique from other tribal nations. In 1904, Superintendent Edwin Minor tore down the "old dilapidated smokehouses" in a crusade to clean up the reservation, ignoring the fact that Makah families relied on these for smoking their winter fish supply. Reflecting the local lack of support for Indian treaty fishing rights, Superintendent A. D. Dodge opined that Makahs should follow state fishing laws: "To strengthen the Indian as a man and citizen I believe that he should be required to fall in line with the rank and file and bear as much of the burden of citizenship as possible." Clarifying his opinion, he argued that the "old treaty rights" did not apply to Indians today. Fortunately, Dodge did not hold this position a few years later when Makahs needed a supportive super-intendent to keep them out of jail when state officials confronted them on the Hoko River. Before he was replaced, though, Dodge made numerous efforts to force Makahs to conform to his assimilation agenda, including traveling down to the Puget Sound fields several times during the hop season in order to "give the Indians the impression that I am there all the time" and using a restraining or-der to shut down the local cannery on Sundays.[68] Recently opened at the end of the nineteenth century, the Neah Bay day school also facilitated control as families moved away from the coastal villages to be near their children. Concen-trating the population at Neah Bay brought more Makahs under the watchful eyes of the reservation superintendent stationed there, allowing him to better enforce prohibitions against speaking their language and engaging in custom-ary songs, dances, potlatches, and other cultural activities.[69]

Others saw the marine economy as hindering the government's assimilation efforts. Raymond Bitney, the superintendent in the early 1930s, complained that "there are a lot of Indians here that will not work as long as they can catch a fish or spear a seal," reflecting his faulty attitude that marine practices were leisure activities. By disconnecting Makah labor from the sea, Bitney trivialized what the People of the Cape valued most, further undercutting a connection under assault by the state's fisheries regulations and officers enforcing them against Na-tives.[70] To discourage Makah marine pursuits, he sent young men away from the reservation to find "good" jobs. In order to substantiate his poor opinion of Makah commercial fishing, on his own initiative Bitney prepared a special re-port in 1932, complete with photographs, condemning them for not caring for their gas- and diesel-powered boats and for not fishing enough with them.[71] He opened his thirty-eight-page report by noting that "one's first impression of Neah Bay and the Makah Indians' possibilities in the fishing industry is very favor-able, especially at the height of the fishing season." Indeed, numerous Indian inspectors had reported this in previous years. Then Bitney's report went through each vessel in the Makah fleet, estimating its value and the profits it had earned its Native owner recently. A typical entry read: "'Ruby'—Owned by Thomas Parker who bought it nine years ago. Boat has nothing wrong with it but has been on the beach for three years. Tom used to fish for halibut in the summer and do quite well. He will not work as long as some one will feed him. Since

Henry T. Markishtum, his brother-in-law, started the grocery store three years ago, Tom has not done any fishing. Boat worth about $300.00 and has been a source of no income." Time and again, he castigated Makahs for letting their boats sit on the beach or for tying them up in a nearby river when they "should be out fishing." Others owners earned his scorn for potlatching instead of fishing like white men. Even those he complimented, such as James Hunter, "one of the best boatmen here and . . . very intelligent," fell short. At this time, Hunter owned three boats, including the diesel-powered *Hunter No. 4*, worth $10,000, that he had contracted out as a mail and passenger vessel. Bitney complained about the "very poorly designed" vessel that was expensive to maintain because "James did not know much about the engine" and kept needing to get it over-hauled in Seattle, where he "would take his whole family along and be gone a week or so on a big time." Of Hunter's two other vessels, the newer one had "never earned its owner a dime," while the other washed ashore during a storm, where it had sat for six months as the owner waited for someone to buy it.

Bitney concluded his report with an overview of the Makah use—or in his mind, squandering—of powerboats. Instead of working a run of fish, "They will make forty or fifty dollars and then lay around 'resting' for a week or two. The White fishermen will be out scooping up the fish and by the time the Indians are 'rested' the run is over and the fish are all gone." Part of the fault came from the fact that "their living comes too easy" because they could simply set a net in a river or fish from a canoe for a few hours to feed themselves. But in Bitney's mind, the main fault was a racial flaw: "The Makah Indian is a canoe fisherman from choice and heredity." As Indians, Makah owners took little care of their boats and engines because "they do not have the pride of ownership nor the sense of responsibility so important in any industry." In this way, Bitney drew upon a tired stereotype—that of the "lazy" Indian—to maintain racial boundaries, implying that the People of the Cape had no one but themselves to blame for white fishers taking salmon and halibut from Makah banks.[72]

But a more careful understanding of the examples Bitney deployed to disparage Makah fishers uncovers various dynamics at work at Neah Bay in the early 1930s. First, Makahs continued to engage in a moditional economy as they had generations earlier, but with some important differences.[73] James Hunter's activities with his boats illustrate this. Not only did he use them for fishing, but he also delivered mail and passengers throughout the Strait of Juan de Fuca; the lighthouse keepers at Tatoosh Island depended on his regular deliveries. Many Makah men mentioned in Bitney's report did not fish as often as the superintendent wanted because they engaged in other money-making opportunities when possible, including logging, running the local grocery store,

Hunter No. 4. James Hunter (Makah) had this built in Tacoma, Washington, in 1926 for $10,000. In addition to using it to fish, he carried mail and passengers around the Strait of Juan de Fuca. Photograph by Raymond H. Bitney, Superintendent at Neah Bay Agency, for a report, "Commercial Fishing by Makah Indians," ca. 1932. From folder 56247-1931, Neah Bay, 155, Central Classified Files, 1907–1939: Neah Bay [Agency], NARA.

and preaching, a profession that cut into the fishing time of Jerry McCarty and Perry Ides. When considering Bitney's report alongside those written by Indian inspectors, a range of labor opportunities emerge, including pelagic sealing—something Makahs were forbidden from using their powerboats for—and basket making, which became an important component to household economies. Perhaps Hunter took his family to Seattle to give them opportunities to sell their baskets at a better price in the city than what the reservation trader would pay.

Second, what whites often considered leisure time remained an important component of the Makah moditional economy. Although Bitney ranted against potlatching and derided Makahs for visiting neighboring communities instead of working, they used these opportunities to maintain important interpersonal linkages throughout the ča·di· borderland and to accomplish a considerable amount of work, such as basket making, which was a social affair. Indigenous borderlanders continued to privilege personal relationships and exchanges that occurred between friends and relatives, which was an integral part of their culture misunderstood by Bitney and non-Natives more generally. Bitney and superintendents before him complained that Makahs went to Tatoosh Island—then off the reservation—or over to Vancouver Island to engage in prohibited practices such as potlatching, dancing, and gambling.[74] Third, Bitney's careful enumeration of vessel ownership and earnings reveals that some families had found ways to make the moditional economy work for them. A few Makah families—such as the Hunters, Claplanhoos, Irvings, Ides, Greenes, Butlers, and Colbys—owned multiple boats and made thousands in a season. Several of these families also continued to fish for ling cod and winter salmon from canoes, earning more money outside the peak fishing season. With these profits, they bought more boats, diversified into other economic activities, and purchased important status items, such as automobiles. Bitney noted that the Claplanhoos made $2,500 a year between their two vessels: "They have a good crew. These people also own several automobiles and visit all the 'potlatches' and celebrations." He missed the ways automobile ownership, potlatches, celebrations, and visits resulted in having a good crew.

Last, Bitney's report highlights some of the structural impediments to Makahs profiting more from the commercial fisheries. He complained about them choosing to fish from canoes rather than powerboats even as he noted that they incurred no expenses when using canoes. Competing against much larger and more expensive purse seiners, long-liners, and trollers, Makah fishers understood that often it was not worth going out in their powerboats. The Claplanhoos told Bitney that "they do not like [the *North*] as it is too big, etc., and the best boat at Neah Bay is left at home." Valued at $3,000, this vessel likely found it challenging at times to compete against non-Native vessels worth ten times its cost. The Claplanhoos and other Makah boat owners understood that it made more sense to use their equipment strategically, not because they were "lazy" but because they did not see the sense in running up high operating expenses for a small profit opportunity. Similarly, the superintendent's photographs show non-Native purse seiners and trolling boats occupying all the moorage spaces, so his complaints about Makah boats lingering on beaches and in rivers ring as disingenuous—where else were cash-strapped families to put their boats when not in use?

Bitney's report failed to detail the efforts Makah families made to maintain the vessels they had and to purchase larger and better vessels so that they could compete against non-Native commercial fishers. For the first few decades of the twentieth century, Makahs sought ways to sell their reservation timber resources in order to invest in modern fishing equipment. In 1907, when reallotting the reservation so that everyone had ten acres of farmland instead of the initial marine-oriented allotments they had received in 1892, the reservation superintendent intended to have another set of forty-acre timber allotments surveyed later. A year later, when the timber allotment survey failed to happen, Makahs petitioned the commissioner of Indian affairs, noting that the ten-acre farming allotments were "wholly inadequate for any of us to make a living on."[75] Many of those signing the petition made their living fishing, so they likely hoped to spend the proceeds on fishing equipment. In his response to the petitioners, Commissioner Francis Leupp outlined how such a sale would benefit the tribe, at least from the perspective of the federal government. The Interior Department would retain the land title of the timber allotments "for the benefit of the tribe." After deducting the expenses for appraisal and sale of the timber, the secretary of the Interior would expend the remaining profit "for the benefit of the Indians in such manner as [he] might deem advisable," which included a water system for Neah Bay, a dam, the purchase of Washington State's right to the tidelands in Neah Bay, and wharves. Through the Neah Bay superintendent, the Interior Department, not Makahs, would define the priorities.[76]

By 1924, the Indian Office had negotiated a timber contract with a paper company, the Zellerbach Corporation, which merged with the Crown Willamette Paper Company in 1928 to form the Crown Zellerbach Corporation, which handled Makah timber for the next several decades. The 1924 contract included twenty thousand acres of spruce, cedar, and hemlock, valued at $715,377 in 1928. But less than 9 percent of this, about $64,000 in timber, was on the 1907 ten-acre farming allotments. It cost Makah allottees from $4,500 to $7,000 to clear their ten acres, and on average they received about $1,300 in profit from their timber, which they usually spent on house improvements, household equipment, and potlatch gifts. Families likely welcomed this one-time infusion of cash, but it was not enough to buy the kinds of vessels they needed to compete in the commercial fisheries. As unionized positions, the logging jobs on the Makah timber concession went to white men who lived in camps some distance in the woods; Makahs occasionally found work cutting cords of firewood. Crown Zellerbach built a railroad to move logs to the edge of the concession in order to float them down the Sail River, thereby destroying one of the few on-reservation salmon spawning grounds, a fact that also went unnoticed in Bitney's report about Makah commercial fishing. In return for occasional labor, a bit of cash, and environmental degradation, the federal government used the money to maintain the streets of Neah Bay and to care for the cemetery and municipal water.[77]

Bitney himself had even blocked Makahs from accessing tribal funds from the timber concession to purchase more expensive fishing vessels. When one Makah asked the superintendent for an $18,000 loan to purchase a purse seiner—probably an older, used one for that price—Bitney denied the request, explaining in a letter to the commissioner that "this particular Indian has lost one boat through his own carelessness and negligence."[78] Instead, Bitney considered that Makahs really only needed boats valued at one-tenth that price, and even these, he noted, were far more expensive than the $600 maximum that the Indian Office allowed for reimbursable loans. He had appended his report on Makah commercial fishing to this letter to prove that loaning tribal money to an Indian fisher was too risky. Bitney also complained about the tendency of Makahs to spend their money on automobiles. He neglected to note that Makah fishers often pulled the engines out and placed them in boats they built themselves. Not a foolish expenditure—and more akin to earlier practices such as repurposing pitchfork tines as fishhooks—this was one of the few ways that some Makahs could acquire a gas-powered fishing vessel.[79] Makahs even appealed to higher authorities, including US senators, to get access to tribal funds. In the early 1930s, Henry Markishtum wrote to Senator A. A. Grorud of the Senate Subcommittee on Indian Affairs requesting that his people have access to five-year reimbursable loans for the purchase of motorboat engines, boat building materials, and new frame houses. Similarly, Mrs. Chestoqua Peterson lobbied Washington's senator C. C. Dill for Makahs to get money from "Tribal Timber." She explained that "children are in need of things, half starved because during fishing season there are thousands of white men come down to fish and in this way they nearly fish out all the fish this people could get for they have first class equipment which our people can[']t buy for they hav[e]n't any money to buy this things. So I think if they could get there [sic] money from Timber and other money that is coming to them why they can compete with white men fishermen and buy good fishing outfit." Again, Bitney blocked this effort, arguing that "these Indians are self supporting and we want to further the incentive to work among the Indians and not kill it by making payments of unearned funds." As Makahs a decade later commented, they believed that "they have as much right to control their funds as any white man." Bitney's actions and the lack of access to their timber moneys left the People of the Cape feeling "oppress[ed]" by the Indian Office and "[helpless] before the tactics of the whites, who . . . find a way to cheat them of their inheritance."[80]

Against this backdrop, the political jurisdiction of fisheries regulations became more complex when the United States and Canada sought ways to conserve halibut and salmon. Beginning in the 1890s, Progressive era fishers from both sides of the Canadian-US border blamed one another for "wanton wastefulness of fish," especially Pacific salmon. Prodded by angry fishers and scientists, US and Canadian politicians began seeking joint efforts for conserving fisheries in the territorial and contiguous waters in North America. Diplomatic discussions over the conservation of Fraser River salmon in 1892, 1909, and 1918 never received much US support because Washington State officials refused to give up any power to regulate fisheries in their waters.[81]

These talks nevertheless laid the groundwork for the successful American-Canadian Sockeye-Salmon Convention of 1930. This established the International Pacific Salmon Fisheries Commission (IPSFC), patterned after the respected International Fisheries Commission, which had been studying and making recommendations about halibut for most of the previous decade. The salmon fisheries commission received wide latitude to establish regulations, but only in an advisory capacity. The convention divided sockeye equally between US and Canadian fishers, and its jurisdiction included the two nations' territorial waters in the Strait of Juan de Fuca, Puget Sound, and the Gulf of Georgia, along with the entire Fraser River, its tributaries, and extraterritorial marine waters between forty-eight and forty-nine degrees latitude west of the entrance to the strait. Although Canada moved to ratify the convention immediately, another seven years passed before the United States did so. One condition the US Senate added was an additional advisory board of five members from each country, representing the branches of the fishery, including the purse seine, gill net, troll, and sports fishers. Noticeably absent was a seat for American Indians or First Nations fishers, even though convention waters included Makah marine fishing banks and those of numerous other indigenous nations. Indeed, the convention, salmon commission, and advisory board reflected no concern for treaty Indian fishing rights. As with the international halibut conventions, the 1930 salmon treaty established a quota system that disadvantaged Native fishers. The season closed when the quota was reached in each area, usually before the best times of the season for Makah fishers and other Indians to catch salmon in waters to which they had access and could use the gear they owned. This depressed their fishing efforts and the meager investments they could make in the commercial industry.[82]

The conservation of Fraser River salmon finally gained the support of Washington State's officials and non-Native commercial fishers, and thereby opening the door to US ratification, through the 1934 passage of Initiative 77, a law that the state fisheries department also used to crack down on American Indian fishers. Sponsored by purse seine, gill net, troll, and sports fishers, the new regulations abolished stationary gear and established a line that closed Puget Sound to all commercial fishers, except treaty Indians fishing on reservations. Those in the commercial fishing fleet supported the initiative because it outlawed fish traps, which had previously taken the largest share of the catch. With the removal of traps from Washington waters, US purse seiners and other vessel fishers found an advantage in the convention terms that would guarantee them an allocation of 50 percent of the catch. The approved initiative also restricted purse seining in certain areas to weekdays and months of October and November, which concentrated this fishing on Makah banks and those of other peoples, such as the Lummi, in the Strait of Juan de Fuca and northern Puget Sound. While Initiative 77 protected treaty Indian fishers on their reservations, state fisheries inspectors interpreted it differently, using it to justify crackdowns on all "young bucks" fishing off-reservation.[83]

After the passage of Initiative 77, Washington's Department of Fisheries also closed the Hoko and Ozette Rivers and other waterways just outside the reservation to all salmon fishing, except for sports fishers using hook and line, thereby preventing Makahs from accessing the critical usual and accustomed grounds on which they had relied for generations. Shortly thereafter, fisheries inspectors arrested Makahs fishing off-reservation and confiscated their gear. Despite these arrests, the People of the Cape continued to fish clandestinely, even using the new road to Neah Bay to their advantage. Inspector E. M. Benn complained in 1937 that he found it impossible to catch two Makah vessels, the *Wyaach* and *Makaah*, rigged for fishing the Hoko's mouth, because two Indians with cars continuously drove along the road to keep tabs on the patrol boat. Despite these efforts at keeping ahead of the fisheries patrols, Makah catches dwindled. Luke Markishtum noted in 1941 that his family dried only twenty-five to thirty fish annually when they had formerly dried hundreds.[84]

By the mid-1930s, the situation at Cape Flattery looked grim. Annually, hundreds of non-Native commercial and sports fishers overwhelmed and overtaxed tribal fishing grounds. This came at the same time that Washington officials tightened their control over fisheries in state waters and seemed to wage war on treaty Indian fishing rights, even when laws exempted Native fishers. During the first three decades of the twentieth century, Makahs sought ways to better participate in the commercial fisheries of salmon and halibut. However, agency superintendents bent on assimilating the People of the Cape away from their customary marine occupations provided serious impediments to their ability to succeed. At best, these officials could sometimes help Makah fishers avoid jail or the confiscation of their gear; at worst, they supported state officials' efforts to arrest Indians. Simultaneously, Makahs found their fisheries regulated by two separate international bodies that set quotas and complicated regulations that disadvantaged American Indian fishing. Their economic options dwindled, as did the amount of fish they could put on household tables. In closing a 1941 meeting of the tribal council and elders, Chester Wanderhard explained, "We Indians are only in this world to live, and we must have this old fishing grounds for our livelihood."[85] As the mid-twentieth century unfolded, the People of the Cape moved to reclaim what they had lost.

THE FIGHT FOR FISHING RIGHTS
AND MAKAH AUTONOMY

Like that of other American Indians during the last three quarters of the twentieth century, the Makah experience with various government branches and agencies resembled that of an erratic pendulum. A gain in one area was often undercut by a loss somewhere else. Few other case studies exemplify this best than what the People of the Cape experienced from changing federal policies and decisions made by county, state, and federal courts. Amid these vicissitudes, though, we should not characterize Makahs as simply responding to forces beyond their control. Instead, this history from the twentieth century illustrates the ways Makah leaders and families took action to retain what was most important to them—the sea and the resources it provided for consumption and commercial purposes.[86]

Across Indian Country, the 1930s were an interesting decade of changes and possibilities, driven by the actions of Native peoples and administrative modifications brought on by the new commissioner of Indian affairs, John Collier. The situation was no different at Neah Bay. About a year into Superintendent Bitney's administration, the People of the Cape decided that they had suffered enough. The tribal council and eighty-five other Makahs petitioned the secretary of the Interior for Bitney's removal. They charged him with malfeasance of duty, declaring that he was repeatedly absent and concerned more with outside affairs than with those of the tribe. Noting that "he is not in sympathy with the affairs of the Makah Indians," they found him antagonistic to their needs, discourteous, and "uneven" in temperament. The petition concluded by declaring that keeping him there "would only mean constant friction and [an] unsatisfactory state of affair[s] as well as mismanagement of the Makah Indians real need." Makahs had complained about agents and superintendents before—their efforts had resulted in the removal of Agent Huntington in 1877—but this was their first petition against a superintendant. Coming just three years after the Presidential Task Force's Meriam Report (1928), which highlighted the dire economic, education, health, and administrative affairs in Indian Country, the petition caught the interest of Commissioner Charles Rhoads, who assigned an Indian Office field representative, Henry Roe Cloud (Ho-Chunk), to investigate.[87]

Arriving at Neah Bay in August 1932, Roe Cloud met with Makah leaders, deposed Bitney, and investigated the actions of W. W. Washburn Jr., the reservation trader. That Roe Cloud's report supported the Makah position should come as no surprise. Through his work in collecting information and writing large portions of the Meriam Report, alongside his efforts at supporting Indian education, Roe Cloud had become a recognized and respected advocate for American Indians.[88] Much of what he observed at Neah Bay seemed to echo the Meriam Report's conclusions. Roe Cloud found that Washburn dominated the Makah reservation by controlling the tribe's timber concession and benefiting from the thousands of non-Native fishers who frequented Neah Bay during the summer. The trader had secured the 1924 bid for tribal timber, which he assigned to the Washington Pulp and Paper Corporation. Not only was the company a subsidiary of the Zellerbach Corporation, but it also employed Washburn as their attorney. Roe Cloud noted, "This key position enabled him to know when an Indian had money coming in, as all records of cuttings by allotments were available to him. By a timely extension of credit to one Indian after another he gradually gained a very strong hand over the Makah Indians. It can be seen how an economic control over tribal affairs such as this can enable a man, in time, to dictate policy in Indian Affairs." Probably erring on the side of diplomacy, Roe Cloud concluded that Washburn also controlled Bitney. "He [Bitney] thunders out authority and commands without obedience from any sources. The Indians see him going about doing the bidding of the trader in the guise of helping the Indians. They see him for what he is—a servant of the trader—and they rend him, not realizing that he, too, is one of the innocent victims of circumstance."[89] Although he lauded Bitney for his education efforts, Roe Cloud condemned him for wielding dictatorial power over the tribe, throwing tribal councils into discord, and allowing Standard Oil (which sold fuel to non-Native fishing vessels) to commandeer Neah Bay's water supply to the detriment of Makah health.

Roe Cloud's recommendations resembled those made two years later when he likely helped write the Wheeler-Howard Act, better known as the Indian Reorganization Act (IRA) of 1934. He outlined his proposed changes as a plan to realize a "new deal" at Neah Bay. First, he advised the commissioner to transfer out Bitney. Second, he advocated a bureaucratic consolidation of Washington State's coastal reservations. Citing a report he had written in April 1933, Roe Cloud urged the Indian Office to position the superintendent at Hoquiam, more than a hundred miles from Neah Bay. Third, the tribe should establish self-governing institutions to replace the once-dictatorial control of the superintendent. This would include an Indian court and a newly organized tribal council headed by "hereditary Chief [Jongie] Claplanhoo," whose authority Bitney had never recognized. Fourth, the Indian Office should install a new village water system for health and fire protection. Fifth, the federal agency should open credit facilities for Makahs, whom he found "capable of fishing on a substantial and large scale," and make available market facilities for them to manage the sale of their own baskets, fish, and timber. In conclusion, Roe Cloud stated that Makahs "can protect their own interests far better through their own council and with a superintendent at Hoquiam who can be . . . more independent of the trader's influence and also, by reason of the distance and new policy and independence for Indians herein recommended." In many ways, these recommendations resembled an early blueprint for the Indian Reorganization Act.[90]

Later that year, Commissioner Collier implemented Roe Cloud's recommendations. He dismissed Bitney and consolidated the Makah reservation with the Quileute, Quinault, and Hoh agencies, forming the Taholah Indian Agency, with a superintendent in Hoquiam. The Indian Office made a $20,000 revolving loan fund available to Makahs to purchase agricultural and fishing equipment to help them become self-sufficient. This was a significant reversal of previous federal management of reservation moneys; however, as Charles Peterson (Makah) testified in 1949, these loans were too meager to accomplish this goal. Considering that the purchase of a single purse seiner would have wiped out the loan in its entirety, this was a fair criticism. Probably reflecting on the positive outcome from their time with Roe Cloud, the newly formed tribal council voted to accept the terms of the Indian Reorganization Act in 1936, and a year later, they implemented a tribal charter that resulted in achieving a fair degree of autonomy.[91] With their new freedom, the tribal council sought legal action to restore some of what they had lost.

The litigation that the Makah Tribal Council pursued both defined and exemplified key issues and concepts related to American Indian treaty rights from the mid-twentieth century on.[92] For Washington's tribal nations, many of these court cases focused on two phrases from the 1855 Stevens treaties: "usual and accustomed grounds and stations" and "in common with all citizens of the United States," both of which appeared in article 4 of the Treaty of Neah Bay. The first phrase referred to places where treaty Indians fished and preserved their catches. Washington State officials, fish trap owners, and non-Native fishers wanted to limit this to fishing grounds located on reservations, while the treaty tribes understood that these grounds included places both on and off the reservation. *United States. v. Winans* (1905), one of the first Supreme Court cases to uphold treaty Indian fishing rights, dealt with this phrase, deciding that usual and accustomed places included fishing grounds beyond reservation boundaries, even when on property owned by non-Natives. *Winans* also defined the right of access as an important dimension to this right. The court determined that the treaty right to usual and accustomed places was meaningless unless Native fishers could reach these locations. The justices grounded their decision in an important interpretation of the treaties, namely that these documents did not grant "special" rights to Indians; instead, treaties acknowledged rights Natives already possessed, ones that they reserved for their current and future uses.[93]

The second phrase—"in common with all citizens of the United States"—proved more challenging for the courts to determine. From the perspective of Washington State officials and non-Natives, this meant that treaty Indians simply possessed an equal opportunity to take fish on similar terms and under the same regulations that applied to everyone. In the 1910s, state fish commissioner Darwin interpreted this phrase to mean that Indians fishing off-reservation must abide by state laws just like whites. From his perspective, anything more connoted "special" or "superior" rights to which Indians were not entitled. As Darwin argued to Cato Sells, commissioner of Indian affairs, "To make further concessions to the Indians than are already made I think would be an unfair discrimination against our whites, who bear the burden of the maintenance of the fisheries department." Subsequent officials even framed the issue as one of state's rights. In 1936, Game Department director Bernard T. McCauley argued that "the current controversy hinges on the point that Indians are infringing on state rights. The state is not infringing on the privileges of Indians."[94] These views shaped Washington's perspective on the meaning of "in common with all citizens of the United States" when facing American Indians in court.[95] The state's tribal nations argued that this phrase meant that they retained the unconditional right to fish off-reservation, although non-Natives could fish in these same places. Nothing in this phrase implied that at some point the state government could abrogate this right. It took the courts most of the twentieth century to determine that the treaty Indian interpretation was correct.

Another key principle shaped the twentieth-century treaty rights cases. In two decisions—*United States. v. Kagama* (1886) and *Seufert Brothers Company v. United States* (1919)—the Supreme Court established the judicial principle that courts should interpret treaty terms as tribal representatives at the treaty councils understood them at the time and in the spirit of the US obligation to protect the interests of a "dependent" people.[96] The following cases illustrate that Makahs and their attorneys relied on this principle in explaining their understanding of what Governor Stevens promised and what rights tribal negotiators reserved in the 1855 Treaty of Neah Bay. Conversely, state officials often groused about this principle, arguing that conditions had changed so much that whatever tribal negotiators had thought back in 1855 no longer mattered.

The People of the Cape began by suing the state in 1940 for arresting Makahs who exercised their treaty rights to fish at the mouth of and along the Hoko River. In their complaint, the Makah asserted "that they had fished this river with all types of commercial gear from the dawn of history until the year 1932, when Inspector Benn had failed to observe their treaty rights and had arrested members of the tribe and confiscated their fishing gear."[97] By referencing "all types of commercial gear," Makahs distinguished that they had always fished the Hoko with "seines, set nets, dip nets and other Indian fishing gear" that state law prohibited.[98] In a US district court decision in 1941, Judge John Bowen granted the injunction to the tribe and ordered the state to quit arresting Makahs for fishing the Hoko. The state appealed through Game Department director McCauley. Although Makah attorneys argued that allowing the state to exercise its power "to take away the Indians' treasured right to fish" did "violence to the Indians' understanding of the right conferred," in *McCauley v. Makah* (1942), Judge Lloyd Black, for the ninth circuit court of appeals, reversed the lower court's decision. Most important, Black cited the recently decided Supreme Court case, *Tulee v. Washington* (1942), to rule that the state's prohibition of set gear was necessary for conservation reasons. Although the court in *Tulee* had ruled that the treaties protected American Indians from state interference, the decision included an important exception for conservation purposes. For this reason Washington State officials at the time saw *Tulee* as a major victory and began using this exception to argue for the necessity of regulating Indian fishing rights off-reservation.[99]

The *McCauley* decision against the Makah caused "considerable dismay." It confirmed their belief that "they are being despoiled by whites and that nothing they can do will prevent it."[100] *McCauley* empowered the state to continue its harassment of Makahs and other treaty Indian fishers, a crusade eagerly followed by Milo Moore, Washington's fisheries director from 1945 to 1949. When the legislature enacted a new fisheries code in 1949 under the urging of Director Moore, it repealed all provisions relating to American Indians, including exemptions for subsistence fishing, following the advice of the state attorney general, who believed that special laws for Indian fishing were unconstitutional now that Natives were US citizens. "All Americans were equal under the law, and from that time forward, everyone would fish 'in common' with each other under the same regulations—state regulations." The People of the Cape understood that this did not reflect the rights guaranteed to them under the Treaty of Neah Bay. Charles Peterson explained to the District Court in 1949 during another unsuccessful litigation effort that "I believe we have a right to fish there [the Hoko River] from things that have been passed on to me from the older people down there. . . . I don't figure I am committing a crime if I go down there and fish, even if I get caught at it." Although some Makahs felt powerless, many more continued to fight the harassment they received at the hands of state officials.[101]

With Judge Black's sudden death in 1950, a new judge headed the ninth circuit court of appeals during the next round of litigation, and Makahs finally began receiving some justice in the courts. In *Makah v. Schoettler* (1951), the tribal council appealed an earlier judgment dismissing a Makah complaint seeking relief from state fishing regulations prohibiting their use of the Hoko River. Catering to sports fishers, the regulations allowed only hook-and-line fishing. The People of the Cape argued that silver salmon, an important source of winter food and income for Makah families, refused to take a hook in the river, so the state regulation prevented them from exercising their treaty right to fish the run. Judge William Denman agreed with the Makah and determined that the regulation was unnecessary for conservation because "the run could be fully preserved by a partial stopping of the fishing" during the spawning season. The state had failed to prove that it needed to enforce their regulations against Makahs for conservation purposes. Although he reaffirmed the conservation exception—state regulations could still displace treaty rights when necessary for conservation—Judge Denman required the state to do more than simply say that regulations were needed. In reversing the district court decision, Judge Denman ordered that court to restrain the Department of Fisheries, then directed by Robert Schoettler, from enforcing regulations against Makahs. Afterward, the tribal council negotiated a voluntary agreement with Director Schoettler to cooperate with the fisheries department by collecting salmon eggs for state hatcheries and removing nets from the Hoko River for three twenty-four hour periods each week to allow escapement for spawning salmon. Invoking the new rule established by *Schoettler*, other tribal nations found relief from anti-Indian state regulations construed as necessary for conservation.[102]

While the Makah fought Washington State in the federal courts in order to regain some salmon fishing rights in state waters, they filed a claim against the federal government through the Indian Claims Commission (ICC) to gain restitution for the loss of their marine fisheries. Established through a congressional act in 1946, the Indian Claims Commission gave tribes five years to file claims. The majority of the Makah claim—$10 million—focused on the destruction of their right to take halibut at usual and accustomed offshore banks, while a smaller portion—another $1 million—sought a settlement for the loss of the right to hunt seals. Although the Makah argued that the International Fisheries Commission's regulations created conditions that cut them out of the fishery, Chief Commissioner Witt ruled against the tribe and sided with the Justice Department, which acted as the defendant in ICC cases. The Makah appealed to the court of claims, which ruled in favor of the commissioner's decision, while noting that there should be a review of the government's payment for the tribe's land cessions and the treaty obligation to supply fishing gear. This outcome resembled those of many ICC cases, illustrating that American Indians still failed to find justice even through programs designed to assist them.[103]

Witt's ruling drew from the conservation exception established by federal courts in treaty Indian fishing cases. The defendant's memorandum argued for dismissing the Makah claims because "conservation could be effected only by concerted action on an international plane and by measures applied to the halibut stock in its natural habitat." Interestingly, the defendant appeared to have some help in framing the argument's substance. Shortly after its loss to the Makah in the federal courts, Washington State's Department of Fisheries—back under the directorship of Milo Moore—coached the Justice Department in its case against the tribe. After the Indian Claims Commission dismissed the tribe's case, Ralph Barney, the department's Indian claims section chief, corresponded with Director Moore to express his "appreciation" for Moore's "tremendous contribution" toward the case: "You will be pleased to observe that your views respecting the necessity and reasonableness of the regulations adopted to conserve these natural resources have been judicially vindicated and that the outstanding success of your efforts has been applauded." Moore probably took some satisfaction from getting back at the tribal nation.[104]

While the Indians Claims Commission deliberated over the Makah claim in the 1950s, the state's fisheries department tried to capitalize on the public's growing anti-Indian attitudes of the Termination Era. In 1953, Congress enacted House Concurrent Resolution 108, which directed federal agencies to terminate the government's trust relationship with American Indian tribes. When signing House Resolution 2828, which terminated the Menominee tribal nation a year later, President Dwight Eisenhower remarked that this bill would help them and others "to realize their full potential as productive citizens of the United States whenever they can advantageously assume complete responsibility for the management of their affairs." Just like Washington State officials who argued that "in common with" meant that treaty Indians shared the same rights as other citizens, his words highlighted the way termination supporters cloaked their intentions with liberation rhetoric. In reality, though, termination sought to remove the few protections tribes had and the rights they had secured for themselves.[105]

In Washington, this took a virulent tone when non-Natives scapegoated American Indians for depleting salmon runs. Local publications ran articles decrying the advantages treaty Indian fishers had over non-Native commercial and sports fishers and cast them as malicious opportunists taking the last salmon valiantly attempting to return upriver to spawn. This attitude had been around for some time; proponents of Initiative 77 (1934) had drawn from this sentiment to exaggerate the effect Indian fishers had on the fishery. Yet as Edward Swindell reported for the Indian Office in 1942, "the extent that the Indian fishing participation in such injury [salmon depletion] has been greatly overemphasized," noting that what Indians caught represented from 2.4 to 6.7 percent of the total catch in Puget Sound from 1938 to 1940. From 1958 to 1967, Native fishers landed just 6.5 percent of salmon in the state, while non-Indian commercial fishers landed 81.3 percent and sports fishers landed 12.2 percent. Despite these findings, Director Moore took to the pages of the *Seattle Times* in 1958 to blame Indian fishers for the fishery's dismal state. Speaking through their attorney, Nathan Richardson, the Makah Tribal Council responded, warning Moore that his statements "will probably antagonize Indian people throughout the State of Washington because . . . [they] leave the impression that the Indian people are depleting the salmon supply in Washington waters. This is of course ridiculous and the article is misleading." Richardson pointed to a collection of factors caused by non-Natives that better explained declining fish runs and castigated Moore for racializing the conflict: "Since that time [of the treaties] of course the hue and cry of those who either do not care to face the facts or are ignorant of the facts still is directed to the Indians. The persons supposedly in the 'know' about things of this matter do not bring in the depletion by mills, dams, deforrested areas, modern fishermen with modern equipment, pulp mills, pol[l]ution and many, many other factors which aid in the destroying and depletion of our fish. Following a pattern, familiar in history, a minority group has been singled out for blame and sportsmen and commercial fishermen throughout the State have a definite idea that the Indians really do seriously affect the supply of salmon in Washington waters. The small amount of fish taken by Indian Fishermen is so insignificant, as compare with other elements involved in depletion that it cannot be considered as a major factor." He reminded the fisheries director that the tribal nation had worked hard at cooperating with the state on salmon conservation.[106]

During the 1960s, Pacific Northwest Native activists responded to the state's increasing arrests of Indian fishers by staging fish-ins that garnered media and celebrity attention. For numerous tribal nations, treaty Indian fishing rights in the Northwest were one of the defining civil rights issues of the decade. Leaders such as Billy Frank Jr. (Nisqually) and Hank Adams (Fort Peck Assiniboine–Sioux) reflected the sentiments of many. Adams asked the government why the state harassed Indian fishers and their families, "while 45,000 non-Indians continue to draw their income from the commercial salmon industry and while half a million non-Indian citizens pleasure themselves in the salmon sports fishery." Although much of the furor and publicity focused on Puget Sound tribes and rivers, Makah fishers also found themselves within the state fisheries department's crosshairs. Thor Tollefson, then director of fisheries, put the Makah Tribal Council on notice for violations of state fishing laws, accusing the People of the Cape for using illegal gear, fishing within preserves and in closed areas, taking salmon out of season, and violating "International Treaties and Compacts, as they affect the Straits of Juan de Fuca." He warned them that "claiming immunity as Indians" would not work and that Makahs would be arrested and prosecuted. Quentin Markishtum, then tribal chairman, responded, noting that Tollefson did not complain that "our fishing activities violate any regulations which are 'necessary for the conservation of fish.'" Markishtum advised the director that his stance that all state fishing regulations applied to American Indians was "ill-advised and unlawful," reminding him that enforcement "would constitute a total deprivation of rights guaranteed to us by treaty and recognized by the courts of this land." He then outlined the long list of court cases affirming the tribal council's position. Markishtum concluded by warning the director, "We must respectfully advise you that we shall resist with every means at our command any effort by your department or any other State law enforcement officials to invade or violate our treaty rights."[107]

Perhaps the new fleet of Makah vessels rather than law-breaking Indians concerned Tollefson. While the fishing wars continued in the courts and on the water, Makahs had sought other means to strengthen their ability to increase their share of salmon and halibut. A major sale of reservation timber in the early 1960s gave the tribal nation some much-needed capital that they invested in commercial fishing. Like other Native communities in the 1960s and 1970s, the Makah Tribal Council took advantage of new federal aid programs to help develop their economy. They applied for and secured a loan from the Small Business Administration through the 1964 Equal Opportunity Loan program for economic development. A large portion went to building a Makah fleet of modern fishing vessels, larger ones capable of competing against non-Native commercial fishers in the Pacific. With this loan, the tribal nation ordered from a Tacoma shipyard nine thirty-six-foot boats and a fifty-six-foot vessel. The Small Business Administration provided half the funds, with in-kind money coming from the recent timber sale. Individual Makahs mortgaged the boats, agreeing to make regular payments. This inaugurated the tribe's modern fishing fleet. Along with many smaller craft, the new Makah vessels gillnetted and trolled for salmon in marine waters. In the 1980s, the fleet began long-lining for halibut and black cod, and in the 1990s they started trawling for whiting and other groundfish species. The current fleet size is 110 marine fishing vessels, including trollers, gill-netters, long-liners, and trawlers. A few of these ships fish for tuna, crab, and other shellfish.[108]

As tensions escalated between American Indian and non-Native fishers in the late 1960s, various stakeholders sought a final court decision affirming or denying the state's control over treaty Indian fishing. Judge Robert Belloni's 1969 decision in *United States v. Oregon* came close to offering a model that treaty rights supporters thought applied as well to Washington State. Although conceding that the state could regulate Indian fishing when "reasonable and necessary for the conservation of the fish resource," Belloni required Oregon to manage its fisheries so that a "fair and equitable share" of fish remained available for Native fishers at their usual and accustomed grounds.[109]

Although this was an important victory for treaty tribes, the question of what constituted a "fair and equitable share" of the fishery remained open, and the state continued to harass Native fishers. At the end of August 1973, the Makah and thirteen other tribal nations again confronted the state and its departments of fisheries and game in the District Court in what became the landmark case *United States v. Washington* (1974). In their interpretation of "fair and equitable," Native fishers contended that they should be able to catch enough fish in order to make a living through this customary practice. George Dysart, the lawyer for the Department of the Interior arguing on behalf of the tribes, argued that Belloni's "fair and equitable" meant that Native fishers were entitled to an equal share of the resource. Washington's Department of Fisheries was willing to go so far as to agree that Indian, non-Native commercial, and sports fishers should each receive one-third of the salmon resource, whereas the Department of Game, which regulated steelhead runs, argued that Natives had no separate privileges or rights greater than those held by non-Natives. The first phase of the trial lasted three weeks and included the testimony of forty-nine witnesses and the filing of hundreds of documents, which Judge George Boldt considered. What became known as *Phase I* of *U.S. v. Washington* examined whether treaty Indian fishers had a right to fish off-reservation and, if so, whether this entitled them to a specific portion of salmon and steelhead in their usual and accustomed places. Handed down on February 12, 1974, the "Boldt decision" affirmed treaty Indian fishing rights. Boldt ruled that tribes indeed have definable rights to salmon, steelhead, and other fish off-reservation and that the state has to consider these rights separately from those of other users. More specifically, he determined that "in common with all citizens of the United States" meant "sharing equally"—or 50 percent of—the amount of harvestable fish. Boldt concurred with previous cases supporting the need for the state to regulate for conservation, but in a major departure, he determined that these regulations had to be carried out in accordance with treaty rights. Additionally, the Boldt decision established the groundwork for eventual comanagement of the resource by recognizing that tribes could manage their share of the fishery. This important distinction helped to "debunk [the] propaganda" of state officials and non-Native sports and commercial fishers who had scapegoated American Indians for destroying salmon runs.[110]

Reactions to the Boldt decision varied. Some Native fishers felt that the judge's decision had not gone far enough, but others celebrated the strong affirmation of treaty fishing rights. Coming down as it did "in a political climate of extreme antagonism directed at Indian fishers," however, the Boldt decision received "unrelenting" resistance from state officials and non-treaty commercial and sports fishing groups.[111] As state attorney general and the lawyer representing the state in *U.S. v. Washington*, Slade Gorton saw overturning the district court's decision as his office's key mission. Probably stemming from both political convictions and personal connections to the commercial fishing industry through Slade Gorton & Co., Inc., a Boston-based seafood company, the attorney general's anti-Indian views prompted him to refer to Natives as "supercitizens" because of rights he felt the court had conferred on them. Non-Native commercial fishers initiated additional court cases to immobilize enacting the equal apportionment, and they also held their own illegal "fish-ins," even burning Boldt's effigy in protest. In affirming *U.S. v. Washington*, the ninth circuit court of appeals in 1975 noted that "except for some desegregation cases . . . , the district court has faced the most concerted official and private efforts to frustrate a decree of a federal court witnessed this century." Yet even this affirmation of *U.S. v. Washington* and the Supreme Court's initial refusal to review the case in 1976 did little to quell the disorder and tensions on the water and in the courts. This led Judge Boldt to assume responsibility of state salmon allocations to ensure that Native fishers received their fair share; still, non-Native illegal fishing and county and state court dismissals of these actions continued. The lower court challenges to the federal court's authority ended up in the Supreme Court. In 1979, the highest court in the land affirmed the Boldt decision, with some slight modifications, and demanded that the state fisheries and game departments adopt and enforce regulations conforming to the district court's decision. This restored state agency control over the fisheries and largely resolved the issue in favor of treaty Indians.[112]

Amid this disorder, *Phase II* of *U.S. v. Washington* began. Having replaced Boldt on the District Court bench, Judge William Orrick presided over this phase of the case that examined the issues of hatchery fish and environmental degradation of salmon habitat. As in the decision in *Phase I*, Judge Orrick ruled in favor of tribal nations, concluding that all hatchery fish must be included in the allocation computations. More important, Judge Orrick ruled that "the treaty-secured fishing right incorporates an environmental right." In poignant language, he ruled that if environmental degradation runs unchecked, "the right to take fish would eventually be reduced to the right to dip one's net into the water . . . and bring it out empty." Under appeal, Orrick's ruling on hatchery fish was upheld, but his decision on the habitat issue was dismissed on procedural grounds.[113] Although this critical issue remains unresolved, the two phases of *U.S. v. Washington* resulted in cooperation among stakeholders in the salmon fishery by the early 1980s. State officials, non-Native commercial and sports fishers, and tribal nations felt by then that this held more promise than litigation. Bolstered by American Indian self-governance movements, state-tribal cooperation became a key component in the 1985 Pacific Salmon Treaty between the United States and Canada and in related legislation.[114]

Phases I and *II* of *U.S. v. Washington* represented a victory for the Makah, specifically salmon fishers. The People of the Cape would no longer suffer harassment at the hands of state officials for exercising their treaty fishing rights on rivers. But this was a limited victory for Makahs. Even though Judge Boldt described the halibut banks and Swiftsure as examples of the tribal nation's usual and accustomed grounds, *Phase I* dealt only with treaty Indian fishing rights in state waters, which did not include the critical marine fisheries located more than three miles offshore. At this time, Makahs continued to have the equal opportunity of access to their halibut fishing banks, although the larger numbers of non-Native commercial and sports fishers, the more highly capitalized non-Native fleet, and dwindling fish stocks constrained them. But even this limited access was about to change.

COMBATTING LINES ON THE WATER

While Makahs and other Washington Indians won substantial acknowledgments of salmon and steelhead fishing rights in the federal courts, international diplomacy around maritime jurisdictional claims swept away the People of the Cape's access to their most lucrative halibut banks. After World War II, pressure mounted for nations to extend their jurisdiction over offshore resources beyond the narrow three-mile coastal zones that had been the normal claims for most of the modern era. Discovery of offshore mineral and oil deposits and the rising catches of long-distance fishing fleets, especially those from Japan and the Soviet Union, along with the threat of pollution from transport ships and oil tankers, increased tensions among nations with maritime claims. Ocean spaces such as the North Pacific then became layered with claims, counterclaims, and sovereignty disputes. First convened in New York in 1973, the Third United Nations Conference on the Law of the Sea aimed to resolve the situation by creating an "effective international regime" for the sea and seafloor. It took eleven sessions over nine years to hammer out what became the United Nations Convention on the Law of the Sea. This "constitution for the seas" covers such issues as territorial sea limits, economic jurisdiction, conservation and management of living marine resources, and protection of the marine environment, among other concerns.[115] In the meantime, most nations extended their jurisdictional claims out two hundred miles through exclusive economic or fishery zones, territorial seas, or some combination thereof. Most relevant for Makahs, both the United States and Canada in 1977 declared two-hundred-mile exclusive fishery zones offshore.[116] This placed the tribal nation's most lucrative halibut fishing banks, Swiftsure and 40-Mile Banks, in Canadian waters, thereby barring Makah fishers from legally accessing these usual and accustomed fishing grounds.

This outcome was anything but inevitable. As early as 1960, the Makah Tribal Council was following the international diplomatic developments. The 1958 Geneva Convention on the Continental Shelf caught the council's attention because it recognized the rights of coastal nations to exercise exclusive jurisdiction over resources of continental shelves; where two neighboring nations share a continental shelf boundary—such as the one underneath Makah marine space and along the boundary between the United States and Canada off the entrance to the Strait of Juan de Fuca—the principle of equidistance determines a maritime boundary, unless there are special interests or factors at play. Understanding this, the Makah Tribal Council passed a resolution in 1960 articulating the special interests—treaty fishing rights to Makah halibut banks—that the United States needed to consider when negotiating a possible sea claim with Canada. They reminded US diplomats that the extension being considered would "deprive the members of the Makah Tribe of Indians their right to fish in their usual and accustomed fishing grounds." Acting on Makah concerns proved unnecessary when the US-Canadian proposal failed to garner enough votes at the conference. Makah actions, though, did bring their concerns into the international arena.[117]

Similarly, the Makah Tribal Council tried diplomatic channels after the United States and Canada declared exclusive fishery zones that encompassed tribal marine space. Through their attorneys in 1978, the tribal council wrote to Ambassador Lloyd Cutler in the State Department, reminding him that critical usual and accustomed fishing grounds then sat under Canadian maritime jurisdiction. Invoking the 1974 Boldt decision, the tribal council stated, "We feel it is imperative upon the government to continue to protect our fishing rights for halibut and other species in the Pacific Ocean and any new agreements which may be reached with the government of Canada. Our rights must, of course, be 'grandfathered in' not only because they are traditional and historic in the normal sense of the word, but also because they have been recognized by treaties with the United States government." But when Ambassador Cutler and others negotiated new agreements with Canada with respect to overlapping claims in the exclusive fishery zone off the Strait of Juan de Fuca, they ignored Makah treaty rights. Instead, in the 1979 protocol, these diplomats secured the access of sports fishers to Swiftsure and other historically Makah banks in Canadian waters. Currently these non-Natives fish former Makah banks and land their catch at Neah Bay. In 1990, this amounted to 105,300 pounds of halibut. To put this number in perspective, that year Makah fishers landed 131,900 pounds of halibut and non-Native commercial fishers caught over 277,000 pounds off the Strait of Juan de Fuca. As a senior fisheries biologist for the Makah noted, the People of the Cape "are deeply concerned by the fact that the United States seems to care more about sport fishermen than treaty Indians when it comes to efforts to secure access to those areas." Outside diplomatic channels, Makahs protested the loss of access to customary marine space by continuing to fish for halibut in the newly claimed Canadian waters during the late 1970s and early 1980s. These actions often resulted in his people having what Greig Arnold called "breakfast on the Queen." What he meant was that Canadian officials arrested these fishers, confiscated their boats and gear, and threw them in jail in Victoria, where they awoke the next morning and received breakfast before being released.[118]

This new line on the water represented another component of the United States' and Canada's long-term efforts at hardening the international border and containing indigenous peoples. In the mid- to late nineteenth century, officials worried about Natives crossing the border at will, buying and selling whiskey, conspiring to attack whites, carrying diseases, and smuggling oil, fish, and other goods.[119] When Washington State and British Columbia, along with federal and dominion forces, increased their abilities to police the border in the early twentieth century, Native peoples who had once easily traversed the čaˑdiˑ borderland found that they sometimes needed new documents, such as passports, simply to visit family on the other side of the strait.[120] Canadian arrests of Makah fishers presented a substantial challenge to maintaining the ča·di· borderland. From the perspective of provincial officials enforcing the exclusive fishery zone, the People of the Cape no longer had any business being in Canadian waters. But from the perspective of indigenous borderlanders who continued to understand the sea as a space of connections, these policies seemed more akin to Cold War politics. In a telling comparison, after the Berlin Wall came down in 1989, "numerous Makah . . . remarked . . . that the Wall was much like the international boundary that the U.S. and Canada imposed on the Makah people and all their linguistic, cultural, and blood relatives in Canada."[121]

While pursuing diplomatic options to secure continued access to ancestral fishing banks then in Canadian waters, Makahs also sought to apply Boldt's fifty-fifty allocation to their marine halibut fisheries under US jurisdiction. Because the Canadian and US establishment of exclusive fishery zones changed what waters fell under the jurisdictional claims of particular countries, the People of the Cape filed new evidence in district court about their marine fishing banks and made a formal request for determination of treaty rights to oceanic fishing grounds. They understood that the court could only rule on Makah claims in US waters.[122] The court agreed with the tribal nation's lawyers and supported their claim to usual and accustomed grounds at sea. However, US halibut regulations, set by the secretary of commerce under the 1953 Halibut Convention, "precluded the Makahs from taking more than a tiny percentage of the available harvest." In 1985, this meant that Makah fishers landed just 2.4 percent of the harvest, far below the 50 percent allocation to which they were entitled. This prompted the tribal council to take the secretary of commerce to court that year. Over the course of six years of litigation, Makahs gained their fair share of the US allocation through a successful partial summary judgment from the district court. They still want the United States either to renegotiate for access to Swiftsure and 40-Mile Banks, just as they did in 1979 for non-Native sports fishers, or to mitigate them for their lost access because the nation neglected to safeguard Makah treaty rights.[123]

Within the context of judicial victories and the American Indian self-determination movement of the 1970s, Makahs also sought a final determination of issues left unsettled from the Indian Claims Commission case from the 1950s, specifically whether the federal government breached its promise to supply $30,000 in fishing gear in return for land cessions. Lawyers for the Makah proved that the government had spent only $265.40 on supporting their fisheries, and the commission agreed to an award of $29,734.60 in 1975.[124] The tribal council contested this the following year, claiming that the real cost of the lack of support was nearly $700,000. Eventually, the federal government settled by accepting the Makah proposal to have Tatoosh and Waadah Islands returned to and incorporated into the reservation. In the nineteenth century, the federal government had seized these islands, building a lighthouse at Tatoosh and a lifesaving station at Waadah. Noting the historical relevance of these islands—Tatoosh was a critical fishing and whaling village that had extensive halibut drying racks in addition to burial grounds, and Makahs had maintained stone tidal fish traps and harvested shellfish on the shores of Waadah—the People of the Cape had always maintained that the federal government had stolen these islands from them.[125] The tribal council worked with Washington State's second district congressman Al Swift to introduce and pass the Makah Claims Settlement Bill in 1984. The legislative report submitted on behalf of the tribe concluded by noting, "Perhaps the most important element of the islands' future change of status will be in the settling of a long-standing controversy with the United States; one which has rankled the Makahs and kept alive a sense of grievance. Every Makah sees Waadah Island every day of his life and Tatoosh Island is a part of the existence of every Makah fisherman. With restoration to the Reservation, those Islands will no longer stand as symbols of injustice, but will become symbols of pride and a mutually respectful relationship between the Makah and the United States government." Coupled with their efforts to restore treaty fishing rights, the restoration of these islands to the People of the Cape illustrated part of their ongoing strategy to reclaim the sea.[126]

Reflecting the constantly changing political climate, the Makah experience with federal and state governments indeed represented an erratic pendulum from the 1930s to the early 1990s. Under BIA policies and congressional acts, the tribal nation made substantial gains: they dismissed one of the worst agency superintendents; achieved some degree of governing autonomy; accessed new forms of credit, thereby inaugurating a fleet of modern fishing vessels; and reclaimed critical islands that restored access to marine space. Yet federal policies also delivered the People of the Cape significant setbacks, such as when the Indian Claims Commission denied their claim for the loss of treaty fishing rights to halibut. Not unexpectedly, until recently Makahs fared far worse when dealing with the state government. Local courts and state fish and game officials sought to limit Makah treaty rights. Like other tribal nations, though, the Makahs generally did well in federal courts, from the district court level to the Supreme Court, with a string of decisions affirming treaty Indian fishing rights. Interestingly, though, they have encountered a lack of support from the Departments of Commerce and State, which ignored their treaty rights when allocating halibut and negotiating for fishing concessions with Canada. Inconsistency characterized their relationship with government officials, branches, and policies through much of the twentieth century.

And inconsistency framed this relationship at the close of the twentieth century and continues to do so. When the tribal nation prepared to return to the water to resume an active whaling practice in the 1990s, they received support from several government agencies, including the National Oceanic and Atmospheric Administration (NOAA), the National Marine Fisheries Service (NMFS), and the US Coast Guard, among others. This support helped them land their first whale in more than seventy years. Yet precisely as Makahs began reaping the benefit of successful relationships with these agencies, another part of the federal government—the judicial branch—swept away the gains they had achieved. Currently, two ninth circuit court decisions block subsequent Makah whale hunts.

In the first court case, Representative Jack Metcalf, who won Al Swift's seat on his retirement in 1994, filed a lawsuit in district court against Secretary of Commerce William Daley, NOAA, and NMFS for violating the National Environmental Policy Act. According to the lawsuit, federal defendants had failed to consider the environmental consequences before approving the 1995 whaling agreement with the Makah. Initially, the district court sided with the defendants, but the ninth circuit court reversed the decision on appeal. The appellate decision in *Metcalf v. Daley* (2000) hinged on the allegation that NOAA and NMFS prepared the environmental assessment too late in the decision-making process. Quoting federal regulations, the court noted that environmental assessments are supposed to be "prepared early enough so that [they] can serve practically as an important contribution to the decision making process and will not be used to rationalize or justify decisions already made."[127] Without evaluating the assessment itself, the court ruled that by making an agreement with the Makah before determining the environmental consequences, NOAA had predisposed itself to issue a finding of "no significant impact" in the assessment. The court then ordered a suspension of Makah whaling and the preparation of a new environmental assessment, a time-consuming and expensive process.

The second ninth circuit court decision, *Anderson v. Evans* (2004), reveals a disturbing trend in the recent jurisprudence of this court to apply legal logic that had been left behind during the heyday of fishing rights cases.[128] In this case, private citizen Will Anderson, along with a collection of animal rights activists, filed suit against Commerce Secretary Donald Evans and other federal defendants for violating the National Environmental Policy Act and the Marine Mammal Protection Act, legislation that bars US citizens from hunting sea mammals. As in the previous case, the district court ruled in favor of the defendants, and the ninth circuit court reversed the decision on appeal. The circuit court held that the National Environmental Policy Act required the government to prepare a more comprehensive environmental impact statement instead of an environmental assessment. More troubling was the court's decision on the Marine Mammal Protection Act, ruling that Makahs, even with a reserved treaty right to whale, were not exempt from the federal law. Seeming to echo the mid-twentieth-century position taken by the State of Washington when it had sought any way to limit Indian fishing rights, the court focused on the treaty phrase, "in common with all citizens of the United States." The justices ruled that such language gave the tribe the right to hunt their "fair share" of whales. Because the Marine Mammal Protection Act gives US citizens no "share" of whales, the Makah quota is also zero. This decision perverts the treaty allocation formula decided by Judge Boldt thirty years earlier and violates the "three principal canons" for understanding treaty rights: treaties should be liberally construed in favor of tribes, treaty provisions should be interpreted as tribal representatives would have understood them at the time, and treaties should be interpreted in a manner that promotes their central purpose.[129] Makah negotiators in 1855 would have never agreed to an interpretation of "in common with" to mean that their rights to hunt whales— one of the central purposes promoted in the Treaty of Neah Bay—could be suspended in this manner.

The history of the Makah relationship with marine space reveals the tenacity, creativity, and adaptability of the People of the Cape in maintaining access to tribal waters and in making a living from the sea. As they had done with whaling and pelagic sealing in the nineteenth century, Makahs turned other customary practices—fishing for halibut and salmon—into lucrative livelihoods in the early twentieth century. Twentieth-century fishing took increasing amounts of capital—something to which Makahs had little access until the mid-1960s, a situation that differed from their experience in the nineteenth century—to remain competitive in an industry that quickly mechanized at many production levels. As in their experience with seal conservation, Makah fishers found that local, national, and international fish conservation efforts privileged non-Natives over indigenous workers and families. Despite these challenges, twentieth-century Makah leaders fought back with a variety of political and legal strategies that resulted in continued access to and even a reclamation of tribal marine space. And these efforts continue. As they have done in the past, the People of the Cape will persevere against current attempts to keep them from the sea.

CONCLUSION: "EVENTS HAPPEN WHEN YOU GET A WHALE"

After having lain still in bed since before dawn on May 17, 1999, Polly Mc-Carty received the news that the whale her partner Theron Parker had harpooned was finally dead. Great-granddaughter of the famed Makah whaler Hišk ʷi ("hish-kwee"), McCarty observed customary rituals that kept her silent and motionless in bed while Parker whaled. Having learned that the whaling crew was on their way home, she and two other women with partners aboard the *Hummingbird* made their way to the Neah Bay waterfront but saw that the massive crowd of people would prevent them from reaching the beach in order to greet the canoe and the whale ashore. As McCarty recalled, family members "gathered around us, one on each side, and they sang the prayer songs with the rattling. . . . It was like parting the Red Sea, everybody moving aside, and we got to go right in the front."[1] Their long day continued as the People of the Cape welcomed ashore the first whale in the past seventy-one years.

Reviving an active whaling practice had benefited the community in many ways. As tribal elder Dale Johnson stated, "Events happen when you get a whale." Families performed songs and dances, and the tribal nation hosted a grand potlatch for guests from across the region and beyond. The 1999 hunt generated interest in other customary marine practices, revitalized Makah culture, and reconnected elders and youth by providing a desire to pass down—and to receive—teachings and tribal histories. It demonstrated the continued cultural importance of tribally specific hunting practices and helped move Makah culture from the museum back onto the water. Dan Greene, a Makah fisher with a whaling lineage, noted that the hunt illustrated that "[whaling] wasn't lost to us."[2] Even the racist backlash against Makah whaling had positive consequences because it brought the community together and encouraged some to take more notice of their heritage, something they had ignored before. Most important, Makahs recognize that the revival of whaling expressed both tribal sovereignty and their identity as the People of the Cape. From the perspective that the sea is their country, the 1999 hunt was part of the tribal nation's continuing efforts to reclaim customary marine space.[3]

On that May morning at the close of the twentieth century, Makah whalers did more than harpoon a whale—they dramatically anchored their nation's identity to the sea, just as generations of ancestors had done. Through spiritual beliefs and customary practices such as whaling, sealing, and fishing, historic Makahs transformed the sea into their sovereign space. They guarded this space from others, reinforcing the understanding that local waters belonged to the People of the Cape. For thousands of years, strategic exploitation of this marine borderland made Makahs a powerful, influential people. During the century after the arrival of non-Natives in this corner of the Pacific Ocean, the Makah relationship with the ocean and their customary marine resources enabled them to participate in global networks of exchange, to resist US assimilation efforts, and to retain greater autonomy than many other land-based reservation communities.

However, from the late nineteenth through early twentieth centuries, overexploitation of marine resources undercut Makah success and power. Efficient Native hunters—Makahs included—nearly exterminated sea otters in local waters by the early nineteenth century, pushing non-Native traders to ply northern regions along the Northwest Coast when seeking valuable "soft gold." By the mid- to late nineteenth century, European, Japanese, and Euro-American hunters exacted a lethal toll on the Pacific's sea mammal species. Hunting any cetacean that provided oil, baleen, and other commodities, whalers brought one species after another to the brink of extinction. Wasteful non-Native overhunting of fur seals triggered national and international conservation efforts. Backed by the London fur industry, influential Euro-Americans harnessed the power of the state to cut out small-scale pelagic sealing operations, such as Makah hunters and schooner owners, while protecting profits earned by large corporations. In the early twentieth century, similar dynamics of overfishing and conservation efforts worked in concert with non-Native fishers with better access to capital to diminish Makah access to tribal marine space and the resources that provided both a livelihood and food for the table. The loss of these customary practices undercut the economic base and autonomy of the People of the Cape at the time that government officials sought to exert more control over Natives. Concern over the dearth of whales off Cape Flattery in the early twentieth century even prompted Makahs to suspend the active practice of

Welcoming the whale home, 1999. Harpooner Theron Parker conducts the
ċi·qa· ("tsee-kah") ceremony to honor the whale. Photograph by Theresa Parker,
courtesy the Makah Cultural and Research Center, Neah Bay, WA.

whaling—an activity at the heart of their cultural identity—until whale populations rebounded. Yet Makahs fought back with various legal and political strategies to reclaim key aspects of the sea and access to marine resources during the second half of the twentieth century. The 1999 whale hunt was a continuation of these efforts.

Focusing on marine rather than terrestrial spaces provides us with a clearer view into the murky waters of the past. First, it reveals that Makah marine space was part of an indigenous borderlands composed of specific networks and socio-political dynamics. Diplomacy, trade, kinship, and violence intertwined the lives of the distinct peoples of the ča·di· borderland. Native borderlands networks were in place long before the arrival of non-Natives to the Northwest Coast, and indigenous power and dynamics shaped the initial phase of cross-cultural interactions. When imperial actors entered the borderlands in the late eighteenth century, they provided new opportunities for conflict within the context of existing tensions among powerful Native chiefs, such as Maquinna (Mowachaht), Wickaninnish (Clayoquot), and Tatoosh (Makah). As the imperial rivalry between the United States and United Kingdom transformed this region into the transnational space known as the Oregon Country during the first half of the nineteenth century, indigenous borderlands dynamics persisted. Powerful Makah chiefs, such as ƛisi·t ("klih-seet") and Yelaƙub ("yeh-luh-koob"), traded whale oil and furs and exploited both indigenous and colonial borderlands networks to maintain the influence of the People of the Cape. Their actions shaped non-Native perceptions of the Makah as a powerful and influential people to respect and even fear. In the later nineteenth century, Makahs such as the Claplanhoo family leveraged existing indigenous borderlands networks to raise the necessary capital and labor to succeed in both the Native and settler-colonial world of the Pacific Northwest through fur sealing. This focus on the regional indigenous borderlands demonstrates that these networks persisted long after the United States and United Kingdom (later Canada) imposed a borderline in 1846.

Borderlands strategists such as Tatoosh, ƛisi·t, Yelaƙub, and the Claplanhoos exploited marine products and social networks to frustrate imperial processes. Tatoosh prevented the British trader John Meares from exploring the Strait of Juan de Fuca and sailing into Puget Sound. By monopolizing much of the maritime fur trade within the strait, the powerful Makah chief expanded his influence in the region and made the People of the Cape a force maritime fur traders respected and feared at times. Although Chiefs ƛisi·t and Yelaƙub embraced divergent strategies for dealing with expanding settler-colonial power, their attitudes of accommodation and intimidation extended Tatoosh's legacy—Makahs were a powerful people colonial authorities needed to appease. Therefore, when

US representatives came to Neah Bay in 1855 to impose a treaty on the tribal nation, Governor Stevens acceded to Makah demands that protected not just tribal lands but also tribal waters and their access to marine resources that had made them an influential people for generations. By whaling, sealing, and fishing—customary practices protected by the Treaty of Neah Bay—Makahs maintained their wealth and influence within both the ča·di· borderland and the settler-colonial world. Makah success allowed them to blunt the worst effects of US assimilation until the end of the nineteenth century.

A focus on marine space reveals a more complete understanding of the ways that indigenous peoples such as Makahs engaged settler-colonialism. During the late eighteenth and early nineteenth centuries, efficient Native hunters and chiefs exploited marine resources and indigenous borderlands trade networks to fill the cargo holds of maritime fur trading vessels and provision crews. The first extractive industry on the Northwest Coast, the maritime fur trade began a process that brought non-Native empires to the region. When the commercial focus shifted to the land-based fur trade, Native peoples and networks remained central to the success of companies, such as the Hudson's Bay Company. The People of the Cape were a key component—perhaps *the* key component—in these early industries. When US and British settlers came to the region, indigenous commodities harvested from the ocean and land provided desperately needed food for the newcomers and made survival possible for underprepared settlers. Native labor and goods also established the foundation for such commercial ventures as logging, whaling, and provisioning. Ironically, Anglos often take pride in these entrepreneurial activities and credit them for taming the wilderness and making this region into the US and Canadian Wests. Yet none of this could have happened without the involvement and support of the indigenous peoples of the Northwest Coast. By the 1880s, Natives like the Makahs did not just work as laborers or hunters for non-Natives in the settler-colonial economy; important financial actors, Makahs invested in the extractive industries of the North Pacific, which contributed to national development. When possible, these investments continued into the twentieth century.

Last, an examination of the relationship of Makahs to marine space and the resources within it demonstrates that the People of the Cape combined customary practices with new opportunities and technologies to succeed on their own terms in the settler-colonial world. By hunting sea otters and trading the pelts and various indigenous commodities, Makahs and other Native peoples of the ča·di· borderland engaged new markets of exchange and brought a bevy of non-Native goods into their communities. These cross-cultural exchanges did not result in dependency, as some scholars conclude. Rather, chiefs funneled the goods and cash into sociocultural networks and employed them to maintain and expand their influence over weaker rivals in the borderlands. By the mid-nineteenth century, Makahs looked to new technologies to expand the range of customary marine practices and participate more closely in the market economy. Makah sealers and fishers in the late nineteenth and twentieth centuries exploited the fur seal, salmon, and halibut fisheries in a commercial capacity, earning cash instead of exchanging goods for their catches. With this money, they bought modern vessels, houses, automobiles, food, and clothing, while still spending large amounts of money on cultural priorities such as potlatches. By adapting non-Native technologies and markets of exchange to fit their specific cultural needs, the People of the Cape maintained their autonomy and controlled tribal spaces—both marine and terrestrial—until the end of the nineteenth century. Although economic and political factors substantially limited Makah marine space and access to ocean resources during the early twentieth century, Makah leaders in the second half of the century fought back in the courts—yet another new avenue for action—to regain some of what they had lost.

A TRADITIONAL FUTURE

The story of Makahs and their relationship to customary marine space seems like a narrative of decline. Basically, Makahs had a good life until Euro-Americans ruined everything. Similar to other American Indian histories, though, the specific contours of this story are particular to the Makah experience. Non-Native diseases decimated but did not destroy the People of the Cape, leaving them susceptible to the nefarious agents of empire. Granted, many Makahs died from disease, including key chiefs in the mid-nineteenth century; however, new leaders emerged to confront the US treaty negotiators who purposefully came hot on the heels of the demographic catastrophe. Still reeling from the deaths of close family members, Makah negotiators protected what was most important to them and their people—the sea. Settler-colonial intrusions also did not automatically ruin Makahs' good lives. Rather, for most of the nineteenth century, the People of the Cape succeeded because they engaged the settler-colonial world, but on their own terms and for their own reasons. This allowed them to maintain enough power to complicate imperial processes such as trade, settlement, treaties, and assimilation, activities that took away the cultures, powers, lands, and resources of so many indigenous peoples elsewhere. Makahs did not experience real trouble until non-Native forces wiped out the resource foundation for Northwest Coast societies and employed the regulatory power of the state to shut out indigenous peoples from customary practices and spaces that had once made them wealthy and powerful. In their newly impoverished condition, the People of the Cape became more susceptible to increased assimilation pressure exerted by dictatorial Indian superintendents.

Older, traditional approaches to American Indian history characterize indigenous peoples as one-dimensional victims. Scholars who assume this perspective shackle indigenous peoples to a static and nostalgic past while giving non-Natives too much power to shape outcomes. This approach ignores the contingent nature of settler-colonial expansion and overlooks how resilient American Indian individuals, communities, and nations adapted and responded to colonialism and its lethal results. The story of the Makah represents an "inclusive and empowering, rather than imperialistic and dominating" history, rebutting simpler stories that we often tell about the indigenous past.[4] Makahs frustrated and engaged settler-colonial processes for their own purposes, and they and other indigenous peoples on both sides of the border proved central to the making of the US and Canadian Wests.

Within the context of indigenous history, narratives of decline continue to problematically frame debates over American Indian identity, sovereignty, and treaty rights in nations today. The controversy over the 1999 whale hunt illustrated this. Critics failed to understand why Makahs continue to value whaling, openly wondering why the tribal nation cannot "get with the twentieth century." As one opponent stated, "With their supermarkets and cars, [Makahs] no longer need to kill a being as sentient as our mammoth whales." Even non-Native supporters of the Makah right to hunt see this as a tribal effort to "return to [a] whaling past."[5] Critics and some supporters alike believe that the Makah nation is trying to turn back the clock, to live in the past, by reviving whaling.

A better understanding of Makah history reveals that we should see the tribal nation's revival of whaling from a different perspective. By pursuing *čitapuk* ("chih-tuh-pook," whales) off Cape Flattery, today's Makahs are articulating a traditional future instead of grasping at a long-lost, static past.[6] Makah-language teacher Crystal Thompson explains that whaling remains important for the future of her people because of the way it restores customary indigenous foodways, encouraging her community to eat "the things we were meant to eat instead of what people brought here for us." Janine Ledford, director of the tribal nation's museum and cultural center, places this within the larger framework of building a "healthy population" for the future, explaining that the preparations young men made to whale, along with the support from their families, strengthened the community.[7] In addition to other marine initiatives pursued by the tribal nation, whaling illustrates that this American Indian nation lives in the present and looks toward the future while retaining what is best about its traditions.[8] This marine practice defines the Makahs as a people distinct from mainstream society.

The 1999 whale hunt and continued whaling efforts are part of a longer Makah strategy to craft a traditional future. During the maritime fur trade, Chief Ta-toosh exploited a customary resource—sea otters—and borderlands networks to extend his authority over neighboring peoples. His successors, such as Chiefs λisi·t and Yelakub, pursued a similar strategy by trading furs, whale oil, and fish with Hudson's Bay Company traders at nearby forts and passing US traders. Even when the chiefs confronted the expanding settler-colonial world in more aggressive ways, they looked toward the future instead of the past. They knew that in order for the People of the Cape to maintain their influence in the nine-teenth century, the newcomers would need to respect Makah power on in-digenous terms. During the treaty negotiations of 1855, Chief Čaqa·wiλ ("tsuh-kah-wihtl") and the other Makah leaders pushed for treaty provisions that protected the tribal nation's rights to customary marine practices and spaces because of their concern over the future. Chief Q̇alču·t ("kuhl-choot") argued that if his people could not take whales, seals, and fish as they had al-ways done, he feared they "would become poor."[9] Today's Makahs note that their ancestors thought of the tribal nation's future welfare when securing whal-ing, sealing, and fishing rights in the Treaty of Neah Bay. When reflecting back on the treaty his ancestors' negotiated, elder Ed Claplanhoo notes that Makah leaders understood that "the land was valuable, but it wasn't as valuable as the water. It wasn't as valuable as the ocean, which had all of the things that we needed to live on."[10]

Makah pelagic sealing during the late nineteenth century exemplified both the benefits and challenges of striving for a traditional future. Combining a cus-tomary practice (hunting seals) with modern opportunities and technologies (global markets and schooners) allowed the People of the Cape to expand their marine space into the Bering Sea and accumulate substantial wealth. This, in turn, strengthened their ability to resist assimilation and shape a Makah future that remained distinct to their identity. Yet conservation concerns over the Prib-ilof fur seal herd resulted in national legislation and international conventions that cut out Makah sealers and other small operators; a similar set of factors worked against Makah fishers a generation later. These conservation efforts codified the stereotype of the Native hunter or fisher who could engage in these customary practices only with premodern equipment and for subsistence purposes. This assumption locked indigenous peoples and their customs in the past and denied them a place in the modern world, extending nineteenth-century racist attitudes into the twentieth century and today.

Current Makah efforts at reviving the active practice of whaling demonstrate the tribal nation's perseverance at articulating a traditional future and the challenges of doing so. During the decades when they were not whaling, the People of the Cape maintained the tradition by including whaling implements in important social events and by performing songs and dances connected to the practice. They clandestinely continued harvesting whale oil, blubber, and meat from drift whales that washed ashore. Because harvesting whale products—even from carcasses that had washed ashore—was illegal, the federal government guarded, buried, and dynamited beached whales to prevent "scavenging" during the 1980s and 1990s. Those living outside the reservation did not see Makah efforts at maintaining the whaling tradition, which caused non-Natives to believe that the community had abandoned the tradition and left it in the past. Critics therefore mistakenly assumed that Makahs were grasping at a nostalgic past when they expressed the intent to revive whaling.[11]

Makahs prepare to embark on the 2005 Tribal Canoe Journeys to the Lower Elwha.
The People of the Cape have been active participants in Tribal Canoe Journeys for many years.
Photograph by Owen Luck. Image supplied courtesy of the Beinecke Rare Book
and Manuscript Library, Yale University.

Ahousahts approach Neah Bay during the 2010 Tribal Canoe Journeys. That year the People
of the Cape hosted the intertribal event, drawing people together from across
the ča·di· borderland. Photograph by Owen Luck. Image supplied courtesy of the
Beinecke Rare Book and Manuscript Library, Yale University.

During the second half of the twentieth century, momentum built for a return to whaling. From the late 1960s until the early 1980s, the archaeological
findings at Ozette, a Makah village just south of Cape Flattery, "sparked a cultural
renaissance" in the community.[12] Several hundred years ago, before the arrival
of non-Natives to this region, a massive mudslide entombed part of Ozette village, one of the principal sea mammal hunting sites along the Northwest Coast.
Most of the forty thousand artifacts and extensive faunal remains dug out of
the mud demonstrated to Western academics what Makahs already knew: they
have always been a people of the sea. Eighty-eight percent of the weight of faunal remains came from harvested whales and demonstrated that Makahs
hunted sea mammals for both subsistence and commercial purposes.[13] The
archaeological work at Ozette uncovered the centrality of whaling to Makah

cultural, subsistence, and commercial activities. George Bowechop, one of the executive directors of the Makah Whaling Commission, points out that the Ozette dig "validated the teachings of our elders to the younger people, at saying that we were whalers."[14] This strengthened the community's ties to its whaling tradition.

Soon after the findings at Ozette, the People of the Cape considered exercising their whaling rights once again. After the federal government removed gray whales from the list of endangered species in 1994, the Makah Tribal Council secured government support to petition the International Whaling Commission for a whaling quota. In 1997, the commission granted the Makah nation a quota of five whales annually, and a year later, the tribal council formed its own whaling commission to oversee the hunt. Responding to animal rights activists concerned that the "traditional" method of hunting was cruel, the tribal whaling commission contracted with a University of Maryland veterinarian to adapt a large-caliber rifle to kill a harpooned whale more humanely and safely. After thousands of hours of physical and ritual preparation, Makah whalers—with key support from their families and community—harpooned and landed their first whale in seventy-one years.[15]

By placing the 1999 whale hunt within the larger context of a Makah narrative that focuses on their connection to marine space, we can see that the People of the Cape have a history of combining customary practices with modern opportunities and technologies. By deciding what constitutes "traditional culture" and how they will practice it, Makahs are exercising self-determination and expressing their identity in today's world.[16] In addition to a revival of canoe culture and participation in the annual Tribal Canoe Journeys, this is just part of a larger strategy of ways that they are reclaiming the sea. Or as Paul Parker, a Makah whaling commissioner, argues, today's whaling efforts are "protecting our identity and protecting what belongs to us . . . as far as culture and our land go."[17] Makahs continue to confront the ongoing effects of colonialism, representing themselves as a modern indigenous community amid national and international pressures. Indigenous traditions and customary practices are not static cultural components frozen in time. They change over time. For Makahs, these changes exemplify "the resilient, adaptive capacity of Indian groups to respond to colonialism in challenging and often deadly circumstances."[18] The People of the Cape are demonstrating that they live in the present and are moving into the future while retaining what they believe is best about their traditions. Or, as one Makah phrased it: "We are whalers. We don't want a Wonder Bread culture."[19]

AFTERWORD

I consider Joshua Reid's work to be a vital contribution to the record of my people. Reid's research takes us on a forensic voyage. He expertly weaves together a multitude of narrative strands, adding an immense amount of depth and breadth to the broad canvas of recorded Makah history. In particular, Reid's work affirms the progression of the transgenerational voyage of perspectives, relative to rich family histories that can be gleaned from the recorded observations of the early sojourners' accounts. Makah futures will be built by strengthening and moving forward the understanding of our historic position in North America. *The Sea Is My Country* fills a vital space between the old ancestors and our elders who have recently passed, offering a considered but succinct appraisal of how Native Makah People have persevered in the tasks of cultural and political self-determination.

My cover art design, an acrylic painting on canvas titled *The Enlightenment of the Great Houses*, finished in the spring of 2014, came to mind while reading Reid's manuscript and reflecting on my own life's work as a living bearer and creator within the traditions and values our ancestors have bequeathed to our current generations. Many Makah and Nuu-chah-nulth families maintain rich intellectual properties—family histories that are in fact the living memory of our Peoples. It is within these teachings that adaptive wisdom sheds light on traditional perspectives moving forward.

The conviction of traditional values in resource management brings to mind a song that is important to us that I'd like to discuss in particular. I was told that my grandfather Jerry McCarty, the first Chairman of the Makah Tribal Council as reestablished under the Indian Reorganization Act, and signatory of the current Makah Constitution, gave the Makah Days Club the right to sing a song composed by *his* father, Hiškʷi. We call it the "knife dance song." It is a favorite during Makah Days, each summer. There is a line in the song that in English might be rendered as, "I come from a House of Great Power." A House of Great Power is simply one that, in the context of strong teachings, is related to many if not most of the other Great Houses of the ča·di·. My painting emerges as if from the canvas sails that became the "family potlatch curtain" for covert potlatches held in spite of past prohibitions on such ceremonies. Under the dark skies of colonialism, on the stormy seas of resistance, the image of a House of Great Power is illuminated by a whaler's moon that holds that face of a thunderbird in man-face form, transposing a "great house." The turbulent seas of those past times of colonial conflict and resistance are juxtaposed in this image with symbols of the persistence of a people who have held onto their rightful places and vital lifeways, through thick and thin. The "sea monster" on the face of the house is a great protector of our oceangoing traditions. While reading Reid's manuscript it was easy to cross-reference rich family and oral histories with his investigative approach to written and oral accounts that so accurately describe the hereditary fortitude of the first resource trustees, a value that still guides Makah treaty policy today. *The Sea Is My Country* bridges the forceful resistance from early colonialists' pilfering of traditional property to foundational Indian case law that led to the "Boldt decision" of 1974.

Forty years after Boldt—and with the recent passing of the famous treaty warrior Billy Frank Jr.—I am reminded of how Makahs and all the tribes of the Northwest Indian Fisheries Commission "case areas" successfully transformed national Indian policy by building on the successes of *U.S. v. Washington* (the Boldt decision) and taking the State of Washington to a Centennial Accord where state and tribal relations are taken beyond "co-management" and into a new era of "intergovernmental relations," where a world-class example of the first and rightful trustees of traditional ecology are in fact doing more to protect the treaty resource environment than the entire rest of the family of governments.

History is and always will be a fundamental attribute of Indian education and related studies. It is the taproot of "who you are and where you come from." In acknowledging the value of new written histories of the Makah (such as the present volume), we must also underline the continuing importance of oral histories and family traditions. As far back as I can remember, my mother, Anne Lunt, would tell me in exquisite detail all of the family teachings that she had learned from my father's family while she lived in Neah Bay. My mother also shared with me her depth of knowledge about her New England roots, including past loyalties to the British crown, so *The Sea Is My Country* has certain special resonances for me and my family. I am also reminded of the countless hours of talking shop with my father as we lived on the sea through sunrises and sunsets, under the same stars and on the same ancestral waters of my people.

Neah Bay and the Makahs' lands and waters have always been a dominant part of my life. Though I attended public schools in Olympia during the school years, I always made it home for the summers, and soon after high school I ultimately made Neah Bay my home. The years after Olympia were filled with a whole new education for me, as I deepened myself among my people as an emerging artist, singer and dancer, fisherman, whaling commissioner, treaty activist, and eventually statesman. Looking back, the superficial and less than half-truth US and Washington State history lessons that I received in public schools contrast sharply to the family histories with which I was raised. May Reid's book give you a truer picture of Makah life in the past, and may your journeys take you to Neah Bay sometime soon, so that you may hear more of those times from my people in person and see the historic landscapes and waters for yourself.

—Micah McCarty, Olympia, Washington, April 2014
Former Councilman and Chairman for Makah from 2004 to 2012;
currently Special Assistant to the President for
Tribal Government Relations at Evergreen State College

Abbreviations

ARCIA	*Annual Report of the Commissioner of Indian Affairs*
BCA	British Columbia Archives, Victoria
BIA	Bureau of Indian Affairs
BSTA	Bering Sea Tribunal of Arbitration
CCF	Central Classified Files
CIA	Commissioner of Indian Affairs
CO	Colonial Office, National Archives, Kew, United Kingdom
DF	Decimal File
HBC	Hudson's Bay Company
HBCA	Hudson's Bay Company Archives, Winnipeg, Manitoba
IPHC	International Pacific Halibut Commission
IWC	International Whaling Commission
LR	Letters Received
MCRC	Makah Cultural and Research Center, Neah Bay, Washington
MTC	Makah Tribal Council, Neah Bay, Washington
NARA	National Archives and Records Administration, Washington, DC
NARA-PNR	National Archives and Records Administration, Pacific Northwest Region, Seattle
NOAA	National Oceanic and Atmospheric Administration
NYT	*New York Times*
PF	*Pacific Fisherman*
PFC	Pacific Fur Company
PRO	Public Records Office, Kew, United Kingdom
ROT	*Record Office Transcripts*, Hudson's Bay Company to Colonial Office
TIA	Taholah Indian Agency, Taholah, Washington
UBCA	University of British Columbia Archives, Vancouver

UBCL	University of British Columbia Library, Vancouver
UW	University of Washington, Seattle
UWSC	University of Washington, Special Collections, Seattle
WSA	Washington State Archives, Olympia
WSHS	Washington State Historical Society, Tacoma

NOTES

INTRODUCTION: JUST WHERE *DOES* ONE GET A LICENSE TO KILL INDIANS?

1. Bowechop, "Contemporary Makah Whaling," 415–19; Sullivan, *Whale Hunt*, 238–65; Sepez, "Political and Social Ecology," 112–97; Miller, "Exercising Cultural Self-Determination"; Miller, "Tribal Cultural Self-Determination"; interviews by Bowechop and Pascua, NOAA Interviews, MCRC; Makah Tribal Council and Makah Whaling Commission, *Makah Nation*; Arnold, interview.

2. Claplanhoo, interview; Greene, interview; US Department of the Interior, Fish and Wildlife Service, and US Department of Commerce, NOAA, "Endangered and Threatened Wildlife and Plants." For a discussion of the IWC negotiations in 1996 and 1997, see Martello, "Negotiating Global Nature and Local Culture," 267–69.

3. Johnson, interview; Mapes, "Celebrating the Whale"; Bowechop, "Contemporary Makah Whaling," 418; Blow, "Great American Whale Hunt"; Gutthiudaschmitt, "Makah Whale Hunt"; Adrienne Bowechop, Janine Bowechop, Micah McCarty, and Crystal Thompson, NOAA Interviews.

4. Blow, "Great American Whale Hunt"; Martello, "Negotiating Global Nature and Local Culture," 267.

5. Ellingson, *Myth of the Noble Savage*, 370; Dan Greene, NOAA Interviews.

6. Wylly quotation from Tizon, "E-Mails, Phone Messages." See also Barton, "'Red Waters,'" 200–218; Marker, "After the Makah Whale Hunt." For more examples, see Mapes, "Celebrating the Whale"; Bowechop, "Contemporary Makah Whaling," 418–419; and Sullivan, *Whale Hunt*.

7. LaDow, *Medicine Line*, 109; Evans, *Borderlands*, 354; Binnema, "Case for Cross-National and Comparative History," 18–19. For a more terrestrial-oriented perspective on the environment of the Northwest Coast, see Suttles, "Environment."

8. Edwards and MacCready, "Strait of Juan de Fuca," 2.

9. For an introduction to indigenous knowledge, see Ellen, Parkes, and Bicker, *Indigenous Environmental Knowledge*; and Gordon and Krech, "Introduction."

10. Favorite and Northwest Fisheries Center, *Ocean Environment*, 28; Roden, "Subarctic-Subtropical Transition Zone."

11. Johnson, interview; Greene, interview; McCarty, interview.

12. Makah fisher Dave Sones speaks of being able to see the change in the ocean when one arrives at the upwelling. See Sones, interview. Today's Makah fishers and whalers simply refer to it as the "Big Eddy."

13. Beak Consultants and Patricia Bay Institute of Ocean Sciences, *Examination*; Purdy, *Summary*, 14; MacFadyen, Hickey, and Cochlan, "Influences of the Juan de Fuca Eddy." Through informal conversations, Makah fishers provided details on how the eddy appears.

14. Favorite and Northwest Fisheries Center, *Ocean Environment*, 48; Berry, Sewell, and Wagenen, "Temporal Trends."

15. Suttles, "Environment," 17–18; Renker and Gunther, "Makah," 422.

16. Suttles, "Introduction"; Thompson and Kinkade, "Languages." For other culture areas, see Walker, *Plateau*; Helm, *Subarctic*; and Heizer, *California*. Throughout the book, I use modern place-names so that we can more easily understand the setting. Where appropriate, I introduce us to indigenous place-names and reference earlier terms used by non-Natives.

17. Lane, "Political and Economic Aspects," 1–13; Stewart, *Indian Fishing*; Stewart, *Cedar*; Taylor, *Making Salmon*, 13–38; Montgomery, *King of Fish*, 39–58; Hewes, "Indian Fisheries Productivity," 136.

18. The complex networks of kinship are discussed in detail in chapters 1 and 2. For an excellent analysis of this topic, see Harmon, *Indians in the Making*. For more on seasonal movements, see Kirk, *Tradition and Change*, 105–38; and Ames and Maschner, *Peoples of the Northwest Coast*, 120–21.

19. Kirk, *Tradition and Change*, 36–56; Donald, *Aboriginal Slavery*; Drucker, *The Northern and Central Nootkan Tribes*, 243–73; Renker and Gunther, "Makah"; Coté, *Spirits of Our Whaling Ancestors*, 22–23.

20. The literature cited earlier discusses the power of chiefs. For a different model on authority within the Northwest Coast, see Miller and Boxberger, "Creating Chiefdoms."

21. For the meaning of the name *Makah*, see Coté, *Spirits of Our Whaling Ancestors*, 18. As with other Northwest Coast characteristics, the literature on potlatches is extensive. For concise overviews, see Drucker, *Northern and Central Nootkan Tribes*, 370–86; Drucker, *Indians of the Northwest Coast*, 123–33; Arima, *West Coast People*, 68–82; Kirk, *Tradition and Change*, 57–69; and Lutz, *Makúk*, 58–61. More than fifty years old, the classic text still remains Codere, "Fighting with Property." For a newer interpretation, see Suttles, "Streams of Property, Armor of Wealth." For a critique of Codere's argument that potlatching replaced warfare, see Lovisek, "Aboriginal Warfare on the Northwest Coast."

22. Lefebvre, *Production of Space*; Tuan, *Space and Place*.

23. "Ratified Treaty No. 286: Documents Relating to the Negotiation of the Treaty of January 31, 1855, with the Makah Indians," p. 2, Documents Relating to the Negotiation of Ratified and Unratified Treaties, NARA-PNR.

24. William Cronon's foreword in Arnold, *Fishermen's Frontier*, x.

25. Limerick, *Legacy of Conquest*, 100.

26. For the classic argument about the role of the federal government, industry, and capital, see White, *"It's Your Misfortune."* For more of an emphasis on commodification of the American West, see Cronon, *Nature's Metropolis.*

27. For a new direction for this scholarship, see Barman and Watson, *Leaving Paradise;* Chang, *Pacific Connections;* and Igler, *Great Ocean.* For the more traditional approach, see Hinckley, "Westward Movement"; Gibson, *Otter Skins;* Gibson, *Yankees in Paradise;* Johnson, *United States in the Pacific;* Heffer, *United States and the Pacific;* Nugent, *Habits of Empire;* and Cumings, *Dominion from Sea to Sea.*

28. For settler-colonialism, see Wolfe, *Settler Colonialism;* Coombes, *Rethinking Settler Colonialism;* Fujikane and Okamura, *Asian Settler Colonialism;* Hoxie, "Retrieving the Red Continent"; Belich, *Replenishing the Earth;* and Byrd, *Transit of Empire.* See also Wolfe, in "Settler Colonialism (1)" and "Settler Colonialism (2)." I would like to thank John Findlay for pushing me to clarify my thinking about how settler-colonialism applies in this case.

29. Trafzer, *Indians, Superintendents, and Councils;* Fisher, *Contact and Conflict;* Harris, *Resettlement of British Columbia;* Asher, *Beyond the Reservation;* Clayton, *Islands of Truth;* Harris, *Making Native Space.* These monographs would have benefitted from looking across the international border, especially when examining periods before the 1846 boundary settlement. Some are beginning to explore cross-border themes in the region. See Seltz, "Embodying Nature"; Harmon, *Power of Promises;* and Wadewitz, *Nature of Borders.* For transnational examples examining the Canadian and US Wests, see Coates, "Matter of Context"; LaDow, *Medicine Line;* Hogue, "Disputing the Medicine Line"; Findlay and Coates, *Parallel Destinies;* McManus, *Line Which Separates;* and Evans, *Borderlands.*

30. Pascua, interview, 2008.

31. In addition to the ones cited in this section, several texts have shaped my borderlands perspective, including Weber, *Spanish Frontier;* Brooks, *Captives and Cousins;* Igler, "Diseased Goods"; Reséndez, *Changing National Identities at the Frontier;* McCrady, *Living with Strangers;* Truett, *Fugitive Landscapes;* St. John, *Line in the Sand;* Hämäläinen and Truett, "On Borderlands"; Chang, *Pacific Connections.*

32. Adelman and Aron, "From Borderlands to Borders," 814–17.

33. Recent scholarship, such as Pekka Hämäläinen's *Comanche Empire,* challenges this core assumption, demonstrating that borderlands also existed where powerful indigenous polities such as the Comanche were the dominant shaping force. Hämäläinen and Jon Wunder addressed this critical flaw in "Of Lethal Places and Lethal Essays." Predating the recent spate of borderlands literature, Jack Forbes makes the case for pre-European borderlands in the American Southwest; see *Apache, Navaho, and Spaniard.*

34. See Swan Papers, 1833–1909.

35. Lutz, *Makúk,* 23–26, 281.

36. Much of the "new Indian history" critiques the traditional "declension and dependency" model of American Indian history. Anderson, *Indian Southwest,* 3–8.

CHAPTER 1: "THE POWER OF WICKANINNISH ENDS HERE"

1. James Swan, one of the earliest non-Native residents of Neah Bay, noted that Makahs painted their faces black for several reasons, including to show their "stout and courageous hearts." Swan, "Indians of Cape Flattery," 17.
2. Meares, *Voyages,* 153–54.
3. Ibid., 156. *Sea power* is defined as "the ability to ensure free movement on the sea for oneself and to inhibit, if need be, a similar capacity in others." Tute and Francis, *Commanding Sea,* 175.
4. Meares, *Voyages,* 165.
5. This incident is analyzed in detail in chapter 2.
6. For an overview of historical changes in Native North America before the intrusion of Europeans, see Salisbury, "Indians' Old World," 453. For the Northwest Coast, see Drucker, *Northern and Central Nootkan Tribes; Drucker Indians of the Northwest Coast;* Arima, *West Coast People;* and McMillan, *Since the Time of the Transformers.* See also *Ahousaht,* 77–90.
7. Said, *Orientalism,* 71.
8. Linton, *What Is Water?,* 5.
9. For late eighteenth-century Anglo perceptions of the sea, see Raban, *Oxford Book of the Sea;* and O'Hara, *Britain and the Sea.*
10. Lefebvre, *Production of Space,* 53. For a sampling of the traditional approach, see Fisher, *Contact and Conflict;* Harris, *Resettlement of British Columbia;* and Harris, *Making Native Space.* For a comparison, see Carter, *Road to Botany Bay.* Arguing that "the imperial fashioning of the Northwest Coast involved an equally complex traffic between a body of Western ideas and a set of local facts and exigencies," geographer Daniel Clayton provides a helpful corrective (*Islands of Truth,* xiii). Histories revisiting American Indians in the North American West continue to uncover similar examples of indigenous peoples able to control space on their own terms and for much longer than traditional narratives assume. See White, "Winning of the West"; Arnold, *Fishermen's Frontier,* 13–74; DeLay, *War of a Thousand Deserts;* and Hämäläinen, *Comanche Empire.*
11. Swan, "Indians of Cape Flattery," 1; Jewitt, *Adventures and Sufferings* (1987), 96; Arima, *Between Ports Alberni and Renfrew,* 12; Ziontz, *Lawyer in Indian Country,* 63; Coté, *Spirits of Our Whaling Ancestors,* 18; entry for October 29, 1859, Diary 2, Swan Papers, 1833–1909. For the importance of "outside resources" to Northwest Coast societies, see Kenyon, *Kyuquot Way,* 35.
12. Drucker, *Northern and Central Nootkan Tribes,* 219–21, 228–31, 240–42.
13. Barker, *Sovereignty Matters,* 21. Joanne Barker (Delaware) and political scientist Taiaiake Alfred (Mohawk) warn that current sovereignty discourse fails to capture the full range of indigenous meanings, perspectives, and identities about law, governance, and culture. Alfred, "Sovereignty," 465. Therefore, it is critical to be historically and culturally specific when discussing terms such as sovereignty. See also Reid, "Indigenous Power in *The Comanche Empire.*"

14. Geographer Robert Galois hints at a similar argument in his introduction to James Colnett's journals of his Northwest Coast voyages. Galois, *Voyage*, 32. For chiefly ownership of drift whales, see Arima, *West Coast People*, 23–24.

15. Beaglehole, *Journals of Cook*, 299; Meares, *Voyages*, 142.

16. Meares, *Voyages*, 136.

17. Galois, *Voyage*, 105; Roquefeuil, *Voyage*, 42.

18. Scholefield and Howay, *British Columbia*, 81–82. Recording this oral history told by Nanaimis and Tsaxawasip's descendant Chief George, Scholefield noted that this referred to the coming of Captain Cook. I believe that this account summarizes several Nuu-chah-nulth encounters with Spanish and British vessels. Because the people of Nootka Sound had already encountered the Spanish at least twice before the arrival of Captain Cook, I find it unlikely that they mistook the *Resolution* and *Discovery* for transformed salmon. Also, this account mentions only a single vessel. It is not uncommon for indigenous oral histories to collapse periods of time into an event that a non-Native scholar interprets as a single, temporal "moment." See Wilson, "Power of the Spoken Word"; Stevenson, "Indigenous Voices, Indigenous Histories, Part I"; Cruikshank, *Social Life of Stories*; and Nabokov, *Forest of Time*. Scholefield's volume on British Columbia celebrates the perspective of Captain Cook's encounter with the peoples of Nootka Sound as the first significant encounter. So his pro-Anglo perspective could have contributed to the framing of this particular oral history as the Nuu-chah-nulth's encounter with Cook.

19. Efrat and Langlois, "Contact Period," 54–55.

20. Beals, *Juan Pérez*, 88–90, 113; Cutter, *California Coast*, 177–83, 255–61 (Peña's quotation of the "mournful tone" is on p. 179). For an overview of Spanish expeditions, see also Cook, *Flood Tide of Empire*, 25–30; Hezeta, *Honor and Country*, 25–26; and Weber, *Spanish Frontier*, 249–53.

21. This initial encounter is summarized from Cook's official account, Riou's log, and Samwell's journal. All three are in Beaglehole, *Journals of Cook*. Cook's account is on pp. 295–296, with an excerpt from Riou's log in note 5 on the same pages; Samwell's version is on p. 1088.

22. Seeking a way to organize varying degrees of outsiders, I have created these conceptual categories. The terms *local outsiders* and *distant outsiders* are mine. For more on the general encounter process between American Indians and Europeans, see Schwartz, *Implicit Understandings*, 1–9; and Lutz, *Myth and Memory*. For a more specific look at Cook's Pacific encounters, see Salmond, *Trial of the Cannibal Dog*.

23. Seemann, *Narrative*, 1:110; Efrat and Langlois, "Contact Period," 58; Arima, *Between Ports Alberni and Renfrew*, 306; Pascua, interview, 2008.

24. Menzies and Newcombe, *Menzies' Journal*, 86–88; Vancouver, *Voyage of Discovery*, 346.

25. For the Nuu-chah-nulth worldview, see Atleo, *Tsawalk*.

26. Efrat and Langlois, "Contact Period," 60.

27. Lamb, "Mystery"; Lamb and Bartroli, "James Hanna and John Henry Cox," 14.

28. For these different protocols, see Meares, *Voyages*, 112–13, 119–20.

29. Gitlin, "Empires of Trade," 104; White, *Middle Ground*; Bockstoce, *Furs and Frontiers*.

30. Meares, *Voyages*, 112–13.

31. Ibid., 139.

32. Captain Cook relied on Tupaia's (Tahitian) knowledge of the South Pacific to navigate through the region. Finney, "James Cook"; Turnbull, "Cook and Tupaia"; Chaplin, *Round about the Earth*, 128–29; Igler, *Great Ocean*, 83.

33. For the role of the Northwest Coast prestige system in gift exchanges and trade, see Clayton, *Islands of Truth*, 98–149.

34. Another British vessel, James Hanna's *Sea Otter*, took Comekala across the Pacific in 1786. Galois, "Voyages of James Hanna," 84–87.

35. Meares, *Voyages*, 109–11, 154.

36. Salisbury, "Indians' Old World," 444; Forbes, *Apache, Navaho, and Spaniard*, 1–28; Brooks, *Captives and Cousins*, 14–15.

37. Donald, *Aboriginal Slavery*, 139–64; Hajda, "Slavery"; Gibson, "Maritime Trade," 375–76.

38. Arnold, interview.

39. Beaglehole, *Journals of Cook*, 301, 1327, 1400; Wilkes, *Narrative*, 4:486.

40. Meares, *Voyages*, 124.

41. Pascua, interview, 2008.

42. Meares, *Voyages*, 125; Espinosa y Tello, *Spanish Voyage*, 34.

43. Howay, *Voyages of the Columbia*, 197; Moziño, *Noticias de Nutka*, 64–65; Jewitt, *Adventures and Sufferings*, 101–8. Salal is an evergreen perennial. Northwest Coasters ate its berries fresh and dried into cakes, an important regional trade good.

44. Pascua, interview, 2008; Swan, "The Coast Tribes of Washington Territory," *Puget Sound Herald*, February 10, 1860, Frank R. and Kathryn M. Stenzel Research Files on Western American Art; Corney and Alexander, *Voyages in the Northern Pacific*, 58; Scouler, "Journal of a Voyage to Northwest America," 195–96; entry for March 14, 1806, in Moulton, *Journals of Lewis and Clark*.

45. Galois, *Voyage*, 404; Espinosa y Tello, *Spanish Voyage*, 32–34; Eggers to Roger Chute, July 27, 1936, Ms 15/58, box 4, Chute Collection.

46. Arnold, interview. For more on the ways indigenous peoples used mobility to inscribe spaces with meaning, see Oetelaar and Meyer, "Movement and Native American Landscapes"; and Hudson, *Creek Paths and Federal Roads*. Henri Lefebvre argues that spaces "attain 'real' existence by virtue of networks and pathways" (*Production of Space*, 84).

47. Beaglehole, *Journals of Cook*, 302–3. For the influence of Cook's third voyage on English interest in the maritime fur trade, see "Proceedings of the Court of Directors 29 April to 10 May 1785 Relative to Secret Proposals for Opening a Trade between the N. W. Coast of America and the Japanese Islands etc.," Home Miscellaneous Series, vol. 494, fols. 359–83. For Russians in North America, see Gibson, "Notable Absence"; Taylor, *American Colonies*, 446–54; Grinev, *Tlingit Indians in Russian America*, 91–106; and Bockstoce, *Furs and Frontiers*.

48. For the Nootka Sound Controversy, see Gormly, "Early Culture Contact," 17–21; Cook, *Flood Tide of Empire*, 129–433; Weber, *Spanish Frontier*, 285–86; and Nokes, *Almost a Hero*, 126–65.

49. Gray, *Making of John Ledyard*. For the maritime fur trade in general, see Fisher, *Contact and Conflict*, 1–23; Gibson, *Otter Skins*; Clayton, *Islands of Truth*, 67–161; and Vaughan and Holm, *Soft Gold*.

50. Howay, *Voyages of the Columbia*, 45, 72.

51. Moziño, *Noticias de Nutka*, 48; Latourette, *Voyages of American Ships*, 255–61. Latourette noted that the lists of US vessels engaged in the maritime fur trade are "avowedly incomplete" due to imperfect archival records.

52. Beals, *Juan Pérez*; Beaglehole, *Journals of Cook*, 302.

53. Meares, *Voyages*, 217.

54. Swan, "Indians of Cape Flattery," 52.

55. Meares, *Voyages*, 196–209; Howay, *Voyages of the Columbia*, 56; Moziño, *Noticias De Nutka*, 71.

56. Howay, "Voyage of the *Hope*," 177.

57. Gibbs, "Notebook: No. 2," p. 32, in Notebooks of Scientific Observations of the Pacific Northwest; Pascua, interview, 2008; Swan, "Indians of Cape Flattery," 7–8; Densmore, *Nootka and Quileute Music*, 109–10; Sapir et al., *Whaling Indians*.

58. Howay, "Yankee Trader," 87; Mathes, "Wickaninnish," 76–79.

59. Galois, *Voyage*, 404.

60. Howay, *Voyages of the Columbia*, 72, 81, 197.

61. Meares, *Voyages*, 146–47, 155.

62. Ibid., 175.

63. Donald, *Aboriginal Slavery*, 232.

64. Jewitt, *Journal*.

65. Salisbury, "Indians' Old World," 453.

66. Howay, "Yankee Trader," 88; Lutz, *Makúk*, 122.

67. Howay, "Four Letters," 135.

68. Howay, *Voyages of the Columbia*, 262–67; Vancouver, *Voyage of Discovery*, 2:254; Jewitt, *Adventures and Sufferings* (1987), 81; Mathes, "Wickaninnish," 17.

69. Claplanhoo, interview; Pascua, interview, 2008; Arima, *Between Ports Alberni and Renfrew*, 303–04; Harmon, *Indians in the Making*, 8.

70. Historians James Brooks and Juliana Barr make a similar case for the southwest colonial and Texas borderlands. Brooks, *Captives and Cousins*; Barr, *Peace Came in the Form of a Woman*.

71. Galois, "Voyages of James Hanna"; Lamb and Bartroli, "James Hanna and John Henry Cox," 12–13.

72. Meares, *Voyages*, 216–17.

73. Curtis, *The Nootka. The Haida*, 34–39; Koppert, "Contributions to Clayoquot Ethnology," 56; Jonaitis and Inglis, *Yuquot Whalers' Shrine*.

74. Meares, *Voyages*, 205; see app. A for Merchant Proprietors, "Instructions of the Merchant Proprietors," December 24, 1787. See also Miller, "Ka'iana, the Once Famous 'Prince of Kauai'"; Nokes, *Almost a Hero*, 33–35, 113–17.

75. Strange, *James Strange's Journal*, 79.

76. Probably impetigo, a bacterial infection encountered in children; this affliction might have been transmitted in the close quarters of the longhouses. For impetigo, see Bryon, "Infections of the Skin."

77. Strange, *James Strange's Journal*, 78, 80–81; Fisher and Bumsted, *Account of a Voyage*, 69–71.

78. Fisher and Bumsted, *Account of a Voyage*, 177–85; Seed, *Ceremonies of Possession*, 16–40.

79. Fisher and Bumsted, *Account of a Voyage*, 180.

80. Ibid., 201; Beresford, *Voyage Round the World*, 232 (quotation); Galois, "Voyages of James Hanna," 87.

81. This was still evident in the mid-nineteenth century. Hancock, *Thirteen Years Residence*, 91–92.

82. Lamb, "Mystery," 41.

83. Richard Cadman Etches, London merchant and supercargo on Dixon and Portlock's 1787 Northwest Coast voyage, believed that Mackay was no master of the Nootkan language as he had made himself out to be. However, even he concluded that Barkley had "found [Mackay] extremely useful in managing the traffic with the natives." Beresford, *Voyage Round the World*, 233. Other traders that season noted Mackay's usefulness to Barkley. See Galois, *Voyage*, 341, n. 121. Some scholars believe that Barkley forcibly removed Mackay from Nootka Sound in order to prevent Strange from benefitting from his assistance. See Ayyar, "Introduction," 11.

84. Jewitt, *Journal*. This is described in more detail in chapter 2.

85. Ibid., 21, 30. For unfree people in the Pacific Northwest, see Igler, "Captive-Taking," 12–17, for details on Jewitt. See also Igler, *Great Ocean*, 73–97.

86. Jewitt, *Journal*, 9, 17, 24, 28, 35, 46–48; Jewitt, *Adventures and Sufferings* (1987). Jewitt wrote several letters and gave them to Indians to pass on to ships—he gave one to Wickaninnish and sent another northward with someone else in a canoe.

87. Gibbs, "Tribes of Western Washington and Northwestern Oregon," 240; Igler, "Captive-Taking," 17–22; Igler, *Great Ocean*, 89–94; Owens and Donnelly, *Wreck of the Sv. Nikolai*, 62 (quotation). Kenneth Owens and Alton Donnelly hypothesize that Mackay, the Irishman left in Nootka Sound in 1786, might have fathered Ulatilla. Other scholars, such as David Igler, have repeated this theory. However, this could not be the case. Jewitt described Ulatilla as being thirty years old in 1804, about thirteen or fourteen years older than he would have been if Mackay had fathered him—surely Jewitt could have told the difference between a sixteen- or seventeen-year-old and a thirty-year-old. Jewitt, *Adventures and Sufferings* (1987), 141. Also, as Mackay himself told Walker in 1788, Maquinna had not given him a wife. Although Mackay could have fathered a child through a less formal liaison, this individual could have risen to become a chief within Makah society only if the mother had been a high-status

Makah. Considering Mackay's disastrous time at Nootka Sound, it seems unlikely that he fathered a Makah chief.

88. Igler writes that Ulatilla "quite possibly viewed these people as lost wanderers in a foreign land and he sought to help them" (*Great Ocean*, 93).

89. Inglis and Haggarty, "Cook to Jewitt," 219–20; Donald, *Aboriginal Slavery*, 27, 96, 103, 39, 277. See also *Ahousaht*, 81–85.

90. For more on this imperial process in the Pacific Northwest, see Clayton, *Islands of Truth*.

91. Historian Beth LaDow characterizes Sitting Bull as a "borderlands strategist," a description that also applies to these Northwest Coast leaders (*Medicine Line*, 60).

CHAPTER 2: INVETERATE WARS AND PETTY PILFERINGS

1. Meares, *Voyages*, 174.

2. Duffin's account of the longboat's brief expedition is included as appendix 4. Meares, *Voyages*, 176, 177.

3. Ibid., 179, 184. In some parts of Native North America, the exchange of body parts represented the strengthening of partnerships against others. See Lipman, "'Meanes to Knitt Them Togeather.'"

4. Meares, *Voyages*, 177.

5. Pearce, *Savagism and Civilization*; Berkhofer, *White Man's Indian*; Ellingson, *Myth of the Noble Savage*.

6. For the complexities of violence from a more indigenous perspective, see Brooks, *Captives and Cousins*; and Blackhawk, *Violence over the Land*. Historian Richard White has also explored these themes. See "Winning of the West"; *Roots of Dependency*; and *Middle Ground*.

7. Fisher, *Contact and Conflict*, 1.

8. Howay, *Outline Sketch of the Maritime Fur Trade*, 12. For a more refined approach to Howay's argument, see Gibson, *Otter Skins*, 158.

9. Clayton, *Islands of Truth*, 86.

10. Nirenberg, *Communities of Violence*.

11. For violence against slaves in Northwest Coast societies, see Donald, *Aboriginal Slavery*, 165–81; and Ernst, *Wolf Ritual*, 6–45, 235–37.

12. Boas, "Tsimshian Mythology," 586–620; McMillan, *Since the Time of the Transformers*, 31–32; McHalsie, Schaepe, and Carlson, "Making the World Right"; and Lutz, *Makúk*, 54. For a Makah oral account of Transformer, see Ulmer, "Deer and the Transformer."

13. Pascua, interview, 2008; Claplanhoo, interview; Arnold, interview. For archaeological and linguistic explanations, see Jacobsen, "Wakashan Comparative Studies," 776; and Samuels, *Ozette Archaeological Project*, 1:11.

14. Coté, *Spirits of Our Whaling Ancestors*, 71–72.

15. Typescript notes from Elizabeth Colson Collection, 105–15, 233, 236–40; and Irvine and Markistun, *How the Makah Obtained Possession of Cape Flattery*. For more oral

histories on conflicts between the Ditidahts and Makahs, see Arima, *Between Ports Alberni and Renfrew*, 300–309.

16. Albert B. Reagan, "Pioneer Makahs Massacred by Quileute Navy," newspaper clipping, ca. 1890, Allison W. Smith Papers.

17. During the mid-nineteenth century, Swan twice noted the Makah belief that Indians who died on the water turned into owls. Entries for July 19, 1862, Diary 6, and January 19, 1865, Diary 9, Swan Papers, 1833–1909.

18. Koppert, "Contributions to Clayoquot Ethnology," 1; Drucker, *Northern and Central Nootkan Tribes*, 240–43. The population estimate is from Meares, *Voyages*, 230.

19. This is where I diverge from traditional borderlands scholarship, which argues that borderlands did not arise until two or more European polities contested and shared a geographic region.

20. Lutz, "First Contact as Spiritual Performance," 30.

21. See "Document No. 19: Journal of Fray Juan Crespi, 5th October 1774," in Cutter, *California Coast*, 263. This smoke likely came from fires Makahs set; they burned berry grounds after the fall harvest. Anderson, "Ozette Prairies of Olympic National Park," 39–56.

22. Campa, *Journal of Explorations*, 41; Hezeta, *Honor and Country*, 76. Today, this site is known as Point Grenville, Washington. *Vara* is approximately the equivalent of a rod, so Hezeta could see only about sixty feet or so into the woods. For Spanish possession ceremonies, see Seed, *Ceremonies of Possession*, 69–99.

23. Sierra, *Fray Benito de La Sierra's Account*, 30.

24. Ibid., 31. In addition to Sierra's account, this attack is detailed in Hezeta, *Honor and Country*, 77–78. See also Campa, *Journal of Explorations*, 42–45; Tovell, *Far Reaches of Empire*, 15–48.

25. Hezeta, *Honor and Country*, 84–85; Sierra, *Fray Benito de La Sierra's Account*, 36; Campa, *Journal of Explorations*, 53–54.

26. Most historical accounts assume that the Spaniards encountered only Quileutes and that these people had perpetrated the violence. See Powell, "Quileute," 435. For Quinault oral histories about this incident, see Storm and Capoeman, *Land of the Quinault*, 84. Whaling done by other non-Makah Washington Indians is still a debated point. Many, including Makahs, claim that only the People of the Cape pursued whales from canoes. However, on July 31, 1861, the Quileutes had whale oil to trade with the crew of the *Sarah Newton*. See James Swan, Bound autograph manuscript journal and memorandum book, 1861–71, Stenzel Research Files on Western American Art (hereafter cited as Manuscript Journal). While teaching Quileute children at a day school at La Push, Washington, in the late 1880s and 1890s, A. W. Smith collected several drawings students made of Quileute whalers (see Allison W. Smith Papers). Quinaults, who only harvested drift whales, would have been unlikely to have whale flesh because this spoils quickly and can be harvested only from a freshly killed whale. Huelsbeck, "Whaling in the Precontact Economy," 7.

27. Beals locates this incident at the Quinault River. Hezeta, *Honor and Country*, 78.

28. Sierra, *Fray Benito de La Sierra's Account*, 29.

29. Beaglehole, *Journals of Cook*, 297 (quotation), 302; Fisher and Bumsted, *Account of a Voyage*, 62. Recent scholarship has begun to reassess the role of violence during Cook's third voyage. Geographer Daniel Clayton argues that although violence was rare, "tension was never far from the surface" (*Islands of Truth*, 32). New Zealand scholar Anne Salmond also reassesses Cook's voyages and the more prominent role violence played than most have assumed (*Trial of the Cannibal Dog*).

30. Rickman, *Journal of Cook's Last Voyage*, 239; Galois, *Voyage*, 107. Non-Native mariners were not the only ones to experience problems with Natives in the region taking things. See Ronda, *Lewis and Clark among the Indians*, 203.

31. Drucker, *Northern and Central Nootkan Tribes*, 313; Moore, "Emergence of Ethnic Roles," 77, 354–55. Enemies and non-kin were sometimes synonymous categories.

32. Galois, *Voyage*, 111; Beaglehole, *Journals of Cook*, 298; Gilje, *Liberty on the Waterfront*, 83.

33. Rickman, *Journal of Cook's Last Voyage*, 236 (quotation). For the fear of attack, see the comment by the expedition's surgeon, David Samwell, in Beaglehole, *Journals of Cook*, 1093. Samwell appeared to have written his Nootka Sound entries while there. Therefore, his observations more accurately present what he and others felt at the time.

34. Rediker, *Between the Devil and the Deep Blue Sea*, 212.

35. Gilje, *Liberty on the Waterfront*, 83.

36. Keel-hauling involved dragging a sailor underneath the ship from one side to the other or from fore to aft. Sailors punished by running the gauntlet had to pass through a double file of men facing each other. Armed with clubs and other weapons, the men struck at individuals running between them. A normal sentence for running the gauntlet was eight to ten passes. Pike, *Penal Servitude in Early Modern Spain*, 132; Volo and Volo, *Daily Life in the Age of Sail*, 131–32.

37. Rediker, *Between the Devil and the Deep Blue Sea*, 207.

38. Beaglehole, *Journals of Cook*, 298.

39. James Trevethen recorded this incident as marginalia in a published volume of Cook's account. See ibid., n. 1.

40. Although this incident is missing from Cook's official account, the expedition's astronomer, William Bayly, recorded it in his journal. See ibid., 307, n. 2.

41. Ibid., 1326; Rickman, *Journal of Cook's Last Voyage*, 236.

42. An account of Barkley's voyage no longer exists. Information comes from contemporary traders who included bits and pieces about his trading expedition. The best assemblage of these scattered fragments is in Lamb, "Mystery of Mrs. Barkley's Diary." Barkley's wife, Frances, was the first Anglo woman to visit the Northwest Coast. Unless otherwise noted, the quotations here are from this article.

43. Details on this incident also appear in Beresford, *Voyage Round the World*, 289–90. The account of Barkely's burning of the Hoh village appears in a 1788 letter the London merchant Etches wrote to Banks. See Howay, "Four Letters," 135. For more on European fears of Northwest Coast cannibals—and vice versa—see Archer, "Cannibalism"; and Thrush, "Vancouver the Cannibal."

44. Meares, *Voyages*, 124.

45. Scholars have noted that the Spanish captain named this island after the liturgical feast of Our Lady of Sorrows (Nuestra Señora de Dolores) because he sailed past it on September 18, close to the date of this Catholic event; however, the Isla de Dolores would have also memorialized the loss of seven crewmembers. See Hayes, *Historical*, 40, map 63.

46. Lamb, "Mystery," 44; Wright, *Lewis and Dryden's Marine History*, 4.

47. Carter, *Road to Botany Bay*, xiv.

48. Meares, *Voyages*, 115.

49. Ibid., 145.

50. Ibid., 155–56.

51. Ibid., 161.

52. Ibid., 209.

53. Moziño, *Noticias de Nutka*, 57.

54. Blackhawk, *Violence over the Land*.

55. Howay, *Voyages of the Columbia*, 72; Espinosa y Tello, *Spanish Voyage*, 36; Howay, "Yankee Trader," 87. For conflicts with their neighbors, see Scouler, "Dr. John Scouler's Journal," 195–96; Sapir and Swadesh, *Native Accounts of Nootka Ethnography*, 381–84, 412–39; Kane, *Wanderings of an Artist*, 229–32; Swan, "Indians of Cape Flattery," 50–51; Renker and Gunther, "Makah," 423.

56. Kendrick, *Voyage of Sutil and Mexicana*, 185.

57. Igler, *Great Ocean*, 84–85.

58. Galois, *Voyage*, 106; Jewitt, *Journal*, 13; Jewitt, *Adventures and Sufferings* (1987), 112. As Stewart notes, no Captain Tawnington appears in the shipping records for the Northwest Coast. Howay thinks this might have been Captain Ewen of the British schooner *Prince William Henry*. He wintered at Friendly Cove in 1792–1793. See Howay, *List of Trading Vessels*, 117.

59. Fisher and Bumsted, *Account of a Voyage*, 199.

60. Jewitt, *Journal*, 13.

61. These quotations appear in a letter "from a gentleman in China" that was published in London's *Daily Universal Register* (precursor to the *London Times*) on August 21, 1787, as reprinted in Galois, "Voyages of James Hanna."

62. As printed in Lamb and Bartroli, "James Hanna and John Henry Cox," 15.

63. Making fictive kin was first discussed in chapter 1. See ibid.; and Galois, "Voyages of James Hanna."

64. Meares, *Voyages*, 118; Moziño, *Noticias de Nutka*, 75–76.

65. Peter Webster, the Nuu-chah-nulth who told this history, noted that Spaniards have never admitted to this horrifying abuse. Efrat and Langlois, "Contact Period," 60.

66. Smith, *Conquest*, 12.

67. Manuel Quimper to Viceroy Conde de Revilla Gigedo, November 13, 1790, in Wagner, *Spanish Explorations*, 80. For Quimper's time with Bodega y Quadra, see Beerman, "Manuel Quimper."

68. Swan, Manuscript Journal, 136.

69. This action earned him reprimands from Bodega y Quadra (Fidalgo's superior at Nootka Sound), the viceroy at San Blas, and even the Spanish king.

70. This section on the Spanish outpost at Neah Bay is assembled from Howay, *Voyages of the Columbia*, 409–16; Howay, "Voyage of the *Hope*," 28; Espinosa y Tello, *Spanish Voyage*, 26–28; Wagner, *Spanish Explorations*, 59–69; and Gormly, "Early Culture Contact," 31–32.

71. Swan, "Coast Tribes of Washington Territory." When Swan first went out to Neah Bay in March 1859, he could find little trace of the Spanish fort (entry for March 18, 1859, Diary 1, Swan Papers, 1833–1909).

72. Jewitt and Thompson's enslavement by Maquinna was discussed in chapter 1. For the most accurate account of Jewitt's time at Yuquot, see his journal. For the heavily revised captivity narrative—written with the help of Richard Alsop, an accomplished writer in Connecticut—see *Narrative of the Adventures and Sufferings*. This is the version that has been republished, edited, and revised over the past two centuries. In this narrative, he complains of the Indians calling him and Thompson Maquinna's "white slaves" (57, 146). For information on the publication of the journal and narrative, along with his 1817 play that ran for three nights in Philadelphia, see Jewitt, *Adventures and Sufferings* (1987), 7, 181–83.

73. Zilberstein, "Objects of Distant Exchange," 610–11. Some examples of this problematic approach include Howay, "Indian Attacks"; Cook, *Flood Tide of Empire*, 432–33; Gough, *Northwest Coast*, 74; and Gibson, *Otter Skins*, 269–78.

74. Clayton, *Islands of Truth*, 114.

75. This argument is also made in Inglis and Haggarty, "Cook to Jewitt," 218–20.

76. Jewitt, *Journal*, 20.

77. Gibson, *Otter Skins*, 205.

78. Mrs. Williams, "Famine," 1–2, Colson Collection; Fisher and Bumsted, *Account of a Voyage*, 181. Nuu-chah-nulth oral histories also mention occasional food shortages before the appearance of Europeans. See Arima, Sapir, and Tyee Bob, *Family Origin Histories*, 151.

79. For an application of dependency theory, see Delâge, *Bitter Feast*, 78–162. For a sample of "new Indian history" studies that turn dependency theory on its head, see White, *Middle Ground*; Anderson, *Indian Southwest*; DuVal, *Native Ground*; Hämäläinen, *Comanche Empire*; and Hyde, *Empires, Nations, and Families*.

80. Jewitt, *Journal*, 13; Efrat and Langlois, "Contact Period," 60.

81. Jewitt, *Adventures and Sufferings* (1987), 100. When the US Exploring Expedition (the Wilkes Expedition) stopped at Neah Bay in 1841, Makahs had many sea otter furs to trade, but they offered such "exorbitantly high prices" that the Euro-Americans refused to buy any. Wilkes, *Narrative*, 4:297, 486.

82. Codere, "Kwakiutl," 363; Clayton, *Islands of Truth*, 126.

83. Jewitt, *Adventures and Sufferings* (1987). Individuals carrying ten muskets might not have been an exaggeration; Jewitt noted that the *Boston* carried three thousand muskets and fowling pieces (35). See also Jewitt, *Journal*, 5.

84. Ibid., 27.

85. Kenyon, *Kyuquot Way*, 124. Interestingly, his reputation did not sully the title of "Maquinna." It is still an important name owned by specific Nuu-chah-nulth families, and only respected individuals can earn the right to call themselves "Maquinna." As of 2010, Chief Michael Maquinna was one of the current members of the Mowachaht/Muchalaht Council of Chiefs. Mowachaht/Muchalaht First Nation, "Contacts."

86. For an overview of the voyage of the *Tonquin*, see Ronda, *Astoria and Empire*, 101–15. One of the passengers kept a journal. See Franchère, *Narrative of a Voyage*, 47–75. Duncan McDougall, supervising partner at Fort Astoria and one of the passengers aboard the *Tonquin* on its voyage from New York to the Columbia River, complained that "the greater part of [Thorn's] Crew were *green hands*" (emphasis in original). Jones, *Annals of Astoria*, 3.

87. The most accurate account of the *Tonquin's* loss came from Joseachal, the Native interpreter Thorn hired. Jones, "Identity of the Tonquin's Interpreter." On June 15–18, 1813, Joseachal told McDougall and others at Fort Astoria about the incident. Jones, *Annals of Astoria*, 191–95 (quotation, 95). Subsequent retellings based on Joseachal's account appear in Franchère, *Narrative of a Voyage*, 179–86; Cox, *Columbia River*, 1:88–96; Irving, *Astoria*, 64–70. The identity of the interpreter is a little unclear. Howay, "Loss of the *Tonquin*," 83–84. Some sources point to him being picked up in the southern part of the ča·di· borderland near Gray's Harbor, while others mention that Thorn picked him up on Vancouver Island near Nootka Sound. For the use of Northwest Coast paddles as convenient weapons, see Arima, *West Coast People*, 36.

88. Reynolds, *Voyage of the New Hazard*, 42.

89. Tla-o-qui-aht (Clayoquot) oral histories number the casualties at eighty. See Cornwall, "Suicide Bomber." In his first telling of the incident to McDougall, Joseachal thought that about a hundred Clayoquots perished in the explosion, and the casualty estimate grew with each retelling during his time at Fort Astoria. Tla-o-qui-aht oral accounts also detail that canoes were towing the *Tonquin* when it exploded. See Tonquin Foundation, "The Mayflower of the West," *The Tonquin Foundation*, http://www.tonquinfoundation.org/ . . . /Mayflower%20of%20the%20West.pdf.

90. Hancock, *Thirteen Years Residence*, 149.

91. Cornwall, "Suicide Bomber."

92. These incidents are discussed in chapter 1. Howay, "Yankee Trader," 87–89; and Mathes, "Wickaninnish," 76–79.

93. Franchère, *Narrative of a Voyage*, 126–27, 187 (quotation). See also Scouler, "Dr. John Scouler's Journal," 205; Jones, *Annals of Astoria*, 40–41.

94. Jewitt, *Journal*, 5, 9; Benito Vivero y Escaño, "Noticias de Nootka y Californias," San Blas, October 22, 1803, fol. 304, Archivo General de la Nación, Mexico City; Vivero y Escaño quoted a letter (Braulio de Otalora y Oquendo, Monterey, August 31, 1803, fol. 306), as referenced in Cook, *Flood Tide of Empire*, 24, 433. Because Brown did not linger in Nootka Sound and interact with Mowachahts or their white slaves, he must have learned of the captives from local Indians. For the initial, brief report, see

the *Columbian Sentinel and Massachusetts Federalist* (Boston), April 25, 1804; and Samuel Hill, "Loss of the Boston (Communicated by Captain Hill from Canton)," *Columbian Sentinel* (Boston), May 20, 1807, both reprinted in Howay, "Early Account of the Loss of the *Boston*," 281–87. See also Jones, *Annals of Astoria*, 29, n. 66; Reynolds, *Voyage of the New Hazard*, 33, 42; *New York Evening Post*, April 22, 1812, as quoted in Giesecke, "Search for the Tonquin (Part 2)," 5; and *Naval Chronicle*, 306–7.

95. Jewitt, *Journal*, 9; Roquefeuil, *Voyage*, 48; Scouler, "Dr. John Scouler's Journal," 195; Reynolds, *Voyage of the New Hazard*, 36–37.

96. Roquefeuil, *Voyage*, 45; Scouler, "Dr. John Scouler's Journal," 192.

97. Roquefeuil, *Voyage*, 118; Scouler, "Dr. John Scouler's Journal," 195.

98. This was an oral history told by Andy Callicum. See Jewitt, *Adventures and Sufferings* (1987), 184.

99. Scouler, "Dr. John Scouler's Journal," 193.

100. Wilkes, *Narrative*, 4:486; Mathes, "Wickaninnish," 90.

101. Jewitt, *Adventures and Sufferings* (1987), 100. Several fur trade accounts also characterized Clayoquots and Makahs as being more successful whalers than the inhabitants of Nootka Sound. Howay, *Voyages of the Columbia*, 70; Galois, *Voyage*, 404. In his journal, Jewitt recorded numerous times that Maquinna went whaling and failed. He often struck whales but lost them when his gear failed him. Jewitt, *Journal*.

CHAPTER 3: "DEPENDING ON THE SUCCESS
OR GOOD-WILL OF THE NATIVES"

1. News of the incident first reached the Anglo world when the *Susan Sturges* arrived at Fort Victoria, not far from Neah Bay. See Rev. Staines [Fort Victoria] to Thomas Boys, July 6, 1852, enclosure in Boys to Desart (Parliamentary Under-Secretary), October 11, 1852, 9263, CO 305/3, p. 495, *Colonial Despatches*. See also James Douglas [chief factor] to Archibald Barclay [HBC secretary], January 3, 1852, *Douglas Letters*, UWSC; Douglas, Gov. Vancouver's Island, to Earl Grey, January 29, 1852, *ROT*, Vol. 726: 1852–1856, pp. 5–10 [microfilm copy in "Correspondence with Hudson's Bay Company," vol. 2, BCA]; *Daily Alta California*, February 14, 1852; *London Daily News*, March 31, 1852; and *New York Daily News*, April 13, 28, 1852. For more information on the *Una's* activities in the Queen Charlottes, see Scholefield and Howay, *British Columbia*, 2:2; and Akrigg and Akrigg, *British Columbia Chronicle*, 44–46. For a comprehensive and detailed list of HBC vessels, see Spoehr, "Nineteenth-Century Chapter," 99. For more on Sudaał, see Boas, "Tsimshian Mythology," 388–89.

2. This appears to have been a common strategy that some indigenous leaders pursued. See Kugel, *To Be the Main Leaders*, 6–7, 84–87.

3. Although Dodd's account never named the chief who resolved the situation at Cape Flattery, this individual was most likely Yelakub. A newspaper article identified Flattery Jack (Yelakub) as the chief who executed ten of the perpetrators. "Oregon." In 1859, one of Yelakub's sons showed Euro-American James Swan, the first government

schoolteacher at Neah Bay, a letter from Douglas to Chief Yelaḱub hailing his efforts at saving the *Una's* property. Entry for November 8, 1859, Diary 2, Swan Papers, 1833–1909.

4. Dodd had been stationed in the Columbia District since 1836 as first mate on several HBC vessels, including the *Beaver* and *Cadborough*, both of which engaged regularly with Makahs and other Northwest Coast peoples. See "Charles Dodd Biographical Sheet (1808–1860) (fl. 1833–1860)," June 1999 (updated July 2005), HBCA, http://www. gov.mb.ca/chc/archives/hbca/biographical/d/dodd_charles.pdf. For more on slave proxies, see Donald, *Aboriginal Slavery*, 103. Other Native North American societies, such as the Osage, engaged in similar proxy practices. DuVal, *Native Ground*, 174. Details on the *Cadborough* expedition appear in James Douglas, Gov. Vancouver's Island, to Earl Grey, February 11, 1852, *ROT, Vol. 726*, 12–13; Douglass [*sic*] to Edmund A. Starling, [Indian agent for Puget Sound District,] February 11, 1852, copy in *ARCIA* (1852), 175–76. Many secondary sources refer to the *Cadborough* as the *Cadboro*. I have elected to use the former spelling because this is what shows up in the ship's logs.

5. Weber, *Vocation Lectures*, 33.

6. Schwantes, *Pacific Northwest*, 97–100.

7. Derived from medieval palimpsests, parchment pages whose previous content had been scraped away to make a mostly clean surface for new words and images, the palimpsest metaphor is "a site where texts have been superimposed onto others in an attempt to displace earlier or competing histories," according to literary scholar Daniel Cooper Alarcón. "Such displacement [by the dominant narrative] is never total; the suppressed material often remains legible, however faintly, challenging the dominant text with an alternate version of events." *Aztec Palimpsest*, xiv. In addition to Cooper Alarcón's fascinating study, I have found the following texts helpful in framing my understanding of palimpsest: Certeau, *Practice of Everyday Life*; Crang, "Envisioning Urban Histories"; and McManus, "Writing the Palimpsest, Again." For applications of the palimpsest to borderlands, see Anzaldúa, *Borderlands*; Truett, *Fugitive Landscapes*, 8; and Richardson, *Kaleidoscopic Odessa*.

8. Adelman and Aron, "From Borderlands to Borders," 840.

9. I have adapted this language from Thrush, *Native Seattle*, 66–79. He describes Seattle of the 1870s and 1880s as a place where Indians and settlers were "imbricated into the urban fabric" (75). A similar process happened earlier and at a more regional level.

10. Historian Gray Whaley describes a similar process for colonial Oregon, where "Native and Western peoples created colonial worlds together through their daily interactions, struggles for power and influence, and accommodations." *Oregon and the Collapse of Illahee*, 19.

11. "Autobiography of James Lawson," http://www.history.noaa.gov/stories_tales/jlaw son.html; "Log of the *Mary Dare* (brig)," October 14, 1852–December 13, 1853, C.1/461, Ship Logs, HBCA; Tolmie, *Journals*, 224, 242–43; Dickey, *Journal*, sec. 1, pp. 40–46; Kane, *Wanderings of an Artist*, 237–39; Gibbs, "Tribes of Western Washington and Northwestern Oregon," 174. Archival sources note differing views on the identity of

Yelakub's father. Kane identified the Makah chief's father as the pilot aboard the *Tonquin*, which Wickaninnish attacked (see chapter 2). Other sources name the pilot as George Ramsey, the son of an English sailor who deserted or was shipwrecked in the late eighteenth century and lived among the Clatsops. Ramsey lived at least until the mid-1840s, more than a decade after the murder of Yelakub's father. For a biography of and summary of sources on Ramsey, see Barry, "Astorians Who Became Permanent Settlers." Due to the nature of intertribal relationships in the borderlands, an indigenous person or group of people from another tribal nation probably murdered the Makah chief's father.

12. Davidson, *Directory for the Pacific Coast*, 112; Lawson, "Autobiography"; Gibbs, "Tribes of Western Washington and Northwestern Oregon," 174–76. For the 1846 murder of Chief George, see Seemann, *Narrative*, 1:106–7. This incident is discussed in more detail later.

13. For race, identity, and colonialism specific to indigenous peoples in the Pacific Northwest, see Harmon, *Indians in the Making*; Lutz, "Making 'Indians' in British Columbia"; and Whaley, *Oregon and the Collapse of Illahee*. These themes are also discussed more generally in Berkhofer, *White Man's Indian*; Smedley, *Race in North America*, 171–74, 330–31; and Kupperman, *Indians and English*.

14. Ronda, *Astoria and Empire*, 243 (quotation). For primary sources on the PFC, see Jones, *Annals of Astoria*; Ross, *Adventures of the First Settlers*, 1–285; Franchère, *Narrative of a Voyage*, 23–204; Seton and Jones, *Astorian Adventure*. For a sampling of the secondary literature, see Irving, *Astoria*; and Dolin, *Fur, Fortune, and Empire*, 189–222.

15. Barman and Watson, *Leaving Paradise*, 34–56.

16. Ross, *Adventures of the First Settlers*, 74 (quotation); Ronda, *Astoria and Empire*, 196–242; Bergmann, "'We Should Lose Much by Their Absence'"; Whaley, *Oregon and the Collapse of Illahee*, 30–50.

17. Whaley, *Oregon and the Collapse of Illahee*, 70.

18. Jones, *Annals of Astoria*, 27 (quotation), 110, 48. For Makah connections to Columbia River peoples, see Pascua, interview, 2008; Swan, "The Coast Tribes of Washington Territory," *Puget Sound Herald*, February 10, 1860, Frank R. and Kathryn M. Stenzel Research Files on Western American Art.

19. Corney and Alexander, *Voyages in the Northern Pacific*, 58. Corney also noted that the Classets were there with Chief Coalpo (Clatsop), who had given his permission for them to be at Baker's Bay. See also Scouler, "Dr. John Scouler's Journal," 195.

20. Kane, *Wanderings of an Artist*, 171–72.

21. Harris, *Resettlement of British Columbia*, 37. For the expansion of the HBC, see Galbraith, *Hudson's Bay Company as an Imperial Factor*, 78–155. Newer scholarship examines the emerging Pacific economy of the nineteenth century and details the role of British fur traders in the Pacific Northwest. Mackie, *Trading beyond the Mountains*. For the placement of Fort Vancouver in an indigenous world, see Hyde, *Empires, Nations, and Families*, 109 (quotation).

22. Howay, "Brig *Owhyhee* in the Columbia"; Maclachlan and Suttles, *Fort Langley Journals*, 23 (quotation); Tolmie, *Journals*, 224.

23. McDonald to John McLeod, January 15, 1832, McLeod Papers, National Archives Canada, as quoted in Mackie, *Trading beyond the Mountains*, 218. In the early 1830s, Chief Factor McLoughlin also shipped packed salmon from the Columbia River to markets in California, Peru, and Chile. McLoughlin, *Letters*, 163, 170, 181. See also Kane, *Wanderings of an Artist*, 221; Mackie, *Trading beyond the Mountains*, 55; Hammatt and Wagner-Wright, *Ships, Furs, and Sandalwood*. For the early nineteenth-century expansion of Pacific trade, see Igler, "Diseased Goods"; and Igler, *Great Ocean*.

24. Corney and Alexander, *Voyages in the Northern Pacific*, 154; Ronda, *Astoria and Empire*, 222–30; Maclachlan and Suttles, *Fort Langley Journals*; Jones, *Annals of Astoria*; Whaley, *Oregon and the Collapse of Illahee*, 24.

25. Mackie, *Trading beyond the Mountains*, 231.

26. See map in Grant, "Description of Vancouver Island." HBC ship logs also reference a Scarborough Point near Neah Bay. See "Log of the *Mary Dare*," November 4, 1853, and "Log of the *Cowlitz* (barque)," July 12, 1850, C.1/265, Ship Logs, HBCA.

27. For Makah sea otter hunting in the 1830s, see Dunn, *History of the Oregon Territory and British North-American Fur Trade*, 231. For examples of HBC vessels trading at Neah Bay, see the "Log of the *Cadborough* (schooner)," June 27, 1827–August 19, 1831, C.1/218; March 25–August 23, 1835, C.1/220; June 25, 1843–August 2, 1850, C.1/221, 222; "Log of the *Columbia* (barque)," September 6, 1842–January 11, 1845, C.1/248; October 4, 1845–May 19, 1848, C.1/250; September 29, 1845–January 29, 1848, C.1/251; September 7, 1848–April 18, 1850, C.1/254; "Log of the *Cowlitz* (barque)," September 20, 1843–February 3, 1846, C.1/259; Private Journal of James Cooper [while aboard the *Cowlitz*], July 19, 1845–June 28, 1846, C.1/262; "Log of the *Dryad* (brig)," March 29, 1832–April 9, 1836, C.1/281, 282; "Log of the *Vancouver* (barque)," September 4, 1841–June 12, 1844, C.1/1063; September 4, 1841–May 23, 1845, C.1/1064; September 2, 1844–July 13, 1847, C.1/1065; and "Log of the *Mary Dare* (brig)," Ship Logs, HBCA. See also Mackie, *Trading beyond the Mountain*, 233. For haˑykʷa harvesting, see Kane, *Wanderings of an Artist*, 238.

28. Howay, "Brig *Owhyhee* in the Columbia," 325–26; Tolmie, *Journals*, 238.

29. Gibbs, *Indian Tribes of Washington Territory*, 35. In 1852, whale oil sold for just over 68 1/4 cents per gallon, so 30,000 gallons represents $20,475 of whale oil. Starbuck, *History of the American Whale Fishery* (1964), 2:660. By comparison, Nuu-chah-nulth whalers of Vancouver Island sold 10,000 gallons of oil to Fort Victoria in 1855. See Pethick, *Victoria*, 124. The number of whales killed is calculated from whaling returns provided by Wha-laltl-as sá buy (also known as Swell) to Swan. Entries for October 29 to November 1, 1859, Diary 2, Swan Papers, 1833–1909. These returns are discussed in more detail in chapter 5.

30. "Log of the *Columbia*," June 15, 1844, C.1/248.

31. Mackie, *Trading beyond the Mountains*, 278 (quotation); Ormsby, "Introduction," xvi; Hyde, *Empires, Nations, and Families*, 133–37.

32. For the construction and early years of Fort Victoria, see Lamb, "Founding of Fort Victoria"; and Ormsby, "Introduction." Historical records of this time called the Lekwungens "Songhees." For this location's importance as a camas field, see Lutz,

Makúk, 67–68. Camas is a perennial that Northwest Coast peoples cultivated and harvested, pit-roasting the bulbs, which resemble an onion. Appropriating Native lands for settler-colonial purposes was a common practice in mid-nineteenth-century Puget Sound. See White, *Land Use, Environment, and Social Change*. For livestock at Victoria, see Douglas to Archibald Barclay, HBC Secretary, September 3, 1849, in Bowsfield, *Fort Victoria Letters*, 45; and Lutz, *Makúk*, 70–84. For use of the name *Camosun*, see "Log of the *Cowlitz* (barque)," C.1/259; Lamb, "Founding of Fort Victoria," 83. Historical geographers have begun to explore the relations among power, maps, and place-names. For a sampling of this literature, see Carter, *Road to Botany Bay*; Harley, "Maps, Knowledge, and Power"; Belyea, "Amerindian Maps"; Belyea, "Inland Journeys, Native Maps"; Turnbull, *Masons, Tricksters and Cartographers*; and Clayton, *Islands of Truth*.

33. Douglas to Simpson, November 16, 1843, D.5/9, HBCA, as quoted in Lamb, "Founding of Fort Victoria," 89–90. Douglas employed Lekwungens and Kanakas to fill the HBC's labor shortage. See Ormsby, "Introduction," xxi. For a general overview of the role of Native Hawai'ian labor in HBC operations in the Pacific Northwest, see Barman and Watson, *Leaving Paradise*, 57–83. Lekwungens maintained a long engagement with Victoria. See Lutz, *Makúk*, 49–117.

34. Seemann, *Narrative*, 1:106. Cape Flattery oil continued to be a common item carried by merchant ships making the seven-month voyage from Fort Victoria to London. Douglas and John Work [Chief Trader] to the [HBC] Governor and Committee [in London], December 7, 1846, in Bowsfield, *Fort Victoria Letters*, 8.

35. Douglas to Lord Russell, Secretary of the State for the Colonies, August 21, 1855, as quoted in Pethick, *Victoria*, 124. Douglas to the Governor and Committee, October 27, 1849, in Bowsfield, *Fort Victoria Letters*, 63. See also Bayley, "Early Life on Vancouver Island," Bancroft; Ormsby, "Introduction," xxx.

36. Maclachlan and Suttles, *Fort Langley Journals*, 67.

37. Finlayson, *History of Vancouver Island*, 68.

38. Seemann, *Narrative*, 1:106.

39. Chief Yelakub related this incident to Paul Kane at Fort Victoria in early 1847. Kane, *Wanderings of an Artist*, 229–32. Makah oral histories still recall this conflict. See Greene, interview.

40. Longstaff and Lamb, "Royal Navy on the Northwest Coast," 123–24.

41. Maclachlan and Suttles, *Fort Langley Journals*, 213; Vincent, *Dungeness Massacre*, 9–12. This McKenzie was not the same individual as Alexander Mackenzie, credited as the first white man to cross North America.

42. McLoughlin to the Governor and Committee, July 10, 1828, B.223/b/4, HBCA, as quoted in Deans, "Hudson's Bay Company and Its Use of Force," 293, n. 14. See also Hyde, *Empires, Nations, and Families*, 113.

43. Dye, "Earliest Expedition against the Puget Sound Indians," 17, 28. See also Maclachlan and Suttles, *Fort Langley Journals*, 214; and "Log of the *Cadborough*," C.1/218.

44. McLoughlin, *Letters*, 18–26, 40–41; Whaley, *Oregon and the Collapse of Illahee*, 84–86. For McLoughlin's failure to develop a consistent policy to deal with Indian-white

violence in the Oregon Country, see Deans, "Hudson's Bay Company and Its Use of Force."

45. There is a little confusion over dating this incident of the enslavement of the Japanese sailors. The clearest dating comes from the entry for June 9, 1834, in Dickey, *Journal*, sec. 1, p. 28. See also Tolmie, "Manuscript Copy of Memo"; Anderson, "Notes on Indian Tribes," 80; Irving and Bonneville, *Rocky Mountains*, 246; Belcher, *Narrative of a Voyage Round the World*, 303–4; Finlayson, *History of Vancouver Island*, 82; Tate, "Japanese Castaways of 1834."

46. Seemann, *Narrative*, 1:106–7; Davidson, *Directory for the Pacific Coast*, 113.

47. Douglas and Work to the Governor and Committee, November 6, 1847, December 5, 1848; Douglas to Archibald Barclay [HBC Secretary], September 1, 1850; all in Bowsfield, *Fort Victoria Letters*, 13, 27, 116.

48. Legal scholar John Phillip Reid argues that the HBC is one of Canada's colonial predecessors. Reid, *Patterns of Vengeance*, 121. I argue that the HBC was also a colonial predecessor for what became the US portion of Oregon Country.

49. "Treaty with Great Britain," June 15, 1846, *Statutes at Large*, 869. For US expansion into the North American West, see Limerick, *Legacy of Conquest*; White, "*It's Your Misfortune*," 57–211; Milner, "National Initiatives"; Nugent, *Habits of Empire*; and Hyde, *Empires, Nations, and Families*, 375, for Polk's stance on the slogan. For the Anglo settling of British Columbia, see Harris, *Resettlement of British Columbia*; Barman, *West beyond the West*, 55–74; and Lutz, *Makúk*, 49–117. For US expansion into the Pacific Northwest, see Schwantes, *Pacific Northwest*, 78–111; and Whaley, *Oregon and the Collapse of Illahee*, 125–226.

50. Seemann, *Narrative*, vol. 1; Gibbs, *Indian Tribes of Washington Territory*, 35; J. H. Jenkins, Agent Report, ARCIA (1858), 237; J. H. Pelly [HBC Governor] to Earl Grey, March 19, 1850, ROT, Vols. 721–725: 1822–1852, 230–33 [microfilm, vol. 1]; G. A. Paige, Agent Report, ARCIA (1857), 331. For these dynamics in other borderlands, see Reséndez, *Changing National Identities at the Frontier*; McManus, *Line Which Separates*; Truett, *Fugitive Landscapes*; and St. John, *Line in the Sand*.

51. "List of Passengers from England per Barque 'Harpooner' 1849," Philip and Helen Akrigg Research Collection; Shortt and Doughty, *Canada and Its Provinces*, 89; Ormsby, "Introduction," xliv–xlvii, xlix.

52. Quotations about Grant are from Douglas to Barclay, 3 September 1849, enclosure in Pelly to Earl Grey, February 28, 1851, ROT, Vols. 721–725, 259–65 [microfilm, vol. 2].

53. Grant, "Report on Vancouvers Island."

54. Grant to Douglas, September 10, 1850, "Vancouver Island—Colonial Surveyor: Correspondence Outward, Original and Transcript"; "Miscellaneous Information Relating to Walter Colquhoun Grant," BCA. See also Blanshard, Gov. of Vancouver's Island, to Earl Grey, September 18, 1850, ROT, Vols. 721–725, 257–58 [microfilm, vol. 1]. Grant left Vancouver Island to fight in the Crimean War (1853–1856), and he died in 1862 in India after falling ill.

55. Gough, *Gunboat Frontier*, 14 (quotation); Harris, *Making Native Space*, 22. For an alternate view on Douglas's interactions with Indians during the early colonial years, see Fisher, *Contact and Conflict*, 49–72.

56. Helmcken [HBC doctor and magistrate at Fort Rupert] to Blanshard, July 17, 1850, CAA 40.3 R2, BCA, as quoted in Gough, *Gunboat Frontier*, 42. See ibid., 32–49, for this incident. Similar to the Makahs deaths at the beginning of this chapter, it is also possible that the Newitty chiefs did not execute any of their people. Perhaps they simply showed to HBC authorities the bodies of three men killed during the shelling.

57. Douglas to Tolmie, August 6, 1851, "Correspondence—Letters to Tolmie from Various Parties, 'D,'" Tolmie Papers.

58. Douglas to Archibald Barclay, January 3, 1852; Douglas to Earl Grey, January 29, 1852.

59. Douglas to Earl Grey, January 29, 1852; Douglass [*sic*] to Starling, February 11, 1852.

60. Douglas to Earl Grey, February 11, 1852.

61. For this classic definition of gunboat diplomacy, see Viscount Palmerston to Sir John Davis, Foreign Office, December 10, 1846, in *Chinese Repository*, 469. Used to awe Indians, see Gough, *Gunboat Frontier*, 211; and Ferris, "SSTR as History," 31.

62. Douglas to Tolmie, January 26, 1853, Tolmie Papers; Douglas to Barclay, January 20, 1853, in Lamb, "Four Letters Relating to the Cruise of the *Thetis*," 205. See also Gough, *Gunboat Frontier*, 50–56; Donald, *Aboriginal Slavery*, 103; and Arnett, *Terror of the Coast*, 40–45.

63. "George Washington Bush and Other Negro Pioneers," Ruby El Hult Papers; Snowden et al., *History of Washington*, vols. 2, 3:421–34; Ayer, "George Bush, Voyageur"; Hult, "Saga of George W. Bush"; Thomas, "George Bush," 2–45, 103–4.

64. Hancock, *Thirteen Years Residence*, 50.

65. Russell to Gov. Stevens, February 6, 1856, Isaac I. Stevens Papers, WSA. For the founding of Seattle, see Thrush, *Native Seattle*, 17–65. For US settler activity in the Oregon Country, see Whaley, *Oregon and the Collapse of Illahee*.

66. Entry for February 11, 1838, in Dickey, *Journal*, sec. 4, p. 11; "Log of the *Cadborough*," November 10, 1845, C.1/221; Grant, "Report on Vancouvers Island," 11; Grant, "Description of Vancouver Island," 285–86. Yelakub was not the only Native individual to direct Grant away from his or her lands. Grant criticized many Indians for misdirection. Similarly, in 1541 Pueblo Indians in the Southwest told the Spanish conquistador Coronado about Quivira, a land east of New Mexico rich in gold, silver, and silks. This misdirection led the Spanish away from the pueblos and into the plains of Kansas. Gutiérrez, *When Jesus Came*, 44–45; Weber, *Spanish Frontier*, 46–49.

67. S. Gordon to Secretary of the Admiralty, October 19, 1845, *ROT*, Vols. 721–725, 66–75 [microfilm, vol. 1]; "Private Journal of Cooper," October 17, 1845; Seemann, *Narrative*, 1:95; Gibbs, "Notebook: Indian Tribes," 50, in Notebooks of Scientific Observations of the Pacific Northwest; Hancock, *Thirteen Years Residence*, 140; Ormsby, "Introduction," l.

68. Hancock, *Thirteen Years Residence*, 89–90.

69. Ibid., 135.

70. Ibid., 137. In one exchange, forty Vancouver Island canoes arrived, and these visitors spent two days trading oil with Hancock. See ibid., 153–54. See also Davidson, *Directory for the Pacific Coast,* 115 (quotation).

71. Hancock, *Thirteen Years Residence,* 134, 140–42.

72. Lawson, Autobiography. Lawson was the topographical aide to Davidson during the Pacific Coast Survey. That Hancock set up this council with Chief X̣isi·t appears to support the notion that this titleholder was the chief sponsoring the trader's presence at Neah Bay.

73. This was a common approach with US officials, too. L. Lea [Commissioner of Indian Affairs], November 30, 1852, *ARCIA* (1852), 4.

74. Lawson, Autobiography. New Zealand historian James Belich explores this topic in the context of Maori-*pakeha* (white) conflicts of the mid-nineteenth century. Belich, *Victorian Interpretation of Racial Conflict.*

75. Lawson, Autobiography (quotations); Hancock, *Thirteen Years Residence,* 153–54; "Indians."

76. "California." See also Gibbs, *Indian Tribes of Washington Territory,* 35.

77. See chapter 2, n. 5.

78. Lawson, Autobiography.

79. Entry for December 9, 1834, in Dickey, *Journal,* sec. 1, p. 46 (first quotation); Tolmie, *Journals,* 243 (second quotation).

80. For information about the Balch brothers' Puget Sound operations, see Albert Balch (San Francisco) to Hiram Balch [Trescott, ME], September 26, 1852, and Francis Balch (San Francisco) to Hiram Balch, February 15, 1854, Hiram A. Balch Papers; Wright, *Lewis and Dryden's Marine History,* 31–32. Sixey appears throughout Swan's diaries as "Captain Balch" and "Billy Balch." See Swan Papers, 1833–1809. As seen later in this chapter and the next, Fowler's ships brought unwelcome cargo to Neah Bay: smallpox (1853) and the US treaty commission (1855).

81. For the cumulative impact of Old World diseases on indigenous peoples, see Crosby, *Columbian Exchange,* 35–63. Crosby explores these topics within the context of ecological imperialism in *Ecological Imperialism.*

82. It is difficult to estimate precise population numbers before the arrival of Europeans and to date the earliest smallpox epidemics. Anthropologist Robert Boyd estimates the pre-encounter number. He also argues that there might have been several localized smallpox epidemics introduced to Northwest Coast peoples in the late eighteenth century: from Kamchatka and the Russians in 1769, from the Spanish in 1775, and from the Plains peoples around 1782. *Coming of the Spirit of Pestilence,* 38.

83. Howay, *Voyages of the Columbia,* 196, 371; Harris, *Resettlement of British Columbia,* 23. Charles Wilkes's US Exploring Expedition estimated that there were a thousand Makah warriors, or approximately four thousand Makahs. Wilkes, *Narrative,* 4:487.

84. Irving, *Astoria,* 1:191–92.

85. Boyd, *Coming of the Spirit of Pestilence,* 45; Tolmie, *Journals,* 238. More than twenty years later, Makahs told British missionary William H. Hills of Dominis's

threat. Hills, "Journal on Board *H.M.S. Portland* and *H.M.S. Virago.*" For Dominis's trading voyages in the Pacific Northwest, see Howay, "Brig *Owhyhee* in the
Columbia."

86. Boyd, *Coming of the Spirit of Pestilence*, 116–60; sections 1 and 2 in Dickey, *Journal*;
Tolmie, *Journals*, 224–43. While at Neah Bay in the early 1860s, Swan frequently
treated scrofula and goiter afflictions among Makahs. For example, see entry for
January 30, 1865, Diary 9, Swan Papers, 1833–1909.

87. Lawson, Autobiography.

88. Entry for November 8, 1853, in Dickey, *Journal*, 43; Gibbs, *Indian Tribes of Washington Territory*, sec. 9, p. 34; Hancock, *Thirteen Years Residence*, 155. For the 1853 epidemic along the Columbia River, see Abigail Malick to children, September 28,
1853, Malick Family Papers. Swan provides a brief account of the epidemic at Shoalwater Bay. *Northwest Coast*, 54–59. For the Banfield quotation, see Arima, *Between
Ports Alberni and Renfrew*, 295.

89. Estimating disease mortalities among indigenous peoples is difficult. Right before
the epidemic struck, members of the US Pacific Coast Survey estimated that 300 to
500 Makah warriors lived at Cape Flattery. For the low number, see Davidson, *Directory for the Pacific Coast*, 115. For the high number, see Lawson, Autobiography. It
seems reasonable to extrapolate from this statistic that there were about 1,200 to 2,000
Makahs alive in 1852. This is close to the Cape Flattery population that HBC traders
approximated in the mid-1840s. See Schafer, "Documents Related to Warre and
Vavasour's Military Reconnaissance," 61. However, the estimates from both HBC
traders and the Pacific Coast Survey appear to have left out those living at Ozette,
about twenty miles south of Cape Flattery. Five hundred people living at Ozette right
before the epidemic would be a conservative estimate. This would give us an estimated
total of at least 1,700–2,500 Makahs. Gibbs noted that 150 Makahs lived at Cape Flattery after the epidemic. *Indian Tribes of Washington Territory*, 35. When the tribal
nation signed the 1855 Treaty of Neah Bay with US representatives, the treaty commission believed that there were approximately 600 Makahs. See "Ratified Treaty
No. 286: Documents Relating to the Negotiation of the Treaty of January 31, 1855,
with the Makah Indians," p. 4, United States, Records of the Bureau of Indian Affairs, Documents Relating to the Negotiation of Ratified and Unratified Treaties
(hereafter cited as Treaty Negotiation Notes). The tribal nation certainly did not rebound from 150 to 600 individuals in just over a year. Instead, Gibbs's estimate of 150
probably left out those living at Ozette, whereas the treaty included those living
there. Makah survivors on Vancouver Island probably returned to Neah Bay after
Gibbs's initial estimate, and they most likely brought other kin with them. Working
with these numbers gives us a mortality rate of around three-fourths. This rate is
similar to mortality estimates of that time. At the end of 1853, Washington Territorial
Indian Agent E. A. Starling reported that the recent smallpox epidemic "has been most
fatal among the Macaws, more than half of the Tribe being carried off by it." Starling to Stevens, December 4, 1853, United States, Records of the Bureau of Indian
Affairs, Records of the Washington Superintendency of Indian Affairs. The leader of

the Pacific Coast Survey had heard that more than two-thirds had fallen victim to the disease. Davidson, *Directory for the Pacific Coast*, 116.

90. Hancock, *Thirteen Years Residence*, 156. Providing food and water did save some lives. More than a decade after the smallpox epidemic, Kichusam, a Saanitch slave owned by Yelakub, credited Hancock for saving his life. Entry for February 8, 1865, Diary 9, Swan Papers, 1833–1909.

91. Lawson complained of Makah "superstition" that led them to believe this. Lawson, Autobiography.

92. Hancock, *Thirteen Years Residence*, 157.

93. Ibid., 183, 185; Kellogg, *History of Whidbey's Island*, 33; Donald, *Aboriginal Slavery*, 180.

94. Hancock, *Thirteen Years Residence*, 156; "Log of the *Mary Dare* (brig)," November 4, 1853; Treaty Negotiation Notes, 2. In the notes detailing the treaty negotiations, Q̓alču·t named the three "Big Chiefs" as Kleh-sitt (λ̓isi·t), Yall-a-coom (Yelakub), and Heh-iks (Halicks).

95. Lawson, Autobiography.

96. In his study on the Plains Sioux experience with US colonialism, historian Jeffrey Ostler warns against presenting chiefs as "taking sides between two rigidly constructed positions." Instead, it is "more productive to realize that Sioux leaders adopted a *range* of strategies based on reasoned assessments of changing conditions and possibilities. Sioux leaders were not always locked into polar antagonisms. Rather, they adjusted their tactics in light of new circumstances and were responsive to changing opinion among their people." This framing of Sioux leadership encouraged me to re-interpret λ̓isi·t and Yelakub's strategies. *Plains Sioux and U.S. Colonialism*, 7.

CHAPTER 4: "I WANT THE SEA"

1. "Ratified Treaty No. 286: Documents Relating to the Negotiation of the Treaty of January 31, 1855, with the Makah Indians," p. 4, United States, Bureau of Indian Affairs, Documents Relating to the Negotiation of Ratified and Unratified Treaties (hereafter cited as Treaty Negotiation Notes).

2. Stevens, *Life of Isaac Ingalls Stevens*, 1:452–53. Other treaty commissioners not present at Neah Bay included High A. Goldsmith and James Doty, the son of a former Wisconsin governor and an individual with experience among the Blackfeet.

3. Treaty Negotiation Notes, 2. All quotations of what was said during the treaty negotiations are from this document and reflect how George Gibbs, Governor Stevens's secretary, understood what various speakers said. While Gibbs knew enough Chinook jargon to publish dictionaries in the trade language in 1863 and 1873, he relied on the linguistic skills of Captain Jack to translate between Makah and Chinook jargon.

4. Today's Makahs remember this canoe excursion on which Čaqá·wiλ insisted. See Makah Tribal Council and Makah Whaling Commission, *Makah Nation*.

5. Swan, *Northwest Coast*, 327–51; Storm and Capoeman, *Land of the Quinault*, 102–3.

6. This point aligns with more recent histories exploring the role of indigenous peoples in the making of colonial spaces. DuVal, *Native Ground*; Thrush, *Native Seattle*; Petrie, *Chiefs of Industry*; Lutz, *Makúk*.

7. Banner, *How the Indians Lost Their Land*, 4.

8. Prucha, *American Indian Treaties*, 129.

9. *Pioneer and Democrat*, February 3, 1855, in Miles, *Michael T. Simmons*, 204. Simmons became the first Indian Agent in the territory. See also Charles J. Russell to Stevens, February 6, 1856, Isaac I. Stevens Papers, 1848–59; Gibbs, *Indian Tribes of Washington Territory*, 35.

10. Brantlinger, *Rule of Darkness*, 8.

11. Treaty Negotiation Notes, 4.

12. Thrush, *Native Seattle*, 47.

13. Entry for December 12, 1846, in Dickey, *Journal*, sec. 5, p. 30.

14. Drew, *Account of the Origin*, 3–7.

15. Richards, "Federal Indian Policy," 29–30.

16. Stevens, "Governor Isaac I. Stevens to the First Annual Session of the Legislative Assembly," 4 (quotation); Stevens to [George W.] Manypenny, [CIA,] December 30, 1854; and Stevens to J. W. Denver, CIA, January 10, 1859, United States, Bureau of Indian Affairs, Records of the Washington Superintendency of Indian Affairs. See also Richards, *Isaac I. Stevens*.

17. Manypenny, November 25, 1854, *ARCIA* (1854), 222. See also Richards, "Federal Indian Policy," 33–40; Seeman, "Treaty and Non-Treaty Coastal Indians," 41–43. For more on federal treaty and reservation policies in the mid-nineteenth century, see Trennert, *Alternative to Extinction*; Prucha, *Great Father*, 108–35; and Prucha, *American Indian Treaties*, 208–60.

18. Richards, "Federal Indian Policy," 54–55; Trafzer, *Indians, Superintendents, and Councils*, 1–6; Richards, "Stevens Treaties of 1854–1855," 7–10. Some scholars point to this ambivalence for causing the failure of the reservation policy in Washington. See Asher, *Beyond the Reservation*, 34–59.

19. Mix, *ARCIA* (1858), 10. See also Asher, *Beyond the Reservation*, 9, 36–37.

20. For a comparison to how boundaries of race, gender, and national identity defined the border in the Albert-Montana borderlands, see McManus, *Line Which Separates*. Hoxie characterizes reservations as "oppressive and unsuccessful instruments of imperial control." "Crow Leadership Amidst Reservation Oppression," 38.

21. Stevens to [Colonel W. J. Hardee, 1850 or 1851], in Stevens, *Life of Isaac Ingalls Stevens*, 1:262 (militia), 297 (HBC concerns); Kappler, *Indian Treaties*, 684; Starling, [Indian Agent for Puget Sound District], Agent Report, *ARCIA* (1852), 173.

22. White, *"It's Your Misfortune,"* 157–70.

23. Starling, "No. 71, Report," 172; [Isaac I. Stevens] to Father [Isaac Stevens, Sr.], November 17, 1838, in Stevens, *Life of Isaac Ingalls Stevens*, 1:55. See also Richards, *Isaac I. Stevens*, 10, 39; and Donald, *Aboriginal Slavery*, 214–24.

24. Hancock, *Thirteen Years Residence*; 164; Sproat, *Scenes and Studies of Savage Life*, 67.

25. Just before the Makah chief Q̇alču·t died, James Swan (then the reservation teacher) facilitated the transfer of the chief's slaves to a relative by making sure that Q̇alču·t's property, including his slaves, was disposed of according to the will the dying title-holder dictated. Entry for January 14, 1863, Diary 6. Agency officials also hired Makah slaves to do various labor and chores. Entry for June 29, 1863, Diary 6. Officials such as Swan and agents assigned to Neah Bay neglected to free slaves, even when a slave requested it. Entries for February 8, 1865, Diary 9; July 13, 1866, Diary 10; January 7, 1879, Diary 24, Swan Papers, 1833–1909. During the 1920s, one Makah described his wife as a slave. See Densmore, *Nootka and Quileute Music*, xv.

26. The first version of this act only voided marriages already solemnized. An amendment to this earlier act prohibited future marriages between whites and those with more than "one-half Indian blood" or individuals with one-fourth or more of "negro blood." See "An Act to Amend an Act, Entitled 'An Act to Regulate Marriage,' Passed April 20th, 1854," in Pierce, *Laws of Washington*, 1:651–52. Although this action ignored interracial common-law marriages, the Marriage Act of 1866 closed this loophole and made these marriages illegal. Ibid., 2:354–57. For fur trade relationships throughout North America, see Van Kirk, *"Many Tender Ties"*; Thorne, *Many Hands of My Relations*; and Hyde, *Empires, Nations, and Families*. Specific to the Pacific Northwest, see Mackie, *Trading beyond the Mountains*, 305–08.

27. Seemann, *Narrative*, 1:104–5; Bayley, "Early Life on Vancouver Island," 5.

28. Stevens to Manypenny, September 16, 1854, in ARCIA (1854), 449–50; Scheuerman, "Territorial Indian Policy and Tribal Relations," 10. Another scholar has argued that Stevens sought to take advantage of the disruptive effects of diseases. Seeman, "Treaty and Non-Treaty Coastal Indians," 45–49.

29. Meeker, *Pioneer Reminiscences of Puget Sound*, 242. See also Blee, *Framing Chief Leschi*, 91, 115.

30. Treaty Negotiation Notes, 2; Richards, *Isaac I. Stevens*, 207.

31. Kappler, *Indian Treaties*, 682–85.

32. The Stevens treaties in western Washington included the Treaty of Medicine Creek (1854), Treaty of Point Elliott (1855), Treaty of Point No Point (1855), and the Treaty of Neah Bay (1855). For more on these treaties, see Richards, *Isaac I. Stevens*, 181–210; Trafzer, *Indians, Superintendents, and Councils*; Marino, "History of Western Washington since 1846," 169–72; Richards, "Stevens Treaties of 1854–1855"; Harmon, *Power of Promises*, 3–31.

33. Treaty Negotiation Notes, 2.

34. "Sample Text of Douglas Treaty." For Douglas's treaties, see Fisher, *Contact and Conflict*, 66–68; and Harris, *Making Native Space*, 17–44 (Lekwungen treaty, 19).

35. Richards argues that Puget Sound Indians knew of the Dart Treaties and about Congress's failure to ratify them, which made chiefs wary of promises made by white officials. Richards, "Federal Indian Policy," 33.

36. Hansen, "Indian Views of the Stevens-Palmer Treaties Today," 11 (Yakama quotation); Barton, "'Red Waters,'" 247 (Makah quotation); Claplanhoo-Martin and Claplanhoo, interview; McCarty, interview.

37. For a concise overview of how land tenure concepts differed among American Indian and "Western" societies, see Sutton, *Indian Land Tenure*, 4–6.

38. For a representation of the scholarship on American Indian land tenure, in addition to works cited in this section, see also White, *Roots of Dependency*; Shipek, *Pushed into the Rocks*; Merrell, *Indians' New World*; Fixico, *Invasion of Indian Country in the Twentieth Century*; and West, *Contested Plains*.

39. For this process in the United States, see Banner, *How the Indians Lost Their Land*.

40. Some indigenous scholars argue a similar case for the Western concept of *sovereignty*. See Alfred, "Sovereignty"; Reid, "Indigenous Power in *The Comanche Empire*," 58.

41. Henry St. Clair, "Land Rights and Other Property," 234–35, Elizabeth Colson Collection; Drucker, *Northern and Central Nootkan Tribes*, 247–73; Kirk, *Tradition and Change*, 43–56; McMillan, *Since the Time of the Transformers*, 16–17; Reid, "Marine Tenure of the Makah."

42. For differing oral accounts, see Pascua, interview, 2009; Johnson, interview; and Claplanhoo-Martin and Claplanhoo, interview. For specific cultural property items, see Coté, *Spirits of Our Whaling Ancestors*, 101–3, 114; Goodman and Swan, *Singing the Songs of My Ancestors*, 112; and Kenyon, *Kyuquot Way*, xi.

43. [Swindell], "Transcript of the Meeting, Oct. 15, 1941—evening meeting," Edward Swindell Jr. Papers.

44. Makahs were not the only people of the ča·di· borderland to express tenure over marine spaces. When Gilbert Malcolm Sproat, a Scottish businessman turned colonial magistrate, attempted to negotiate cessions from Tseshaht chiefs of Barkely Sound in 1860, he found them unwilling to sell their land or water. Sproat, *Scenes and Studies of Savage Life*, 4.

45. Suttles, "Coping with Abundance," 58. See the Introduction for a more complete explanation of the region's oceanography.

46. Lefebvre, *Production of Space*, 116; Tuan, *Space and Place*, 83 (quotation).

47. Nietschmann, "Traditional Sea Territories," 60. For ways people use their ecological and environmental understandings to configure inshore waters into specific regimes of local sea tenure, see Cordell, *Sea of Small Boats*, 1–32.

48. Atleo, *Tsawalk*, 21.

49. Treaty Negotiation Notes, 2.

50. Basso, *Wisdom Sits in Places*; Nietschmann, "Traditional Sea Territories," 83; McHalsie, "Halq'eméylem Place Names in Stó:Lō Territory," 135. Similarly, historian William Bauer notes that tribally specific stories and places coupled Round Valley Indians in California to their landscapes. *We Were All Like Migrant Workers Here*, 16. For the importance of place-names, see Thornton, "Anthropological Studies of Native American Place Naming."

51. Espinosa y Tello, *Spanish Voyage*, 32–37. For late twentieth-century Makah recollections of Vancouver Island place-names, see Arima, *Between Ports Alberni and Renfrew*, 270–76.

52. Bernard Nietschmann makes a similar argument for Torres Strait Islanders. See Nietschmann, "Traditional Sea Territories," 83. Entry for October 7, 1880, Diaries 28

and 29, Swan Papers, 1833–1909; and T. T. Waterman, "Geography of the Makah," [n.d.], in Erna Gunther Papers, 1887–1977. Unfortunately, Waterman's incomplete manuscript rarely noted the history or stories behind specific place-names. Others have criticized it for its terrestrial focus. Lane, "Makah Economy circa 1855." For information on place-naming among the Tseshaht, Nuu-chah-nulth relatives of the Makah, see Coté, *Spirits of Our Whaling Ancestors*, 75–95.

53. For this name, see Elliot Anderson [Makah] to Roger Chute, 19 June 1937, Ms 15/23, George Roger Chute Collection. While at Neah Bay for three months in 1852, members of the US Coast Survey noted this name as "opichuk't" (Hupačakt). Davidson, *Directory for the Pacific Coast*, 111. The other original Makah name is *ča·di·*. For this name, see Pascua, interview, 2008.

54. Entry for November 24, 1859, Diary 2, Swan Papers, 1833–1909.

55. See Gibbs, "Notebook: No. 2," in Notebooks of Scientific Observations of the Pacific Northwest.

56. This incident was detailed in chapter 2. See also Irvine and Markistun, *How the Makah Obtained Possession of Cape Flattery*; and Waterman, "Geography of the Makah," 13.

57. For information on Makah navigation techniques, see "Exhibit HH: Written Testimony of Nora Barker, Makah Elder and Teacher of Makah History, [August 23, 1977]," Legal Case C85-1606M, Makah v. U.S., MTC Collection; "Memorandum—Information Obtained from Robert Lee as to Sealing," December 22, 1938, Seals and Sealskins—Reports, etc. (Original Neah Bay Agency), DF 927.0, TIA, NARA-PNR (hereafter cited as Robert Lee Info); Hancock, *Thirteen Years Residence*, 154; Waterman, "Whaling Equipment of the Makah Indians," 47; Johnson, interview; McCarty, interview; and Greene, interview.

58. Oral histories detail these skills. Sones, interview; James Swan, Bound autograph manuscript journal and memorandum book (hereafter cited as Manuscript Journal), Stenzel Research Files on Western American Art (hereafter cited as Stenzel Files); entry for December 21, 1878, Diary 23, Swan Papers, 1833–1909.

59. Swan, "Cape Flattery"; entry for September 25, 1865, Diary 9, Swan Papers, 1833–1909.

60. Treaty Negotiation Notes, 2–3. Anthropologist Faith Harrington makes a similar argument for seventeenth-century New England, arguing that English development of cod fisheries in the northeast Atlantic was an expression of their national territoriality. "Sea Tenure in Seventeenth Century New England." For a concise explanation of how people know nature through their labor, see White, "'Are You an Environmentalist or Do You Work for a Living?'" 172.

61. Robert Lee Info; E. M. Gibson, Agent Report, *ARCIA* (1873), 308; entry for November 16, 1859, Diary 2, Swan Papers, 1833–1909. Huntington, *Memoir, 1899*, 133.

62. Like many Northwest Coast peoples, Makahs had specialized canoes for specific purposes. Waterman and Coffin, *Types of Canoes on Puget Sound*; Waterman, "Whaling Equipment of the Makah Indians," 11–26.

63. Capt. Clarke, "Pelagic Sealing," pp. 4–9, vol. 40, Ser. B: Miscellaneous—Pelagic Sealing [reel A01765], Newcombe Family Papers; Swan, "Fur Seal Industry of Cape

Flattery and the Vicinity" [1883?], Stenzel Files; Robert Lee Info; "Pelagic Seal Hunting by Makah and Quilleute Indians" [ca. 1930s], Seals and Sealskins—Reports, etc. (Original Neah Bay Agency), DF 927.0, TIA, NARA-PNR; McCarty, interview. Circus Jim (James Sly), a noted Makah sealer, spoke about getting two seals with one throw. See BSTA, *Fur Seal Arbitration*, 380.

64. TIA, "Elliott Anderson: The Last Surviving Member of the Ozette Tribe and Ozette Reservation," Ms 15/21, George Roger Chute Collection.

65. Charles Huntington, Agent Report, *ARCIA* (1875), 362–64.

66. Diaries 1–6, Swan Papers, 1833–1909; Coté, *Spirits of Our Whaling Ancestors*, 30–31; Barton, "'Red Waters,'" 86. Archaeological evidence has also confirmed these harvests. Huelsbeck, "Whaling in the Precontact Economy." Although Huelsbeck hypothesizes that Makahs harvested sperm whales and orcas only as drift whales, Swan's diaries referenced several specific killings of orcas. His informants also told him that they sometimes harvested sperm whales, but his diaries never noted a sperm whale hunt. Swan, Manuscript Journal, 73. Oral histories also imply that Makahs hunted a wide range of whales. See Sones, interview; and Mrs. Williams, "Lazy Boy," 62–67, Colson Collection. Information about whales Makahs hunted also appears in letters Swan wrote to Professor Spencer Baird of the Smithsonian, November 6, December 12, 1882, Letterbook, 6:309–11, 339–40, Swan Papers, 1852–1907.

67. Samuel Morse, Agent Report, *ARCIA* (1897), 291–92; Hancock, *Thirteen Years Residence*, 139; Swan, "Indian Method of Killing Whales"; Waterman, "Whaling Equipment of the Makah Indians," 44 (quotation); Anderson to Chute, June 19, 1937, Ms 15/23, Chute Collection; Lewis, "Whale Hunters of Neah Bay"; Kirk and Daugherty, *Hunters of the Whale*, 44–50. Makah oral histories also recount ancestral whaling techniques. Sones, interview; Claplanhoo-Martin and Claplanhoo, interview; Greene, interview; and Bowechop and Pascua, NOAA Interviews, MCRC.

68. Robert Lee Info; Henry St. Clair, "Sealing," 19–20, Colson Collection; Charles Willoughby, Agent Report, *ARCIA* (1880), 155–56; John C. Keenan, Agent Report, *ARCIA* (1896), 313; Swan, "Indian Method of Killing Whales"; entry of July 6, 1879, Diary 10, Swan Papers, 1833–1909; BSTA, *Fur Seal Arbitration*, 381; Beaglehole, *Journals of Cook*, 302; Swan, "Indians of Cape Flattery," 21; Waterman, "Whaling Equipment of the Makah Indians," 34–36. The Makah trade in sealskins during the late nineteenth century is detailed in chapter 5.

69. The Ozette archaeological dig uncovered over a thousand tools (25 percent) made of whalebone. Huelsbeck, "Whaling in the Precontact Economy," 7, 9–10. See also Henry St. Clair, "Tuna and the Pelican," 17–18, Colson Collection; entries for October 29, 1859, Diary 2, and December 25, 1864, Diary 8, Swan Papers, 1833–1909; Swan, "Indians of Cape Flattery," 22; and Squire, *Resources and Development of Washington Territory*, 37.

70. Williams, "Ideas of Nature," 83. I have adapted his statement: "We have mixed our labor with the earth, our forces with its forces too deeply to be able to separate each other out." Cordell calls this "a special fraternity with the sea." Cordell, *Sea of Small Boats*, 2.

71. Kosek, *Understories*, 119; Krech, *Ecological Indian.*

72. This perspective still shapes Makahs' understanding of marine tenure. Sones, interview.

73. Donald, *Aboriginal Slavery*, 272–308.

74. Thrush and Ludwin, "Finding Fault," 6. For the unity of the spiritual and physical realms, see Atleo, *Tsawalk.* Similarly, family heads among the Lekwungens across the strait on Vancouver Island acted as stewards who managed the use of these resources. "This was both a right, with benefits attached, and a responsibility," administered through special regulations and protocols. Lutz, *Makúk*, 55.

75. Fixico, *American Indian Mind in a Linear World*, 7.

76. Harrod, *Animals Came Dancing*, xiv.

77. Swan, Manuscript Journal, December 4, 1863.

78. Wa and Uukw, *Spirit in the Land*, 7. For the Northwest Coast belief that animals are people and the importance of protocols governing relationships, see Atleo, *Tsawalk*, 59–64.

79. Entry for September 24, 1861, Diary 5, Swan Papers, 1833–1909; Swan, Manuscript Journal, 63.

80. Penned in October 1878, a notation about Cedakanim's story appears on p. 172 in Swan's annotated volume of Meares's account of his voyages. Available at UWSC. This was—and continues to be—a common belief among Northwest Coast peoples. See Wa and Uukw, *Spirit in the Land*, 7.

81. Entry for March 10, 1879, Diary 25, Swan Papers, 1833–1909.

82. In Chinook jargon, a trade language Makahs used when speaking with whites on the Northwest Coast in the mid-nineteenth century, *Skookum* meant "strength," especially supernatural strength. Gibbs, *Dictionary of the Chinook Jargon.* For whaling powers, see Curtis, *The Nootka. The Haida*, 16–18, 38–40; Densmore, *Nootka and Quileute Music*, 47–53; Colson, *Makah Indians*, 242; Atleo, *Tsawalk*, 72–74; and Coté, *Spirits of Our Whaling Ancestors*, 23–24.

83. Waterman, "Geography of the Makah," 30; Swan, 22 January 1865, Manuscript Journal (quotation); entry for September 23, 1866, Diary 10, Swan Papers, 1833–1909.

84. Waterman, "Whaling Equipment of the Makah Indians," 38–39; Webster and Campbell River Museum and Archives Society, *As Far as I Know*; Atleo, *Tsawalk*, 17; Coté, *Spirits of Our Whaling Ancestors*, 23–35.

85. Atleo, *Tsawalk*, x (quotation). Other indigenous societies also believe that animals agree to become food because of the shared bond of kinship between humans and nonhuman people. Harrod, *Animals Came Dancing*, xii; Vitebsky, *Reindeer People*, 259–84. For the role of wives, see Waterman, "Whaling Equipment of the Makah Indians," 46; Gunther, "Reminiscences of a Whaler's Wife"; Atleo, *Tsawalk*, 113; and Coté, *Spirits of Our Whaling Ancestors*, 26–27.

86. Colson, *Makah Indians*, 250; McMillan, *Since the Time of the Transformers*, 132; Coté, *Spirits of Our Whaling Ancestors*, 27, 34. Information on whaling names is from the entry for December 21, 1878, Diary 23, Swan Papers, 1833–1909; and Micah McCarty, email to author, October 13, 2004.

87. Entry for April 25, 1861, Diary 4, Swan Papers, 1833–1909. He also judged the butchering process a "most filthy sight." Entry for March 9, 1862, Diary 5. See also Swan, "Indian Method of Killing Whales"; Waterman, "Whaling Equipment of the Makah Indians," 45–46; Swan, "Visit to Tatooche Island," *Washington Standard*, 20 July 1861, in Katz, *Almost Out of the World*, 120; Swan, "Indians of Cape Flattery," 22–23; Testimony of Joe Sly, October 15, 1941, "Old Fishing Locations, October 1941," Swindell Papers; and Atleo, *Tsawalk*, 103 (quotation).

88. Entry for January 1, 1864, Diary 6, Swan Papers, 1833–1909; Hancock, *Thirteen Years Residence*, 143. For the importance of such demonstrations during betrothal, see Atleo, *Tsawalk*, 50–57. For marriage ceremonies of Makah whalers, see Curtis, *The Nootka. The Haida*, 64–65; and Densmore, *Nootka and Quileute Music*, 247–50.

89. Jackson, "Water Is Not Empty," 87. For a critique of the separation of spaces, see Lefebvre, *Production of Space*.

90. Treaty Negotiation Notes, 1.

91. Richards, *Isaac I. Stevens*, 69–91; Stevens, *Life of Isaac Ingalls Stevens*, 1:241–79.

92. Jackson, "Water Is Not Empty," 89. For concise overviews of the general "Western" concept of the sea as commons, see Harrington, "Sea Tenure in Seventeenth Century New England," 36–41; Cordell, *Sea of Small Boats*, 12–13; and Steinberg, *Social Construction of the Ocean*, 90–98. In the 1840s, "Western" nation-states began constructing coastal waters as territorial seas that belonged to specific countries. Steinberg, *Social Construction of the Ocean*, 137.

93. Angell, *Treatise on the Common Law*. Richards notes that Stevens purchased this copy for the territorial library. "Federal Indian Policy," 6–7.

94. Writing about indigenous marine peoples of Australia, Cordell explains that "indigenous fishing and maritime communities were thought [by settler-colonial whites] to be analogous to hunters-gatherers. It was widely assumed such economies precluded the formation of property rights." See "Indigenous Peoples' Coastal Marine Domains," 2.

95. Treaty Negotiation Notes, 2.

96. Entries for April 6, September 7–9, 1863, Diary 6, Swan Papers, 1833–1909.

97. Entries for June 15, 20, July 12, 1865, Diary 9; August 20, 25, 1866, July 17, 18, 1879, Diary 10, ibid.

98. Although the metaphorical spatial boundaries he differentiates among Pacific islands and beaches do not fit the Makah, Greg Dening explores similar themes in his fascinating work: *Islands and Beaches*, 3–34; *Performances*, 64–78; and "Deep Times, Deep Spaces."

99. For more information about Swan, see Swan, *Northwest Coast*; McDonald, *Swan among the Indians*; Doig, *Winter Brothers*; and Miles, *James Swan*. Many of Swan's newspaper articles are collected in Katz, *Almost Out of the World*. See Swan's Manuscript Journal, 39–66, for detailed notes about the first census Swan took of the Makah reservation. The bulk of his diaries compose the Swan Papers, 1833–1909. Other Swan notebooks from this time are part of the Stenzel Files.

100. I adapted this method from Certeau, "Walking in the City," in *The Practice of Every-day Life*, 91–110. In this piece, the French scholar mapped "pedestrian speech acts" to analyze the real systems and networks that spatialize a city. For a similar method applied to South Pacific Islanders and how their voyages reveal ways they "encompassed" the sea, see Dening, "Geographical Knowledge of the Polynesians"; and Dening, "Deep Times, Deep Spaces," 27. I compiled the 951 observations Swan made from Diaries 1 through 10, Swan Papers, 1833–1909.

101. Jenkins, Agent Report, 237; Henry A. Webster, Agent Report, *ARCIA* (1862), 410.

102. Entries for September 18, 1859, Diary 2; April 5, 6, 22, May 4, 1864, Diary 8, Swan Papers, 1833–1909. For Jackson, see Manuscript Journal, 56. For Q̓i·tap, see Pascua, interview, 2008; Arnold, interview; Morse and Marr, *Portrait in Time*, 35; and Barton, "'Red Waters,'" 240.

103. At this time, Ozette was not part of the reservation, so I have included it as an off-reservation, indigenous village. Ozette gained reservation status in 1893 through an ex-ecutive order, and Makahs and US officials considered it part of the Makah reservation.

104. Entry for May 9, 1862, Diary 5, Swan Papers, 1833–1909. Brown often made trips to Vancouver Island villages to purchase oil.

105. Entry for October 7, 1863, ibid. Swan noted the Cedakanim family genealogy that connected them to Wickaninnish in the entry for September 8, 1880, Diary 29.

106. Entry for March 6, 1863, Diary 6, ibid.

107. See Diary 4, ibid., for information on Wha-laltl's murder. Swan also detailed this incident in "Murder of Wha-lathl, or 'Swell,'" to readers of the *Washington Standard* on March 30, 1861. See Katz, *Almost Out of the World*, 100–104.

108. Katz, *Almost Out of the World*, 107.

109. Manuscript Journal, 37.

110. Ibid., 54.

111. Entry for October 6, 1861, Diary 5, Swan Papers, 1833–1909; Manuscript Journal, 55.

112. John T. Knox, Sub-Agent Report, *ARCIA* (1866), 69–70; entries for March 7, 1862, Diary 5; August 1, 1863, February 4, 1864, Diary 6; February 20, April 6, 1866, Diary 9, Swan Papers, 1833–1909. The thirty-three soldiers probably represented the entire gar-rison at Fort Steilacoom. By the 1860s, it had become difficult to recruit soldiers for outposts so distant from the battlefields of the Civil War. In 1862, only twenty-seven volunteers were stationed at Steilacoom. Snowden et al., *History of Washington*, 4:108.

113. By the fall of 1866, Swan had relocated to Port Townsend after resigning as the reser-vation teacher, so it is difficult to date exactly when territorial authorities released Brown and the rest. Swan noted that Agent Webster sent Brown, the reservation's policeman, to apprehend two Makah women who had run off with some white coalminers to Victoria. Entry for October 3, 1867, Diary 11, Swan Papers, 1833–1909. Brown held this position throughout the tenure of several Indian agents and still worked as an agency policeman in 1879. Entry for 18 November 1879, Diary 10.

114. Asher, *Beyond the Reservation*, 34–59.

CHAPTER 5: "AN ANOMALY IN THE INDIAN SERVICE"

1. Henry Webster, Agent Report, *ARCIA* (1865), 91; Swan, "Two Months with the Makahs," *San Francisco Evening Bulletin*, October 22, 1860, quoted in Katz, *Almost Out of the World*, 73–74.

2. Prucha, *Great Father*, 193–95, 217–21; Lewis, *Neither Wolf nor Dog*, 7–21; Usner, *Indian Work*, 18–41.

3. For a more complete introduction to this dichotomy, see Raibmon, *Authentic Indians*.

4. The classic work on this stereotype still remains Berkhofer, *White Man's Indian*.

5. O'Neill, "Rethinking Modernity," 12.

6. Trachtenberg, *Incorporation of America*, 37 (quotation). See also Busch, *War against the Seals*, 95–157; McEvoy, *Fisherman's Problem*, 19–119; Gibson, *Otter Skins*; Dorsey, *Dawn of Conservation Diplomacy*, 105–64; and Dolin, *Fur, Fortune, and Empire*. Recent literature—much of it cited in this chapter—has begun to counter this trend.

7. Hosmer, *American Indians in the Marketplace*; O'Neill, *Working the Navajo Way*; Raibmon, *Authentic Indians*; Lutz, *Makúk*; and Bauer, *We Were All Like Migrant Workers Here*.

8. "Heirship Report for Chestoqua Peterson," December 2, 1926 [Probate No. 17954/21 and 56084/26], folder 17954-21; and "Heirship Report for Quata Moore," September 11, 1930 [Probate No. 56334/30], folder 56334-30, box 350, CCF, NARA. See also Swan's diaries in Swan Papers, 1833–1909; Family Group Sheets, MCRC; Claplanhoo-Martin and Claplanhoo, interview; and McCarty, interview.

9. Non-Natives have always had difficulty writing indigenous names. "Klah-pe at hoo" is an approximation of Claplanhoo. "Ratified Treaty No. 286: Documents Relating to the Negotiation of the Treaty of January 31, 1855, with the Makah Indians," p. 2, United States, Bureau of Indian Affairs, Documents Relating to the Negotiation of Ratified and Unratified Treaties, NARA-PNR (hereafter cited as Treaty Negotiation Notes).

10. For the dangers of romanticizing Indian agency, see Hosmer, *American Indians in the Marketplace*, 223.

11. "New Bedford Shipping List: Whaling in the North Pacific," as printed in Starbuck, *History of the American Whale Fishery* (1964), 1:104. During the whaling industry, there was no standard for gallons per barrel. Each barrel of whale oil contained from thirty to thirty-five gallons. Scoresby, *Account of the Arctic Regions*, 2:397–415, 525–28. See chapter 3 for an explanation about Makah whaling returns in the mid-nineteenth century.

12. McCarty, interview. In anthropologist Erna Gunther's genealogical notes on Makahs, Hiškʷi shows up as xicka, or "John (Old Man) McCarty." McCarty Genealogy Notes, Erna Gunther Papers, 1882–1981.

13. The exact origins of non-Native whaling in the North Pacific are unclear. Historians point to the 1835 voyage of Captain Folger's *Ganges* from Nantucket as the first whaler to hunt north of 49°N and east of 170°W. But there were probably earlier voyages, including the *Eleanora* from Providence, Rhode Island (1802); the *Minerva* from Norfolk, Virginia (1805); Benjamin Worth, a Nantucket whaling master, who claimed to have whaled along the Northwest Coast as far north as 59°N before 1824;

and at least one French whaler (*Gange*) in 1834. Webb, *On the Northwest*, 15, 35–36; Brandt, *Whale Oil*, vii (quotation).

14. Committee on Rosin Oil, *Report on Rosin Oil*, 5.

15. Except where otherwise noted, information about the early decades of Pacific whaling is from Jenkins, *History of the Whale Fisheries*, 207–55; Scammon, *Marine Mammals of the North-Western Coast*, 212–15; and Starbuck, *History of the American Whale Fishery* (1964), 1:90–98.

16. George W. R. Bailey (green hand), keeper, "The Journal of the *Caroline* on the Northwest Coast, September 1843," MS 596, Kendall Whaling Museum, Sharon, MA, as excerpted in Webb, *On the Northwest*, 287–95, quotation on p. 294. See also S. Gordon (Captain of H.M.S. *America*) to Secretary of the Admiralty, October 19, 1845, *ROT, Vols.* 721–725: 1822–1852, 723:5–10 [microfilm copy in "Correspondence with Hudson's Bay Company," vol. 1, BCA]; "Log of the *Cowlitz* (barque)," October 16, 1845, C.1/259, Ship Logs, HBCA.

17. James Douglas and John Work to [HBC] Governor and Committee, November 6, 1847, in Bowsfield, *Fort Victoria Letters*, 13; Webb, *On the Northwest*, 125–32.

18. Culin, "Summer Trip among the Western Indians," 151–52; Barton, "'Red Waters,'"240. For more on Q̓iˑtap (David Fischer), see Pascua, interview, 2008; Arnold, interview; Morse and Marr, *Portrait in Time*, 35.

19. "Later from the West Coast—More about the Mysterious Wreck—The Whaling Expedition," *British Colonist*, March 31, 1869; Webb, *On the Northwest*, 127.

20. Historian David Arnold makes a similar argument for Haida and Tlingit fishers in southeast Alaska during the late nineteenth and early twentieth centuries. *Fishermen's Frontier*, 130.

21. Webb, *On the Northwest*, 70–72.

22. Starbuck, *History of the American Whale Fishery* (1964), 1:102–3; Springer et al., "Whales and Whaling in the North Pacific Ocean and Bering Sea," 246. Springer estimates that "aboriginal whaling" in the Pacific had reduced the number of grays to twelve thousand by 1846. Japanese shore whaling, which intensified from the seventeenth to nineteenth centuries, also caused this reduction. For historical Japanese whaling, see Kalland and Moeran, *Japanese Whaling*, 65–94; and Watanabe, *Japan's Whaling*. For the early hunt in Magdalena Bay along the Baja coastline, see Igler, *Great Ocean*, 117–24.

23. Songini, *Lost Fleet*, 287–342. For an overview of the 1870s decline of the Yankee whaling industry, see Starbuck, *History of the American Whale Fishery* (1964), 1:109–13, quotation on p. 112. For more on the price of whale oil versus petroleum, see Brandt, *Whale Oil*, 50–54. In 1881, the federal government switched from whale oil to "coal oil" (petroleum) to fuel the nation's lighthouse lamps, a change noted by those acquainted with lighthouses on the Olympic Peninsula. Entry for June 7, 1881, Diary 29, Swan Papers, 1833–1909.

24. Brandt, *Whale Oil*, 54.

25. Ibid., 51–52; Webb, *On the Northwest*, 221–87.

26. Swan, "Indians of Cape Flattery," 7–8; entries for November 24, 1859, Diary 2; April 6, 1866, Diary 9; September 23, 1866, Diary 10, Swan Papers, 1833–1909.

27. M. T. Simmons, Agent Report, *ARCIA* (1858), 232; entry for July 15, 1891, Diary 55, Swan Papers, 1833–1909.

28. For the 1860s censuses, see Swan, Bound autograph manuscript journal and memorandum book (hereafter cited as Manuscript Journal), Frank R. and Kathryn M. Stenzel Research Files on Western American Art. For details on these economic activities, see the Swan Diaries, especially 5, 6, 8, and 9. John's continued status among the People of the Cape was noted in December 21, 1878, and January 23, 24, 1879, Diary 23, Swan Papers, 1833–1909.

29. Entries for October 29, November 1, 1859, Diary 2, Swan Papers, 1833–1909. This represents an average of 2,300 gallons of oil per whale, a number that I use in estimating indigenous whaling returns of this period.

30. No returns were recorded from 1871 to 1874 due to the disaster of ships crushed by Arctic ice in 1871. San Francisco's oil imports dwindled to 1,200 barrels (or about 39,000 gallons) in 1875 and dipped even lower—675 barrels (or about 21,938 gallons)—a year later. But in 1877, the city imported its highest amount yet, 4,520 barrels (or about 146,900 gallons) of oil; however, no oil imports were recorded from 1878 to 1883 with the collapse of the sail-powered Yankee whaling industry in the late 1870s. Beginning in the 1880s, steam-powered whaling ships began embarking from San Francisco to ply the North Pacific and Arctic. Working from more efficient steamships and armed with a new darting gun (combination of bomb lance and harpoon), non-Native whalers realized large returns, and oil imports in San Francisco peaked at 29,870 barrels (nearly 1 million gallons) in 1887. Starbuck, *History of the American Whale Fishery* (1964), 2:697; Tower, *History of the American Whale Fishery*, 130. In this period, the number of gallons per barrel of whale oil varied from 30 to 35 gallons; when estimating the amount of gallons based on barrel statistics, I have used the average of 32.5 gallons per barrel.

31. They processed more oil in 1889 because the whales they landed were larger than the ones from the previous year. "Report of A. B. Alexander, Fishery Expert," enclosure in Tanner, "Report," 278. For more on the history of the San Simeon Bay whaling station, see Pavlik, "Shore Whaling at San Simeon Bay."

32. "Whalers in the Pacific." For the estimate of twenty barrels, see economist Lester Lave's estimate that nineteenth-century whalers harvested this amount of oil per whale. Kovarick, "Whale Oil Myth." For the estimate of thirty barrels, see Coté, *Spirits of Our Whaling Ancestors*, 62. See also Lord Cornbury to Board of Trade, July 1708, as quoted in Starbuck, *History of the American Whale Fishery* (1878), 1:26; Hammond, "Lubrication of Cutting Tools—3," 607.

33. Claplanhoo-Martin and Claplanhoo, interview. During the interview, Pug associated Jongie's last whale with the year of the Alaska-Yukon-Pacific Exposition. Jongie's great-grandfather, Che-ya-te-toh, probably made this harpoon and added the first notches to it. See also Boalt, "Indian Canoemen." For the last Makah whale hunt of the 1920s, see Laut, "Who Wants a Whale Steak?"; Webb, *On the Northwest*, 287; and Collins, "Subsistence and Survival," 183. The IWC granted protection for gray whales in 1947. In some parts of the West Coast, grays were protected beginning in

1937. See Dedina, *Saving the Gray Whale,* 26; and US House Committee on Merchant Marine and Fisheries, *Saving the Gray and Bowhead Whales.*

34. Entry for March 27, 1862, Diary 5, Swan Papers, 1833–1909; William A. Newell, US Indian Inspector, "Neah Bay Agency, W.T., Inspector's Report," November 18, 1884, United States, Records of the Bureau of Indian Affairs, Inspection of Field Jurisdiction Neah Bay.

35. Entry for February 24, 1880, Diary 10, Swan Papers, 1833–1909. See also Morse and Marr, *Portrait in Time,* 29; Barton, "'Red Waters,'" 115; Webster, *ARCIA* (1865), 90–93; Henry Webster, Agent Report, *ARCIA* (1867), 41–45; E. M. Gibson, Agent Report, *ARCIA* (1873), 306–9; and Charles Huntington, Agent Report, *ARCIA* (1875), 362–64.

36. CIA to Wood, December 11, 1884, p. 273, Finance Division, vol. 108, 8 November 1884 to 17 December 1884, United States, Office of Indian Affairs Correspondence. See also Wood to CIA, January 14, 1885, no. 2053, United States, Letters Received (hereafter cited as LR). Steamships in the Pacific Northwest hired Native deckhands at fifty to sixty dollars a month plus board. See I. W. Powell (Indian superintendent of British Columbia), *Annual Report of the Department of Indian Affairs* (1886), 107. In the first part of the twentieth century, white California fishers followed a similar pattern, relying on technological advances of motorized vessels to open up deepwater fisheries. See McEvoy, *Fisherman's Problem,* 123–55.

37. Entries for September 24, 1861, Diary 5; May 27, 1879, Diary 25, Swan Papers, 1833–1909; "Exciting Whale Hunt," June 15, 1905, *Victoria Daily Colonist,* 8; Lewis, "Whale Hunters of Neah Bay."

38. "It is precisely because stories of wealthy Indians deviate from the familiar chronicle of economic decline that they deserve to be told." Harmon, *Rich Indians,* 9.

39. When Swan initially wrote of James, he described him as John's nephew. Later diary entries described him as John's son. See entries for December 2, 1863, Diary 6; November 6, 1864, Diary 8, Swan Papers, 1833–1909. A 1930 heirship report clarified the Claplanhoo genealogy, showing that James was Halick's son and that John was his uncle. With Halick's death from smallpox in 1853, John married his brother's wife and adopted James. See Heirship Report for Quata Moore. For information on James's whaling activities, see Claplanhoo-Martin and Claplanhoo, interview.

40. Stewart, "Practical Advice on the Choice of Furs No. 3."

41. E. M. Gibson, Agent Report, *ARCIA* (1871), 280; Gibson, *ARCIA* (1873), 308; and Charles Huntington, Agent Report, *ARCIA* (1874), 332; Swan, "Report of Investigations at Neah Bay," 205. The Swan report noted that Makah sealers and local whites involved in the industry believed that Cape Flattery fur seals differed from the migratory fur seal herds and, at the very least, represented a local breeding population. Recent archaeological studies confirm this possibility. See Crockford, Frederick, and Wigen, "Cape Flattery Fur Seal." I have estimated the number of sealers from Huntington's report. He counted 174 Makah males. Some of the oldest males did not hunt, while some of the older boys (counted as children) accompanied male relatives on seal hunts. For sealing done by older boys, see the Alanson Wesley Smith Papers (microfilm, roll 3).

42. Entries for January 15, 1879, Diary 23; March 12, 1879, Diary 24; January 29, 1881, Diary 29, Swan Papers, 1833–1909; Charles Willoughby, Agent Report, *ARCIA* (1880), 155–56; Charles Willoughby, Agent Report, *ARCIA* (1882), 155; A. W. Vowell, Indian Superintendent [of British Columbia], to Theo Davie, Attorney General [of BC], August 3, 1894 (1030/94); and Hammersly and Hamilton, barristers, to Arthur G. Smith, Deputy Attorney General [of BC], September 11, 1894 (1277/94), box 3, file 2: Correspondence Inward, 1894, British Columbia, Attorney General [microfilm B09318], BCA; Swan, "Fur Seal Industry of Cape Flattery and the Vicinity" [1880?], Stenzel Collection. Nuu-chah-nulth sealers also made similar labor arrangements. Guillod, Journal; William Stone to Mr. Daykin, June 12, 1895, file 2254, part 1, Canada, Department of Marine and Fisheries Central Registry Records [reel B-11112], BCA. See also Murray, *Vagabond Fleet*, 16–17; and Lutz, *Makúk*, 189, 199.

43. For details related to purchasing the *Lottie*, see entries for April 16, 1885, Diary 38; January 17, February 3, 8, 1886, Diary 39, Swan Papers, 1833–1909. Entries from February through July in Diary 39 include details about James's first season as owner of the *Lottie*. See also Isaac Powell, Agent Report, *ARCIA* (1886), 235.

44. Entries for March 26, 1881, Diary 29; October 17, 1885, Diary 38; September 17, October 18, 1886, Diary 40; December 9, 1893, Diary 59, Swan Papers, 1833–1909. For Indian agents' information on Makah schooner ownership, see Oliver Wood, Agent Report, *ARCIA* (1885), 188; Powell, Agent Report, *ARCIA* (1887), 210; and Powell to CIA, August 21, 1889, no. 24364, LR. See also "Deposition of Charlie, Nitnat Indian sealer," and "Deposition of Moses, Nitnat Indian sealer," April 27, 1892, BSTA, *Fur Seal Arbitration*, 3:304, 308. The *British Colonist* also tracked Makah-owned schooners: April 10, 1887, September 4, 1889, October 28, 1892, February 2, 1893. Information on Makah ownership of schooners also appears in Lohbrunner, "Reminiscences of B.C. Sealing Industry," BCA; Collins, "Report on the Fisheries of the Pacific Coast," 254; and Costello, *Siwash*, 121.

45. Costello, *Siwash*, 116.

46. Harmon, *Rich Indians*, 134–35 (quotation). See also Hosmer, *American Indians in the Marketplace*; O'Neill, *Working the Navajo Way*; and Arnold, *Fishermen's Frontier*. This analysis is adapted from Patricia Albers's findings about American Indian laborers and markets of exchange. Albers, "Marxism and Historical Materialism," 279.

47. Powell to CIA, March 8, 1886, no. 7920, LR; C. S. Fairchild, Acting Secretary of the Treasury, to Secretary of the Interior, April 5, 1886, no. 9425, LR; Powell to CIA, March 10, 1887, no. 7376, LR; entries for March 9, 1880, Diary 10; September 7, 1887, Diary 41; August 31, September 1, 1889, Diary 48, Swan Papers, 1833–1909; Murray, *Vagabond Fleet*, 155; Stewart, "Practical Advice on the Choice of Furs No. 3."

48. For information on the Claplanhoo fleet's expansion, see *British Colonist*, October 28, 1892, and January 28, 1893. See also October 25, 1891, Diary 55; December 15, 1892, Diary 58; January 22, March 30, December 9, 1893, Diary 59; January 3, 1897, Diary 63, Swan Papers, 1833–1909. For Deeah genealogical information, see January 13, 1863, Diary 6. Many entries in the Swan diaries note Makah owners maintaining and insuring their vessels: November 21, 1886, Diary 40; February 22, 1890, Diary

50; July 11, 1890, Diary 51; May 14, 1891, Diary 55; June 7, 1892, Diary 56; January 29, February 3, 1893, Diary 59.

49. Harry Guillod, Indian Agent (West Coast Agency), September 23, 1901, *Annual Report of the Department of Indian Affairs* (1901), 268; Jordan, *Fur Seals and Fur-Seal Islands*, part 1, 217; Knight, *Indians at Work*, 158.

50. Harmon, *Rich Indians*, 9.

51. Charles Adie, ["Bill of Sale,"] December 26, 1891, enclosed in letter from McGlinn to CIA, December 30, 1891, no. 608, LR; entry for September 7, 1891, Diary 55, Swan Papers, 1833–1909; McGlinn, Agent Report, *ARCIA* (1892), 495 (quotation). For Koba·li's ownership of the Hotel Classet, see Culin, "Summer Trip among the Western Indians," 147, 152. See also Lutz, *Makúk*, 191; Knight, *Indians at Work*, 163; and Hosmer, *American Indians in the Marketplace*, 109–211.

52. Information for this description of nineteenth-century Makah sealing is taken from a collection of depositions made by Makah sealers and schooner owners on April 27, 1892, as evidence for the Bering Sea Tribunal of Arbitration. Sealers making statements included Peter Brown, his son Chestoqua, James Claplanhoo, and eighteen others. See "Testimony Taken among the Makah Indians," BTSA, *Fur Seal Arbitration*, 3:376–99. See also entries for February 24, 1880, Diary 10; December 31, 1878, Diary 23, Swan Papers, 1833–1909.

53. For the dates of the two sealing seasons during the 1880s and 1890s, see Diaries 25–62, Swan Papers, 1833–1909.

54. For Chestoqua's Makah sealer count, see entry for June 15, 1892, Diary 56, Swan Papers, 1833–1909. The Makah Indian agent counted 141 males above age eighteen and 59 ages six to sixteen. Assuming that 21 of the 59 were boys ages ten to sixteen (three boys/age year), brings the total to 162 males ages ten and above. Conservatively assuming that 10 of these were simply too old to seal brings the total to 152 sealing-aged males. For census data and income from the coastal sealing season, see McGlinn, *ARCIA* (1892), 496. For the age range of sealers, see the depositions from Makah and Nuu-chah-nulth sealers in BSTA, *Fur Seal Arbitration*, 3:304–98.

55. Entry for 14 July 1896, Diary 62, Swan Papers; Lutz, *Makúk*, 95, 187.

56. Swan made numerous references to these other purposes. See entries for February 6, July 13, August 21, 1887, Diary 41; June 23, July 5, 1890, Diary 51; December 1, 1890, Diary 53; January 25, 1892, Diary 56, Swan Papers, 1833–1909. For hop pickers, see Raibmon, *Authentic Indians*, 74–134. For similar cases, both terrestrial and maritime, see Knight, *Indians at Work*; Shepherd, "Land, Labor, and Leadership"; O'Neill, *Working the Navajo Way*; Thrush, *Native Seattle*, 66–78; Lutz, *Makúk*; Arnold, *Fishermen's Frontier*; and Bauer, *We Were All Like Migrant Workers Here*.

57. Swan described a more complete range of these goods and services. See Diaries 39–64, covering the years 1886–98, Swan Papers, 1833–1909.

58. Except for the first year of their lease, when they only took about 23,000 seals, in fifteen of the twenty years, ACC hunters exceeded the 100,000 quota by up to 10,000 seals. The 1870 number is from Tomasevich, *International Agreements*, 74. Data for 1871–95 are from "United States No. 2 (1898): Joint Statement of Conclusions Signed

by the British, Canadian, and United States' Delegates Respecting the Fur-Seal Herd Frequenting the Pribyloff Islands in Behring Sea," in BSTA, *Bering Sea Arbitration Papers*, 5:4. Data for 1896–97 are from Jordan, *Fur Seals and Fur-Seal Islands*, part 1. For the Pribilof herd, see also Baird, "Status Report on the Northern Fur Seal," 4–5; Scammon, *Marine Mammals of the North-Western Coast*, 141–63; Paterson, "North Pacific Seal Hunt," 98; and Dorsey, *Dawn of Conservation Diplomacy*, 114.

59. Wright, *Lewis and Dryden's Marine History*, 427. This is probably a more accurate number than the two thousand to three thousand identified in Jordan, *Fur Seals and Fur-Seal Islands*, part 1.

60. "Deposition of Osly, Makah Indian sealer," April 27, 1892, in BSTA, *Fur Seal Arbitration*, 3:391 (quotation). The fur seal statistics for the AAC, NACC, and pelagic catches are from "United States No. 2 (1898): Joint Statement of Conclusions," 4; and Jordan, *Fur Seals and Fur-Seal Islands*, part 1. Jordan argued for a more complete tabulation of the cost of pelagic sealing on the Pribilof herd (170–72). Although he did not estimate the number lost by hunting with shotguns and rifles, he did note that there must have been a "great loss by sinking" of seals shot and not recovered (143). For a more complete discussion on the environmental cost of North Pacific sealing, see Dorsey, *Dawn of Conservation Diplomacy*, 105–64; and Busch, *War against the Seals*, 95–157.

61. Huntington, *ARCIA* (1875), 362–64; Rufus Calhoun, Master of the *Buena Vista*, to CIA, March 23, 1882, no. 10292, LR; *British Colonist*, June 13, 1883 (quotation). For examples of maritime accidents involving Makah sealers and schooners, see *British Colonist*, May 17, 1882, April 10, 1887, April 19, 1895.

62. September 7, 1887, Diary 41, Swan Papers, 1833–1909; Fairchild to Secretary of the Interior, April 5, 1886, no. 9425, LR; Powell to CIA, March 10, 1887, no. 7376, LR.

63. Scott, *Seeing Like a State*, 2.

64. Wright, *Lewis and Dryden's Marine History*, 426.

65. "Behring Sea Arbitration Award of the Tribunal of Arbitration, Constituted under Article 1 of the Treaty Concluded at Washington on the 19th February, 1892, between Her Britannic Majesty and the United States of America" (London: Harrison and Sons, August 1893), in West Coast Agency—Decision of Tribunal of Arbitration, vol. 3873, file 89,849, part 2 [microfilm C-10154], Library and Archives Canada, Ottawa; Wright, *Lewis and Dryden's Marine History*, 429 (quotation).

66. Guillod to Vowell, August 17, 1898, West Coast Agency—Decision of Tribunal of Arbitration (quotation); entry for March 26, 1889, Diary 47, Swan Papers, 1833–1909. For an overview of the diplomatic troubles, see Paterson, "North Pacific Seal Hunt"; Busch, *War against the Seals*, 123–57; Murray, *Vagabond Fleet*; and Dorsey, *Dawn of Conservation Diplomacy*, 105–64.

67. July 31, August 31, 1889, Diary 48, Swan Papers, 1833–1909; George H. Shields, Assistant Attorney General, to Secretary of the Interior, December 21, 1889, enclosed in letter from Secretary of the Interior to CIA, December 21, 1889, no. 36992, LR.

68. Powell to CIA, August 21, 1889, no. 24364, LR; Shields to Secretary of the Interior, December 21, 1889, enclosed in letter from Secretary of the Interior to CIA,

December 21, 1889, no. 36992, LR. Examples of Euro-American vessels seized include the *San Diego* and the *Sierra*. See Murray, *Vagabond Fleet*, 62.

69. Powell to CIA, November 13, 1893, no. 43351, LR. See also Swan's filed objection, "Exceptions to the Ruling of the Court in *U.S. v. Schooner* James G. Swan," April 7, 1892, enclosed in Powell's letter (quotation). Ironically, Swan's logic on the inability of Congress to turn the Bering Sea into a *mare clausum* aligned with the decision handed down by the Paris Tribunal in 1894. See also entries for September 21, 1889, Diary 48; April 4, 1890, Diary 50; April 19, 1890, Diary 51, Swan Papers, 1833–1909.

70. See Charles H. Tupper to Foster, May 26, 1893, enclosure 1 in no. 65, and John W. Foster to Tupper, 27 May 1893, enclosure 2 in no. 65, "United States, No. 11 (1893): Papers Relating to the Proceedings of the Tribunal of Arbitration," in BTSA, *Bering Sea Arbitration Papers*, 5:50–51.

71. Powell, Agent Report, *ARCIA* (1894), 316; *British Colonist*, January 3, July 2, 1894; December 9, 30, 1893, Diary 59, Swan Papers, 1833–1909. Koatslanhoo was also known as Washington Irving or Albert.

72. See William H. Brinker, US Attorney, to John C. Keenan, October 26, 1895, and [newspaper clipping, 1895], enclosed in letter from Keenan, US Indian Agent at Neah Bay Agency, to CIA, November 1, 1895, no. 45552, LR. See also *Mountain Democrat*, June 22, 1895; and *Weekly Gazette and Stockman*, February 27, 1896.

73. The closed season covered the Pacific north of 35°N latitude and east of 180° longitude. Other tribunal recommendations included a sixty-mile no-sealing zone around Saint Paul and Saint George Island and a new requirement for the licensing of sealing vessels. See Paterson, "North Pacific Seal Hunt," 103; and Dorsey, *Dawn of Conservation Diplomacy*, 122.

74. Powell to Capt. D. F. Tozier of the [Revenue] Steamer Grant, June 4, 1894, enclosed in letter from Powell to CIA, June 4, 1894, no. 22501, LR; Acting Secretary of the Interior to CIA, October 4, 1894, no. 38575, LR. See also Powell, *ARCIA* (1894), 316; December 9, 1893, Diary 59; June 26, July 15, 1894, Diary 60, Swan Papers, 1833–1909. James Claplanhoo owned a share of the *Puritan*.

75. [Newspaper clipping, excerpt], *Daily Columbian*, December 9, 1893, West Coast Agency—Decision of Tribunal of Arbitration.

76. Powell, *ARCIA*, 1894, 316; John C. Keenan, Agent Report, *ARCIA* (1896), 313; October 7, 1895, Diary 61; October 7, 1896, Diary 62, Swan Papers, 1833–1909.

77. Tomasevich, *International Agreements*, 88; Paterson, "North Pacific Seal Hunt," 101; Busch, *War against the Seals*, 123–25. For the act that President McKinley signed into law on December 29, 1897, see Jordan, *Fur Seals and Fur-Seal Islands*, part 1. For more on McKinley-era Republican politics, see Cherny, *American Politics in the Gilded Age*, 94–138; and Rauchway, *Murdering McKinley*.

78. Cushing to Robert McClelland, Secretary of the Interior, July 5, 1856, in Andrews, *Official Opinions of the Attorneys General*, 7:749; Judson Harmon to the Secretary of the Treasury, January 5, 1897, in Brandenburg, *Official Opinions of the Attorneys-General*, 21:468; WA Const., art. 6, § 1.

79. Harmon, *Indians in the Making*, 160–89.

80. Prucha, *Great Father,* 230.
81. James Claplanhoo, Capt. John Claplanhoo, et al., Petition, [December] 1897, no. 53731, LR. For a similar strategy deployed by American Indians in other parts of the nation, see Lewis, *Neither Wolf nor Dog;* and Bauer, *We Were All Like Migrant Workers Here.*
82. Claplanhoo-Martin and Claplanhoo, interview. A precursor to the US Coast Guard, the Life-Saving Service established the Neah Bay Station in 1877 on reservation land that the Department of the Interior let the service use. See "Station Neah Bay, Washington." In 1889, John Claplanhoo had complained to Swan about the appropriated land, and he purchased part of it back from the Life-Saving Service in 1891. See entries for April 4, 1877, Diary 22; May 18, 1889, Diary 47; June 15, 1891, Diary 55, Swan Papers, 1833–1909.
83. Chestoqua Peterson to Swan, May 5, 1899, series B.1.2.1, [UW microfilm A8576, reel 4], Swan Papers, 1852–1907.
84. Morse to CIA, July 2, 1900, no. 32541, LR. For an overview of Nuu-chah-nulth sealing from 1866 to 1916, see Lutz, *Makúk,* 198–201. For the use of shipping articles in Victoria, see documents in File 2254, Part 1: Sealing—Efforts of U.S. Vessels to Enlist Indian Crews and Protests of Victoria Sealing Company against Same, 1895–99, Department of Marine and Fisheries, Documents Relating to B.C. [microfilm reel B-11112], BCA.
85. For a complete examination of the diplomatic efforts to bring about this convention, see Busch, *War against the Seals,* 123–57; Tomasevich, *International Agreements;* and Dorsey, *Dawn of Conservation Diplomacy,* 105–64.
86. BSTA, *Fur Seal Arbitration,* 7:130–31.
87. Costello, *Siwash,* 116.
88. Anthropologist Katherine Reedy-Maschner makes a similar argument relative to the Alaska Native Claims Settlement Act (1971) and Aleut communities. "Deprivations amid Abundance," 115.
89. N. O. Nicholson, Taholah Superintendent, to Western Weekly, Inc., September 10, 1934, File 927.0 Seals and Sealskins—Reports, etc. (Original Neah Bay Agency), box 171: Decimal File 921.5–936, TIA.
90. For an explanation about the development of this stereotype, see Usner, *Indian Work,* 8–12. I have estimated the schooner investment figure from Swan's records. See Diaries 39–63, Swan Papers, 1833–1909. This figure does not include money spent on canoes, sealing gear, upkeep, moorage, or insurance.
91. Jangi James to Swan, February 24, 1899, series B.1.2.3, Swan Papers, 1852–1907; Colfax to Frank K. Lane, Secretary of the Interior, December 9, 1919; Colfax to Cato Sells, CIA, 9 December 1919; E. B. Meritt, Assistant Commissioner [of Indian Affairs] to Colfax, January 8, 1920; Smith, Commissioner of Fisheries, to CIA, December 30, 1919, folder 106911-1919, box 115, CCF; Murray, *Vagabond Fleet,* 160.
92. Raymond H. Bitney, Superintendent of Neah Bay Agency, to CIA, January 20, 1932, folder 69742-1931, box 155, CCF; Claplanhoo-Martin and Claplanhoo, interview.
93. Morse, Agent Report, *ARCIA* (1899), 356.

94. Tomasevich, *International Agreements*, 107. Environmental historian Kurkpatrick Dorsey concludes, "The end of pelagic sealing had given the fur seal a new life." *Dawn of Conservation Diplomacy*, 162.

95. Lutz, *Makúk*, 23–26.

96. For perspectives on Swan's reputation, see Roger Chute, Assistant Fish Economist, to Erna Gunther, Director of the Washington State Museum at the University of Washington, April 22, 1937, Ms 15/106, George Roger Chute Collection; and Huntington, *Memoir, 1899*, 127. For biographic information on Swan during these years, see "Guide to the James Gilchrist Swan Papers, 1833–1909"; and McDonald, *Swan among the Indians*, 169–79. For an assessment of his importance to Smithsonian collections, see Cole, *Captured Heritage*, 9–47; and Miles, *James Swan*, 25–36. The more than thirteen hundred times Swan noted someone coming to or leaving the reservation are from Diaries 10 and 23–30, Swan Papers, 1833–1909. I also consulted Wright to determine the Pacific ports of specific vessels. Wright, *Lewis and Dryden's Marine History*.

97. Entries for July 26, 1879, Diary 10; July 10, 15, 21, August 2, 6, 13, 1880, Diary 28; July 10, August 9, 1880, June 25, July 23, 1881, Diary 29; March 5, 1879, Diary 25; October 22, 1879, Diary 23, Swan Papers, 1833–1909.

98. "Deadly Embrace of a Devil-Fish."

99. Entries for December 5, 8, 1879, Diary 10; February 26, 1879, Diary 25; April 23, 1880, Diary 28, Swan Papers, 1833–1909; Wright, *Lewis and Dryden's Marine History*, 142, 430; Swan, "Report of Investigations at Neah Bay," 203.

100. For the development of Puget Sound and Washington Territory, along with the rise of specific towns and industries, see Snowden et al., *History of Washington*, 4:137–254; Meany, *History of the State of Washington*, 220–79; Bagley, *History of Seattle*, 1:100–134; Morgan, *Last Wilderness*, 29–82; Russell, *Jimmy Come Lately, History of Clallam County*; Martin and Brady, *Port Angeles, Washington*, 13–71; Thrush, *Native Seattle*, 17–78; Klingle, *Emerald City*, 12–85.

101. Entries for August 30, October 7, 8, 1879, January 24, 1880, Diary 10; October 4, 11, 1880, Diary 28; October 2, 4, 11, 17, 20, July 18, 1880, Diary 29; September 11, 1881, Diary 30; October 10, 14, September 2, 1884, Diary 36, Swan Papers, 1833–1909; Raibmon, *Authentic Indians*, 74–134.

102. Entries for December 11, 1863, Diary 6; October 10, 1864, Diary 8; July 2, 1880, Diary 28, Swan Papers, 1833–1909; Wright, *Lewis and Dryden's Marine History*, 256.

103. Entries for March 16, 1880, Diary 10; May 26, 1880, Diary 28, Swan Papers, 1833–1909.

104. Entries for April 18, 1881, Diary 29; January 17, February 3, 8, 1886, Diary 39; May 26, 1887, Diary 41; March 1, 1889, Diary 46; May 15, June 7, 1892, Diary 56; December 15, 1892, Diary 58; January 23, March 30, 1893, Diary 59; October 19, 1894, Diary 60, Swan Papers, 1833–1909.

105. Entries for December 1878, Diary 23, Swan Papers, 1833–1909; Claplanhoo-Martin and Claplanhoo, interview.

106. Swan, "History of the Commencement of the Makah Indian Agency at Neah Bay, W.T.," April 5, 1881; August 30, September 26, 1865, Diary 9, Swan Papers, 1833–1909. For more on Indians making opportunities from education, see Collins, "Future with a Past."

107. Entries for November 28, 1864, Diary 8, and May 6, 1865, Diary 9, Swan Papers, 1833–1909; Swan, 22 January 1865, Manuscript Journal.
108. McGlinn to CIA, 25 January 1892, No. 3889, LR; "Indian Potlatch."
109. Entries for March 1, 1889, Diary 46; March 26, 27, 1889, Diary 47, Swan Papers, 1833–1909. James hired another son-in-law, Luke Gilbert, as master of the *Emmett Felitz*. Entry for April 4, 1893, Diary 59. At least one other historian has claimed that Makah schooner purchases meant that they left behind expensive indigenous practices such as potlatching. See Murray, *Vagabond Fleet*, 156. He comes to this conclusion based upon the 1893 words of Chief Peter Brown, who claimed that they had abandoned the potlatch so that they could buy schooners. Perhaps Chief Brown told the inspector what he wanted to hear. As father of James's son-in-law and business associate Chestoqua Peterson, Chief Brown would have been a familiar participant in these potlatches. The McGlinn report that Murray cites also has no mention of this interview with Chief Brown. McGlinn, Agent Report, *ARCIA* (1893), 325–27. However, this was certainly what McGlinn wanted to believe. McGlinn to CIA, January 25, 1892, no. 3889, LR.
110. Entries for July 11, 1881, Diary 29; June 12, 1885, Diary 38, Swan Papers, 1833–1909; Adie, ["Bill of Sale"]; McGlinn to CIA, December 30, 1891, no. 609, LR; Claplanhoo-Martin and Claplanhoo, interview.
111. For the unsuitability of other Indian reservation lands for agriculture, see Schusky, "Lower Brule Sioux Reservation"; Pennington, "Government Policy and Indian Farming"; Wessel, "Agent of Acculturation"; Lewis, *Neither Wolf nor Dog*; Ostler, *Plains Sioux and U.S. Colonialism*, 56, 138; and Ficken, "After the Treaties."
112. Willoughby, *ARCIA* (1882), 155.
113. Charles Huntington, Agent Report, *ARCIA* (1876), 133–35; J. H. Hays, Agent Report, *ARCIA* (1870), 36; Daniel W. Quedessa, [Makah], to A. W. Smith, April 1885, Alanson Wesley Smith Papers (microfilm roll 3); Gibson, *ARCIA* (1873), 308.
114. McGlinn's letter to the commissioner exemplifies this. McGlinn to CIA, January 25, 1892, no. 3889, LR.
115. Stevens, *Life of Isaac Ingalls Stevens*, 1:477.
116. For their initial lack of interest in allotment, see McGlinn, Agent Report, *ARCIA* (1890), 222–25. For Makah support of ten-acre, waterfront allotments, see McGlinn, *ARCIA* (1892), 494.
117. Said, *Orientalism*, 54.
118. Claude C. Covey, Agent Report, *ARCIA* (1903), 333.
119. Daniel Dorchester, Superintendent of Indian Schools, to CIA, October 4, 1890, no. 31461, LR; Acting Secretary of the Interior Department to CIA, October 4, 1894, no. 38575, LR.
120. "Special Meeting of the Makah Tribe and Council," January 23, 1956, Erna Gunther Papers, 1871–1962; Jim Terry (Stanford University), Ed Claplanhoo, Ione Bowechop, and Vivian Lawrence, "Analysis of Schools and Education on Our Makah People," [1973], Erna Gunther Papers, 1887–1980; Claplanhoo-Martin and Claplanhoo, interview; McCarty, interview; Mrs. Jerry McCarty Testimony, [Swindell], "Transcript of

the Meeting, Oct. 15, 1941—evening meeting," pp. 5–6, Edward Swindell Jr. Papers; Testimony of Perry Ides, Makah, July 14, 1949, "Official Reporter's Transcript of Trial Proceedings," p. 111, 98-A-234, box 158: file 15216—Makah Indian Tribe vs. Milo Moore, Dir. of Fisheries, 1 of 3, Attorney General Files, WSA; Coté, *Spirits of Our Whaling Ancestors*, 50–52; Colson, *Makah Indians*, 18–21, 77–78.

121. Recent scholarship is beginning to explore this new narrative. For a North American perspective, see Foster, *Being Comanche*; Hosmer and O'Neill, *Native Pathways*; Deloria, *Indians in Unexpected Places*; Raibmon, *Authentic Indians*; and Harmon, *Rich Indians*. Scholars outside the North American context have also developed this narrative. See Petrie, *Chiefs of Industry*.

CHAPTER 6: "EVERYTHING IS PLAYED OUT HERE"

1. *Makah v. U.S.*; John Geisness, Samuel B. Bassett, and J. Duane Vance, Attorneys for Petitioners [Makahs], *Amended Petition for [Docket] No. 60: Before the Indian Claims Commission of the United States of America—Makah Indian Tribe v. United States of America* (Seattle: Argus Press, n.d.), p. 9 (quotation), folder: Makah Litigation, docket 60, box 20, Department of Fisheries, MCRC.

2. *Makah v. U.S.*

3. Estelle Reel, [Superintendent of Indian Schools], to William A. Jones, May 19, 1900, Estelle Reel Collection.

4. For another case study examining the Tlingit and Haida of southeast Alaska, see Arnold, *Fishermen's Frontier*.

5. IPHC, "Pacific Halibut," 4–13; Tomasevich, *International Agreements on Conservation of Marine Resources*, 127–29; Bell, *Pacific Halibut*.

6. Barbara Lane, "Makah Traditional Fisheries at the Entrance of the Juan de Fuca Strait and Northwestward—Halibut," April 1991, 2; "Written Testimony of Nora Barker, Makah Elder and Teacher of Makah History, [August 23, 1977]," 2; testimony of Oliver Ward Ides and Harry McCarthy [probably McCarty] from "Transcript, Hearing of Sep. 7, 1977, before Magistrate Cooper," 18, 21–23; "Affidavit of Dale Johnson re: Makah Request for Ocean Fishing Places, Sep. 28, 1982," 1–2; "Affidavit of Charles Peterson re: Makah Request for Ocean Fishing Places, Sep. 28, 1982," 2; John. A Thomas and Ann M. Renker, "Halibut Fishing, [ca. 1991]," 1; Ann M. Renker, "Report of the MCRC Halibut Research Team," May 1991, 7; exhibits; folder: Legal Case C85-1606M, Makah v. U.S., box 14, Makah Tribe, MTC Collection. [Swindell], "Transcript of the Meeting, Oct. 15, 1941—Evening Meeting," and "Place Names, 24 November 1941," Edward Swindell Jr. Papers; James Swan to Governor Miles C. Moore, August 30, 1889, box 1P-1-2: folder—Fishing, Washington State, Governors Papers, Miles C. Moore Papers; Testimony of Charles E. Peterson, Makah, July 13,1949, "Official Reporter's Transcript of Trial Proceedings," p. 14, in 98-A-234, box 158: file 15216—Makah Indian Tribe vs. Milo Moore, Dir. of Fisheries, 1 of 3, Washington State, Attorney General Files, WSA (hereafter cited as Peterson Testimony); La Pérouse, *Voyage Round the World*, 182–83. Roger Chute heard the oral

history about the discovery of the banks from James Hunter. See "Hunter, James; John Markishtum and James Hunter (Makah Indians, Neah Bay), June 25, 1936," Ms 15/57, George Roger Chute Collection (hereafter cited as Markishtum and Hunter); Irving, interview; Greene, interview.

7. Irving, interview; "Joint Affidavit of Randolph Parker, Chester Wanderhard, Henry St. Clair, Luke Markishtum, Henry Markishtum and Arthur Johnson—Makah Indian Tribe," May 11, 1942, in Swindell, "Report," 195; Transcript of the Meeting, 3–29; Chute Interview of St. Clair, June 25, 1936, Ms 15/2, 15/74, Chute Collection; Wessen, "Prehistory of the Ocean Coast of Washington," 419; Renker and Gunther, "Makah," 425. For the life history of Pacific salmon, see Lichatowich, *Salmon without Rivers*, 9–23. For a map of salmon migration routes through the region, see Wadewitz, *Nature of Borders*, 5.

8. Markishtum, *Seattle Mail and Herald*, December 9, 1905. Additional information on Makah halibut fishing comes from Peter Eggers, Oral Testimony Collected by Roger Chute, 29 May 1936, Ms 15/58, Chute Collection (hereafter cited as Eggers Testimony); Markishtum and Hunter; James Swan, Bound autograph manuscript journal and memorandum book, p. 76, Stenzel Collection, Beinecke; Renker, "Report of the MCRC Halibut Research Team"; Testimony of Perry Ides, Makah, July 14, 1949, "Official Reporter's Transcript of Trial Proceedings," p. 110 (hereafter cited as Ides Testimony); Thomas and Renker, "Halibut Fishing," 4–7; Claplanhoo-Martin and Claplanhoo, interview; and Swan, "Indians of Cape Flattery," 93–106.

9. In addition to the Markishtum article, sources on halibut processing include Chute to Henry St. Clair, Neah Bay, November 1, 1937, Ms 15/71, and Washburn testimony, July 24, 1936, Ms 15/21, Chute Collection; Chute Interview of St. Clair; Renker, "Report of the MCRC Halibut Research Team," 6; E. M. Gibson, Agent Report, *ARCIA* (1873), 307; Samuel G. Morse, Agent Report, *ARCIA* (1902), 357; and Collins, "Report on the Fisheries of the Pacific Coast," 266.

10. Irving, interview; Kelez, "Troll Fishery," 749; Chute Interview of St. Clair; McCarthy [McCarty] Testimony, 22; Daniel William Quedessa to Sister Mary, May 5, 1926, Kenneth G. Smith Papers; "Written Testimony of Nora Barker," 1–2.

11. Swan to Miles C. Moore [governor, Washington Territory], August 30, 1889, "Fishing," box 1P-1-2, Moore Papers. Swan drew this statistic from a fisheries report he sent to Spencer Baird at the Smithsonian in October 1880. He also noted 154 family heads at Neah Bay. For the population statistic, see *ARCIA*, 1880, 252. See also Chute Interview of St. Clair; and Chute Interview of LaChester, June 26, 1936, Ms 15/53, Chute Collection. LaChester noted that salmon were bigger back then, normally weighing around twenty pounds.

12. Smith, "Report on the Division of Methods and Statistics of the Fisheries," 163.

13. "Joint Affidavit of Randolph Parker, et al.," 195. Swindell also met with tribal elders and leaders earlier at Neah Bay to hear about their usual and accustomed fishing grounds. See Transcript of the Meeting.

14. For intertribal trade, see Transcript of the Meeting, 18; Banfield, *Daily Victoria Gazette*, August 14, 1858; Peter Eggers to Chute, July 27, 1936, Ms 15/58, James Hunter's

reply to Chute's letter dated November 1, 1937, Ms 15/71, Chute Collection; Eggers Testimony; Chute Interview of St. Clair; and Swan, "Visit to Tatooche Island," *Washington Standard*, 20 July 1861, in Katz, *Almost Out of the World*, 121.

15. Renker, "Report of the MCRC Halibut Research Team," 5–6.

16. Howay, *Voyages of the "Columbia,"* 74, 197, 371–72, 380–81, 394; Testimony of Joe Sly, Henry St. Clair, and Luke Markishtum, Transcript of the Meeting, 16, 18, 22. See chapter 2 for sales to the HBC.

17. Banfield, *Daily Victoria Gazette*, September 3, 1858; M. T. Simmons, Agent Report, ARCIA (1858), 232; Swan, "Two Months with the Makahs," October 22, 1860, in Katz, *Almost Out of the World*, 73–74; Bancroft, *History of Washington, Idaho and Montana*, 346. By 1859, only two of the original four remained: Webster and C. L. Strong, a fisheries entrepreneur from San Francisco.

18. Henry A. Webster, Agent Report, ARCIA (1863), 444–45; entries for July 6, 7, 17, August 29, 1864, Diary 8, Swan Papers, 1833–1909; "Our Fisheries" (quotation).

19. Charles Huntington, Agent Report, ARCIA (1874), 332; Charles Huntington, Agent Report, ARCIA (1876), 134; Charles Willoughby, Agent Report, ARCIA (1881), 162; Charles Willoughby, Agent Report, ARCIA (1882), 155.

20. Testimony of Henry St. Clair, Transcript of the Meeting, 18 (hereafter St. Clair Testimony); W. L. Powell, Agent Report, ARCIA (1886), 235; W. L. Powell, Agent Report, ARCIA (1888), 225; Collins, "Report on the Fisheries of the Pacific Coast," 249; Bell, *Pacific Halibut*, 21.

21. *Pacific Fisherman* 3, no. 7 (1905): 16; Collins, "Report on the Fisheries of the Pacific Coast," 260–64, quotation on p. 261; Thompson and Freeman, "History of the Pacific Halibut Fishery," 18–20; Bell, *Pacific Halibut*, 21–28; "Closed Season on Halibut," 11. Swan had traveled to the East Coast a decade earlier to encourage Gloucester fishers to make use of Northwest Coast fisheries. See his entries for February 1867, Diary 11; see also February, March, June 1888, Diary 43, and March 30, 1889, Diary 47, Swan Papers, 1833–1909, for information about these schooners. Due to an accident at sea, the *Edward E. Webster*—also owned by Capt. Jacobs—arrived too late in 1888 to engage in halibut fishing that year. Owners sold the *Oscar and Hattie* in Victoria to a sealer who renamed it the *E. P. Marvin*.

22. Thompson and Freeman, "History of the Pacific Halibut Fishery," 16, 18; Bell, *Pacific Halibut*, 24, 41; Collins, "Report on the Fisheries of the Pacific Coast," 266.

23. Cheseboro, "Looking Backwards"; John P. McGlinn, Agent Report, ARCIA (1891), 448 (quotation). See also "Fish of the Pacific." "North Pacific Fisheries" (quotation).

24. For Makah population statistics, see M. T. Simmons, Agent Report, ARCIA (1857), 335; and Powell, Agent Report, ARCIA (1888), 225. For non-Native statistics, see US Census Office, *United States in 1860*, 4; and US Census Office, *Report on the Populations: 1890*, 14.

25. Powell, ARCIA (1888), 225; McGlinn, Agent Report, ARCIA (1890), 222, 225; McGlinn, ARCIA (1891), 448.

26. Bell, Dunlop, and Freeman, "Pacific Coast Halibut Landings," 10; McGlinn, Agent Report, ARCIA (1892), 495; Bell, *Pacific Halibut*, 22–49, 57–60, 75–78, 80–81; This-

tle, "'As Free of Fish,'" 107–8; "Halibut Fishing"; "Growth of the Halibut Industry"; Bower, *Report*, 36; Alexander, "Notes on the Halibut Fishery," 142; Thompson and Freeman, "History of the Pacific Halibut Fishery," 44–45.

27. Names of Pacific salmon can get confusing, especially when drawn from numerous archival accounts. Spring salmon (*O. tscawytscha*) also go by the name Chinook, king, quinnat, and tyee; sockeye (*O. nerka*) is sometimes called "red" salmon; humpbacks (*O. gorbuscha*) are also known as pinks; silvers (*O. kisutch*) are coho salmon; and chum (*O. keta*) are sometimes called dog or keta salmon. Newell, *Tangled Webs of History*, 13. See also Sword, "Annual Report," 106; Scholefield and Howay, *British Columbia*, 2:585; and Cobb, *Pacific Salmon Fisheries*, 18–22, 152.

28. Bower, *Report*, 37–39; Barbare Bros.: Boat Builders and Designers, Catalog (Tacoma, WA: Stanley Bell Printing, 1915), in box 2H-2-50: folder—Fish Commission—1914, Washington State, Governors Papers, Ernest Lister Papers; Cobb, *Pacific Salmon Fisheries*, 75–90; Kelez, "Troll Fishery," 749–53; Boxberger, *To Fish in Common*, 63–68; Wadewitz, *Nature of Borders*, 75–81.

29. "Huge Fishing Fleet at Neah Bay"; "Mild Curing at Neah Bay"; "New Gorman Cannery"; "Floating Cannery for Neah Bay."

30. Ides Testimony, 112; Testimony of Arthur Johnson, Transcript of the Meeting, 28; Collins, "Report on the Fisheries of the Pacific Coast," 266; Kelez, "Troll Fishery," 749; James Crawford, "Report of [the State] Fish Commissioner," November 1, 1892, 18; box 1P-1-2: Folder—Fishing; Moore Papers; Wilcox, "Fisheries of the Pacific Coast," 289; Samuel G. Morse, Agent Report, *ARCIA* (1897), 292; Morse, Agent Report, *ARCIA* (1898), 300; Morse, Agent Report, *ARCIA* (1900), 396; Morse, Agent Report, *ARCIA* (1901), 385 (quotation); Claude C. Covey, Agent Report, *ARCIA* (1903), 333; Edwin Minor, Agent Report, *ARCIA* (1905), 358; Minor, Agent Report, *ARCIA* (1906), 375; Peter Eggers to Chute, August 30, 1937, and Theo Eggers, interview by Chute, transcript, June 19, 1936, Ms 15/58, Chute Collection; D. W. Manchester, Special Agent, "Report on Neah Bay, Washington, Agency," February 1902 (quotation), no. 9638, LR; "News Items from the Fisheries Districts"; "News Items from the Fisheries Districts: Puget Sound"; "Mild Curing at Neah Bay."

31. Peterson Testimony, 37, 52–53; St. Clair Testimony, 19; Lida W. Quimby, "Report of the Field Matron, Neah Bay Agency," August 15, 1901, *ARCIA* (1901), 388 (quotation); Minor, *ARCIA* (1905), 358; Morse, *ARCIA* (1897), 292 (quotation). Some fishers still use the *čibu·d* today. See also "Old Indian Goes into Halibut Business"; Peter Eggers to Chute, July 27, December 12, 1936, Ms 15/58, Chute Collection; Raymond H. Bitney, "Commercial-Fishing by Makah Indians at Neah Bay, Wash.," [1932], p. 34, folder 56247-1931, Neah Bay, 155, United States, Records of the Bureau of Indian Affairs, CCF.

32. McEvoy, *Fisherman's Problem*, 10 (quotation). McEvoy's integration of environment and society differs from Hardin, "Tragedy of the Commons." See also Fr. Howerd Bell, interview by Roger Chute, January 20, 1936 (quotation), Ms 15/84, Chute Collection.

33. Renker, "Report of the MCRC Halibut Research Team," 6. Southeast Alaskan fisheries also experienced the replacement of carefully controlled indigenous ownership

with a new system of unregulated property rights brought by non-Natives. See Arnold, *Fishermen's Frontier*.

34. Sproat, *Scenes and Studies of Savage Life*, 225.

35. Alexander, "Notes on the Halibut Fishery," 142; Rathbun, "Review of the Fisheries," 260 (quotation); "Halibut Fishing," 39; "Flattery Fishing Is Poor" (quotation). For contested claims of overfishing, see Thistle, "'As Free of Fish,'" 109–14.

36. "Closed Season on Halibut"; A. C. Little, "Report of A. C. Little, State Fish Commissioner," January 1, 1902, p. 25, and T. R. Kershaw, "Report of Fish and Game Commissioner, 1902," December 1, 1902, p. 101, box 2D-1-4: folder—Fish Commission, Washington State, Governors Papers, Henry McBride Papers; John L. Riseland, "Twentieth Annual Report of the State Fish Commissioner and Ex Officio Game Warden, 1909," April 1, 1910, box 2G-2-14: folder—Fish Commission, 1909, Washington State, Governors Papers, Marion E. Hay Papers; Thompson, "Statistics of the Halibut Fishery in the Pacific."

37. Roosevelt, "State of the Union Address." There is a wealth of literature about Pacific salmon overfishing and conservation efforts. See McEvoy, *Fisherman's Problem*; Newell, *Tangled Webs of History*; Taylor, *Making Salmon*; Lichatowich, *Salmon without Rivers*; Harris, *Fish, Law, and Colonialism*; Montgomery, *King of Fish*; and Harris, *Landing Native Fisheries*. For a comparison to Atlantic salmon and Atlantic fisheries in general, see Jenkins, "Atlantic Salmon," 845–52; and Bolster, *Mortal Sea*.

38. "Closed Season on Halibut"; Thompson, "Statistics of the Halibut Fishery in the Pacific"; Thompson, "Regulation of the Halibut Fishery of the Pacific"; Thistle, "'As Free of Fish,'" 114–19.

39. Taylor, "Negotiating Nature," 337.

40. *Report of the America-Canadian Fisheries Conference, 1918* (Washington, DC: GPO, 1920), p. 33 (quotation), box 2J-1-19: folder—Fisheries Commission, 1924, Washington State, Governors Papers, Louis F. Hart Papers; Tomasevich, *International Agreements*, 142–43; Thistle, "'As Free of Fish,'" 121–23.

41. Newell, *Tangled Webs of History*, 183. For more on this treaty, see Bell, *Pacific Halibut*, 149–50.

42. Babcock et al., "Report of the International Fisheries Commission," 7.

43. Thistle, "'As Free of Fish,'" 124.

44. Tomasevich, *International Agreements*, 154–55 (quotation); Thompson and Freeman, "History of the Pacific Halibut Fishery," 12; Babcock et al., "Report of the International Fisheries Commission"; Bell, *Pacific Halibut*, 151.

45. Frank Heward Bell, interview by Roger Chute, 20 January 1936 (quotation); and Notes by Roger Chute from the National Recovery Administration Code Hearing, [ca. 1933–1935], "Notes," Ms 15/84, Chute Collection. See also Thompson and Freeman, "History of the Pacific Halibut Fishery," 12, 46–47; Tomasevich, *International Agreements*, 150; Bell, *Pacific Halibut*, 76, 84; Babcock et al., "Report of the International Fisheries Commission," 10–13.

46. Tomasevich, *International Agreements*, 155–62; Bell, *Pacific Halibut*, 136–37, 51–59.

47. *Pacific Fisherman* 32, no. 5 (1934): 37; and *Pacific Fisherman* 32, no. 7 (1934): 35; Tomase-vich, *International Agreements*, 171–85; Bell, *Pacific Halibut*, 139–42; "Bureau of Fisher-ies Completes 70 Years of Service," June 15, 1940, p. 10, Ms 15/56, Chute Collection.

48. John Markishtum and Henry St. Clair, interviews by Roger Chute, June 25, 1936, Ms 15/95, 15/74, Chute Collection; "Joint Affidavit of Randolph Parker, et al.," 197.

49. Two letters from the Makah Boat Owners Association to N. O. Nicholson, TIA, Janu-ary 19, 1938, and Paul J. Brodersen, Sub-Agent, Neah Bay, to N. O. Nicholson, Super-intendent, January 21, 1938, file 921: Hunting and Fishing [1 of 3], box 170: Decimal File 916–921, United States. Records of the Bureau of Indian Affairs, Talolah Indian Agency (hereafter TIA). In 1974, Makah lawyers investigated the federal govern-ment's expenditures on Makah fishing since 1855—they found nothing tied to this 1938 request. See Alvin J. Ziontz, "Plaintiff's Requested Findings of Fact on the Issue of the Oral Promises of the United States to Furnish Aid and Support for Makah Fisheries," December 16, 1974, 13–16, Legal Case 60-A, Makah v. U.S., ICC, MTC.

50. Colson, *Makah Indians*, 154.

51. Ibid., 123 ("old men" quotation); Peterson Testimony, 19 (quotation); *Amended Peti-tion before the Indian Claims Commission of the United States of America, No. 60: Makah Indian Tribe v. United States of America* (Seattle: Argus Press, [1952]), pp. 9–10, 98-A-234, box 158: file 15216—Makah Indian Tribe vs. Milo Moore, Dir. of Fisheries, 3 of 3, Attorney General Files, WSA.

52. St. Clair Interview; Markishtum, interview; Transcript of the Meeting, 1.

53. Taylor, "Negotiating Nature," 337. For buffalo comparison, see Calloway, *Our Hearts Fell to the Ground*, 121–32; West, *Contested Plains*, 90; and Zontek, *Buffalo Nation*, 21.

54. White, *"It's Your Misfortune."* For a helpful introduction to conflicts over American Indian treaty rights, see Wilkins and Lomawaima, *Uneven Ground*, 117–42.

55. Wadewitz, *Nature of Borders*, 84; Boxberger, *To Fish in Common*, 90.

56. Boxberger, *To Fish in Common*, 90.

57. *Seattle Post-Intelligencer*, August 3, 1915; Darwin, "Annual Reports," 42.

58. *State v. Towessnute; State v. Alexis; Kennedy v. Becker;* Cato Sells, ARCIA (1916), 66; Cohen, *Treaties on Trial*, 56–58.

59. Ides Testimony, 113 (quotation); clipping, "State Arrests Indian Fishers," *Seattle Post-Intelligencer*, October 14, [1924], and Boyd, Superintendent and Physician, Neah Bay Indian Agency, to CIA, January 12, 1925, folder 88716-1924, box 115, CCF.

60. As quoted in Boyd to CIA, January 12, 1925.

61. "State Arrests Indian Fishers."

62. Irving to Commissioner, February 25, 1925, folder 88716-1924, box 115, CCF; Boyd to CIA, January 12, 1925.

63. Boyd to CIA, March 2, 1925, folder 88716-1924, box 115, CCF.

64. Estep to CIA, 2 December 1924—folder 88716-1924, CCF; Charles H. Burke, Com-missioner, to Hubert Work, Secretary of the Interior, 16 February 1925—folder 88716-1924, box 115, CCF.

65. Goodall, Supervisor, "Report of Inspection of the Neah Bay School and Agency," July 9, 1916, pp. 17–18, folder 26652-1915, box 910, CCF; Sells, *ARCIA* (1916), 81, 105, 129, 195. For more on Makah basketry, see Thompson and Marr, "Evolution of Makah Basketry."

66. Henderson, "Report on the Neah Bay Indian Agency, Washington," January 7, 1929, pp. 12–15, 21, folder 150: Inspections, Investigations, Reports, etc. (Neah Bay Agency), box 102: decimal file 137–150, TIA; Bitney, "Commercial-Fishing," 37; US Department of Commerce, Bureau of Economic Analysis, http://www.bea.gov.

67. Hoxie, *Final Promise*.

68. Minor, Agent Report, *ARCIA* (1904), 352; A. D. Dodge, Superintendent, US Indian School Neah Bay, to CIA, July 26, 1920, folder 49747-1920, box 115, CCF; F. W. Buhram, Anacortes Fisheries, to CIA, telegram, July 17, 1919, folder 60721-1919, box 124, CCF; [Dodge] to CIA, August 7, 1922, folder 38838-1922, box 175, CCF.

69. This development was discussed in chapter 5.

70. I have adapted this idea from White, "'Are You an Environmentalist?,'" 174.

71. Bitney, "Commercial-Fishing." See also Bitney, "1932 Annual Report," September 7, 1932, p. 3, folder 00-1932, box 31, CCF.

72. For more on the use of this stereotype, see Lutz, *Makúk*, 32–37.

73. Ibid., 23–26. See chapter 5 for a discussion of the late nineteenth-century Makah moditional economy.

74. Superintendent of U.S. Indian School, Neah Bay, to CIA, August 27, 1923, folder 8: Letter (8–27–1923), box 103: decimal file 150–160, TIA; Bitney to CIA, March 3, 1931, Folder 150: Inspections, Investigations, Reports, etc. (Neah Bay Agency), Box 102: Decimal File 137–150, TIA; Claplanhoo, interview; Pascua, interview, 2009; Claplanhoo-Martin and Claplanhoo, interview. For the importance of leisure time in a moditional economy, see Lutz, *Makúk*, 303.

75. C. L. Woods, Superintendent and Physician, "Report of Superintendent in Charge of Neah Bay Agency," August 14, 1907, folder 71405-1907, box 31, CCF. For confirmation from the CIA on this plan, see Francis E. Leupp to Secretary of the Interior, March 21, 1907, box 2E-2-13: folder—Fed. Depts.—Indian Service, Washington State, Governors Papers, Albert E. Mead Papers. See also Woods to CIA, June 20, 1908, folder 93252-1907, Neah Bay, box 13, CCF.

76. [Francis E. Leupp,] CIA, to Schuyler Colfax, James Hunter, and Others, July 6, 1908, folder 93252-1907, box 13, CCF; Leupp, *ARCIA* (1909), 64–65. For the federal government's management of tribal resources, see Fixico, *Invasion of Indian Country*.

77. Henderson, "Report on the Neah Bay Agency," 19–20; Bitney, "1932 Annual Report," 4–5. For Crown Zellerbach's history, see "Guide to the Crown Zellerbach Corporation Records."

78. Bitney, Superintendent, Neah Bay Agency, to CIA, January 22, 1932, file 150 Inspections, Investigations, Reports, etc. (Neah Bay Agency), box 102: decimal file 130–150, TIA.

79. McCarty, interview.

80. Mrs. C. Peterson, [Makah], to T. W. Hauff [c/o Senator C. C. Dill], November 24, 1931; and Bitney to CIA, January 20 1932, folder 69742-1931, box 155, CCF; Colson, *Makah Indians*, 124.

81. [Rathbun and Wakeham], *Preservation of the Fisheries*; Tomasevich, *International Agreements*, 250–56; Dorsey, *Dawn of Conservation Diplomacy*, 40–53, 76–104; Boxberger, *To Fish in Common*, 98–99; Wadewitz, *Nature of Borders*, 158–62, quotation on p. 159. For an introduction to Progressive era conservation, see Hays, *Conservation and the Gospel of Efficiency*; and Koppes, "Efficiency/Equity/Esthestics."

82. Beaulieu, "Fishing Activities of Indians," 1; Tomasevich, *International Agreements*, 257–68; Boxberger, *To Fish in Common*.

83. Boddy, "Enforcing Observance of Game Laws," 19 (quotation); Cohen, *Treaties on Trial*, 44; Boxberger, *To Fish in Common*, 103–5. For an overview of the fisheries politics of this time and an economic analysis, see Barsh, *Washington Fishing Rights Controversy*.

84. E. M. Benn to Director of Fisheries, November 9, 1937, and S. P. Phillips, Acting Supervisor, Fisheries Patrol, to Robert J. Schoettler, Director [of Fisheries], August 24, 1951, folder: Makah, Copy 1855 Treaty, Tribal Fishing, 1936–1951, box 20: Makah, 1936–197; Department of Fisheries—Indian Affairs Files, WSA; Beaulieu, "Fishing Activities of Indians," 1; Transcript of the Meeting, 4, 23, 29; Peterson Testimony, 18; McCarty, interview; Colson, *Makah Indians*, 44.

85. Transcript of the Meeting, 29.

86. I have borrowed the pendulum idea from Boxberger, *To Fish in Common*. For similar examples, see Wunder, *"Retained by the People"*; Iverson, *We Are Still Here*; Hosmer and O'Neill, *Native Pathways*; Raibmon, *Authentic Indians*, 135–97; Fisher, *Shadow Tribe*; and Fixico, *Indian Resilience and Rebuilding*.

87. Exhibit #6: Petition to Secretary of the Interior against Raymond H. Bitney, Superintendent, 5 November 1931, enclosed in Henry Roe Cloud, "Report of Henry Roe Cloud, Field Representative, on Removal of Raymond H. Bitney, Neah Bay [and] Quileute Jurisdictions," [1933?], folder 10: 160 Personnel, Miscellaneous (1927–1936), box 103: decimal file 150–160, TIA. For the Meriam Report, see Wunder, *"Retained by the People,"* 54–63.

88. Crum, "Henry Roe Cloud"; Ramirez, "Henry Roe Cloud."

89. "Report of Henry Roe Cloud," 1, 10–11.

90. Ibid., 11–12. For more on the IRA, see Deloria and Lytle, *Nations Within*; and Rusco, *Fateful Time*.

91. Peterson Testimony, 24–32; Makah Tribe, *Constitution and Bylaws*; Colson, *Makah Indians*, 21–22; Ruby, Brown, and Collins, *Guide to the Indian Tribes of the Pacific Northwest*, 180.

92. For Pacific Northwest fishing rights cases, see Ziontz, "History of Treaty Fishing Rights in the Northwest"; Cohen, *Treaties on Trial*; Harmon, *Indians in the Making*, 218–44; Wilkinson, *Messages from Frank's Landing*; Wilkinson, *Blood Struggle*, 167–73; Mulier, "Recognizing the Full Scope"; Duthu, *American Indians and the Law*, 99–105; Ziontz, *Lawyer in Indian Country*; and Wilkinson, *People Are Dancing Again*.

93. _U.S. v. Winans._ The Winans brothers had purchased land on the Washington side of the Columbia River, built fish wheels on the river, and erected fences around their operation, shutting out the Yakama tribal nation from its usual and accustomed grounds. On behalf of the Yakama tribe, the United States sued the Winans brothers.

94. Darwin to G. H. Best, Editor of _The Herald_, [1914], folder: Indian Fishing Rights, box 2H-2–59, and Darwin to Cato Sells, June 2, 1917, folder: Indian Fishing, box 2H-2-113, Lister Papers; Boddy, "Enforcing Observance of Game Laws," 19.

95. Statement of Alvin J. Ziontz, Attorney for Makah Tribe, 79, LAL 4: Treaty Rights, Opinions, Statements, Magnuson Bill [1964], box 9: MTC Records.

96. _U.S. v. Kagama; Seufert Brothers Company v. U.S._

97. Phillips to Schoettler, August 24, 1951.

98. _McCauley v. Makah._

99. For the Makah position, see Vanderveer, Bassett and Geisness, Attorneys for the Makah, Appellee's Brief for _McCauley v. Makah_ (1942), folder 1: Law—Fishing Case—Makah Tribe v. State of Washington [1 of 2], box 554: Correspondence Relating to Indian Fishing Rights, 1931–45, TIA. See also _Tulee v. Washington_; Beaulieu, "Fishing Activities of Indians"; Swindell, "Report," 189; Woods, "Who's in Charge of Fishing?," 419.

100. Colson, _Makah Indians_, 125.

101. Woods, "Who's in Charge of Fishing?," 420; Peterson Testimony, 64.

102. _Makah v. Schoettler_ (quotation); Nathan G. Richardson, [Makah attorney], to Milo Moore, Director, Department of Fisheries, October 15, 1958, folder: Makah Administrative Correspondence, box 20, Department of Fisheries, MCRC; Woods, "Who's in Charge of Fishing?," 420–22.

103. _Makah v. U.S._; Geisness, et al., _Amended Petition for [Docket] No. 60_; Ruby, Brown, and Collins, _Guide to the Indian Tribes of the Pacific Northwest_, 180–81. For the ICC, see Wunder, _"Retained by the People,"_ 89–93; and Wilkins, _Hollow Justice._

104. Defendant's Memorandum for [Docket] No. 60: Makah Indian Tribe v. United States of America, [n.d.], 26, folder: Makah Litigation, Docket 60, box 20, Department of Fisheries; Ralph A. Barney, US Department of Justice, to Milo Moore, May 4, 1959, Makah Administrative Correspondence, Department of Fisheries, MCRC.

105. Dwight Eisenhower, "Statement by the President upon Signing Bill Concerning Termination of Federal Supervision over the Menominee Indian Tribe," June 17, 1954, Peters and Woolley, _The American Presidency Project,_ http://www.presidency.ucsb.edu/ws/?pid=9927. For termination, see Wunder, _"Retained by the People,"_ 97–105; and Fixico, _Termination and Relocation._

106. Swindell, "Report," 96; American Friends Service Committee, _Uncommon Controversy_, 127; Richardson to Moore.

107. Adams, Projects Director [for the Survival of the American Indians Association], to President Lyndon B. Johnson, December 17, 1968, reproduced in Duwors, "Documents from the Indian Fishing Rights Controversy"; Tollefson to MTC, October 19, 1965, and Markishtum to Tollefson, November 8, 1965, MTC Collection.

108. Personal communication with Jerry Lucas, Makah manager of the SBA loan in the 1960s and 1970s, March 4, 2014; personal communication with Russell Svec, Fisheries Director for the Makah Fisheries Management Department, May 9, 2014. See also *U.S. v. Washington*. For more on ways Native peoples accessed new federal programs for economic development, see LaGrand, *Indian Metropolis*; and Cobb, *Native Activism in Cold War America*.

109. *Richard Sohappy v. McKee Smith* and *U.S. v. Oregon* (1969).

110. *U.S. v. Washington*. For summaries of the Boldt decision, see Cohen, *Treaties on Trial*, 3–14, quotation on p. 13; Wilkinson, *Messages from Frank's Landing*, 49–65; Woods, "Who's in Charge of Fishing?," 426–30; Mulier, "Recognizing the Full Scope," 58–67.

111. Northwest Indian Fisheries Commission, *Treaty Fishing Rights*; Brown, "Treaty Rights," 3; Mulier, "Recognizing the Full Scope," 59, 69 (quotations).

112. *U.S. v. Washington* (1975); *U.S. v. Washington* (1976); Cohen, *Treaties on Trial*, 15, 87–93, 100; Woods, "Who's in Charge of Fishing?," 430–31; *Washington v. Washington Commercial Passenger Fishing Vessel Association* (1979).

113. *U.S. v. Washington (Phase II)* (1980); *U.S. v. Washington (Phase II)* (1985).

114. Woods, "Who's in Charge of Fishing?," 433–35. For an alternate view on the 1985 treaty, see Boxberger, "Lummi Indians." For contemporary perspectives on self-governance and self-determination, see Minugh, Morris, and Ryser, *Indian Self-Governance*; O'Brien, *American Indian Tribal Governments*; Ambler, *Breaking the Iron Bonds*; and Castile, *Taking Charge*.

115. United Nations, Division for Ocean Affairs and the Law of the Sea, "The United Nations Convention on the Law of the Sea." UNCLOS went into effect in 1994 after the sixtieth nation signed it. Although the United States signed the treaty, the US Senate has yet to ratify it.

116. Johnson and Langdon, "Two Hundred Mile Zones"; Smith, *Exclusive Economic Zone Claims*, 21, 31, 223; Thompson, "Canadian Foreign Policy and Straddling Stocks," 221. In 1983, the United States upgraded its maritime jurisdictional claims from an exclusive fishery zone to an exclusive economic zone. These boundary expansions only applied to the jurisdictional claims of nation-states; Washington State's jurisdiction still only extends out three miles offshore.

117. Department of State, "Maritime Boundary Negotiations with Canada," September 1976, enclosed in David A. Colson, attorney in the Office of the Assistant Legal Adviser for Oceans, Environment and Science, to Steven S. Anderson, [lawyer for the Makah Tribal Council,] October 21, 1976, Legal Case C85-1606M, MTC Collection; Resolution No. 20 of the Makah Indian Tribe, [1960]; and Milo Moore to Quentin Markishtum, Makah Chairman, 15 March 1960 (quotation), Makah Administrative Correspondence, Department of Fisheries, MCRC; Smith, *Exclusive Economic Zone Claims*, 9.

118. "Statement of Makah Tribe to Ambassador Lloyd Cutler Concerning United States–Canadian Talks on Halibut and Other Species," July 31, 1978, Affidavit of Stephen H. Joner, May 6, 1991, and Alvin Ziontz, et al., [attorneys for Makah Tribe,]

"Plaintiff's Memorandum in Support of Motion for Partial Summary Judgment and in Response to Federal Defendants' Motion for Partial Summary Judgment," May 6, 1991, pp. 61–63, Legal Case C85-1606M, MTC Collection; Arnold, interview.

119. Edmund A. Starling, Agent Report, *ARCIA* (1852), 173; A. C. Elliot, [BC Attorney General], to K. W. Scott, [Canadian] Secretary of State, August 30, 1879, box 1, file 7: Correspondence Inward, 1878, British Columbia, Attorney General [microfilm B09318], BCA; Henry A. Webster to [Territorial Governor] E. P. Ferry, September 9, 1879, Indian Affairs Folder, box 1K-1-3, Washington State, Governors Papers, Elisha P. Ferry Papers; Seltz, "Epidemics, Indians, and Border-Making."

120. Willie Clallam to Thomas Bishop, care of Senator Miles Poindexter, January 7, 1919; T. G. Bishop to CIA, February 8, 1919; and E. B. Merith, Asst. Commissioner, to T. G. Bishop, February 14, 1919, folder 11986-1919, box 116, CCF. For the ways US borders hardened in the early twentieth century, see St. John, *Line in the Sand*, 90–118; and Wadewitz, *Nature of Borders*, 144–67.

121. Thomas and Renker, "Halibut Fishing," 8, n. 17.

122. "Transcript, Hearing of Sep. 7, 1977, before Magistrate Cooper," and George D. Dysart, Asst. Regional Solicitor, Department of the Interior Counsel for the United States, "U.S. Memorandum re: Makah Request for Determination of Ocean Fishing Grounds," August 31, 1977, Legal Case C85-1606M, Makah v. U.S., MTC Collection.

123. "Plaintiff's Memorandum," quotation on p. 1.

124. Alvin J. Ziontz, "Plaintiff's Requested Findings of Fact on the Issue of the Oral Promises of the United States to Furnish Aid and Support for Makah Fisheries, and Plaintiff's Brief," December 16, 1974, Legal Case No. 60-A, MTC Collection.

125. For the cultural importance of the islands, see Barbara Lane, "Brief Report on the History of Tatoosh Island and Its Cultural Significance to the Makah Indians," August 1982, and "Brief Report on the History of Waadah Island and Its Cultural Significance to the Makah Indians," August 1982, Legal: Laws, U.S., MTC Collection.

126. 98 Stat. 179 and Public Law 98–282; "The Makah Claims Settlement Bill: An Honorable and Practical Resolution of 34 Years of Litigation," 1984, pp. 15–16, folder: Legal—Laws, U.S., MTC Collection.

127. *Metcalf, et al. v. Daley, et al.*

128. *Anderson, et al. v. Evans, et al.*

129. Mulier, "Recognizing the Full Scope," 89.

CONCLUSION: "EVENTS HAPPEN WHEN YOU GET A WHALE"

1. Polly McCarty, interview by Bowechop and Pascua, NOAA Interviews.

2. Johnson, interview; Dan Greene, NOAA Interviews.

3. These benefits are summarized from various sources, including Sones, interview; McCarty, interview; NOAA Interviews; Bowechop, "Contemporary Makah Whaling"; Barton, "'Red Waters'"; Sepez, "Political and Social Ecology"; Renker, "Whale Hunting and the Makah Tribe"; Coté, *Spirits of Our Whaling Ancestors*, 140–41, 149. See the Introduction for more on the whale hunt and the reactions to it.

4. Richter, "Whose Indian History?" 389. Vine Deloria Jr. criticized supposedly inclusive US histories for simply adding the stereotypical trappings of various minority groups—"a few feathers, woolly heads, and sombreros"—to the dominant white narrative of "manifest destiny." *We Talk, You Listen*, 39.

5. Kershaw, "In Petition to Government."

6. American Indian scholar Jace Weaver brought this concept to the attention of the field in "More Light Than Heat," 249. He credits the following for developing the concept: Smith, Burke, and Ward, "Globalisation and Indigenous Peoples"; Gough, "History, Representation, Globalisation and Indigenous Cultures." See also Clifford, "Traditional Futures."

7. Crystal Thompson and Janine Bowechop (Ledford), NOAA, interviews.

8. The Makah have partnered with the Olympic Coast National Marine Sanctuary to protect marine resources, including whales, halibut, black cod, whiting, and seals. See Vincent Cooke (Makah) and George Galasso (Olympic National Marine Sanctuary), "Challenges and Opportunities for the Makah Tribe and Olympic National Marine Sanctuary," [2000?], *National Sea Grant Library Website*, accessed July 2009, http://nsgd.gso.uri.edu/riu/ riuco4001/riuco4001_part4.pdf.

9. "Ratified Treaty No. 286: Documents Relating to the Negotiation of the Treaty of January 31, 1855, with the Makah Indians," p. 2, Documents Relating to the Negotiation of Ratified and Unratified Treaties, NARA-PNR.

10. *Makah Nation*, produced by the MTC and Makah Whaling Commission; Greene, NOAA Interviews.

11. See Pascua, interview, 2008; Sepez, "Political and Social Ecology," 109; Coté, *Spirits of Our Whaling Ancestors*, 69–114.

12. Ibid., 127–29. See also Erikson, *Voices of a Thousand People*, 119–34.

13. Huelsbeck, "Whaling in the Precontact Economy," 9.

14. *Makah Nation*.

15. For citations about the 1999 hunt, see the Introduction.

16. This is drawn from Robert Miller's definition of "self-determination." Miller, "Tribal Cultural Self-Determination," 123.

17. *Makah Nation*.

18. Blackhawk, "Recasting the Narrative of America," 1168.

19. Barton, "'Red Waters,'" 190 (quotation). Nuu-chah-nulth scholar Charlotte Coté characterizes the 1999 whale hunt as an indigenous action striking back at "culinary imperialism," a power dynamic that dictates what counts as acceptable food, especially with respect to what indigenous peoples are allowed to produce and eat. *Spirits of Our Whaling Ancestors*, 163. For a brief history on the "Western hegemonic control of food production and food consumption," see Barsh, "Food Security, Food Hegemony, and Charismatic Animals." For a discussion of culinary imperialism applied to the Third World, see Narayan, *Dislocating Cultures*. Culinary imperialism is not limited to the Third World; the Japanese have complained about US culinary imperialism as applied to consuming whale products. See Sims, "Japan, Feasting on Whale."

BIBLIOGRAPHY

Adelman, Jeremy, and Stephen Aron. "From Borderlands to Borders: Empires, Nation-States, and the Peoples in between in North American History." *American Historical Review* 104 (1999): 814–41.

Ahousaht Indian Band and Nation v. Canada (Attorney General). 2009 BCSC 1494.

Akrigg, G. P. V., and Helen B. Akrigg. *British Columbia Chronicle, 1847–1871: Gold and Colonists.* Vancouver: Discovery Press, 1977.

Akrigg, Philip and Helen. Research Collection. UBCA.

Albers, Patricia C. "Marxism and Historical Materialism in American Indian History." In *Clearing a Path: Theorizing the Past in Native American Studies*, edited by Nancy Shoemaker, 107–36. New York: Routledge, 2002.

Alexander, A. B. "Notes on the Halibut Fishery of the Northwest Coast in 1895." *Bulletin of the United States Fish Commission* 17 (1897): 141–44. Washington, DC: GPO, 1898.

Alfred, Taiaiake. "Sovereignty." In *A Companion to American Indian History*, edited by Philip J. Deloria and Neal Salisbury, 460–74. Malden, MA: Blackwell , 2002.

Ambler, Marjane. *Breaking the Iron Bonds: Indian Control of Energy Development.* Lawrence: University Press of Kansas, 1990.

American Friends Service Committee. *Uncommon Controversy: Fishing Rights of the Muckleshoot, Puyallup, and Nisqually Indians.* Seattle: University of Washington Press, 1970.

Ames, Kenneth M., and Herbert D. G. Maschner. *Peoples of the Northwest Coast: Their Archaeology and Prehistory.* London: Thames and Hudson, 1999.

Anderson, Alexander Caulfield. "Notes on Indian Tribes of British North America and the North West Coast." *Historical Magazine*, March 1863, 73–81.

Anderson, Gary Clayton. *The Indian Southwest, 1580–1830: Ethnogenesis and Reinvention.* Norman: University of Oklahoma Press, 1999.

Anderson, M. Kat. "The Ozette Prairies of Olympic National Park: Their Former Indigenous Uses and Management." Port Angeles, WA: Olympic National Park, 2009.

Andrews, C. C., ed. *Official Opinions of the Attorneys General of the United States, Advising the President and Heads of Departments, in Relation to Their Official Duties, and*

Expounding the Constitution, Treaties with Foreign Governments and with Indian Tribes, and the Public Laws of the Country. Vol. 7. Washington, DC: Robert Farnham, 1856.

Angell, Joseph Kinnicut. *A Treatise on the Common Law, in Relation to Water Courses: Intended More Particularly as an Illustration of the Rights and Duties of the Owners and Occupants of Water Privileges: To Which Is Added an Appendix, Containing the Principal Adjudged Cases.* Boston: Wells and Lilly, 1824.

Anzaldúa, Gloria. *Borderlands: The New Mestiza=La Frontera* [in English and Spanish]. 2nd ed. San Francisco: Aunt Lute Books, 1999.

Archer, Christon I. "Cannibalism in the Early History of the Northwest Coast: Enduring Myths and Neglected Realities." *Canadian Historical Review* 61, no. 4 (1980): 453–79.

Arima, Eugene Y. *Between Ports Alberni and Renfrew: Notes on West Coast Peoples.* Hull, QC: Canadian Museum of Civilization, 1991.

———. *The West Coast People: The Nootka of Vancouver Island and Cape Flattery.* Victoria: British Columbia Provincial Museum, 1983.

Arima, Eugene Y., Edward Sapir, and Tyee Bob. *Family Origin Histories: The Whaling Indians: West Coast Legends and Stories, Part 11 of the Sapir-Thomas Nootka Texts* [Text in English and Nookta; abstract in French]. Gatineau, QC: Canadian Museum of Civilization, 2009.

Arnett, Chris. *The Terror of the Coast: Land Alienation and Colonial War on Vancouver Island and the Gulf Islands, 1849–1863.* Burnaby, BC: Talonbooks, 1999.

Arnold, David F. *The Fishermen's Frontier: People and Salmon in Southeast Alaska.* Seattle: University of Washington Press, 2008.

Arnold, Greig. Interview by author. Digital audio recording, October 14, 2008. MCRC.

Asher, Brad. *Beyond the Reservation: Indians, Settlers, and the Law in Washington Territory, 1853–1889.* Norman: University of Oklahoma Press, 1999.

Atleo, Eugene Richard. *Tsawalk: A Nuu-Chah-Nulth Worldview.* Vancouver: University of British Columbia Press, 2004.

Ayer, John Edwin. "George Bush, Voyageur." *Washington Historical Quarterly* 7, no. 1 (1916): 40–45.

Ayyar, A. V. Venkatarama. "Introduction: An Adventurous Madras Citizen: James Strange, 1753–1840." In *James Strange's Journal and Narrative of the Commercial Expedition from Bombay to the Northwest Coast of America*, 7–13. Fairfield, WA: Ye Galleon Press, 1982.

Babcock, John Pease, William A. Found, Miller Freeman, and Henry O'Malley. "Report of the International Fisheries Commission Appointed under the Northern Pacific Halibut Treaty." Report no. 1. Seattle: International Fisheries Commission, 1931.

Bagley, Clarence. *History of Seattle from the Earliest Settlement to the Present Time.* 3 vols. Chicago: S. J. Clarke, 1916.

Baird, Robin W. "Status Report on the Northern Fur Seal, *Callorhinus ursinus*, in Canada." Ottawa: Committee on the Status of Endangered Wildlife in Canada, 1996.

Balch, Hiram A. Papers (Coll. 90). Mystic Seaport Collections Research Center, Mystic, CT.

Bancroft, Hubert Howe. *History of Washington, Idaho and Montana, 1845–1889.* San Francisco: History Company, 1890.

Banner, Stuart. *How the Indians Lost Their Land: Law and Power on the Frontier.* Cambridge, MA: Belknap Press of Harvard University Press, 2005.

Barker, Joanne. *Sovereignty Matters: Locations of Contestation and Possibility in Indigenous Struggles for Self-Determination.* Lincoln: University of Nebraska Press, 2005.

Barman, Jean. *The West beyond the West: A History of British Columbia.* 3rd ed. Toronto: University of Toronto Press, 2007.

Barman, Jean, and Bruce McIntyre Watson. *Leaving Paradise: Indigenous Hawaiians in the Pacific Northwest, 1787–1898.* Honolulu: University of Hawai'i Press, 2006.

Barr, Juliana. *Peace Came in the Form of a Woman: Indians and Spaniards in the Texas Borderlands.* Chapel Hill: University of North Carolina Press, 2007.

Barry, J. Nielson. "Astorians Who Became Permanent Settlers." *Washington Historical Quarterly* 24, no. 4 (1933): 282–301.

Barsh, Russell Lawrence. "Food Security, Food Hegemony, and Charismatic Animals." In *Toward a Sustainable Whaling Regime,* edited by Robert L. Friedheim, 147–79. Seattle: University of Washington Press, 2001.

———. *The Washington Fishing Rights Controversy: An Economic Critique.* 2nd ed. Seattle: University of Washington, Graduate School of Business Administration, 1979.

Barton, Karen Samantha. "'Red Waters': Contesting Marine Space as Indian Place in the U.S. Pacific Northwest." PhD diss., University of Arizona, 2000.

Basso, Keith H. *Wisdom Sits in Places: Landscape and Language among the Western Apache.* Albuquerque: University of New Mexico Press, 1996.

Bauer, William J. *We Were All Like Migrant Workers Here: Work, Community, and Memory on California's Round Valley Reservation, 1850–1941.* Chapel Hill: University of North Carolina Press, 2009.

Bayley, C. A. "Early Life on Vancouver Island." 1878. Microfilm P-C 3. Bancroft Library, Berkeley, CA.

Beaglehole, J. C., ed. *The Journals of Captain James Cook on His Voyages of Discovery.* Rochester, NY: Boydell Press, 1999.

Beak Consultants and Patricia Bay Institute of Ocean Sciences. *An Examination of the Variability of Upwelling on the West Coast of Vancouver Island and Its Relationship to the Flushing of Alberni Inlet.* Sidney, BC: Institute of Ocean Sciences, Patricia Bay, 1979.

Beals, H. K. *Juan Pérez on the Northwest Coast: Six Documents of His Expedition in 1774.* Portland: Oregon Historical Society Press, 1989.

Beerman, Eric. "Manuel Quimper: Un Marino Limeño En Las Costa Oeste De Canadá." *Derroteros de la Mar del Sur* 4 ([n.d.]). http://derroteros.perucultural.org.pe/nume4.shtml.

Belcher, Edward. *Narrative of a Voyage Round the World: Performed in Her Majesty's Ship Sulphur during the Years 1836–1842: Including Details of the Naval Operations in China from Dec. 1840 to Nov. 1841.* London: H. Colburn, 1843.

Belich, James. *Replenishing the Earth: The Settler Revolution and the Rise of the Anglo-World, 1783–1939.* Oxford: Oxford University Press, 2009.

———. *The Victorian Interpretation of Racial Conflict: The Maori, the British, and the New Zealand Wars.* Kingston, ON: McGill-Queen's University Press, 1990.

Bell, Frederick Heward. *The Pacific Halibut: The Resource and the Fishery.* Anchorage: Alaska Northwest, 1981.

Bell, Frederick Heward, Henry A. Dunlop, and Norman L. Freeman. "Pacific Coast Halibut Landings 1888 to 1950 and Catch According to Area of Origin." Seattle: n.p., 1952.

Belyea, Barbara. "Amerindian Maps: The Explorer as Translator." *Journal of Historical Geography* 18, no. 3 (1992): 267–77.

———. "Inland Journeys, Native Maps." *Cartographica* 33, no. 2 (1996): 1–16.

Beresford, William. *A Voyage Round the World; but More Particularly to the North-West Coast of America: Performed in 1785, 1786, 1787, and 1788, in the King George and Queen Charlotte, Captains Portlock and Dixon.* 2nd ed. London: n.p., 1789.

Bergmann, Mathais D. "'We Should Lose Much by Their Absence': The Centrality of Chinookans and Kalapuyans to Life in Frontier Oregon." *Oregon Historical Quarterly* 109, no. 1 (2008): 34–59.

Bering Sea Tribunal of Arbitration (BSTA). *Bering Sea Arbitration Papers.* 5 vols. London: Harrison and Sons, 1890–98.

———. *Fur Seal Arbitration. Proceedings of the Tribunal of Arbitration, Convened at Paris, under the Treaty between the United States . . . and Great Britain, Concluded at Washington, February 29, 1892, for the Determination of Questions between the Two Governments Concerning the Jurisdictional Rights of the United States in the Waters of Bering Sea.* 16 vols. Washington, DC: GPO, 1895.

Berkhofer, Robert F. *The White Man's Indian: Images of the American Indian from Columbus to the Present.* New York: Alfred A. Knopf, 1978.

Berry, Helen, Amy Sewell, and Bob Van Wagenen. "Temporal Trends in the Areal Extent of Canopy-Forming Kelp Beds along the Strait of Juan de Fuca and Washington's Outer Coast." In 2001 *Puget Sound Research Conference.* Bellevue, WA: Puget Sound Action Team, 2002.

Binnema, Theodore. "The Case for Cross-National and Comparative History: The Northwestern Plains as Bioregion." In *Borderlands of the American and Canadian Wests: Essays on Regional History of the Forty-Ninth Parallel,* edited by Sterling Evans, 17–41. Lincoln: University of Nebraska Press, 2006.

Biographical Sheets. Hudson's Bay Company Archives (HBCA). http://www.gov.mb.ca/chc/archives/hbca/biographical/.

Blackhawk, Ned. "Recasting the Narrative of America: The Rewards and Challenges of Teaching American Indian History." *Journal of American History* 93 (2007): 1165–70.

———. *Violence over the Land: Indians and Empires in the Early American West.* Cambridge, MA: Harvard University Press, 2006.

Blee, Lisa. *Framing Chief Leschi: Narratives and the Politics of Historical Justice.* Chapel Hill: University of North Carolina Press, 2014.

Blow, Richard. "The Great American Whale Hunt." *Mother Jones,* September–October 1998.

Boalt, Fred L. "Indian Canoemen Outspeed Power Boats in Whaling on West Coast." *Muskogee Times Democrat,* September 29, 1915.

Boas, Franz. "Tsimshian Mythology (Based on Texts Recorded by Henry W. Tate)." *Thirty-First Annual Report of the Bureau of Ethnology for the Years 1909–1910* 31 (1916): 29–1037.

Bockstoce, John R. *Furs and Frontiers in the Far North: The Contest among Native and Foreign Nations for the Bering Strait Fur Trade.* New Haven: Yale University Press, 2009.

Boddy, Herbert R. N. "Enforcing Observance of Game Laws by the Indians." *Washington Sportsman*, April–May 1936.

Bolster, W. Jeffrey. *The Mortal Sea: Fishing the Atlantic in the Age of Sail.* Cambridge, MA: Belknap Press of Harvard University Press, 2012.

Bowechop, Janine. "Contemporary Makah Whaling." In *Coming to Shore*, edited by Marie Mauzé, Michael E. Harking, and Sergei Kan, 407–19. Lincoln: University of Nebraska Press, 2000.

Bowechop, Janine, and Maria Pascua, Interviewers for National Oceanic and Atmospheric Administration Oral Interviews. Digital audio recordings, 2008. MCRC.

Bower, George M. *Report of the Commissioner of Fisheries for the Fiscal Year 1912 and Special Papers.* Washington, DC: GPO, 1914.

Bowsfield, Hartwell, ed. *Fort Victoria Letters, 1846–1851.* Winnipeg, MB: Hudson's Bay Record Society, 1979.

Boxberger, Daniel L. "The Lummi Indians and the Canadian/American Pacific Salmon Treaty." *American Indian Quarterly* 12, no. 4 (1988): 299–311.

———. *To Fish in Common: The Ethnohistory of Lummi Indian Salmon Fishing.* Seattle: University of Washington Press, 1999.

Boyd, Robert T. *The Coming of the Spirit of Pestilence: Introduced Infectious Diseases and Population Decline among Northwest Coast Indians, 1774–1874.* Vancouver: University of British Columbia Press, 1999.

Brandenburg, E. C., ed. *Official Opinions of the Attorneys-General of the United States, Advising the President and Heads of Departments in Relation to Their Official Duties, and Expounding the Constitution, Treaties with Foreign Government and with Indian Tribes, and the Public Laws of the Country.* Vol. 21. Washington, DC: GPO, 1898.

Brandt, Karl. *Whale Oil: An Economic Analysis.* [Palo Alto, CA]: Stanford University Press, 1940.

Brantlinger, Patrick. *Rule of Darkness: British Literature and Imperialism, 1830–1914.* Ithaca, NY: Cornell University Press, 1988.

British Columbia Attorney General. Correspondence Inward, 1872–1910. Microfilm B09318-B09324. BCA.

Brooks, James F. *Captives and Cousins: Slavery, Kinship, and Community in the Southwest Borderlands.* Chapel Hill: University of North Carolina Press, 2002.

Brown, Jovana J. "Treaty Rights: Twenty Years after the Boldt Decision." *Wicazo Sa Review* 10, no. 2 (1994): 1–16.

Bryon, Charles. "Infections of the Skin and Its Appendages, Muscles, Bones, and Joints." In *Microbiology and Immunology On-Line*, edited by Richard Hunt. Columbia: Board of Trustees of the University of South Carolina, 2007. http://pathmicro.med.sc.edu /Infectious%20Disease/Skin%20Bone.htm.

Busch, Briton C. *The War against the Seals: A History of the North American Seal Fishery*. Kingston, ON: McGill-Queen's University Press, 1985.

Byrd, Jodi A. *The Transit of Empire: Indigenous Critiques of Colonialism*. Minneapolis: University of Minnesota Press, 2011.

"California: Further Extracts from Our Pacific Files." *New York Daily Times*, November 30, 1852.

Calloway, Colin G. *Our Hearts Fell to the Ground: Plains Indian Views of How the West Was Lost*. Boston: Bedford Books of St. Martin's Press, 1996.

Campa, Miguel de la. *A Journal of Explorations: Northward along the Coast from Monterey in the Year 1775*, edited by John Galvin. San Francisco: John Howell, 1964.

Canada. Department of Indian Affairs. *Annual Reports*. Ottawa: McLean, Roger, 1885–1901.

——. Department of Indian Affairs. West Coast Agency—Decision of Tribunal of Arbitration Concerning the Bering Sea Award. RG 10. BCA.

——. Department of Marine and Fisheries. Central Registry Records, 1895–1914. Microfilm B11064-B11147. BCA.

——. Department of Marine and Fisheries. Documents Relating to B.C., 1895–1914. Microfilm B11112. BCA.

Carter, Paul. *The Road to Botany Bay: An Essay in Spatial History*. London: Faber and Faber, 1987.

Castile, George Pierre. *Taking Charge: Native American Self-Determination and Federal Indian Policy, 1975–1993*. Tucson: University of Arizona Press, 2006.

Certeau, Michel de. *The Practice of Everyday Life*. Berkeley: University of California Press, 1984.

Chang, Kornel S. *Pacific Connections: The Making of the U.S.-Canadian Borderlands*. Berkeley: University of California Press, 2012.

Chaplin, Joyce E. *Round about the Earth: Circumnavigation from Magellan to Orbit*. New York: Simon and Schuster, 2012.

Cherny, Robert W. *American Politics in the Gilded Age, 1868–1900*. Wheeling, WV: Harlan Davidson, 1997.

Cheseboro, Samuel Z. "Looking Backwards." *Fishing Gazette* 88 (March 1924).

The Chinese Repository. Vol. 16. Canton: Printed for the Proprietors, 1847.

Chute, George Roger. Manuscript Collection. WSHS (MCRC photocopies from originals).

Claplanhoo, Ed. Interview by author. Digital audio recording. October 13, 2008. MCRC.

Claplanhoo-Martin, Mary Ann, and Charles "Pug" Claplanhoo. Interview by author. Digital audio recording, May 19, 2009. MCRC.

Clayton, Daniel W. *Islands of Truth: The Imperial Fashioning of Vancouver Island*. Vancouver: University of British Columbia Press, 2000.

Clifford, James. "Traditional Futures." In *Questions of Tradition*, edited by Mark Salber Phillips and Gordon Schochet, 152–68. Toronto: University of Toronto Press, 2004.

"A Closed Season on Halibut." *Pacific Fisherman* 14, no. 1 (1916): 11.

Coates, Ken S. "A Matter of Context: The Pacific Northwest in World History." In *Terra Pacifica: People and Place in the Northwest States and Western Canada*, edited by Paul W. Hirt, 109–33. Pullman: Washington State University Press, 1998.

Cobb, Daniel M. *Native Activism in Cold War America: The Struggle for Sovereignty*. Lawrence: University Press of Kansas, 2008.

Cobb, John N. *Pacific Salmon Fisheries*. Washington, DC: GPO, 1921.

Codere, Helen. "Fighting with Property: A Study of Kwakiutl Potlatching and Warfare, 1792–1930. With Tribal and Linguistic Map of Vancouver Island and Adjacent Territory." MA thesis, Columbia University, 1950.

———. "Kwakiutl: Traditional Culture." In *Northwest Coast*, edited by Wayne Suttles, 359–77. Vol. 7 of *The Handbook of North American Indians*. Washington, DC: Smithsonian Institution, 1990.

Cohen, Fay G. *Treaties on Trial: The Continuing Controversy over Northwest Indian Fishing Rights*. Seattle: University of Washington Press, 1986.

Cole, Douglas. *Captured Heritage: The Scramble for Northwest Coast Artifacts*. Norman: University of Oklahoma Press, 1985.

Collins, Cary C. "A Future with a Past: Hazel Pete, Cultural Identity, and the Federal Indian Education System." *Pacific Northwest Quarterly* 92, no. 1 (2000–2001): 15–28.

———. "Subsistence and Survival: The Makah Indian Reservation, 1855–1933." *Pacific Northwest Quarterly* 87, no. 4 (1996): 180–93.

Collins, Joseph William. "Report on the Fisheries of the Pacific Coast of the United States." In *Report of the Commissioner for 1888*, edited by US Commission of Fish and Fisheries, 3–269. Washington, DC: GPO, 1892.

Colonial Despatches: The Colonial Despatches of Vancouver Island and British Columbia, 1846–1871. Digital archive. http://bcgenesis.uvic.ca/index.htm.

Colson, Elizabeth. Collection. Typescript notes. MCRC.

———. *The Makah Indians: A Study of an Indian Tribe in Modern American Society*. Minneapolis: University of Minnesota Press, 1953.

Committee on Rosin Oil. *A Report on Rosin Oil*. Lowell, MA: S. J. Varney, 1852.

Cook, Warren L. *Flood Tide of Empire: Spain and the Pacific Northwest, 1543–1819*. New Haven: Yale University Press, 1973.

Coombes, Annie E., ed. *Rethinking Settler Colonialism: History and Memory in Australia, Canada, Aotearoa New Zealand and South Africa*. Manchester, UK: Manchester University Press, 2006.

Cooper Alarcón, Daniel. *The Aztec Palimpsest: Mexico in the Modern Imagination*. Tucson: University of Arizona Press, 1997.

Cordell, John. "Indigenous Peoples' Coastal Marine Domains: Some Matters of Cultural Documentation." In *Turning the Tide: Conference on Indigenous Peoples and Sea Rights*. Darwin, Australia: Faculty of Law, Northern Territory University, 1993.

———. *A Sea of Small Boats*. Cambridge, MA: Cultural Survival, 1989.

Corney, Peter, and William DeWitt Alexander. *Voyages in the Northern Pacific: Narrative of Several Trading Voyages from 1813 to 1818, between the Northwest Coast of America, the Hawaiian Islands and China, with a Description of the Russian Establishments on the Northwest Coast.* Honolulu: T. G. Thrum, 1896.

Cornwall, Claudia. "The Suicide Bomber of Clayoquot Sound, Revived." *Tyee*, March 14, 2008.

Costello, J. A. *Siwash: Their Life, Legends, and Tales.* Seattle: Calvert, 1895.

Coté, Charlotte June. "'It's Who We Are': Makah and Nuu-Chah-Nulth Whaling." PhD diss., University of California, Berkeley, 2002.

——. *Spirits of Our Whaling Ancestors: Revitalizing Makah and Nuu-Chah-Nulth Traditions.* Seattle: University of Washington Press, 2010.

Cox, Ross. *The Columbia River; or, Scenes and Adventures during a Residence of Six Years on the Western Side of the Rocky Mountains among Various Tribes of Indians Hitherto Unknown; Together with a Journey across the American Continent.* 2nd ed. London: H. Colburn and R. Bentley, 1832.

Crang, Mike. "Envisioning Urban Histories: Bristol as Palimpsest, Postcards, and Snapshots." *Environment and Planning A* 28, no. 3 (1996): 429–52.

Crockford, Susan J., S. Gay Frederick, and Rebecca J. Wigen. "The Cape Flattery Fur Seal; an Extinct Species of *Callorhinus* in the Eastern North Pacific?" *Canadian Journal of Archaeology/Journal Canadien d'Archéologie* 26 (2002): 152–74.

Cronon, William. *Nature's Metropolis: Chicago and the Great West.* New York: W. W. Norton, 1991.

Crosby, Alfred W. *The Columbian Exchange: Biological and Cultural Consequences of 1492.* Westport, CT: Greenwood, 1972.

——. *Ecological Imperialism: The Biological Expansion of Europe, 900–1900.* Cambridge: Cambridge University Press, 1986.

Cruikshank, Julie. *The Social Life of Stories: Narrative and Knowledge in the Yukon Territory.* Lincoln: University of Nebraska Press, 1998.

Crum, Steven J. "Henry Roe Cloud, a Winnebago Indian Reformer: His Quest for American Indian Education." *Kansas History* 11, no. 3 (1988): 171–84.

Culin, Stewart. "A Summer Trip among the Western Indians." *Bulletin [of the] Free Museum of Science and Art, Department of Archaeology, University of Pennsylvania* 3, no. 3 (1901): 143–75.

Cumings, Bruce. *Dominion from Sea to Sea: Pacific Ascendancy and American Power.* New Haven: Yale University Press, 2009.

Curtis, Edward S. *The Nootka. The Haida.* Volume 11 of *The North American Indian.* Edited by Frederick Webb Hodge. Cambridge, MA: Harvard University Press, 1916.

Cutter, Donald C., ed. *The California Coast: A Bilingual Edition of Documents from the Sutro Collection.* Norman: University of Oklahoma Press, 1969.

Darwin, L. H. "Annual Reports of the State Fish Commissioner to the Governor of the State of Washington, April 1, 1913, to March 31, 1915." Olympia, WA: Frank M. Lamborn, 1916.

Davidson, George. *Directory for the Pacific Coast of the United States: Reported to the Superintendent of the U. S Coast Survey.* [Washington, DC?]: n.p., 1862.

"The Deadly Embrace of a Devil-Fish." *New York Times*, January 19, 1878.

Deans, Jonathan R. "The Hudson's Bay Company and Its Use of Force, 1828–1829." *Oregon Historical Quarterly* 98, no. 3 (1997): 262–95.

Dedina, Serge. *Saving the Gray Whale: People, Politics, and Conservation in Baja California.* Tucson: University of Arizona Press, 2000.

Delâge, Denys. *Bitter Feast: Amerindians and Europeans in Northeast North America, 1600–1664.* Translated by Jane Brierley. Vancouver: University of British Columbia Press, 1993.

DeLay, Brian. *War of a Thousand Deserts: Indian Raids and the U.S.-Mexican War.* New Haven: Yale University Press, 2008.

Deloria, Philip J. *Indians in Unexpected Places.* Lawrence: University Press of Kansas, 2004.

Deloria, Vine. *We Talk, You Listen: New Tribes, New Turf.* New York: Macmillan, 1970.

Deloria, Vine, and Clifford M. Lytle. *The Nations Within: The Past and Future of American Indian Sovereignty.* Austin: University of Texas Press, 1998.

Dening, Greg. "Deep Times, Deep Spaces." In *Sea Changes: Historicizing the Ocean,* edited by Bernhard Klein and Gesa Mackenthun, 13–35. New York: Routledge, 2004.

———. "The Geographical Knowledge of the Polynesians and the Nature of Inter-Island Contact." In *Polynesian Navigation,* edited by Jack Golson, 102–53. Wellington, NZ: Polynesian Society, 1972.

———. *Islands and Beaches: Discourse on a Silent Land, Marquesas, 1774–1880.* Honolulu: University Press of Hawaii, 1980.

———. *Performances.* Chicago: University of Chicago Press, 1996.

Densmore, Frances. *Nootka and Quileute Music.* Washington, DC: GPO, 1939.

Dickey, George. *The Journal of Occurrences at Fort Nisqually: Commencing May 30, 1833; Ending September 27, 1859.* Tacoma, WA: Fort Nisqually Association, 1993.

Doig, Ivan. *Winter Brothers: A Season at the Edge of America.* New York: Harcourt Brace Jovanovich, 1980.

Dolin, Eric Jay. *Fur, Fortune, and Empire: The Epic History of the Fur Trade in America.* New York: W. W. Norton, 2010.

Donald, Leland. *Aboriginal Slavery on the Northwest Coast of North America.* Berkeley: University of California Press, 1997.

Dorsey, Kurkpatrick. *The Dawn of Conservation Diplomacy: U.S.-Canadian Wildlife Protection Treaties in the Progressive Era.* Seattle: University of Washington Press, 1998.

Drew, Charles S. *An Account of the Origin and Early Prosecution of the Indian War in Oregon.* Fairfield, WA: Ye Galleon Press, 1973.

Drucker, Philip. *Indians of the Northwest Coast.* New York: McGraw-Hill, 1955.

———. *The Northern and Central Nootkan Tribes.* Washington, DC: GPO, 1951.

Dunn, John. *History of the Oregon Territory and British North-American Fur Trade: With an Account of the Habits and Customs of the Principal Native Tribes on the Northern Continent.* London: Edwards and Hughes, 1844.

Duthu, N. Bruce. *American Indians and the Law.* New York: Viking, 2008.

DuVal, Kathleen. *The Native Ground: Indians and Colonists in the Heart of the Continent.* Philadelphia: University of Pennsylvania Press, 2006.

Duwors, Richard, ed. "Documents from the Indian Fishing Rights Controversy in the Pacific Northwest." *Pacific Northwest Quarterly* 99, no. 2 (2008): 55–65.

Dye, Eva Emery. "Earliest Expedition against the Puget Sound Indians." *Washington Historical Quarterly* 1, no. 2 (1907): 16–29.

Edwards, Kathleen A., and Parker MacCready. "The Strait of Juan de Fuca as Seen from Satellite." In *2001 Puget Sound Research Conference*. Bellevue, WA: Puget Sound Action Team, 2002.

Efrat, Barbara S., and W. J. Langlois. "The Contact Period as Recorded by Indian Oral Traditions." *Sound Heritage* 7, no. 1 (1978): 54–61.

Ellen, R. F., Peter Parkes, and Alan Bicker, eds. *Indigenous Environmental Knowledge and Its Transformations: Critical Anthropological Perspectives*. Amsterdam: Harwood Academic, 2000.

Ellingson, Ter. *Myth of the Noble Savage*. Berkeley: University of California Press, 2001.

Erikson, Patricia Pierce. *Voices of a Thousand People: The Makah Cultural and Research Center*. Lincoln: University of Nebraska Press, 2002.

Ernst, Alice Henson. *Wolf Ritual of the Northwest Coast*. 1952; reprint ed., Eugene: University of Oregon Press, 2001.

Espinosa y Tello, Josef. *A Spanish Voyage to Vancouver and the North-West Coast of America: Being the Narrative of the Voyage Made in the Year 1792 by the Schooners Sutil and Mexicana to Explore the Strait of Fuca*. London: Argonaut, 1930.

Evans, Sterling. *The Borderlands of the American and Canadian Wests: Essays on Regional History of the Forty-Ninth Parallel*. Lincoln: University of Nebraska Press, 2006.

Family Group Sheets. MCRC.

Favorite, F., and Northwest Fisheries Center. *The Ocean Environment*. Seattle: Northwest Fisheries Center, National Marine Fisheries Center, and National Oceanic and Atmospheric Administration, 1975.

Ferris, John. "SSTR as History: The British Royal Navy Experience, 1815–1930." In *Naval Peacekeeping and Humanitarian Operations: Stability from the Sea*, edited by Jeffrey A. Larsen and James J. Wirtz, 26–41. New York: Routledge, 2009.

Ficken, Robert E. "After the Treaties: Administering Pacific Northwest Indian Reservations." *Oregon Historical Quarterly* 106, no. 3 (2005): 442–61.

Findlay, John M., and Kenneth Coates. *Parallel Destinies: Canadian-American Relations West of the Rockies*. Seattle: University of Washington Press, 2002.

Finlayson, Roderick. *History of Vancouver Island and the Northwest Coast*. N.p., 1879.

Finney, Ben. "James Cook and the European Discovery of Polynesia." In *From Maps to Metaphors: The Pacific World of George Vancouver*, edited by Robin Fisher and Hugh Johnston, 19–34. Vancouver: University of British Columbia Press, 1993.

"Fish of the Pacific." *New York Times*, 7 June 1891.

Fisher, Andrew H. *Shadow Tribe: The Making of Columbia River Indian Identity*. Seattle: University of Washington Press, 2010.

Fisher, Robin. *Contact and Conflict: Indian-European Relations in British Columbia, 1774–1890*. 2nd ed. Vancouver: University of British Columbia Press, 1992.

Fisher, Robin, and J. M. Bumsted, eds. *An Account of a Voyage to the North West Coast of North America in 1785 and 1786 by Alexander Walker*. Vancouver: Douglas and McIntyre, 1982.

Fixico, Donald Lee. *The American Indian Mind in a Linear World: American Indian Studies and Traditional Knowledge*. New York: Routledge, 2003.

——. *Indian Resilience and Rebuilding: Indigenous Nations in the Modern American West*. Tucson: University of Arizona Press, 2013.

——. *The Invasion of Indian Country in the Twentieth Century: American Capitalism and Tribal Natural Resources*. Niwot: University Press of Colorado, 1998.

——. *Termination and Relocation: Federal Indian Policy, 1945–1960*. Albuquerque: University of New Mexico Press, 1986.

"Flattery Fishing Is Poor." *Pacific Fisherman* 4, no. 8 (1906): 22.

"Floating Cannery for Neah Bay." *Pacific Fisherman* 10, no. 5 (1912): 12.

Forbes, Jack D. *Apache, Navaho, and Spaniard*. 2nd ed. Norman: University of Oklahoma Press, 1994.

Foster, Morris W. *Being Comanche: A Social History of an American Indian Community*. Tucson: University of Arizona Press, 1991.

Franchère, Gabriel. *Narrative of a Voyage to the Northwest Coast of America in the Years 1811, 1812, 1813, and 1814; or, the First American Settlement of the Pacific*. Translated and edited by J. V. Huntington. New York: Redfield, 1854.

Fujikane, Candace, and Jonathan Y. Okamura, eds. *Asian Settler Colonialism: From Local Governance to the Habits of Everyday Life in Hawai'i*. Honolulu: University of Hawai'i Press, 2008.

Galbraith, John S. *The Hudson's Bay Company as an Imperial Factor, 1821–1869*. Berkeley: University of California Press, 1957.

Galois, Robert. "The Voyages of James Hanna to the Northwest Coast: Two Documents." *British Columbia Studies*, no. 103 (1994): 83–88.

——, ed. *A Voyage to the North West Side of America: The Journals of James Colnett, 1786–89*. Vancouver: University of British Columbia Press, 2004.

Gibbs, George. *Dictionary of the Chinook Jargon, or Indian Trade Language, Now in General Use on the Northwest Coast, Adapted for General Business*. Olympia, WA: T. G. Lowe, 1873.

——. *Indian Tribes of Washington Territory*. Fairfield, WA: Ye Galleon Press, 1972.

——. Notebooks of Scientific Observations of the Pacific Northwest, 1853–1858 (WA MSS S-1810). Beinecke Rare Book and Manuscript Library, Yale University, New Haven.

——. "Tribes of Western Washington and Northwestern Oregon." *Contributions to North American Ethnology* 1, no. 2 (1877): 157–361.

Gibson, Arrell Morgan. *Yankees in Paradise: The Pacific Basin Frontier*. Albuquerque: University of New Mexico Press, 1993.

Gibson, James R. "A Notable Absence: The Lateness and Lameness of Russian Discovery and Exploration in the North Pacific, 1693–1803." In *From Maps to Metaphors: The Pacific World of George Vancouver*, edited by Robin Fisher and Hugh Johnston, 85–103. Vancouver: University of British Columbia Press, 1993.

——. "The Maritime Trade of the North Pacific Coast." In *History of Indian-White Relations*, edited by Wilcomb E. Washburn, 375–90. Vol. 4 of *The Handbook of North American Indians*. Washington, DC: Smithsonian Institution, 1988.

———. *Otter Skins, Boston Ships, and China Goods: The Maritime Fur Trade of the North-west Coast, 1758–1841.* Seattle: University of Washington Press, 1992.

Giesecke, Eberhard W. "Search for the *Tonquin* (Part 2)." *Cumtux: Clatsop County His-torical Society Quarterly* 10, no. 4 (1990): 3–14.

Gilje, Paul A. *Liberty on the Waterfront: American Maritime Culture in the Age of Revolu-tion.* Philadelphia: University of Pennsylvania Press, 2004.

Gitlin, Jay. "Empires of Trade, Hinterlands of Settlement." In *The Oxford History of the American West,* edited by Clyde A. Milner, Carol A. O'Connor, and Martha A. Sand-weiss, 79–113. Oxford: Oxford University Press, 1994.

Goodman, Linda, and Helma Swan. *Singing the Songs of My Ancestors: The Life and Music of Helma Swan, Makah Elder.* Norman: University of Oklahoma Press, 2003.

Gordon, David, and Shepard Krech III. "Introduction: Indigenous Knowledge and the Environment." In *Indigenous Knowledge and the Environment in Africa and North Amer-ica,* edited by David Gordon and Shepard Krech III, 1–24. Athens: Ohion University Press, 2012.

Gormly, Mary. "Early Culture Contact on the Northwest Coast, 1774–1795: Analysis of Spanish Source Material." MA thesis, University of Idaho, 1959.

Gough, Barry M. *Gunboat Frontier: British Maritime Authority and Northwest Coast Indians, 1846–1890.* Vancouver: University of British Columbia Press, 1984.

———. *The Northwest Coast: British Navigation, Trade, and Discoveries to 1812.* Rev. ed. Vancouver: University of British Columbia Press, 1992.

Gough, Julie. "History, Representation, Globalisation and Indigenous Cultures: A Tasma-nian Perspective." In *Indigenous Cultures in an Interconnected World,* edited by Claire Smith and Graehme K. Ward, 89–107. Vancouver: University of British Columbia Press, 2000.

Grant, William Colquhoun. "Description of Vancouver Island." *Journal of the Royal Geo-graphic Society of London* 27 (1857): 268–320.

———. "Report on Vancouvers Island." October 25, 1849. BCA.

———. "Vancouver Island—Colonial Surveyor: Correspondence Outward, Original and Transcript." September 10, 1850. BCA.

Gray, Edward G. *The Making of John Ledyard: Empire and Ambition in the Life of an Early American Traveler.* New Haven: Yale University Press, 2007.

Great Britain. Colonial Office. Correspondence with Hudson's Bay Company Relating to Conveyance, Settlement, and Reconveyence of Vancouver Island. Vols. 1 and 2. Mi-crofilm B16916–B16917 (copied from originals in the Public Records Office, London [PRO series CO 134]).

Greene, Dan. Interview by author. Digital audio recording. October 19, 2010. MCRC.

Grinev, A. V. *The Tlingit Indians in Russian America, 1741–1867.* Lincoln: University of Nebraska Press, 2005.

"The Growth of the Halibut Industry of the Pacific Coast." *Pacific Fisherman* 3, no. 7 (1905): 16.

"Guide to the Crown Zellerbach Corporation Records, ca. 1876–1986." BANC MSS 88/215 cp. Bancroft Library, Berkeley, CA. http://www.oac.cdlib.org/findaid/ark:/13030/tf7z09n9mr/admin/.

"Guide to the James Gilchrist Swan Papers, 1833–1909." 2004. UWSC.

Guillod, Harry. Journal—September 1, 1881–1906. Microfilm A01000(6). BCA.

Gunther, Erna. Papers, 1871–1962. UWSC.

———. Papers, 1882–1981. UWSC.

———. Papers, 1887–1980. UWSC.

———. "Reminiscences of a Whaler's Wife." *Pacific Northwest Quarterly* 33 (1942): 65–69.

Gutiérrez, Ramón A. *When Jesus Came, the Corn Mothers Went Away: Marriage, Sexuality, and Power in New Mexico, 1500–1846.* Stanford, CA: Stanford University Press, 1991.

Gutthiudaschmitt, Lieff. "Makah Whale Hunt Scores Victory for Rights of Indigenous People." *The Militant*, June 28, 1999.

Hajda, Yvonne P. "Slavery in the Great Lower Columbia Region." *Ethnohistory* 52, no. 3 (2005): 563–88.

"Halibut Fishing." *Pacific Fisherman* 3, no. 7 (1905): 35–39.

Hämäläinen, Pekka. *The Comanche Empire.* New Haven: Yale University Press, 2008.

Hämäläinen, Pekka, and Samuel Truett. "On Borderlands." *Journal of American History* 98 (2011): 338–61.

Hammatt, Charles H., and Sandra Wagner-Wright. *Ships, Furs, and Sandalwood: A Yankee Trader in Hawai'i, 1823–1825.* Honolulu: University of Hawai'i Press, 1999.

Hammond, Edward K. "Lubrication of Cutting Tools—3." *Machinery* 23 (1917): 595–607.

Hancock, Samuel. *Thirteen Years Residence on the North-West Coast: Containing an Account of Travels and Adventures among the Indians, Their Manners and Customs, Their Treatment of Prisoners, and also a Description of the Country* (1860). Unpublished manuscript version. Hancock Papers. UWSC.

Hansen, Clark. "Indian Views of the Stevens-Palmer Treaties Today." *Oregon Historical Quarterly* 106, no. 3 (2005): 475–89.

Hardin, Garrett. "The Tragedy of the Commons." *Science* 162 (1968): 1243–48.

Harley, J. Brian. "Maps, Knowledge, and Power." In *The Iconography of Landscape*, edited by Denis Cosgrove and Stephen Daniels, 277–312. Cambridge: Cambridge University Press, 1988.

Harmon, Alexandra. *Indians in the Making: Ethnic Relations and Indian Identities.* Berkeley: University of California Press, 1998.

———. *The Power of Promises: Rethinking Indian Treaties in the Pacific Northwest.* Seattle: Center for the Study of the Pacific Northwest in association with University of Washington Press, 2008.

———. *Rich Indians: Native People and the Problem of Wealth in American History.* Chapel Hill: University of North Carolina Press, 2010.

Harrington, Faith. "Sea Tenure in Seventeenth Century New England: Native Americans and Englishmen in the Sphere of Marine Resources, 1600–1630." PhD diss., University of California, Berkeley, 1985.

Harris, Cole. *Making Native Space: Colonialism, Resistance, and Reserves in British Columbia*. Vancouver: University of British Columbia Press, 2002.

———. *The Resettlement of British Columbia: Essays on Colonialism and Geographical Change*. Vancouver: University of British Columbia Press, 1997.

Harris, Douglas C. *Fish, Law, and Colonialism: The Legal Capture of Salmon in British Columbia*. Toronto: University of Toronto Press, 2001.

———. *Landing Native Fisheries: Indian Reserves and Fishing Rights in British Columbia, 1849–1925*. Vancouver: University of British Columbia Press, 2008.

Harrod, Howard L. *The Animals Came Dancing: Native American Sacred Ecology and Animal Kinship*. Tucson: University of Arizona Press, 2000.

Hayes, Derek. *Historical Atlas of the Pacific Northwest: Maps of Exploration and Discovery: British Columbia, Washington, Oregon, Alaska, Yukon*. Seattle: Sasquatch Books, 1999.

Hays, Samuel P. *Conservation and the Gospel of Efficiency: The Progressive Conservation Movement, 1890–1920*. Cambridge, MA: Harvard University Press, 1959.

Heffer, Jean. *The United States and the Pacific: History of a Frontier*. Translated by W. Donald Wilson. Notre Dame, IN: University of Notre Dame Press, 2002.

Heizer, Robert, ed. *California*. Volume 8 of *The Handbook of North American Indians*, edited by William C. Sturtevant. Washington, DC: Smithsonian Institution, 1978.

Helm, June, ed. *Subarctic*. Volume 6 of *The Handbook of North American Indians*, edited by William C. Sturtevant. Washington, DC: Smithsonian Institution, 1981.

Hewes, Gordon Winant. "Indian Fisheries Productivity in Pre-Contact Times in the Pacific Salmon Area." *Northwest Anthropological Research Notes* 7, no. 2 (1973): 133–55.

Hezeta, Bruno de. *For Honor and Country: The Diary of Bruno De Hezeta*. Translated by Herbert K. Beals. Portland, OR: Western Imprints, 1985.

Hills, William. "Journal onboard H.M.S. *Portland* and H.M.S. *Virago*." 1852–1853. UBCL.

Hinckley, Thomas. "The Westward Movement and Historical Involvement of the Americas in the Pacific Basin; Conference Proceedings." Paper presented at the Conference on the Westward Movement and Historical Involvement of the Americas in the Pacific Basin, San Jose State College, CA, 1965.

Hogue, Michel. "Disputing the Medicine Line: The Plains Crees and the Canadian-American Border, 1876–1885." *Montana* 52 (Winter 2002): 2–17.

Home Miscellaneous Series, ca. 1600 to ca. 1900, India Office Records, British Library, London.

Hosmer, Brian C. *American Indians in the Marketplace: Persistence and Innovation among the Menominees and Metlakatlans, 1870–1920*. Lawrence: University Press of Kansas, 1999.

Hosmer, Brian C., and Colleen M. O'Neill. *Native Pathways: American Indian Culture and Economic Development in the Twentieth Century*. Boulder: University Press of Colorado, 2004.

Howay, Frederic William. "Brig *Owhyhee* in the Columbia, 1827." *Oregon Historical Quarterly* 34, no. 4 (1933): 324–29.

——. "An Early Account of the Loss of the *Boston* in 1803." *Washington Historical Quarterly* 17, no. 4 (1926): 280–88.

——. "Four Letters from Richard Cadman Etches to Sir Joseph Banks, 1788–92." *British Columbia Historical Quarterly* 6, no. 2 (1942): 125–39.

——. "Indian Attacks upon the Maritime Traders of the North-West Coast, 1785–1805." *Canadian Historical Review* 6 (1925): 287–309.

——. *A List of Trading Vessels in Maritime Fur Trade, 1785–1825*. Ottawa: Royal Society of Canada, 1930.

——. "The Loss of the *Tonquin*." *Washington Historical Quarterly* 13, no. 2 (1922): 83–92.

——. *An Outline Sketch of the Maritime Fur Trade*. Ottawa: F. A. Acland, 1932.

——. "The Voyage of the *Hope*, 1790–1792." *Washington Historical Quarterly* 11, no. 1 (1920): 3–28.

——, ed. *Voyages of the Columbia to the Northwest Coast, 1787–1790 and 1790–1793*. 2nd ed. Portland: Oregon Historical Society Press, 1990.

——. "A Yankee Trader on the Northwest Coast, 1791–1795." *Washington Historical Quarterly* 21, no. 2 (1930): 83–94.

Hoxie, Frederick E. "Crow Leadership amidst Reservation Oppression." In *State and Reservation: New Perspectives on Federal Indian Policy*, edited by George Pierre Castile and Robert L. Bee, 38–60. Tucson: University of Arizona Press, 1992.

——. *A Final Promise: The Campaign to Assimilate the Indians, 1880–1920*. Cambridge: Cambridge University Press, 1984.

——. "Retrieving the Red Continent: Settler Colonialism and the History of American Indians in the U.S." *Ethnic and Racial Studies* 31, no. 6 (2008): 1153–67.

Hudson, Angela Pulley. *Creek Paths and Federal Roads: Indians, Settlers, and Slaves and the Making of the American South*. Chapel Hill: University of North Carolina Press, 2010.

Huelsbeck, David R. "Whaling in the Precontact Economy of the Central Northwest Coast." *Arctic Anthropology* 25, no. 1 (1988): 1–15.

"Huge Fishing Fleet at Neah Bay." *Pacific Fisherman* 10, no. 8 (1912): 12.

Hult, Ruby El. Papers, 1910–2003. UWSC.

——. "The Saga of George W. Bush." *Negro Digest*, September 1962, 88–96.

Huntington, Charles A. *Memoir, 1899*. Beinecke Rare Book and Manuscript Library, Yale University, New Haven.

Hyde, Anne Farrar. *Empires, Nations, and Families: A History of the North American West, 1800–1860*. Lincoln: University of Nebraska Press, 2011.

Igler, David. "Captive-Taking and Conventions of Encounters on the Northwest Coast, 1789–1810." *Southern California Quarterly* 91, no. 1 (2009): 3–25.

——. "Diseased Goods: Global Exchanges in the Eastern Pacific Basin, 1770–1850." *American Historical Review* 109, no. 3 (2004): 693–719.

——. *The Great Ocean: Pacific Worlds from Captain Cook to the Gold Rush*. Oxford: Oxford University Press, 2013.

"An Indian Potlatch: When a Northwestern Savage Sets It Up for Glory That's a Potlatch." *Logansport Journal*, August 15, 1893.

"The Indians." *New York Daily Times*, October 14, 1852.

Inglis, Richard I., and James C. Haggarty. "Cook to Jewitt: Three Decades of Change in Nootka Sound." In *"Le Castor Fait Tout": Selected Papers of the Fur Trade Conference, 1985*, edited by Bruce G. Trigger, Toby Morantz, and Louise Dechêne, 193–222. [Montreal]: Lake St. Louis Historical Society, 1985.

International Pacific Halibut Commission (IPHC). "The Pacific Halibut: Biology, Fishery, and Management." Technical Report No. 16. Seattle: IPHC, 1978.

Irvine, Albert, and Luke Markistun. *How the Makah Obtained Possession of Cape Flattery*. New York: Museum of the American Indian, 1921.

Irving, Hillary "Zab." Interview by Dave Huelsbeck and Barbara Schmieden. Transcript. November 23, 1982. MCRC.

Irving, Washington. *Astoria; or, Enterprise beyond the Rocky Mountains*. London: Richard Bentley, 1836.

———. *The Rocky Mountains; or, Scenes, Incidents, and Adventures in the Far West*. 2 vols. Philadelphia: Carey, Lea, and Blanchard, 1837.

Iverson, Peter. *We Are Still Here: American Indians in the Twentieth Century*. Wheeling, WV: Harlan Davidson, 1998.

Jack Metcalf, et al. v. William Daley, et al. 214 F.3d 1135 (2000).

Jackson, S. E. "The Water Is Not Empty: Cross-Cultural Issues in Conceptualising Sea Space." *Australian Geographer* 26, no. 1 (1995): 87–96.

Jacobsen, William H., Jr. *First Lessons in Makah*. Rev. ed. Neah Bay, WA: Makah Cultural and Research Center, 1999.

———. "Wakashan Comparative Studies." In *Languages of Native America: Historical and Comparative Assessment*, edited by Lyle Campbell and Marianne Mithun, 766–91. Austin: University of Texas Press, 1979.

Jenkins, David. "Atlantic Salmon, Endangered Species, and the Failure of Environmental Policies." *Comparative Studies in Society and History* 45 (2003): 843–72.

Jenkins, J. T. *A History of the Whale Fisheries, from the Basque Fisheries of the Tenth Century to the Hunting of the Finner Whale at the Present Date*. London: H. F. and G. Witherby, 1921.

Jewitt, John R. *Adventures and Sufferings of John R. Jewitt, Only Survivor of the Ship Boston, during a Captivity of Nearly Three Years among the Savages of Nootka Sound; with an Account of the Manners, Mode of Living, and Religious Opinions of the Natives*. Edinburgh: Archibald Constable, 1824.

———. *The Adventures and Sufferings of John R. Jewitt: Captive of Maquinna*. Annotated by Hilary Stewart. Seattle: University of Washington Press, 1987.

———. *A Journal, Kept at Nootka Sound, . . . One of the Surviving Crew of the Ship Boston, of Boston, John Salter, Commander, Who Was Massacred on the 22nd of March, 1803; Interspersed with Some Account of the Natives, Their Manners and Customs*. Boston: n.p., 1807.

———. *A Narrative of the Adventures and Sufferings, of John R. Jewitt: Only Survivor of the Crew of the Ship Boston, during a Captivity of Nearly Three Years among the Savages of Nootka Sound: With an Account of the Manners, Mode of Living, and Religious Opinions of the Natives*. Middletown: Loomis and Richards, 1815.

Johnson, Barbara, and Frank Langdon. "Two Hundred Mile Zones: The Politics of North Pacific Fisheries." *Pacific Affairs* 49, no. 1 (1976): 5–27.

Johnson, Dale. Interview by author. Digital audio recording. May 18, 2009. MCRC.

Johnson, Donald D. *The United States in the Pacific: Private Interests and Public Policies, 1784–1899.* Westport, CT: Praeger, 1995.

Jonaitis, Aldona, and Richard Inglis. *The Yuquot Whalers' Shrine.* Seattle: University of Washington Press, 1999.

Jones, Robert Francis, ed. *Annals of Astoria: The Headquarters Log of the Pacific Fur Company on the Columbia River, 1811–1813.* New York: Fordham University Press, 1999.

———. "The Identity of the Tonquin's Interpreter." *Oregon Historical Quarterly* 98, no. 3 (Fall 1997): 296–314.

Jordan, David Starr. *The Fur Seals and Fur-Seal Islands of the North Pacific Ocean.* 4 vols. Washington, DC: GPO, 1898.

Kalland, Arne, and Brian Moeran. *Japanese Whaling: End of an Era?* London: Curzon, 1992.

Kane, Paul. *Wanderings of an Artist among the Indians of North America: From Canada to Vancouver's Island and Oregon through the Hudson's Bay Company's Territory and Back Again.* London: Longman, Brown, Green, Longmans, and Roberts, 1859.

Kappler, Charles J., ed. *Indian Treaties, 1778–1883.* New York: Interland, 1972.

Katz, William A., ed. *Almost Out of the World: Scenes from Washington Territory.* Tacoma: Washington State Historical Society, 1971.

Kelez, George B. "The Troll Fishery." In *The Salmon and Salmon Fisheries of Swiftsure Bank, Puget Sound, and the Fraser River,* edited by George A. Rounsefell and George B. Kelez, 749–53. Washington, DC: GPO, 1938.

Kellogg, George Albert. *A History of Whidbey's Island (Whidbey Island) State of Washington.* Oak Harbor, WA: G. B. Astel, 1934.

Kendrick, John, ed. *The Voyage of Sutil and Mexicana, 1792: The Last Spanish Exploration of the Northwest Coast of America.* Spokane, WA: Arthur H. Clark, 1991.

Kennedy v. Becker. 241 U.S. 556 (1916).

Kenyon, Susan Mary. *The Kyuquot Way: A Study of a West Coast (Nootkan) Community.* Ottawa: National Museums of Canada, 1980.

Kershaw, Sarah. "In Petition to Government, Tribe Hopes for Return to Whaling Past." *New York Times,* September 19, 2005.

Kirk, Ruth. *Tradition and Change on the Northwest Coast: The Makah, Nuu-Chah-Nulth, Southern Kwakiutl and Nuxalk.* Seattle: University of Washington Press, 1986.

Kirk, Ruth, and Richard D. Daugherty. *Hunters of the Whale: An Adventure in Northwest Coast Archaeology.* New York: William Morrow, 1974.

Klingle, Matthew W. *Emerald City: An Environmental History of Seattle.* New Haven: Yale University Press, 2007.

Knight, Rolf. *Indians at Work: An Informal History of Native Labour in British Columbia, 1848–1930.* Vancouver: New Star Books, 1996.

Koppert, Vincent Aloysius. "Contributions to Clayoquot Ethnology." PhD diss., Catholic University of America, 1930.

Koppes, Clayton R. "Efficiency/Equity/Esthestics: Towards a Reinterpretation of American Conservation." *Environmental Review* 11, no. 2 (1987): 127–46.

Kosek, Jake. *Understories: The Political Life of Forests in Northern New Mexico*. Durham, NC: Duke University Press, 2006.

Kovarick, Bill. "The Whale Oil Myth." *The Source*, Fall 2008, http://sustainablehistory. wordpress.com/bioenergy/the-whale-oil-myth/.

Krech III, Shepard. *The Ecological Indian: Myth and History*. New York: W. W. Norton, 1999.

Kugel, Rebecca. *To Be the Main Leaders of Our People: A History of Minnesota Ojibwe Politics, 1825–1898*. East Lansing: Michigan State University Press, 1998.

Kupperman, Karen Ordahl. *Indians and English: Facing Off in Early America*. Ithaca, NY: Cornell University Press, 2000.

LaDow, Beth. *The Medicine Line: Life and Death on a North American Borderland*. New York: Routledge, 2001.

LaGrand, James B. *Indian Metropolis: Native Americans in Chicago, 1945–75*. Urbana: University of Illinois Press, 2002.

Lamb, W. Kaye, and Tomás Bartroli. "The Founding of Fort Victoria." *British Columbia Historical Quarterly* 7, no. 2 (1943): 71–92.

———. "Four Letters Relating to the Cruise of the *Thetis*, 1852–1853." *British Columbia Historical Quarterly* 6, no. 3 (1942): 189–206.

———. "James Hanna and John Henry Cox: The First Maritime Fur Trader and His Sponsor." *British Columbia Studies* 84 (Winter 1989–1990): 3–36.

———. "The Mystery of Mrs. Barkley's Diary: Notes on the Voyage of the 'Imperial Eagle,' 1786–87." *British Columbia Historical Quarterly* 6, no. 1 (1942): 31–47.

Lane, Barbara. "Makah Economy circa 1855 and the Makah Treaty—A Cultural Analysis" [1972]. MTC Collection, MCRC.

———. "Political and Economic Aspects of Indian-White Culture Contact in Western Washington in the Mid-Nineteenth Century." May 10, 1973. Washington State Library, Olympia.

La Pérouse, Jean-François de Galaup. *A Voyage Round the World, in the Years 1785, 1786, 1787, and 1788*. 3 vols. London: J. Johnson, 1799.

Latourette, Kenneth Scott. *Voyages of American Ships to China, 1784–1844*. New Haven: Connecticut Academy of Arts and Sciences, 1927.

Laut, Agnes C. "Who Wants a Whale Steak? The Exciting Enterprise of Catching a Whale." *Mentor*, September 1928, 33–35.

Lawson, James S. Autobiography. 1879. National Oceanic and Atmospheric Administration Central Library, Silver Spring, MD. http://www.history.noaa.gov/stories_tales/jlawson .html.

Lefebvre, Henri. *The Production of Space*. Translated by Donald Nicholson-Smith. Malden, MA: Blackwell, 1974.

Lewis, David Rich. *Neither Wolf nor Dog: American Indians, Environment, and Agrarian Change*. New York: Oxford University Press, 1994.

Lewis, Lucien M. "The Whale Hunters of Neah Bay: How on Occasion the Makah Indians Paddle out to Sea in Their Dugout Canoes and Kill 'Chit-up-Puk.'" *Field and Stream*, April 1906, 1223–27 [clipping available at BCA].

Lichatowich, Jim. *Salmon without Rivers: A History of the Pacific Salmon Crisis*. Washington, DC: Island Press, 1999.

Limerick, Patricia Nelson. *The Legacy of Conquest: The Unbroken Past of the American West*. New York: W. W. Norton, 1987.

Linton, Jamie. *What Is Water? The History of a Modern Abstraction*. Vancouver: University of British Columbia Press, 2010.

Lipman, Andrew. "'A Meanes to Knitt Them Togeather': The Exchange of Body Parts in the Pequot War." *William and Mary Quarterly*, 3rd ser., 65 (2008): 3–28.

Lohbrunner, Max. "Reminiscences of B.C. Sealing Industry." Interview by Imbert Orchard. Audiocassette. 1967. BCA.

Longstaff, F. V., and W. Kaye Lamb. "The Royal Navy on the Northwest Coast, 1813–1850, Part II." *British Columbia Historical Quarterly* 9, no. 2 (1945): 113–28.

Lovisek, Joan A. "Aboriginal Warfare on the Northwest Coast: Did the Potlatch Replace Warfare?" In *North American Indigenous Warfare and Ritual Violence*, edited by Richard J. Chacon and Rubén G. Mendoza, 58–73. Tucson: University of Arizona Press, 2007.

Lutz, John S. "First Contact as Spiritual Performance: Encounters on the North American West Coast." In *Myth and Memory: Stories of Indigenous-European Contact*, edited by John Lutz, 30–45. Seattle: University of Washington Press, 2008.

———. "Making 'Indians' in British Columbia." In *Power and Place in the North American West*, edited by Richard White and John M. Findlay, 61–84. Seattle: University of Washington Press, 1999.

———. *Makúk: A New History of Aboriginal-White Relations*. Vancouver: University of British Columbia Press, 2008.

———, ed. *Myth and Memory: Stories of Indigenous-European Contact*. Vancouver: University of British Columbia Press, 2008.

MacFadyen, Amy, Barbara Hickey, and William Cochlan. "Influences of the Juan de Fuca Eddy on Circulation, Nutrients, and Phytoplankton Production in the Northern California Current System." *Journal of Geophysical Research* 113 (2008): C08008.

Mackie, Richard. *Trading beyond the Mountains: The British Fur Trade on the Pacific, 1793–1843*. Vancouver: University of British Columbia Press, 1997.

Maclachlan, Morag, and Wayne Suttles. *The Fort Langley Journals, 1827–30*. Vancouver: University of British Columbia Press, 1998.

Makah Indian Tribe v. Schoettler, Director of the Department of Fisheries. 192 F.2d 244 (1951).

Makah Indian Tribe v. The United States of America. 7 Ind. Cl. Com. 477 (1959).

Makah Tribal Council and Makah Whaling Commission. *Makah Nation: A Whaling People*. VHS. Neah Bay, WA: Makah Tribe, 2002. http://access.nwifc.org/newsinfo/streaming.asp.

Makah Tribe. *Constitution and Bylaws of the Makah Indian Tribe of the Makah Indian Reservation, Washington.* Washington, DC: GPO, 1936.

——. Department of Fisheries (M043). MCRC.

——. Makah Tribal Council Collection (M010). MCRC.

——. Makah Tribal Council Records. RG MAK. NARA-PNR.

Malick Family. Papers, 1848–1869 (WA MSS S-1298). Beinecke Rare Book and Manuscript Library, Yale University, New Haven.

Manis, Jim. *State of the Union Addresses by United States Presidents.* Hazleton: Pennsylvania State University-Hazleton, 2003. http://www2.hn.psu.edu/faculty/jmanis/uspressu.htm.

Mapes, Lynda. "Celebrating the Whale—Native Peoples from All Over Share Makah Potlatch," *Seattle Times*, May 23, 1999.

Marino, Cesare. "History of Western Washington since 1846." In *Northwest Coast*, edited by Wayne Suttles, 169–79. Vol. 7 of *The Handbook of North American Indians*. Washington, DC: Smithsonian Institute, 1990.

Marker, Michael. "After the Makah Whale Hunt: Indigenous Knowledge and Limits to Multicultural Discourse." *Urban Education* 41, no. 5 (2006): 482–505.

Martello, Marybeth Long. "Negotiating Global Nature and Local Culture: The Case of Makah Whaling." In *Earthly Politics: Local and Global in Environmental Governance*, edited by Sheila Jasanoff and Maybeth Long Martello, 263–84. Cambridge, MA: MIT Press, 2004.

Martin, Paul J., and Peggy Brady. *Port Angeles, Washington: A History.* Port Angeles, WA: Peninsula, 1983.

Mathes, Valerie L. "Wickaninnish, a Vancouver Island Chieftain: His Life as Told by Foreign Visitors." MA thesis, University of New Mexico, 1965.

McCarty, John. Interview by author. Digital audio recording. May 19, 2009. MCRC.

McCauley v. Makah. 128 F.2d 867 (1942).

McCrady, David G. *Living with Strangers: The Nineteenth-Century Sioux and the Canadian-American Borderlands.* Lincoln: University of Nebraska Press, 2006.

McDonald, Lucile. *Swan among the Indians: Life of James G. Swan, 1818–1900.* Portland, OR: Binfords Mort, 1972.

McEvoy, Arthur F. *The Fisherman's Problem: Ecology and Law in the California Fisheries, 1850–1980.* Cambridge: Cambridge University Press, 1986.

McHalsie, Albert (Sonny), David M. Schaepe, and Keith Thor Carlson. "Making the World Right through Transformations." In *A Stó:lō Coast Salish Historical Atlas*, edited by Keith Thor Carlson and Albert (Sonny) McHalsie, 6–7. Vancouver: Douglas and McIntyre, 2001.

McLoughlin, John. *Letters of Dr. John Mcloughlin, Written at Fort Vancouver, 1829–1832.* Edited by Burt Brown Barker. Portland, OR: Binfords and Mort, 1948.

McManus, Phil. "Writing the Palimpsest, Again; Rozelle Bay and the Sydney 2000 Olympic Games." *Urban Policy and Research* 22, no. 2 (2004): 157–67.

McManus, Sheila. *The Line which Separates: Race, Gender, and the Making of the Alberta-Montana Borderlands.* Lincoln: University of Nebraska Press, 2005.

McMillan, Alan D. *Since the Time of the Transformers: The Ancient Heritage of the Nuu-Chah-Nulth, Ditidaht, and Makah.* Vancouver: University of British Columbia Press, 1999.

Meany, Edmond Stephen. *History of the State of Washington.* New York: Macmillan, 1909.

Meares, John. *Voyages Made in the Years 1788 and 1789 from China to the North-West Coast of America.* Amsterdam: Da Capo, 1967.

Meeker, Ezra. *Pioneer Reminiscences of Puget Sound: The Tragedy of Leschi.* Seattle: Lowman and Hanford, 1905.

Menzies, Archibald, and C. F. Newcombe. *Menzies' Journal of Vancouver's Voyage, April to October, 1792.* Victoria: Archives of British Columbia, 1923.

Merrell, James Hart. *The Indians' New World: Catawbas and Their Neighbors from European Contact through the Era of Removal.* Chapel Hill: University of North Carolina Press, 1989.

"Mild Curing at Neah Bay." *Pacific Fisherman* 10, no. 8 (1912): 22.

Miles, Charles. *Michael T. Simmons.* [Seattle]: V. E. Bower, 1980.

Miles, George A. *James Swan, Cha-Tic of the Northwest Coast: Drawings and Watercolors from the Franz and Kathryn Stenzel Collection of Western American Art.* New Haven: Yale University Press, 2003.

Miller, Bruce G., and Daniel L. Boxberger. "Creating Chiefdoms: The Puget Sound Case." *Ethnohistory* 41, no. 2 (1994): 267–93.

Miller, David O. "Ka'iana, the Once Famous 'Prince of Kauai.'" *Hawaiian Journal of History* 22 (1988): 1–19.

Miller, Robert J. "Exercising Cultural Self-Determination: The Makah Indian Tribe Goes Whaling." *American Indian Law Review* 25, no. 2 (2002): 165–273.

———. "Tribal Cultural Self-Determination and the Makah Whaling Culture." In *Sovereignty Matters: Locations of Contestation and Possibility in Indigenous Struggles for Self-Determination,* edited by Joanne Barker, 123–51. Lincoln: University of Nebraska Press, 2005.

Milner, Clyde A. "National Initiatives." In *Oxford History of the American West,* edited by Clyde A. Milner, Carol A. O'Connor, and Martha A. Sandweiss, 155–93. Oxford: Oxford University Press, 1994.

Minugh, Carol J., Glenn T. Morris, and Rudolph C. Ryser, eds. *Indian Self-Governance: Perspectives on the Political Status of Indian Nations in the United States of America.* Kenmore, WA: Center for World Indigenous Studies, 1989.

"Miscellaneous Information Relating to Walter Colquhoun Grant." BCA.

Montgomery, David R. *King of Fish: The Thousand-Year Run of Salmon.* Boulder, CO: Westview, 2003.

Moore, Turrell Adcock. "The Emergence of Ethnic Roles and the Beginning of Nootkan Native-Overseas European Relations, 1774–1789." PhD diss., University of Oregon, 1977.

Morgan, Murray Cromwell. *The Last Wilderness.* New York: Viking, 1955.

Morse, Samuel G., and Carolyn Marr. *Portrait in Time: Photographs of the Makah by Samuel G. Morse, 1896–1903.* Neah Bay, WA: Makah Cultural and Research Center, 1987.

Moulton, Gary E., ed. *The Journals of the Lewis and Clark Expedition.* Lincoln: University of Nebraska Press/University of Nebraska-Lincoln Libraries-Electronic Text Center, 2005. http://lewisandclarkjournals.unl.edu/index.html.

Mowachaht/Muchalaht First Nation. "Contacts." http://www.yuquot.ca/contacts.html.

Moziño, José Mariano. *Noticias de Nutka: An Account of Nootka Sound in 1792.* Translated by Iris Higbie Wilson. Seattle: University of Washington Press, 1970.

Mulier, Vincent. "Recognizing the Full Scope of the Right to Take Fish under the Stevens Treaties: The History of Fishing Rights Litigation in the Pacific Northwest." *American Indian Law Review* 31, no. 1 (2006–2007): 41–92.

Murray, Peter. *The Vagabond Fleet: A Chronicle of the North Pacific Sealing Schooner Trade.* Victoria, BC: Sono Nis Press, 1988.

Nabokov, Peter. *A Forest of Time: American Indian Ways of History.* Cambridge: Cambridge University Press, 2002.

Narayan, Uma. *Dislocating Cultures: Identities, Traditions, and Third-World Feminism.* New York: Routledge, 1997.

The Naval Chronicle. Vol. 30. London: J. Gold, 1813.

Newcombe Family. Papers, 1870–1955. BCA.

Newell, Dianne. *Tangled Webs of History: Indians and the Law in Canada's Pacific Coast Fisheries.* Toronto: University of Toronto Press, 1993.

"New Gorman Cannery." *Pacific Fisherman* 10, no. 5 (1912): 12.

"News Items from the Fisheries Districts." *Pacific Fisherman* 8, no. 1 (1910): 19.

"News Items from the Fisheries Districts: Puget Sound." *Pacific Fisherman* 9, no. 5 (1911): 17.

Nietschmann, Bernard. "Traditional Sea Territories, Resources and Rights in Torres Strait." In *A Sea of Small Boats,* edited by John Cordell, 60–93. Cambridge, MA: Cultural Survival, 1989.

Nirenberg, David. *Communities of Violence: Persecution of Minorities in the Middle Ages.* Princeton, NJ: Princeton University Press, 1996.

Nokes, J. Richard. *Almost a Hero: The Voyages of John Meares, R.N., to China, Hawaii, and the Northwest Coast.* Pullman: Washington State University Press, 1998.

"North Pacific Fisheries: Fresh Salmon and Halibut Now Sent to the East." *New York Times,* December 1, 1891.

Northwest Indian Fisheries Commission. *Treaty Fishing Rights and the Northwest Indian Fisheries Commission.* Olympia, WA: [Northwest Indian Fisheries] Commission, 1980.

Nugent, Walter T. K. *Habits of Empire: A History of American Expansion.* New York: Alfred A. Knopf, 2008.

O'Brien, Sharon. *American Indian Tribal Governments.* Norman: University of Oklahoma Press, 1989.

O'Hara, Glen. *Britain and the Sea.* Basingstoke, UK: Palgrave Macmillan, 2010.

O'Neill, Colleen M. "Rethinking Modernity and the Discourse of Development in American Indian History, an Introduction." In *Native Pathways: American Indian Culture and Economic Development in the Twentieth Century,* edited by Brian C. Hosmer and Colleen O'Neill, 1–24. Boulder: University Press of Colorado, 2004.

———. *Working the Navajo Way: Labor and Culture in the Twentieth Century.* Lawrence: University Press of Kansas, 2005.

Oetelaar, Gerald A., and David Meyer. "Movement and Native American Landscapes: A Comparative Approach." *Plains Anthropologist* 51, no. 199 (2006): 355–74.

"Old Indian Goes into Halibut Business." *Pacific Fisherman* 4, no. 6 (1905): 16.

"Oregon." *New York Daily Times* April 28, 1852.

Ormsby, Margaret A. "Introduction." In *Fort Victoria Letters, 1846–1851,* edited by Hartwell Bowsfield, xi–xcix. Winnipeg, MB: Hudson's Bay Record Society, 1979.

Ostler, Jeffrey. *The Plains Sioux and U.S. Colonialism from Lewis and Clark to Wounded Knee.* Cambridge: Cambridge University Press, 2004.

"Our Fisheries." *Puget Sound Argus,* August 1, 1878.

Owens, Kenneth N., and Alton S. Donnelly, eds. *The Wreck of the Sv. Nikolai: Two Narratives of the First Russian Expedition to the Oregon Country, 1808–1810.* Portland, OR: Western Imprints, 1985.

Pascua, Maria. Interview by author. Digital audio recording. October 13, 2008. MCRC.

———. Interview by author. Digital audio recording. May 18, 2009. MCRC.

Paterson, D. G. "The North Pacific Seal Hunt, 1886–1910: Rights and Regulations." *Explorations in Economic History* 14, no. 2 (1977): 97–119.

Pavlik, Robert C. "Shore Whaling at San Simeon Bay." *Sea Letters* [San Francisco Maritime National Park Association], Fall–Winter 1990.

Pearce, Roy Harvey. *Savagism and Civilization: A Study of the Indian and the American Mind.* 1953; reprint ed., Berkeley: University of California Press, 1988.

Pennington, William D. "Government Policy and Indian Farming on the Cheyenne and Arapaho Reservation: 1869–1880." *Chronicles of Oklahoma* 57, no. 2 (1979): 171–89.

Pethick, Derek. *Victoria: The Fort.* Vancouver: Mitchell Press, 1968.

Petrie, Hazel. *Chiefs of Industry: Maori Tribal Enterprise in Early Colonial New Zealand.* Auckland, NZ: Auckland University Press, 2007.

Pierce, Frank. *Laws of Washington; a Publication of the Session Laws of Washington Territory, Including the General Laws and Resolutions of the Years 1854 to 1888 Inclusive; the Federal and Colonial Orders, Treaties, Acts and Ordinances Affecting Land Titles in Washington.* 5 vols. Seattle: Tribune Printing, 1895.

Pike, Ruth. *Penal Servitude in Early Modern Spain.* Madison: University of Wisconsin Press, 1983.

Powell, James V. "Quileute." In *Northwest Coast,* edited by Wayne Suttles, 431–37. Volume 7 of *The Handbook of North American Indians,* edited by William C. Sturtevant. Washington, DC: Smithsonian Institution, 1990.

Prucha, Francis Paul. *American Indian Treaties: The History of a Political Anomaly.* Berkeley: University of California Press, 1994.

———. *The Great Father: The United States Government and the American Indians.* Abridged ed. Lincoln: University of Nebraska Press, 1986.

Purdy, David F. *A Summary of the Physical Oceanography of the Pacific Northwest Coast.* OCS Information Report. [Washington, DC]: US Department of the Interior, Minerals Management Service, Pacific OCS Region, 1990.

Raban, Jonathan. *The Oxford Book of the Sea*. Oxford: Oxford University Press, 1992.

Raibmon, Paige. *Authentic Indians: Episodes of Encounter from the Late-Nineteenth-Century Northwest Coast*. Durham, NC: Duke University Press, 2005.

Ramirez, Renya. "Henry Roe Cloud: A Granddaughter's Native Feminist Biographical Account." *Wicazo Sa Review* 24, no. 2 (2009): 77–103.

Rathbun, Richard. "A Review of the Fisheries in the Contiguous Waters of the State of Washington and British Columbia." In *Report of the Commissioner for the Year Ending June 30, 1899*, edited by US Commission of Fish and Fisheries, 251–350. Washington, DC: GPO, 1900.

[Rathbun, Richard, Representative on Behalf of the United States, and William Wakeham, Representative on Behalf of Great Britain.] *Preservation of the Fisheries in Waters Contiguous to the United States and Canada*. H. Doc. no. 54–315, at 14–15 and 174 (February 24, 1897).

Rauchway, Eric. *Murdering Mckinley: The Making of Theodore Roosevelt's America*. New York: Hill and Wang, 2003.

Rediker, Marcus. *Between the Devil and the Deep Blue Sea: Merchant Seamen, Pirates, and the Anglo-American Maritime World, 1700–1750*. Cambridge: Cambridge University Press, 1987.

Reedy-Maschner, Katherine. "Deprivations Amid Abundance: The Role of Salmon and 'Other Natural Resources' in Sustaining Indigenous Aleut Communities." In *Keystone Nations: Indigenous Peoples and Salmon across the North Pacific*, edited by Benedict J. Colombi and James F. Brooks, 109–32. Santa Fe, NM: School for Advanced Research, 2012.

Reel, Estelle. Collection. Northwest Museum of Arts and Culture/Eastern Washington State Historical Society, Spokane.

Reid, John Phillip. *Patterns of Vengeance: Crosscultural Homicide in the North American Fur Trade*. [Pasadena, CA]: Ninth Judicial Circuit Historical Society, 1999.

Reid, Joshua L. "Indigenous Power in *The Comanche Empire*." *History and Theory* 52, no. 1 (2013): 54–59.

———. "Marine Tenure of the Makah." In *Indigenous Knowledge and the Environment in Africa and North America*, edited by David Gordon and Shepard Krech III, 243–58. Athens: Ohio University Press, 2012.

Renker, Ann M. "Whale Hunting and the Makah Tribe: A Needs Statement." 80. [Impington, UK]: International Whaling Commission, 2007.

Renker, Ann M., and Erna Gunther. "Makah." In *Northwest Coast*, edited by Wayne Suttles, 422–30. Volume 7 of *The Handbook of North American Indians*, edited by William C. Sturtevant. Washington, DC: Smithsonian Institution, 1990.

Reséndez, Andrés. *Changing National Identities at the Frontier: Texas and New Mexico, 1800–1850*. Cambridge: Cambridge University Press, 2004.

Reynolds, Stephen. *The Voyage of the New Hazard to the Northwest Coast, Hawaii and China, 1810–1813*. Salem, MA: Peabody Museum, 1938.

Richard Sohappy v. McKee A. Smith, and U.S. v. Oregon. 302 F.Supp. 899 (1969).

Richards, Kent. "Federal Indian Policy, Isaac I. Stevens, and the Western Washington Treaties, 1854–1855." 1991. In Sue Lean Donation. WSA.

———. *Isaac I. Stevens: Young Man in a Hurry*. Provo, UT: Brigham Young University Press, 1979.

———. "The Stevens Treaties of 1854–1855, an Introduction." *Oregon Historical Quarterly* 106, no. 3 (Fall 2005).

Richardson, Tanya. *Kaleidoscopic Odessa: History and Place in Contemporary Ukraine*. Toronto: University of Toronto Press, 2008.

Richter, Daniel K. "Whose Indian History?" *William and Mary Quarterly*, 3rd ser., 50 (1993): 379–93.

Rickman, John. *Journal of Captain Cook's Last Voyage to the Pacific Ocean*. New York: Da Capo, 1967.

Roden, Gunnar I. "Subarctic-Subtropical Transition Zone of the North Pacific: Large-Scale Aspects and Mesoscale Structure." In *Biology, Oceanography, and Fisheries of the North Pacific Transition Zone and Subarctic Frontal Zone: Papers from the North Pacific Transition Zone Workshop, Honolulu, Hawaii, 9–11 May 1988*, edited by Jerry A. Wetherall, 1–38. Honolulu: US Department of Commerce, National Oceanic and Atmospheric Administration, 1991.

Ronda, James P. *Astoria and Empire*. Lincoln: University of Nebraska Press, 1990.

Roosevelt, Theodore. "State of the Union Address," December 8, 1908. In *State of the Union Addresses by Theodore Roosevelt*, ed. Ed Manis, pp. 378–79, http://www2.hn.psu.edu/faculty/jmanis/poldocs/uspressu/SUaddressTRoosevelt.pdf.

Roquefeuil, Camille de. *Voyage around the World between the Years 1816–1819, and Trading for Sea Otter Fur on the Northwest Coast of America*. Fairfield, WA: Ye Galleon Press, 1981.

Ross, Alexander. *Adventures of the First Settlers on the Oregon or Columbia River: Being a Narrative of the Expedition Fitted out by John Jacob Astor to Establish the Pacific Fur Company: With an Account of Some Indian Tribes on the Coast of the Pacific*. London: Smith, Elder, 1849.

Ruby, Robert H., John A. Brown, and Cary C. Collins. *A Guide to the Indian Tribes of the Pacific Northwest*. 3rd ed. Norman: University of Oklahoma Press, 2010.

Rusco, Elmer R. *A Fateful Time: The Background and Legislative History of the Indian Reorganization Act*. Reno: University of Nevada Press, 2000.

Russell, Jervis, ed. *Jimmy Come Lately, History of Clallam County: A Symposium*. Port Angeles, WA: Clallam County Historical Society, 1971.

Said, Edward. *Orientalism*. New York: Vintage Books, 1978.

Salisbury, Neal. "The Indians' Old World: Native Americans and the Coming of Europeans." *William and Mary Quarterly*, 3rd ser., 53 (1996): 435–58.

Salmond, Anne. *The Trial of the Cannibal Dog: Captain Cook in the South Seas*. London: Allen Lane, 2003.

"Sample Text of Douglas Treaty: Swengwhung Tribe—Victoria Peninsula, South of Colquitz." *Province of British Columbia Website*, http://www.gov.bc.ca/arr/treaty/land mark/douglas/sample.html.

Samuels, Stephan R. *Ozette Archaeological Project Research Reports.* 2 vols. Pullman: Department of Anthropology, Washington State University, 1991.

Sapir, Edward, and Morris Swadesh. *Native Accounts of Nootka Ethnography.* Bloomington: Indiana University, Research Center in Anthropology, Folklore, and Linguistics, 1955.

Sapir, Edward, Katherine Robinson, Terry Klokeid, and Eugene Y. Arima. *The Whaling Indians: West Coast Legends and Stories: Tales of Extraordinary Experience.* Hull: Canadian Museum of Civilization, 2000.

Scammon, Charles Melville. *The Marine Mammals of the North-Western Coast of North America and the American Whale Fishery.* Riverside, CA: Manessier, 1969.

Schafer, Joseph. "Documents Related to Warre and Vavasour's Military Reconnaissance in Oregon, 1845–46." *Oregon Historical Quarterly* 10, no. 1 (1909): 1–99.

Scheuerman, Richard D. "Territorial Indian Policy and Tribal Relations, 1850–1856." In *Indians, Superintendents, and Councils: Northwestern Indian Policy, 1850–1855,* edited by Clifford E. Trafzer, 7–18. Lanham, MD: University Press of America, 1986.

Scholefield, Ethelbert Olaf Stuart, and Frederic William Howay. *British Columbia from the Earliest Times to the Present.* Vancouver: S. J. Clarke, 1914.

Schusky, Ernest L. "The Lower Brule Sioux Reservation: A Century of Misunderstanding." *South Dakota History* 7, no. 4 (1977): 422–37.

Schwantes, Carlos A. *The Pacific Northwest: An Interpretive History.* Lincoln: University of Nebraska Press, 1989.

Schwartz, Stuart B., ed. *Implicit Understandings: Observing, Reporting and Reflecting on the Encounters between Europeans and Other Peoples in the Early Modern Era.* New York: Cambridge University Press, 1994.

Scoresby, William. *An Account of the Arctic Regions, with a History and Description of the Northern Whale-Fishery.* 1820; reprint ed., [New York]: Newton Abbot, David and Charles, 1969.

Scott, James C. *Seeing Like a State: How Certain Schemes to Improve the Human Condition Have Failed.* New Haven: Yale University Press, 1998.

Scouler, John. "Dr. John Scouler's Journal of a Voyage to Northwest America (1824–25–26)." *Quarterly of the Oregon Historical Society* 6 (1905): 54–75, 159–205, 276–87.

Seed, Patricia. *Ceremonies of Possession: Europe's Conquest of the New World, 1492–1640.* Cambridge: Cambridge University Press, 1995.

Seeman, Carole. "The Treaty and Non-Treaty Coastal Indians." In *Indians, Superintendents, and Councils: Northwestern Indian Policy, 1850–1855,* edited by Clifford E. Trafzer, 37–67. Lanham, MD: University Press of America, 1986.

Seemann, Berthold. *Narrative of the Voyage of H.M.S. Herald during the Years 1845–1851: under the Command of Captain Henry Kellett Being a Circumnavigation of the Globe, and Three Cruizes to the Arctic Regions in Search of Sir John Franklin.* 2 vols. London: Reeve, 1853.

Seltz, Jennifer. "Embodying Nature: Health, Place, and Identity in Nineteenth-Century America." PhD diss., University of Washington, 2005.

——. "Epidemics, Indians, and Border-Making in the Nineteenth-Century Pacific Northwest." In *Bridging National Borders in North America: Transnational and Com-*

parative Histories, edited by Benjamin Johnson and Andrew Graybill, 91–115. Durham, NC: Duke University Press, 2010.

Sepez, Jennifer. "Political and Social Ecology of Contemporary Makah Subsistence Hunting, Fishing and Shellfish Collecting Practices." PhD diss., University of Washington, 2001.

Seton, Alfred, and Robert Francis Jones. *Astorian Adventure: The Journal of Alfred Seton, 1811–1815*. New York: Fordham University Press, 1993.

Seufert Brothers Company v. United States. 249 U.S. 194 (1919).

Shepherd, Jeffrey P. "Land, Labor, and Leadership: The Political Economy of Hualapai Community Building, 1910–1940." In *Native Pathways: American Indian Culture and Economic Development in the Twentieth Century*, edited by Brian C. Hosmer and Colleen O'Neill, 209–37. Boulder: University Press of Colorado, 2004.

Shipek, Florence Connolly. *Pushed into the Rocks: Southern California Indian Land Tenure, 1769–1986*. Lincoln: University of Nebraska Press, 1987.

Ship Logs. HBCA.

Shortt, Adam, and Arthur G. Doughty, eds. *Canada and Its Provinces: A History of the Canadian People and Their Institutions*. Vol. 21. Toronto: Glasgow, Brook, 1914.

Sierra, Benito de la. *Fray Benito De La Sierra's Account of the Hezeta Expedition to the Northwest Coast in 1775*. San Francisco: [California Historical Society], 1930.

Sims, Calvin. "Japan, Feasting on Whale, Sniffs at 'Culinary Imperialism' of U.S." *New York Times*, August 10, 2000.

Smedley, Audrey. *Race in North America: Origin and Evolution of a Worldview*. 2nd ed. Boulder: Westview Press, 1999.

Smith, Alanson Wesley. Papers. Microfilm. NARA-PNR.

Smith, Allison W. Papers, 1878–1907. Beinecke Rare Book and Manuscript Library, Yale University, New Haven.

Smith, Andrea. *Conquest: Sexual Violence and American Indian Genocide*. Cambridge, MA: South End Press, 2005.

Smith, Claire, Heather Burke, and Graehme K. Ward. "Globalisation and Indigenous Peoples: Threat or Empowerment?" In *Indigenous Cultures in an Interconnected World*, edited by Claire Smith and Graehme K. Ward, 1–24. Vancouver: University of British Columbia Press, 2000.

Smith, Hugh M. "Report on the Division of Methods and Statistics of the Fisheries." In *Report of the United States Commissioner of Fish and Fisheries for the Fiscal Year Ending June 30, 1892*. Washington, DC: GPO, 1894.

Smith, Kenneth G. Papers, 1884–1939. UWSC.

Smith, Robert W. *Exclusive Economic Zone Claims: An Analysis and Primary Documents*. Dordrecht: Martinus Nijhoff Publishers, 1986.

Snowden, Clinton A., et al. *History of Washington: The Rise and Progress of an American State*. 4 vols. New York: Century History, 1909.

Sones, Dave. Interview by author. Digital audio recording. May 19, 2009. MCRC.

Songini, Marc L. *The Lost Fleet: A Yankee Whaler's Struggle against the Confederate Navy and Arctic Disaster*. New York: St. Martin's, 2007.

Spoehr, Alexander. "Nineteenth-Century Chapter in Hawaiʻi's Maritime History: Hudson's Bay Company Merchant Shipping, 1829–1859." *Hawaiian Journal of History* 22 (1988): 70–100.

Springer, Alan M., Gus B. Van Vliet, John F. Piatt, and Eric M. Danner. "Whales and Whaling in the North Pacific Ocean and Bering Sea: Oceanographic Insights and Ecosystem Impacts." In *Whales, Whaling, and Ocean Ecosystems*, edited by James A. Estes, et al., 245–61. Berkeley: University of California Press, 2006.

Sproat, Gilbert Malcolm. *Scenes and Studies of Savage Life*. London: Smith, Elder, 1868.

Squire, Watson C. *Resources and Development of Washington Territory: Message and Report of Watson C. Squire, Governor of Washington Territory to the Legislative Assembly, Session 1885–6*. Seattle: Lowman and Hanford Stationary and Printing, 1886.

St. John, Rachel. *Line in the Sand: A History of the Western U.S.-Mexico Border*. Princeton, NJ: Princeton University Press, 2011.

Starbuck, Alexander. *History of the American Whale Fishery, from Its Earliest Inception to the Year 1876*. 2 vols. New York: Argosy-Antiquarian, 1964.

"Station Neah Bay, Washington." *U.S. Coast Guard Website*, January 2001, http://www.uscg.mil/history/stations/NEAHBAY.pdf.

State v. Alexis. 89 Wash. 492 (1916).

State v. Towessnute. 89 Wash. 478 (1916).

Statutes at Large and Treaties of the United States of America. Vol. 9, *December 1, 1845—March 3, 1851*. Boston: Little, Brown, 1862.

Steinberg, Phil. *The Social Construction of the Ocean*. Cambridge: Cambridge University Press, 2001.

Stenzel, Frank R. and Kathryn M., Research Files on Western American Art. Series 2, James G. Swan, 1870–1979, Beinecke Rare Book and Manuscript Library, Yale University, New Haven.

Stevens, Hazard. *The Life of Isaac Ingalls Stevens*. 2 vols. Boston: Houghton, Mifflin, 1900.

Stevens, Isaac I. "Governor Isaac I. Stevens to the First Annual Session of the Legislative Assembly, February 28, 1854." In *Messages of the Governors of the Territory of Washington to the Legislative Assembly, 1854–1889*, edited by Charles M. Gates, 3–9. Seattle: University of Washington Press, 1940.

——. Papers, 1848–1859. Beinecke Rare Book and Manuscript Library, Yale University, New Haven.

——. Papers. WSA.

Stevenson, Winona. "Indigenous Voices, Indigenous Histories, Part I: The Othering of Indigenous History." *Saskatchewan History* 50, no. 2 (1998): 24–27.

Stewart, Hilary. *Cedar: Tree of Life to the Northwest Coast Indians*. Seattle: University of Washington Press, 1984.

——. *Indian Fishing: Early Methods on the Northwest Coast*. Seattle: University of Washington Press, 1977.

Stewart, Mrs. Fitzroy. "Practical Advice on the Choice of Furs No. 3—Sealskins." In *Every Woman's Encyclopedia*. London: 23–29 Bouverie Street, 1910.

Storm, Jacqueline M., and Pauline K. Capoeman. *Land of the Quinault*. 2nd ed. Taholah, WA: Quinault Indian Nation, 1991.

Strange, James. *James Strange's Journal and Narrative of the Commercial Expedition from Bombay to the Northwest Coast of America*. Fairfield, WA: Ye Galleon Press, 1982.

Sullivan, Robert. *A Whale Hunt: Two Years on the Olympic Peninsula with the Makah and Their Canoe*. New York: Scribner, 2000.

Suttles, Wayne. "Coping with Abundance: Subsistence on the Northwest Coast." In *Man the Hunter*, edited by Richard B. Lee and Irven DeVore, 56–68. Chicago: Aldine, 1968.

———. "Environment." In *Northwest Coast*, edited by Wayne Suttles, 16–29. Volume 7 of *The Handbook of North American Indians*, edited by William C. Sturtevant. Washington, DC: Smithsonian Institution, 1990.

———. "Introduction." In *Northwest Coast*, edited by Wayne Suttles, 1–15. Volume 7 of *The Handbook of North American Indians*, edited by William C. Sturtevant. Washington, DC: Smithsonian Institution, 1990.

———. "Streams of Property, Armor of Wealth: The Traditional Kwakiutl Potlatch." In *Chiefly Feasts: The Enduring Kwakiutl Potlatch*, edited by Aldona Jonaitis, 71–133. Seattle: University of Washington Press, 1991.

Sutton, Imre. *Indian Land Tenure: Bibliographical Essays and a Guide to the Literature*. New York: Clearwater, 1975.

Swan, James. "Cape Flattery." *Washington Standard*, June 20, 1863.

———. "Indian Method of Killing Whales," *Port Townsend Register*, May 20, 1860.

———. "The Indians of Cape Flattery, at the Entrance to the Strait of Juan de Fuca, Washington Territory." In *Smithsonian Contributions to Knowledge*, edited by Smithsonian Institution, 108. Washington: Smithsonian Institution, 1870.

———. "Murder of Wha-lathl, or 'Swell.'" *Washington Standard*, March 30, 1861.

———. *The Northwest Coast; or, Three Years' Residence in Washington Territory*. Seattle: University of Washington Press, 1972.

———. Papers, 1833–1909. UWSC.

———. Papers, 1852–1907. UBC.

———. "Report of Investigations at Neah Bay, Wash., Respecting the Habits of Fur Seals of That Vicinity, and to Arrange for Procuring Specimens of Skeletons of Cetacea." *Bulletin of the United States Fish Commission* 3 (1883): 201–7.

Swindell, Edward Jr. Papers (M005). MCRC.

———. "Report on Source, Nature and Extent of the Fishing, Hunting and Miscellaneous Related Rights of Certain Indian Tribes in Washington and Oregon: Together with Affidavits Showing Location of a Number of Usual and Accustomed Fishing Grounds and Stations." Los Angeles: Division on Forestry and Grazing, 1942.

Sword, C. B., Inspector of Fisheries. "Annual Report on the Fisheries of British Columbia for the Year 1901," January 22, 1902. In *Thirty-Fifth Annual Report of the Department of Marine and Fisheries*, 1902. Ottawa: S. E. Dawson, 1903.

Tanner, Z. L. "Report upon the Investigations of the U.S. Fish Commission Steamer *Albatross* from July 1, 1889, to June 30, 1891." In *Report of the Commissioner [of Fish and Fisheries] for 1889 to 1891*. Washington, DC: GPO, 1893.

Tate, Cassandra. "Japanese Castaways of 1834: The Three Kichis." *HistoryLink.Org Online Encyclopedia of Washington State History.* http://www. historylink.org/index .cfm?DisplayPage=output.cfm&file _id=9065.

Taylor, Alan. *American Colonies: The Settling of North America.* New York: Penguin Books, 2001.

Taylor III, Joseph E. *Making Salmon: An Environmental History of the Northwest Fisheries Crisis.* Seattle: University of Washington Press, 1999.

———. "Negotiating Nature through Science, Sentiment, and Economics." *Diplomatic History* 25, no. 2 (March 2001): 335–39.

Thistle, John. "'As Free of Fish as a Billiard Ball Is of Hair': Dealing with Depletion in the Pacific Halibut Fishery, 1899–1924." *BC Studies*, no. 142/143 (2004): 105–25.

Thomas, Paul F. "George Bush." MA thesis, University of Washington, 1965.

Thompson, Alexander. "Canadian Foreign Policy and Straddling Stocks: Sustainability in an Interdependent World." *Policy Studies Journal* 28, no. 1 (2000): 219–35.

Thompson, Laurence C., and M. Dale Kinkade. "Languages." In *Northwest Coast*, edited by Wayne Suttles, 30–51. Volume 7 of *The Handbook of North American Indians*, edited by William C. Sturtevant. Washington, DC: Smithsonian Institution, 1990.

Thompson, Nile R., and Carolyn J. Marr. "The Evolution of Makah Basketry." In *From the Hands of a Weaver: Olympic Peninsula Basketry through Time*, edited by Jacilee Wray, 111–41. Norman: University of Oklahoma Press, 2012.

Thompson, William F. "The Regulation of the Halibut Fishery of the Pacific." In *Report of the British Columbia Commissioner of Fisheries for 1916*, 28–34. Victoria, BC: King's Printer, 1917.

———. "Statistics of the Halibut Fishery in the Pacific: Their Bearing on the Biology of the Species and the Condition of the Banks." In *Report of the British Columbia Commissioner of Fisheries for 1915*, 65–126. Victoria, BC: King's Printer, 1916.

Thompson, William F., and Frederick Heward Bell. "Biological Statistics of the Pacific Halibut Fishery: Effect of Changes in Intensity upon Total Yield and Yield Per Unit of Gear." Report no. 8. Seattle: International Fisheries Commission, 1934.

Thompson, William F., and Norman L. Freeman. "History of the Pacific Halibut Fishery." Report no. 5. Seattle: International Fisheries Commission, 1930.

Thorne, Tanis C. *The Many Hands of My Relations: French and Indians on the Lower Missouri.* Columbia: University of Missouri Press, 1996.

Thornton, Thomas F. "Anthropological Studies of Native American Place Naming." *American Indian Quarterly* 21, no. 2 (1997): 209–28.

Thrush, Coll. *Native Seattle: Histories from the Crossing-Over Place.* Seattle: University of Washington Press, 2007.

———. "Vancouver the Cannibal: Cuisine, Encounter, and the Dilemma of Difference on the Northwest Coast, 1774–1808." *Ethnohistory* 58, no. 1 (2011): 1–35.

Thrush, Coll, and Ruth S. Ludwin. "Finding Fault: Indigenous Seismology, Colonial Science, and the Rediscovery of Earthquakes and Tsunamis in Cascadia." *American Indian Culture and Research Journal* 31, no. 4 (2007): 1–24.

Tizon, Alex. "E-Mails, Phone Messages Full of Threats, Invective." *Seattle Times*, May 22, 1999.

Tolmie, William Fraser. *The Journals of William Fraser Tolmie, Physician and Fur Trader.* Vancouver: Mitchell Press, 1963.

———. "Manuscript Copy of Memo in Reference to Japanese Junk Wrecked at Cape Flattery, W.T. in Winter of 1834–35." Beinecke Rare Book and Manuscript Library, Yale University, New Haven.

———. Papers, 1833–1865. UWSC.

Tomasevich, Jozo. *International Agreements on Conservation of Marine Resources, with Special Reference to the North Pacific.* Stanford, CA: Stanford University, Food Research Institute, 1943.

Tonquin Foundation. "The Mayflower of the West." *The Tonquin Foundation*, http://www .tonquinfoundation.org/ . . . /Mayflower%20of%20the%20West.pdf.

Tovell, Freeman. *At the Far Reaches of Empire: The Life of Juan Francisco de la Bodega y Quadra.* Vancouver: University of British Columbia Press, 2008.

Tower, Walter Sheldon. *A History of the American Whale Fishery.* Philadelphia: [University of Pennsylvania], 1907.

Trachtenberg, Alan. *The Incorporation of America: Culture and Society in the Gilded Age.* New York: Hill and Wang, 2007.

Trafzer, Clifford E. *Indians, Superintendents, and Councils: Northwestern Indian Policy, 1850–1855.* Lanham, MD: University Press of America, 1986.

Trennert, Robert A. *Alternative to Extinction: Federal Indian Policy and the Beginnings of the Reservation System, 1846–51.* Philadelphia: Temple University Press, 1975.

Truett, Samuel. *Fugitive Landscapes: The Forgotten History of the U.S.-Mexico Borderlands.* New Haven: Yale University Press, 2006.

Tuan, Yi-Fu. *Space and Place: The Perspective of Experience.* Minneapolis: University of Minnesota Press, 1977.

Tulee v. Washington. 315 U.S. 681 (1942).

Turnbull, David. "Cook and Tupaia, a Tale of Cartographic Méconnaissance?" In *Science and Exploration in the Pacific: European Voyages to the Southern Oceans in the Eighteenth Century*, edited by Margarette Lincoln, 117–31. Suffolk, UK: Boydell Press, 1998.

———. *Masons, Tricksters and Cartographers: Comparative Studies in the Sociology of Scientific and Indigenous Knowledge.* Amsterdam: Harwood Academic, 2000.

Tute, Warren, and Claire Francis, eds. *The Commanding Sea: Six Voyages of Discovery.* London: Book Club Associates, 1981.

Ulmer, Vera. "Deer and the Transformer" [n.d.]. Gunther Papers. UWSC.

United Nations. Office of Legal Affairs. Division for Ocean Affairs and the Law of the Sea. Office of Legal Affairs. "The United Nations Convention on the Law of the Sea: A Historical Perspective," prepared for the International Year of the Ocean, 1998. [New York]: United Nations, 2012. http://www.un.org/Depts/los/convention_agreements/con vention_historical_perspective.htm.

United States. Census Office. *Report on the Population of the United States at the Eleventh Census: 1890.* Washington, DC: GPO, 1895.

——. *The United States in 1860; Compiled from the Original Returns of the Eighth Census, under the Direction of the Secretary of the Interior, by Joseph C. G. Kennedy, Superintendent of the Census.* Washington, DC: GPO, 1864.

United States. Department of the Interior. *Annual Report of the Commissioner of Indian Affairs.* Washington, DC: GPO, 1852–1916.

United States. Department of the Interior, Fish and Wildlife Service, and US Department of Commerce, National Oceanic and Atmospheric Administration. "Endangered and Threatened Wildlife and Plants; Final Rule to Remove the Eastern North Pacific Population of the Gray Whale from the List of Endangered Wildlife." *Federal Register*, vol. 59, no. 115 (June 16, 1994), Rules and Regulations, 31094–95.

United States. House of Representatives. Committee on Merchant Marine and Fisheries. *Saving the Gray and Bowhead Whales: Report to Accompany H. Resolution 15445.* 94th Cong., 2nd sess., 1976. No. 94–1574.

United States. Office of Indian Affairs Correspondence. RG 75. NARA.

United States. Records of the Bureau of Indian Affairs. Central Classified Files for Neah Bay Agency [CCF]. RG 75. NARA.

——. Documents Relating to the Negotiation of Ratified and Unratified Treaties with Various Tribes of Indians, 1801–1869. RG 75. Microfilm T-494, reel 5. NARA-PNR.

——. Inspection of Field Jurisdiction, Neah Bay, 1881–1897. Microfilm M-1070, roll 28. NARA-PNR.

——. Letters Received [LR], 1881–1907. RG 75. NARA.

——. Records of the Washington Superintendency of Indian Affairs, 1853–1874. National Archives Microfilm Publications No. 5. RG 75. NARA.

——. Talolah Indian Agency [TIA]. RG 75. NARA-PNR.

United States v. Kagama. 118 U.S. 375 (1886).

United States v. Washington. 384 F.Supp. 312 (1974).

United States v. Washington. 590 F.2d 676 (1975).

United States v. Washington. 423 U.S. 1086 (1976).

United States v. Washington (Phase II). 506 F.Supp. 187 (1980).

United States v. Washington (Phase II). 759 F.2d 1353 (1985).

United States v. Winans. 198 U.S. 371 (1905).

Usner, Daniel H. *Indian Work: Language and Livelihood in Native American History.* Cambridge, MA: Harvard University Press, 2009.

Van Kirk, Sylvia. *"Many Tender Ties": Women in Fur-Trade Society, 1670–1870.* Norman: University of Oklahoma Press, 1980.

Vancouver, George. *A Voyage of Discovery to the North Pacific Ocean and Round the World, 1791–1795: With an Introduction and Appendices.* 4 vols. London: Hakluyt Society, 1984.

Vaughan, Thomas, and Bill Holm. *Soft Gold: The Fur Trade and Cultural Exchange on the Northwest Coast of America.* 2nd ed. Portland: Oregon Historical Society Press, 1990.

Vincent, Mary Ann Lambert. *Dungeness Massacre and Other Regional Tales.* N.p.: Mary Ann Lambert, 1961.

Vitebsky, Piers. *The Reindeer People: Living with Animals and Spirits in Siberia*. Boston: Houghton Mifflin, 2005.

Volo, Dorothy Denneen, and James M. Volo. *Daily Life in the Age of Sail*. Westport, CT: Greenwood, 2002.

Wa, Gisday, and Delgam Uukw. *The Spirit in the Land: Statements of the Gitksan and Wet'suwet'en Hereditary Chiefs in the Supreme Court of British Columbia, 1987–1990*. Gabriola: Reflections, 1992.

Wadewitz, Lissa K. *The Nature of Borders: Salmon, Boundaries, and Bandits on the Salish Sea*. Seattle: University of Washington Press, 2012.

Wagner, Henry Raup. *Spanish Explorations in the Strait of Juan de Fuca*. Santa Ana: Fine Arts Press, 1933.

Walker, Deward E., ed. *Plateau*. Volume 12 of *The Handbook of North American Indians*, edited by William C. Sturtevant. Washington, DC: Smithsonian Institution, 1998.

Washington State. Attorney General Files. WSA.

Washington State. Department of Fisheries—Indian Affairs Files. WSA.

Washington State. Governors Papers. Elisha P. Ferry Papers. WSA.

———. Louis F. Hart Papers. WSA.

———. Marion E. Hay Papers. WSA.

———. Ernest Lister Papers. WSA.

———. Henry McBride Papers. WSA.

———. Albert E. Mead Papers. WSA.

———. Miles C. Moore Papers. WSA.

Washington v. Washington Commercial Passenger Fishing Vessel Association. 443 U.S. 658 (1979).

Watanabe, Hiroyuki. *Japan's Whaling: The Politics of Culture in Historical Perspective*. Translated by Hugh Clarke. Melbourne: Trans Pacific Press, 2009.

Waterman, T. T. "The Whaling Equipment of the Makah Indians." *University of Washington Publications in Anthropology* 1, no. 1 (June 1920): 1–67.

Waterman, T. T., and Geraldine Coffin. *Types of Canoes on Puget Sound*. New York: Museum of the American Indian, Heye Foundation, 1920.

Weaver, Jace. "More Light Than Heat: The Current State of Native American Studies." *American Indian Quarterly* 31, no. 2 (Spring 2007): 233–55.

Webb, Robert Lloyd. *On the Northwest: Commercial Whaling in the Pacific Northwest, 1790–1967*. Vancouver: University of British Columbia Press, 1988.

Weber, David J. *The Spanish Frontier in North America*. New Haven: Yale University Press, 1992.

Weber, Max, David S. Owen, and Tracy B. Strong. *The Vocation Lectures*. Translated by Rodney Livingstone. Indianapolis: Hackett Pub., 2004.

Webster, Peter S., and Campbell River Museum and Archives Society. *As Far as I Know: Reminiscences of an Ahousat Elder*. Campbell River: Campbell River Museum and Archives, 1983.

Wessel, Thomas R. "Agent of Acculturation: Farming on the Northern Plains Reservations, 1880–1910." *Agricultural History* 60, no. 2 (Spring 1986): 233–45.

Wessen, Gary. "Prehistory of the Ocean Coast of Washington." In *Northwest Coast*, edited by Wayne Suttles, 412–21. Volume 7 of *The Handbook of North American Indians*, edited by William C. Sturtevant. Washington, DC: Smithsonian Institution, 1990.

West, Elliot. *The Contested Plains: Indians, Goldseekers, and the Rush to Colorado*. Lawrence: University Press of Kansas, 1998.

"Whalers in the Pacific [30 August]." *New York Times*, September 7, 1891.

Whaley, Gray H. *Oregon and the Collapse of Illahee: U.S. Empire and the Transformation of an Indigenous World, 1792–1859*. Chapel Hill: University of North Carolina Press, 2010.

White, Richard. "'Are You an Environmentalist or Do You Work for a Living?': Work and Nature." In *Uncommon Ground: Rethinking the Human Place in Nature*, edited by William Cronon, 171–85. New York: W. W. Norton, 1996.

——. *"It's Your Misfortune and None of My Own": A History of the American West*. Norman: University of Oklahoma Press, 1991.

——. *Land Use, Environment, and Social Change: The Shaping of Island County, Washington*. Seattle: University of Washington Press, 1992.

——. *The Middle Ground: Indians, Empires, and Republicans in the Great Lakes Region, 1650–1815*. Cambridge: Cambridge University Press, 1991.

——. *Roots of Dependency: Subsistence, Environment, and Social Change among the Choctaws, Pawnees, and Navajos*. Lincoln: University of Nebraska Press, 1983.

——. "The Winning of the West: The Expansion of the Western Sioux in the Eighteenth and Nineteenth Centuries." *Journal of American History* 65, no. 2 (1978): 319–43.

Wilcox, William A. "Fisheries of the Pacific Coast." In *Report of the Commissioner [of Fish and Fisheries] for the Year Ending June 30, 1893*. Washington, DC: GPO, 1895.

Wilkes, Charles. *Narrative of the United States Exploring Expedition during the Years 1838, 1839, 1840, 1841, 1842*. 5 vols. Philadelphia: Lea and Blanchard, 1845.

Wilkins, David E. *Hollow Justice: A History of Indigenous Claims in the United States*. New Haven: Yale University Press, 2013.

Wilkins, David E., and K. Tsianina Lomawaima. *Uneven Ground: American Indian Sovereignty and Federal Law*. Norman: University of Oklahoma Press, 2001.

Wilkinson, Charles F. *Blood Struggle: The Rise of Modern Indian Nations*. New York: W. W. Norton, 2005.

——. *Messages from Frank's Landing: A Story of Salmon, Treaties, and the Indian Way*. Seattle: University of Washington Press, 2000.

——. *The People Are Dancing Again: The History of the Siletz Tribe of Western Oregon*. Seattle: University of Washington Press, 2010.

Will Anderson, et al. v. Donald Evans, et al. 371 F.3d 475 (2004).

Williams, Raymond. "Ideas of Nature." In *Problems in Materialism and Culture*, edited by Raymond Williams, 67–85. London: Verso, 1980.

Wilson, Angela Cavender. "Power of the Spoken Word: Native Oral Traditions in American Indian History." In *Rethinking American Indian History*, edited by Donald Lee Fixico, 101–16. Albuquerque: University of New Mexico Press, 1997.

Wolfe, Patrick, ed. "Settler Colonialism and Indigenous Alternatives in a Global Context (1): The Settler Complex." Special issue, *American Indian Culture and Research Journal* 37, no. 2 (2013): 1–232.

———, ed. "Settler Colonialism and Indigenous Alternatives in a Global Context (2): Recuperating Binarism." Special issue, *Settler Colonial Studies* 4, no. 3–4 (2013): 257–450.

———. *Settler Colonialism and the Transformation of Anthropology: The Politics and Poetics of an Ethnographic Event.* London: Cassell, 1999.

Woods, Fronda. "Who's in Charge of Fishing?" *Oregon Historical Quarterly* 106, no. 3 (2005): 412–41.

Wright, E. W. *Lewis and Dryden's Marine History of the Pacific Northwest.* Portland, OR: Lewis and Dryden, 1895.

Wunder, John R. *"Retained by the People": A History of American Indians and the Bill of Rights.* New York: Oxford University Press, 1994.

Wunder, John R., and Pekka Hämäläinen. "Of Lethal Places and Lethal Essays." *American Historical Review* 104, no. 4 (1999): 1229–34.

Zilberstein, Anya. "Objects of Distant Exchange: The Northwest Coast, Early America, and the Global Imagination." *William and Mary Quarterly*, 3rd ser., 114 (2007): 591–620.

Ziontz, Alvin J. "History of Treaty Fishing Rights in the Northwest." In *Tribal Report to the Presidential Task Force on Treaty Fishing Rights in the Northwest,* edited by Northwest Indian Fisheries Commission, 4–55. Olympia: The Commission, 1977.

———. *A Lawyer in Indian Country: A Memoir.* Seattle: University of Washington Press, 2009.

Zontek, Ken. *Buffalo Nation: American Indian Efforts to Restore the Bison.* Lincoln: University of Nebraska Press, 2007.

Index

Note: Italic page numbers refer to illustrations.